The Winter's Tale

Texts and Contexts

—⟩✦⟨—

DISCARDED

WILLIAM SHAKESPEARE

The Winter's Tale

Texts and Contexts

>·<

Edited by

MARIO DIGANGI

City University of New York

Bedford / St. Martin's　　　BOSTON　◆　NEW YORK

For Bedford/St. Martin's

Editorial Assistant: Marisa Feinstein
Senior Production Supervisor: Joe Ford
Production Associate: Sarah Ulicny
Executive Marketing Manager: Jenna Bookin Barry
Project Management: DeMasi Design and Publishing Services
Text Design: Claire Seng-Niemoeller
Cover Design: Donna Lee Dennison
Cover Art: Harvest (detail from the lid of a harpsichord) by Frederick van
  Valckenborch. Courtesy of Scala/Art Resource, NY.
Composition: TexTech
Printing and Binding: RR Donnelley & Sons Company

President: Joan E. Feinberg
Editorial Director: Denise B. Wydra
Editor in Chief: Karen S. Henry
Director of Marketing: Karen Melton Soeltz
Director of Editing, Design, and Production: Marcia Cohen
Manager, Publishing Services: Emily Berleth

Library of Congress Control Number: 2007929147

Manufactured in the United States of America.

2 1 0 9 8 7
f e d c b a

For information, write: Bedford/St. Martin's, 75 Arlington Street, Boston, MA 02116
(617-399-4000)

ISBN-10: 0-312-16704-0
ISBN-13: 978-0-312-16704-2

Published and distributed outside North America by

PALGRAVE MACMILLAN

Houndmills, Basingstoke, Hampshire RG21 6XS and London
Companies and representatives throughout the world.

ISBN-10: 1-4039-9793-4
ISBN-13: 978-1-4039-9793-7

A catalog record for this book is available from the British Library.

About the Series

Shakespeare wrote his plays in a culture unlike, though related to, the culture of the emerging twenty-first century. The Bedford Shakespeare Series resituates Shakespeare within the sometimes alien context of the sixteenth and seventeenth centuries while inviting students to explore ways in which Shakespeare, as text and as cultural icon, continues to be part of contemporary life. Each volume frames a Shakespearean play with a wide range of written and visual material from the early modern period, such as homilies, polemical literature, emblem books, facsimiles of early modern documents, maps, woodcut prints, court records, other plays, medical tracts, ballads, chronicle histories, and travel narratives. Selected to reveal the many ways in which Shakespeare's plays were connected to the events, discourses, and social structures of his time, these documents and illustrations also show the contradictions and the social divisions in Shakespeare's culture and in the plays he wrote. Engaging critical introductions and headnotes to the primary materials help students identify some of the issues they can explore by reading these texts with and against one another, setting up a two-way traffic between the Shakespearean text and the social world these documents help to construct.

Jean E. Howard
Columbia University
Series Editor

About This Volume

———————————————✕—————————————————

Like the other volumes in the Bedford Shakespeare Series, this book is guided by the premise that reading Shakespeare's plays in the context of their original culture can be abundantly rewarding. Although such an approach acknowledges Shakespeare's talent for transforming the raw material of English Renaissance culture into brilliant theater, it also recognizes that the historical moment in which Shakespeare lived necessarily imposed certain limits on what he thought and wrote.

In its historical emphasis, this volume thus departs from conventional accounts that treat Shakespeare's texts in isolation from the shaping pressures of their particular time and place. Too often, Shakespeare's plays have been regarded as self-contained vessels of poetic beauty and universal truth elevated high above the messy contingencies of political or social struggle. Proponents of this idealistic attitude tend to view the plays as "works": finely wrought objects, much like the venerated royal crowns in Shakespeare's tragedies and history plays. Revered as a brilliant crown, the Shakespeare play shines all the more brightly when it is held up against (what is presumed to be) the dim backdrop of contemporary writing or when it is extricated altogether from the confused bustle of history. This book insists, on the contrary, that the artistry and power of Shakespeare's plays should be understood not in spite of but because of their being embedded in the ebb and flow of English Renaissance culture. The metaphor of culture as ebb and flow suggests an alternative way of thinking about literature in its relationship to history — one that emphasizes fluid process over static product, one that imagines the borders between a literary text and its innumerable contexts to be permeable and ever-shifting.

To begin with, even the fundamental questions of how we should identify a "context" or how we should understand the relationship between "text" and "context" have no definitive answers. We might narrowly identify contexts for *The Winter's Tale* as works of imaginative literature from sixteenth- and seventeenth-century England, including plays, poems, pamphlets, ballads, and romances. More broadly, we might define contexts to include contemporary texts that are not typically classified as literature but that nonetheless share thematic, ideological, or stylistic traits with literary texts: religious sermons, medical treatises, political polemics, social satires, financial records, royal proclamations, and so on. Some of the contexts through which we inevitably read Shakespeare's plays also derive from modern historical narratives that shape our perceptions about the Renaissance (or, as historians tend to call it, the "early modern" period). To support their claims about "typical" early modern views on subjects as diverse as monarchical government and sexual reproduction, modern historical narratives both build upon the evidence of sixteenth- and seventeenth-century texts and impose a certain order upon those texts — drawing links and patterns among them, accentuating certain details and occluding others. These historical narratives might be regarded as convenient fictions that can help us to appreciate the broad differences between present and past societies. Yet any claims to know "what Shakespeare's contemporaries thought" about such multifaceted topics as politics, religion, or sexuality should be taken with a healthy dose of skepticism.

In thus straddling the disciplinary boundaries of literature and history, *The Winter's Tale: Texts and Contexts* requires a kind of double vision from its readers. On the one hand, this book acknowledges the value of *The Winter's Tale* as an imaginative text that repays our sustained attention to its distinctive language, characterization, and exploration of fundamental questions about love, power, loss, and faith. On the other hand, this book insists that we approach *The Winter's Tale* as one text among many — in other words, that we understand and evaluate its literary, theatrical, political, and philosophical meanings in conversation with other texts within the broader fields of Renaissance literature, theater, politics, and philosophy.

At the most basic level, this endeavor involves reading a lot of other texts from the sixteenth and seventeenth centuries, some familiar and some obscure. Students of English Renaissance literature and history will find among the contextual documents some of the usual suspects: Sir Philip Sidney's eloquent critical treatise, *The Defense of Poesy* (Chapter 1); Arthur Golding's vastly influential translation of Ovid's *Metamorphoses* (Chapters 1 and 5); and King James's aggressive justification of royal prerogative in *The True Law of Free Monarchies* (Chapter 3). Other texts reproduced in the pages that follow are virtually unknown today, and have never before been acknowledged as relevant contexts for *The Winter's Tale*: examples include Robert Allyne's *Funeral Elegies* (Chapter 2) and Gerrit de Veer's *True and Perfect Description of Three Voyages* (Chapter 4). In some cases the temporal proximity of a set of documents to *The Winter's Tale* suggests that a certain issue was becoming a flashpoint in the larger culture. For instance, the act 3 debate between Leontes and Paulina over the legitimacy of female speech anticipates the pamphlet war that broke out in London shortly after the play's first performances, as represented in Chapter 3 by Joseph Swetnam's *Arraignment of Lewd . . . Women* (1615) and by Rachel Speght's response, *A Muzzle for Melastomus* (1617). Likewise, the play's concluding scene of devotion to Hermione's statue points to contemporary debates between Catholics and Protestants over the legitimacy of praying to saints and their images (addressed in Chapter 5).

Whereas many of the Renaissance texts reproduced in this volume were originally published slightly prior to or roughly at the same time as the first performances of *The Winter's Tale* (1610–11), others were published later, and thus cannot be regarded as direct or indirect "sources" of the play. In the case of direct sources such as Arthur Golding's translation of Ovid's *Metamorphoses* (1567) and Robert Greene's tale *Pandosto* (1588), we will consider how Shakespeare borrowed from and transformed previous texts in composing *The Winter's Tale*. The primary purpose of this edition, however, is not to identify the sources that Shakespeare might have consciously or unconsciously drawn upon in writing the play, but to place the play in dialogue with historically proximate texts that address similar problems and concerns. For this reason, it is not necessary to limit the contextual documents to those that Shakespeare or his original audiences knew or might have known. Documents that postdate the play can also offer valuable perspectives on ideas that were in circulation or controversies that were raging when *The Winter's Tale* was first staged. For instance, William Gouge's *Of Domestical Duties* (1622) and Milton's *Paradise Lost* (1674), both included in Chapter 2, provide influential articulations of certain Protestant positions on marriage that had been emerging since the mid-sixteenth century, positions that make their mark on *The Winter's Tale*. The texts of Gouge and Milton serve to remind us that the contextual documents reproduced in this volume are intended not to provide a stable "background" on which to fix the meaning of *The Winter's Tale*, but to suggest that many different meanings might have been available to Shakespeare's contemporaries in their encounters with the play.

For most of the documents transcribed in this volume, I consulted the original printed texts at the Folger Shakespeare Library or the electronic versions of the original texts available on Early English Books Online (EEBO). EEBO is a database that makes available approximately 100,000 digital facsimile versions of virtually every book published in the English language between 1473 and 1700. Considerations of space in this volume necessitated the use of relatively concise selections from sixteenth- and seventeenth-century texts, some of which run for hundreds of pages, but readers with access to EEBO through a university or public library are strongly encouraged to explore the originals for themselves. Almost all the texts transcribed in this volume can be easily found on EEBO by doing a search using the *Short-Title Catalogue* (STC) number that has been provided in the source footnote for each document. (The STC is the standard list of all surviving books printed in English up to 1640.)

There is much to be learned about Shakespeare's culture, and the place of *The Winter's Tale* within it, by studying original texts in greater depth. With the obvious and important exception of their material form, the texts reproduced on EEBO appear as they did in their own day. Unlike modernized editions of a Shakespeare play such as this one, each text on EEBO retains its original spelling, punctuation, typefaces, layout, and printing errors, with no explanatory footnotes, glosses, introductions, or any other modern editorial interventions. Although EEBO cannot provide us with an "authentic" early modern reading experience — given the vast differences between seventeenth-century and twenty-first-century culture, no amount of technological ingenuity can recreate such an experience — access to original documents does allow us to appreciate much about the form in which Shakespeare and his contemporaries encountered these texts.

Editorial Policy

For each text included in this volume, I have generally transcribed the first published edition. To provide a sense of the contemporary popularity of a text, the headnotes indicate the frequency and number of editions of that text published during the sixteenth and seventeenth centuries. I have modernized the texts according to the following principles:

1. Spelling has been modernized to reflect American usage. However, I have retained archaic verb endings (e.g., *-eth*) and certain archaic words (e.g., *reciprock* instead of *reciprocal*), which retain the distinctive tang of early modern language without affecting clarity. Modern spellings of obsolete words come from the *Oxford English Dictionary*, which I have also used for the definitions that appear in the glosses. I consulted the *Dictionary of National Biography* for much of the biographical data about authors that appears in headnotes. Foreign words have been retained in the main body of the texts but are translated in the notes.

2. Punctuation has been lightly modernized to clarify meaning and facilitate reading. For instance, where the early modern texts use a colon to signify a full stop, I have silently changed the colon to a period. While attempting to respect the characteristic style of each text, I have aimed to improve syntactical and rhetorical comprehension by breaking up long sentences into smaller units, adding semicolons to separate long series of phrases, and adding paragraph divisions to emphasize shifts in topic. Whereas early modern texts typically use italics to indicate direct speech, I have removed the italics and added quotation marks.

3. I have generally not retained the occasional use of emphatic capitalization and italics in the original texts.

4. I have modernized the titles of texts according to the above principles of spelling and punctuation. When referring to the texts in the Introduction and the contextual chapters, I use shortened versions of the original titles, which can be very elaborate. The source footnote that accompanies each text often gives a fuller version of the original title.

5. In citing sixteenth- and seventeenth-century texts, I have used signature numbers rather than page numbers when appropriate. Signature numbers, a now-obsolete method of pagination, indicate how large sheets of paper were folded and bound in the creation of a book. To create a *folio* or *F* volume, a printer would fold large sheets of paper into two. For a smaller *quarto* or *Q* volume, pages were folded into four, and for a yet smaller *octavo* or *O* volume into eight. The printer would use a letter to identify all the pages printed on each large single sheet, followed by a number indicating the order of each page in that "gathering," followed by an "r" (for *recto* or "front") or a "v" (for *verso* or "back") to distinguish the front side and back side of each page. Thus a marking of "B3v" at the bottom of a page indicates that the page is located in the second gathering of folded sheets, on the third page, on the inverse side of the page.

6. For dates, I have used the more neutral B.C.E. (Before Common Era) and C.E. (Common Era) instead of the equivalent B.C. and A.D.

7. In the Introduction and chapter commentaries, I have cited from David Bevington's edition of *The Winter's Tale* reprinted in this volume. Citations from other Shakespeare plays come from *The Norton Shakespeare*, edited by Stephen J. Greenblatt (New York: Norton, 1997).

Acknowledgments

Jean E. Howard, editor of this series, has long amazed me with her level-headed professionalism, intellectual generosity, and appreciation for what's at stake in the academic work we do. I am deeply grateful to Karen S. Henry, editor in chief, not only for her patience and guidance with this project, but for the vision and direction that have led to so many wonderful volumes in the Bedford Shakespeare Series. At various stages, Frances E. Dolan (whose own edition of *The Taming of the Shrew* set a high standard for the series) was an extremely perceptive and generous reader. I am also indebted to Mary Ellen Lamb, Lori Newcomb, Rick Rambuss, and Valerie Wayne, who will, I hope, recognize their salutary influence on the choice of topics, selection of texts, and framing of issues.

Producing a book is a collaborative endeavor. I was fortunate to work with the dedicated and professional staff at Bedford/St. Martin's, including production coordinator Emily Berleth, Linda DeMasi of DeMasi Design and Publishing Services, and copyeditor Kate Cohen, who asked the right questions and often read my writing with a sharper eye than I did. Persistent and resourceful, Jennifer Blanksteen did a fantastic job of tracking down illustrations and securing permissions, and Marisa Feinstein helped with this task.

In conjunction with Jennifer Blanksteen, several people went out of their way to locate the images that grace this book. My sincere thanks to Jennie Rathbun of the Houghton Library, Harvard University; Bettina Smith, image request coordinator of the Folger Shakespeare Library; Stephen Tabor, curator of early printed books at the Huntington Library; and Helen Trompeteler, picture librarian at the National Portrait Gallery in London.

While working on this book, I explored the relationship between Shakespearean texts and contexts in two courses taught at Columbia University and at the CUNY Graduate Center. Among the many bright and dedicated students who participated in those courses, I would like to acknowledge, from the Graduate Center, Linda Neiberg and Louise Geddes (who continue to be passionate interlocutors for the kinds of questions raised in this book); and, from Columbia, Garth Brown, Justin Klein, Zoë Ferraris, and, especially, Ian Nussbaum. At the Graduate Center, Brenda Henry-Offor and Robert Azzarello were capable and dedicated research assistants; Joost Burgers and Mark Cirino generously gave of their knowledge and resources. I have benefited greatly from the support and kindness of Steve Kruger.

The research for this book was generously supported by a George N. Shuster Faculty Development Program Award, a Lehman College Fellowship Award, and a PSC-CUNY Award. As head of the English department at Lehman College, Walter Blanco made it easier for me to devote time to my research.

Many wonderful friends have provided invaluable advice about this project over the course of its development: Mary Bly, Julie Crawford, Will Fisher, Bonnie Gordon, and Natasha Korda. Bianca Calabresi and Adam Zucker also provided incisive readings of early chapters.

George Mayer alerted me to the resources of the TOFT library at the New York Public Library; the ability to review a tape of the Propeller performance of *The Winter's Tale* made possible the last document in this book.

The Winter's Tale is about the forces that drive a family apart and bring them back together; fortunately, my own parents, Franco and Christine DiGangi, have always been there to encourage, tease, and inspire me. During the writing of this book, my partner, John Antosca, was "all my exercise, my mirth, my matter."

Jean Howard, David Scott Kastan, and Jim Shapiro introduced me to the pleasures and challenges of reading historically. This book is dedicated to them.

Mario DiGangi
City University of New York

Contents

><

→ 4. *Encountering Nature*   300

→ 5. *Hermione's Statue*   360

Illustrations

⸎

Introduction

><

Shakespeare wrote *The Winter's Tale* (1610–11) late in his career. It is not surprising, then, that in this mature play Shakespeare revisits many of the social, political, and philosophical questions, as well as distinctive character types and dramatic situations, that had long occupied his imagination. For example, Hermione is not the first of Shakespeare's women to face a false charge of sexual infidelity: she is preceded in this by Hero, from the comedy *Much Ado about Nothing* (1598), and Desdemona, from the tragedy *Othello* (1604). Paulina, with her sharp tongue and righteous indignation, might be an older and wiser version of Katherine, the assertive "shrew" of *The Taming of the Shrew* (1592). Like Katherine, Paulina vigorously challenges the limitations placed on female speech by a patriarchal society. The courtship of Perdita and Florizel expresses the ardor of young love that Shakespeare celebrated in comedies such as *A Midsummer Night's Dream* (1595) and *As You Like It* (1599). Conversely, Leontes' fear and rage align him with Shakespeare's tragic protagonists: as a furiously jealous husband, he recalls Othello; as a rash and domineering patriarch, he recalls King Lear. Through Leontes' tyrannical behavior, moreover, Shakespeare raises the issue of the limits of monarchical power, as he had done in his English history plays of the 1590s. In many ways, then, *The Winter's Tale* has the feel of a familiar "old tale" (5.3.118).

At the same time, *The Winter's Tale* also tells an outlandish story, one that stretches credulity by asking us to imagine a world in which terrible losses and betrayals do not preclude restoration, forgiveness, and reconciliation. To the degree that *The Winter's Tale* exploits elements of the implausible, it operates as a fable: a fairy tale about a wicked king and a virtuous queen; a dead woman who comes back to life; a prophecy fulfilled; a princess raised as a shepherdess and unexpectedly reunited with her family many years later. It would be a mistake, however, to reduce *The Winter's Tale* to the familiar outlines and archetypes of a fairy tale, for the play's wonderfully rich texture derives from its active engagement with debates about political authority, gender roles, and religious faith, among other issues, that are specific to the culture of early modern England in which Shakespeare lived and worked.

The London citizen Simon Forman, who recorded his attendance at a performance of *The Winter's Tale* at the Globe Playhouse in May 1611, seems to have responded most keenly to the play's representation of just such culturally specific matters. In his journal entry about the play, Forman fails to mention what many regard as its most distinctive theatrical traits: the bear that chases Antigonus across the stage and the "statue" of Hermione that appears to come to life before our eyes. After summarizing the major episodes of the plot, Forman focuses instead on the clever thief Autolycus, whose real-life counterpart he might have encountered on the streets outside the Globe:

> Remember also the rogue that came in all tattered like colt-pixie, and how he feigned him sick and to have been robbed of all that he had, and how he cozened the poor man of all his money, and after came to the sheep-shear with a pedlar's pack and there cozened them again all of their money, and how he changed apparel with the King of Bohemia his son, and then how he turned courtier, etc. Beware of trusting feigned beggars or fawning fellows.   (quoted in Orgel, *Winter's Tale* 233)

What Forman takes away from *The Winter's Tale* is not the lesson about forgiveness and redemption to which many critics have attributed the play's universal significance and appeal, but the decidedly pragmatic lesson about avoiding con artists. Forman's complete neglect of the remarkable statue scene has even led to speculation that he saw an earlier version of the play in which that scene did not appear (Bergeron, "Apollo" 160). In any case, we should not regard Forman's response to the play as somehow "representative" of all seventeenth-century playgoers, any more than we would regard one individual's response to a performance of *The Winter's Tale* in 2007 as the representative experience of all twenty-first-century theater audiences.

Precisely because of its resistance to a singular, transparent interpretation, Forman's journal entry illustrates that approaching *The Winter's Tale* through sixteenth- and seventeenth-century documents, as this book does, will not reveal any single "contemporary understanding" of the play's meaning or resolve its ambiguities. The purpose of reading the play alongside contemporary documents is not to fix its meaning through reference to a supposedly stable or coherent "historical context." Rather, reading the play in the context of multiple, sometimes contradictory, historical records and narratives should enable us to ask more penetrating questions — and hence to formulate more complex answers — about the social, philosophical, and aesthetic issues that engaged Renaissance audiences and that continue to speak to us. Thus while the documents in this edition will not yield definitive interpretations, they will suggest particular frameworks for interpretation. For instance, the presence of a bear in *The Winter's Tale* seems less arbitrary in the context of a contemporary travel narrative that describes sailors' terrifying (but often exhilarating) adventures with polar bears in the northern seas. In different ways, both the travel narrative and the play raise compelling questions about the pleasures and dangers of human encounters with the natural world, and about our habit of transforming animals into art, using them as symbols of our dual capacity for "savage" destruction or "natural" compassion.

The contextual documents that comprise Part Two of this edition are divided into five chapters. Each chapter pursues an avenue of interpretation that might have been available to a contemporary playgoer and that can enrich our own experience of *The Winter's Tale*. The arrangement of the chapters roughly follows the movement of the play from Sicilia to Bohemia and back to Sicilia. Addressing the play's broad generic traits, the first chapter, "Romance and Tragicomedy," examines the elements of fantasy and the large leaps of time and place typical of romance. The dissolution of Leontes' family and court in acts 1 through 3 is covered in "Gender, Sexuality, and the Family," and "Authority and Resistance." The documents in these chapters reveal the deep interconnection of private and public life for Renaissance families, especially aristocratic ones. In Chapter 2, for instance, accounts of the elaborate ceremonies performed at the birth of a royal child in seventeenth-century England can help us to appreciate the terribly anomalous circumstances surrounding the birth of Perdita in the play. In Chapter 3, texts that address contemporary controversies about the limits of monarchical power and of women's speech elucidate Paulina's double role as both royal counselor and domestic shrew. Chapter 4, "Encountering Nature," considers the hardships and pleasures of rural life as depicted in the play's Bohemian episodes, which feature not only the remarkable bear, but also the remarkably long sheep-shearing festival. The final chapter, "Hermione's Statue," explores the significance of Hermione's return as a living statue in terms of Renaissance understanding of the social, erotic, and religious functions of art. The remainder of this introduction provides a more detailed account of the relationship of *The Winter's Tale* both to Shakespeare's other plays and to the broad thematic rubrics under which the documents in this edition are organized.

Romance and Tragicomedy

> They looked as they had heard of a world ransomed, or one destroyed
>
> (5.2.11–12)

By providing a general set of conventions for structuring a story, generic categories impose certain boundaries on our experience of literary texts. We expect a comedy to begin with strife and end with celebration, typically in the form of reconciled family members and a marriage (or, as frequently in Shakespearean comedies, multiple marriages). We expect a tragedy to depict the suffering and death that accompanies the fall of a great leader. In the words of the above epigraph from *The Winter's Tale*, comedy tells us of a "world ransomed" and tragedy of a world "destroyed." Yet the flexible nature of generic categories also allows for significant variations in style, tone, and plot structure among texts in the same genre. Some texts, moreover, seem deliberately to blur the distinctions between genres, producing hybrid forms such as "tragicomedies" that might thwart our expectations.

The titles of Shakespeare's plays often signal their genres, as in *The Comedy of Errors* or *The Tragedy of Macbeth*. While the title *The Winter's Tale* alerts us to expect a certain kind of story, it does not specify the generic parameters of this story. What kind of "winter's tale" are we going to be told? "Winter" evokes the season conventionally associated with hardship, decline, and death — the stuff of tragedy — and the echo of the play's title in the brief domestic scene between Mamillius and his mother confirms this somber association. Just moments after Mamillius tells Hermione that "a sad tale's best for winter," Leontes violently bursts in upon their intimate conversation, forever severing the boy from his mother (2.1.25). Shakespeare's own "sad tale" of winter begins, then, with the tragic decline of Leontes, his family, and his court.

Yet *The Winter's Tale* is not the tragedy of King Leontes in the same way that *Macbeth* can be considered the tragedy of Macbeth. Like a fairy tale,

The Winter's Tale allows time, fortune, and the virtues of patience, loyalty, and faith to bring a tragic course of events to a spectacular, seemingly miraculous, conclusion. In these ways, *The Winter's Tale* is typical of the literary genre of romance: "a success story in which difficulties of any number of kinds are overcome, and a tall story in which they are overcome against impossible odds or by miraculous means" (Felperin 10). "Impossible odds" and "miraculous means" aptly describe the implausible series of events by which *The Winter's Tale* achieves its relatively happy ending. Perdita not only survives the bear attack that kills Antigonus, she is discovered and raised by a kind shepherd, falls in love with the prince who is the son of her father's estranged childhood friend, and ends up back at her father's court, sixteen years later, during which time her mother has secretly "preserved" herself in order to fulfill an oracle's promise of her daughter's return (5.3.128).

That Shakespeare must introduce the choral figure of Time to explain the passage of sixteen years between acts 3 and 4 is evidence of the strain that romance, with its emphasis on the miraculous and its enormous spans of time and place, places on the resources of theater. Chapter 1 opens with Sir Philip Sidney's *The Defense of Poesy* (1595), an important work of literary criticism that accuses contemporary English dramatists of violating the rules of classical genres. Instead of producing "right tragedies" or "right comedies," Sidney laments, English playwrights produce only "mongrel tragi-comedy." Ridiculing these plays' reliance on shipwrecks, monsters, lost children, immense passages of time, and sudden shifts of exotic locale, Sidney enumerates some of the most notable features of romance and tragicomedy that would characterize *The Winter's Tale* many years later. *The Defense of Poesy* articulates a conventional standard of what is appropriate for different dramatic genres against which we can evaluate the sometimes surprising dramaturgical choices Shakespeare makes in *The Winter's Tale*.

The other documents in Chapter 1 provide further perspectives on the generic hybridity of *The Winter's Tale*. When John Fletcher published his theatrical flop *The Faithful Shepherdess* in 1610, he included a preface that instructed his readers on what to expect from the unfamiliar genre of "pastoral tragicomedy." Recently imported from Italy, pastoral tragicomedy was an erudite mixture of tragedy, comedy, and pastoral, a literary mode that presented idealized portraits of shepherds as gentle lovers and poets. It is tempting to speculate on the generic expectations that London playgoers — perhaps some of the same ones who rejected Fletcher's play — brought to *The Winter's Tale* in 1611, and to consider how these expectations might have shifted as the play progressed. How might the playgoing public's knowledge (or lack of knowledge) of "pastoral tragicomedy" have shaped its responses to *The Winter's Tale*? While we do not know the answers to such questions, Fletcher's effort to define the proper characteristics and aims of tragicomedy shows just how fluid this genre was for playwrights and audiences at this time.

The only document in this edition that can be considered a direct "source" for *The Winter's Tale* is Robert Greene's prose romance *Pandosto. The Triumph of Time* (1588), from which Shakespeare borrows his basic plot and characters. Yet Shakespeare also significantly departs from his source material, inventing a central character, Paulina, and achieving a more subtle balance between tragedy and comedy. Certain differences between *Pandosto* and *The Winter's Tale* reflect the differences between prose narrative and drama as modes of storytelling. *Pandosto* has a narrator who shapes the story, provides interpretative commentary, and gives direct access into characters' private thoughts. Although Shakespeare also provides access into characters' private thoughts through soliloquies, the lack of an omniscient narrative voice in drama as well as the specific choices made by actors and directors in performance can produce radically different accounts of characters' behaviors and motives. Comparing *The Winter's Tale* with *Pandosto* foregrounds the exciting openness of dramatic interpretation.

Whereas a prose story can easily convey long passages of time — the narrator simply need inform us how many years have gone by — a play cannot. Shakespeare's recourse to a personification of Time not only underlines the implausibility of the romance narrative on stage, but also emphasizes the crucial role that time plays in the resolution of that narrative. Although not a direct source in the manner of *Pandosto*, the myth of Proserpina, as recounted by Ovid in his great compilation of classical mythology, the *Metamorphoses* (1567), provides a model for the story of loss and return that structures *The Winter's Tale*. Proserpina, daughter of the harvest goddess Ceres, is picking flowers in the Sicilian countryside one day when Dis, god of the underworld, abducts her and hales her back to his infernal kingdom as his bride. Ceres finally negotiates an arrangement with Jove whereby Proserpina spends six months with her husband in the underworld (the winter season) and six months with her mother in Sicily (the summer season). This story of mother-daughter reunion is also a myth of seasonal time that explains the endless cycle of winter and summer, death and rebirth, loss and restoration. Like *The Winter's Tale*, then, the Proserpina myth might be classified as a tragicomedy. Unlike Ceres and Proserpina, however, Hermione and Perdita are mortals subject to the strict laws of time: Hermione has recovered her daughter, but can never recover the sixteen years during which they were separated. For different readers or viewers, then, recognizing the Proserpina myth as a subtext for *The Winter's Tale* might emphasize the comic, tragic, or tragicomedic traits of the play.

The texts in Chapter 1, themselves representative of different genres, demonstrate how *The Winter's Tale* draws on the traditions of comedy, tragedy, tragicomedy, pastoral, and romance. To recognize the workings of different generic traditions in the play facilitates a deeper understanding of the social and aesthetic codes that literary genres help to organize, however loosely or provisionally. Paying attention to how various generic traits blend and clash in the play helps us to perceive the broad outlines of certain social, political, and ideological issues that subsequent chapters explore in greater detail.

Gender, Sexuality, and the Family

> Should all despair
> That have revolted wives, the tenth of mankind
> Would hang themselves (1.2.198–200)

Of the five chapters in this edition, Chapter 2 covers the broadest territory. Every Shakespearean play contains a family of one kind or another; in every play, too, ideas about gender and sexuality centrally inform the psychology of selfhood and the dynamics of social interaction. Nonetheless, *The Winter's Tale* is among the very few plays in which Shakespeare depicts a complete family unit containing a mother, father, and children. In most of the comedies, one of the parents (usually the mother) is missing: the daughters in *The Taming of the Shrew*, *A Midsummer Night's Dream*, and *The Merchant of Venice* are all motherless, whereas Bertram and Helena in *All's Well That Ends Well* are fatherless. With the important exceptions of *Romeo and Juliet* and *Hamlet*, the central families in the tragedies are either motherless (*King Lear*, *Othello*), fatherless (*Coriolanus*), or childless (*Macbeth*). Along with *Pericles*, moreover, *The Winter's Tale* is one of only two Shakespearean plays in which a mother gives birth in the course of the play and in which her child is shown years later as a young woman herself on the threshold of adult sexuality. As indicated above, destructively jealous men also appear in *Much Ado about Nothing* and *Othello*, but only *The Winter's Tale* depicts the horrific impact of a father's jealousy upon his children.

For all these reasons, *The Winter's Tale* focuses with unusual intensity on how gender identity and sexual desire affect the formation — and the dissolution — of the family. The documents in Chapter 2 will not provide a definitive explanation for Leontes' sudden outbreak of jealousy, which has often troubled readers and critics of the play. Rather, by broadly addressing the points of stress in early modern ideologies of gender and sexuality, the documents will suggest multiple ways of understanding the possible causes, consequences, and implications of Leontes' jealousy.

In an unsettling mixture of tones that might be considered characteristic of tragicomedy, the first three acts of *The Winter's Tale* present us with the sudden death of one child, Mamillius, and the birth and banishment of another child, Perdita. Since the lives of infants and young children in early modern England revolved around female caregiving, it is important to understand the gendered implications of contemporary notions and customs surrounding childbirth. From the onset of the mother's labor, to her post-delivery recovery (or "lying-in") period, to the churching ceremony through which she formally re-entered society approximately four weeks later, women organized the practical, symbolic, and social aspects of childbirth. Two of the documents in Chapter 2 address early modern beliefs about the responsibility of women — not only mothers, but also midwives and nurses — for the physical and mental well-being of infants and young children of both sexes. This responsibility gave women power in the household, but could also be the occasion for blame, suspicion, and resentment by men who were largely excluded from the processes of childbirth, nursing, and early childrearing. In his compendious manual *Of Domestical Duties* (1622), the Puritan minister William Gouge describes childbirth as a tense and even dangerous period in the life of a family. Gouge rebukes husbands who, like Leontes, destabilize their marriages by neglecting or psychologically abusing their pregnant wives; at the same time, he blames unsuccessful pregnancies on maternal neglect and abuse. In *Childbirth; Or, the Happy Delivery of Women* and *The Nursing of Children* (1612), the French physician Jacques Guillemeau acknowledges that midwives and nurses can have a positive or negative impact on young children; for this reason, he argues, it is crucial to make sure that only women of decent moral and physical character have contact with children.

Hermione, of course, is not only a mother but a queen. In early modern England, the birth of a royal child was greeted with great ceremony, as when Queen Anne gave birth in 1605 to Princess Mary. Recording the elaborate rituals and enormous costs surrounding Mary's delivery and christening, the seventeenth-century documents published by the nineteenth-century antiquaries John Nichols and Frederick Devon provide fascinating contexts for analyzing the political implications of the degrading circumstances in which Hermione gives birth. By calling public attention to the queen's supposed sexual transgression and labeling his daughter a bastard, Leontes sullies the symbolic display of sovereign power that usually attended a royal birth.

Chapter 2 further addresses the importance of female chastity in *The Winter's Tale* and in the patriarchal culture of early modern England by examining instances of breakdown in conjugal harmony. In John Milton's *Paradise Lost* (1674), a fallen Adam bitterly articulates the principle of male vulnerability to female seduction and betrayal — a culturally pervasive anxiety that helps to explain Leontes' seemingly baseless suspicions of Hermione. Leontes' intense fear of being publicly shamed by the sexual infidelity of his wife is illuminated by Benedetto Varchi's treatise on the causes and effects of jealousy, the *Blazon of Jealousy* (1615). Once he makes his own suspicions public, Leontes subjects Hermione to the putatively objective legal mechanisms for defining and punishing crimes such as treason. A narrative of the early-sixteenth-century trial of Henry VIII's wife Anne Boleyn, who was executed for adultery and treason, provides a historical model for the trial of Hermione. We will also consider how English laws about treason and "petty treason" (the murder of a husband by a wife or servant) reflect ideologies of gender that disadvantaged wives who were accused of crimes against their husbands.

The Winter's Tale is one of the few Shakespearean plays in which a child dies. In early modern England, as the birth of a royal child was greeted with public celebration, so the death of a royal child was met with public grieving. England witnessed an outpouring of such grief in 1612, about a year after the first performances of *The Winter's Tale*, when Prince Henry, King James's oldest son and heir to the throne, died suddenly at the age of eighteen. Robert Allyne's *Funeral Elegies* (1613), a poem that extravagantly laments the political consequences of Prince Henry's death, foregrounds the strikingly muted response to Mamillius's death in *The Winter's Tale*. The recollections of Prince Henry's behavior as a young boy recorded in William Haydon's *True Picture and Relation of Prince Henry* (1634) establish a context for understanding Mamillius's role in the domestic and political life of the royal family. That Leontes does not protect his young son from knowledge of his mother's supposed sexual transgression might make better sense (though not better parenting) when we understand King James's eagerness to cultivate Prince Henry's identity as a little man, a miniature image of his own royal manhood. Finally, Ben Jonson's verses on the deaths of his infant daughter and young son provide insight, poetically mediated though it be, into one seventeenth-century father's attempts to come to terms with such terrible loss.

Authority and Resistance

> that ever I
> Had squared me to thy counsel! (5.1.51–52)

If *The Winter's Tale* lacks the tragic grandeur and horror of a *King Lear* or *Macbeth*, it also avoids the sharp focus on matters of state characteristic of Shakespeare's political tragedies and English history plays. In the tragedies and histories, formal speeches and soliloquies often serve to lay out moral and political positions about sovereignty. For instance, in *Macbeth*, Malcolm explicitly defines the "king-becoming graces" as "justice, verity, temperance, stableness, / Bounty, perseverance, mercy, [and] lowliness" (4.3.93–95). The actions of the kings in the histories and tragedies, then, can be judged not only against conventional ideas about sovereignty, but also against their own claims about what kings are and do. Characters in *The Winter's Tale* do not articulate theories of monarchical authority so directly; nonetheless, the conflicts between Leontes and his counselors evoke contemporary political debates about the limits of royal prerogative and the role of counsel. The documents in Chapter 3 address such debates from various perspectives, royalist to republican.

When King James VI of Scotland became King James I of England in 1603, he bestowed on Shakespeare's playing company the honor of serving as his official troupe, the King's Men. Consequently, many critics have argued that the tragedies and romances Shakespeare wrote after 1603 reflect — albeit indirectly and incompletely — the tastes, interests, and political philosophies of his royal patron. Whether Shakespeare takes a royalist line in any of his plays is certainly debatable, but it is true that his later plays address political issues that deeply concerned the king. One productive context for *The Winter's Tale* is provided by King James's own political treatise *The True Law of Free Monarchies* (1598), which argues that monarchy, "resembling the divinity, approacheth nearest to perfection" (see p. 240). James's exposition of the monarch's extremely broad powers lays bare some of the reasoning behind Leontes' assumption of his own infallibility in the face of his counselors' imprecations and demands.

As James's own theory of monarchy reveals, however, the human capacity for error lies in the unbridgeable gap between "approaching" divinity and being divine. Constance Jordan suggests that the "most important theme" of Shakespeare's romances as a group concerns "the ruler's status as a mortal rather than a god or godlike creature" (12–13). Leontes' capacity for error — the possibility that he is wrong about Hermione's infidelity — is the constant theme of his counselors, yet he recognizes this truth too late. In his essay "Of Counsel" (1612), Sir Francis Bacon, a Member of Parliament and a powerful minister under King James, takes a moderate line on monarchical power, instructing the king on the wise use of political advisers. Assured of his god-like ability to penetrate the secret plots of his wife and subjects, Leontes refuses to heed the warnings of his counselors who have the interests of the kingdom in mind. In his political treatise *De Jure Regni apud Scotos* (1579), the republican theorist George Buchanan goes further than Bacon in advocating violent resistance to a king who rules unjustly. Although no one in *The Winter's Tale* voices such a politically radical position, it is important to realize that such positions were being expressed in Shakespeare's culture. Not everybody was convinced of the transparent truth of arguments for the divinity of kings and the wickedness of rebellion. By evoking contemporary debates about tyranny and resistance, Shakespeare (whether deliberately or inadvertently) exposes King James's position as just that — an ideological position in a debate, not an absolute and universal "law" that admits no possible alternatives. Simply to reveal that James's position is neither natural nor inevitable is already to weaken its metaphysical claims.

The most vocal dissident against Leontes' absolutism is Paulina. Readers of the play have often admired Paulina's courage, integrity, and plain-spoken exposure of Leontes' folly, yet assertive and outspoken women were not always regarded with sympathy in early modern England. Paulina's overt resistance to Leontes' authority as husband and king sharply evokes contemporary debates over the legitimacy of female speech. From the very first scene of the play, in which Leontes charges Hermione to persuade Polixenes to remain in Sicilia, the potency and danger of female speech in a patriarchal culture is at issue in *The Winter's Tale*.

To begin with, the play's title alludes to the familiar domestic scenario of children gathered around a winter fire, attending to a tale told by a mother, nurse, or maid (Figure 1). In *Oral and Literate Culture in England 1500–1700*, Adam Fox explains that in early modern England "the world of the household in which gender roles often conditioned women to operate and in which children were nurtured had a rich and distinctive oral tradition of its own," including "old wives' stories" enjoyed "around that hub of domestic life and focus of narrative tradition, the winter fireside" (174, 188). On this count, Fox cites the seventeenth-century writer John Aubrey, who remembers the days when "the fashion was for old women and maids to tell fabulous stories nighttimes, and of sprites and walking of ghosts, etc." (quoted in Fox 188). As Sara Mendelson and Patricia Crawford observe, women "were repositories of oral traditions of all sorts: literary, musical, poetical, magical,

FIGURE I *Frontispiece from Charles Perrault*, Histoires du temps passé, ou les contes de ma mere l'oye *(1786). Originally published in France in 1697, Charles Perrault's collection of fairy tales included "Little Red Riding-Hood," "Sleeping Beauty," and "Puss in Boots." The frontispiece illustration to this edition of 1786 depicts an archetypal scenario of the "winter's tale": an old servant spinning by the hearth, telling a story to three enthralled children. A sign on the wall reads "Contes de Ma Mere L'oye," or "Mother Goose Tales."*

pragmatic, mythical, and historical." For women, in fact, speech was the "primary medium for transmitting not only superstitions and magical lore, but collective feminine experience about housewifery, medicine (particularly gynecology and obstetrics), gardening, cookery, childcare, textile and other work skills, and a host of philosophical as well as practical concerns" (Mendelson and Crawford 217).

Despite the importance and scope of verbally transmitted female knowledge, women's speech could be trivialized through the condescending notion of "old wives' tales." Mary Ellen Lamb explains that the phrase "old wives' tales" served an ideological function in early modern England, marking a value-laden distinction between "literate male culture" and "oral female culture" that belied the existence of illiterate men and literate women ("Old Wives' Tales" 28–29). Quick to dismiss the popular lore of women as superstitious nonsense, John Aubrey writes of "silly wenches" who, led by "foolish curiosity," perform magical love rituals "they have received by tradition from their mother, perhaps, or nurse" (quoted in Fox 180). Significantly, Leontes' rejection of the truthful speech of Hermione and Paulina launches the play into tragedy; the possibility for a comic ending depends on Leontes' capacity for change, his developing the ability to value female language and the autonomous selfhood it expresses.

The documents in Chapter 3 provide evidence of a vibrant and vigorous debate over the legitimacy of female speech in early modern England. In his wedding sermon *A Bride Bush: Or, A Direction for Married Persons* (1619), the Puritan minister William Whately insists that the virtuous Christian wife must speak with reverence to her husband. Although Leontes shares Whately's loathing of outspoken women, his own boisterous railing against Paulina makes him sound less like a moralizing preacher and more like the unruly pamphleteer Joseph Swetnam, whose misogynistic diatribe *The Arraignment of Lewd, Idle, Froward, and Unconstant Women* (1615) ignited a heated controversy about gender relations. In *A Muzzle for Melastomus* (1617), Rachel Speght, the nineteen-year-old daughter of a London minister, published a passionate defense of women that challenged Swetnam's outrageous caricature of women as sharp-tongued, manipulative shrews. Like Paulina, Speght metaphorically arms herself to battle a slanderer of women, all the while insisting that her aims are to restore, not to subvert, social and domestic order. Finally, we will look at a popular ballad, "A Merry Dialogue Betwixt a Married Man and his Wife" (1628), in which a husband and wife negotiate with each other for a fair balance of authority and respect within the household.

Encountering Nature

> Come on,
> And bid us welcome to your sheep-shearing,
> As your good flock shall prosper   (4.4.68–70)

Like Shakespeare's late plays *Pericles* (1607–08) and *The Tempest* (1611), *The Winter's Tale* contains the typical romance episode of an adventure — and loss — at sea. In romances, the forces of nature can seem capriciously destructive, but the suffering they cause is often revealed to play a role in a larger drama of familial reconciliation and reconstitution. Pericles, for instance, believes that his wife has perished during a terrible storm at sea, but years later a dream sent by the goddess Diana directs him to reunite with her. *The Tempest* opens with a violent storm that shipwrecks the Neapolitan court, separating the king from his son. However, Prospero, who has magically caused the tempest, uses the occasion to orchestrate a familial and political reconciliation with his former enemies. In *The Winter's Tale*, Antigonus and the sailors who bring the infant Perdita to Bohemia all perish, but Perdita survives, and her fortunate discovery by an Old Shepherd ensures that, in the words of Apollo's oracle, "that which is lost" will one day be found (3.2.131).

Yet not everything that has been lost will be restored. Perdita's safe return to Sicilia sixteen years later seals for Paulina the painful truth that her husband is "never to be found again" (5.3.136), and recalls for the audience the horror of the earlier scene in which Antigonus is devoured by a bear. The first two documents in Chapter 4 provide contexts for understanding the strange appearance of a ravenous bear in *The Winter's Tale*. Edward Topsell's account of the typical behavior and character of bears in the *History of Four-Footed Beasts* (1607), a compilation of historical, zoological, and mythical knowledge, suggests why Shakespeare might have chosen this particular beast (as opposed, say, to a lion or wolf) as the instrument of Antigonus's demise. *The True and Perfect Description of Three Voyages* (1609), a popular travel narrative by the Dutch writer Gerrit de Veer, is a very different kind of text from Topsell's *History*. Graphically describing deadly encounters between bears and sailors adventuring in the northern seas, de Veer conveys the danger and excitement of journeys to unknown lands, a staple of the romance genre of which *The Winter's Tale* is a part.

Through its pastoral setting and emphasis on youthful romance, the sheep-shearing festival that dominates act 4 of *The Winter's Tale* looks back to earlier Shakespearean comedies such as *A Midsummer Night's Dream* and *As You Like It*. The central scenes of these comedies take place in the forest or the pasture: the "green world" environment of holiday escape from the more rigid, legalistic, confines of the city and the court. In *As You Like It*, the holiday atmosphere is epitomized by the Fool's reliance on the word "if": a kind of shorthand for experiences that are conditional, provisional, or experimental, and that consequently encourage a perception of truth as relative or contingent. Shakespearean green worlds typically operate under the premise of *what if . . . ?* During the sheep-shearing festival of *The Winter's Tale*, the premise of "what if?" suggests that the tragic course of events in Sicilia was not inevitable: jealous husbands and tyrannous kings need not always succeed in imposing their destructive wills upon their families and subjects. Hence the King of Bohemia is not the central figure at the sheep-shearing feast. Here, Perdita is queen, and no matter how brutal the enraged king's threats, the shepherdess comprehends a higher truth of human dignity in observing that the "selfsame sun that shines upon [the king's] court / Hides not his visage" from her humble cottage (4.4.424–425). In the Bohemian countryside, against the background of a fertile landscape warmed by a summer sun, conflicts between men and women, fathers and children, and kings and subjects play out in a more hopeful register than they do in the wintry Sicilian court.

For the sunny optimism of the sheep-shearing episode, Shakespeare draws upon the familiar conventions of Renaissance pastoral poetry. Pastoral poetry, which idealizes the innocence and harmony of rural life, does not, of course, portray the actual experiences of shepherds and farmers. Rather, it provides a highly stylized venue for distinguishing the values of the country from those of the city or the court, and for staging debates about the rival claims of nature and art. The archetypical pastoral debate between Perdita and Polixenes concerning the superiority of art or nature is illuminated by *The Art of English Poesy* (1589), in which George Puttenham explains how poets can use art to enhance the natural beauty of language. Both the sheep-shearing festival and the play's final scene in Paulina's chapel revolve around the power of art, as an instrument of redemption or betrayal. If one sees art as deceptive "artifice," one might consider pastoral poetry to be a kind of lie, in that it presents the dirty and strenuous life of shepherds as one of contemplation and ease. Michael Drayton's *Ninth Eclogue* (1606), a poetic rendition of an English sheep-shearing festival, exemplifies this idealization of the social, moral, and political virtues of rural life. In contrast, John Fitzherbert's *Book of Husbandry* (1598 ed.), a practical manual for farmers, describes the unpleasant jobs of washing and shearing sheep. Whereas Drayton celebrates the innocence of pastoral play and Fitzherbert presents the drudgery of pastoral work, Philip Stubbes's *Anatomy of Abuses* (1583) strenuously objects to the theatrical artifice and moral abandon typical of holiday celebrations. Strangely enough, perhaps, in *The Winter's Tale* it is Perdita who similarly objects to her complicity in the theatrical deceptions of the sheep-shearing festival.

Chapter 4 concludes with documents about rogues and peddlers that address Autolycus's role in the play. From one perspective, Autolycus, whose name means "the wolf himself," is a dangerous interloper in a pastoral environment: he even calls the simple country folk on whom he preys "the herd" (4.4.585). During the reigns of Elizabeth and James, parliamentary statues and royal proclamations attempted to distinguish rogues — masterless men with no fixed abode or vocation — from industrious peddlers, who traveled through small towns and rural areas selling clothes, household goods, and recreational items. But in practice it was sometimes difficult to tell a wandering peddler from a wandering rogue, and both kinds of men, through their geographical mobility and their facility at role-playing, could provoke fears about the transgression of social hierarchy. The Elizabethan statute (1597) and Jacobean royal proclamation (1618) excerpted in Chapter 4 speak to the anxiety and hostility directed at masterless vagrants such as Autolycus.

As the Elizabethan statute's grouping of peddlers with "common players" and "minstrels" indicates, however, Autolycus might be defined not simply as a dangerous criminal, but also as a popular entertainer. At the sheep-shearing festival, he sings and hawks entertaining ballads about women who give birth to money-bags. Chapter 4 includes a sixteenth-century ballad, *The Description of a Rare or Rather Most Monstrous Fish* (1566), in which a sensationalistic natural wonder is saddled with a typically moralistic commentary that interprets monsters as signs of divine wrath. A ballad-seller like Autolycus could be scorned as a purveyor of ridiculous lies or appreciated as a messenger of moral truths that were available to those who could interpret properly. Autolycus also plays a double role in furnishing the sheep-shearing revelers with colorful ribbons and garments that might be regarded either as worthless trash or as harmless signs of holiday cheer. Whereas Autolycus himself mocks the shepherds for snatching up his trifles, Polixenes (disguised as a guest of the feast) chides Florizel for not having "ransacked / The peddler's silken treasury" for "knacks" that would convey his affection for Perdita (4.4.327–328). The 1618 Proclamation reproduced in Chapter 4 reflects a similar ambivalence about peddlers as those who furnish both "superstitious trumpery" and necessary household items.

While entertaining the Bohemian revelers with ballads and knickknacks, Autolycus entertains us by wittily fleecing the doltish Clown. Robert Greene's pamphlets, the *Second* and *Third and Last Part of Cony-Catching* (1592), describe the tricks used by clever London con artists to rob similarly unsuspecting gulls. Although Greene publishes these pamphlets under the pretense of revealing criminal scams to the public, the tales encourage us to admire the improvisational wit of the rogues and thereby imply that laughter at a well-played trick, rather than horror at criminal activity, might be the appropriate response to such knavery. Like Greene's talented cut-purses, Autolycus functions as a theatrical entertainer — a double of the talented comic actor who played his part at the Globe — and as a skilled rhetorician who can pass himself off as a victim of robbery, an industrious peddler, or a haughty courtier.

Hermione's Statue

> Her natural posture!
> Chide me, dear stone, that I may say indeed
> Thou art Hermione   (5.3.23–5)

Each of the four late Shakespearean romances ends with a family reunion orchestrated through the intervention of a god or a character with godlike powers. In *The Tempest*, Prospero uses magic to shipwreck his brother on the island where he and his daughter have lived in exile for twelve years. In *Cymbeline*, a dream vision of the god Jupiter assures Posthumus that his suffering will soon end; Jupiter's promise is fulfilled in the final scene when Posthumous is reunited with his estranged wife, Innogen. The eponymous hero of *Pericles* mistakenly believes that his wife Thaisa has died in childbirth and that his daughter Marina has died while in the care of a foster family. Pericles mourns for years until a chance encounter reunites him with Marina; father and daughter are subsequently reunited with Thaisa after a dream vision of the goddess Diana reveals her location.

For characters as well as audience members, the implausible events of romance typically evoke wonder, "the natural effect of miracles, real or apparent" (Cunningham 78). In *The Winter's Tale* as in the other romances, wonder is often the response to unexpectedly happy turns of fortune or providence, as with Perdita's return to Sicilia. Stunned into silence by the revelation of Perdita's identity, Leontes and Camillo, we are told, manifest the "passion of wonder," yet "the wisest beholder, that knew no more but seeing, could not say if th'importance were joy or sorrow" (5.2.12–14). As the "shocked limit of feeling," wonder expresses an emotional tension entirely appropriate for the tragicomic tonality of Shakespearean romance (Cunningham 92).

The harmonious endings of Shakespeare's romances depend upon wonderful recognitions and reunions, but deception and artifice play an unusually large role in the resolution of *The Winter's Tale*. In *Cymbeline*, Innogen disguises herself as a boy while separated from her husband, but Hermione allows her husband to live for sixteen years under the misapprehension that she is dead. Whereas in *Pericles* the audience but not Pericles knows that Thaisa has survived her near-death experience, Shakespeare hides Hermione's survival from the audience as well as from Leontes. And whereas Prospero needs magic to regain his lost dukedom, Paulina only pretends to use magic: Hermione's "resurrection" is not a supernatural event but a scripted theatrical spectacle. Nonetheless, when Hermione's statue suddenly begins to move, we, too, are likely to experience wonder at the mystery of a living work of art.

The documents in Chapter 5 examine wonder as an effect of religious faith. As an object of hushed admiration in Paulina's chapel, Hermione's statue resembles the sculpted and painted images of saints, particularly the Virgin Mary, to which early modern Catholics paid devotion. Whereas Protestant reformers regarded such practices as idolatry — the superstitious worship of senseless images — Catholics believed that saints could work physical and spiritual miracles for the faithful who visited their shrines and chapels. The Sicilian court's homage to a stone image in a chapel thus speaks to theological controversies between Catholics and Protestants concerning the existence of miracles in the modern world. Could paying devotion to saints produce genuine miracles, as Catholic writers such as A. G. claimed in *The Widow's Mite* (1619), or were such miracles really just tricks, delusions, and lies, as the Protestant William Crashaw charged in *The Jesuits' Gospel* (1610)? Because Hermione's possibly miraculous "resurrection" represents the culmination of Leontes' sixteen-year ritual of penitent devotion at her tomb, the statue scene raises comparable questions about the efficacy of repentance. Chapter 5 addresses such questions through the Elizabethan *Homily of Repentance* (1563), the Anglican Church's orthodox statement of the relationship between outward ceremonies and inward faith.

Although questions of faith are certainly pertinent to the scene in Paulina's chapel, from another perspective what Paulina provides her audience is a shocking, and possibly illicit, spectacle: the resurrection of a woman who has been dead for sixteen years. The second set of documents in Chapter 5 confronts the aura of transgressive desecration that heightens the tension of the statue scene. Paulina's insistence that she is neither "assisted / By wicked powers" nor engaged in "unlawful business" reveals the delicacy of her position (5.3.90–91, 96). It is hardly surprising that Paulina disavows any connection with witchcraft, considering that in *The Discovery of Witchcraft* (1584) Reginald Scot accuses supposed "witches" of using theatrical tricks to perform false miracles such as raising the dead. From Scot's skeptical position, Paulina's promise to animate Hermione's statue might be regarded as a form of pseudo-witchcraft, a blasphemous claim to possess powers that belong to God alone. Although Paulina does not actually raise Hermione from the grave, Thomas Middleton's sensationalistic *Second Maiden's Tragedy* (1611), performed in the same year as *The Winter's Tale*, depicts the desecration of a woman's corpse. When the Lady in Middleton's tragedy commits suicide in order to preserve her chastity, the lustful Tyrant who has brought her to this end disinters her body and brings it to his private chambers. But whereas the display of a dead woman's body in Middleton's tragedy constitutes a shocking violation of moral, political, and spiritual virtues, the theatrical resurrection of a "dead" woman in Shakespeare's romance brings to a tragic sequence of events the opportunity for redemption and forgiveness.

The myth of the sculptor Pygmalion, recounted in Ovid's *Metamorphoses*, hovers precariously between taboo sexuality and transformative love. Like the Tyrant in *The Second Maiden's Tragedy*, Pygmalion seeks to enjoy a forbidden object of desire: not a dead woman but a "dead" piece of ivory he has carved into the likeness of a woman. Yet Pygmalion loves his ivory lady so deeply that Venus, the goddess of love, rewards his devotion by giving the statue life. The parallel between the vivification of Hermione's statue and the vivification of Pygmalion's statue might imply that Leontes is similarly rewarded for his sincere penitence and his pious acceptance of Paulina's advice to trust in providence. Nonetheless, the transformation of Pygmalion's statue into a living woman seems to reflect a male fantasy of designing the perfect wife — a fantasy that is particularly troubling in the context of *The Winter's Tale*. Has Hermione become such an ideal woman to be (re)possessed by Leontes? Or might Paulina and Hermione be debunking the fantasy of possessing the ideal woman by showing Leontes that such a "miracle" can only be achieved as a temporary theatrical illusion?

The myth of Pygmalion also concerns the power and value of art. The artistic contexts of the statue scene will be illuminated by Henry Peacham's discussion in "Of Antiquities" (1634) of the value of collecting ancient statues. When *The Winter's Tale* was staged in 1611, art collecting was just beginning to be recognized in England as a legitimate aristocratic pursuit. Peacham associates the cultural status of connoisseurship with the social status of aristocratic rank when he praises one of the most notable art collectors of the age, the Earl of Arundel (Figure 2), for being "as great for his noble patronage of arts and ancient learning, as for his birth and place" (see p. 413). Peacham's treatise encourages us to consider the possible social implications of Paulina's role as an art connoisseur, the owner of a "gallery" full of "singularities" that she displays to privileged visitors (5.3.10, 12). Hermione might have her own reasons for wishing to return to public life as

FIGURE 2 *Daniel Mytens,* Lord Arundel *(1618). Arundel points to the classical statuary displayed in his gallery.*

a "royal piece" of art (5.3.38), but what does Paulina have to gain from presenting herself as the patron of the "rare Italian master, Julio Romano" and as the owner of his "[m]asterly" statue (5.2.74, 5.3.65)?

The tragicomic tone of *The Winter's Tale* is perhaps most poignantly rendered in its final scenes, where the joy of reunion is tempered by the regret that accompanies memories of betrayal, loss, and separation. When Hermione returns to life, she embraces Leontes but does not speak to him, and her silence makes it difficult to assess whether or not she has fully forgiven him. It is a critical commonplace that Shakespeare's late plays conclude with an emphasis on "reconciliation and reunion" (Frye 18). But in performance, the choices made by the director, actors, and designers of a particular production can significantly affect an audience's experience of the delicate balance between harmony and dissonance, redemption and suffering, that usually concludes a Shakespearean romance. Examining accounts of notable performances of the statue scene from the nineteenth, twentieth, and twenty-first centuries will provide an opportunity to consider how different staging choices might change the balance of comedy and tragedy in *The Winter's Tale*.

This edition will have served its purpose if the documents help readers to appreciate how *The Winter's Tale* is not what Hermione's statue initially appears to be: a cold, inert aesthetic object to be admired in passive wonder. Rather, like that statue's transformation into a moving, speaking subject, this remarkable play might be better understood as a process, a site of contact between past and present that stimulates our imagination and demands our engagement.

PART ONE

WILLIAM SHAKESPEARE

The Winter's Tale

Edited by David Bevington

The Winter's Tale

><

[MOPSA, } *Shepherdesses.*]
[DORCAS, }

[A MARINER
A JAILER
Two LADIES *attending Hermione*
Two SERVANTS *attending Leontes*
One or more LORDS *attending Leontes*
An OFFICER *of the court*
A GENTLEMAN *attending Leontes*
Three GENTLEMEN *of the court of Sicilia*
A SERVANT *of the Old Shepherd*

TIME, *as Chorus*]

Other Lords and Gentlemen, [*Ladies, Officers,*] *and Servants; Shepherds and
Shepherdesses;* [*Twelve Countrymen disguised as Satyrs*]

SCENE: *Sicilia, and Bohemia.*]

ACT 1, SCENE 1°

Enter Camillo and Archidamus.

ARCHIDAMUS: If you shall chance, Camillo, to visit Bohemia on the like
occasion whereon my services are now on foot,° you shall see, as I have
said, great difference betwixt our Bohemia and your Sicilia.

CAMILLO: I think this coming summer the King of Sicilia means to pay
Bohemia° the visitation which he justly owes him.   5

ARCHIDAMUS: Wherein our entertainment shall shame us, we will be justified in our loves;° for indeed —

CAMILLO: Beseech you —

ARCHIDAMUS: Verily, I speak it in the freedom of my knowledge.° We cannot with such magnificence — in so rare — I know not what to say. We   10
will give you sleepy° drinks, that your senses, unintelligent° of our insuffi-
cience, may, though they cannot praise us, as little accuse us.

ACT 1, SCENE 1. **Location:** Sicilia. The court of Leontes.   **1–2. on the . . . foot:** on an occasion like this one that I am engaged in (attending on King Polixenes).   **5. Bohemia:** the
King of Bohemia. (Also at line 16.)   **6–7. Wherein . . . loves:** in whatever way our attempts
to entertain you will shame us by falling short, we will make up for by our affection.
9. in . . . knowledge: as my knowledge entitles me to speak.   **11. sleepy:** sleep-inducing.
unintelligent: unaware.

CAMILLO: You pay a great deal too dear for what's given freely.

ARCHIDAMUS: Believe me, I speak as my understanding instructs me and as mine honesty puts it to utterance. 15

CAMILLO: Sicilia° cannot show himself overkind to Bohemia. They were trained together in their childhoods, and there rooted betwixt them then such an affection which cannot choose but branch° now. Since their more mature dignities and royal necessities made separation of their society,° their encounters, though not personal,° hath been royally at- 20 torneyed° with interchange of gifts, letters, loving embassies, that they have seemed to be together though absent, shook hands as over a vast,° and embraced as it were from the ends of opposed winds.° The heavens° continue their loves!

ARCHIDAMUS: I think there is not in the world either malice or matter 25 to alter it. You have an unspeakable comfort of° your young prince Mamillius. It is a gentleman of the greatest promise that ever came into my note.°

CAMILLO: I very well agree with you in the hopes of him. It is a gallant child, one that indeed physics the subject,° makes old hearts fresh. They 30 that went on crutches ere he was born desire yet their life° to see him a man.

ARCHIDAMUS: Would they else be content to die?

CAMILLO: Yes, if there were no other excuse why they should desire to live.

ARCHIDAMUS: If the King had no son, they would desire to live on 35 crutches till he had one.°   *Exeunt.*

ACT 1, SCENE 2°

Enter Leontes, Hermione, Mamillius, Polixenes, Camillo.

POLIXENES:

Nine changes of the wat'ry star° hath been
The shepherd's note° since we° have left our throne

---

16. **Sicilia:** the King of Sicilia.   18. **branch:** put forth new growth, flourish. (Also perhaps with opposite and unconscious suggestion of "divide.")   19–20. **their society:** their being together.   20. **personal:** in person.   20–21. **attorneyed:** carried out by deputy.   22. **vast:** boundless space.   23. **ends . . . winds:** i.e., opposite ends of the earth.   **The heavens:** may the heavens.   26. **of:** in the person of.   28. **note:** observation.   30. **physics the subject:** brings health to the subjects of this kingdom.   31. **their life:** to continue living.   35–36. **If . . . one:** even if there were no living heir to the throne, these old people would still wish to go on living in hopes of one.   ACT 1, SCENE 2. **Location:** The same.   1. **wat'ry star:** moon.   2. **note:** observation.   **we:** I. (The royal "we.")

Without a burden.° Time as long again
Would be filled up, my brother, with our thanks,
And yet we should for perpetuity°   5
Go hence in debt. And therefore, like a cipher,
Yet standing in rich place,° I multiply
With one "We thank you" many thousands more
That go before it.

LEONTES: Stay your thanks awhile
And pay them when you part.

POLIXENES: Sir, that's tomorrow.   10
I am questioned by my fears of what may chance
Or breed upon our absence, that may blow
No sneaping winds at home to make us say,
"This is put forth too truly."° Besides, I have stayed
To tire your royalty.

LEONTES: We are tougher, brother,   15
Than you can put us to't.°

POLIXENES: No longer stay.

LEONTES:
One sev'nnight° longer.

POLIXENES: Very sooth,° tomorrow.

LEONTES:
We'll part the time° between 's, then, and in that
I'll no gainsaying.°

POLIXENES: Press me not, beseech you, so.
There is no tongue that moves, none, none i' th' world   20
So soon as yours could win me. So it should now,
Were there necessity in your request, although
'Twere needful I denied it. My affairs
Do even drag me homeward, which to hinder
Were in your love a whip° to me, my stay   25
To you a charge° and trouble. To save both,
Farewell, our brother.

---

3. **burden:** occupant. 5. **for perpetuity:** forever. 6–7. **like . . . place:** like a zero at the end of a number, increasing its value by powers of ten, though of itself without value. 11–14. **I am . . . truly:** I am anxious about what may happen in my absence, especially a stirring up of envy and backbiting that would cause me to say my fears were all too plausible. 16. **Than . . . to't:** than anything you can do to try me. 17. **sev'nnight:** week. **Very sooth:** truly. 18. **part the time:** split the difference, i.e., divide a week in two. 19. **I'll no gainsaying:** I won't take "no" for an answer. 25. **Were . . . whip:** would be a punishment to me, though done through love. 26. **charge:** expense, burden.

LEONTES: Tongue-tied, our Queen? Speak you.

HERMIONE:

I had thought, sir, to have held my peace until
You had drawn oaths from him not to stay.° You, sir,
Charge him too coldly. Tell him you are sure   30
All in Bohemia's well; this satisfaction
The bygone day proclaimed.° Say° this to him,
He's beat from his best ward.°

LEONTES: Well said, Hermione.

HERMIONE:

To tell° he longs to see his son were strong.°
But let him say so then, and let him go.   35
But let him swear so and he shall not stay;°
We'll thwack him hence with distaffs.°
[*To Polixenes*] Yet of your royal presence I'll adventure°
The borrow° of a week. When at Bohemia
You take my lord, I'll give him my commission   40
To let him there a month behind the gest
Prefixed for 's parting.° — Yet, good deed,° Leontes,
I love thee not a jar o' th' clock behind
What lady she her lord.° — You'll stay?

POLIXENES: No, madam.

HERMIONE:

Nay, but you will?

POLIXENES: I may not, verily.   45

HERMIONE:

Verily?
You put me off with limber° vows; but I,
Though you would seek t'unsphere the stars with oaths,
Should yet say, "Sir, no going." Verily,
You shall not go. A lady's "verily" is   50
As potent as a lord's. Will you go yet?

28–29. I . . . to stay: i.e., I almost thought that you were going to get him to swear he *won't* stay, before I got a chance to say anything. **31–32.** this . . . proclaimed: yesterday brought news to satisfy on that score. **32.** Say: if you say. **33.** ward: defensive posture. (A fencing term.) **34.** tell: tell us that. strong: a strong argument. **36.** he shall not stay: i.e., we wouldn't let him stay even if he wanted to. **37.** distaffs: sticks used in spinning, here employed as a domestic kind of weapon. **38.** adventure: risk. **39.** borrow: borrowing. **41–42.** To . . . parting: to let him stay there a month longer than the originally agreed-upon time for his departure. **42.** good deed: indeed. **43–44.** I love . . . lord: I love you not even a tiny bit (literally, a tick of the clock) less than any noble lady loves her husband. **47.** limber: limp.

Force me to keep you as a prisoner,
Not like a guest: so you shall pay your fees°
When you depart, and save your thanks. How say you?
My prisoner or my guest? By your dread "verily,"   55
One of them you shall be.

POLIXENES: Your guest, then, madam.
To be your prisoner should import offending,°
Which is for me less easy to commit
Than you to punish.

HERMIONE: Not your jailer, then,
But your kind hostess. Come, I'll question you   60
Of my lord's tricks and yours when you were boys.
You were pretty lordings then?

POLIXNES: We were, fair Queen,
Two lads that thought there was no more behind°
But such a day tomorrow as today,
And to be boy eternal.

HERMIONE: Was not my lord   65
The verier wag° o'th' two?

POLIXENES:
We were as twinned lambs that did frisk i'th' sun
And bleat the one at th'other. What we changed°
Was innocence for innocence; we knew not
The doctrine of ill-doing, nor dreamed   70
That any did. Had we pursued that life,
And our weak spirits ne'er been higher reared
With stronger blood,° we should have answered heaven
Boldly "Not guilty," the imposition cleared
Hereditary ours.°

HERMIONE: By this we gather   75
You have tripped since.

POLIXENES: Oh, my most sacred lady,
Temptations have since then been born to 's, for
In those unfledged° days was my wife a girl;

---

53. **fees:** payments demanded by jailers of prisoners at the time of their release.   57. **import offending:** imply my having offended.   63. **behind:** still to come.   66. **The verier wag:** truly the more mischievous.   68. **changed:** exchanged.   73. **stronger blood:** mature sexual passions.   74–75. **the imposition . . . ours:** i.e., being freed from original sin itself (if we had continued in that state); or, excepting of course the original sin that is the common condition of all mortals.   78. **unfledged:** not yet feathered, i.e., immature.

Your precious self had then not crossed the eyes
Of my young playfellow.

HERMIONE: Grace to boot!°   80
Of this make no conclusion,° lest you say
Your queen and I are devils. Yet go on.
Th'offenses we have made you do we'll answer,
If you first sinned with us, and that with us
You did continue fault, and that you slipped not   85
With any but with us.

LEONTES: Is he won yet?°

HERMIONE:
He'll stay, my lord.

LEONTES: At my request he would not.
Hermione, my dearest, thou never spok'st
To better purpose.

HERMIONE: Never?

LEONTES: Never but once.

HERMIONE:
What? Have I twice said well? When was 't before?   90
I prithee, tell me. Cram 's with praise and make 's
As fat as tame things. One good deed dying tongueless°
Slaughters a thousand waiting upon that.°
Our praises are our wages. You may ride 's
With one soft kiss a thousand furlongs ere   95
With spur we heat° an acre. But to th' goal:°
My last good deed was to entreat his stay.
What was my first? It has an elder sister,
Or I mistake you. Oh, would her name were Grace!
But once before I spoke to the purpose. When?   100
Nay, let me have 't; I long.

LEONTES: Why, that was when
Three crabbèd months had soured themselves to death
Ere I could make thee open thy white hand
And clap° thyself my love. Then didst thou utter,
"I am yours forever."

---

80. **Grace to boot!**: Heaven help me!   81. **Of . . . conclusion**: don't follow your implied line of reasoning to its logical conclusion.   86. **Is he won yet?**: (Leontes has been out of hearing for much of their conversation.)   92. **tongueless**: unpraised, unsung.   93. **Slaughters . . . that**: i.e., will inhibit many other good deeds that would have been inspired by that praise. 96. **heat**: traverse as in a race. **to th' goal**: to come to the point.   104. **clap**: clasp hands, pledge.

HERMIONE: 'Tis grace indeed.   105
  Why, lo you now, I have spoke to th' purpose twice:
  The one forever earned a royal husband,
  Th'other for some while a friend.   [*She gives her hand to Polixenes.*]
  LEONTES: [*aside*]   Too hot, too hot!
  To mingle friendship far is mingling bloods.°
  I have *tremor cordis*° on me. My heart dances,   110
  But not for joy, not joy. This entertainment°
  May a free face° put on, derive a liberty
  From heartiness, from bounty, fertile bosom,°
  And well become the agent.° 'T may, I grant.
  But to be paddling palms and pinching fingers,   115
  As now they are, and making practiced smiles
  As in a looking glass, and then to sigh, as 'twere
  The mort° o'th' deer; oh, that is entertainment
  My bosom likes not, nor my brows.° — Mamillius,
  Art thou my boy?
  MAMILLIUS: Ay, my good lord.
  LEONTES: I'fecks,°   120
  Why, that's my bawcock.° What, hast smutched thy nose?
  They say it is a copy out of mine. Come, captain,
  We must be neat; not neat, but cleanly,° captain.
  And yet the steer, the heifer, and the calf
  Are all called neat. — Still virginaling°   125
  Upon his palm? — How now, you wanton° calf?
  Art thou my calf?
  MAMILLIUS: Yes, if you will, my lord.
  LEONTES:
  Thou want'st a rough pash and the shoots that I have°
  To be full° like me. Yet they say we are
  Almost as like as eggs. Women say so,   130

---

109. **mingling bloods:** (Sexual intercourse was thought to produce a mingling of bloods.) 110. *tremor cordis:* fluttering of the heart. 111. **entertainment:** i.e., of Polixenes by Hermione. 112. **free face:** innocent appearance. 113. **fertile bosom:** i.e., generous affection. 114. **well . . . agent:** do credit to the doer. 118. **mort:** note sounded on a horn at the death of the hunted deer. 119. **brows:** (Alludes to cuckolds' horns, the supposed badge of men whose wives are unfaithful.) 120. **I'fecks:** in faith. 121. **bawcock:** i.e., fine fellow. (French *beau coq*.) 123. **not . . . cleanly:** (Leontes changes the word because *neat* also means "cattle" and hence reminds him of cuckolds' horns.) 125. **virginaling:** touching hands, as in playing on the virginals, a keyboard instrument. 126. **wanton:** frisky. 128. **Thou . . . have:** you lack a shaggy head and the horns that I have. (Again alluding to cuckolds' horns.) 129. **full:** fully.

That will say anything. But were they false
As o'erdyed blacks,° as wind, as waters, false
As dice are to be wished by one that fixes
No bourn twixt his and mine,° yet were it true
To say this boy were like me. Come, sir page,   135
Look on me with your welkin° eye. Sweet villain!
Most dear'st! My collop!° Can thy dam?° — may't be? —
Affection, thy intention stabs the center.
Thou dost make possible things not so held,
Communicat'st with dreams — how can this be? —   140
With what's unreal thou coactive art,
And fellow'st nothing. Then 'tis very credent
Thou mayst cojoin with something;° and thou dost,
And that beyond commission,° and I find it,
And that to the infection of my brains   145
And hard'ning of my brows.

POLIXENES: What means Sicilia?°

HERMIONE:
He something° seems unsettled.

POLIXENES: How, my lord?
What cheer? How is't with you, best brother?

HERMIONE: You look
As if you held a brow of much distraction.
Are you moved,° my lord?

LEONTES: No, in good earnest.   135
How sometimes nature° will betray its folly,
Its tenderness, and make itself a pastime°
To harder bosoms!° Looking on the lines
Of my boy's face, methoughts° I did recoil°

---

132. **o'erdyed blacks:** black garments that have been weakened by too much dye or that have been dyed over another color (thereby betraying a falseness in the mourner). 132–34. **false . . . mine:** as false as dice are wished false by one who intends to cheat me, and who respects no boundary between what is his and mine. 136. **welkin:** sky-blue. 137. **collop:** small piece of meat; i.e., of my own flesh. **dam:** mother. 138–43. **Affection . . . something:** strong passion, your intense power pierces to the very center, the soul. You make possible things normally considered fantastic, partaking as you do of the nature of dreams. How can this be? You collaborate with unreality and imagined fantasies. It's all the likelier, then, that such imaginings may also fasten on a real object. 144. **commission:** what is lawful. 146. **What means Sicilia?:** why is the King of Sicilia looking so distracted? 147. **something:** somewhat. 150. **moved:** angry. 151. **nature:** i.e., affectionate feeling between parent and child. 152. **pastime:** occasion for amusement. 153. **To harder bosoms:** for persons who are less tender-hearted. 154. **methoughts:** it seemed to me. **recoil:** i.e., go back in memory.

Twenty-three years, and saw myself unbreeched,° 155
In my green velvet coat, my dagger muzzled°
Lest it should bite its master and so prove,
As ornaments oft do, too dangerous.
How like, methought, I then was to this kernel,
This squash,° this gentleman. — Mine honest° friend, 160
Will you take eggs for money?°

MAMILLIUS:
No, my lord, I'll fight.

LEONTES:
You will? Why, happy man be 's dole!° — My brother,
Are you so fond of your young prince as we
Do seem to be of ours?

POLIXENES: If at home, sir, 165
He's all my exercise, my mirth, my matter,°
Now my sworn friend and then mine enemy,
My parasite,° my soldier, statesman, all.
He makes a July's day short as December,
And with his varying childness° cures in me 170
Thoughts that would thick my blood.°

LEONTES: So stands this squire
Officed° with me. We two will walk, my lord,
And leave you to your graver steps. Hermione,
How thou lov'st us, show in our brother's welcome.
Let what is dear in Sicily be cheap.° 175
Next to thyself and my young rover, he's
Apparent° to my heart.

HERMIONE: If you would seek us,
We are yours i'th' garden. Shall 's° attend you there?

LEONTES:
To your own bents dispose you.° You'll be found,

155. **unbreeched:** not yet wearing breeches. 156. **muzzled:** i.e., sheathed. (With phallic suggestion.) 160. **squash:** unripe peascod or pea pod. **honest:** worthy. 161. **take eggs for money:** i.e., be imposed upon, taken advantage of, cheated. (Proverbial.) 163. **happy . . . dole:** may good fortune be his lot. (Proverbial.) 166. **matter:** concern. 168. **parasite:** a flatterer or obsequious courtier. 170. **childness:** childlike ways. 171. **thick my blood:** (Melancholy thoughts were supposed to thicken the blood.) 172. **Officed:** placed in particular function. 174–75. **How . . . cheap:** (A hidden second meaning in these lines may be intentional: show just how much you love me by the way you encourage Polixenes's attentions and thereby cheapen the most precious thing in Sicily.) 177. **Apparent:** heir apparent (perhaps with a suggestion too of "evident, revealed"). 178. **Shall 's:** shall we. 179. **To . . . dispose you:** act according to your inclinations. (With more bitter double meaning, continued in *You'll be found,* i.e., found out.)

Be you beneath the sky. [*Aside*] I am angling now,   180
Though you perceive me not how I give line.°
Go to,° go to!
How she holds up the neb,° the bill to him,
And arms her with° the boldness of a wife
To her allowing° husband!   [*Exeunt Polixenes and Hermione.*]
                    Gone already!   185
Inch thick, knee-deep, o'er head and ears a forked° one! —
Go play, boy, play.° Thy mother plays,° and I
Play° too, but so disgraced a part, whose issue°
Will hiss me to my grave. Contempt and clamor
Will be my knell. Go play, boy, play. There have been,   190
Or I am much deceived, cuckolds ere now;
And many a man there is, even at this present,
Now while I speak this, holds his wife by th' arm,
That little thinks she has been sluiced° in 's absence
And his pond fished by his next neighbor, by   195
Sir Smile, his neighbor. Nay, there's comfort in't
Whiles other men have gates° and those gates opened,
As mine, against their will. Should all despair
That have revolted° wives, the tenth of mankind
Would hang themselves. Physic° for't there's none.   200
It is a bawdy planet,° that will strike°
Where 'tis predominant;° and 'tis powerful, think it,°
From east, west, north, and south. Be it concluded,
No barricado° for a belly. Know't,°
It will let in and out the enemy   205
With bag and baggage.° Many thousand on 's°
Have the disease and feel't not. — How now, boy?

---

181. **give line:** pay out line (to let the fish hook itself well).   182. **Go to:** (An expression of remonstrance.)   183. **neb:** beak, i.e., nose, mouth.   184. **arms her with:** assumes.   185. **allowing:** approving.   186. **forked:** horned.   187. **play:** play games.   **plays:** i.e., in a sexual liaison.   188. **Play:** play a role.   **issue:** outcome. (With a pun on the sense of "offspring" and "theatrical exit.")   194. **sluiced:** drawn off, as by a sluice. (The water in his pond, so to speak, has been drawn off by a cheating neighbor.)   197. **gates:** sluice gates, suggestive of the wife's chastity that has been opened and robbed.   199. **revolted:** unfaithful.   200. **Physic:** medicine.   201. **It . . . planet:** i.e., this unchastity is like the planet Venus.   **strike:** blast, destroy by a malign influence.   202. **predominant:** in the ascendant. (Said of a planet.)   **think it:** be assured of this.   204. **barricado:** barricade.   **Know't:** be certain of this.   206. **bag and baggage:** all the property of an army. (To complete a campaign *with bag and baggage* is to win decisively, with nothing surrendered.) (With sexual suggestion as earlier in *dagger* [line 156], *sluiced, gates, let in and out,* etc.)   **on 's:** of us.

MAMILLIUS:

   I am like you, they say.

LEONTES: Why, that's some comfort.

   What, Camillo there?

CAMILLO: [*coming forward*]   Ay, my good lord.

LEONTES:

   Go play, Mamillius; thou'rt an honest man.   [*Exit Mamillius.*] 210

   Camillo, this great sir will yet stay longer.

CAMILLO:

   You had much ado to make his anchor hold.

   When you cast out, it still came home.°

LEONTES: Didst note it?

CAMILLO:

   He would not stay at your petitions, made

   His business more material.°

LEONTES: Didst perceive it?   215

   [*Aside*] They're here with me already,° whisp'ring, rounding,°

   "Sicilia is a so-forth."° 'Tis far gone

   When I shall gust° it last. — How came't, Camillo,

   That he did stay?

CAMILLO: At the good Queen's entreaty.

LEONTES:

   "At the Queen's" be't. "Good" should be pertinent,°   220

   But so it is,° it is not. Was this taken°

   By any understanding pate but thine?

   For thy conceit is soaking,° will draw in

   More than the common blocks.° Not noted is't,

   But of the finer natures?° By some severals°   225

   Of headpiece extraordinary? Lower messes°

   Perchance are to this business purblind?° Say.

CAMILLO:

   Business, my lord? I think most understand

   Bohemia stays here longer.

---

213. **still came home:** always came back to the ship, failed to hold.   215. **material:** important.
216. **They're . . . already:** people are already onto my situation.   **rounding:** whispering, gossiping.   217. **a so-forth:** a so-and-so, a you-know-what.   218. **gust:** taste, i.e., hear of.   220.
pertinent: i.e., appropriately applied.   221. **so it is:** as things stand.   **taken:** perceived.   223.
conceit is soaking: understanding is receptive.   224. **blocks:** blockheads.   225. **But . . .
natures:** except by those of rarefied intellect.   **severals:** individuals.   226. **Lower messes:**
those who sit lower at table, i.e., inferior persons.   227. **purblind:** totally blind.

LEONTES: Ha?

CAMILLO: Stays here longer.

LEONTES: Ay, but why? 230

CAMILLO:
To satisfy Your Highness and the entreaties
Of our most gracious mistress.

LEONTES: Satisfy?°
Th'entreaties of your mistress? Satisfy?
Let that suffice. I have trusted thee, Camillo,
With all the nearest things to my heart, as well 235
My chamber councils,° wherein, priestlike, thou
Hast cleansed my bosom. I from thee departed
Thy penitent reformed. But we have been
Deceived in thy integrity, deceived
In that which seems so.

CAMILLO: Be it forbid,° my lord! 240

LEONTES:
To bide upon't, thou art not honest; or,
If thou inclin'st that way, thou art a coward,
Which hoxes honesty behind, restraining
From course required;° or else thou must be counted
A servant grafted in my serious trust° 245
And therein negligent; or else a fool
That see'st a game played home,° the rich stake drawn,°
And tak'st it all for jest.

CAMILLO: My gracious lord,
I may be negligent, foolish, and fearful;
In every one of these no man is free
But that his negligence, his folly, fear, 250
Among the infinite doings of the world
Sometime puts forth.° In your affairs, my lord,
If ever I were willful-negligent,

---

232. **Satisfy?:** (Leontes takes the word in a sexual sense.) 235–36. **as well . . . councils:** as well as with my private affairs. 240. **Be it forbid:** i.e., God forbid I should do such a thing. 241–44. **To bide . . . required:** if you hold back from saying what you think, you are not being honest; or, if you would like to speak but remain silent, you are a coward, allowing frankness to be hamstrung or shackled from carrying out the duty it should perform. 245. **grafted . . . trust:** taken into my complete confidence. (*Grafted* means "deeply embedded," like a graft.) 247. **home:** i.e., for keeps, in earnest. (With perhaps a sexual double meaning, continued in *rich stake drawn*.) **drawn:** won. 253. **Sometime puts forth:** sometimes shows itself.

It was my folly; if industriously°   255
I played the fool, it was my negligence,
Not weighing well the end; if ever fearful
To do a thing where I the issue doubted,°
Whereof the execution did cry out
Against the nonperformance,° 'twas a fear   260
Which oft infects the wisest. These, my lord,
Are such allowed° infirmities that° honesty
Is never free of. But, beseech Your Grace,
Be plainer with me. Let me know my trespass
By its own visage.° If I then deny it,   265
'Tis none of mine.

LEONTES: Ha' not you seen, Camillo —
But that's past doubt; you have, or your eyeglass°
Is thicker than a cuckold's horn° — or heard —
For to a vision so apparent,° rumor
Cannot be mute — or thought — for cogitation   270
Resides not in that man that does not think° —
My wife is slippery?° If thou wilt confess,
Or else be impudently negative
To have nor eyes° nor ears nor thought, then say
My wife's a hobbyhorse,° deserves a name   275
As rank as any flax-wench° that puts to°
Before her trothplight.° Say't and justify't.°

CAMILLO:
I would not be a stander-by to hear
My sovereign mistress clouded so without
My present° vengeance taken. 'Shrew° my heart,   280
You never spoke what did become you less
Than this, which to reiterate were sin
As deep as that, though true.°

255. **industriously:** deliberately.   258. **the issue doubted:** feared the outcome.   259–60. **Where-of . . . nonperformance:** in which the completion of the task showed how wrong I was in being reluctant to undertake it.   262. **allowed:** acknowledged.   **that:** as.   265. **visage:** face, i.e., plain appearance.   267. **eyeglass:** lens of the eye.   268. **cuckold's horn:** (A thin sheet of horn can be seen through like a lens, though a cuckold's horn is another matter.)   269. **to a vision so apparent:** about something so plainly visible.   271. **think:** i.e., think so.   272. **slippery:** unchaste.   273–74. **Or . . . eyes:** or, as the only possible alternative, insist impudently that you have neither eyes.   275. **hobbyhorse:** wanton woman.   276. **flax-wench:** common slut.   **puts to:** engages in sex.   277. **trothplight:** promise of marriage.   **justify't:** affirm it.   280. **present:** immediate.   **'Shrew:** beshrew, curse.   282–83. **which . . . true:** i.e., to repeat which accusation would be to sin as deeply as her supposed adultery, even if it were true (which it isn't).

LEONTES: Is whispering nothing?
Is leaning cheek to cheek? Is meeting noses?
Kissing with inside lip? Stopping the career°   285
Of laughter with a sigh — a note infallible
Of breaking honesty?° Horsing foot on foot?°
Skulking in corners? Wishing clocks more swift,
Hours minutes,° noon midnight? And all eyes
Blind with the pin and web° but theirs, theirs only,   290
That would unseen be wicked? Is this nothing?
Why, then the world and all that's in't is nothing,
The covering sky is nothing, Bohemia nothing,
My wife is nothing, nor nothing have these nothings,
If this be nothing.
CAMILLO: Good my lord, be cured   295
Of this diseased opinion, and betimes,°
For 'tis most dangerous.
LEONTES: Say it be,° 'tis true.
CAMILLO:
No, no, my lord.
LEONTES: It is. You lie, you lie!
I say thou liest, Camillo, and I hate thee,
Pronounce thee a gross lout, a mindless slave,   300
Or else a hovering temporizer,° that
Canst with thine eyes at once see good and evil,
Inclining to them both.° Were my wife's liver
Infected as her life,° she would not live
The running of one glass.°
CAMILLO: Who does infect her?   305
LEONTES:

Why, he that wears her like her medal,° hanging
About his neck, Bohemia — who, if I
Had servants true about me, that bare° eyes
To see alike mine honor as their profits,
Their own particular thrifts,° they would do that   310

---

285. **career:** full gallop.   287. **honesty:** chastity.   **Horsing foot on foot:** placing one's foot on that of another person and then moving the feet up and down together.   289. **Hours minutes:** wishing hours were minutes.   290. **pin and web:** cataract of the eye. (The lovers wish to think themselves unobserved.)   296. **betimes:** quickly.   297. **Say it be:** even if it is dangerous. 301. **hovering temporizer:** wavering time-server.   303. **Inclining . . . both:** being tolerant of evil along with the good.   304. **Infected as her life:** as full of disease as is her moral conduct. 305. **glass:** hourglass.   306. **like her medal:** like a miniature portrait of her, worn in a locket. 308. **bare:** bore, had.   310. **thrifts:** gains.

Which should undo° more doing. Ay, and thou,
His cupbearer — whom I from meaner form°
Have benched° and reared to worship,° who mayst see
Plainly as heaven sees earth and earth sees heaven
How I am galled° — mightst bespice a cup   315
To give mine enemy a lasting wink,°
Which draft to me were cordial.°

CAMILLO: Sir, my lord,
I could do this, and that with no rash° potion,
But with a ling'ring dram that should not work
Maliciously° like poison. But I cannot   320
Believe this crack° to be in my dread° mistress,
So sovereignly° being honorable.
I have loved thee —

LEONTES: Make that thy question, and go rot!°
Dost think I am so muddy,° so unsettled,
To appoint myself in this vexation,° sully   325
The purity and whiteness of my sheets —
Which to preserve is sleep, which being spotted
Is goads, thorns, nettles, tails of wasps —
Give scandal to the blood o' th' prince my son,
Who I do think is mine and love as mine,   330
Without ripe moving to't?° Would I do this?
Could man so blench?°

CAMILLO: I must believe you, sir.
I do, and will fetch off° Bohemia for't;
Provided that, when he's removed, Your Highness
Will take again your queen as yours at first,   335
Even for your son's sake, and thereby for sealing°
The injury of tongues in courts and kingdoms
Known and allied to yours.

---

311. **undo:** prevent. 312. **meaner form:** humbler station. 313. **benched:** placed on the bench of authority. **worship:** dignity, honor. 315. **galled:** rubbed, chafed. 316. **lasting wink:** everlasting closing of the eyes (in death). 317. **were cordial:** would be restorative. 318. **rash:** quick-acting (and therefore easily detected). 320. **Maliciously:** virulently. 321. **crack:** flaw. **dread:** worthy of awe. 322. **sovereignly:** supremely. 323. **Make . . . rot!:** i.e., If you're going to question my accusations, may you rot in hell! 324. **muddy:** muddle-headed. 325. **To . . . vexation:** to give myself this vexation. 331. **ripe moving to't:** having been moved to do it by full knowledge and wise judgment. 332. **blench:** swerve (from sensible conduct). 333. **fetch off:** do away with; or, with deliberate ambiguity, rescue. (As also in *removed* in the next line.) 336. **for sealing:** for the sake of silencing. (Some editors prefer *forsealing*, sealing up tight.)

LEONTES: Thou dost advise me
Even so as I mine own course have set down.
I'll give no blemish to her honor, none.   340

CAMILLO:
My lord,
Go then, and with a countenance as clear
As friendship wears at feasts, keep° with Bohemia
And with your queen. I am his cupbearer.
If from me he have wholesome beverage,   345
Account me not your servant.

LEONTES: This is all.
Do't and thou hast the one half of my heart;
Do't not, thou splitt'st thine own.

CAMILLO: I'll do't, my lord.

LEONTES:
I will seem friendly, as thou hast advised me.   *Exit.*

CAMILLO:
Oh, miserable lady! But, for me,   350
What case stand I in? I must be the poisoner
Of good Polixenes, and my ground to do't
Is the obedience to a master, one
Who in rebellion with himself will have
All that are his so too.° To do° this deed,   355
Promotion follows. If ° I could find example
Of thousands that had struck anointed kings
And flourished after, I'd not do't; but since
Nor brass, nor stone, nor parchment bears not one,°
Let villainy itself forswear't. I must   360
Forsake the court. To do't or no° is certain
To me a breakneck.° Happy° star reign now!
Here comes Bohemia.

Enter Polixenes.

POLIXENES: [*to himself*]   This is strange. Methinks
My favor here begins to warp.° Not speak?° —

---

343. **keep:** remain in company.   355. **All . . . too:** i.e., all his followers like him in rebelling against the best in themselves and in obeying his worst self.   **To do:** if I do.   356. **If:** even if.
358–59. **but . . . one:** but since recorded history shows no instances of persons who have killed a king and prospered afterwards.   361. **To do't or no:** i.e., either to kill Polixenes or not to kill him.   362. **breakneck:** destruction, ruin.   **Happy:** propitious, favorable.   364. **warp:** change, shrivel, grow askew (as wood warps).   **Not speak:** (Leontes has just passed by Polixenes without speaking.)

Good day, Camillo.

CAMILLO: Hail, most royal sir! 365

POLIXENES:
What is the news i'th' court?

CAMILLO: None rare,° my lord.

POLIXENES:
The King hath on him such a countenance
As° he had lost some province and a region
Loved as he loves himself. Even now I met him
With customary compliment, when he, 370
Wafting his eyes to th' contrary° and falling°
A lip of much contempt, speeds from me, and
So leaves me to consider what is breeding°
That changeth thus his manners.

CAMILLO:
I dare not know, my lord. 375

POLIXENES:
How, dare not? Do not?° Do you know, and dare not?
Be intelligent° to me. 'Tis thereabouts,°
For to yourself what you do know you must,
And cannot say you dare not.° Good Camillo,
Your changed complexions are to me a mirror 380
Which shows me mine changed too; for I must be
A party in this alteration,° finding
Myself thus altered with't.

CAMILLO: There is a sickness
Which puts some of us in distemper, but
I cannot name the disease; and it is caught 385
Of° you that yet are well.

POLIXENES: How? Caught of me?
Make me not sighted° like the basilisk.°
I have looked on thousands who have sped° the better
By my regard,° but killed none so. Camillo,

---

366. rare: noteworthy.   368. As: as if.   371. Wafting . . . contrary: averting his eyes.   fall-ing: letting fall.   373. breeding: hatching.   376. Do not?: i.e., or do you mean you don't know?   377. intelligent: intelligible.   'Tis thereabouts: it must be something of this sort, i.e., that you know and dare not tell.   378–79. For . . . dare not: i.e., for in your heart, what-ever it is you know, you must in fact know, and can't claim it's a matter of not daring to know.   381–82. for . . . alteration: i.e., for my looks must have changed, too, reflecting this change in my position.   386. Of: from.   387. sighted: provided with a gaze.   basilisk: a fabled serpent whose gaze was fatal.   388. sped: prospered.   389. regard: look.

As you are certainly a gentleman, thereto   390
Clerklike experienced, which no less adorns
Our gentry than our parents' noble names,
In whose success we are gentle,° I beseech you,
If you know aught which does behoove my knowledge
Thereof to be informed, imprison't not   395
In ignorant concealment.°

CAMILLO: I may not answer.

POLIXENES:
A sickness caught of me, and yet I well?
I must be answered. Dost thou hear, Camillo?
I conjure thee, by all the parts° of man
Which honor does acknowledge, whereof the least   400
Is not° this suit of mine, that thou declare
What incidency° thou dost guess of harm
Is creeping toward me; how far off, how near;
Which way to be prevented, if to be;°
If not, how best to bear it.

CAMILLO: Sir, I will tell you,   405
Since I am charged in honor and by him°
That I think honorable. Therefore mark my counsel,
Which must be even as swiftly followed as
I mean to utter it, or both yourself and me
Cry lost, and so good night!°

POLIXENES: On, good Camillo.   410

CAMILLO:
I am appointed him° to murder you.

POLIXENES:
By whom, Camillo?

CAMILLO: By the King.

POLIXENES: For what?

CAMILLO:
He thinks, nay, with all confidence he swears,
As he had seen't or been an instrument

390–93. **thereto . . . gentle:** in addition to which you are a cultivated and educated person —
something that graces our gentlemanlike condition no less than the worthy name of our an-
cestors, by succession from whom we are made noble.   396. **ignorant concealment:** concealment that would keep me ignorant or that would proceed from pretended ignorance on your
part.   399. **parts:** obligations.   400–01. **whereof . . . not:** not the least of which is (to answer).   402. **incidency:** likely incident.   404. **if to be:** if it can be (prevented).   406. **by
him:** i.e., by you yourself.   410. **good night:** i.e., this is the end.   411. **him:** by him (Leontes),
or, the one.

To vice° you to't, that you have touched his queen   415
Forbiddenly.
POLIXENES: Oh, then my best blood turn
To an infected jelly, and my name
Be yoked with his that did betray the Best!°
Turn then my freshest reputation to
A savor° that may strike the dullest nostril   420
Where I arrive, and my approach be shunned,
Nay, hated too, worse than the great'st infection
That e'er was heard or read!
CAMILLO: Swear his thought over°
By each particular star in heaven and
By all their influences, you may as well   425
Forbid the sea for to° obey the moon
As or by oath remove or° counsel shake
The fabric° of his folly, whose foundation
Is piled upon his faith and will continue
The standing of his body.°
POLIXENES: How should this grow?°   430
CAMILLO:
I know not. But I am sure 'tis safer to
Avoid what's grown than question how 'tis born.
If therefore you dare trust my honesty,
That lies enclosèd in this trunk° which you
Shall bear along impawned,° away tonight!   435
Your followers I will whisper to° the business,
And will by twos and threes at several posterns°
Clear them o'th' city. For myself, I'll put
My fortunes to your service, which are here
By this discovery° lost. Be not uncertain,   440
For, by the honor of my parents, I
Have uttered truth, which if you seek to prove,°

415. **vice:** force, as with a carpenter's tool, or, impel, tempt. (The *Vice* was a tempter in the morality play.)   418. **his . . . Best:** the name of him (Judas) who betrayed Christ.   420. **savor:** stench.
423. **Swear . . . over:** i.e., even if you should deny his suspicion with oaths.   426. **for to:** to.
427. **or . . . or:** either . . . or.   428. **fabric:** edifice.   428–30. **whose . . . body:** the foundation of which is built upon an unshaken conviction and which will last as long as his body exists.
430. **How . . . grow?:** how could this suspicion have arisen?   434. **trunk:** body. (With a suggestion too of a traveling trunk.)   435. **impawned:** i.e., as a pledge of good faith.   436. **whisper to:** secretly inform of and urge.   437. **posterns:** rear gates.   440. **discovery:** revelation, disclosure.   442. **prove:** test.

I dare not stand by;° nor shall you be safer
Than one condemned by the King's own mouth, thereon
His execution sworn.

POLIXENES: I do believe thee;   445
I saw his heart in 's face. Give me thy hand.
Be pilot to me, and thy places shall
Still neighbor mine.° My ships are ready, and
My people did expect my hence departure
Two days ago. This jealousy   450
Is for a precious creature. As she's rare,
Must it be great; and as his person's mighty,
Must it be violent; and as he does conceive
He is dishonored by a man which ever
Professed° to him, why, his revenges must   455
In that be made more bitter. Fear o'ershades me.
Good expedition be my friend, and comfort
The gracious Queen, part of his theme, but nothing
Of his ill-ta'en suspicion!° Come, Camillo,
I will respect thee as a father if   460
Thou bear'st my life off.° Hence! Let us avoid.°

CAMILLO:
It is in mine authority to command
The keys of all the posterns. Please Your Highness
To take the urgent hour. Come, sir, away.   *Exeunt.*

Act 2, Scene 1°

Enter Hermione, Mamillius, [and] Ladies.

HERMIONE:
Take the boy to you. He so troubles me,
'Tis past enduring.

FIRST LADY: [*taking Mamillius from the Queen*]
                    Come, my gracious lord,
Shall I be your playfellow?

---

443. **stand by:** affirm publicly; stay.   447–48. **thy . . . mine:** your official position will always be near to me.   455. **Professed:** openly professed friendship.   457–59. **Good . . . suspicion!:** may good speed befriend me, and may my quick departure ease the predicament of the gracious Queen, who is the object of the King's suspicions but who is guiltless of them!   461. **bear'st my life off:** can get me out of this alive.   **avoid:** depart.   Act 2, Scene 1. **Location:** Sicilia. The royal court.

MAMILLIUS:
No, I'll none of you.°

FIRST LADY: Why, my sweet lord?

MAMILLIUS:
You'll kiss me hard and speak to me as if   5
I were a baby still. — I love you better.

SECOND LADY:
And why so, my lord?

MAMILLIUS: Not for because°
Your brows are blacker; yet black brows, they say,
Become some women best, so° that there be not
Too much hair there, but in a semicircle,   10
Or a half-moon made with a pen.

SECOND LADY: Who taught'° this?

MAMILLIUS:
I learned it out of women's faces. Pray now,
What color are your eyebrows?

FIRST LADY: Blue, my lord.

MAMILLIUS:
Nay, that's a mock. I have seen a lady's nose
That has been blue, but not her eyebrows.

FIRST LADY: Hark ye,   15
The Queen your mother rounds apace.° We shall
Present our services to a fine new prince
One of these days, and then you'd wanton° with us,
If we would have you.

SECOND LADY: She is spread of late
Into a goodly bulk. Good time encounter her!°   20

HERMIONE: [calling to her women]
What wisdom stirs amongst you? — Come, sir, now
I am for you° again. Pray you, sit by us
And tell 's a tale.

MAMILLIUS: Merry or sad shall 't be?

HERMIONE:
As merry as you will.

MAMILLIUS:
A sad tale's best for winter. I have one   25

---

4. **none of you:** have nothing to do with you.   7. **for because:** because.   9. **so:** provided.
11. **taught:** taught you.   16. **rounds apace:** is quickly becoming round.   18. **wanton:** sport,
play.   20. **Good . . . her!:** may she have a happy issue!   22. **for you:** ready for you.

Of sprites and goblins.

HERMIONE: Let's have that, good sir.
Come on, sit down. Come on, and do your best
To fright me with your sprites. You're powerful at it.

MAMILLIUS:
There was a man —

HERMIONE: Nay, come sit down, then on.   [*Mamillius sits.*]

MAMILLIUS:
Dwelt by a churchyard. I will tell it softly;   30
Yond crickets° shall not hear it.

HERMIONE:
Come on, then, and give't me in mine ear.   [*They converse privately.*]

[*Enter*] *Leontes, Antigonus, Lords,* [*and others*].

LEONTES:
Was he met there? His train? Camillo with him?

A LORD:
Behind the tuft of pines I met them. Never
Saw I men scour° so on their way. I eyed them   35
Even to their ships.

LEONTES: How blest am I
In my just censure,° in my true opinion!
Alack, for lesser knowledge!° How accurst
In being so blest!° There may be in the cup
A spider° steeped, and one may drink, depart,   40
And yet partake no venom, for his knowledge
Is not infected; but if one present
Th'abhorred ingredient to his eye, make known
How he hath drunk, he cracks his gorge,° his sides,
With violent hefts.° I have drunk, and seen the spider.   45
Camillo was his help in this, his pander.
There is a plot against my life, my crown.
All's true that is mistrusted.° That false villain
Whom I employed was pre-employed by him.
He has discovered° my design, and I   50

---

31. **crickets:** i.e., the court ladies, tittering and laughing.   35. **scour:** scurry.   37. **censure:** judgment.   38. **Alack . . . knowledge!:** would that there were less for me to know!   39. **blest:** i.e., with knowledge (that causes unhappiness).   40. **A spider:** (The superstition referred to here is that the drinker is not poisoned by the spider in the cup unless the spider is known to be there.)   44. **gorge:** throat.   45. **hefts:** heavings, retchings.   48. **mistrusted:** suspected.   50. **discovered:** disclosed.

Remain a pinched° thing, yea, a very trick°
For them to play° at will. How came the posterns
So easily open?

A LORD: By his great authority,
Which often hath no less prevailed than so
On your command.   55

LEONTES:
I know't too well.
[*To Hermione*] Give me the boy. I am glad you did not nurse him.
Though he does bear some signs of me, yet you
Have too much blood in him.

HERMIONE: What is this? Sport?°

LEONTES: [*to a Lord*]
Bear the boy hence; he shall not come about her.   60
Away with him! And let her sport herself
With that she's big with, [*to Hermione*] for 'tis Polixenes
Has made thee swell thus.   [*Mamillius is led out.*]

HERMIONE: But I'd° say he had not,
And I'll be sworn you would believe my saying,
Howe'er you lean to th' nayward.°

LEONTES: You, my lords,   65
Look on her, mark her well. Be but about
To say "She is a goodly° lady," and
The justice of your hearts will thereto add
"'Tis pity she's not honest,° honorable."
Praise her but for this her without-door° form,   70
Which on my faith deserves high speech, and straight°
The shrug, the hum or ha, these petty brands°
That calumny doth use — oh, I am out,°
That mercy does,° for calumny will sear
Virtue itself — these shrugs, these hums and ha's,   75
When you have said she's goodly, come between°
Ere you can say she's honest. But be't known,
From him that has most cause to grieve it should be,
She's an adulteress.

---

51. **pinched:** tortured, ridiculous. **trick:** plaything. 52. **play:** play with. 59. **Sport?:** a joke?
63. **I'd:** I need only. 65. **th' nayward:** the contrary. 67. **goodly:** attractive. 69. **honest:** chaste.
70. **without-door:** outward, external. 71. **straight:** straightaway, at once. 72. **brands:** i.e.,
signs, stigmas. 73. **out:** wrong, in error. 74. **does:** uses. (Leontes's point is that no one
commits calumny by suggesting with a shrug that Hermione is unchaste; calumny attacks
virtue itself, whereas Hermione has only the false appearance of virtue.) 76. **come between:**
interrupt.

HERMIONE: Should a villain say so,
  The most replenished° villain in the world, 80
  He were as much more villain.° You, my lord,
  Do but mistake.
LEONTES: You have mistook,° my lady,
  Polixenes for Leontes. Oh, thou thing!
  Which I'll not call a creature of thy place,°
  Lest barbarism, making me the precedent 85
  Should a like° language use to all degrees°
  And mannerly distinguishment leave out°
  Betwixt the prince and beggar. I have said
  She's an adult'ress; I have said with whom.
  More, she's a traitor, and Camillo is 90
  A fedarie° with her, and one that knows
  What she should shame to know herself
  But with her most vile principal,° that she's
  A bed-swerver,° even as bad as those
  That vulgars give bold'st titles,° ay, and privy° 95
  To this their late° escape.
HERMIONE: No, by my life,
  Privy to none of this. How will this grieve you,
  When you shall come to clearer knowledge, that
  You thus have published° me! Gentle my° lord,
  You scarce can right me throughly then to say° 100
  You did mistake.
LEONTES: No. If I mistake
  In those foundations which I build upon,
  The center° is not big enough to bear
  A schoolboy's top. — Away with her to prison!
  He who shall speak for her is afar off° guilty 105
  But that he speaks.°
HERMIONE: There's some ill planet reigns.

---

80. **replenished:** complete.   81. **He . . . villain:** his saying so would double his villainy.   82. **mistook:** taken wrongfully. (Playing bitterly on *mistake*, "misapprehend.")   84. **Which . . . place:** whose exalted rank I will not desecrate by calling you what you really are.   86. **like:** similar **degrees:** social ranks.   87. **And . . . out:** and leave out proper distinctions.   91. **fedarie:** confederate.   92–93. **to know . . . principal:** to acknowledge privately even with her contemptible partner.   94. **bed-swerver:** adulteress.   95. **That . . . titles:** that common people call by the rudest names.   **privy:** in on the secret.   96. **late:** recent.   99. **published:** proclaimed. **Gentle my:** my noble.   100. **You . . . say:** you scarcely can do me full justice then merely by saying.   103. **center:** earth.   105. **afar off:** indirectly.   106. **But . . . speaks:** merely by speaking.

I must be patient till the heavens look
With an aspect more favorable. Good my lords,
I am not prone to weeping, as our sex
Commonly are, the want° of which vain dew   110
Perchance shall dry your pities; but I have
That honorable grief lodged here which burns
Worse than tears drown. Beseech you all, my lords,
With thoughts so qualified° as your charities
Shall best instruct you, measure° me; and so   115
The King's will be performed!

LEONTES: Shall I be heard?°

HERMIONE:
Who is't that goes with me? Beseech Your Highness
My women may be with me, for you see
My plight requires it. — Do not weep, good fools;°
There is no cause. When you shall know your mistress   120
Has deserved prison, then abound in tears
As I come out.° This action I now go on
Is for my better grace.° — Adieu, my lord.
I never wished to see you sorry; now
I trust I shall. My women, come, you have leave.°   125

LEONTES:
Go, do our bidding. Hence!   [Exit Queen, guarded, with Ladies.]

A LORD:
Beseech Your Highness, call the Queen again.

ANTIGONUS:
Be certain what you do, sir, lest your justice
Prove violence, in the which three great ones suffer:
Yourself, your queen, your son.

A LORD: For her, my lord,   130
I dare my life lay down and will do't, sir,
Please you t'accept it, that the Queen is spotless
I'th'eyes of heaven and to you — I mean
In this which you accuse her.

ANTIGONUS: If it prove

---

110. want: lack.   114. qualified: tempered.   115. measure: judge.   116. heard: i.e., obeyed.
119. fools: (Here, a term of endearment.)   122. come out: am released from prison.
122–23. The action . . . grace: what I now must undergo will ultimately make me seem more
gracious in others' eyes and ennoble me by suffering.   125. leave: permission (to attend me).

She's otherwise, I'll keep my stables where   135
I lodge my wife.° I'll go in couples° with her;
Than when I feel and see her no farther trust her.°
For every inch of woman in the world,
Ay, every dram of woman's flesh is false,
If she° be.

LEONTES: Hold your peaces.

A LORD: Good my lord —   140

ANTIGONUS:
It is for you we speak, not for ourselves.
You are abused,° and by some putter-on°
That will be damned for't. Would I knew the villain;
I would land-damn° him. Be she honor-flawed,
I have three daughters — the eldest is eleven,   145
The second and the third, nine and some° five —
If this prove true, they'll pay for't. By mine honor,
I'll geld° 'em all! Fourteen they shall not see
To bring false generations.° They are co-heirs,°
And I had rather glib° myself than they   150
Should not produce fair issue.°

LEONTES: Cease, no more!
You smell this business with a sense as cold
As is a dead man's nose; but I do see't and feel't
As you feel doing thus,° and see withal
The instruments that feel.°

ANTIGONUS: If it be so,   155
We need no grave to bury honesty;
There's not a grain of it the face to sweeten
Of the whole dungy earth.

135–36. I'll . . . wife: (If Hermione is an adulteress, says Antigonus, then all women are no better than animals, to be penned up and guarded suspiciously.)   136. in couples: i.e., like two hounds leashed together and hence inseparable.   137. Than . . . her: trust her no further than I can feel her next to me and actually see her.   140. she: i.e., Hermione.   142. abused: deceived. putter-on: instigator.   144. land-damn: lambaste. (? Meaning uncertain.)   146. some: about. 148. geld: sterilize, de-sex.   149. bring false generations: have illegitimate children.   They are co-heirs: i.e., they will share my inheritance (since I have no son to inherit all).   150. glib: castrate, geld.   151. fair issue: legitimate offspring.   154. thus: (Leontes presumably grasps Antigonus by the arm or pinches him or tweaks his nose.)   154–55. and see . . . feel: i.e., just as you and I see these fingers that pinch, I see in my mind's eye the amorous touching of Hermione and Polixenes. (*Withal* means "in addition.")

LEONTES: What? Lack I credit?°

A LORD:

I had rather you did lack than I, my lord,
Upon this ground;° and more it would content me   160
To have her honor true than your suspicion,
Be blamed for't how you might.

LEONTES: Why, what need we°

Commune with you of this, but rather follow
Our forceful instigation?° Our prerogative
Calls not your counsels, but our natural goodness   165
Imparts this;° which if you — or° stupefied
Or seeming so in skill° — cannot or will not
Relish° a truth like us, inform yourselves
We need no more of your advice. The matter,
The loss, the gain, the ordering on't,° is all   170
Properly ours.

ANTIGONUS: And I wish, my liege,

You had only in your silent judgment tried it,
Without more overture.°

LEONTES: How could that be?

Either thou art most ignorant by age,°
Or thou wert born a fool. Camillo's flight,   175
Added to their familiarity —
Which was as gross as ever touched conjecture,°
That lacked sight only, naught for approbation°
But only seeing, all other circumstances
Made up° to th' deed — doth push on° this proceeding.   180
Yet, for a greater confirmation —
For in an act of this importance 'twere
Most piteous to be wild° — I have dispatched in post°
To sacred Delphos,° to Apollo's temple,
Cleomenes and Dion whom you know   185

---

158. **credit:** credibility.   160. **Upon this ground:** in this matter.   162. **we:** I. (The royal "we.")
164. **Our . . . instigation:** my own strong inclination.   164–66. **Our prerogative . . . this:** My
royal prerogative is under no obligation to consult you, but rather out of natural generosity
I inform you of the matter.   166. **or:** either.   167. **Or . . . skill:** or pretending to be stupefied out of cunning.   168. **Relish:** savor, appreciate.   170. **on't:** of it.   173. **overture:** public
disclosure.   174. **by age:** through the folly of old age.   177. **as gross . . . conjecture:** as palpably evident as any conjecture ever touched upon and verified.   178. **approbation:** proof.
180. **Made up:** added up.   **push on:** urge onward.   183. **wild:** rash.   **post:** haste.   184. **Delphos:** Delphi, an ancient Greek city and site of the famous oracle of the sun-god Apollo.

Of stuffed sufficiency.° Now from the oracle
They will bring all,° whose spiritual counsel had°
Shall stop or spur me. Have I done well?

A LORD:
Well done, my lord.

LEONTES:
Though I am satisfied, and need no more   190
Than what I know, yet shall the oracle
Give rest to th' minds of others, such as he°
Whose ignorant credulity will not
Come up to° th' truth. So have we thought it good
From° our free° person she should be confined,   195
Lest that the treachery of the two fled hence
Be left her to perform. Come, follow us.
We are to speak in public, for this business
Will raise° us all.

ANTIGONUS: [aside]   To laughter, as I take it,
If the good truth were known.   *Exeunt.*   200

ACT 2, SCENE 2°

Enter Paulina, a Gentleman, [and attendants].

PAULINA:
The keeper of the prison, call to him.
Let him have knowledge who I am.   [*The Gentleman goes to the door.*]
                                   Good lady,°
No court in Europe is too good for thee;
What dost thou then in prison?

[*Enter*] *Jailer.*

                              Now, good sir,
You know me, do you not?

JAILER: For a worthy lady   5
And one who much I honor.

PAULINA: Pray you then,

---

186. **Of stuffed sufficiency:** abundantly qualified and trustworthy.   187. **all:** the whole truth.
had: having been obtained.   192. **he:** any person (such as Antigonus).   194. **Come up to:**
face.   195. **From:** away from.   **free:** accessible.   199. **raise:** rouse.   ACT 2, SCENE 2. Location: Sicilia. A prison.   2. **Good lady:** (Addressed to the absent Hermione.)

Conduct me to the Queen.

JAILER: I may not, madam.
To the contrary I have express commandment.

PAULINA:
Here's ado, to lock up honesty and honor from
Th'access of gentle visitors! Is't lawful, pray you,   10
To see her women? Any of them? Emilia?

JAILER: So please you, madam,
To put apart° these your attendants, I
Shall bring Emilia forth.

PAULINA: I pray now, call her. —
Withdraw yourselves.   [*Gentleman and attendants withdraw.*] 15

JAILER:
And, madam,
I must be present at your conference.

PAULINA:
Well, be't so, prithee.   [*Exit Jailer.*]
Here's such ado, to make no stain a stain
As passes coloring.°

[*Enter Jailer, with*] *Emilia.*

                 Dear gentlewoman,   20
How fares our gracious lady?

EMILIA:
As well as one so great and so forlorn
May hold together. On° her frights and griefs —
Which° never tender lady hath borne greater —
She is something° before her time delivered.   25

PAULINA:
A boy?

EMILIA: A daughter, and a goodly babe,
Lusty° and like° to live. The Queen receives
Much comfort in't, says, "My poor prisoner,
I am innocent as you."

PAULINA: I dare be sworn.
These dangerous unsafe lunes° i'th' King, beshrew them! 30

---

13. **put apart:** dismiss. **19–20. to make . . . coloring:** to make out of no stain at all a besmirching of honor that surpasses any justification. (Expressed in a metaphor of dyeing and painting.) **23. On:** in consequence of. **24. Which:** than which. **25. something:** somewhat. (Also in line 55.) **27. Lusty:** vigorous. **like:** likely. **30. lunes:** fits of lunacy.

He must be told on't,° and he shall. The office
Becomes° a woman best; I'll take't upon me.
If I prove honeymouthed, let my tongue blister°
And never to my red-looked° anger be
The trumpet any more. Pray you, Emilia,   35
Commend° my best obedience to the Queen.
If she dares trust me with her little babe,
I'll show't the King and undertake to be
Her advocate to th' loud'st.° We do not know
How he may soften at the sight o'th' child.   40
The silence often of pure innocence
Persuades when speaking fails.

EMILIA: Most worthy madam,
Your honor and your goodness is so evident
That your free° undertaking cannot miss
A thriving issue.° There is no lady living   45
So meet° for this great errand. Please° Your Ladyship
To visit the next room, I'll presently°
Acquaint the Queen of your most noble offer,
Who but today hammered of° this design,
But durst not tempt° a minister of honor   50
Lest she should be denied.

PAULINA: Tell her, Emilia,
I'll use that tongue I have. If wit° flow from't
As boldness from my bosom, let 't not be doubted
I shall do good.

EMILIA: Now be you blest for it!
I'll to the Queen — Please you, come something nearer.°   55

JAILER:
Madam, if 't please the Queen to send the babe,
I know not what I shall incur to pass it,°
Having no warrant.

PAULINA: You need not fear it, sir.
This child was prisoner to the womb and is
By law and process of great Nature thence   60

---

31. **on't:** of it. 32. **Becomes:** suits. 33. **blister:** (It was popularly supposed that lying blistered the tongue.) 34. **red-looked:** red-faced. 36. **Commend:** deliver. 39. **to th' loud'st:** as loudly as I can. 44. **free:** generous. 45. **thriving issue:** successful outcome. 46. **meet:** suited. **Please:** if it please. 47. **presently:** at once. 49. **hammered of:** mused upon. 50. **tempt:** solicit (to serve as ambassador in such a case). 52. **wit:** wisdom. 55. **come . . . nearer:** i.e., come into the next room (as in lines 46–7). 57. **to pass it:** if I let it pass.

Freed and enfranchised, not a party to
The anger of the King nor guilty of —
If any be — the trespass of the Queen.

JAILER:
I do believe it.

PAULINA:
Do not you fear. Upon mine honor, I   65
Will stand betwixt you and danger.   *Exeunt.*

ACT 2, SCENE 3°

Enter Leontes.

LEONTES:
Nor night nor day, no rest! It is but weakness
To bear the matter thus, mere weakness. If
The cause were not in being° — part o'th' cause,
She th'adulteress, for the harlot° King
Is quite beyond mine arm, out of the blank   5
And level° of my brain, plot-proof, but she
I can hook° to me — say that she were gone,
Given to the fire,° a moiety° of my rest
Might come to me again. — Who's there?

[Enter a] Servant.

SERVANT: My lord?

LEONTES:
How does the boy?   10

SERVANT:
He took good rest tonight;° 'tis hoped
His sickness is discharged.

LEONTES: To see his nobleness!
Conceiving° the dishonor of his mother,
He straight° declined, drooped, took it deeply,
Fastened and fixed the shame on't° in himself,   15

ACT 2, SCENE 3. **Location:** Sicilia. The royal court. **3. not in being:** dead. **4. harlot:** lewd. (Originally applied to either sex.) **5–6. out . . . level:** beyond the range. (Archery terms: *blank* is the center of the target or the close range needed for a direct shot at it, as in "pointblank"; *level* is the action of aiming.) **7. hook:** (As with grappling hooks.) **8. Given to the fire:** burned at the stake (as a traitor conspiring against the King). **moiety:** portion. **11. tonight:** last night. **13. Conceiving:** grasping the enormity of. **14. straight:** immediately. **15. on't:** of it.

Threw off his spirit, his appetite, his sleep,
And downright languished. — Leave me solely.° Go,
See how he fares.   [*Exit Servant.*]
                    Fie, fie! No thought of him.°
The very thought of my revenges that way
Recoil upon me — in himself too mighty,   20
And in his parties, his alliance.° Let him be,
Until a time may serve. For present vengeance,
Take it on her. Camillo and Polixenes
Laugh at me, make their pastime at my sorrow.
They should not laugh if I could reach them, nor   25
Shall she, within my power.

Enter Paulina [with a baby]; Antigonus and Lords [trying to hold her back].

A LORD: You must not enter.
PAULINA:
  Nay, rather, good my lords, be second to° me.
  Fear you his tyrannous passion more, alas,
  Than the Queen's life? A gracious innocent soul,
  More free° than he is jealous.
ANTIGONUS: That's enough.   30
SERVANT:
  Madam, he hath not slept tonight, commanded
  None should come at him.
PAULINA: Not so hot, good sir.
  I come to bring him sleep. 'Tis such as you,
  That creep like shadows by him and do sigh
  At each his needless heavings,° such as you   35
  Nourish the cause of his awaking.° I
  Do come with words as medicinal as true,
  Honest as either, to purge him of that humor°
  That presses him from sleep.
LEONTES: What noise there, ho?
PAULINA:
  No noise, my lord, but needful conference   40
  About some gossips° for Your Highness.
LEONTES: How?

17. **solely:** alone. 18. **him:** i.e., Polixenes. 21. **his parties . . . alliance:** his supporters and allies. 27. **be second to:** aid, second. 30. **free:** innocent. 35. **heavings:** sighs or groans. 36. **awaking:** inability to sleep. 38. **humor:** distemper. 41. **gossips:** godparents for the baby at its baptism.

Away with that audacious lady! Antigonus,
I charged thee that she should not come about me.
I knew she would.

ANTIGONUS: I told her so, my lord,
On your displeasure's peril and on mine,   45
She should not visit you.

LEONTES: What, canst not rule her?

PAULINA:
From all dishonesty he can. In this,
Unless he take the course that you have done —
Commit° me for committing honor — trust it,
He shall not rule me.

ANTIGONUS: La you now, you hear!°   50
When she will take the rein I let her run,
But she'll not stumble.

PAULINA: Good my liege, I come —
And, I beseech you hear me, who professes
Myself your loyal servant, your physician,
Your most obedient counselor, yet that dares   55
Less appear so in comforting your evils
Than such as most seem yours° — I say, I come
From your good queen.

LEONTES:
Good queen?

PAULINA:
Good queen, my lord, good queen, I say good queen,   60
And would by combat° make° her good, so were I
A man, the worst° about you.

LEONTES: [*to Lords*]   Force her hence.

PAULINA:
Let him that makes but trifles of his eyes
First hand me. On mine own accord I'll off,
But first I'll do my errand. The good Queen,   65
For she is good, hath brought you forth a daughter —
Here 'tis — commends it to your blessing.   [*She lays down the baby.*]

LEONTES: Out!

---

49. **Commit:** i.e., to prison.   50. **La . . . hear!:** i.e., there now, you hear how she will go on talking!   56–57. **in comforting . . . yours:** when it comes to encouraging your evil courses than those flatterers who seem to be your most loyal servants.   61. **by combat:** by trial by combat. **make:** prove.   62. **worst:** least manly, or, lowest in rank.

ACT 2, SCENE 3 | 59

A mankind° witch! Hence with her, out o' door!
A most intelligencing bawd!°
PAULINA: Not so.
  I am as ignorant in that as you   70
  In so entitling me, and no less honest
  Than you are mad; which is enough, I'll warrant,
  As this world goes, to pass for honest.
LEONTES: [*to Lords*]   Traitors!
  Will you not push her out? [*To Antigonus*] Give her the bastard.
  Thou dotard, thou art woman-tired,° unroosted°   75
  By thy Dame Partlet° here. Take up the bastard!
  Take't up, I say. Give't to thy crone.
PAULINA: [*to Antigonus*]   Forever
  Unvenerable be thy hands if thou
  Tak'st up the Princess by that forcèd baseness°
  Which he has put upon't!
LEONTES: He dreads his wife.   80
PAULINA:
  So I would you did. Then 'twere past all doubt
  You'd call your children yours.
LEONTES: A nest of traitors!
ANTIGONUS:
  I am none, by this good light.°
PAULINA: Nor I, nor any
  But one that's here, and that's himself; for he
  The sacred honor of himself, his queen's,   85
  His hopeful son's, his babe's, betrays to slander,
  Whose sting is sharper than the sword's; and will not —
  For, as the case now stands, it is a curse
  He cannot be compelled to't — once remove
  The root of his opinion,° which is rotten   90
  As ever oak or stone was sound.
LEONTES: A callet°
  Of boundless tongue, who late° hath beat her husband

---

68. **mankind:** masculine, behaving like a man.   69. **intelligencing bawd:** acting as go-between and spy (for the Queen and Polixenes).   75. **woman-tired:** henpecked. (From *tire* in falconry, meaning "tear with the beak.")   **unroosted:** driven from perch.   76. **Partlet:** or Pertilote, a common name for a hen (as in *Reynard the Fox* and in Chaucer's "Nun's Priest's Tale").   79. **by that forcèd baseness:** under that wrongfully imposed name of bastard.   83. **by this good light:** by the light of day. (A common oath.)   88–90. **as . . . opinion:** i.e., since he is King, he regrettably can't be compelled to change his deeply rooted opinion.   91. **callet:** scold.   92. **late:** recently.

And now baits° me! This brat is none of mine;
It is the issue of Polixenes.
Hence with it, and together with the dam   95
Commit them to the fire!
PAULINA: It is yours;
And, might we lay th'old proverb to your charge,
So like you, 'tis the worse.° Behold, my lords,
Although the print be little, the whole matter
And copy of the father — eye, nose, lip,   100
The trick° of 's frown, his forehead, nay, the valley,°
The pretty dimples of his chin and cheek, his smiles,
The very mold and frame of hand, nail, finger.
And thou, good goddess Nature, which hast made it
So like to him that got° it, if thou hast   105
The ordering of the mind too, 'mongst all colors
No yellow° in't, lest she suspect, as he does,
Her children not her husband's!
LEONTES: A gross hag!
And, lozel,° thou art worthy to be hanged,
That wilt not stay° her tongue.
ANTIGONUS: Hang all the husbands   110
That cannot do that feat, you'll leave yourself
Hardly one subject.
LEONTES: Once more, take her hence.
PAULINA:
A most unworthy and unnatural lord
Can do no more.
LEONTES: I'll ha' thee burnt.
PAULINA: I care not.
It is an heretic that makes the fire,   115
Not she which burns in't.° I'll not call you tyrant;
But this most cruel usage of your queen,

---

93. **baits:** (With a pun on *beat* in the previous line, pronounced "bate.") 98. **So . . . worse:** Paulina alludes to the proverb: "he's so like you that he fares the worse for it." 101. **trick:** characteristic expression. **valley:** cleft above the upper lip. 105. **got:** begot. 107. **No yellow:** let there be no yellow, i.e., the color of jealousy. (A chaste woman could hardly expect that her own children are illegitimate, but Paulina may be hyperbolically ridiculing Leontes's suspicions.) 109. **lozel:** worthless person, scoundrel. (Addressed to Antigonus.) 110. **stay:** restrain. 115–16. **It is . . . in't:** i.e., in burning me, you who would be making or building the fire are the heretic, not me (since loss of faith in innocence is a kind of heresy), or, you can burn a woman if you like, but it's a heretic's fire only if she is, in fact, a heretic.

Not able° to produce more accusation
Than your own weak-hinged fancy, something savors
Of tyranny and will ignoble make you,   120
Yea, scandalous to the world.
LEONTES: [*to Antigonus*]   On your allegiance,
    Out of the chamber with her! Were I a tyrant,
    Where were her life?° She durst not call me so
    If she did know me one. Away with her!
PAULINA:
    I pray you, do not push me; I'll be gone.   125
    Look to your babe, my lord; 'tis yours. Jove send her
    A better guiding spirit! — What needs these hands?°
    You that are thus so tender o'er his follies
    Will never do him good, not one of you.
    So, so. Farewell, we are gone.   *Exit.* 130
LEONTES: [*to Antigonus*]
    Thou, traitor, hast set on thy wife to this.
    My child? Away with't! Even thou, that hast
    A heart so tender o'er it, take it hence
    And see it instantly consumed with fire;
    Even thou and none but thou. Take it up straight.   135
    Within this hour bring me word 'tis done,
    And by good testimony, or I'll seize thy life,
    With what thou else call'st thine. If thou refuse
    And wilt encounter with my wrath, say so;
    The bastard brains with these my proper° hands   140
    Shall I dash out. Go, take it to the fire,
    For thou set'st on thy wife.
ANTIGONUS: I did not, sir.
    These lords, my noble fellows, if they please,
    Can clear me in't.
LORDS: We can. My royal liege,
    He is not guilty of her coming hither.   145
LEONTES:
    You're liars all.
A LORD:
    Beseech Your Highness, give us better credit.°

---

118. **Not able:** you not being able.   123. **Where . . . life?:** how could she escape execution at
my command?   127. **What . . . hands?:** what need is there to push me?   140. **proper:** own.
147. **credit:** belief.

We have always truly served you, and beseech'°
So to esteem of us; and on our knees we beg,
As recompense of our dear° services   150
Past and to come, that you do change this purpose,
Which being so horrible, so bloody, must
Lead on to some foul issue. We all kneel.

LEONTES:
I am a feather for each wind that blows.
Shall I live on to see this bastard kneel   155
And call me father? Better burn it now
Than curse it then. But be it; let it live.
It shall not neither. [*To Antigonus*] You, sir, come you hither,
You that have been so tenderly officious
With Lady Margery,° your midwife there,   160
To save this bastard's life — for 'tis a bastard,
So sure as this beard's° gray. What will you adventure
To save this brat's life?

ANTIGONUS: Anything, my lord,
That my ability may undergo
And nobleness impose. At least thus much: 165
I'll pawn the little blood which I have left
To save the innocent — anything possible.

LEONTES: [*holding his sword*]
It shall be possible. Swear by this sword
Thou wilt perform my bidding.

ANTIGONUS: [*his hand on the hilt*]   I will, my lord.

LEONTES:
Mark and perform it, see'st thou;° for the fail°   170
Of any point in't shall not only be
Death to thyself but to thy lewd-tongued wife,
Whom for this time we pardon. We enjoin thee,
As thou art liegeman° to us, that thou carry
This female bastard hence, and that thou bear it   175
To some remote and desert place quite out
Of our dominions, and that there thou leave it,
Without more mercy, to it° own protection
And favor of the climate. As by strange fortune

---

148. **beseech:** beseech you.   150. **dear:** loyal, heartfelt.   160. **Margery:** (A derisive term, evidently equivalent to *Partlet* in line 76.)   162. **this beard's:** (Probably Antigonus's.)   170. **see'st thou:** i.e., do you hear.   **fail:** failure.   174. **liegeman:** loyal subject.   178. **it:** its.

It came to us, I do in justice charge thee,   180
On thy soul's peril and thy body's torture,
That thou commend it strangely to some place°
Where chance may nurse or end it. Take it up.

ANTIGONUS: [*taking up the baby*]
I swear to do this, though a present death
Had been more merciful. — Come on, poor babe.   185
Some powerful spirit instruct the kites and ravens
To be thy nurses! Wolves and bears, they say,
Casting their savageness aside, have done
Like offices of pity. — Sir, be prosperous
In more° than this deed does require!° — And blessing   190
Against this cruelty fight on thy side,
Poor thing, condemned to loss!°   *Exit* [*with the baby*].

LEONTES: No, I'll not rear
Another's issue.

Enter a Servant.

SERVANT: Please Your Highness, posts°
From those you sent to th'oracle are come
An hour since. Cleomenes and Dion,   195
Being well arrived from Delphos, are both landed,
Hasting to th' court.

A LORD: So please you, sir, their speed
Hath been beyond account.°

LEONTES: Twenty-three days
They have been absent. 'Tis good speed, foretells
The great Apollo suddenly° will have   200
The truth of this appear. Prepare you, lords.
Summon a session,° that we may arraign
Our most disloyal lady; for, as she hath
Been publicly accused, so shall she have
A just and open trial. While she lives   205
My heart will be a burden to me. Leave me,
And think upon my bidding.   *Exeunt* [*separately*].

---

182. **commend . . . place**: commit it to some foreign place. 190. **more**: i.e., more ways, more extent. **require**: deserve. 192. **loss**: destruction. 193. **posts**: messengers. 198. **beyond account**: unprecedented, or, beyond explanation. 200. **suddenly**: at once. 202. **session**: trial.

ACT 3, SCENE 1°

Enter Cleomenes and Dion.

CLEOMENES:
    The climate's delicate, the air most sweet,
    Fertile the isle,° the temple much surpassing
    The common praise it bears.
DION: I shall report,
    For most it caught me, the celestial habits° —
    Methinks I so should term them — and the reverence   5
    Of the grave wearers. Oh, the sacrifice!
    How ceremonious, solemn, and unearthly
    It was i'th'offering!
CLEOMENES: But of all, the burst
    And the ear-deaf'ning voice o'th'oracle,
    Kin to Jove's thunder, so surprised° my sense   10
    That I was nothing.
DION: If th'event° o'th' journey
    Prove as successful to the Queen — O, be't so! —
    As it hath been to us rare, pleasant, speedy,
    The time is worth the use on't.°
CLEOMENES: Great Apollo
    Turn all to th' best! These proclamations,   15
    So forcing faults upon Hermione,
    I little like.
DION: The violent carriage° of it
    Will clear or end the business. When the oracle,
    Thus by Apollo's great divine° sealed up,
    Shall the contents discover,° something rare   20
    Even then will rush to knowledge. Go. Fresh horses!
    And gracious be the issue!   *Exeunt.*

ACT 3, SCENE 1. **Location:** Sicilia. On the way to Leontes court.   **2. isle:** The city of Delphos [see 2.1.184] to which Leontes' ambassadors have been sent was often confused with the island of Delos, the birthplace of Apollo.   **4. habits:** vestments.   **10. surprised:** overwhelmed.   **11. th'event:** the outcome.   **14. is worth . . . on't:** has been well employed.   **17. carriage:** execution, management.   **19. great divine:** chief priest.   **20. discover:** reveal.

ACT 3, SCENE 2°

Enter Leontes, Lords, [and] Officers.

LEONTES:
This sessions, to our great grief we pronounce,
Even pushes 'gainst our heart: the party tried
The daughter of a king, our wife, and one
Of us° too much beloved. Let us be cleared
Of being tyrannous, since we so openly   5
Proceed in justice, which shall have due course
Even to the guilt or the purgation.°
Produce the prisoner.

OFFICER:
It is His Highness' pleasure that the Queen
Appear in person here in court. Silence!   10

[Enter] Hermione, as to her trial, [Paulina, and] Ladies.

LEONTES:
Read the indictment.

OFFICER: [*reads*] "Hermione, Queen to the worthy Leontes, King of Sicilia, thou art here accused and arraigned of high treason, in committing adultery with Polixenes, King of Bohemia, and conspiring with
Camillo to take away the life of our sovereign lord the King, thy royal   15
husband; the pretense° whereof being by circumstances partly laid open,
thou, Hermione, contrary to the faith and allegiance of a true subject,
didst counsel and aid them, for their better safety, to fly away by night."

HERMIONE:
Since what I am to say must be but that
Which contradicts my accusation, and   20
The testimony on my part no other
But what comes from myself, it shall scarce boot° me
To say "not guilty." Mine integrity,
Being counted falsehood, shall, as I express it,
Be so received. But thus: if powers divine   25
Behold our human actions, as they do,

ACT 3, SCENE 2. **Location:** Sicilia. A place of justice, probably at court.   4. **Of us:** by me.
7. **purgation:** acquittal.   16. **pretense:** purpose, design.   22. **boot:** avail.

I doubt not then but innocence shall make
False accusation blush and tyranny
Tremble at patience. You, my lord, best know,
Who least will seem to do so, my past life   30
Hath been as continent, as chaste, as true
As I am now unhappy; which is more
Than history° can pattern,° though devised
And played to take° spectators. For behold me —
A fellow of the royal bed, which owe°   35
A moiety° of the throne, a great king's daughter,
The mother to a hopeful prince — here standing
To prate and talk for life and honor 'fore
Who please° to come and hear. For life, I prize it
As I weigh grief, which I would spare. For honor,   40
'Tis a derivative from me to mine,
And only that I stand for.° I appeal
To your own conscience,° sir, before Polixenes
Came to your court, how I was in your grace,
How merited to be so; since he came,   45
With what encounter so uncurrent I
Have strained t'appear thus;° if one jot beyond
The bound of honor, or in act or will
That way inclining, hardened° be the hearts
Of all that hear me, and my near'st of kin   50
Cry "Fie" upon my grave!
LEONTES: I ne'er heard yet
That any of these bolder vices wanted
Less° impudence to gainsay what they did
Than to perform it first.
HERMIONE: That's true enough,
Though 'tis a saying, sir, not due° to me.   55
LEONTES:
You will not own it.

---

33. **history:** story, drama. **pattern:** show a similar example for. 34. **take:** please, charm.
35. **which owe:** who owns. 36. **moiety:** share. 39. **Who please:** whoever chooses.
39–42. **For . . . stand for:** As for life, I value it as I value grief, and would as willingly do without; as for honor, it is transmitted from me to my descendants, and that only I make a stand for.
43. **conscience:** consideration, inward knowledge. 46–47. **With . . . thus:** (I ask) by what behavior so unacceptable I have transgressed so that I appear thus (in disgrace and on trial).
49. **hardened:** hardened against me. 52–53. **wanted Less:** were more lacking in. 55. **due:** applicable.

HERMIONE: More than mistress of
Which comes to me in name of fault, I must not
At all acknowledge.° For° Polixenes,
With whom I am accused, I do confess
I loved him as in honor he required;°   60
With such a kind of love as might become
A lady like me; with a love even such,
So, and no other, as yourself commanded;
Which not to have done I think had been in me
Both disobedience and ingratitude   65
To you and toward your friend, whose love had spoke,
Even since it could speak, from an infant, freely
That it was yours.° Now, for conspiracy,
I know not how it tastes, though it be dished°
For me to try how. All I know of it   70
Is that Camillo was an honest man;
And why he left your court, the gods themselves,
Wotting° no more than I, are ignorant.

LEONTES:
You knew of his departure, as you know
What you have underta'en to do in 's absence.   75

HERMIONE:
Sir,
You speak a language that I understand not.
My life stands in the level° of your dreams,
Which° I'll lay down.

LEONTES: Your actions are my dreams.°
You had a bastard by Polixenes,   80
And I but dreamed it. As you were past all shame —
Those of your fact° are so — so past all truth,
Which to deny concerns more than avails;° for as
Thy brat hath been cast out, like to itself,°

56–58. More . . . acknowledge: I must not acknowledge more faults than I actually have.
58. For: as for.   60. required: deserved.   66–68. your friend . . . yours: i.e., Polixenes, who
professed love for you from earliest childhood (as you for him).   69. though . . . dished:
even if it were to be served up.   73. Wotting: supposing they know.   78. level: aim, range.
79. Which: i.e., my life.   Your . . . dreams: i.e., you have performed what I have fantasized,
and what you have done preys on my mind.   82. Those of your fact: All those who do what
you did.   83. Which . . . avails: your denial of which is understandable, but it won't do you
any good.   84. like to itself: as an outcast, fatherless brat ought to be.

No father owning it — which is indeed   85
More criminal in thee than it — so thou
Shalt feel our justice, in whose easiest passage
Look for no less than death.°

HERMIONE: Sir, spare your threats.
The bug° which you would fright me with I seek.
To me can life be no commodity.°   90
The crown and comfort of my life, your favor,
I do give° lost, for I do feel it gone,
But know not how it went. My second joy
And firstfruits of my body, from his presence
I am barred, like one infectious. My third comfort,   95
Starred most unluckily,° is from my breast,
The innocent milk in it° most innocent mouth,
Haled out to murder; myself on every post°
Proclaimed a strumpet; with immodest° hatred
The childbed privilege denied, which longs°   100
To women of all fashion;° lastly, hurried
Here to this place, i'th'open air, before
I have got strength of limit.° Now, my liege,
Tell me what blessings I have here alive
That I should fear to die? Therefore proceed.   105
But yet hear this; mistake me not. No life,°
I prize it not a straw. But for mine honor,
Which I would free,° if I shall be condemned
Upon surmises, all proofs sleeping else
But what your jealousies awake, I tell you   110
'Tis rigor° and not law. Your Honors all,
I do refer me to the oracle.
Apollo be my judge!

A LORD: This your request
Is altogether just. Therefore bring forth,
And in Apollo's name, his oracle.   [*Exeunt certain Officers.*]   115

87–88. **in whose . . . death:** i.e., which will impose the death sentence at least, perhaps torture also. 89. **bug:** bugbear, bogey, imaginary object of terror. 90. **commodity:** asset. 92. **give:** reckon as, or give up for. 96. **Starred most unluckily:** born under a most unlucky star. 97. **it:** its. 98. **post:** posting place for public notices. 99. **immodest:** immoderate. 100. **The childbed . . . longs:** denied the privilege of bedrest after giving birth, something that is the right. 101. **all fashion:** every rank. 103. **got . . . limit:** regained my strength after having borne a child. 106. **No life:** i.e., I do not ask for life. 108. **free:** vindicate. 111. **rigor:** tyranny.

HERMIONE:
The Emperor of Russia was my father.
Oh, that he were alive and here beholding
His daughter's trial! That he did but see
The flatness° of my misery, yet with eyes
Of pity, not revenge!   120

[*Enter Officers, with*] Cleomenes [*and*] Dion.

OFFICER: [*holding a sword*]
You here shall swear upon this sword of justice
That you, Cleomenes and Dion, have
Been both at Delphos, and from thence have brought
This sealed up oracle, by the hand delivered
Of great Apollo's priest, and that since then   125
You have not dared to break the holy seal.
Nor read the secrets in't.
CLEOMENES, DION: All this we swear.
LEONTES:
Break up° the seals and read.
OFFICER: [*reads*] "Hermione is chaste, Polixenes blameless, Camillo a true
    subject, Leontes a jealous tyrant, his innocent babe truly begotten, and 130
    the King shall live without an heir if that which is lost be not found."
LORDS:
Now blessèd be the great Apollo!
HERMIONE: Praised!
LEONTES:
Hast thou read truth?
OFFICER: Ay, my lord, even so
As it is here set down.
LEONTES:
There is no truth at all i'th'oracle.   135
The sessions shall proceed. This is mere falsehood.

[*Enter a Servant.*]

SERVANT:
My lord the King, the King!
LEONTES: What is the business?
SERVANT:
Oh, sir, I shall be hated to report° it!

119. **flatness:** boundlessness.   128. **up:** open.   138. **to report:** for reporting.

The Prince your son, with mere conceit and fear°
Of the Queen's speed,° is gone.

LEONTES: How? Gone?

SERVANT: Is dead.   140

LEONTES:

Apollo's angry, and the heavens themselves
Do strike at my injustice. [*Hermione swoons.*] How now there?

PAULINA:

This news is mortal to the Queen. Look down
And see what death is doing.

LEONTES: Take her hence.
Her heart is but o'ercharged; she will recover.   145
I have too much believed mine own suspicion.
Beseech you, tenderly apply to her
Some remedies for life.   [*Exeunt Paulina and Ladies, with Hermione.*]
                              Apollo, pardon
My great profaneness 'gainst thine oracle!
I'll reconcile me to Polixenes,   150
New woo my queen, recall the good Camillo,
Whom I proclaim a man of truth, of mercy;
For, being transported by my jealousies
To bloody thoughts and to revenge, I chose
Camillo for the minister to poison   155
My friend Polixenes; which had been done,
But that the good mind of Camillo tardied°
My swift command, though I with death and with
Reward did threaten and encourage him,
Not doing it and being done.° He, most humane   160
And filled with honor, to my kingly guest
Unclasped my practice,° quit his fortunes here,
Which you knew great, and to the hazard
Of all incertainties himself commended,°
No richer than° his honor. How he glisters   165
Through my rust!° And how his piety
Does my deeds make the blacker!

---

139. **conceit and fear:** i.e., anxious concern.   140. **speed:** fate, fortune.   157. **tardied:** delayed.   160. **Not . . . done:** i.e., death if he did not do it and reward if he did.   162. **Unclasped my practice:** disclosed my plot.   164. **himself commended:** entrusted himself.   165. **No richer than:** with no riches except.   165–66. **How . . . rust!:** how he shines in contrast with my fault!

[*Enter Paulina.*]

PAULINA: Woe the while!
  Oh, cut my lace,° lest my heart, cracking it,
  Break too!
A LORD: What fit is this, good lady?
PAULINA:
  What studied° torments, tyrant, hast for me?   170
  What wheels, racks, fires? What flaying,° boiling
  In leads or oils? What old or newer torture
  Must I receive, whose every word deserves
  To taste of thy most worst?° Thy tyranny,
  Together working with thy jealousies —   175
  Fancies too weak for boys, too green and idle°
  For girls of nine — oh, think what they have done,
  And then run mad indeed, stark mad! For all
  Thy bygone fooleries were but spices° of it.
  That thou betrayed'st Polixenes, 'twas nothing;   180
  That did but show thee, of° a fool, inconstant
  And damnable ingrateful. Nor was 't much
  Thou wouldst have poisoned good Camillo's honor,
  To have° him kill a king — poor° trespasses,
  More monstrous standing by;° whereof I reckon   185
  The casting forth to crows° thy baby daughter
  To be or none° or little, though a devil
  Would have shed water out of fire° ere done't.
  Nor is't directly laid to thee, the death
  Of the young Prince, whose honorable thoughts,   190
  Thoughts high for one so tender,° cleft the heart
  That could conceive° a gross and foolish sire
  Blemished his gracious dam.° This is not, no,
  Laid to thy answer.° But the last — Oh, lords,
  When I have said,° cry woe! The Queen, the Queen,   195

---

168. **my lace:** the lace of my stays.   170. **studied:** ingeniously devised.   171. **wheels . . . flaying:** (Various methods of torture: being stretched on a wheel or rack until the bones are broken or pulled apart at the joints, being burned or skinned alive.)   173–74. **whose . . . worst?:** I, whose every word seems to invite your severest punishment?   176. **idle:** foolish.   179. **spices:** foretastes, samples.   181. **of:** for.   184. **To have:** by having.   **poor:** slight.   185. **More . . . by:** when more monstrous sins are at hand for comparison.   186. **crows:** carrion birds.   187. **or none:** either none.   188. **shed . . . fire:** wept from his fiery eyes or while surrounded by hell-fire.   191. **tender:** young.   192. **conceive:** apprehend that.   193. **dam:** mother.   194. **Laid . . . answer:** presented as a charge that you must answer.   195. **said:** finished speaking.

The sweet'st, dear'st creature's dead, and vengeance for't
Not dropped down yet.

A LORD: The higher powers forbid!

PAULINA:

I say she's dead. I'll swear't. If word nor oath
Prevail not, go and see. If you can bring
Tincture° or luster in her lip, her eye,   200
Heat outwardly or breath within, I'll serve you
As I would do the gods. But, O thou tyrant!
Do not repent these things, for they are heavier
Than all thy woes can stir.° Therefore betake thee
To nothing but despair. A thousand knees   205
Ten thousand years together, naked, fasting,
Upon a barren mountain, and still° winter
In storm perpetual, could not move the gods
To look that way thou wert.°

LEONTES: Go on, go on.
Thou canst not speak too much. I have deserved   210
All tongues to talk their bitt'rest.

A LORD: [to Paulina]   Say no more.
Howe'er the business goes, you have made fault
I'th' boldness of your speech.

PAULINA: I am sorry for't.
All faults I make,° when I shall come to know them,
I do repent. Alas, I have showed too much   215
The rashness of a woman! He is touched
To th' noble heart. What's gone and what's past help
Should be past grief — Do not receive affliction
At my petition.° I beseech you, rather
Let me be punished, that have minded you°   220
Of what you should forget. Now, good my liege,
Sir, royal sir, forgive a foolish woman.
The love I bore your queen — lo, fool again!
I'll speak of her no more, nor of your children;
I'll not remember° you of my own lord,   225
Who is lost too. Take your patience to you,°
And I'll say nothing.

---

200. Tincture: color.   204. woes can stir: penance can remove.   207. still: always.   209. To look . . . wert: to regard you.   214. I make: that I make.   218–19. Do . . . petition: do not afflict yourself with remorse at my urging.   220. minded you: put you in mind.   225. remember: remind.   226. Take . . . you: Arm yourself with patience.

LEONTES: Thou didst speak but well
When most the truth, which I receive much better
Than to be pitied of thee. Prithee, bring me
To the dead bodies of my queen and son.　　　　　　　230
One grave shall be for both. Upon them shall
The causes of their death appear, unto
Our shame perpetual. Once a day I'll visit
The chapel where they lie, and tears shed there
Shall be my recreation.° So long as nature°　　　　235
Will bear up with this exercise, so long
I daily vow to use it. Come and lead me
To these sorrows.　　　　　　　　　　　*Exeunt.*

Act 3, Scene 3°

Enter Antigonus [and] a Mariner, [with a] babe.

ANTIGONUS:
Thou art perfect° then, our ship hath touched upon
The deserts of Bohemia?°
MARINER: Ay, my lord, and fear
We have landed in ill time. The skies look grimly,
And threaten present° blusters. In my conscience,°
The heavens with that we have in hand are angry　　　5
And frown upon 's.
ANTIGONUS:
Their sacred wills be done! Go, get aboard;
Look to thy bark.° I'll not be long before
I call upon thee.
MARINER: Make your best haste, and go not
Too far i'th' land. 'Tis like° to be loud° weather.　　　10
Besides, this place is famous for the creatures
Of prey that keep upon't.°
ANTIGONUS: Go thou away.
I'll follow instantly.

---

235. **my recreation:** (1) my sole diversion (2) my spiritual regeneration.　**nature:** my physical being.　**Act 3, Scene 3. Location:** Bohemia. The seacoast.　1. **perfect:** certain.　2. **deserts of Bohemia:** i.e., deserted region on the coast. (Shakespeare follows his primary source, Robert Greene's prose romance *Pandosto,* in erroneously giving a seacoast to Bohemia, a landlocked European nation.)　4. **present:** immediate.　**conscience:** opinion.　8. **bark:** ship.　10. **like:** likely.　**loud:** stormy.　12. **keep upon't:** inhabit it.

MARINER: I am glad at heart
 To be so rid o'th' business.   *Exit.*

ANTIGONUS: Come, poor babe.
 I have heard, but not believed, the spirits o'th' dead   15
 May walk again. If such thing be, thy mother
 Appeared to me last night, for ne'er was dream
 So like a waking. To me comes a creature,
 Sometimes her head on one side, some another,°
 I never saw a vessel of like sorrow,   20
 So filled and so becoming.° In pure white robes,
 Like very sanctity, she did approach
 My cabin where I lay, thrice bowed before me,
 And, gasping to begin some speech, her eyes
 Became two spouts. The fury spent, anon   25
 Did this break from her: "Good Antigonus,
 Since fate, against thy better disposition,
 Hath made thy person for the thrower-out
 Of my poor babe, according to thine oath,
 Places remote enough are in Bohemia;   30
 There weep and leave it crying. And, for° the babe
 Is counted lost forever, Perdita,°
 I prithee, call't. For this ungentle° business
 Put on thee by my lord, thou ne'er shalt see
 Thy wife Paulina more." And so, with shrieks,   35
 She melted into air. Affrighted much,
 I did in time collect myself and thought
 This was so and no slumber. Dreams are toys;°
 Yet for this once, yea, superstitiously,
 I will be squared° by this. I do believe   40
 Hermione hath suffered death, and that
 Apollo would, this being indeed the issue
 Of King Polixenes, it should here be laid,
 Either for life or death, upon the earth
 Of its right father. Blossom, speed thee well! *[He lays down the baby.]* 45
 There lie, and there thy character;° there these,°

---

19. **some another:** sometimes the other. 21. **So . . . becoming:** i.e., so filled with sorrow and able to bear it so gracefully. 31. **for:** because. 32. **Perdita:** i.e., the lost one. 33. **ungentle:** ignoble. 38. **toys:** trifles. 40. **squared:** directed in my course. 46. **thy character:** the written account of you (i.e., the one that subsequently will serve to identify Perdita). **these:** i.e., the gold and jewels found by the Shepherd, also later used to identify her.

[*He places a box and a fardel° beside the baby.*]
Which may, if fortune please, both breed thee,° pretty,°
And still rest thine.° [*Thunder.*] The storm begins. Poor wretch,
That for thy mother's fault art thus exposed
To loss and what may follow! Weep I cannot,°   50
But my heart bleeds; and most accurst am I
To be by oath enjoined to this. Farewell!
The day frowns more and more. Thou'rt like to have
A lullaby too rough. I never saw
The heavens so dim by day. A savage clamor!   55
Well may I get aboard! This is the chase.
I am gone forever!   *Exit, pursued by a bear.*

[*Enter a*] Shepherd.

SHEPHERD: I would there were no age between ten and three-and-twenty,
or that youth would sleep out the rest, for there is nothing in the between but getting wenches with child, wronging the ancientry,° steal-   60
ing, fighting — Hark you now, would any but these boiled brains° of
nineteen and two-and-twenty hunt this weather? They have scared away
two of my best sheep, which I fear the wolf will sooner find than the
master. If anywhere I have them, 'tis by the seaside, browsing of ivy.
Good luck, an't be thy will!° [*Seeing the child.*] What have we here? Mercy   65
on 's, a bairn,° a very pretty bairn! A boy or a child,° I wonder? A pretty
one, a very pretty one. Sure some scape.° Though I am not bookish, yet
I can read waiting-gentlewoman in the scape. This has been some stair-
work, some trunk-work, some behind-door-work.° They were warmer
that got° this than the poor thing is here. I'll take it up for pity. Yet I'll   70
tarry till my son come; he hallooed but even now. — Whoa, ho, hoa!

Enter Clown.°

CLOWN: Hilloa, loa!

46.1. *box, fardel*: (The box, containing gold and jewels, is later produced by the old Shepherd
and the Clown; see 4.4.708. They also have a *fardel*, or "bundle," consisting evidently of the
bearing cloth [3.3.99] and/or mantle [5.2.24] in which the babe was found.)   47. **breed thee:**
keep you, pay for your support.   **pretty:** pretty one.   48. **And still rest thine:** i.e., and still
provide a heritage with what is unspent.   50. **Weep I cannot:** i.e., I cannot weep as the Queen
instructed me (line 31).   60. **ancientry:** old people.   61. **boiled brains:** addlepated youths.
65. **Good . . . will!:** i.e., may God grant me good luck in finding my sheep!   66. **bairn:** child.
66. **child:** i.e., female infant.   67. **scape:** sexual escapade.   68–69. **stair-work . . . behind-
door-work:** i.e., sexual liaisons under or behind the stairs or using a room or a trunk for concealment.   70. **got:** begot.   71.1. *Clown:* country fellow, rustic.

SHEPHERD: What, art so near? If thou'lt see a thing to talk on when thou art dead and rotten, come hither. What ail'st thou, man?

CLOWN: I have seen two such sights, by sea and by land! But I am not to 75
say it is a sea, for it is now the sky; betwixt the firmament and it you cannot thrust a bodkin's° point.

SHEPHERD: Why, boy, how is it?

CLOWN: I would you did but see how it chafes, how it rages, how it takes
up° the shore! But that's not to the point. Oh, the most piteous cry of the 80
poor souls! Sometimes to see 'em, and not to see 'em; now the ship boring the moon with her mainmast, and anon swallowed with yeast° and froth, as you'd thrust a cork into a hogshead.° And then for the land service,° to see how the bear tore out his shoulder bone; how he cried to me for help and said his name was Antigonus, a nobleman. But to make an 85
end of the ship: to see how the sea flapdragoned° it! But first, how the poor souls roared and the sea mocked them, and how the poor gentleman roared and the bear mocked him, both roaring louder than the sea or weather.

SHEPHERD: Name of mercy, when was this, boy? 90

CLOWN: Now, now. I have not winked° since I saw these sights. The men are not yet cold under water, nor the bear half dined on the gentleman. He's at it now.

SHEPHERD: Would I had been by, to have helped the old man!

CLOWN: I would you had been by the ship side, to have helped her. There 95
your charity would have lacked footing.°

SHEPHERD: Heavy matters, heavy matters! But look thee here, boy. Now bless thyself. Thou met'st with things dying, I with things newborn. Here's a sight for thee; look thee, a bearing cloth° for a squire's child! Look thee here; take up, take up, boy. Open't. So, let's see. It was told me 100
I should be rich by the fairies. This is some changeling.° Open't. What's within, boy?   [*The Clown opens the box.*]

CLOWN: You're a made old man. If the sins of your youth are forgiven you, you're well to live.° Gold, all gold!

---

77. **bodkin's:** needle's. (A *bodkin* can also be a dagger, awl, etc.)   79–80. **takes up:** (1) contends with, rebukes (2) swallows.   82. **yeast:** foam.   83. **hogshead:** large barrel. (The image is of a cork swimming in a turbulent expanse of frothing liquid.)   83–84. **land service:** (1) dish of food served on land (2) military service on land (as distinguished from naval service); here, the doings on land.   86. **flapdragoned:** swallowed as one would a flapdragon, i.e., a raisin or the like swallowed out of burning brandy in the game of snapdragon.   91. **winked:** blinked an eye.   96. **footing:** (1) foothold (2) establishment of a charitable foundation, one that would provide *charity* (line 96).   99. **bearing cloth:** rich cloth or mantle in which a child was carried to its baptism.   101. **changeling:** child left or taken by fairies.   104. **well to live:** well-to-do.

SHEPHERD: This is fairy gold, boy, and 'twill prove so. Up with't, keep it 105
close.° Home, home, the next° way. We are lucky, boy, and to be so still°
requires nothing but secrecy.° Let my sheep go. Come, good boy, the next
way home.

CLOWN: Go you the next way with your findings. I'll go see if the bear be
gone from the gentleman, and how much he hath eaten. They are never 110
curst° but when they are hungry. If there be any of him left, I'll bury it.

SHEPHERD: That's a good deed. If thou mayest discern by that which is
left of him what he is,° fetch me to th' sight of him.

CLOWN: Marry,° will I; and you shall help to put him i'th' ground.

SHEPHERD: 'Tis a lucky day, boy, and we'll do good deeds on't. *Exeunt.* 115

ACT 4, SCENE I

Enter Time, the Chorus.

TIME:
I, that please some, try° all, both joy and terror
Of good and bad, that makes and unfolds error,°
Now take upon me, in the name of Time,
To use my wings. Impute it not a crime
To me or my swift passage that I slide 5
O'er sixteen years and leave the growth untried°
Of that wide gap, since it is in my power
To o'erthrow law° and in one self-born° hour
To plant and o'erwhelm custom. Let me pass
The same I am ere ancient'st order was 10
Or what is now received.° I witness to
The times that brought them° in; so shall I do
To th' freshest things now reigning, and make stale
The glistering° of this present as my tale

---

106. **close:** secret. **next:** nearest. **still:** on a continuing basis. 106–07. **to be . . . secrecy:** (To talk about fairy gifts would be to more properly ensure bad luck.) 111. **curst:** mean, fierce. 113. **what he is:** what is his identity or rank. 114. **Marry:** i.e., indeed. (Originally an oath, "by the Virgin Mary.") ACT 4, SCENE I. 1. **try:** test. 2. **that . . . error:** i.e., I who make error, thus bringing joy to the bad and terror to the good, and then at last unfold or disclose error, thus bringing joy to the good and terror to the bad. 6. **growth untried:** developments unexplored. 8. **law:** any established order (including the rule of the unity of time in a dramatic performance, conventionally limiting the action to twenty-four hours). **self-born:** selfsame, or born of myself (since hours are the creations of Time). 9–11. **Let . . . received:** let me continue as I have been from before the beginning of time to the present. 12. **them:** i.e., law and custom. 14. **glistering:** glittering shine.

Now seems to it.° Your patience this allowing,   15
I turn my glass° and give my scene such growing
As° you had slept between. Leontes leaving
Th' effects of his fond° jealousies, so grieving
That he shuts up himself, imagine me,
Gentle spectators, that I now may be   20
In fair Bohemia. And remember well
I mentioned a son o'th' King's, which Florizel
I now name to you; and with speed so pace°
To speak of Perdita, now grown in grace
Equal with wond'ring.° What of her ensues   25
I list not° prophesy; but let Time's news
Be known when 'tis brought forth. A shepherd's daughter,
And what to her adheres,° which follows after,
Is th' argument° of Time. Of this allow,
If ever you have spent time worse ere now;   30
If never, yet that° Time himself doth say
He wishes earnestly you never may.   *Exit.*

ACT 4, SCENE 2°

Enter Polixenes and Camillo.

POLIXENES: I pray thee, good Camillo, be no more importunate. 'Tis a
sickness denying thee anything, a death to grant this.

CAMILLO: It is fifteen° years since I saw my country. Though I have for the
most part been aired abroad,° I desire to lay my bones there. Besides, the
penitent King, my master, hath sent for me, to whose feeling° sorrows I   5
might be some allay° — or I o'erween° to think so — which is another
spur to my departure.

POLIXENES: As thou lov'st me, Camillo, wipe not out the rest of thy services by leaving me now. The need I have of thee thine own goodness
hath made. Better not to have had thee than thus to want° thee. Thou,   10
having made me businesses which none without thee can sufficiently

---

15. **seems to it:** seems (stale) when compared with the present.   16. **glass:** hourglass.   17. **As:**
as if.   18. **fond:** foolish.   23. **pace:** proceed.   24–25. **now . . . wond'ring:** now grown so
gracious (and graceful) as to inspire wonderment.   26. **list not:** do not care to.   28. **to her
adheres:** concerns her.   29. **th'argument:** the subject matter.   31. **yet that:** i.e., yet allow that.
ACT 4, SCENE 2. **Location:** Bohemia. The court of Polixenes.   3. **fifteen:** (Compare "sixteen" at 4.1.6.)   4. **been aired abroad:** lived abroad.   5. **feeling:** heartfelt.   6. **allay:** means
of abatement.   **o'erween:** am presumptuous enough.   10. **want:** lack.

manage, must either stay to execute them thyself or take away with thee the very services thou hast done; which if I have not enough consid-ered° — as too much I cannot — to be more thankful to thee shall be my study, and my profit therein the heaping friendships.° Of that fatal country, Sicilia, prithee, speak no more, whose very naming punishes me with the remembrance of that penitent, as thou call'st him, and rec-onciled King, my brother, whose loss of his most precious queen and children are even now to be afresh lamented. Say to me, when saw'st thou the Prince Florizel, my son? Kings are no less unhappy, their issue not being gracious,° than they are in losing them when they have approved° their virtues. 15

20

CAMILLO: Sir, it is three days since I saw the Prince. What his happier affairs may be are to me unknown; but I have missingly° noted he is of late much retired from court and is less frequent to° his princely exercises than formerly he hath appeared. 25

POLIXENES: I have considered so much,° Camillo, and with some care, so far that I have eyes under my service which look upon his removedness;° from whom I have this intelligence,° that he is seldom from° the house of a most homely° shepherd — a man, they say, that from very nothing, and beyond the imagination of his neighbors, is grown into an unspeakable° estate. 30

CAMILLO: I have heard, sir, of such a man, who hath a daughter of most rare note.° The report of her is extended more than can be thought to begin from such a cottage. 35

POLIXENES: That's likewise part of my intelligence; but, I fear, the angle° that plucks our° son thither. Thou shalt accompany us to the place, where we will, not appearing what we are, have some question° with the shep-herd; from whose simplicity I think it not uneasy° to get the cause of my son's resort thither. Prithee, be my present partner in this business, and lay aside the thoughts of Sicilia. 40

CAMILLO: I willingly obey your command.

POLIXENES: My best Camillo! We must disguise ourselves.

Exit [with Camillo].

13–14. **considered:** rewarded.   15. **heaping friendships:** accumulation of your kind services and our mutual affection.   20-21. **their . . . gracious:** if their children behave ungraciously. 21. **approved:** proved.   24. **missingly:** being aware that he is missing.   25. **frequent to:** devoted to.   27. **so much:** as much.   28. **eyes . . . removedness:** spies who keep an eye on him in his absence.   29. **intelligence:** news.   **from:** away from.   30. **homely:** simple.   31. **un-speakable:** beyond description.   34. **note:** distinction.   36. **angle:** baited fishhook.   37. **our:** (The royal plural; also in *us*, line 37.)   38. **question:** talk.   39. **uneasy:** difficult.

Act 4, Scene 3°

Enter Autolycus, singing.

AUTOLYCUS:
When daffodils begin to peer,°
  With heigh, the doxy° over the dale!
Why, then comes in the sweet o'the year,
  For the red blood reigns in the winter's pale.°

The white sheet bleaching on the hedge,   5
  With heigh, the sweet birds, oh, how they sing!
Doth set my pugging tooth on edge,°
  For a quart of ale° is a dish for a king.

The lark, that tirralirra chants,
  With heigh, with heigh, the thrush and the jay!   10
Are summer songs for me and my aunts,°
  While we lie tumbling in the hay.

I have served Prince Florizel and in my time wore three-pile,° but now I
am out of service.

But shall I go mourn for that,° my dear?   15
  The pale moon shines by night,
And when I wander° here and there,
  I then do most go right.°

If tinkers may have leave to live,°
  And bear the sow-skin budget,°   20
Then my account° I well may give,
  And in the stocks avouch it.°

Act 4, Scene 3. **Location:** Bohemia. A road near the Shepherd's cottage. **1. peer:** peep out, appear. **2. doxy:** beggar's wench. **4. pale:** (1) paleness (2) domain, region of authority. (The image is of red blood restoring vitality to a pale complexion.) **7. set . . . on edge:** i.e., whets the appetite of my thieving tooth, my taste for thieving. (To *pug* is to "pull, tug.") **8. quart of ale:** (To be paid for perhaps with profits from theft of sheets.) **11. aunts:** i.e., whores. **13. three-pile:** velvet having very rich pile or nap. **15. for that:** i.e., for being out of service. **17. wander:** (i.e., as a thief). **18. most go right:** i.e., live the life that is meant for me. **19. leave to live:** permission to practice their trade. **20. budget:** tool bag. **21. my account:** an account of myself. **22. in . . . avouch it:** i.e., affirm that I am a tinker if I find myself sitting in the stocks, where vagabonds often end up. (Autolycus passes himself off as a tinker to mask his real calling of thief.)

My traffic is sheets; when the kite builds, look to lesser linen.° My father named me Autolycus,° who,° being, as I am, littered under Mercury,° was likewise a snapper-up of unconsidered° trifles. With die and drab I purchased this caparison, and my revenue is the silly cheat.° Gallows and knock are too powerful on the highway; beating and hanging are terrors to me.° For° the life to come, I sleep out the thought of it.° A prize,° a prize! 25

Enter Clown.

CLOWN: Let me see: every 'leven wether tods;° every tod yields pound and odd shilling; fifteen hundred shorn, what comes the wool to? 30
AUTOLYCUS: [*aside*]   If the springe° hold, the cock's° mine.
CLOWN: I cannot do't without counters.° Let me see; what am I to buy for our sheep-shearing feast? Three pound of sugar, five pound of currants, rice — what will this sister of mine do with rice? But my father hath made her mistress of the feast, and she lays it on. She hath made me° four-and-twenty nosegays° for the shearers — three-man-song men° all, and very good ones; but they are most of them means° and basses, but one Puritan amongst them, and he sings psalms to hornpipes.° I must have saffron to color the warden° pies; mace; dates? — none, that's out of my note;° nutmegs, seven; a race° or two of ginger, but that I may beg; four pound of prunes, and as many of raisins o'th' sun.° 35 40
AUTOLYCUS: Oh, that ever I was born! [*He grovels on the ground.*]
CLOWN: I'th' name of me!°

---

23. when . . . linen: (The kite, a bird of prey, was thought to carry off small pieces of linen with which to construct its nest, whereas Autolycus makes off with larger linen or sheets hung out to dry.)   **24. Autolycus:** (Like his namesake, Ulysses's grandfather, the son of Mercury, this Autolycus is an expert thief.)   **who:** (Refers ambiguously to Autolycus and "My father"; see next note.)   **littered under Mercury:** (1) sired by Mercury, the god of thieves (2) born when the planet Mercury was in the ascendant.   **25. unconsidered:** left unattended, not worth thinking about.   **25–26. With . . . cheat:** gambling and whoring have brought me to the wearing of these tattered rags, and my source of income is petty trickery used to cheat simpletons.   **26–28. Gallows . . . to me:** i.e., hanging and being beaten, the ordinary hazards of being a highwayman, are too much for me; I'll stick to being a petty thief.   **28. For:** as for.   **sleep . . . it:** i.e., don't give a thought to punishment in the next world.   **prize:** booty.   **30. every . . . tods:** every eleven sheep yield a *tod*, i.e., a bulk of wool weighing twenty-eight pounds.   **32. springe:** snare.   **cock:** woodcock. (A proverbially stupid bird.)   **33. counters:** metal disks used in reckoning.   **36. made me:** made. (*Me* is used colloquially.)   **37. nosegays:** bouquets.   **three-man-song men:** singers of songs for three male voices: bass, tenor, and treble.   **38. means:** tenors.   **38–39. but . . . hornpipes:** (Puritans were often laughed at for their pious singing; this Puritan is imagined as singing hymns even to the sounds of raucous merriment at a fair.)   **40. warden:** made of the warden pear.   **40–41. out of my note:** not on my list.   **41. race:** root.   **42. o'th' sun:** dried in the sun.   **44. I'th' name of me!:** (An unusual and perhaps comic oath.)

AUTOLYCUS: Oh, help me, help me! Pluck but off these rags, and then   45
death, death!

CLOWN: Alack, poor soul! Thou hast need of more rags to lay on thee,
rather than have these off.

AUTOLYCUS: Oh, sir, the loathsomeness of them offend me more than the
stripes I have received, which are mighty ones and millions.   50

CLOWN: Alas, poor man! A million of beating may come to a great matter.

AUTOLYCUS: I am robbed, sir, and beaten; my money and apparel ta'en
from me, and these detestable things put upon me.

CLOWN: What, by a horseman° or a footman?°

AUTOLYCUS: A footman, sweet sir, a footman.   55

CLOWN: Indeed, he should be a footman by the garments he has left with
thee. If this be a horseman's coat, it hath seen very hot service. Lend me
thy hand; I'll help thee. Come, lend me thy hand. [*He helps him up.*]

AUTOLYCUS: Oh, good sir, tenderly. Oh!

CLOWN: Alas, poor soul!   60

AUTOLYCUS: Oh, good sir, softly, good sir! I fear, sir, my shoulder blade is out.

CLOWN: How now? Canst stand?

AUTOLYCUS: [*picking his pocket*] Softly, dear sir; good sir, softly. You ha' done
me a charitable office.

CLOWN: [*reaching for his purse*] Dost lack any money? I have a little money   65
for thee.°

AUTOLYCUS: No, good sweet sir; no, I beseech you, sir. I have a kinsman
not past three quarters of a mile hence, unto whom I was going; I shall
there have money or anything I want. Offer me no money, I pray you.
That kills my heart.   70

CLOWN: What manner of fellow was he that robbed you?

AUTOLYCUS: A fellow, sir, that I have known to go about with troll-my-
dames.° I knew him once a servant of the Prince. I cannot tell, good sir, for
which of his virtues it was, but he was certainly whipped out of the court.

CLOWN: His vices, you would say. There's no virtue whipped out of the   75
court. They cherish it to make it stay there; and yet it will no more but
abide.°

---

54. **horseman:** highwayman.   **footman:** a robber on foot. (As the Clown observes in line 56, a
common robber on foot would have poorer clothes than a mounted highwayman.)   **65–66. I
have . . . thee:** (The Clown reaches for his money and might have discovered the robbery if
Autolycus had not quickly begged him not to bother.)   **72–73. troll-my-dames:** or troll-
madams (from the French *trou-madame*), a game in which the object was to *troll* balls through
arches set on a board. (Autolycus uses the word to suggest women who *troll* or saunter about.)
76–77. no more but abide: make only a temporary or unwilling stay.

AUTOLYCUS: Vices, I would say, sir. I know this man well. He hath been since an ape bearer,° then a process server,° a bailiff. Then he compassed a motion° of the Prodigal Son and married a tinker's wife within a mile where my land and living° lies, and, having flown over many knavish professions, he settled only in rogue. Some call him Autolycus.

CLOWN: Out upon him! Prig,° for my life, prig! He haunts wakes,° fairs, and bearbaitings.

AUTOLYCUS: Very true, sir. He, sir, he. That's the rogue that put me into this apparel.

CLOWN: Not a more cowardly rogue in all Bohemia. If you had but looked big and spit at him, he'd have run.

AUTOLYCUS: I must confess to you, sir, I am no fighter. I am false° of heart that way, and that he knew, I warrant him.

CLOWN: How do you now?

AUTOLYCUS: Sweet sir, much better than I was. I can stand and walk. I will even take my leave of you and pace softly° towards my kinsman's.

CLOWN: Shall I bring thee on the way?°

AUTOLYCUS: No, good-faced sir, no, sweet sir.

CLOWN: Then fare thee well. I must go buy spices for our sheep-shearing.

Exit.

AUTOLYCUS: Prosper you, sweet sir!° Your purse is not hot enough to purchase your spice.° I'll be with you at your sheep-shearing too. If I make not this cheat bring out° another, and the shearers prove sheep, let me be unrolled° and my name put in the book of virtue!

Song.

Jog on, jog on, the footpath way,
  And merrily hent° the stile-a;
A merry heart goes all the day,
  Your sad tires in a mile-a.

Exit.

---

79. **ape bearer:** one who carries a trained monkey about for exhibition. **process server:** sheriff's officer who serves processes or summonses. 79–80. **compassed a motion:** devised a puppet show. 81. **living:** property. 83. **Prig:** thief. **wakes:** village festivals. 89. **false:** cowardly. 93. **softly:** slowly. 94. **bring . . . way:** go part of the way with you. 97. **Prosper . . . sir!** (Said to the departing Clown.) 97–98. **Your . . . spice:** i.e., you'll find but a cold purse to pay for your hot spices; an empty purse is a cold one. (Said after the Clown's departure.) 99. **cheat bring out:** swindle lead to. 100. **unrolled:** taken off the roll (of rogues and vagabonds). 102. **hent:** take hold of (as a means of leaping over).

ACT 4, SCENE 4°

Enter Florizel [in shepherd's garb, and] Perdita [in holiday attire].

FLORIZEL:

    These your unusual weeds° to each part of you
    Does give a life; no shepherdess, but Flora°
    Peering in April's front.° This your sheep-shearing
    Is as a meeting of the petty° gods,
    And you the queen on't.

PERDITA: Sir, my gracious lord,   5
    To chide at your extremes° it not becomes me.
    Oh, pardon that I name them! Your high self,
    The gracious mark o'th' land,° you have obscured
    With a swain's wearing,° and me, poor lowly maid,
    Most goddesslike pranked up.° But that our feasts   10
    In every mess have folly, and the feeders
    Digest it with a custom,° I should blush
    To see you so attired, swoon, I think,
    To show myself a glass.°

FLORIZEL: I bless the time
    When my good falcon made her flight across   15
    Thy father's ground.

PERDITA: Now Jove afford you cause!°
    To me the difference forges dread;° your greatness
    Hath not been used to fear. Even now I tremble
    To think your father by some accident
    Should pass this way as you did. Oh, the Fates!   20
    How would he look to see his work, so noble,
    Vilely bound up?° What would he say? Or how

ACT 4, SCENE 4. **Location:** Bohemia. The Shepherd's cottage. (See lines 181–82, 185, etc.) 1. **unusual weeds:** special, holiday attire. 2. **Flora:** goddess of flowers. 3. **Peering ... front:** peeping forth in early April, or, in April's countenance or garb. 4. **petty:** minor. 6. **extremes:** extravagant statements. 8. **mark o'th' land:** one who is noted and used as a model by everyone. 9. **wearing:** garb. 10. **pranked up:** bedecked. 10–12. **But ... custom:** were it not that whenever folks gather for merry feasting one encounters some folly, which the guests take in their stride as to be expected. 14. **To show ... glass:** if I were to see myself in a mirror. 16. **Jove ... cause!:** may Jove grant that you have good reason to be thankful! 17. **To me ... dread:** to me, the difference in our social rank is a source of dread. 21–22. **How ... bound up?:** what would he think to see the nobly-born son he created so vilely outfitted? (The *work*, Florizel, is metaphorically a piece of writing, and his garments are the binding of the book.)

Should I, in these my borrowed flaunts,° behold
The sternness of his presence?

FLORIZEL: Apprehend
Nothing but jollity. The gods themselves,   25
Humbling their deities to love, have taken
The shapes of beasts upon them. Jupiter
Became a bull, and bellowed; the green Neptune
A ram, and bleated; and the fire-robed god,
Golden Apollo, a poor humble swain,°   30
As I seem now. Their transformations
Were never for a piece of beauty rarer,
Nor in a way° so chaste, since my desires
Run not before mine honor, nor my lusts
Burn hotter than my faith.

PERDITA: Oh, but sir,   35
Your resolution cannot hold when 'tis
Opposed, as it must be, by th' power of the King.
One of these two must be necessities,
Which then will speak: that you must change this purpose
Or I my life.°

FLORIZEL: Thou dearest Perdita,   40
With these forced° thoughts, I prithee, darken not
The mirth o'th' feast. Or° I'll be thine, my fair,
Or not my father's. For I cannot be
Mine own, nor anything to any, if
I be not thine. To this I am most constant,   45
Though destiny say no. Be merry, gentle!°
Strangle such thoughts as these with anything
That you behold the while.° Your guests are coming.
Lift up your countenance as° it were the day
Of celebration of that nuptial which   50
We two have sworn shall come.

PERDITA: O Lady Fortune,
Stand you auspicious!

---

23. **flaunts:** finery.   27–30. **Jupiter . . . swain:** (Jupiter in the guise of a bull wooed Europa, Neptune disguised as a ram deceived Bisaltes or Theophane [Ovid, *Metamorphoses*, 6.117], and Apollo took the guise of a humble shepherd to enable Admetus to woo Alcestis.)   33. **in a way:** i.e., pursuing a purpose.   40. **Or I my life:** i.e., or I will be threatened with loss of life (as Polixenes indeed threatens at lines 414–21).   41. **forced:** farfetched, unnatural.   42. **Or:** either.   46. **gentle:** i.e., my gentle love.   47–48. **Strangle . . . while:** i.e., put down such thoughts by attending to matters at hand.   49. **as:** as if.

FLORIZEL: See, your guests approach.
Address° yourself to entertain them sprightly,
And let's be red with mirth.

[*Enter*] *Shepherd, Clown; Polixenes, Camillo* [*disguised*]*; Mopsa, Dorcas; servants.*

SHEPHERD:
Fie, daughter! When my old wife lived, upon   55
This day she was both pantler,° butler, cook,
Both dame° and servant; welcomed all, served all;
Would sing her song and dance her turn; now here,
At upper end o'th' table, now i'th' middle;
On his shoulder, and his;° her face afire   60
With labor, and the things she took to quench it
She would to each one sip.° You are retired,
As if you were a feasted one and not
The hostess of the meeting. Pray you, bid
These unknown friends to 's° welcome, for it is   65
A way to make us better friends, more known.°
Come, quench your blushes and present yourself
That which you are, mistress o'th' feast. Come on,
And bid us welcome to your sheep-shearing,
As your good flock shall prosper.
PERDITA: [*to Polixenes*]   Sir, welcome.   70
It is my father's will I should take on me
The hostess-ship o'th' day [*To Camillo*] You're welcome, sir. —
Give me those flowers there, Dorcas. — Reverend sirs,
For you there's rosemary and rue; these keep
Seeming° and savor all the winter long.   75
Grace and remembrance° be to you both,
And welcome to our shearing!   [*Giving them flowers.*]
POLIXENES: Shepherdess —
A fair one are you — well you fit our ages
With flowers of winter.
PERDITA: Sir, the year growing ancient,°

---

53. **Address:** prepare.   56. **pantler:** pantry servant.   57. **dame:** mistress of the household.
60. **On his . . . his:** at one person's . . . another's.   61–62. **and . . . sip:** and she would toast each
one with the drink she took to quench the fire of her labor.   65. **to 's:** each to his.   66. **more
known:** better acquainted.   75. **Seeming:** outward appearance, color.   76. **Grace and remembrance:** divine grace and remembrance after death. (Equated respectively with rue and
rosemary.)   79. **the year . . . ancient:** i.e., when autumn arrives.

Not yet on summer's death nor on the birth 80
Of trembling winter, the fairest flow'rs o'th' season
Are our carnations and streaked gillyvors,°
Which some call nature's bastards.° Of that kind
Our rustic garden's barren, and I care not
To get slips° of them.
POLIXENES: Wherefore, gentle maiden, 85
Do you neglect them?
PERDITA: For° I have heard it said
There is an art° which in their piedness° shares
With great creating nature.
POLIXENES: Say there be;
Yet nature is made better by no mean°
But° nature makes that mean. So, over that art 90
Which you say adds to nature is an art
That nature makes. You see, sweet maid, we marry
A gentler° scion to the wildest stock,
And make conceive a bark of baser kind
By bud of nobler race. This is an art 95
Which does mend nature — change it, rather — but
The art itself is nature.
PERDITA: So it is.
POLIXENES:
Then make your garden rich in gillyvors,
And do not call them bastards.
PERDITA: I'll not put
The dibble° in earth to set one slip of them, 100
No more than, were I painted,° I would wish
This youth should say 'twere well, and only therefore
Desire to breed by me. Here's flowers for you: [*giving them flowers*]
Hot° lavender, mints, savory, marjoram,
The marigold, that goes to bed wi'th' sun 105
And with him rises weeping. These are flowers

---

82. **gillyvors:** gillyflowers, a kind of carnation.   83. **nature's bastards:** i.e., the result of artificial breeding. (See lines 86–88.)   85. **slips:** cuttings.   86. **For:** because.   87. **art:** i.e., of crossbreeding.   **piedness:** particolored appearance. (Perdita disclaims the art of crossbreeding, since it infringes on what nature itself does so well.)   89. **mean:** means.   90. **But:** unless. (Polixenes's point is that the art of improving on nature is itself natural.)   93. **gentler:** nobler, more cultivated.   100. **dibble:** trowel.   101. **painted:** made artificially beautiful by cosmetics.   104. **Hot:** eager, ardent, aromatic (?). (Spices were classified as hot or cold.)

Of middle summer,° and I think they are given
To men of middle age. You're very welcome.

CAMILLO:
I should leave grazing, were I of your flock,
And only live by gazing.

PERDITA: Out,° alas!   110
You'd be so lean that blasts of January
Would blow you through and through. [*To Florizel*] Now, my fair'st friend,
I would I had some flow'rs o'th' spring that might
Become your time of day; [*to the Shepherdesses*] and yours, and yours,
That wear upon your virgin branches yet   115
Your maidenheads growing. O Proserpina,°
For the flow'rs now that, frighted, thou let'st fall
From Dis's wagon! Daffodils,
That come before the swallow dares, and take°
The winds of March with beauty; violets dim,°   120
But sweeter than the lids of Juno's eyes
Or Cytherea's° breath; pale primroses,
That die unmarried ere they can behold
Bright Phoebus° in his strength — a malady
Most incident to maids;° bold oxlips and   125
The crown imperial,° lilies of all kinds,
The flower-de-luce° being one. Oh, these I lack°
To make you garlands of, and my sweet friend,°
To strew him o'er and o'er!

FLORIZEL: What, like a corpse?

PERDITA:
No, like a bank for Love to lie and play on,°   130
Not like a corpse; or if,° not to be buried,

---

107. **middle summer**: (Having no autumn flowers in any case [lines 79–82], since it is too early in the season, Perdita flatters her older guests by giving them flowers appropriate to *middle age*.) 110. **Out**: (An exclamation of dismay.) 116. **Proserpina**: daughter of Ceres, stolen away by Pluto (*Dis*) and taken to Hades when, according to Ovid, she was gathering flowers. 119. **take**: charm. 120. **dim**: with hanging head. 122. **Cytherea's**: Venus's. 124. **Phoebus**: the sun-god. 124–25. **a malady . . . maids**: (Young maids, suffering from greensickness, a kind of anemia, are pale like the primrose.) 126. **crown imperial**: flower from the Levant, cultivated in English gardens. 127. **flower-de-luce**: fleur-de-lis. **I lack**: (Because the season is too late for them.) 128. **To . . . friend**: to make garlands of them for you (Polixenes and Camillo) and for my sweet friend (Florizel). 130. **like . . . play on**: as if one were strewing a bank where Cupid himself might lie in amorous play. 131. **or if**: or if like a corpse, that is, a living body.

But quick° and in mine arms. Come, take your flowers.   [*Giving flowers.*]
Methinks I play as I have seen them do
In Whitsun pastorals.° Sure this robe of mine
Does change my disposition.

FLORIZEL: What you do   135
Still betters what is done.° When you speak, sweet,
I'd have you do it ever. When you sing,
I'd have you buy and sell so, so give alms,
Pray so; and, for the ord'ring your affairs,
To sing them too. When you do dance, I wish you   140
A wave o'th' sea, that you might ever do
Nothing but that — move still, still so,
And own no other function. Each your doing,°
So singular° in each particular,
Crowns what you are doing in the present deeds,°   145
That all your acts are queens.

PERDITA: Oh, Doricles,°
Your praises are too large.° But that° your youth,
And the true blood which peeps fairly through't
Do plainly give you out° an unstained shepherd,
With wisdom I might fear, my Doricles,   150
You wooed me the false way.

FLORIZEL: I think you have
As little skill° to fear as I have purpose
To put you to't.° But come, our dance, I pray.
Your hand, my Perdita. So turtles° pair,
That never mean to part.

PERDITA: I'll swear for 'em.°   [*They speak apart.*] 155

POLIXENES: [*to Camillo*]
This is the prettiest lowborn lass that ever

---

132. **quick:** alive.   134. **Whitsun pastorals:** plays (including Robin Hood plays) and English
morris dances often performed at Whitsuntide, seven Sundays after Easter. (The part of Maid
Marian strikes Perdita as immodest for her usual behavior.)   136. **Still . . . done:** gets better
and better.   143. **Each your doing:** each thing you do and how you do it.   144. **singular:**
unique and peerless.   145. **Crowns . . . deeds:** makes whatever you are doing at the moment seem supremely wonderful.   146. **Doricles:** (Florizel's disguise name.)   147. **large:** lavish.   **But that:** were it not that.   149. **give you out:** proclaim you to be.   152. **skill:** reason.
153. **To . . . to't:** i.e., to woo you "the false way," with intent to seduce you.   154. **turtles:**
turtledoves, as symbols of faithful love.   155. **I'll swear for 'em:** i.e., I'll be sworn they do.

Ran on the greensward.° Nothing she does or seems
But smacks of something greater than herself,
Too noble for this place.

CAMILLO: He tells her something
That makes her blood look out.° Good sooth, she is   160
The queen of curds and cream.

CLOWN: Come on, strike up!

DORCAS:
Mopsa must be your mistress.° Marry, garlic,
To mend her kissing° with!

MOPSA: Now, in good time!°

CLOWN:
Not a word, a word. We stand upon° our manners.
Come, strike up!   [*Music.*] *Here a dance*° *of shepherds and*   165
                                             shepherdesses.

POLIXENES:
Pray, good shepherd, what fair swain is this
Which dances with your daughter?

SHEPHERD:
They call him Doricles, and° boasts himself
To have a worthy feeding;° but I have it
Upon his own report and I believe it.
He looks like sooth.° He says he loves my daughter.   170
I think so too, for never gazed the moon
Upon the water as he'll stand and read,
As 'twere, my daughter's eyes; and, to be plain,
I think there is not half a kiss to choose   175
Who loves another° best.

POLIXENES: She dances featly.°

SHEPHERD:
So she does anything — though I report it
That should be silent. If young Doricles
Do light upon° her, she shall bring him that
Which he not dreams of.   180

Enter Servant.

---

157. **greensward:** grassy turf.   160. **makes . . . out:** makes her blush.   162. **mistress:** i.e.,
partner in the dance.   163. **kissing:** i.e., bad breath. (Dorcas jests that even garlic would improve Mopsa's breath.)   **in good time:** (An expression of indignation.)   164. **stand upon:** set
store by.   165.1. *dance:* (Probably a morris dance.)   168. **and:** i.e., and they say he.   169. **feeding:** pasturage, lands.   171. **He . . . sooth:** he appears to be honest.   176. **another:** the other.
featly: gracefully.   179. **light upon:** choose.

SERVANT: Oh, master, if you did but hear the peddler at the door, you would never dance again after a tabor° and pipe; no, the bagpipe could not move you. He sings several° tunes faster than you'll tell° money. He utters them as° he had eaten ballads and all men's ears grew to his tunes.

CLOWN: He could never come better.° He shall come in. I love a ballad but even too well,° if it be doleful matter merrily set down, or a very pleasant° thing indeed and sung lamentably.°   185

SERVANT: He hath songs for man or woman, of all sizes.° No milliner° can so fit his customers with gloves. He has the prettiest love songs for maids, so without bawdry, which is strange, with such delicate bur- 190 dens° of dildos and fadings,° "Jump her and thump her"; and where some stretchmouthed° rascal would, as it were, mean mischief and break a foul gap into the matter,° he makes the maid to answer, "Whoop, do me no harm, good man"; puts him off, slights him, with "Whoop, do me no harm, good man."   195

POLIXENES: This is a brave° fellow.

CLOWN: Believe me, thou talkest of an admirable conceited° fellow. Has he any unbraided° wares?

SERVANT: He hath ribbons of all the colors i'th' rainbow; points° more than all the lawyers in Bohemia can learnedly handle, though they come 200 to him by th' gross; inkles, caddisses, cambrics, lawns.° Why, he sings 'em over as they were gods or goddesses; you would think a smock° were a she-angel, he so chants to the sleevehand° and the work about the square on't.°

CLOWN: Prithee, bring him in, and let him approach singing.   205

PERDITA: Forewarn him that he use no scurrilous words in 's tunes.

[The Servant goes to the door.]

CLOWN: You have of these peddlers° that have more in them than you'd think, sister.

PERDITA: Ay, good brother, or go about° to think.

---

182. **tabor:** small drum.   183. **several:** various.   **tell:** count.   184. **as:** as if. (Also in line 202.) 185. **better:** at a better time.   185–86. **but even too well:** all too well.   186. **pleasant:** merry. 187. **lamentably:** mournfully.   188. **sizes:** sorts.   **milliner:** vendor of fancy ware and apparel, including gloves, ribbons, and bonnets.   190–91. **burdens:** refrains.   191. **dildos and fadings:** words used as part of the refrains of ballads. (But with sexually suggestive double meaning unperceived by the servant, as also in *jump her, thump her, do me no harm*, etc.)   192. **stretch-mouthed:** widemouthed, foulmouthed.   192–93. **break . . . matter:** insert some gross obscenity into the song, or, act in a suggestive way.   196. **brave:** excellent.   197. **admirable conceited:** wonderfully witty and clever.   198. **unbraided:** not shopworn, new.   199. **points:** (1) laces for fastening clothes (2) headings in an argument.   201. **inkles . . . lawns:** linen tapes, worsted tape used for garters, fine heavy linen fabrics, fine sheer linens.   202. **smock:** petticoat.   203. **sleevehand:** wristband.   204. **square on't:** embroidered bosom or yoke of the garment.   207. **You . . . peddlers:** you'll find peddlers.   209. **go about:** intend, wish.

Enter Autolycus,° singing.

AUTOLYCUS:

> Lawn as white as driven snow,   210
> Cyprus° black as e'er was crow,
> Gloves as sweet° as damask roses,
> Masks for faces and for noses,
> Bugle bracelet,° necklace amber,
> Perfume for a lady's chamber,   215
> Golden coifs° and stomachers,°
> For my lads to give their dears,
> Pins and poking-sticks° of steel,
> What maids lack from head to heel,
> Come buy of me, come. Come buy, come buy.   220
> Buy, lads, or else your lasses cry.
> Come buy.

CLOWN: If I were not in love with Mopsa, thou shouldst take no money of me, but being enthralled as I am, it will also be the bondage° of certain ribbons and gloves.   225

MOPSA: I was promised them against° the feast, but they come not too late now.

DORCAS: He hath promised you more than that, or there be liars.°

MOPSA: He hath paid you all he promised you. Maybe he has paid you more,° which will shame you to give him again.°   230

CLOWN: Is there no manners left among maids? Will they wear their plackets° where they should bear their faces?° Is there not milking time, when you are going to bed, or kilnhole,° to whistle° of these secrets, but you must be tittle-tattling before all our guests? 'Tis well they are whisp'ring. Clamor° your tongues, and not a word more.   235

209.1. *Enter Autolycus:* (Apparently he is wearing a false beard; later in this scene, he removes it to impersonate a courtier to the Clown and Shepherd.) **211. Cyprus:** crepe. **212. sweet:** i.e., perfumed. (Also in line 237.) **214. Bugle bracelet:** bracelet of black glossy beads. **216. coifs:** close-fitting caps. **stomachers:** embroidered fronts for ladies' dresses. **218. poking-sticks:** rods used for ironing and stiffening the plaits of ruffs. (With sexual suggestion.) **224. it will . . . bondage:** it will mean the taking into custody (by means of purchase and tying up into a parcel). **226. against:** in anticipation of, in time for. **228. He . . . liars:** i.e., He promised to marry you, too, or else rumor is a liar. **229–30. paid you more:** i.e., made you pregnant. **230. which . . . again:** i.e., which will shame you by giving birth to his child. **232. plackets:** slits in petticoats. (With sexual suggestion of the pudendum, as in line 586.) **231–32. Will . . . faces?:** i.e., will they always be talking and revealing personal secrets? **233. kilnhole:** fire hole of a baking oven (where maids might gossip). **whistle:** whisper. **235. Clamor:** i.e., silence.

MOPSA: I have done. Come, you promised me a tawdry lace° and a pair of sweet gloves.

CLOWN: Have I not told thee how I was cozened° by the way and lost all my money?

AUTOLYCUS: And indeed, sir, there are cozeners abroad; therefore it behooves men to be wary.   240

CLOWN: Fear not thou, man, thou shalt lose nothing here.

AUTOLYCUS: I hope so, sir, for I have about me many parcels of charge.°

CLOWN: What hast here? Ballads?

MOPSA: Pray now, buy some. I love a ballad in print alife,° for then we are   245
sure they are true.

AUTOLYCUS: Here's one to a very doleful tune, how a usurer's wife was brought to bed of twenty money-bags at a burden,° and how she longed to eat adders' heads and toads carbonadoed.°

MOPSA: Is it true, think you?   250

AUTOLYCUS: Very true, and but a month old.

DORCAS: Bless° me from marrying a usurer!

AUTOLYCUS: Here's the midwife's name to't, one Mistress Taleporter,° and five or six honest wives that were present. Why should I carry lies abroad?   255

MOPSA: Pray you now, buy it.

CLOWN: Come on, lay it by, and let's first see more ballads. We'll buy the other things anon.

AUTOLYCUS: Here's another ballad, of a fish that appeared upon the coast on Wednesday the fourscore° of April, forty thousand fathom° above   260
water, and sung this ballad against the hard hearts of maids. It was thought she was a woman and was turned into a cold fish for she would not exchange flesh° with one that loved her. The ballad is very pitiful and as true.

DORCAS: Is it true too, think you?   265

AUTOLYCUS: Five justices' hands at it,° and witnesses more than my pack will hold.

CLOWN: Lay it by too. Another.

AUTOLYCUS: This is a merry ballad, but a very pretty one.

MOPSA: Let's have some merry ones.   270

---

236. **tawdry lace:** cheap and showy lace, or, neckerchief. (So called from St. Audrey's Fair.)   238. **cozened:** cheated.   243. **parcels of charge:** valuable items.   245. **alife:** on my life.   248. **at a burden:** in one childbirth.   249. **carbonadoed:** scored across and grilled.   52. **Bless:** God protect, keep.   253. **Taleporter:** i.e., talebearer, gossip.   260. **fourscore:** eightieth (!). **forty thousand fathom:** 240,000 feet.   263. **exchange flesh:** have sex.   266. **hands at it:** signatures on it.

AUTOLYCUS: Why, this is a passing° merry one and goes to the tune of
"Two Maids Wooing a Man." There's scarce a maid westward° but she
sings it. 'Tis in request, I can tell you.

MOPSA: We can both sing it. If thou'lt bear a part, thou shalt hear; 'tis in
three parts.

DORCAS: We had the tune on't° a month ago.   275

AUTOLYCUS: I can bear my part; you must know 'tis my occupation. Have
at it° with you.

Song.

AUTOLYCUS:
 Get you hence, for I must go
 Where it fits not you to know.   280
DORCAS:
  Whither?
MOPSA: Oh, whither?
DORCAS: Whither?
MOPSA:
 It becomes thy oath full well,
 Thou to me thy secrets tell.
DORCAS:
 Me too. Let me go thither.
MOPSA:
 Or° thou goest to th' grange° or mill.   285
DORCAS:
 If to either, thou dost ill.
AUTOLYCUS:
 Neither.
DORCAS: What, neither?
AUTOLYCUS: Neither.
DORCAS:
 Thou hast sworn my love to be.
MOPSA:
 Thou hast sworn it more to me.
 Then whither goest? Say, whither?   290
CLOWN: We'll have this song out° anon by ourselves. My father and the

---

271. **passing:** surpassingly.   272. **westward:** in the West Country.   276. **on't:** of it.
277–78. **Have at it:** here goes.   285. **Or:** either.   **grange:** farm.   291. **have this song out:**
finish this song.

gentlemen are in sad° talk, and we'll not trouble them. Come, bring away
thy pack after me. Wenches, I'll buy for you both. Peddler, let's have the
first choice. Follow me, girls.   [*Exit with Dorcas and Mopsa.*]

AUTOLYCUS: And you shall pay well for 'em.   [*He follows singing.*]   295

       Song.

      Will you buy any tape,
      Or lace for your cape,
   My dainty duck, my dear-a?
      Any silk, any thread,
      And toys° for your head,   300
 Of the new'st and fin'st, fin'st wear-a?
      Come to the peddler;
      Money's a meddler,°
 That doth utter° all men's ware-a.   *Exit.*

[*Enter a Servant.*]

SERVANT: Master, there is three carters,° three shepherds, three neatherds,°   305
three swineherds, that have made themselves all men of hair.° They call
themselves saultiers,° and they have a dance which the wenches say is a
gallimaufry° of gambols, because they are not in't; but they themselves
are o'th' mind, if it be not too rough for some that know little but bowling,° it will please plentifully.   310

SHEPHERD: Away! We'll none on't. Here has been too much homely° fool-
ery already. — I know, sir, we weary you.

POLIXENES: You weary those that refresh us. Pray, let's see these four
threes of herdsmen.

SERVANT: One three° of them, by their own report, sir, hath danced before   315
the King, and not the worst of the three but jumps twelve foot and a half
by the square.°

SHEPHERD: Leave° your prating. Since these good men are pleased, let
them come in; but quickly now.

SERVANT: Why, they stay at door, sir.   [*He goes to the door.*]   320

---

292. **sad:** serious.   300. **toys:** trifles.   303. **meddler:** i.e., go-between in commercial transac-
tions.   304. **utter:** put on the market.   305. **carters:** cart drivers.   **neatherds:** cowherds.
306. **of hair:** dressed in skins.   307. **saultiers:** leapers or vaulters. (With perhaps a play on
Saltiers as a blunder for "satyrs.")   308. **gallimaufry:** jumble.   309–10. **bowling:** (A more
gentle sport than the vigorous satyr dancing.)   311. **homely:** unpolished.   315. **three:** three-
some.   317. **by the square:** precisely.   318. **Leave:** leave off.

Here a dance of twelve Satyrs.

POLIXENES: [*to the Shepherd*]
   Oh, father, you'll know more of that hereafter.°
   [*To Camillo*] Is it not too far gone? 'Tis time to part them.
   He's simple° and tells much. [*To Florizel*] How now, fair shepherd?
   Your heart is full of something that does take
   Your mind from feasting. Sooth, when I was young   325
   And handed° love as you do, I was wont
   To load my she with knacks. I would have ransacked
   The peddler's silken treasury and have poured it
   To her acceptance;° you have let him go,
   And nothing marted with° him. If your lass   330
   Interpretation should abuse° and call this
   Your lack of love or bounty, you were straited°
   For a reply, at least if you make a care
   Of happy holding her.°
FLORIZEL: Old sir, I know
   She prizes not such trifles as these are.   335
   The gifts she looks° from me are packed and locked
   Up in my heart, which I have given already,
   But not delivered.° [*To Perdita*] Oh, hear me breathe my life°
   Before this ancient sir,° who, it should seem,
   Hath sometime loved! I take thy hand, this hand,   340
   As soft as dove's down and as white as it,
   Or Ethiopian's tooth, or the fanned° snow that's bolted°
   By th' northern blasts twice o'er.   [*He takes her hand.*]
POLIXENES: What follows this?
   How prettily the young swain seems to wash
   The hand was° fair before! I have put you out.°   345
   But to your protestation,° let me hear
   What you profess.
FLORIZEL: Do, and be witness to't.

---

321. Oh, . . . hereafter: (Polixenes completes the conversation he has been having with the old Shepherd during the dance. *Father* is a respectful term of address for older men.)   323. He's simple: the old Shepherd is guileless.   326. handed: handled, dealt in.   329. To her acceptance: for her to choose.   330. nothing marted with: have done no business with.   331. Interpretation should abuse: should interpret wrongly.   332. were straited: would be hard-pressed.   334. happy holding her: keeping her happy.   336. looks: looks for.   338. But not delivered: i.e., but I have not confirmed it by a solemn vow before witnesses, making binding the contract. breathe my life: i.e., pronounce eternal vows.   339. this ancient sir: Polixenes.   342. fanned: blown.   bolted: sifted.   345. was: that was.   put you out: interrupted what you were saying.   346. to your protestation: on with your public affirmation.

POLIXENES:
And this my neighbor too?

FLORIZEL: And he, and more
Than he, and men — the earth, the heavens, and all:
That, were I crowned the most imperial monarch,   350
Thereof most worthy,° were I the fairest youth
That ever made eye swerve,° had force and knowledge
More than was ever man's, I would not prize them
Without her love; for her employ them all,
Commend them and condemn them to her service   355
Or to their own perdition.°

POLIXENES: Fairly offered.

CAMILLO:
This shows a sound affection.

SHEPHERD: But, my daughter,
Say you the like to him?

PERDITA: I cannot speak
So well, nothing so well; no, nor mean better.
By th' pattern of mine own thoughts I cut out   360
The purity of his.°

SHEPHERD: Take hands, a bargain!
And, friends unknown, you shall bear witness to't:
I give my daughter to him and will make
Her portion equal his.

FLORIZEL: Oh, that must be
I' th' virtue of your daughter. One being dead,°   365
I shall have more than you can dream of yet;
Enough then for your wonder.° But come on:
Contract us 'fore these witnesses.

SHEPHERD: Come, your hand;
And, daughter, yours.

POLIXENES: Soft,° swain, awhile, beseech you.
Have you a father?   370

FLORIZEL:
I have, but what of him?

351. **Thereof most worthy:** the most worthy of monarchs.   352. **swerve:** turn in my direction (out of awe and respect).   355–56. **Commend . . . perdition:** either commend them to her service, or, failing that, condemn them to deserved destruction.   360–61. **By . . . of his:** by the purity of my own thoughts I can define the purity of his. (A metaphor of clothesmaking, Perdita has formed her own thoughts on the model of his.)   365. **One being dead:** when a certain person dies.   367. **Enough . . . wonder:** there will be enough then for you to wonder at.   369. **Soft:** wait a minute.

POLIXENES:
   Knows he of this?
FLORIZEL:
   He neither does nor shall.
POLIXENES:
   Methinks a father
   Is at the nuptial of his son a guest   375
   That best becomes the table. Pray you, once more,
   Is not your father grown incapable
   Of reasonable affairs?° Is he not stupid
   With age and altering rheums?° Can he speak? Hear?
   Know man from man? Dispute° his own estate?°   380
   Lies he not bedrid, and again does nothing
   But what he did being childish?°
FLORIZEL: No, good sir,
   He has his health and ampler strength indeed
   Than most have of his age.
POLIXENES: By my white beard,
   You offer him, if this be so, a wrong   385
   Something° unfilial. Reason my son°
   Should choose himself a wife, but as good reason
   The father, all whose joy is nothing else
   But fair posterity, should hold some counsel°
   In such a business.
FLORIZEL: I yield° all this;   390
   But for some other reasons, my grave sir,
   Which 'tis not fit you know, I not acquaint
   My father of this business.
POLIXENES: Let him know't.
FLORIZEL:
   He shall not.
POLIXENES: Prithee, let him.
FLORIZEL: No, he must not.
SHEPHERD:
   Let him, my son. He shall not need to grieve   395

---

378. **reasonable affairs:** matters requiring the use of reason.   379. **altering rheums:** weakening catarrhs or other diseases.   380. **Dispute:** discuss.   **estate:** affairs, condition.   382. **being childish:** when he was a child.   386. **Something:** somewhat.   **Reason my son:** it is reasonable that my son. (The disguised Polixenes seems to be speaking hypothetically, using himself as an example, but of course the application to Florizel is direct.)   389. **hold some counsel:** be consulted.   390. **yield:** concede.

At knowing of thy choice.

FLORIZEL: Come, come, he must not.
Mark our contract.

POLIXENES: [*discovering himself*] Mark your divorce, young sir,
Whom son I dare not call. Thou art too base
To be acknowledged. Thou a scepter's heir,
That thus affects° a sheephook? — Thou old traitor,   400
I am sorry that by hanging thee I can
But shorten thy life one week. — And thou, fresh piece
Of excellent witchcraft, who of force° must know
The royal fool thou cop'st° with —

SHEPHERD: Oh, my heart!

POLIXENES:
I'll have thy beauty scratched with briers and made   405
More homely° than thy state. — For thee, fond° boy,
If I may ever know thou dost but sigh
That thou no more shalt see this knack° — as never
I mean thou shalt — we'll bar thee from succession,
Not hold thee of our blood, no, not our kin,   410
Farre than Deucalion off.° Mark thou my words.
Follow us to the court. — Thou churl,° for this time,
Though full of our displeasure, yet we free thee
From the dead° blow of it. — And you, enchantment,°
Worthy enough a herdsman — yea, him too,   415
That makes himself, but for our honor therein,
Unworthy thee° — if ever henceforth thou
These rural latches to his entrance open,
Or hoop his body more with thy embraces,
I will devise a death as cruel for thee   420
As thou art tender to't.   *Exit.*

PERDITA: Even here undone!
I was not much afeard; for once or twice
I was about to speak and tell him plainly
The selfsame sun that shines upon his court

---

400. **affects:** desires, shows inclination for. 403. **of force:** of necessity. 404. **thou cop'st:** you deal. 406. **homely:** (1) unattractive (2) humble. **fond:** foolish. 408. **knack:** trifle, schemer.
411. **Farre . . . off:** farther [*farre* = more far] in kinship than Deucalion (the Noah of classical legend and hence the primal, distant ancestor of the whole human race). 412. **churl:** i.e., the Shepherd. 414. **dead:** deadly. **enchantment:** i.e., Perdita. 415–17. **him too . . . thee:** worthy indeed of him (Florizel) whose behavior renders him unworthy even of you, if we were to set aside for the moment the question of the dignity of our royal house.

Hides not his visage from our cottage, but 425
Looks on alike.° Will't please you, sir, begone?
I told you what would come of this. Beseech you,
Of your own state take care. This dream of mine —
Being now awake, I'll queen it no inch farther,
But milk my ewes and weep.

CAMILLO: Why, how now, father? 430
Speak ere thou diest.°

SHEPHERD: I cannot speak, nor think,
Nor dare to know that which I know. [*To Florizel*] Oh, sir,
You have undone a man of fourscore three,
That thought to fill his grave in quiet, yea,
To die upon the bed my father died,° 435
To lie close by his honest bones; but now
Some hangman must put on my shroud and lay me
Where no priest shovels in dust. [*To Perdita*] Oh, cursed wretch,
That knew'st this was the Prince, and wouldst adventure
To mingle faith° with him! Undone, undone! 440
If I might die within this hour, I have lived
To die when I desire.   *Exit.*

FLORIZEL: [*to Perdita*]   Why look you so upon me?
I am but sorry, not afeard; delayed,
But nothing altered. What I was, I am,
More straining on for plucking back,° not following 445
My leash unwillingly.

CAMILLO: Gracious my lord,
You know your father's temper. At this time
He will allow no speech, which I do guess
You do not purpose to him; and as hardly
Will he endure your sight as yet, I fear. 450
Then, till the fury of His Highness settle,
Come not before him.

FLORIZEL: I not purpose it.
I think Camillo?

CAMILLO: Even he, my lord.

---

426. alike: both alike.   **431. ere thou diest:** before you die of grief (?). (Although Polixenes has relented of his threat to hang the Shepherd, the Shepherd is gloomily sure it will come to a hanging, lines 437–38.)   **435. died:** died on.   **440. mingle faith:** exchange pledges.
445. More . . . back: i.e., like a hound on the leash, all the more eager to go forward for being restrained.

PERDITA:

How often have I told you 'twould be thus?
How often said my dignity° would last   455
But till 'twere known?

FLORIZEL: It cannot fail but by
The violation of my faith; and then°
Let nature crush the sides o'th' earth together
And mar the seeds within!° Lift up thy looks.
From my succession wipe me, father;° I   460
Am heir to my affection.°

CAMILLO: Be advised.°

FLORIZEL:

I am, and by my fancy.° If my reason
Will thereto be obedient, I have reason;°
If not, my senses, better pleased with madness,
Do bid it welcome.

CAMILLO: This is desperate, sir.   465

FLORIZEL:

So call it, but it does fulfill my vow;
I needs must think it honesty. Camillo,
Not for Bohemia nor the pomp that may
Be thereat gleaned, for all the sun sees or
The close earth wombs° or the profound seas hides   470
In unknown fathoms, will I break my oath
To this my fair beloved. Therefore, I pray you,
As you have ever been my father's honored friend,
When he shall miss me — as, in faith, I mean not
To see him any more — cast your good counsels   475
Upon his passion.° Let myself and fortune
Tug° for the time to come. This you may know
And so deliver.° I am put to sea
With her who° here I cannot hold on shore;
And most opportune to our need I have   480

---

455. my dignity: i.e., the new status this marriage would have offered. **457. then:** when that happens. **459. mar the seeds within:** i.e., destroy the very sources of life of earth (since all material life was thought to be derived from *seeds*). **460. From . . . father:** (Florizel addresses the absent Polixenes.) **460–61. I . . . affection:** i.e., I will be content with my passionate love for Perdita in place of my inheritance. **461. Be advised:** think carefully, be receptive to wise advice. **462. fancy:** love. **463. have reason:** (1) will be reasonable (2) will be sane. **470. wombs:** encloses, conceals. **476. passion:** anger. **477. Tug:** contend. **478. deliver:** report. **479. who:** whom.

A vessel rides° fast by, but° not prepared
For this design. What course I mean to hold
Shall nothing benefit your knowledge nor
Concern me the reporting.°
CAMILLO: Oh, my lord,
I would your spirit were easier for° advice,   485
Or stronger for your need.
FLORIZEL: Hark, Perdita.
[*To Camillo*] I'll hear you by and by.   [*He draws Perdita aside.*]
CAMILLO: [*aside*]   He's irremovable,°
Resolved for flight. Now were I happy if
His going I could frame° to serve my turn,
Save him from danger, do him love and honor,   490
Purchase the sight again of dear Sicilia
And that unhappy king, my master, whom
I so much thirst to see.
FLORIZEL: Now, good Camillo,
I am so fraught with curious° business that
I leave out ceremony.°
CAMILLO: Sir, I think   495
You have heard of my poor services i'th' love
That I have borne your father?
FLORIZEL: Very nobly
Have you deserved. It is my father's music
To speak your deeds, not little of his care
To have them recompensed as thought on.°
CAMILLO: Well, my lord,   500
If you may please to think I love the King
And through him what's nearest to him, which is
Your gracious self, embrace but my direction,°
If your more ponderous° and settled project
May suffer° alteration. On mine honor,   505
I'll point you where you shall have such receiving
As shall become Your Highness,° where you may

481. rides: that rides at anchor. but: though. 483–84. Shall . . . reporting: would not behoove you to know nor me to report. 485. easier for: more open to. 487. irremovable: immovable. 489. frame: shape. 494. curious: demanding care. 495. I . . . ceremony: (Florizel apologizes for failing to observe proper ceremony toward Camillo under the pressures of the present crisis). 500. as thought on: as deservingly as they merit. 503. embrace . . . direction: simply follow my advice. 504. ponderous: weighty. 505. suffer: permit. 507. become Your Highness: suit your royal rank, suit Your Highness.

Enjoy your mistress — from the whom I see
There's no disjunction to be made but by,
As heavens forfend,° your ruin — marry her, 510
And, with° my best endeavors in your absence
Your discontenting° father strive to qualify°
And bring him up to liking.°
FLORIZEL: How, Camillo,
May this, almost a miracle, be done,
That I may call thee something more than man, 515
And after° that trust to thee?
CAMILLO: Have you thought on
A place whereto you'll go?
FLORIZEL: Not any yet.
But as th'unthought-on accident is guilty
To what we wildly do,° so we profess
Ourselves to be the slaves of chance and flies° 520
Of every wind that blows.
CAMILLO: Then list to me.
This follows, if you will not change your purpose
But undergo this flight: make for Sicilia,
And there present yourself and your fair princess —
For so I see she must be — 'fore Leontes. 525
She shall be habited° as it becomes
The partner of your bed. Methinks I see
Leontes opening his free° arms and weeping
His welcomes forth; asks thee there "Son, forgiveness!"
As 'twere i'th' father's person; kisses the hands 530
Of your fresh° princess; o'er and o'er divides him
Twixt his unkindness and his kindness.° Th'one
He chides to hell, and bids the other grow
Faster° than thought or time.
FLORIZEL: Worthy Camillo,

---

510. **forfend:** forbid.   511. **with:** together with.   512. **discontenting:** discontented, displeased.
qualify: appease, pacify.   513. **bring . . . liking:** get him to the point of approval.   516. **after:**
ever after.   518–19. **as . . . wildly do:** just as the unexpected happening (e.g., of our being discovered by the King) is responsible for what we rashly do at this point.   520. **flies:** i.e.,
insignificant insects, blown about by the winds of chance.   526. **habited:** (richly) dressed.
528. **free:** generous, noble.   531. **fresh:** young and beautiful.   531–32. **divides . . . kindness:**
divides his speech between his former unkindness (which he condemns) and his present intention of kindness.   534. **Faster:** firmer; also, more swiftly.

What color° for my visitation shall I   535
Hold up before° him?
CAMILLO: Sent° by the King your father
To greet him and to give him comforts. Sir,
The manner of your bearing towards him, with
What you, as from your father, shall deliver° —
Things known betwixt us three — I'll write you down,   540
The which shall point you forth° at every sitting°
What you must say, that he shall not perceive
But that you have your father's bosom° there
And speak his very heart.
FLORIZEL: I am bound to you.
There is some sap° in this.
CAMILLO: A course more promising   545
Than a wild dedication of yourselves
To unpathed waters, undreamed shores, most certain
To miseries enough; no hope to help you,
But as you shake off one° to take° another;
Nothing° so certain as your anchors, who   550
Do their best office if they can but stay you
Where you'll be loath to be.° Besides, you know
Prosperity's the very bond of love,
Whose fresh complexion and whose heart together
Affliction alters.°
PERDITA: One of these is true: 555
I think affliction may subdue the cheek,°
But not take in° the mind.
CAMILLO: Yea, say you so?
There shall not at your father's° house these seven years°
Be born another such.
FLORIZEL: My good Camillo,

---

535. color: excuse, pretext.   536. Hold up before: present to.   Sent: i.e., say you are sent.
539. deliver: say.   541. point you forth: indicate to you.   sitting: conference.   543. bosom:
inmost thoughts.   545. sap: the vital juice in plants; hence, life or hope.   549. one: one misery, one misfortune.   take: encounter.   550. Nothing: not at all.   550–52. who . . . to be:
which are doing as well as can be hoped if they simply hold you in some undesirable place
(rather than allowing you to proceed on toward even greater disaster).   553–55. Prosperity's . . . alters: i.e., young love flourishes while things are going well but loses its fresh complexion and strength of feeling under the test of adversity.   556. subdue the cheek: make the
complexion look pale and wasted.   557. take in: overcome.   558. your father's: (Said either to
Florizel or Perdita.)   these seven years: i.e., for a long time to come. (Camillo's point is that
she is a nonpareil.)

She's as forward of her breeding° as she is   560
I'th' rear 'our° birth.

CAMILLO: I cannot say 'tis pity
She lacks instructions,° for she seems a mistress°
To most that teach.

PERDITA: Your pardon, sir; for this
I'll blush you thanks.

FLORIZEL: My prettiest Perdita!
But oh, the thorns we stand upon! Camillo,   565
Preserver of my father, now of me,
The medicine of our house, how shall we do?
We are not furnished like Bohemia's son,
Nor shall appear so in Sicilia.

CAMILLO:
My lord,   570
Fear none of this. I think you know my fortunes
Do all lie there. It shall be so my care
To have you royally appointed° as if
The scene you play were mine. For instance, sir,
That you may know you shall not want, one word.   [*They talk aside.*]   575

Enter Autolycus.

AUTOLYCUS: Ha, ha, what a fool Honesty is! And Trust, his sworn brother,
a very simple gentleman! I have sold all my trumpery; not a counterfeit
stone, not a ribbon, glass, pomander,° brooch, table book,° ballad, knife,
tape, glove, shoe tie, bracelet, horn ring, to keep my pack from fasting.°
They throng who should buy first, as if my trinkets had been hallowed°   580
and brought a benediction to the buyer; by which means I saw whose
purse was best in picture,° and what I saw, to my good use I remembered.
My clown, who wants but something° to be a reasonable man, grew so in
love with the wenches' song that he would not stir his pettitoes° till he
had both tune and words, which so drew the rest of the herd to me that   585
all their other senses stuck in ears.° You might have pinched a placket,° it

---

560. **forward . . . breeding:** far in advance of her lowly upbringing.   561. **I'th rear 'our:** below me in.   562. **instructions:** formal schooling.   **a mistress:** a teacher.   573. **appointed:**
equipped, outfitted.   578. **pomander:** scent-ball.   **table book:** notebook.   579. **from fasting:** i.e., from being empty.   580. **hallowed:** made sacred, like a relic.   582. **best in picture:**
i.e., best to look at, most promising.   583. **wants but something:** lacks one thing only (i.e.,
intelligence).   584. **pettitoes:** pig's toes; here, toes.   586. **stuck in ears:** were occupied with
hearing.   **placket:** (Literally, slit in a petticoat; with sexual suggestion.)

was senseless.° 'Twas nothing to geld a codpiece of a purse.° I could have
filed keys off that hung in chains. No hearing, no feeling, but my sir's°
song, and admiring the nothing° of it. So that in this time of lethargy I
picked and cut most of their festival purses; and had not the old man   590
come in with hubbub against his daughter and the King's son and scared
my choughs° from the chaff, I had not left a purse alive in the whole
army.

[*Camillo, Florizel, and Perdita come forward.*]

CAMILLO:
Nay, but my letters, by this means being there
So soon as you arrive, shall clear that doubt.   595

FLORIZEL:
And those that you'll procure from King Leontes —

CAMILLO:
Shall satisfy your father.

PERDITA: Happy be you!
All that you speak shows fair.

CAMILLO: [*seeing Autolycus*]   Who have we here?
We'll make an instrument of this, omit
Nothing° may give us aid.   600

AUTOLYCUS: [*aside*]   If they have overheard me now, why, hanging.

CAMILLO: How now, good fellow? Why shak'st thou so? Fear not, man,
here's no harm intended to thee.

AUTOLYCUS: I am a poor fellow, sir.

CAMILLO: Why, be so still. Here's nobody will steal that from thee. Yet   605
for the outside of thy poverty° we must make an exchange. Therefore
discase° thee instantly — thou must think° there's a necessity in't — and
change garments with this gentleman. Though the pennyworth° on his
side be the worst, yet hold thee, there's some boot.°   [*He gives money.*]

AUTOLYCUS: I am a poor fellow, sir. [*Aside*] I know ye well enough.   610

CAMILLO: Nay, prithee, dispatch.° The gentleman is half flayed° already.

AUTOLYCUS: Are you in earnest, sir? [*Aside*] I smell the trick on't.

---

587. **senseless:** insensible.   **geld . . . purse:** cut a purse loose from the pouch worn at the
front of a man's breeches.   588. **my sir's:** i.e., the Clown's.   589. **nothing:** (1) vacuity (2) noting, tune. (*Nothing* and *noting* were sounded alike in Elizabethan English.)   592. **choughs:**
jackdaws.   600. **Nothing:** nothing that.   606. **the outside . . . poverty:** i.e., your ragged
clothing.   607. **discase:** undress.   **think:** understand.   608. **pennyworth:** i.e., value of the
bargain.   609. **some boot:** something in addition.   611. **dispatch:** hurry. (Also in line 613.)
flayed: skinned, i.e., undressed.

FLORIZEL: Dispatch, I prithee.

AUTOLYCUS: Indeed, I have had earnest,° but I cannot with conscience
take it.   615

CAMILLO: Unbuckle, unbuckle.   [*Florizel and Autolycus exchange garments.*]
Fortunate mistress — let my prophecy
Come home to ye!° — you must retire yourself
Into some covert.° Take your sweetheart's hat
And pluck it o'er your brows, muffle your face,   620
Dismantle you, and, as you can, disliken
The truth of your own seeming,° that you may —
For I do fear eyes° — over to shipboard
Get undescried.

PERDITA: I see the play so lies
That I must bear a part.

CAMILLO: No remedy. —   625
Have you done there?

FLORIZEL: Should I now meet my father,
He would not call me son.

CAMILLO: Nay, you shall have no hat.
                                                       [*He gives it to Perdita.*]
Come, lady, come. Farewell, my friend.

AUTOLYCUS: Adieu, sir.

FLORIZEL:
Oh, Perdita, what have we twain forgot?
Pray you, a word.   [*They speak aside.*]   630

CAMILLO: [*aside*]
What I do next shall be to tell the King
Of this escape and whither they are bound;
Wherein my hope is I shall so prevail
To force him after, in whose company
I shall re-view° Sicilia, for whose sight   635
I have a woman's longing.

FLORIZEL: Fortune speed us!
Thus we set on, Camillo, to th' seaside.

CAMILLO:
The swifter speed the better.   *Exit* [*with Florizel and Perdita*].

---

614. **earnest:** advance payment. (Playing on *in earnest* in line 612.)   **617–18. let . . . to ye!:** i.e.,
let my prophecy that you, Perdita, will be fortunate be fulfilled for you!   **619. covert:** hidden
place.   **621–22. as you . . . seeming:** as much as you can, disguise your outward appearance.
623. eyes: spying eyes.   **635. re-view:** see again.

AUTOLYCUS: I understand the business; I hear it. To have an open ear, a
quick eye, and a nimble hand is necessary for a cutpurse; a good nose is   640
requisite also, to smell out work for th' other senses. I see this is the time
that the unjust man doth thrive. What an exchange had this been without boot!° What a boot° is here with this exchange! Sure the gods do this
year connive at° us, and we may do anything extempore. The Prince himself is about° a piece of iniquity, stealing away from his father with his   645
clog° at his heels. If I thought it were a piece of honesty to acquaint the
King withal,° I would not do't. I hold it the more knavery to conceal it;
and therein am I constant to my profession.

Enter Clown and Shepherd [carrying a bundle and a box].

Aside, aside! Here is more matter for a hot brain. Every lane's end, every
shop, church, session,° hanging, yields a careful man work.   650

                                            [He stands aside.]

CLOWN: See, see, what a man you are now! There is no other way but to
tell the King she's a changeling° and none of your flesh and blood.

SHEPHERD: Nay, but hear me.

CLOWN: Nay, but hear me.

SHEPHERD: Go to,° then.   655

CLOWN: She being none of your flesh and blood, your flesh and blood has
not offended the King, and so your flesh and blood is not to be punished
by him. Show those things you found about her, those secret things, all
but what she has with her. This being done, let the law go whistle, I warrant you.   660

SHEPHERD: I will tell the King all, every word, yea, and his son's pranks
too; who, I may say, is no honest man, neither to his father nor to me, to
go about° to make me the King's brother-in-law.

CLOWN: Indeed, brother-in-law was the farthest off you could have been
to him, and then your blood had been the dearer by I know not how   665
much an ounce.

AUTOLYCUS: [*aside*]   Very wisely, puppies!

SHEPHERD: Well, let us to the King. There is that in this fardel° will make
him scratch his beard.

AUTOLYCUS: [*aside*]   I know not what impediment this complaint may be to   670
the flight of my master.°

642–3. **without boot:** i.e., even without added payment.   643. **What a boot:** what a profit.
644. **connive at:** look indulgently at.   645. **about:** engaged in.   646. **clog:** encumbrance
(i.e., Perdita).   647. **withal:** with it.   652. **session:** court session.   652. **changeling:** child
left by the fairies.   655. **Go to:** go ahead. (Or, an expression of impatience.)   663. **go about:**
make it his object.   668. **fardel:** bundle.   671. **my master:** i.e., Florizel. (See 4.3.13.)

CLOWN: Pray heartily he be at° palace.

AUTOLYCUS: [aside]   Though I am not naturally honest, I am so sometimes
by chance. Let me pocket up my peddler's excrement.° [He takes off his false
beard.] How now, rustics, whither are you bound?   675

SHEPHERD: To the palace, an it like° Your Worship.

AUTOLYCUS: Your affairs there, what, with whom, the condition° of that
fardel, the place of your dwelling, your names, your ages, of what having,°
breeding, and anything that is fitting to be known, discover.°

CLOWN: We are but plain° fellows, sir.   680

AUTOLYCUS: A lie; you are rough and hairy. Let me have no lying. It becomes none but tradesmen, and they often give us soldiers the lie,° but
we pay them for it with stamped coin, not stabbing steel; therefore they
do not give° us the lie.

CLOWN: Your Worship had like° to have given us one, if you had not taken   685
yourself with the manner.°

SHEPHERD: Are you a courtier, an't like you, sir?

AUTOLYCUS: Whether it like me or no, I am a courtier. See'st thou not the
air of the court in these enfoldings?° Hath not my gait in it the measure°
of the court? Receives not thy nose court odor from me? Reflect I not   690
on thy baseness court contempt? Think'st thou, for that I insinuate to
toze from thee thy business,° I am therefore no courtier? I am courtier
cap-à-pie,° and one that will either push on or pluck back thy business
there. Whereupon I command thee to open° thy affair.

SHEPHERD: My business, sir, is to the King.   695

AUTOLYCUS: What advocate hast thou to him?

SHEPHERD: I know not, an't like you.

CLOWN: [aside to Shepherd]   "Advocate" 's the court word for a pheasant.° Say
you have none.

SHEPHERD: None, sir. I have no pheasant, cock nor hen.   700

---

672. at': at the.   674. excrement: outgrowth of hair, beard.   676. an it like: if it please.
677. condition: nature.   678. having: property.   679. discover: reveal.   680. plain: simple.
(But Autolycus plays on the meaning "smooth.")   682. give . . . lie: i.e., cheat us. (But *giving
the lie* also means to accuse a person to his face of lying, an affront which a soldier would repay
with *stabbing steel*.)   684. give: (Autolycus punningly observes that, since soldiers pay tradesmen for their wares, the tradesmen cannot be said to have *given* the lie, and so a duel is avoided.)
685. had like: was about.   685–86. taken . . . manner: i.e., caught yourself in the act, stopped
short. (The Clown observes that Autolycus has once again avoided the "giving of the lie"
and its consequences in a duel by his clever equivocation. Compare with Touchstone in *As You
Like It*, 5.4.)   689. enfoldings: clothes.   measure: stately tread.   691–92. for that . . . business: because I undertake to pry out of you what your business may be.   693. cap-à-pie: from
head to foot.   694. open: reveal.   698. pheasant: (The rustics suppose that Autolycus has
asked them what gift they propose to present as a bribe, as one might do to a judge in a court
of law.)

AUTOLYCUS: [*aside*]

How blessed are we that are not simple men!

Yet nature might have made me as these are;

Therefore I will not disdain.

CLOWN: [*to Shepherd*]   This cannot be but a great courtier.

SHEPHERD: His garments are rich, but he wears them not handsomely.   705

CLOWN: He seems to be the more noble in being fantastical.° A great man,

I'll warrant. I know by the picking on's teeth.°

AUTOLYCUS: The fardel there? What's i'th' fardel? Wherefore that box?

SHEPHERD: Sir, there lies such secrets in this fardel and box which none

must know but the King, and which he shall know within this hour if I   710

may come to the speech of him.

AUTOLYCUS: Age,° thou hast lost thy labor.

SHEPHERD: Why, sir?

AUTOLYCUS: The King is not at the palace. He is gone aboard a new ship

to purge melancholy and air himself; for, if thou be'st capable of° things   715

serious, thou must know the King is full of grief.

SHEPHERD: So 'tis said, sir; about his son, that should have married a shep-

herd's daughter.

AUTOLYCUS: If that shepherd be not in handfast,° let him fly. The curses he

shall have, the tortures he shall feel, will break the back of man, the heart   720

of monster.

CLOWN: Think you so, sir?

AUTOLYCUS: Not he alone shall suffer what wit° can make heavy and

vengeance bitter, but those that are germane° to him, though removed

fifty times, shall all come under the hangman — which, though it be   725

great pity, yet it is necessary. An old sheep-whistling° rogue, a ram ten-

der, to offer° to have his daughter come into grace?° Some say he shall be

stoned; but that death is too soft for him, say I. Draw our throne into a

sheepcote?° All deaths are too few, the sharpest too easy.

CLOWN: Has the old man e'er a son, sir, do you hear, an't like you, sir?   730

AUTOLYCUS: He has a son, who shall be flayed alive; then, 'nointed over

with honey, set on the head of a wasp's nest; then stand till he be three-

quarters and a dram° dead; then recovered again with aqua vitae° or some

---

706. **fantastical:** eccentric.   707. **picking on's teeth:** (A stylish affectation in Shakespeare's time.)   712. **Age:** old man.   715. **be'st capable of:** know anything about.   719. **handfast:** custody. (With a play on "betrothal.")   723. **wit:** ingenuity (in devising tortures).   724. **germane:** related.   726. **sheep-whistling:** tending sheep by whistling after them.   727. **offer:** dare.   **grace:** favor.   729. **sheepcote:** pen for sheep.   733. **a dram:** i.e., a small amount, a fraction.   **aqua vitae:** brandy.

other hot infusion; then, raw as he is, and in the hottest day prognostica-
tion° proclaims, shall he be set against a brick wall, the sun looking with a   735
southward eye upon him, where he° is to behold him with flies blown° to
death. But what° talk we of these traitorly rascals, whose miseries are to
be smiled at, their offenses being so capital? Tell me, for you seem to be
honest plain men, what you have to° the King. Being something gently
considered,° I'll bring you where he is aboard, tender your persons° to his   740
presence, whisper him in your behalfs; and if it be in man besides the
King to effect your suits, here is man shall do it.

CLOWN: [*to Shepherd*]   He seems to be of great authority. Close with him,°
give him gold; and though authority be a stubborn bear, yet he is oft led
by the nose with gold. Show the inside of your purse to the outside of his   745
hand, and no more ado. Remember — "stoned," and "flayed alive."

SHEPHERD: An't please you, sir, to undertake the business for us, here is
that gold I have. [*He offers money.*] I'll make it as much more and leave this
young man in pawn° till I bring it you.

AUTOLYCUS: After I have done what I promised?   750

SHEPHERD: Ay, sir.

AUTOLYCUS: [*taking the money*]   Well, give me the moiety.° [*To the Clown*] Are
you a party in this business?

CLOWN: In some sort, sir. But, though my case° be a pitiful one, I hope I
shall not be flayed out of it.   755

AUTOLYCUS: Oh, that's the case of the shepherd's son. Hang him, he'll be
made an example.

CLOWN: [*to Shepherd*]   Comfort, good comfort! We must to the King and
show our strange sights. He must know 'tis none of your daughter nor my
sister; we are gone else.° — Sir, I will give you as much as this old man   760
does when the business is performed, and remain, as he says, your pawn
till it be brought you.

AUTOLYCUS: I will trust you. Walk before toward the seaside; go on the
right hand. I will but look upon the hedge° and follow you.

CLOWN: [*to Shepherd*]   We are blessed in this man, as I may say, even blessed.   765

SHEPHERD: Let's before, as he bids us. He was provided to do us good.

Exeunt [Shepherd and Clown].

---

735. **prognostication:** forecasting (in the almanac).   736. **he:** i.e., the sun.   **blown:** swollen.
737. **what:** i.e., why.   739. **what you have to:** what business you have with.   739–40. **Being . . . considered:** i.e., (1) being a gentleman of some influence (2) if I receive a gentlemanly
consideration, a bribe.   740. **tender your persons:** introduce you.   743. **Close with him:**
accept his offer.   749. **in pawn:** as security.   752. **moiety:** half.   754. **case:** (1) cause (2) skin.
760. **gone else:** undone otherwise.   764. **look . . . hedge:** i.e., relieve myself.

AUTOLYCUS: If I had a mind to be honest, I see Fortune would not suffer
me; she drops booties in my mouth. I am courted now with a double
occasion:° gold, and a means to do the Prince my master good, which
who knows how that may turn back° to my advancement? I will bring   770
these two moles, these blind ones, aboard him.° If he think it fit to shore°
them again and that the complaint they have to the King concerns him
nothing,° let him call me rogue for being so far officious, for I am proof
against° that title and what shame else belongs to't. To him will I present
them. There may be matter in it.   [*Exit.*]   775

ACT 5, SCENE 1°

Enter Leontes, Cleomenes, Dion, Paulina, [and] servants.

CLEOMENES:
Sir, you have done enough, and have performed
A saintlike sorrow. No fault could you make
Which you have not redeemed — indeed, paid down
More penitence than done trespass. At the last,
Do as the heavens have done: forget your evil.   5
With them, forgive yourself.
LEONTES: Whilst I remember
Her and her virtues, I cannot forget
My blemishes in them,° and so still think of
The wrong I did myself, which was so much
That heirless it hath made my kingdom and   10
Destroyed the sweet'st companion that e'er man
Bred his hopes out of. True?
PAULINA: Too true, my lord.
If one by one you wedded all the world,
Or from the all that are° took something good
To make a perfect woman, she you killed   15
Would be unparalleled.
LEONTES: I think so. Killed?
She I killed? I did so, but thou strik'st me
Sorely to say I did. It is as bitter

---

769. **occasion:** opportunity. 770. **turn back:** redound. 771. **aboard him:** i.e., to him (Prince
Florizel) aboard his ship. **shore:** put ashore. 773. **nothing:** not at all. 773–74. **proof against:**
invulnerable to. ACT 5, SCENE 1. **Location:** Sicilia. The royal court. 8. **in them:** in comparison with them. 14. **the all that are:** all the women that there are.

Upon thy tongue as in my thought. Now, good now,°
Say so but seldom.

CLEOMENES: Not at all, good lady.   20
You might have spoken a thousand things that would
Have done the time more benefit and graced
Your kindness better.

PAULINA: You are one of those
Would have him wed again.

DION: If you would not so,
You pity not the state nor the remembrance°   25
Of his most sovereign name, consider° little
What dangers by His Highness' fail of issue°
May drop upon his kingdom and devour
Incertain° lookers-on. What were more holy
Than to rejoice the former queen is well?°   30
What holier than, for royalty's repair,
For present comfort and for future good,
To bless the bed of majesty again
With a sweet fellow to't?

PAULINA: There is none worthy,
Respecting° her that's gone. Besides, the gods   35
Will have fulfilled their secret purposes;°
For has not the divine Apollo said,
Is't not the tenor of his oracle,
That King Leontes shall not have an heir
Till his lost child be found? Which that it shall   40
Is all as monstrous to our human reason
As° my Antigonus to break his grave
And come again to me, who, on my life,
Did perish with the infant. 'Tis your counsel°
My lord should to the heavens be contrary,   45
Oppose° against their wills. [To Leontes] Care not for° issue.
The crown will find an heir. Great Alexander

---

19. **good now:** i.e., if you please.   25. **nor the remembrance:** i.e., nor give consideration to the perpetuation (through bearing a child and heir).   26. **consider:** you consider.   27. **fail of issue:** failure to produce an heir.   29. **Incertain:** not knowing what to think or do (about the royal succession).   30. **well:** happy, at rest (in heaven).   35. **Respecting:** in comparison with.   36. **Will . . . purposes:** are determined to have their secret purposes fulfilled.   42. **As:** as for.   44. **'Tis your counsel:** it's your advice that.   46. **Oppose:** oppose himself.   **Care not for:** do not be anxious about.

Left his to th' worthiest;° so his successor
Was like to be the best.

LEONTES: Good Paulina,
Who hast the memory of Hermione,   50
I know, in honor, oh, that ever I
Had squared me° to thy counsel! Then even now
I might have looked upon my queen's full eyes,
Have taken treasure from her lips —

PAULINA: And left them
More rich for what they yielded.

LEONTES: Thou speak'st truth.   55
No more such wives, therefore no wife. One worse,
And better used,° would make her° sainted spirit
Again possess her corpse,° and on this stage,
Where we're offenders now, appear soul-vexed,
And begin, "Why to me?"°

PAULINA: Had she such power,   60
She had just cause.

LEONTES: She had,° and would incense° me
To murder her I married.

PAULINA: I should so.°
Were I the ghost that walked, I'd bid you mark
Her eye and tell me for what dull part in't
You chose her. Then I'd shriek, that even your ears   65
Should rift° to hear me, and the words that followed
Should be, "Remember mine."°

LEONTES: Stars,° stars,
And all eyes else° dead coals! Fear thou no wife;
I'll have no wife, Paulina.

PAULINA: Will you swear
Never to marry but by my free leave?   70

LEONTES:
Never, Paulina, so be blest my spirit!

---

48. **Left . . . worthiest:** (When Alexander the Great died in 323 B.C.E., his son Alexander was yet unborn, necessitating the choice of an heir.)   52. **squared me:** adjusted or regulated myself.   56–57. **One . . . used:** i.e., If I took a new, less excellent wife and treated her better.   57. **her:** Hermione's.   58. **possess her corpse:** i.e., return to earth (*this stage*) in Hermione's human shape.   60. **Why to me?:** why this offense to me?   61. **had:** would have.   **incense:** stir up, incite.   62. **should so:** would similarly incite you.   66. **rift:** rive, split.   67. **mine:** my eyes.   **Stars:** i.e., her eyes were stars.   68. **all eyes else:** all other eyes.

PAULINA:
Then, good my lords, bear witness to his oath.

CLEOMENES:
You tempt° him overmuch.

PAULINA: Unless another,
As like Hermione as is her picture,
Affront° his eye.

CLEOMENES: Good madam —

PAULINA: I have done.   75
Yet if my lord will marry — if you will, sir,
No remedy, but you will — give me the office
To choose you a queen. She shall not be so young
As was your former, but she shall be such
As, walked your first queen's ghost,° it should take joy°   80
To see her in your arms.

LEONTES: My true Paulina,
We shall not marry till thou bidd'st us.

PAULINA: That
Shall be when your first queen's again in breath;
Never till then.

Enter a Gentleman.°

GENTLEMAN:
One that gives out himself° Prince Florizel,   85
Son of Polixenes, with his princess — she
The fairest I have yet beheld — desires access
To your high presence.

LEONTES: What° with him? He comes not
Like to° his father's greatness. His approach,
So out of circumstance° and sudden, tells us   90
'Tis not a visitation framed,° but forced
By need and accident. What train?°

GENTLEMAN: But few,
And those but mean.°

LEONTES: His princess, say you, with him?

---

73. tempt: bear down on.   **75. Affront:** confront.   **80. walked . . . ghost:** if your first queen's ghost were to walk.   **take joy:** be overjoyed.   **84.1. *Enter a Gentleman*:** (He is called a "Servant" in the Folio text, but his writing poetry in lines 100–04 is more consistent with his being a courtier. Any such person at court is a servant of the king.)   **85. gives out himself:** reports himself to be.   **88. What:** what retinue.   **89. Like to:** in a manner consistent with.   **90. out of circumstance:** without ceremony.   **91. framed:** planned.   **92. train:** retinue.   **93. mean:** lowly.

GENTLEMAN:
Ay, the most peerless piece of earth, I think,
That e'er the sun shone bright on.

PAULINA: Oh, Hermione,   95
As every present time doth boast itself
Above a better gone, so must thy grave
Give way to what's seen now!° [*To the Gentleman*] Sir, you yourself
Have said and writ so, but your writing now
Is colder than that theme.° She had not been   100
Nor was not to be equaled° — thus your verse
Flowed with her beauty once. 'Tis shrewdly ebbed°
To say you have seen a better.

GENTLEMAN: Pardon, madam.
The one I have almost forgot — your pardon!
The other, when she has obtained your eye,   105
Will have your tongue° too. This is a creature,
Would she begin a sect, might quench the zeal
Of all professors else,° make proselytes
Of who she but bid follow.°

PAULINA: How? Not women!°

GENTLEMAN:
Women will love her that she is a woman   110
More worth than any man; men, that she is
The rarest of all women.

LEONTES: Go, Cleomenes.
Yourself, assisted with your honored friends,
Bring them to our embracement.   *Exit* [*Cleomenes with others*].
                        Still, 'tis strange
He thus should steal upon us.

PAULINA: Had our prince,   115
Jewel of children, seen this hour, he had paired
Well with this lord. There was not full a month
Between their births.

96–98. **As . . . now!:** As every present age boasts its superiority to past times that were in point of fact better, so you, long dead, must give way to present fashion! 100. **that theme:** i.e., Hermione, the subject of your verses. 100–01. **She . . . equaled:** the poet evidently had written that Hermione had not been nor was not to be equaled in beauty. 102. **'Tis shrewdly ebbed:** i.e., you've egregiously gone back on your word. 106. **tongue:** i.e., approval. 108. **professors else:** believers in other sects or deities. 109. **Of . . . follow:** of all those whom she merely told to follow her. **How? Not women!:** What do you mean? Surely women wouldn't become converts!

LEONTES:
Prithee, no more, cease. Thou know'st
He dies to me again when talked of. Sure,   120
When I shall see this gentleman, thy speeches
Will bring me to consider that which may
Unfurnish° me of reason. They are come.

Enter Florizel, Perdita, Cleomenes, and others.

Your mother was most true to wedlock, Prince,
For she did print your royal father off,   125
Conceiving you. Were I but twenty-one,
Your father's image is so hit° in you,
His very air, that I should call you brother,
As I did him, and speak of something wildly
By us performed before. Most dearly welcome!   130
And your fair princess — goddess! Oh! Alas,
I lost a couple that twixt heaven and earth
Might thus have stood begetting wonder as
You, gracious couple, do. And then I lost —
All mine own folly — the society,   135
Amity too, of your brave° father, whom,
Though bearing misery, I desire my life°
Once more to look on him.°
FLORIZEL: By his command
Have I here touched Sicilia, and from him
Give you all greetings that a king, at friend,°   140
Can send his brother; and but° infirmity,
Which waits upon worn times,° hath something seized
His wished ability,° he had himself
The lands and waters twixt your throne and his
Measured° to look upon you, whom he loves —   145
He bade me say so — more than all the scepters
And those that bear them living.°
LEONTES: O my brother!
Good gentleman, the wrongs I have done thee stir

---

123. **Unfurnish:** deprive, divest.   127. **hit:** exactly reproduced.   136. **brave:** noble.   137. **my life:** i.e., to live long enough.   138. **him:** (Redundant in modern syntax.)   140. **at friend:** in friendship.   141. **but:** were it not that.   142. **waits . . . times:** attends old age.   142–43. **something . . . ability:** to some extent taken away his ability (to travel) as he wishes.   145. **Measured:** traversed.   147. **those . . . living:** those living kings who bear scepters.

Afresh within me, and these thy offices,°
So rarely° kind, are as interpreters   150
Of my behindhand slackness.° Welcome hither,
As is the spring to th'earth. And hath he too
Exposed this paragon to th' fearful usage —
At least ungentle — of the dreadful Neptune,°
To greet a man not worth her pains, much less   155
Th'adventure° of her person?
FLORIZEL: Good my lord,
She came from Libya.
LEONTES: Where the warlike Smalus,
That noble honored lord, is feared and loved?
FLORIZEL:
Most royal sir, from thence, from him, whose daughter
His tears proclaimed his, parting with her.° Thence,   160
A prosperous south wind friendly, we have crossed,
To execute the charge my father gave me
For visiting Your Highness. My best train
I have from your Sicilian shores dismissed,
Who for Bohemia bend,° to signify   165
Not only my success in Libya, sir,
But my arrival and my wife's in safety
Here where we are.
LEONTES: The blessèd gods
Purge all infection from our air whilst you
Do climate° here! You have a holy father,   170
A graceful° gentleman, against whose person,
So sacred as it is, I have done sin,
For which the heavens, taking angry note,
Have left me issueless; and your father's blest,
As he from heaven merits it, with you,   175
Worthy his goodness. What might I have been,
Might I a son and daughter now have looked on,
Such goodly things as you?

Enter a Lord.

---

149. **offices:** messages of good will, courteous attentions.   150. **rarely:** exceptionally.
150–51. **are . . . slackness:** are like commentators on my slowness in greeting you.   154. **Neptune:** god of the sea.   156. **Th'adventure:** the hazard.   159–60. **whose . . . her:** whose tears, as he parted with her, proclaimed her to be his daughter.   165. **bend:** direct their course.
170. **climate:** dwell, reside (in this clime).   171. **graceful:** full of grace, gracious.

LORD: Most noble sir,
That which I shall report will bear no credit
Were not the proof so nigh. Please you, great sir, 180
Bohemia greets you from himself by me;
Desires you to attach° his son, who has —
His dignity and duty° both cast off —
Fled from his father, from his hopes, and with
A shepherd's daughter.

LEONTES: Where's Bohemia? Speak. 185

LORD:
Here in your city. I now came from him.
I speak amazedly, and it becomes
My marvel and my message.° To your court
Whiles he was hast'ning — in the chase, it seems,
Of this fair couple — meets he on the way 190
The father of this seeming lady and
Her brother, having both their country quitted
With this young prince.

FLORIZEL: Camillo has betrayed me,
Whose honor and whose honesty till now
Endured all weathers.

LORD: Lay't so to his charge.° 195
He's with the King your father.

LEONTES: Who? Camillo?

LORD:
Camillo, sir. I spake with him, who now
Has these poor men in question.° Never saw I
Wretches so quake. They kneel, they kiss the earth,
Forswear themselves as often as they speak. 200
Bohemia stops his ears and threatens them
With divers deaths° in death.

PERDITA: Oh, my poor father!
The heaven sets spies upon us, will not have
Our contract celebrated.

LEONTES: You are married?

---

182. **attach:** arrest. 183. **dignity and duty:** princely dignity and filial duty. 187–88. **I . . . message:** i.e., I speak perplexedly as befits my perplexity and my astonishing news. 195. **Lay't . . . charge:** confront him with it directly. 198. **in question:** under interrogation. 202. **deaths:** i.e., tortures.

FLORIZEL:

We are not, sir, nor are we like° to be.   205
The stars, I see, will kiss the valleys first;
The odds for high and low's alike.°

LEONTES: My lord,
Is this the daughter of a king?

FLORIZEL: She is,
When once she is my wife.

LEONTES:

That "once," I see, by your good father's speed   210
Will come on very slowly. I am sorry,
Most sorry, you have broken from his liking
Where you were tied in duty, and as sorry
Your choice is not so rich in worth° as beauty,
That you might well enjoy her.

FLORIZEL: [to Perdita]   Dear, look up.   215
Though Fortune, visible an enemy,
Should chase us with my father,° power no jot
Hath she to change our loves. — Beseech you, sir,
Remember since you owed no more to time
Than I do now.° With thought of such affections,°   220
Step forth mine advocate. At your request
My father will grant precious things as trifles.

LEONTES:

Would he do so, I'd beg your precious mistress,
Which he counts but a trifle.

PAULINA: Sir, my liege,
Your eye hath too much youth in't. Not a month   225
'Fore your queen died, she was more worth such gazes
Than what you look on now.

LEONTES: I thought of her
Even in these looks I made. [To Florizel] But your petition
Is yet unanswered. I will to your father.
Your honor not o'erthrown by your desires,°   230

---

205. like: likely.   207. The odds . . . alike: fortune treats high and low alike.   214. worth:
rank.   216–17. Though . . . father: though the goddess Fortune herself were to manifest herself as our enemy and join my father in chasing us.   219–20. since . . . now: when you were no
older than I am now.   220. With . . . affections: recalling what it was to be in love at that age.
230. Your . . . desires: if your chaste honor has not been overcome by sexual desire, or, if what
you want in this match is compatible with your royal honor.

I am friend to them and you. Upon which errand
I now go toward him. Therefore follow me,
And mark what way° I make. Come, good my lord.   *Exeunt.*

ACT 5, SCENE 2°

Enter Autolycus and a Gentleman.

AUTOLYCUS: Beseech you, sir, were you present at this relation?°

FIRST GENTLEMAN: I was by at the opening of the fardel, heard the old
shepherd deliver° the manner how he found it; whereupon, after a little
amazedness, we were all commanded out of the chamber. Only this,
methought, I heard the shepherd say: he found the child.   5

AUTOLYCUS: I would most gladly know the issue° of it.

FIRST GENTLEMAN: I make a broken° delivery of the business, but the
changes I perceived in the King and Camillo were very notes of admiration.° They seemed almost, with staring on one another, to tear the cases
of their eyes.° There was speech in their dumbness, language in their very   10
gesture. They looked as° they had heard of a world ransomed, or one
destroyed. A notable passion of wonder appeared in them, but the wisest
beholder, that knew no more but seeing,° could not say if th'importance°
were joy or sorrow; but in the extremity of the one° it must needs be.

Enter another Gentleman.

Here comes a gentleman that haply° knows more. — The news, Rogero?   15

SECOND GENTLEMAN: Nothing but bonfires. The oracle is fulfilled; the
King's daughter is found. Such a deal° of wonder is broken out within
this hour that ballad makers cannot be able to express it.

Enter another Gentleman.

Here comes the Lady Paulina's steward. He can deliver you more. —
How goes it now, sir? This news which is called true is so like an old tale   20
that the verity of it is in strong suspicion. Has the King found his heir?

THIRD GENTLEMAN: Most true, if ever truth were pregnant by circumstance.° That which you hear you'll swear you see, there is such unity in

---

233. **way:** progress. ACT 5, SCENE 2. Location: At court. 1. **relation:** narrative, account.
3. **deliver:** report. 6. **issue:** outcome. 7. **broken:** disjointed, fragmented. 8–9. **very notes
of admiration:** veritable marks of wonderment. 9–10. **cases of their eyes:** eyelids. 11. **as:**
as if. 13. **no . . . seeing:** nothing except what he could see. **th'importance:** the import,
meaning. 14. **of the one:** of one or the other. 15. **haply:** perhaps. 17. **deal:** huge quantity.
22–23. **pregnant by circumstance:** made apparent by circumstantial evidence.

the proofs. The mantle of Queen Hermione's, her jewel about the neck
of it, the letters of Antigonus found with it which they know to be his   25
character,° the majesty of the creature in resemblance of the mother, the
affection of° nobleness which nature shows above her breeding,° and
many other evidences proclaim her with all certainty to be the King's
daughter. Did you see the meeting of the two kings?

SECOND GENTLEMAN: No.   30

THIRD GENTLEMAN: Then have you lost a sight which was to be seen,
cannot be spoken of. There might you have beheld one joy crown
another, so and in such manner that it seemed Sorrow wept to take leave
of them, for their joy waded in tears. There was casting up of eyes, holding up of hands, with countenance° of such distraction that they were to   35
be known by garment, not by favor.° Our king, being ready to leap out of
himself for joy of his found daughter, as if that joy were now become a
loss, cries, "Oh, thy mother, thy mother!" then asks Bohemia forgiveness;
then embraces his son-in-law; then again worries he° his daughter with
clipping° her; now he thanks the old shepherd, which stands by like a   40
weather-bitten conduit of many kings' reigns.° I never heard of such
another encounter, which lames report to follow it and undoes description to do it.°

SECOND GENTLEMAN: What, pray you, became of Antigonus, that carried
hence the child?   45

THIRD GENTLEMAN: Like an old tale still, which will have matter to
rehearse° though credit° be asleep and not an ear open. He was torn to
pieces with° a bear. This avouches° the shepherd's son, who has not only
his innocence,° which seems much, to justify him, but a handkerchief
and rings of his° that Paulina knows.   50

FIRST GENTLEMAN: What became of his bark and his followers?

THIRD GENTLEMAN: Wrecked the same instant of their master's death
and in the view of the shepherd; so that all the instruments which aided
to expose the child were even then lost when it was found. But oh, the
noble combat that twixt joy and sorrow was fought in Paulina! She had   55
one eye declined for the loss of her husband, another elevated that the

---

26. **character:** handwriting.   27. **affection of:** natural disposition to.   **breeding:** rearing.
35. **countenance:** bearing, demeanor.   36. **favor:** features.   39. **worries he:** he pesters.
40. **clipping:** embracing.   40–41. **which . . . reigns:** who stands by weeping like a weather-
beaten fountain that has stood there over the course of many kings' reigns.   42–43. **which . . .
do it:** which makes any account of it seem inadequate and beggars the powers of description in an attempt to do justice to it.   47. **rehearse:** relate.   **credit:** belief.   48. **with:** by.
avouches: confirms, corroborates.   49. **innocence:** simplemindedness (such that he would
seem unable to invent such a story).   50. **his:** Antigonus's.

oracle was fulfilled.° She lifted the Princess from the earth, and so locks her in embracing as if she would pin her to her heart, that she might no more be in danger of losing.°

FIRST GENTLEMAN: The dignity of this act was worth the audience of kings and princes, for by such was it acted. 60

THIRD GENTLEMAN: One of the prettiest touches of all, and that which angled for mine eyes — caught the water, though not the fish — was when, at the relation of the Queen's death, with the manner how she came to't bravely confessed and lamented by the King, how attentiveness° wounded his daughter; till, from one sign of dolor° to another, she did, with an "Alas!" I would fain say, bleed tears, for I am sure my heart wept blood. Who was most marble° there changed color; some swooned, all sorrowed. If all the world could have seen't, the woe had been universal. 65

FIRST GENTLEMAN: Are they returned to the court? 70

THIRD GENTLEMAN: No. The Princess hearing of her mother's statue, which is in the keeping of Paulina — a piece many years in doing and now newly performed° by that rare Italian master, Julio Romano,° who, had he himself eternity and could put breath into his work, would beguile° Nature of her custom,° so perfectly he is her ape;° he so near to Hermione hath done Hermione that they say one would speak to her and stand in hope of answer — thither with all greediness of affection° are they gone, and there they intend to sup.° 75

SECOND GENTLEMAN: I thought she had some great matter there in hand, for she hath privately twice or thrice a day, ever since the death of Hermione, visited that removed° house. Shall we thither and with our company piece° the rejoicing? 80

FIRST GENTLEMAN: Who would be thence that has the benefit of access? Every wink of an eye some new grace will be born. Our absence makes us unthrifty to° our knowledge. Let's along. *Exeunt [Gentlemen].* 85

AUTOLYCUS: Now, had I not the dash of my former life in me, would preferment drop on my head.° I brought the old man and his son aboard

---

55–57. **She . . . fulfilled:** i.e., she wept and laughed at the same time. 59. **losing:** being lost. 65–66. **attentiveness:** listening to it. 66. **dolor:** grief. 68. **Who . . . marble:** even the most hardhearted. 74. **performed:** completed. **Julio Romano:** Italian painter and sculptor of the sixteenth century, better known as a painter (and an anachronism in this play). 76. **beguile:** deprive, cheat. **custom:** trade. **ape:** imitator. 78. **greediness of affection:** eagerness born of love. 79. **sup:** i.e., feed their hungry eyes (?) or, perhaps, have a commemorative banquet (?). 82. **removed:** sequestered. 83. **piece:** add to, augment. 86. **unthrifty to:** passing up an opportunity to increase. 87–88. **had I . . . head:** if it weren't for the lingering reputation of petty thievery that hangs about me, royal favor would be sure to fall to my lot.

the Prince,° told him I heard them talk of a fardel and I know not what. But he at that time overfond of the shepherd's daughter — so he then took her to be — who began to be much seasick, and himself little better, extremity of weather continuing, this mystery remained undiscovered. But 'tis all one° to me, for had I been the finder out of this secret, it would not have relished° among my other discredits. 90

Enter Shepherd and Clown, [dressed in finery].

Here come those I have done good to against my will, and already appearing in the blossoms of their fortune. 95

SHEPHERD: Come, boy. I am past more children, but thy sons and daughters will be all gentlemen born.

CLOWN: [*to Autolycus*]   You are well met, sir. You denied to fight with me this other° day because I was no gentleman born. See you these clothes? Say you see them not and think me still no gentleman born. You were best say these robes are not gentlemen born. Give me the lie,° do, and try whether I am not now a gentleman born. 100

AUTOLYCUS: I know you are now, sir, a gentleman born.

CLOWN: Ay, and have been so any time these four hours. 105

SHEPHERD: And so have I, boy.

CLOWN: So you have. But I was a gentleman born before my father; for the King's son took me by the hand and called me brother; and then the two kings called my father brother; and then the Prince my brother and the Princess my sister called my father father; and so we wept, and there was the first gentlemanlike tears that ever we shed. 110

SHEPHERD: We may live, son, to shed many more.

CLOWN: Ay, or else 'twere hard luck, being in so preposterous° estate as we are.

AUTOLYCUS: I humbly beseech you, sir, to pardon me° all the faults I have committed to Your Worship, and to give me your good report to the Prince my master. 115

SHEPHERD: Prithee, son, do; for we must be gentle,° now we are gentlemen.

CLOWN: [*to Autolycus*]   Thou wilt amend thy life?

AUTOLYCUS: Ay, an it like° Your good Worship. 120

CLOWN: Give me thy hand. I will swear to the Prince thou art as honest a true° fellow as any is in Bohemia.

---

89. **the Prince:** the Prince's ship.   93. **'tis all one:** it's all the same.   94. **relished:** tasted well, suited.   99–100. **this other:** the other.   102. **Give me the lie:** accuse me to my face of lying (an insult that requires a challenge to a duel).   113. **preposterous:** (blunder for "prosperous.")   115. **me:** on my behalf.   118. **gentle:** nobly generous.   120. **an it like:** if it please.   121–22. **honest a true:** worthy an honest.

SHEPHERD: You may say it, but not swear it.

CLOWN: Not swear it, now I am a gentleman? Let boors° and franklins° say
it; I'll swear it.   125

SHEPHERD: How if it be false, son?

CLOWN: If it be ne'er so false, a true gentleman may swear it in the behalf
of his friend. — And I'll swear to the Prince thou art a tall fellow of thy
hands° and that thou wilt not be drunk; but I know thou art no tall fellow
of thy hands and that thou wilt be drunk. But I'll swear it, and I would   130
thou wouldst be a tall fellow of thy hands.

AUTOLYCUS: I will prove so, sir, to my power.°

CLOWN: Ay, by any means prove a tall fellow. If I do not wonder how thou
dar'st venture to be drunk, not being a tall fellow, trust me not. Hark, the
kings and the princes, our kindred, are going to see the Queen's picture.°   135
Come, follow us. We'll be thy good masters.   *Exeunt.*

ACT 5, SCENE 3°

Enter Leontes, Polixenes, Florizel, Perdita, Camillo, Paulina, lords, etc.

LEONTES:
O grave and good Paulina, the great comfort
That I have had of thee!

PAULINA: What,° sovereign sir,
I did not well, I meant well. All my services
You have paid home.° But that you have vouchsafed,
With your crowned brother and these your contracted   5
Heirs of your kingdoms, my poor house to visit,
It is a surplus of your grace which never
My life may last to answer.°

LEONTES: O Paulina,
We honor you with trouble.° But we came
To see the statue of our queen. Your gallery   10
Have we passed through, not without much content
In many singularities;° but we saw not
That which my daughter came to look upon,

---

124. **boors:** peasants.   **franklins:** farmers owning their own small farms.   128–29. **tall . . .
hands:** brave fellow.   132. **my power:** the best of my ability. (Autolycus slyly promises
to use his hands well—in picking pockets.)   135. **picture:** i.e., likeness, painted statue.
ACT 5, SCENE 3. Location: Sicilia. Paulina's house.   2. **What:** whatever.   4. **home:** fully.
7–8. **which . . . answer:** which I can never live long enough to be able to repay.   9. **We . . .
trouble:** i.e., we trouble you with the demands of hospitality, though you are kind enough to
call it an honor.   12. **singularities:** rarities, curiosities.

The statue of her mother.

PAULINA: As she lived peerless,
So her dead likeness, I do well believe,   15
Excels whatever yet you looked upon
Or hand of man hath done. Therefore I keep it
Lonely,° apart. But here it is. Prepare
To see the life as lively mocked° as ever
Still° sleep mocked death. Behold, and say 'tis well.   20

                    [*Paulina draws a curtain, and discovers*]
                    Hermione [*standing*] *like a statue.*

I like your silence; it the more shows off
Your wonder. But yet speak; first, you, my liege.
Comes it not something° near?

LEONTES: Her natural posture!
Childe me, dear stone, that I may say indeed
Thou art Hermione; or rather, thou art she   25
In thy not chiding, for she was as tender
As infancy and grace. But yet, Paulina,
Hermione was not as much wrinkled, nothing°
So agèd as this seems.

POLIXENES: Oh, not by much.

PAULINA:

So much the more our carver's excellence,   30
Which lets go by some sixteen years and makes her
As she° lived now.

LEONTES: As now she might have done,
So much to my good comfort as it is
Now piercing to my soul. Oh, thus she stood,
Even with such life of majesty — warm life,   35
As now it coldly stands — when first I wooed her!
I am ashamed. Does not the stone rebuke me
For being more stone than it? O royal piece!°
There's magic in thy majesty, which has
My evils conjured to remembrance and   40
From thy admiring° daughter took the spirits,°
Standing like stone with thee.

PERDITA: And give me leave,
And do not say 'tis superstition, that

---

18. **Lonely:** isolated.   19. **as lively mocked:** as realistically counterfeited.   20. **Still:** motion-less.   23. **something:** somewhat.   28. **nothing:** not at all.   32. **As she:** as if she.   38. **piece:** work of art.   41. **admiring:** filled with wonder.   **spirits:** vital spirits.

I kneel and then implore her blessing. Lady,   [*kneeling*]
Dear Queen, that ended when I but began,   45
Give me that hand of yours to kiss.

PAULINA: Oh, patience!
The statue is but newly fixed;° the color's
Not dry.

CAMILLO:
My lord, your sorrow was too sore° laid on,
Which sixteen winters cannot blow away,   50
So many summers dry.° Scarce any joy
Did ever so long live; no sorrow
But killed itself much sooner.

POLIXENES: Dear my brother,
Let him° that was the cause of this have power
To take off so much grief from you as he   55
Will piece up in himself.°

PAULINA: Indeed, my lord,
If I had thought the sight of my poor image
Would thus have wrought° you — for the stone is mine —
I'd not have showed it.

LEONTES: Do not draw the curtain.

PAULINA:
No longer shall you gaze on't, lest your fancy   60
May think anon it moves.

LEONTES: Let be, let be.
Would I were dead but that methinks already —
What was he that did make it? See, my lord,
Would you not deem it breathed? And that those veins
Did verily bear blood?

POLIXENES: Masterly done.   65
The very life seems warm upon her lip.

LEONTES:
The fixture of her eye has motion in't,°
As we are mocked with art.°

PAULINA: I'll draw the curtain.

---

47. **fixed:** made fast in its color.   49. **sore:** heavily.   51. **So . . . dry:** i.e., and sixteen summers cannot dry up. (Camillo tells the King that he has imposed too heavy a sorrow on himself if even sixteen years' time cannot end it.)   54. **him:** i.e., myself (as an innocent cause, but still a cause).   56. **piece up in himself:** add to his own burden.   58. **wrought:** affected.   67. **The fixture . . . in't:** i.e., her eye, though motionless, gives the appearance of motion.   68. **As . . . art:** in such a way that we are fooled by artistic illusion.

My lord's almost so far transported that
He'll think anon it lives.

LEONTES: Oh, sweet Paulina,   70
Make me to think so twenty years together!
No settled senses of the world° can match
The pleasure of that madness. Let't alone.

PAULINA:
I am sorry, sir, I have thus far stirred you; but
I could afflict you farther.

LEONTES: Do, Paulina;   75
For this affliction has a taste as sweet
As any cordial° comfort. Still methinks
There is an air comes from her. What fine chisel
Could ever yet cut breath? Let no man mock me,
For I will kiss her.

PAULINA: Good my lord, forbear.   80
The ruddiness upon her lip is wet;
You'll mar it if you kiss it, stain your own
With oily painting.° Shall I draw the curtain?

LEONTES:
No, not these twenty years.

PERDITA: So long could I
Stand by, a looker on.

PAULINA: Either forbear,   85
Quit presently° the chapel, or resolve you
For more amazement. If you can behold it,
I'll make the statue move indeed, descend
And take you by the hand. But then you'll think —
Which I protest against — I am assisted   90
By wicked powers.

LEONTES: What you can make her do
I am content to look on, what to speak
I am content to hear; for 'tis as easy
To make her speak as move.

PAULINA: It is required
You do awake your faith. Then all stand still.
On; those° that think it is unlawful business   95
I am about, let them depart.

---

72. **No settled . . . world:** no calm mind in the world.   77. **cordial:** restorative, heartwarming.
83. **painting:** paint.   86. **presently:** immediately.   96. **On; those:** (Often emended to *Or those.*)

LEONTES: Proceed.
  No foot shall stir.
PAULINA: Music, awake her; strike!°   [*Music.*]
  'Tis time. Descend. Be stone no more. Approach.
  Strike all that look upon° with marvel. Come,   100
  I'll fill your grave up. Stir, nay, come away,
  Bequeath to death your numbness, for from him°
  Dear life redeems you. — You perceive she stirs.   [*Hermione comes down.*]
  Start not. Her actions shall be holy as
  You hear my spell is lawful. Do not shun her   105
  Until you see her die again, for then
  You kill her double.° Nay, present your hand.
  When she was young you wooed her. Now in age
  Is she become the suitor?   [*Leontes touches her.*]
LEONTES: Oh, she's warm!
  If this be magic, let it be an art   110
  Lawful as eating.
POLIXENES:
  She embraces him.
CAMILLO:
  She hangs about his neck.
  If she pertain to life,° let her speak too.
POLIXENES:
  Ay, and make it manifest where she has lived,   115
  Or how stol'n from the dead.
PAULINA: That she is living,
  Were it but told you, should be hooted at
  Like an old tale; but it appears she lives,
  Though yet she speak not. Mark a little while.
  [*To Perdita*] Please you to interpose, fair madam.° Kneel,   120
  And pray your mother's blessing. — Turn, good lady;
  Our Perdita is found.
HERMIONE: You gods, look down
  And from your sacred vials pour your graces
  Upon my daughter's head! — Tell me, mine own,
  Where hast thou been preserved? Where lived? How found   125
  Thy father's court? For thou shalt hear that I,

98: **strike:** strike up.   100. **upon:** on.   102. **him:** i.e., death.   105–07. **Do . . . double:** i.e., if you ever shun her during the rest of her life, you will kill her again.   114. **pertain to life:** be truly alive.   120. **madam:** (Addressed to Perdita as Princess and affianced to be married.)

Knowing by Paulina that the oracle
Gave hope thou wast in being, have preserved
Myself to see the issue.°

PAULINA:
There's time enough for that,   130
Lest they desire upon this push to trouble
Your joys with like relation.° Go together,
You precious winners all; your exultation
Partake to° everyone. I, an old turtle,°
Will wing me to some withered bough and there   135
My mate, that's never to be found again,
Lament till I am lost.°

LEONTES: Oh, peace, Paulina!
Thou shouldst a husband take by my consent,
As I by thine a wife. This is a match,
And made between 's by vows. Thou hast found mine,   140
But how is to be questioned, for I saw her,
As I thought, dead, and have in vain said many
A prayer upon her grave. I'll not seek far —
For° him, I partly know his mind — to find thee
An honorable husband. Come, Camillo,   145
And take her by the hand, whose° worth and honesty
Is richly noted° and here justified°
By us, a pair of kings. Let's from this place.
[_To Hermione_] What? Look upon my brother. Both your pardons,
That e'er I put between your holy looks   150
My ill suspicion. This'° your son-in-law
And son unto the King, whom, heavens directing,
Is trothplight° to your daughter. Good Paulina,
Lead us from hence, where we may leisurely
Each one demand and answer to his part   155
Performed in this wide gap of time since first
We were dissevered. Hastily lead away.   _Exeunt._

FINIS

129. **the issue:** (1) the outcome (2) my child.   131–32. **Lest . . . relation:** lest they (bystanders) insist, at this critical juncture, on interrupting this moment of joy with your relating of your story or with their telling what has happened to them.   134. **Partake to:** share with, communicate.   **turtle:** turtledove.   136–37. **My mate . . . lost:** grieve for my lost mate until I die.   144. **For:** as for.   146. **whose:** i.e., Camillo's.   147. **richly noted:** abundantly acknowledged.   **justified:** avouched.   151. **This':** this is.   153. **trothplight:** betrothed.

THE WINTER'S TALE

Copy text: the First Folio. Characters' names are grouped at the heads of scenes throughout the play. Act and scene divisions are as marked in the Folio.
DRAMATIS PERSONAE. [printed in F at the end of the play]
ARCHIDAMUS [after *Autoclycus* in F]
ACT 1, SCENE 1. 6. us, we: vs: we.
ACT 1, SCENE 2. 104. And: a. 121. hast: has't. 137–38. be? — / Affection, thy: be / Affection? thy. 148. What . . . brother: [assigned in F to Leontes]. 151–53. its folly, . . . Its tenderness, . . . bosoms! it's folly? . . . It's tenderness? . . bosomes? 158. do: do's. 202–03. powerful, think it, . . . south. Be: powrefull: thinke it: . . . South, be. 208. you, they: you. 253. forth. In . . . lord: forth in . . . (my Lord.) 275. hobbyhorse: Holy-Horse. 386. How? Caught: how caught. 461. off. Hence!: off, hence.
ACT 2, SCENE 1. 2. [and throughout scene] FIRST LADY: *Lady.* 91. fedarie: federarie.
ACT 2, SCENE 2. 32–3. me. / If . . . blister: me, / If . . . blister.
ACT 2, SCENE 3. 2. thus, mere weakness. If: thus: meere weaknesse, if. 39. What: who. 61. good, so: good so.
ACT 3, SCENE 2. 10. Silence!: [printed in F as a s.d.]. 10.1. *Hermione, as to her trial . . . Ladies:* [at start of scene in F, as generally with the s.d. in this play]. 30. Who: whom. 96. Starred: star'd. 151. woo: woe.
ACT 3, SCENE 3. 62. scared: scarr'd. 103. made: mad.
ACT 4, SCENE 2. 10. thee. Thou: thee, thou.
ACT 4, SCENE 3. 1. AUTOLYCUS [not in F]. 7. on: *an.* 10. With heigh, with heigh: *with heigh.* 34. currants: currence.
ACT 4, SCENE 4. 12. Digest it: digest. 13. swoon: sworne. 60. afire: o'fire. 83. bastards. Of: bastards) of. 93. scion: sien. 98. your: you. 160. out: on't. 210. AUTOLYCUS: [not in F]. 233. kilnhole: kill-hole. 277. AUTOLYCUS: [in F, appears at line 278]. 281. Whither: whether [and similarly throughout song]. 292. gentleman: gent. 297. cape: crpe. 317. square: squire. 333. reply, at least: reply at least. 339. who: whom. 399. acknowledged: acknowledge. 403. who: whom. 408. see: neuer see. 419. hoop: hope. 447. your: my. 450. sight as yet, I fear: sight, as yet I feare. 462–63. fancy. If . . . obedient, I: fancie, if . . . obedient: I. 480. our: her. 587. could: would. 588. filed: fill'd. off: of. 611. flayed: fled. 665. know not: know. 691. to: at. 767.1. s.d. *Exeunt:* [at 775 in F].
ACT 5, SCENE 1. 6. Whilst: whilest [also at line 169]. 59. Where . . . appear: (Where we Offendors now appeare). 61. just: just such. 75. I have done: [assigned in F to Cleomenes]. 84.1. s.d. *Gentleman: Servant.* 85. [and through line 110] GENTLEMAN: *Ser.* 114. s.d. *Exit:* [after "us" in line 115 in F]. 160. his, parting: his parting.
ACT 5, SCENE 2. 86. s.d. *Exeunt: Exit.*
ACT 5, SCENE 3. 18. Lonely: louely. 67. fixture: fixure.

PART TWO

Cultural Contexts

CHAPTER I

Romance and Tragicomedy

>‹

Like an old tale still . . . (5.2.46)

Modern one-volume editions of Shakespeare usually classify *The Winter's Tale* as a "romance" and group it with three other plays written late in the playwright's career: *Pericles*, *The Tempest*, and *Cymbeline*. Because these plays are generally not as well known as, say, *A Midsummer Night's Dream*, *Hamlet*, or *Henry IV*, *Part 1*, the genre of romance is at first perhaps recognized more by what it is not — comedy, tragedy, or history — than by what it is.

We can begin to define Shakespearean dramatic romance, however, by identifying the three literary traditions that conveyed romance themes and conventions to English Renaissance readers: Hellenistic (Greek) prose romances written in the third century C.E.; medieval chivalric romances such as Thomas Malory's *Mort D'Arthur*; and late medieval morality plays and miracle plays that dramatized the lives of Christian saints. The characteristics of romance are particularly visible in the Hellenistic romances, three of which were first translated into English in the sixteenth century: Achilles Tatius's *Clitophon and Leucippe* (tr. 1597 and 1638); Heliodorus's *Aethiopica* (tr. 1569); and Longus's *Daphnis and Chloe* (tr. 1587). Maurice Hunt explains that Hellenistic romance typically consists of

> an episodic journey, of a hero's or pair of separated lovers' wandering toward home or reunion. Along the way, they endure a series of hardships,

including shipwrecks and seizure by pirates, as well as marvels and the intervention in their lives of deities. Essentially the characters are idealized — pious and chaste — although accounts of the young couple's interaction sometimes [have] an erotic quality that appealed to Elizabethans fond of Ovid. Usually the hero or heroine must disguise himself or herself, almost always as a person of a lower social class, at one or more moments during the quest. A token or mark generally precipitates the final union of romance between strangers, made so by lapsed time, great distances, and disfiguring suffering, who discover they are husband and wife or lovers. Hellenistic romance thus reaffirms the reality of a providential outcome for suffering, presumably as a reward for virtue maintained though beset by temptation and adversity, and often involving the fulfillment of the riddling terms of an early oracle or prophecy.   (385)

The Winter's Tale has a lost child, sea journey, oracle, shipwreck, and various hardships eventually leading to discovery and reunion. Certain details of the play seem to follow closely the romance pattern described by Hunt. For instance, the Bohemian sheep-shearing festival of act 4 focuses on the erotic intrigue of young lovers, including a shepherdess unaware of her royal birth. The young lovers disguise themselves and take a sea voyage that ends with the reunion of a long-separated family (Figure 3). Yet Shakespeare invests the basic romance plot of separation and return with a characteristic emotional intensity: the hardships Leontes endures are not the shipwreck or captivity typically suffered by the romance hero, but psychological anguish and political strife. Like a virtuous romance heroine, Hermione is finally rewarded for her patience in waiting for the fulfillment of the oracle, yet the only journey she takes involves sequestering herself on Paulina's estate.

Although *The Winter's Tale* incorporates features of Hellenistic romance, Shakespeare's contemporaries reserved the term "romance" primarily for medieval "verse tales of chivalry"; they labeled plays such as *The Winter's Tale* "histories," "comedies," or "tales" (Mowat, "Tragicomedy" 133; Hunt 384). In 1623, when members of Shakespeare's company published the First Folio (a large volume that collected thirty-five of his plays), they divided the plays into three groups: Comedies, Histories, and Tragedies. The relegation of *The Tempest* and *The Winter's Tale* to the borders of the Comedies category perhaps indicates that the Folio editors recognized the traits that distinguished these plays from Shakespeare's other comedies (Figure 4). For instance, the typical romance situation of a prince or princess falling in love with a commoner "does not occur in the Shakespeare canon" outside *The Tempest*, *The Winter's Tale*, *Pericles*, and *Cymbeline* (Mowat, "Tragicomedy" 140). Such distinctive traits led later editors and critics, beginning in the Victorian period, to designate these four late plays as romances. Other

FIGURE 3 *Frontispiece of Achilles Tatius's prose romance,* The Loves of Clitophon and Leucippe *(tr. Anthony Hodges, 1638). The image depicts the typical romance scenario of noble lovers on a tempest-tossed ship: the sail carries the words* Navis Amantibus Portus *("the ship harbors the lovers"). In romance, hardships at sea, such as the shipwreck that accompanies Perdita's abandonment in Bohemia, often precede the eventual reunion of family members or lovers.*

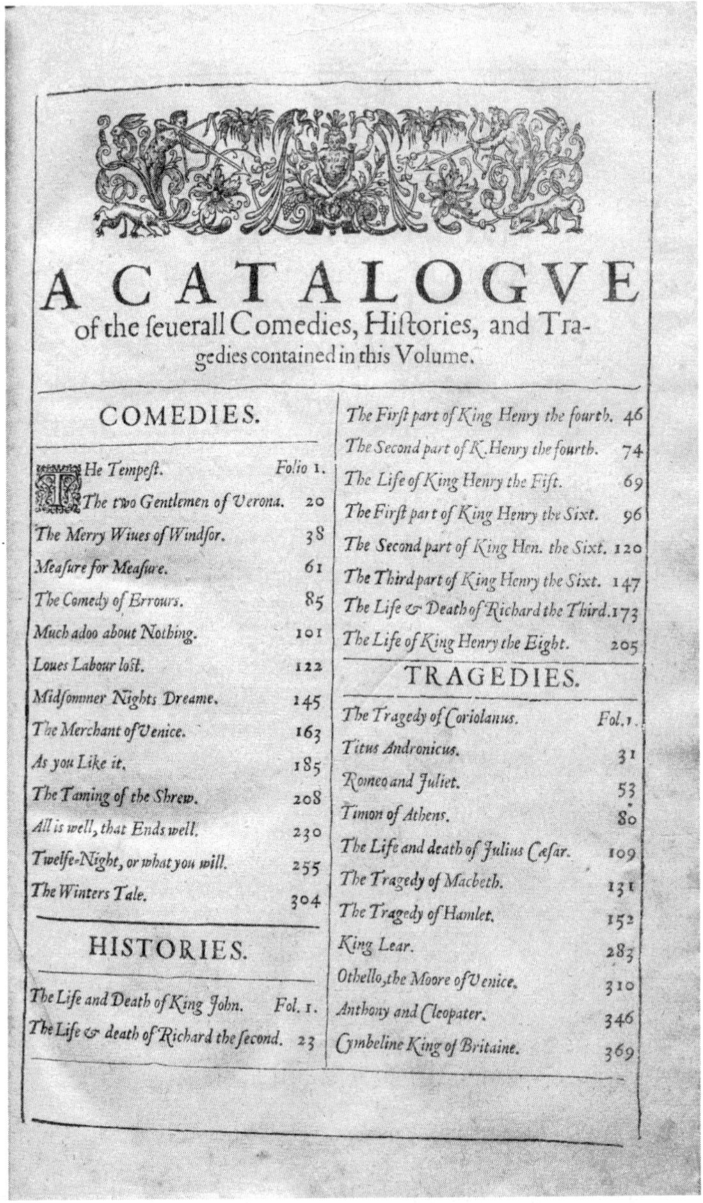

A CATALOGVE

of the feuerall Comedies, Hiftories, and Tragedies contained in this Volume.

COMEDIES.

He Tempeſt.	Folio 1.
The two Gentlemen of Verona.	20
The Merry Wiues of Windſor.	38
Meaſure for Meaſure.	61
The Comedy of Errours.	85
Much adoo about Nothing.	101
Loues Labour loſt.	122
Midſomner Nights Dreame.	145
The Merchant of Venice.	163
As you Like it.	185
The Taming of the Shrew.	208
All is well, that Ends well.	230
Twelfe-Night, or what you will.	255
The Winters Tale.	304

HISTORIES.

The Life and Death of King John.	Fol. 1.
The Life & death of Richard the ſecond.	23
The Firſt part of King Henry the fourth.	46
The Second part of K. Henry the fourth.	74
The Life of King Henry the Fiſt.	69
The Firſt part of King Henry the Sixt.	96
The Second part of King Hen. the Sixt.	120
The Third part of King Henry the Sixt.	147
The Life & Death of Richard the Third.	173
The Life of King Henry the Eight.	205

TRAGEDIES.

The Tragedy of Coriolanus.	Fol. 1.
Titus Andronicus.	31
Romeo and Juliet.	53
Timon of Athens.	80
The Life and death of Julius Cæſar.	109
The Tragedy of Macbeth.	131
The Tragedy of Hamlet.	152
King Lear.	283
Othello, the Moore of Venice.	310
Anthony and Cleopater.	346
Cymbeline King of Britaine.	369

FIGURE 4 *"Catalogue of the Several Comedies, Histories, and Tragedies contained in this Volume," from* Mr. William Shakespeare's Comedies, Histories, and Tragedies *(1623).*

labels that have been suggested for these plays include "late Shakespearean comedy," "romantic tragicomedy," or "tragicomic romance" (Mowat, "Tragicomedy" 134).

If Shakespeare and his contemporaries did not have a specific category to distinguish plays like *The Winter's Tale* and *The Tempest* from comedies more generally, they were nonetheless able to identify the characteristics that such plays had in common. Because of its fairy tale characteristics — a focus on heroes from faraway places and legendary times — romance has sometimes been discredited as an escapist or frivolous literary mode. Indeed, Shakespeare's use in *The Winter's Tale* and *The Tempest* of typical romance elements such as storms, shipwrecks, oracles, gods, ghosts, and magic elicited a condescending remark from Ben Jonson, one of the most important playwrights and critics of the age. In the induction to Jonson's *Bartholomew Fair* (1614), a comedy set in contemporary London, the audience is warned not to expect any fantastic adventures, for Jonson is "loth to make Nature afraid in his plays, like those that beget *Tales*, *Tempests*, and such like drolleries" (12). Years later, disappointed by the cold reception of his play *The New Inn* (1631), Jonson ridiculed the poor taste of playgoers who preferred a "mouldy tale / Like *Pericles*" to his more refined theatrical fare (quoted in Hattaway 206).

The documents in this chapter address the generic contexts through which a seventeenth-century audience might have understood and (if Jonson is right) enjoyed dramatic romances such as *The Winter's Tale*. Like Jonson, Sir Philip Sidney did not care for dramatic romance. Sidney's *Defense of Poesy* pronounces judgment on dramatic romance from the perspective of classical rules about what legitimate drama should be and do. Whereas Sidney critiques the "gross absurdities" of using romance elements on stage, John Fletcher, in the preface to his play *The Faithful Shepherdess*, justifies his attempt to write a play according to the rules of "pastoral tragicomedy." Fletcher's preface suggests how *The Winter's Tale* might be positioned within the development of the new kind of tragicomedy Fletcher was popularizing at that time. Robert Greene's Elizabethan prose romance *Pandosto* is the only document in this chapter that can be considered a direct "source" for *The Winter's Tale*, although the Hellenistic romances should themselves be acknowledged as sources for Greene (Gillespie 229). Like *The Winter's Tale*, *Pandosto* is a generically hybrid text: is it a comedy, tragedy, or tragicomedy? Examining Shakespeare's alterations to his source provides significant insight into the generic complexity of *The Winter's Tale*. Finally, the myth of Proserpina, as told in Ovid's *Metamorphoses*, can be considered an indirect source or analogue for Shakespeare's representation of time in terms of seasonal cycles of loss and return. The cyclical nature of the seasons might be regarded as a "tragicomic" model of time, in that the winter is always followed by the spring, but *The Winter's Tale* also bears witness to a competing model of time as linear, and of the past as unrecoverable.

→ SIR PHILIP SIDNEY

From The Defense of Poesy   *1595*

One of the most celebrated figures of the Elizabethan age, Sir Philip Sidney was a courtier, soldier, scholar, and author of three extremely influential works, all published posthumously: a prose romance, *The Countess of Pembroke's Arcadia* (1590); a sonnet sequence, *Astrophil and Stella* (1591); and a theoretical treatise, the *Defense of Poesy* (written at some point after 1579 and published in two editions in 1595). The *Defense* stands as the definitive statement of literary theory produced in Renaissance England. Sidney might have written it to refute the *School of Abuse* (1579) by Stephen Gosson, a Puritan who dedicated to Sidney his attack on poets and plays.

Sidney defends literature (to which he generally refers as poesy or "poetry") in terms of its imaginative freedom and ability to create a "golden" world more perfect than the "brazen" world of nature in which we live. Echoing an ancient commonplace, he also praises imaginative literature for its ability "to teach and delight." In making his case, Sidney cites ancient authorities such as Aristotle and Virgil; subdivides poetry into various kinds (such as lyric, tragic, comic, and satiric); distinguishes poetry from the disciplines of history and philosophy; and describes the current state of English literature. Although Sidney himself wrote a prose romance, he rejects the use of romance elements on the popular stage.

Sidney grounds his criticism of dramatic romance in the Renaissance commonplace that tragedies should observe the "unities" of time (the action should take place in one day), of place (in one locale), and of action (through one plot). This rule of three unities was thought, mistakenly, to derive from the classical authority of Aristotle's *Poetics*, which actually specifies only unity of action as a requirement of dramatic composition. Although most English Renaissance plays, including those of Shakespeare, fail to comply with the stringent requirements of the three unities (*The Tempest* is a notable exception), dramatic romances in particular typically refuse to restrict their action to a single place or time, and further stretch plausibility with their emphasis on marvels and the supernatural.

In his discussion of dramatic genres, Sidney begins by defining the two genres with the strongest classical pedigrees, comedy and tragedy, known to educated

Sir Philip Sidney, *The Defense of Poesy* (London, 1595); STC 22534.5; sigs. F2r–F4r, I4v–K2v.

Renaissance readers primarily through the ancient Roman comic dramatists Terence and Plautus and the ancient Roman tragedian Seneca. Sidney then launches into a critique of the current practice of English playwrights. In reading the selection below, consider how Sidney's objections to romance and tragicomedy combine aesthetic, social, and moral issues. Why should tragicomedy raise greater objections for Sidney than either comedy or tragedy?

Sidney was not alive to see *The Winter's Tale*, but it is instructive to imagine what he would have thought about it. For instance, we might analyze and evaluate the "tragic" aspects of the play (such as Leontes' tyrannical behavior) in terms of Sidney's general requirements for tragedy. How, according to Sidney's prescriptions, might the mixture of comedic and tragic elements in the first three acts affect an audience's responses to the play? Does the mixture of genres in *The Winter's Tale* dilute or intensify comic pleasure and tragic pity? We might also consider how such broad questions derived from *The Defense* fail to take into account differences of gender, age, or social status among audience members, differences that might significantly influence individual responses to particular characters and episodes.

Sidney's *Defense* can also be used to examine certain dramaturgical choices Shakespeare makes. For instance, Sidney advocates the poet's "liberty" to alter historical narratives, but at the same time he insists that the "laws" of poetry require a dramatist to limit his story to one locale and one day. Obviously, *The Winter's Tale* does not meet these expectations, but what if it did? What would be lost or gained if Shakespeare had the events of *The Winter's Tale*, like those of *The Tempest*, transpire over the course of a single day? How might such a compression of time be accomplished? In the play as it stands, the choric figure of Time reports events that have occurred in the sixteen-year gap between acts 3 and 4, and thus cannot be staged; yet Shakespeare also refuses to stage the emotional reunion between Leontes and Perdita that takes place in the present. What might Sidney say about a play that has no qualms about leaping sixteen years into the future, but that keeps off-stage a crucial scene happening in the present moment?

From *The Defense of Poesy*

By these therefore examples and reasons, I think it may be manifest that the poet, with that same hand of delight, doth draw the mind more effectually than any other art doth, and so a conclusion not unfitly ensueth: that as virtue is the most excellent resting place for all worldly learning to make his end of, so poetry, being the most familiar to teach it, and most princely to move towards it, in the most excellent work, is the most excellent workman.

But I am content not only to decipher him by his works (although works in commendation or dispraise, must ever hold a high authority), but more narrowly will examine his parts; so that (as in a man) though altogether may carry a presence full of majesty and beauty, perchance in some one defectious[1] piece, we may find a blemish.

Now in his parts, kinds, or species (as you list[2] to term them), it is to be noted that some poesies have coupled together two or three kinds, as tragical and comical, whereupon is risen the tragi-comical. Some in the like manner have mingled prose and verse, as Sanazzaro and Boethius.[3] Some have mingled matters heroical and pastoral. But that cometh all to one in this question,[4] for, if severed they be good, the conjunction cannot be hurtful. Therefore, perchance forgetting some, and leaving some as needless to be remembered, it shall not be amiss in a word to cite the special kinds, to see what faults may be found in the right use of them. . . . [Sidney describes and refutes objections to pastoral, elegiac, and satiric poetry.]

No, perchance it is the comic [which is disliked], whom naughty playmakers and stage-keepers have justly made odious. To the argument of abuse, I will answer after. Only thus much now is to be said: that the comedy is an imitation of the common errors of our life, which he representeth in the most ridiculous and scornful sort that may be. So as it is impossible that any beholder can be content to be such a one. Now, as in geometry the oblique[5] must be known as well as the right, and in arithmetic the odd as well as the even, so in the actions of our life who seeth not the filthiness of evil wanteth[6] a great foil[7] to perceive the beauty of virtue. This doth the comedy handle so in our private and domestical matters, as with hearing it we get as it were an experience what is to be looked for of a niggardly Demea,[8] of a crafty Davus,[9] of a flattering Gnatho,[10] of a vainglorious Thraso;[11] and not only to know what effects are to be expected, but to know who be such, by the signifying badge given them by the comedian. And little reason hath any man to say that men learn evil by seeing it so set out, sith[12] as I said before, there is no man living but by the force truth hath in nature, no sooner seeth these men play their parts, but wisheth them *in pistrinum*.[13] Although perchance the sack[14] of his own faults lie so behind

---

[1] **defectious:** defective. [2] **list:** desire. [3] **Sanazzaro and Boethius:** Jacopo Sannazaro (1457–1530), a Neapolitan poet and author of the immensely influential pastoral romance, *Arcadia* (1504); Boethius (c. 480–524), a Roman statesman and philosopher best known for *The Consolation of Philosophy*. [4] **cometh all to one in this question:** comes to the same thing in this matter. [5] **oblique:** an angle less than 180 degrees, but not equal to a right angle, or one of 90 degrees. [6] **wanteth:** lacks. [7] **foil:** a thin leaf of metal placed under a precious stone to increase its brilliancy. [8] **Demea:** the stingy father in Terence's comedy *Adelphi* (160 B.C.E.). [9] **Davus:** a cunning slave in Terence's *Andria* (166 B.C.E.). [10] **Gnatho:** a parasitic guest in Terence's *Eunuchus* (161 B.C.E.). [11] **Thraso:** the boastful soldier in *Eunuchus*. [12] **sith:** since. [13] *in pistrinum*: at hard labor [Latin]. [14] **sack:** large bag carried on the back.

his back that he seeth not himself dance the same measure, whereto yet nothing can more open his eyes than to find his own actions contemptibly set forth.

So that the right use of comedy will (I think) by nobody be blamed, and much less of the high and excellent tragedy, that openeth the greatest wounds, and showeth forth the ulcers that are covered with tissue; that maketh kings fear to be tyrants, and tyrants manifest their tyrannical humors; that with stirring the affects of admiration and commiseration,[15] teacheth the uncertainty of this world, and upon how weak foundations gilden roofs are builded. . . .

Our tragedies and comedies (not without cause cried out against), observing rules neither of honest civility nor of skillful poetry, excepting *Gorboduc*[16] (again, I say, of those that I have seen), which notwithstanding as it is full of stately speeches and well sounding phrases, climbing to the height of Seneca[17] his style, and as full of notable morality, which it doth most delightfully teach, and so obtain the very end of poesy; yet in truth it is very defectious in the circumstances, which grieveth me, because it might not remain as an exact model of all tragedies. For it is faulty both in place and time, the two necessary companions of all corporeal actions. For where the stage should always represent but one place, and the uttermost time presupposed in it should be, both by Aristotle's precept[18] and common reason, but one day, there is both many days and many places, inartificially[19] imagined.

But if it be so in *Gorboduc*, how much more in all the rest, where you shall have Asia of the one side, and Afric of the other, and so many other underkingdoms, that the player, when he cometh in, must ever begin with telling where he is, or else the tale will not be conceived. Now ye shall have three ladies walk to gather flowers, and then we must believe the stage to be a garden. By and by, we hear news of a shipwreck in the same place, and then we are to blame if we accept it not for a rock. Upon the back of that comes out a hideous monster with fire and smoke, and then the miserable beholders are bound to take it for a cave. While in the meantime two armies fly in, represented with four swords and bucklers, and then what hard heart will not receive it for a pitched field?

---

[15] **commiseration:** pity, compassion.   [16] *Gorboduc:* one of the first English tragedies, first produced in 1561, by Thomas Norton (1532–1584) and Thomas Sackville (1536–1608).   [17] **Seneca:** Lucius Anneaus (55 B.C.E.–39 C.E.), Roman rhetorician and tragedian.   [18] **Aristotle's precept:** refers to the Aristotelean unities of time, place, and action. In the *Poetics*, Aristotle actually specifies only unity of action as a requirement of drama.   [19] **inartificially:** artlessly, clumsily.

Now, of time they are much more liberal. For ordinary it is that two young princes[20] fall in love; after many traverses,[21] she is got with child, delivered of a fair boy; he is lost, groweth a man, falls in love, and is ready to get another child; and all this in two hours' space: which how absurd it is in sense, even sense may imagine, and art hath taught, and all ancient examples justified, and at this day, the ordinary players in Italy will not err in. Yet will some bring in an example of *Eunuchus* in Terence, that containeth matter of two days, yet far short of twenty years. True it is, and so was it to be played in two days, and so fitted to the time it set forth. And though Plautus[22] hath in one place done amiss, let us hit with him, and not miss with him.

But they will say, how then shall we set forth a story which containeth both many places and many times? And do they not know that a tragedy is tied to the laws of poesy, and not of history; not bound to follow the story, but having liberty either to feign a quite new matter, or to frame the history to the most tragical conveniency? Again, many things may be told which cannot be showed, if they know the difference betwixt reporting and representing. As for example, I may speak (though I am here) of Peru, and in speech digress from that to the description of Calicut,[23] but in action I cannot represent it without Pacolet's horse;[24] and so was the manner the ancients took, by some *Nuncius*[25] to recount things done in former time or other place.

Lastly, if they will represent a history, they must not (as Horace saith) begin *ab ovo*,[26] but they must come to the principal point of that one action which they will represent. By example this will be best expressed. I have a story of young Polydorus, delivered for safety's sake, with great riches, by his father Priam[27] to Polymnestor, king of Thrace, in the Trojan war time. He, after some years, hearing the overthrow of Priam, for to make the treasure his own, murdereth the child. The body of the child is taken up by Hecuba;[28] she, the same day, findeth a sleight[29] to be revenged most cruelly

---

[20] **two young princes**: "prince" could refer to male or female royalty.   [21] **traverses**: obstacles, impediments.   [22] **Plautus**: Titus Maccius (c. 250–184 B.C.E.), Roman comic playwright. Sidney is probably referring to Plautus's *Captivi* (prisoners of war) as the play that violates the unity of time.   [23] **Calicut**: a seaport in southwest India.   [24] **Pacolet's horse**: in the story of *Valentine and Orson*, an early French romance that appeared in English about 1510, Pacolet is a dwarf messenger who has a little magic horse of wood that conveys him instantly wherever he wishes.   [25] *Nuncius*: a messenger.   [26] *ab ovo*: literally, from the egg, i.e., the very beginning. In *Ars Poetica* (*The Art of Poetry*), Horace observes that the epic poet properly begins his story not *ab ovo* (from the beginning) but *in medias res* (in the middle of things).   [27] **Priam**: the king of Troy at the time of its destruction by the Greeks under Agamemnon.   [28] **Hecuba**: the wife of Priam.   [29] **sleight**: a cunning trick.

of the tyrant. Where now would one of our tragedy writers begin, but with the delivery of the child? Then should he sail over into Thrace, and so spend I know not how many years, and travel numbers of places. But where doth Euripides?[30] Even with the finding of the body, leaving the rest to be told by the spirit of Polydorus. This need no further to be enlarged; the dullest wit may conceive it.

But besides these gross absurdities, how all their plays be neither right tragedies, nor right comedies, mingling kings and clowns, not because the matter so carrieth it, but thrust in clowns by head and shoulders to play a part in majestical matters, with neither decency nor discretion. So as neither the admiration and commiseration, nor the right sportfulness, is by their mongrel tragi-comedy obtained. I know Apuleius[31] did somewhat so, but that is a thing recounted with space of time, not represented in one moment; and I know the ancients have one or two examples of tragi-comedies, as Plautus hath *Amphitruo*.[32] But if we mark them well, we shall find that they never, or very daintily, match hornpipes and funerals. So falleth it out that, having indeed no right comedy, in that comical part of our tragedy, we have nothing but scurrility,[33] unworthy of any chaste ears, or some extreme show of doltishness,[34] indeed fit to lift up a loud laughter, and nothing else. Where the whole tract of a comedy should be full of delight, as the tragedy should be still maintained in a well-raised admiration. But our comedians think there is not delight without laughter, which is very wrong, for though laughter may come with delight, yet cometh it not of delight, as though delight should be the cause of laughter; but well may one thing breed both together. Nay, rather in themselves they have as it were a kind of contrariety: for delight we scarcely do but in things that have a conveniency to ourselves, or to the general nature; laughter almost ever cometh of things most dispro-portioned to ourselves and nature. Delight hath a joy in it, either permanent or present. Laughter hath only a scornful tickling.

---

[30] **Euripides:** (c. 480–406 B.C.E.), Greek dramatist and last of the trio of important tragedians after Aeschylus and Sophocles; author of *Hecuba* (424 B.C.E.), whose plot Sidney recounts here.
[31] **Apuleius:** (born c. 123 C.E.), Roman writer, born in Africa, whose *Golden Ass* includes both bawdy and religious episodes. [32] *Amphitruo*: the Roman playwright Plautus's *tragico-comedia* (c. 195 B.C.E.), an adaptation of the mythical subject of the cuckolding of Amphitryon.
[33] **scurrility:** coarseness or indecency of language, especially in invective and jesting.
[34] **doltishness:** stupidity.

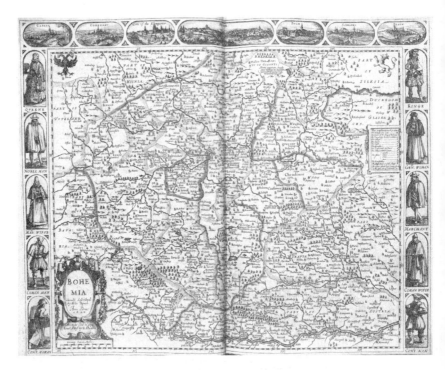

FIGURE 5 *Map of Bohemia, from John Speed,* A Prospect of the Most Famous Parts of the World *(London, 1631). By bringing together clowns and kings, act 4 of* The Winter's Tale *evokes not only Sidney's attacks against "mongrel tragi-comedy," but also the practice of seventeenth-century cartographers who identified national characteristics through culturally specific markers of social status. For instance, the maps in John Speed's* Prospect of the Most Famous Parts of the World *are bordered by figures of different ranks, genders, and professions. What does the visual arrangement of the ten figures imply about their status or importance in the nation? How does Speed's depiction of the Country Woman and Country Man compare to Shakespeare's depiction of the Bohemian shepherds?*

QVEENE   KINGE   NOBLE MAN   GEN̄. WOMAN

MĀR. WIFFE   MARCHANT   COMAN MAN   COMAN WIFFE

CON̄T. WOMAN   CON̄T. MAN

→ JOHN FLETCHER

From The Faithful Shepherdess   *1610*

The son of a prominent clergyman, John Fletcher attended Cambridge University and the Inns of Court, London's law schools. In 1608, he began collaborating with his fellow law student Francis Beaumont, and together they produced many popular tragicomedies and tragedies for the London stage. Having collaborated with Shakespeare on *Henry VIII* (1613) and *The Two Noble Kinsmen* (1613–14), Fletcher became chief dramatist of the King's Men after Shakespeare's death in 1616. At his death in 1625, Fletcher had authored or co-authored close to fifty plays, and was largely responsible for having established tragicomedy as "the most important dramatic phenomenon in England between 1610 and 1650" (Hunt 395).

"Tragicomedy" was not a generic label much in use during the earlier seventeenth century. The 1647 first folio of Beaumont and Fletcher's works identifies the plays simply as tragedies and comedies; the second folio of 1679 identifies ten plays as tragicomedies (Hunt 395). Nonetheless, many Beaumont and Fletcher plays are aptly described as tragicomic. Ending on a note of celebration and restoration, these plays are essentially comic in structure, yet they achieve social harmony through tonally tragic episodes involving incest, political strife, physical and psychological abuse, narrowly averted deaths, tormented consciences, and so on. A similar tragicomic sensibility informs the four romances Shakespeare wrote between 1608 and 1612, including an emphasis on "the theatrical and sensational type of scene," a "playing on suspense and surprise," and a "dissipation of emotion through verbal decorativeness," all of which might be taken to describe the statue scene that concludes *The Winter's Tale* (Pettet 176, 181).

The Faithful Shepherdess (1609) was Fletcher's first and only play in the style of pastoral tragicomedy popularized by the Italian writer Giambattista Guarini. Guarini's *Il Pastor Fido, Tragicommedia Pastorale* (The Faithful Shepherd, a Pastoral Tragicomedy) was originally published in Italian in 1590 and later translated into English. Influenced by Guarini, Fletcher's *Faithful Shepherdess* explores the sexual intrigues of shepherds and shepherdesses who live in an elegant, ultimately comic world punctuated with episodes of violence and dark passion. *The Faithful Shepherdess* was a failure on stage, and in the document below, a preface appended to the published edition of the play in 1610, Fletcher expresses his chagrin at playgoers who did not understand the nature of "pastoral tragicomedy." Unlike Sidney, Fletcher does not set out the formal laws and didactic aims of various dramatic kinds; rather, by attaching a narrow definition to both pastoral and tragicomedy, he seeks to establish the legitimacy of his play.

John Fletcher, *The Faithful Shepherdess* (London, 1610); STC 11068; sig. A2v.

We can use Fletcher's preface to assess the particular generic choices Shakespeare makes in *The Winter's Tale*. Concerning pastoral, Fletcher insists that the shepherds in his play are drawn from literary tradition, not from accurate observation of the English countryside. Why is Fletcher so eager to establish that "pastoral" refers to a literary convention, and how might his discussion of pastoral convention illuminate *The Winter's Tale*? If Shakespeare had written a preface to *The Winter's Tale* explaining his theory of "pastoral tragicomedy," how might his account resemble or differ from Fletcher's? Another set of questions raised by Fletcher concerns the social status of characters. In *The Winter's Tale*, to what degree do commoners, kings, and gods interact, and what role do characters of different status play in bringing about a tragicomic resolution? What position, if any, does the play seem to take on the intermingling of social classes? Such questions are difficult to answer because the interaction of social classes and value systems in *The Winter's Tale* is more complex than Fletcher's confident pronouncements about the accommodation of aristocrats and commoners in tragicomedy would imply (Henke 176–81).

Like Fletcher's preface, *The Winter's Tale* also raises questions about the degree to which the comic and the tragic can be successfully integrated in tragicomedy. By including the deaths of Mamillius and Antigonus, does *The Winter's Tale* skew irretrievably toward the tragic? Ultimately, if we accept that divine providence, in the form of Apollo's oracle, has somehow brought about this conclusion, might we be left wondering at the justice of such a deity? Although Hermione beseeches the gods to "look down" and pour their "graces" on Perdita's head (5.3.122–23), her prayer for a purely comic, providential future is not the last word in the play. The play ends with Leontes' desire to recount collectively the events that occurred in "this wide gap of time since first / We were dissevered" (5.3.156–57). He asks, that is, for another telling of this tragicomic winter's tale.

From *The Faithful Shepherdess*

To the Reader

If you be not reasonably assured of your knowledge in this kind of poem,[1] lay down the book or read this, which I would wish had been the prologue. It is a pastoral tragi-comedy, which the people seeing when it was played, having ever had a singular gift in defining, concluded to be a play of country hired shepherds, in gray cloaks, with curtailed dogs in strings, sometimes laughing together, and sometimes killing one another; and missing

---

[1] **poem:** i.e., *The Faithful Shepherdess*; plays were often referred to as "poems" in this period.

Whitsun ales,[2] cream, wassail[3] and morris-dances,[4] began to be angry. In their error I would not have you fall, lest you incur their censure. Understand therefore a pastoral to be a representation of shepherds and shepherdesses, with their actions and passions, which must be such as may agree with their natures, at least not exceeding former fictions, and vulgar traditions: they are not to be adorned with any art, but such improper ones as nature is said to bestow, as singing and poetry, or such as experience may teach them, as the virtues of herbs and fountains, the ordinary course of the sun, moon, and stars, and such like. But you are ever to remember shepherds to be such as all the ancient poets and modern of understanding have received them: that is, the owners of flocks and not hirelings.[5] A tragicomedy is not so called in respect of mirth and killing, but in respect it wants deaths, which is enough to make it no tragedy, yet brings some near it, which is enough to make it no comedy, which must be a representation of familiar people with such kind of trouble as no life be questioned. So that a god is as lawful in this as in a tragedy, and mean[6] people as in a comedy. Thus much I hope will serve to justify my poem and make you understand it. To teach you more for nothing I do not know that I am in conscience bound.

[2] **Whitsun ales:** festivities surrounding Pentecost. [3] **wassail:** spiced ale or mulled wine drunk during celebrations for Twelfth Night and Christmas Eve. [4] **morris-dances:** traditional English dances often performed on festive occasions. [5] **hirelings:** laborers hired for wages. [6] **mean:** low in rank.

➔ ROBERT GREENE

From Pandosto. The Triumph of Time   1588

Educated at Cambridge University, Robert Greene published some twenty-five works, including plays, short tales, romances, pamphlets, and autobiographies. Greene's influence on *The Winter's Tale* is visible not only in the source text *Pandosto*, but also in the pamphlets about roguery (excerpted in Chapter 4) that describe the methods of con artists such as Autolycus. *Pandosto* has been a remarkably popular and enduring work. Printed in at least twenty-four editions by 1740 (Newcomb 21), it spawned multiple versions of the story of Dorastus and Fawnia, including two prose translations and two tragicomedies in French by 1631. The passages excerpted below come from the beginning and end of

Robert Greene, *Pandosto. The Triumph of Time* (London, 1588); STC 12285; sigs. A3r–B1r; B4r–B4v; C3r–C4r; G1v–G4r.

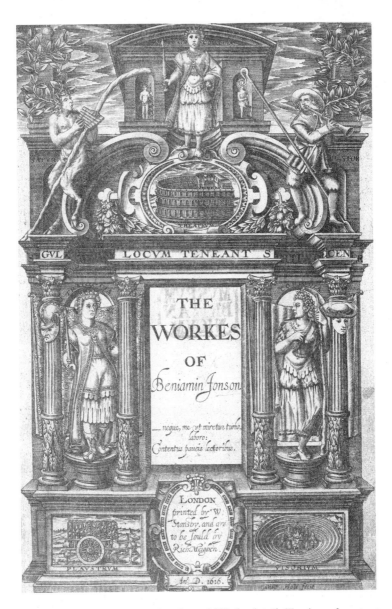

FIGURE 6 *In the frontispiece to Ben Jonson's* Works *(1616), Tragicomedy rests upon the more prominent canonical figures of Tragedy and Comedy, and is flanked by two figures from the pastoral tradition, the shepherd and the satyr (associated in the Renaissance with satire). While Tragicomedy is smaller in size than Comedy and Tragedy, it is placed above them. This ambiguous arrangement might imply that comedy and tragedy "are the source of [tragicomedy's] prestige, that it is their abstract and purely formal synthesis or that it constitutes the historical product, the child, of their stock" (Loewenstein 33).*

151

Pandosto. Corresponding to the Sicilian episodes that frame the action of *The Winter's Tale*, these passages allow us to appreciate how Shakespeare molded his sources to his own ends.

In an obvious alteration of his source text, Shakespeare reverses locales, making Pandosto (the Leontes character) King of Bohemia and Egistus (the Polixenes character) King of Sicilia. Shakespeare does not invest these locales with sharply identifiable political, social, or geographical traits. Notoriously, he follows Greene in giving a seacoast to Bohemia, a landlocked country in what today is the Czech Republic. Shakespeare also omits contemporary references to religious or political affairs that might have elicited strong biases in an audience, such as Bohemia's reputation for "staunch and embattled Protestantism" (Orgel, *Winter's Tale* 38; Ellison 176, 179), or Sicily's status as a territory of Catholic Spain, a nation which many of Shakespeare's contemporaries regarded with deep apprehension and hostility. Arguably, then, Sicilia and Bohemia function in the play not as dramatic reflections of these seventeenth-century states but as emblematic sites through which to organize basic conceptual oppositions: winter and summer, tragic constraint and pastoral expansiveness, courtly treachery and country festivity. Upon closer examination, Bohemia appears less the antithesis than a distorting mirror of Sicilia, a place where the same kinds of political and sexual conflicts encountered earlier in the play can be directed toward more harmonious ends, thus facilitating the comic redemption of the last act.

Of the many changes Shakespeare made to *Pandosto*, his invention of new names is worth noting for the insight it provides into characters' moral and symbolic qualities. Pandosto becomes Leontes, a name that suggests the leonine qualities of wrath and royal pride; Garinter becomes Mamillius, a name that links the young boy, through the Latin root *mamillia* (breast), with his mother. Mamillia is also the name of the female protagonist in Greene's courtly romance *Mamillia* (1580–81). Shakespeare transforms Greene's pastoral names Fawnia and Dorastus into the Latinate Perdita ("the lost one") and Florizel, a name evocative of the flowering countryside in which their romance develops. Perhaps most importantly, Shakespeare invents the character of Paulina and makes her essential to the play's resolution. Paulina's role also contributes to the generic ambiguity of the play, for whereas her loyal care of Hermione softens the tragic implications of the queen's sixteen-year sequestration, it might also indicate the difficulty Hermione will have reestablishing an intimate bond with Leontes.

An examination of the structure of *Pandosto* illuminates the tragicomic mixture of genres in *The Winter's Tale*. Opening with the observation that jealousy can convert "joy" into "bloody revenge," Greene frames his story within the generic boundaries of tragedy. He explicitly blames Pandosto's fall on the conventional enemy of happy lovers in romance, the inconstant goddess Fortune, who "turned her wheel and darkened their bright sun of prosperity with the misty clouds of mishap and misery" (see p. 155). The image of Fortune spinning her wheel to topple great men from the heights of prosperity derives from the

FIGURE 7 *Map of the Mediterranean Sea, from George Sandys,* A Relation of a Journey Begun An. Dom. 1610 *(1621). In 1610, Sandys traveled to various Mediterranean locales, such as Sicily, typically found in the ancient Greek tales that influenced Shakespeare's dramatic romances. Shakespeare's first romance,* Pericles *(1607–08), is set in the eastern Mediterranean cities of Tyre, Antioch, Pentapolis, Tarsus, Ephesus, and Mytilene. Not visible on Sandys' map, Bohemia is far from this exotic Mediterranean world.*

medieval tradition of tragedy known as *de casibus virorum illustrium* (of the falls of famous men). How does the notion of a tragic fall play out in *Pandosto*? In what ways does *The Winter's Tale* soften the tragic features of *Pandosto*, and in what ways does it retain or emphasize them? At the end of the play, do Leontes and Hermione achieve a reconciliation that allows them to transcend the losses of the past, or do they still seem haunted by tragedy?

While a comparison of parallel episodes elicits many noteworthy differences, the larger question of literary genre can productively be addressed in terms of the differences between prose narration and drama as kinds of storytelling. How does Shakespeare use the particular resources of theater to depict psychological, social, and political conflict? For instance, we might ask how Shakespeare's depiction of the interaction between Hermione and Polixenes suggests a different perspective on the causes of Leontes' jealousy than the narration of the analogous episode in *Pandosto*. Without an omniscient narrator explaining characters' inner thoughts and attributing causality to forces such as fortune, how can readers of *The Winter's Tale* make sense of the chain of events that leads to the destruction and reunion of the royal family?

From *Pandosto. The Triumph of Time*

Among all the passions wherewith human minds are perplexed, there is none that so galleth[1] with restless despite[2] as the infectious sore of jealousy. For all other griefs are either to be appeased with sensible persuasions, to be cured with wholesome counsel, to be relieved in want, or by tract of time to be worn out — jealousy only excepted, which is sauced with suspicious doubts and pinching mistrust, that whoso seeks by friendly counsel to raze out this hellish passion, it forthwith suspecteth that he giveth this advice to cover his own guiltiness. Yea, whoso is pained with this restless torment doubteth all, distrusteth himself, is always frozen with fear and fired with suspicion, having that wherein consisteth all his joy to be the breeder of his misery. Yea, it is such a heavy enemy to that holy estate of matrimony, sowing between the married couples such deadly seeds of secret hatred, as love being once razed out by spiteful distrust, there oft ensueth bloody revenge, as this ensuing history manifestly proveth: wherein Pandosto (furiously incensed by causeless jealousy) procured the death of his most loving and loyal wife, and his own endless sorrow and misery.

In the country of Bohemia[3] there reigned a king called Pandosto, whose fortunate success in wars against his foes and bountiful courtesy towards his friends in peace made him to be greatly feared and loved of all men. This Pandosto had to wife a lady called Bellaria, by birth royal, learned by education, fair by nature, by virtues famous, so that it was hard to judge whether her beauty, fortune, or virtue won the greatest commendations. These two, linked together in perfect love, led their lives with such fortunate content that their subjects greatly rejoiced to see their quiet disposition. They had

---

[1] **galleth:** makes sore with chafing or rubbing.   [2] **despite:** contempt.   [3] **Bohemia:** a region of Central Europe; today the western part of the Czech Republic.

not been married long, but Fortune (willing to increase their happiness) lent them a son so adorned with the gifts of nature as the perfection of the child greatly augmented the love of the parents, and the joys of their commons.

In so much that the Bohemians, to show their inward joys by outward actions, made bonfires and triumphs throughout all the kingdom, appointing jousts[4] and tourneys[5] for the honor of their young prince, whither resorted not only his nobles, but also divers[6] kings and princes which were his neighbors, willing to show their friendship they owed to Pandosto, and to win fame and glory by their prowess and valor. Pandosto, whose mind was fraught with princely liberality, entertained the kings, princes, and noblemen with such submiss[7] courtesy and magnifical bounty that they all saw how willing he was to gratify their good wills, making a general feast for his subjects, which continued by the space of twenty days; all which time the jousts and tourneys were kept to the great content both of the lords and ladies there present. This solemn triumph being once ended, the assembly taking their leave of Pandosto and Bellaria, the young son (who was called Garinter) was nursed up in the house to the great joy and content of the parents.

Fortune, envious of such happy success, willing to show some sign of her inconstancy, turned her wheel and darkened their bright sun of prosperity with the misty clouds of mishap and misery. For it so happened that Egistus, King of Sicilia, who in his youth had been brought up with Pandosto, desirous to show that neither tract of time nor distance of place could diminish their former friendship, provided a navy of ships and sailed into Bohemia to visit his old friend and companion, who hearing of his arrival, went himself in person and his wife Bellaria, accompanied with a great train of lords and ladies, to meet Egistus. And espying him, alighted[8] from his horse, embraced him very lovingly, protesting that nothing in the world could have happened more acceptable to him than his coming, wishing his wife to welcome his old friend and acquaintance; who (to show how she liked him whom her husband loved) entertained him with such familiar courtesy, as Egistus perceived himself to be very well welcome. After they had thus saluted and embraced each other, they mounted again on horseback and rode toward the city, devising and recounting how being children they had passed their youth in friendly pastimes, where, by the means of the citizens, Egistus was received with triumphs and shows in such sort, that he marveled how on so small a warning they could make such preparation. Passing the streets thus with such rare sights, they rode on to the palace,

---

[4] **jousts:** contests in which two opponents on horseback fight with lances. [5] **tourneys:** tournaments. [6] **divers:** various. [7] **submiss:** submissive. [8] **alighted:** jumped down.

where Pandosto entertained Egistus and his Sicilians with such banqueting and sumptuous cheer, so royally, as they all had cause to commend his princely liberality. Yea, the very basest slave that was known to come from Sicilia was used[9] with such courtesy, that Egistus might easily perceive how both he and his were honored for his friend's sake.

Bellaria (who in her time was the flower of courtesy), willing to show how unfeignedly[10] she loved her husband by his friend's entertainment, used him likewise so familiarly that her countenance bewrayed[11] how her mind was affected towards him: oftentimes coming herself into his bed-chamber to see that nothing should be amiss to mislike[12] him. This honest familiarity increased daily more and more betwixt them, for Bellaria, noting in Egistus a princely and bountiful mind adorned with sundry and excellent qualities, and Egistus, finding in her a virtuous and courteous disposition, there grew such a secret uniting of their affections, that the one could not well be without the company of the other. In so much that when Pandosto was busied with such urgent affairs that he could not be present with his friend Egistus, Bellaria would walk with him into the garden, where they two in private and pleasant devices[13] would pass away the time to both their contents.

This custom still continuing betwixt them, a certain melancholy passion entering the mind of Pandosto drove him into sundry and doubtful thoughts. First, he called to mind the beauty of his wife Bellaria, the comeliness and bravery of his friend Egistus, thinking that love was above all laws, and therefore to be stayed[14] with no law; that it was hard to put fire and flax[15] together without burning; that their open pleasures might breed his secret displeasures. He considered with himself that Egistus was a man, and must needs love; that his wife was a woman, and therefore subject unto love; and that where fancy[16] forced, friendship was of no force. These and such like doubtful thoughts a long time smothering in his stomach began at last to kindle in his mind a secret mistrust, which, increased by suspicion, grew at last to be a flaming jealousy that so tormented him as he could take no rest. He then began to measure all their actions and to misconstrue of their too private familiarity, judging that it was not for honest affection but for disordinate[17] fancy, so that he began to watch them more narrowly, to see if he could get any true or certain proof to confirm his doubtful suspicion. While thus he noted their looks and gestures, and suspected their thoughts and meanings, they two silly[18] souls who doubted[19] nothing of this his

---

[9] used: treated. [10] unfeignedly: sincerely. [11] bewrayed: revealed. [12] mislike: displease. [13] devices: familiar conversations. [14] stayed: stopped. [15] flax: the wick of a candle. [16] fancy: love. [17] disordinate: immoderate. [18] silly: innocent. [19] doubted: feared, suspected.

treacherous intent frequented daily each other's company, which drove him into such a frantic passion that he began to bear a secret hate to Egistus and a louring[20] countenance to Bellaria, who, marveling at such unaccustomed frowns, began to cast beyond the moon and to enter into a thousand sundry thoughts which way she should offend[21] her husband. But finding in herself a clear conscience, ceased to muse until such time as she might find fit opportunity to demand the cause of his dumps. In the meantime Pandosto's mind was so far charged with jealousy that he did no longer doubt but was assured (as he thought) that his friend Egistus had entered a wrong point in his tables,[22] and so had played him false play.

Whereupon desirous to revenge so great an injury, he thought best to dissemble the grudge with a fair and friendly countenance, and so under the shape of a friend to show him the trick of a foe. Devising with himself a long time how he might best put away Egistus without suspicion of treacherous murder, he concluded at last to poison him, which opinion pleasing his humor,[23] he became resolute in his determination; and the better to bring the matter to pass he called unto him his cupbearer, with whom in secret he brake the matter, promising to him for the performance thereof to give him a thousand crowns of yearly revenues. His cupbearer, either being of a good conscience or willing for fashion's sake to deny such a bloody request, began with great reasons to persuade Pandosto from his determinate mischief, showing him what an offense murder was to the gods, how such unnatural actions did more displease the heavens than men, and that causeless cruelty did seldom or never escape without revenge. He laid before his face that Egistus was his friend, a king, and one that was come into his kingdom to confirm a league of perpetual amity[24] betwixt them; that he had and did show him a most friendly countenance; how Egistus was not only honored of his own people by obedience, but also loved of the Bohemians for his courtesy. And that if he now should without any just or manifest cause poison him, it would not only be a great dishonor to his majesty, and a means to sow perpetual enmity between the Sicilians and the Bohemians, but also his own subjects would repine at[25] such treacherous cruelty.

[Franion the cupbearer, unable to dissuade Pandosto from his determination to have Egistus murdered, reveals the plot to Egistus. A few days later, Franion and Egistus flee Bohemia. Taking their flight as evidence of guilt, Pandosto imprisons Bellaria and makes a public proclamation accusing her of adultery and

---

[20] louring: scowling. [21] she should offend: she had offended. [22] had entered . . . tables: had cheated (the metaphor comes from backgammon). [23] humor: disposition. [24] amity: friendship. [25] repine at: complain about.

conspiracy to murder him. In prison, Bellaria laments her harsh treatment and reveals that she is with child.]

The jailor, pitying these her heavy passions, thinking that if the king knew she were with child he would somewhat appease his fury and release her from prison, went in all haste and certified Pandosto what the effect of Bellaria's complaint was. Who no sooner heard the jailor say she was with child but, as one possessed with a frenzy, he rose up in a rage, swearing that she and the bastard brat she was withal should die if the gods themselves said no, thinking assuredly by computation of time that Egistus, and not he, was father to the child. This suspicious thought galled afresh this half-healed sore, in so much as he could take no rest until he might mitigate his choler[26] with a just revenge, which happened presently after.

For Bellaria was brought to bed of a fair and beautiful daughter, which no sooner Pandosto heard but he determined that both Bellaria and the young infant should be burnt with fire. His nobles, hearing of the king's cruel sentence, sought by persuasions to divert him from this bloody determination, laying before his face the innocency of the child and virtuous disposition of his wife, how she had continually loved and honored him so tenderly that without due proof he could not nor ought not to appeach[27] her of that crime. And if she had faulted, yet it were more honorable to pardon with mercy then to punish with extremity, and more kingly to be commended of pity than accused of rigor. And as for the child, if he should punish it for the mother's offense it were to strive against nature and justice; and that unnatural actions do more offend the gods than men; how causeless cruelty nor innocent blood never scapes[28] without revenge.

These and such like reasons could not appease his rage, but he rested resolute in this: that Bellaria being an adulteress, the child was a bastard, and he would not suffer that such an infamous brat should call him father. Yet at last (seeing his noblemen were importunate[29] upon him) he was content to spare the child's life, and yet to put it to a worser death. For he found out this device, that seeing (as he thought) it came by Fortune, so he would commit it to the charge of Fortune, and therefore he caused a little cock-boat[30] to be provided wherein he meant to put the babe and then send it to the mercy of the seas and the destinies.

[The infant is placed in a small boat and abandoned at sea. When Pandosto denies Bellaria's demand for a trial, Bellaria asks him to send some noblemen to

---

[26] **choler:** bile, or one of the "four humors" of early physiology supposed to cause irascibility of temper.   [27] **appeach:** accuse.   [28] **scapes:** escapes.   [29] **importunate:** persistent, pressing.   [30] **cock-boat:** very small, light boat.

the oracle of Apollo to ascertain the truth. In the presence of the lords and commons of Bohemia, Bellaria is called to the judgment hall to hear the contents of Apollo's scroll.]

. . . the king commanded that one of his dukes should read the contents of the scroll, which after the commons had heard they gave a great shout, rejoicing and clapping their hands that the queen was clear of that false accusation. But the king, whose conscience was a witness against him of his witless fury and false suspected jealousy, was so ashamed of his rash folly that he entreated his nobles to persuade Bellaria to forgive and forget these injuries, promising not only to show himself a loyal and loving husband, but also to reconcile himself to Egistus and Franion, revealing then before them all the cause of their secret flight and how treacherously he thought to have practiced his death, if the good mind of his cupbearer had not prevented his purpose. As thus he was relating the whole matter, there was word brought him that his young son Garinter was suddenly dead, which news so soon as Bellaria heard, surcharged before with extreme joy and now suppressed with heavy sorrow, her vital spirits[31] were so stopped that she fell down presently dead and could never be revived.

This sudden sight so appalled the king's senses that he sank from his seat in a sound,[32] so as he was fain[33] to be carried by his nobles to his palace, where he lay by the space of three days without speech. His commons were as men in despair, so diversely distressed. There was nothing but mourning and lamentation to be heard throughout all Bohemia: their young prince dead, their virtuous queen bereaved of her life, and their king and sovereign in great hazard. This tragical discourse of fortune so daunted them as they went like shadows, not men; yet somewhat to comfort their heavy hearts, they heard that Pandosto was come to himself and had recovered his speech, who as in a fury brayed out[34] these bitter speeches:

"O miserable Pandosto, what surer witness than conscience? What thoughts more sour than suspicion? What plague more bad than jealousy? Unnatural actions offend the gods more than men, and causeless cruelty never scapes without revenge. I have committed such a bloody fact[35] as repent I may but recall I cannot. Ah jealousy, a hell to the mind and a horror to the conscience, suppressing reason and inciting rage, a worse passion than frenzy, a greater plague than madness. Are the gods just? Then let them revenge such brutish cruelty: my innocent babe I have drowned in the seas; my loving wife I have slain with slanderous suspicion; my trusty friend I

---

[31] **vital spirits:** highly-refined fluids that issue from the heart and sustain the body. [32] **sound:** swoon. [33] **fain:** obliged. [34] **brayed out:** cried out in grief and pain. [35] **fact:** deed.

have sought to betray, and yet the gods are slack to plague such offenses. Ah unjust Apollo, Pandosto is the man that hath committed the fault; why should Garinter, silly child, abide the pain? Well, sith[36] the gods mean to prolong my days to increase my dolor,[37] I will offer my guilty blood a sacrifice to those sackless[38] souls whose lives are lost by my rigorous folly."

And with that he reached at a rapier to have murdered himself, but his peers being present stayed him from such a bloody act, persuading him to think that the commonwealth consisted on his safety and that those sheep could not but perish that wanted a shepherd; wishing that if he would not live for himself, yet he should have care of his subjects, and to put such fancies out of his mind, sith in sores past help, salves do not heal but hurt, and in things past cure, care is a corrosive. With these and such like persuasions the king was overcome and began somewhat to quiet his mind, so that as soon as he could go abroad, he caused his wife to be embalmed and wrapped in lead with her young son Garinter; erecting a rich and famous sepulcher wherein he entombed them both, making such solemn obsequies[39] at her funeral as all Bohemia might perceive he did greatly repent him of his forepassed folly, causing this epitaph to be engraven on her tomb in letters of gold:

> The Epitaph.
> Here lies entombed Bellaria fair,
> Falsely accused to be unchaste;
> Cleared by Apollo's sacred doom,[40]
> Yet slain by jealousy at last.
>
> What ever thou be that passest by,
> Curse him that caused this queen to die.

This epitaph being engraven, Pandosto would once a day repair to the tomb and there with watery plaints[41] bewail his misfortune, coveting no other companion but sorrow, nor no other harmony but repentance. But leaving him to his dolorous passions, at last let us come to show the tragical discourse of the young infant.

[After two days at sea, the boat carrying the infant arrives on the coast of Sicilia. A shepherd, Porrus, discovers the infant (along with the gold and jewels accompanying her) and brings her home to his wife; they name her Fawnia and raise her as their own. One day, when she is sixteen years old, Fawnia is serving as the mistress of the shepherds' feast when Dorastus spies her and falls in love.

---

[36] sith: since.   [37] dolor: pain.   [38] sackless: innocent.   [39] obsequies: rites or ceremonies.   [40] doom: sentence.   [41] watery plaints: tearful laments.

Understanding that Egistus would never approve of their marriage, Dorastus and Fawnia determine to flee Sicilia. When Porrus's neighbors inform him that Dorastus has been courting Fawnia, he determines to reveal to Egistus the mystery of her identity. Dorastus's servant Capnio intercepts Porrus on his way to the king and tricks him into coming aboard Dorastus's ship. A few days later, a tempest forces them to land in Bohemia. Disguising their identities, Dorastus (calling himself Meleagrus) and Fawnia present themselves to Pandosto, who commits Dorastus to prison and attempts to seduce Fawnia. Although Fawnia resists his advances, Pandosto persists.]

But again to Pandosto, who broiling at the heat of unlawful lust could take no rest but still felt his mind disquieted with his new love, so that his nobles and subjects marveled greatly at this sudden alteration, not being able to conjecture the cause of this his continued care. Pandosto, thinking every hour a year till he had talked once again with Fawnia, sent for her secretly into his chamber, whither though Fawnia unwillingly coming, Pandosto entertained her very courteously, using these familiar speeches, which Fawnia answered as shortly in this wise.

PANDOSTO: Fawnia, are you become less willful[42] and more wise, to prefer the love of a king before the liking of a poor knight? I think ere this you think it is better to be favored of a king than of a subject.

FAWNIA: Pandosto, the body is subject to victories, but the mind not to be subdued by conquest; honesty is to be preferred before honor; and a dram[43] of faith weigheth down a ton of gold. I have promised Meleagrus to love, and will perform no less.

PANDOSTO: Fawnia, I know thou art not so unwise in thy choice as to refuse the offer of a king, nor so ungrateful as to despise a good turn. Thou art now in that place where I may command, and yet thou seest I entreat. My power is such as I may compel by force, and yet I sue by prayers. Yield, Fawnia, thy love to him which burneth in thy love. Meleagrus shall be set free, thy countrymen discharged, and thou both loved and honored.

FAWNIA: I see, Pandosto, where lust ruleth it is a miserable thing to be a virgin; but know this, that I will always prefer fame before life, and rather choose death than dishonor.

Pandosto, seeing that there was in Fawnia a determinate courage to love Meleagrus and a resolution without fear to hate him, flung away from her in a rage, swearing if in short time she would not be won with reason, he would forget all courtesy and compel her to grant by rigor. But these threatening

---

[42] willful: obstinate.   [43] dram: a tiny amount, ⅛ of a fluid ounce.

words no whit[44] dismayed Fawnia, but that she still both despited[45] and despised Pandosto.

While thus these two lovers strove — the one to win love, the other to live in hate — Egistus heard certain news by merchants of Bohemia that his son Dorastus was imprisoned by Pandosto, which made him fear greatly that his son should be but hardly entreated.[46] Yet considering that Bellaria and he was cleared by the Oracle of Apollo from that crime wherewith Pandosto had unjustly charged them, he thought best to send with all speed to Pandosto, that he should set free his son Dorastus and put to death Fawnia and her father Porrus. Finding this by the advice of counsel the speediest remedy to release his son, he caused presently two of his ships to be rigged and thoroughly furnished with provision of men and victuals,[47] and sent divers of his nobles ambassadors into Bohemia, who, willing to obey their king and receive their young prince, made no delays for fear of danger but with as much speed as might be sailed towards Bohemia. The wind and seas favored them greatly, which made them hope of some good hap,[48] for within three days they were landed, which Pandosto no sooner heard of their arrival but he in person went to meet them, entreating them with such sumptuous and familiar courtesy that they might well perceive how sorry he was for the former injuries he had offered to their king and how willing (if it might be) to make amends.

As Pandosto made report to them how one Meleagrus, a knight of Trapolonia, was lately arrived with a lady called Fawnia in his land, coming very suspiciously, accompanied only with one servant and an old shepherd, the ambassadors perceived by the half what the whole tale meant, and began to conjecture that it was Dorastus, who for fear to be known had changed his name. But dissembling the matter, they shortly arrived at the court, where after they had been very solemnly and sumptuously feasted, the noblemen of Sicilia being gathered together, they made report of their embassage: where they certified Pandosto that Meleagrus was son and heir to the king Egistus and that his name was Dorastus; how contrary to the king's mind he had privily[49] conveyed away that Fawnia, intending to marry her, being but daughter to that poor shepherd Porrus; whereupon the king's request was that Capnio, Fawnia, and Porrus might be murdered and put to death, and that his son Dorastus might be sent home in safety.

Pandosto, having attentively and with great marvel heard their embassage, willing to reconcile himself to Egistus and to show him how greatly he esteemed his favor, although love and fancy forbad him to hurt Fawnia, yet

---

[44] no whit: not at all. [45] despited: showed contempt for. [46] hardly entreated: treated harshly.
[47] victuals: food and supplies. [48] hap: chance or fortune. [49] privily: secretly, privately.

in despite of love he determined to execute Egistus' will without mercy. And therefore he presently sent for Dorastus out of prison, who, marveling at this unlooked for courtesy, found at his coming to the king's presence that which he least doubted of, his father's ambassadors, who no sooner saw him but with great reverence they honored him, and Pandosto embracing Dorastus set him by him very lovingly in a chair of estate. Dorastus, ashamed that his folly was bewrayed, sat a long time as one in a muse till Pandosto told him the sum of his father's embassage, which he had no sooner heard but he was touched at the quick for the cruel sentence that was pronounced against Fawnia. But neither could his sorrow nor persuasions prevail, for Pandosto commanded that Fawnia, Porrus, and Capnio should be brought to his presence; who were no sooner come but Pandosto, having his former love turned to a disdainful hate, began to rage against Fawnia in these terms:

"Thou disdainful vassal, thou currish kite,[50] assigned by the destinies to base fortune and yet with an aspiring mind gazing after honor, how durst thou presume, being a beggar, to match with a prince? By thy alluring looks to enchant the son of a king to leave his own country to fulfill thy disordinate lusts? Oh, despiteful mind, a proud heart in a beggar is not unlike to a great fire in a small cottage, which warmeth not the house, but burneth it. Assure thyself that thou shalt die, and thou, old doting fool, whose folly hath been such as to suffer thy daughter to reach above thy fortune, look for no other meed[51] but the like punishment. But Capnio, thou which has betrayed the king and has consented to the unlawful lust of thy lord and master, I know not how justly I may plague thee: death is too easy a punishment for thy falsehood, and to live (if not in extreme misery) were not to show thee equity. I therefore award that thou shall have thine eyes put out, and continually while thou diest, grind in a mill like a brute beast."

The fear of death brought a sorrowful silence upon Fawnia and Capnio, but Porrus, seeing no hope of life, burst forth into these speeches:

"Pandosto, and ye noble ambassadors of Sicilia, seeing without cause I am condemned to die, I am yet glad I have opportunity to disburden my conscience before my death. I will tell you as much as I know, and yet no more than is true. Whereas I am accused that I have been a supporter of Fawnia's pride and she disdained as a vile beggar, so it is that I am neither father unto her nor she daughter unto me. For so it happened that I being a poor shepherd in Sicilia, living by keeping other men's flocks, one of my sheep straying down to the seaside, as I went to seek her, I saw a little boat

---

[50] **currish kite:** quarrelsome person who preys upon others.   [51] **meed:** recompense.

driven upon the shore wherein I found a babe of six days old, wrapped in a mantle of scarlet, having about the neck this chain. I, pitying the child and desirous of the treasure, carried it home to my wife, who with great care nursed it up and set it to keep sheep. Here is the chain and the jewels, and this Fawnia is the child whom I found in the boat. What she is or of what parentage I know not, but this I am assured: that she is none of mine."

Pandosto would scare suffer him to tell out his tale, but that he inquired the time of the year, the manner of the boat, and other circumstances, which when he found agreeing to his count, he suddenly leapt from his seat and kissed Fawnia, wetting her tender cheeks with his tears and crying, "My daughter Fawnia, ah, sweet Fawnia, I am thy father, Fawnia." This sudden passion of the king drove them all into a maze,[52] especially Fawnia and Dorastus. But when the king had breathed himself[53] a while in this new joy, he rehearsed before the ambassadors the whole matter how he had entreated his wife Bellaria for jealousy, and that this was the child whom he sent to float in the seas.

Fawnia was not more joyful that she had found such a father than Dorastus was glad he should get such a wife. The ambassadors rejoiced that their young prince had made such a choice, that those kingdoms which through enmity had long time been dissevered should now through perpetual amity be united and reconciled. The citizens and subjects of Bohemia (hearing that the king had found again his daughter which was supposed dead, joyful that there was an heir apparent to his kingdom), made bonfires and shows throughout the city. The courtiers and knights appointed jousts and tourneys to signify their willing minds in gratifying the king's hap.

Eighteen days being past in these princely sports, Pandosto, willing to recompense old Porrus, of a shepherd made him a knight. Which done, providing a sufficient navy to receive him and his retinue,[54] accompanied with Dorastus, Fawnia, and the Sicilian ambassadors, he sailed towards Sicilia, where he was most princely entertained by Egistus, who, hearing this comical event, rejoiced greatly at his son's good hap and without delay (to the perpetual joy of the two young lovers) celebrated the marriage. Which was no sooner ended but Pandosto (calling to mind how first he betrayed his friend Egistus, how his jealousy was the cause of Bellaria's death, that contrary to the law of nature he had lusted after his own daughter) moved with these desperate thoughts, he fell into a great melancholy fit, and, to close up the comedy with a tragical stratagem, he slew himself. Whose death being many days bewailed of Fawnia, Dorastus, and his dear friend Egistus,

---

[52] drove them all into a maze: amazed them all.   [53] breathed himself: expressed himself.
[54] retinue: a company of followers.

Dorastus taking his leave of his father went with his wife and the dead corpse into Bohemia, where after they were sumptuously entombed, Dorastus ended his days in contented quiet.

→ OVID

From Metamorphoses 1567

Translated by Arthur Golding

The great Roman poet Publius Ovidius Naso (43 B.C.E.–17 C.E.), or Ovid, tells the story of Proserpina in Book 5 of the *Metamorphoses*, an enormously influential poetic compendium of classical mythology. The *Metamorphoses* was a staple text in the grammar school curriculum of Shakespeare's England. In 1565, Arthur Golding published an English translation of the first four books of *Metamorphoses*; two years later, he published the first complete English translation of all fifteen books. Reprinted in 1575, 1584, 1587, 1593, 1603, and 1612, Golding's version exerted a wide influence on Elizabethan authors, including Spenser, Marlowe, and, of course, Shakespeare.

In the myth of Proserpina, Ovid describes how a young woman is violently taken from and ultimately restored to her mother. Although Perdita does not realize until the end of the play that she, too, has been forcefully separated from her mother, she evokes the traumatic scene of Proserpina's abduction: "O Proserpina, / For the flow'rs now that, frighted, thou let'st fall / From Dis's wagon!" (4.4.116–18). While gathering flowers one day in the Sicilian countryside, Proserpina, daughter of Ceres, goddess of the harvest, is abducted by Dis, king of the underworld. Ceres eventually elicits a promise from Jove, king of the gods and Proserpina's father, to allow Proserpina to return to earth for six months each year. The six months Proserpina spends in Sicily with her mother are summer; those she spends in the underworld with Dis are winter. Shakespeare's reversal of the locales of Bohemia and Sicilia in Greene's *Pandosto* suggests that he might have had the Proserpina myth in mind as a model for Perdita's banishment from and homecoming to Sicilia. In fact, when Florizel and Perdita arrive in Sicilia, Leontes declares that they are as welcome "[a]s is the spring to th'earth" (5.1.152).

Read as an allegory of seasonal change, the Proserpina myth points to the importance of time in the romance narrative of *The Winter's Tale*. Like the Proserpina myth, Shakespeare's play powerfully evokes a seasonal model of cyclical time: we can take comfort in knowing that each year moves from spring (the

Ovid, *The XV Books of P. Ovidius Naso, Entitled Metamorphoses, Translated out of Latin into English Meter by Arthur Golding, Gentleman, a Work Very Pleasant and Delectable* (London, 1567); STC 18956; sigs. J6r–K1v.

period of birth) through summer and autumn (periods of growth and maturity) to winter (the period of death) and then back to spring. In terms of plot, *The Winter's Tale* enacts this comic, essentially redemptive, cyclical view of time through the narrative of Perdita's exile from and eventual return to Sicilia.

With the act 5 revelation of Perdita's identity as the daughter of Leontes and Hermione, *The Winter's Tale* also alludes to an alternative understanding of time as a linear process instead of a cyclical rotation. The redemptive implications of time's power to "unfold" secrets and reveal errors are best embodied in the Latin proverb *veritas filia temporis* (truth is the daughter of time) (Figure 8).

In Medieval and Renaissance literature, the notion of truth as time's daughter is sometimes associated with the story of the slandered wife who is imprisoned or exiled until the passage of time vindicates her chastity (Iwasaki 253), as Hermione and Perdita are exonerated from the false charges of adultery and bastardy. This proverb was sometimes given explicitly political applications during the period. For instance, Peter Pett's poem "Time's Journey to Seek his Daughter Truth" (1599) associates the figure of Truth with Queen Elizabeth, who defeats Envy (her Catholic sister Mary Tudor) and expels Superstition (Roman Catholicism) from England. As a slandered queen whose chastity is ultimately vindicated, Hermione might have nostalgically recalled Queen Elizabeth for some members of Shakespeare's original audience. Even more than *Pandosto*, which is subtitled *The Triumph of Time* and includes the motto *veritas filia temporis* on its title page, *The Winter's Tale* points to the redemptive power of time by uniting Perdita, the lost daughter, with her mother, the true wife.

Nonetheless, the aging of Hermione, etched in her wrinkled visage, forces us to recognize the destructive aspects of the linear progression of time, as expressed in the Latin proverb *tempus edax rerum* (time devours all). Time was often personified as an old man holding an hourglass and scythe, representing transience and death. Thus even though Perdita and Hermione are eventually reunited, the play does not allow us to forget the origin of their separation in Perdita's banishment from Sicilia, which resonates with Proserpina's traumatic abduction from the Sicilian countryside (Figure 9). As the "mythological country of classical literature," Sicily boasted a lushly fertile landscape, but it was also a violent place inhabited by "monsters, giants, and cyclops where tyrannous kings and malignant gods imposed their will and pleasures on a subservient and terrified population" (Marrapodi 214–15). Is the tyrannous king Leontes a version of the malignant god Dis? Especially when we consider that the word "rape" derives from the Latin *rapere*, to take or seize by force, might we regard Dis's rape of Proserpina as an analogue for Leontes' violent treatment of his daughter? How might our memory of that primal scene of violence affect our response to Leontes' reunion with his daughter sixteen years later?

As a narrative of rape, the Proserpina myth also evokes the disturbing subtext of sexual danger to women that runs throughout *The Winter's Tale*. Justifying his use of a shepherd disguise to court Perdita, Florizel cites as precedent the Ovidian gods who, "[h]umbling their deities to love," took the shapes of animals

FIGURE 8 *Jost Amman (1539–1591),* Allegory of Truth and Time *(1562). In this allegorical woodcut, Time finally sets his daughter free from the dark cave in which the wicked powers of Envy and Slander have imprisoned her.*

to seduce mortal women (4.4.26). Perdita's costume as Flora, moreover, alludes to yet another mythological tale of rape, recounted in Ovid's poem *Fasti,* in which Zephyrus, the west wind, rapes the nymph Chloris. Zephyrus then compensates Chloris by giving her dominion over flowers as the goddess Flora. In its tragicomic structuring of the relationship between sexuality and time, we might consider how *The Winter's Tale* reflects possibly contradictory cultural notions about women's assertion of their erotic agency.

Ultimately, the subtext of the Proserpina myth alerts us to the generic instability of *The Winter's Tale,* its delicate and perhaps precarious balance between the comic and the tragic. Though the Proserpina myth concludes with a joyful recovery, Hermione and Perdita are subject to different rules of time than those at work in the *Metamorphoses.* The tragicomic journey from separation to reunion in *The Winter's Tale* powerfully raises the question of what Ceres, demanding justice for the loss of her daughter, calls "restitution." Does Hermione receive "restitution" for the violent abduction of her daughter or for the loss of the sixteen years during which they have been separated? Does she ask for such restitution or expect to receive it? Unlike Ceres and Proserpina, Hermione and Perdita are mortal women subject to the process of time. How much time do Hermione and Perdita have left to share with each other?

FIGURE 9 *Alessandro Varotari (Il Padovanino) (1588–1648)*, The Rape of Proserpina. *What perspective does this painting provide on Dis's desire for Proserpina?*

From *Metamorphoses*

Dame Ceres first to break the earth with plough the manner found,
She first made corn[1] and stover[2] soft to grow upon the ground,
She first made laws: for all these things we are to Ceres bound.
Of her must I as now entreat: would God I could resound
Her worthy laud:[3] she doubtless is a goddess worthy praise.   5
Because the giant Typhon[4] gave presumptuously assays
To conquer Heaven, the hougy[5] Isle of Trinacris[6] is laid
Upon his limbs, by weight whereof perforce he down is weighed.

---

[1] **corn**: grain.   [2] **stover**: fodder for cattle.   [3] **laud**: praise.   [4] **Typhon**: a giant who rose up against the Olympian gods and was buried under Sicily.   [5] **hougy**: huge.   [6] **Isle of Trinacris**: Island of Sicily.

He strives and struggles for to rise full many a time and oft.
But on his right hand toward Rome Pelorus stands aloft: 10
Pachynus stands upon his left: his legs with Lilybe[7]
Are pressed down: his monstrous head doth under Aetna[8] lie.
From whence he lying bolt upright with wrathful mouth doth spit
Out flames in fire. He wrestleth oft and walloweth[9] for to wit[10]
And if he can remove the weight of all that mighty land   15
Or tumble down the towns and hills that on his body stand.
By means whereof it comes to pass that oft the earth doth shake:
And even the King of Ghosts[11] himself for very fear doth quake,
Misdoubting[12] lest the earth should cleave so wide that light of day
Might by the same pierce down to Hell and there the ghosts affray.[13]   20
Forecasting this, the Prince of Fiends forsook his darksome hole,
And in a Chariot drawn with steeds as black as any coal
The whole foundation of the Isle of Sicil warily viewed.
When thoroughly he had searched each place that harm had none ensued,
As carelessly he ranged abroad, he chanced to be seen   25
Of Venus[14] sitting on her hill: who taking straight between
Her arms her winged Cupid, said: "My son, mine only stay,[15]
My hand, mine honor and my might, go take without delay
Those tools[16] which all wights[17] do subdue, and strike them in the heart
Of that same god that of the world enjoys the lowest part.   30
The gods of Heaven, and Jove[18] himself, the power of sea and land
And he that rules the powers on earth obey thy mighty hand:
And wherefore then should only Hell still unsubdued stand?
Thy mother's empire and thine own why dost thou not advance?
The third part of all the world now hangs in doubtful chance.   35
And yet in heaven too now, their deeds thou seest me fain[19] to bear.
We are despised: the strength of love with me away doth wear.
See'st not the Darter Diane[20] and dame Pallas[21] have already
Exempted them from my behests? and now of late so heady
Is Ceres' daughter too, that if we let her have her will,   40
She will continue all her life a maid unwedded still.

---

[7] **Pelorus, Pachynus, Lilybe:** promontories of northeastern, southeastern, and southern Sicily, respectively.   [8] **Aetna:** Mt. Etna, the volcano.   [9] **walloweth:** rolls about.   [10] **to wit:** to discover.   [11] **King of Ghosts:** Dis or Pluto, god of the underworld.   [12] **Misdoubting:** fearing.   [13] **affray:** frighten.   [14] **Venus:** goddess of love and mother of Cupid.   [15] **stay:** support.   [16] **tools:** weapons, i.e., Cupid's arrows, which induce love.   [17] **wights:** people, beings.   [18] **Jove:** king of the gods and of heaven.   [19] **fain:** willing under the circumstances.   [20] **Diane:** Diana, goddess of the hunt (hence "the Darter") and of virginity.   [21] **Pallas:** Minerva, goddess of arts and sciences, and a virgin.

For that is all her hope, and mark whereat she minds to shoot.
But thou (if ought this gracious turn[22] our honor may promote,
Or ought our empire beautify which jointly we do hold,)
This damsel to her uncle join."[23] No sooner had she told   45
These words, but Cupid opening straight his quiver chose therefro
One arrow (as his mother bade) among a thousand mo.
But such a one it was, as none more sharper was than it,
Nor none went straighter from the bow the aimed mark to hit.
He set his knee against his bow and bent it out of hand,   50
And made his forked arrow's steel in Pluto's heart to stand.
          Near Enna[24] walls there stands a lake: Pergusa is the name.
          Cayster[25] heareth not mo songs of swans than doth the same.
A wood environs every side the water round about,
And with his leaves as with a veil doth keep the sun heat out.   55
The boughs do yield a cool fresh air: the moistness of the ground
Yields sundry flowers: continual spring is all the year there found.
While in this garden Proserpine was taking her pastime,
In gathering either violets blew, or lilies white as lime,
And while of maidenly desire she filled her maund[26] and lap,   60
Endeavoring to outgather her companions there, by hap
Dis spied her; loved her; caught her up: and all at once well near.
So hasty, hot, and swift a thing is love as may appear.
The lady with a wailing voice affright did often call
Her mother and her waiting maids, but mother most of all.   65
And as she from the upper part her garment would have rent,
By chance she let her lap slip down, and out her flowers went.
And such a silly[27] simpleness her childish age yet bears,
That even the very loss of them did move her more to tears.
The Catcher drives his chariot forth, and calling every horse   70
By name, to make away apace he doth them still enforce:
And shakes about their necks and manes their rusty bridle reins
And through the deepest of the lake perforce he them constrains. . . .

[A water nymph, Cyane, attempts to stop Dis from taking Proserpine, but he
uses his mace to make a hole through which to enter into Hell. Ceres searches
the world for her daughter, and eventually returns to Sicily, where she discovers
Proserpine's girdle.]

---

[22] turn: favor.   [23] This damsel . . . join: join this damsel (Proserpine) to her uncle (Dis).
[24] Enna: city in the center of Sicily.   [25] Cayster: river in Lydia famous for swans.   [26] maund:
woven basket.   [27] silly: innocent.

For when she saw it, by and by as though she had but than
Been new advertised of her chance,[28] she piteously began   155
To rend her ruffled hair, and beat her hands against her breast.
As yet she knew not where she was. But yet with rage oppressed,
She curst all lands, and said they were unthankful everich one,[29]
Yea and unworthy of the fruits bestowed them upon.
But bitterly above the rest she banned[30] Sicily,   160
In which the mention of her loss she plainly did espy.
And therefore there with cruel hand the earing ploughs she brake,
And man and beast that tilled the ground to death in anger strake.
She marred the seed, and eke[31] forbade the fields to yield their fruit.
The plenteousness of that same isle of which there went such brute[32]   165
Through all the world, lay dead: the corn was killed in the blade:
Now too much drought, now too much wet did make it for to fade.
The stars and blasting winds did hurt, the hungry fowls did eat
The corn in ground: the tines[33] and briars did overgrow the wheat.
And other wicked weeds the corn continually annoy,   170
Which neither tilth[34] nor toil of man was able to destroy. . . .

[Arethusa, a water nymph from Pisa, asks Ceres to cease her revenge on the land.]

"A time will one day come when you to mirth may better frame,
And have your heart more free from care, which better serve me may
To tell you why I from my place so great a space do stray,
And unto Ortygie[35] am brought through so great seas and waves.   190
The ground doth give me passage free, and by the lowest caves
Of all the earth I make my way, and here I raise my head,
And look upon the stars again near out of knowledge fled.
Now while I underneath the earth the Lake of Styx[36] did pass,
I saw your daughter Proserpine with these same eyes. She was   195
Not merry, neither rid of fear as seemed by her cheer.[37]
But yet a queen, but yet of great god Dis the stately fere:[38]
But yet of that same droopy[39] realm the chief and sovereign peer."
        Her mother stood as stark as stone, when she these news did hear,
        And long she was like one that in another world had been.   200

---

[28] chance: fate.   [29] everich one: every one.   [30] banned: cursed.   [31] eke: also.   [32] brute: fame.
[33] tines: strangling weeds.   [34] tilth: cultivation.   [35] Ortygie: the island of Delos.   [36] Styx: a
river in the underworld.   [37] cheer: deportment.   [38] fere: partner.   [39] droopy: dejected.

But when her great amazedness by greatness of her teen[40]
Was put aside, she gets her to her chariot by and by
And up to heaven in all post haste immediately doth sty.[41]
And there beslobbered all her face: her hair about her ears,
To royal Jove in way of plaint[42] this spiteful tale she bears: 205
"As well for thy blood as for mine a suitor unto thee
I hither come. If no regard may of the mother be
Yet let the child her father move,[43] and have not lesser care
Of her (I pray) because that I her in my body bare.[44]
Behold our daughter whom I sought so long is found at last: 210
If finding you it term,[45] when of recovery means is past.
Or if you finding do call to have a knowledge where
She is become. Her ravishment we might consent to bear,
So restitution might be made. And though there were to me
No interest in her at all, yet forasmuch as she   215
Is yours, it is unmeet she be bestowed upon a thief."
Jove answered thus: "My daughter is a jewell dear and lief.[46]
A collop[47] of mine own flesh cut as well as out of thine.
But if we in our hearts can find things rightly to define,
This is not spite but love. And yet madam in faith I see   220
No cause of such a son-in-law ashamed for to be,
So you contented were therewith. For put the case that he
Were destitute of all things else, how great a matter ist
Jove's brother for to be? But sure in him is nothing missed.[48]
Nor he inferior is to me save only that by lot[49]   225
The Heavens to me, the Hells to him the destinies did allot.
But if you have so sore desire your daughter to divorce,
Though she again to Heaven repair I do not greatly force.[50]
But yet conditionally that she have tasted there no food:
For so the destinies have decreed." He ceased. And Ceres stood   230
Full bent to fetch her daughter out: but destinies her withstood,
Because the maid had broke her fast[51] . . .

[Since Proserpine has eaten some pomegranate seeds while in the underworld,
she cannot return unconditionally to earth. Nonetheless, Jove reaches a compro-
mise between Ceres and Dis.]

---

[40] teen: anger, grief.   [41] sty: ascend.   [42] plaint: complaint.   [43] move: influence.   [44] bare: bore.
[45] If finding you it term: if you can call it "finding" her when I am unable to bring her back (i.e.,
she is still lost to me).   [46] lief: beloved.   [47] collop: piece of flesh.   [48] missed: lacking.   [49] lot:
fate.   [50] force: care.   [51] broke her fast: while in Hell, Proserpine had eaten.

But mean[52] between his brother and his heavy[53] sister goth
God Jove, and parteth equally the year between them both.
And now the goddess Proserpine indifferently doth reign   270
Above and underneath the earth, and so doth she remain
One half year with her mother and the resdue[54] with her fere.
Immediately she altered is as well in outward cheer
As inward mind. For where her look might late before appear
Sad even to Dis, her countenance now is full of mirth and grace   275
Even like as Phoebus[55] having put the watery clouds to chase,
Doth show himself a conqueror with bright and shining face.

---

[52] **mean:** intermediary.   [53] **heavy:** sad.   [54] **resdue:** residue, rest.   [55] **Phoebus:** Apollo, god of
the sun.

CHAPTER 2

Gender, Sexuality, and the Family

———————————————— ⭥ ————————————————

That the family at the center of *The Winter's Tale* is also a royal family brings into sharp relief the commonplace Renaissance analogy between the family and the state. In theory, just as the king ruled over obedient subjects in an orderly commonwealth, so the father ruled over an obedient family in an orderly household. To promote this domestic ideal, conduct books by Puritan ministers such as William Gouge (*Of Domestical Duties*), William Perkins (*Christian Economy*), and John Dod and Robert Cleaver (*A Godly Form of Household Government*) carefully outlined the roles and responsibilities of each member of the household. As might be expected, these guides promoted orthodox social and religious doctrines that enjoined children to honor their parents, servants to obey their masters, and wives to submit to their husbands. The subordinate status of wives was justified by the *a priori* "natural" difference of gender: authors of conduct books "consistently based their case for household patriarchy upon women's inferiority, as evidenced by the Fall, and upon God's direction" (Fletcher 76). As such, the conduct books took their place in a long tradition of philosophical, medical, and satiric literature that advanced the notion of women as "weaker vessels" unable to control their emotions and sexual appetites.

The widespread belief in the inherent superiority of men sat uncomfortably, however, with the emergent Protestant ideal of the affectionate "companionate marriage," which assumed a measure of equality and compatibility between husband and wife. Furthermore, while ultimately accountable to their husbands, wives typically managed the daily affairs of the household, including the care of infants and young children. Given the evidence of women's competence in running domestic affairs, conduct book authors at the very least had to acknowledge their rationality and intelligence. John Dod and Robert Cleaver thus affirm, albeit somewhat condescendingly, that women "are as men are reasonable creatures," who possess "flexible wits both to good and evil the which with use, discretion and good counsel may be altered and turned" (quoted in Fletcher 77). The women of *The Winter's Tale* do indeed have "flexible wits": tragedy occurs because a powerful man refuses to allow his inflexible judgment to be "turned" by "discretion and good counsel." Leontes' radical failure to conform to the model of the virtuous husband described in the conduct books represents one of the many ways that Shakespeare's play engages contemporary discourses about the importance (and difficulty) of establishing marital harmony.

By offering multiple, sometimes competing, perspectives on the sources and consequences of domestic disorder, the documents in this chapter shed light on the unraveling of Leontes' household. In the first part of the chapter, documents drawn from theological, political, and medical contexts attest to the gendered divisions that structured the experiences of pregnancy, childbirth, and early childhood for English men and women. These documents reveal the great responsibility given to women for the delivery and care of children. At the same time, they reveal patriarchal anxieties about the unusual degree of autonomy women exercised in these matters, and they articulate fears about women's capacity to neglect or abuse their power over the lives of infants. Documents in the second section of the chapter address various "conjugal faultlines" that shake the foundations of Leontes' marriage: the Renaissance valuation of male friendship over companionship with women; the misogynist assumption that wives will readily cuckold their husbands; and the gender bias of the legal institutions responsible for correcting domestic disorder. A final section on the death of children presents two texts concerning Prince Henry, son and heir to King James and Queen Anne, who died in 1612 at the age of eighteen. *The Winter's Tale* was first mounted at the Globe Theater in 1610 or 1611, before Henry's death, but when it was revived at court in 1613, the depiction of Mamillius's death must have evoked painful memories of the royal family's recent tragedy. Leontes' taciturn response to the death of his son and loss of his daughter is all the more striking in the context of Ben Jonson's tender poems grieving the death of a son and daughter of approximately the same ages as Mamillius and Perdita.

Gender Division in Childbirth and Childhood

The childbed privilege denied, which longs
To women of all fashion;   (3.2.100–01)

In Shakespeare's age no less than today, having a child could bring husbands and wives together in feelings of anxiety, joy, or grief. The experience of childbirth in early modern England, however, also sharply emphasized the gender differences commonly presumed to divide men from women. For a seventeenth-century audience, as well as for Leontes, the sight of Hermione's pregnant body at the beginning of *The Winter's Tale* could have graphically evoked commonplace beliefs regarding the "natural" weakness and instability of all women. Women's bodies were thought to produce more fluids than men's bodies, and as a result women were often described as "leaky vessels" unable to control or contain the flow of blood, urine, tears, and milk (Paster, *Body* 25). This perceived anatomical deficiency was used to justify beliefs about women's lack of emotional, moral, and sexual self-control.

Likewise, medical texts and guidebooks about childbirth, almost all of which were written by men, hardly conveyed the neutral facts of scientific knowledge. Instead, they displayed a "discomfort with the fluids and processes of female physiology and . . . with the technical events of birth" (Paster, *Body* 173). Regarding the womb "as a kind of quasi-independent force in the female body," these medical writers typically conceptualized pregnancy — even normal, successful pregnancy — "as a disease state" (Paster, *Body* 175, 182). In an era before modern gynecology and obstetrics, to be sure, labor could be a perilous experience for both mother and child. As David Cressy remarks, childbirth's "pain and peril — Eve's legacy and nature's course — was a rite of violence through which all mothers passed and which a minority would not survive" (*Birth* 28).

As the excerpts from Jacques Guillemeau's treatises on childbirth and nursing amply reveal, the work of childbearing and early childrearing in early modern Europe was squarely in women's hands, and the ceremonies surrounding "the protocols of pregnancy, midwifery, and female fellowship around the childbed" were "deeply embedded" in the culture (Cressy, *Birth* 15). Although *The Winter's Tale* provides only brief glimpses of these ceremonies and practices, it is important to understand the implications of what Leontes denies Hermione by causing her to give birth in prison and forcing her to stand trial during the "childbed privilege" of her lying-in month (3.2.100). The community of women that typically formed around the pregnant woman provided comfort, advice, care, and camaraderie. This community usually comprised a midwife, who delivered the baby; a nurse, who cared for the wife during her lying-in period; and neighbors and relatives who assisted at the birth and later visited the mother during her recovery (Figure 10). To recover from the physical and emotional stress of delivery, women were advised to be merry, and their female relatives, friends, and neighbors — collectively called "gossips" — would visit the lying-in chamber to eat, drink, and talk. At the end of the mother's lying-in month, her gossips would accompany her to a churching ceremony (for a description of Queen's Anne's churching ceremony, see the document on p. 192).

The woman-centered activities surrounding childbirth could sometimes incite male anxiety and marital tension. David Cressy explains that "[f]rom the viewpoint of ministers and physicians, and perhaps too for many husbands, the gathering of women at childbirth was exclusive, mysterious, and

FIGURE 10 *Jacob Rüff,* De Conceptu et Generatione Hominis *(1580). This image depicts a lying-in chamber following a birth. What activities appear to be taking place? How does this representation of women's participation in the childbirth process compare to what we see in* The Winter's Tale*?*

potentially unruly" (*Birth* 55). Arguably, the person with the most power in the household during childbirth was the midwife, who "took charge as soon as she arrived, and expected to remain in charge thereafter" (Wilson 72). Aside from being the only person authorized to deliver the baby, the midwife was required to determine the true identity of the child's father (if necessary, by persistently questioning the mother during her most intense labor pains); to swaddle the infant; and to present it, along with the true report of its paternity, to the waiting father. A midwife might choose to hide the truth about an illegitimate birth or, conversely, to dispute a father's suspicions of illegitimate paternity. Caroline Bicks suggests that Leontes angrily calls Paulina a "midwife" (2.3.160) precisely because her report of the infant's paternity contradicts his own (52). Leontes also attacks Paulina's credibility by accusing her of possessing the illicit knowledge of socially transgressive women: the "mankind witch" and "intelligencing bawd" (2.3.68–69).

Leontes' complaints against Paulina recall those found in contemporary satires of the unruly antics of gossips. The husband was customarily excluded from gossips' visits to the wife during her lying-in month. Satirical accounts of lying-in celebrations such as that in *The Bachelor's Banquet* (1603) ridicule disorderly women who spread rumors, drink excessively, and stir up domestic strife by convincing the wife of her husband's inadequacies. From Leontes' perspective, Paulina might resemble a dissention-spreading gossip when she harasses him with "audacious" reproaches and berates him for "cruel usage" of his wife (2.3.42, 117). Later in the play, Autolycus's ballad about the usurer's wife who gives birth to twenty money-bags provides another satirical portrait of untrustworthy childbed attendants. Autolycus ironically bases the credibility of this absurd story on the testimony of the midwife Mistress "Taleporter" — an untrustworthy carrier of tales — "and five or six honest wives that were present" (4.4.253–54).

While satires comically exaggerated the foibles of midwives and the gossips who gathered around the childbed, other kinds of texts emphasized the dangers that women ostensibly posed to newborns and infants. In *The Winter's Tale*, the depiction of a father who endangers the lives of his children goes against the grain of the predominant cultural belief that mothers posed the greatest threat to the safety of young children. Valerie Fildes' recent study of child abandonment patterns in sixteenth- and seventeenth-century London reveals that mothers might have had pragmatic, even charitable, reasons for relinquishing a child, such as "widowhood during or soon after pregnancy and desertion by the husband, both resulting in the mother's poverty and inability to support the child" (153). Nonetheless, sensationalist news pamphlets of the period told stories of women who, acting from a perverse sense of maternal responsibility, killed their children "in order to save them from religious falsehood, from starvation, and occasionally, from the mother's own desperate psychological state" (Staub 335).

While we might feel sympathy for the plight of such women, the official response was unforgiving. In 1624, Parliament passed a statute against infanticide that ignored "the many ways of and motives for eliminating children," criminalizing only unmarried women's murder of their illegitimate newborns (Dolan, *Dangerous* 123). The statute reads as follows:

> Whereas many lewd women that have been delivered of bastard children, to avoid their shame and to escape punishment do secretly bury or conceal the death of their children, and after, if the child be found dead, the said women do allege that the said child was born dead, whereas it falleth out sometimes (although hardly it is to be proved) that the said child or children were murdered by the said women, their lewd mothers, or by their assent or procurement.
>
> For the preventing therefore of this great mischief, be it enacted by the authority of this present parliament, that if any woman after one month next ensuing the end of this session of parliament be delivered of any issue of her body, male or female, which being born alive should by the laws of this realm be a bastard, and that she endeavor privately, either by drowning, or secret burying thereof, or any other way either by her self or the procuring of others so to conceal the death thereof, as that it may not come to light, whether it were born alive or not, but be concealed; in every such case, the said mother so offending shall suffer death, as in case of murder, except such mother can make proof by one witness at the least that the child (whose death was by her so intended to be concealed) was born dead. (*A Collection of Sundry Statutes*, p. 1409)

When Shakespeare's Old Shepherd discovers Perdita, he likewise assumes that an unmarried serving woman has abandoned her bastard infant in order to conceal her sexual transgression. He is mistaken, and Perdita does not in any case die, but under the 1624 law a woman who concealed even the *accidental* death of a bastard infant could be executed for murder because the law presumed that, absent a witness to the contrary, the very concealment of the burial implied guilt of murder.

The Winter's Tale does not overtly endorse the view, articulated in the 1624 statute (and by the puritan minister William Gouge in the first text on p. 182), that "lewd women" are the primary perpetrators of violence against children. Instead, the play emphasizes a father's ruthless violence in tearing a "bastard" infant from its mother and haling it out to murder (3.2.80). Nevertheless, Frances Dolan argues that *The Winter's Tale* "prepares for forgiveness by sparing Leontes the direct, criminalized agency associated with murderous mothers" in early modern culture and by "helping us to repress our knowledge of his crucial role in 'losing' his children" (*Dangerous* 167). In giving us the latitude either to indict or to exonerate Leontes for the "loss" of his children, does the play fail to engage the larger question of the causes and consequences of the predominant cultural belief in maternal violence?

The play's refusal to indict Leontes directly for the death of Mamillius and the loss of Perdita might have something to do with his elevated status as king. As the following documents relating to the birth of Princess Mary suggest, the symbolic power of a royal family depended on maintaining an orderly public image and guaranteeing a pure lineage. Although these unique political circumstances prevent us from taking Leontes' family as typical of Renaissance families, dominant cultural notions concerning gender difference and sexual reproduction informed the experiences of pregnancy, childbirth, and caregiving for women of all social levels, from commoner to queen. As Naomi Miller observes, "In a variety of early modern texts and images associated with female caregivers, mothers and others offer the potential for both nurture and rejection, sustenance and destruction" (6). By examining such varied and sometimes contradictory notions of maternity in the documents that follow, we can better appreciate how *The Winter's Tale* represents the experience of childbirth in terms of familial continuity as well as familial dissolution.

→ WILLIAM GOUGE

From Of Domestical Duties   *1622*

As an orthodox Calvinist (or "puritan") minister in London, William Gouge earned a reputation for his impressive sermons and published several theological tracts, beginning in 1617 with *The Whole-Armor of God* and *A Short Catechism*. *Of Domestical Duties* (1622), his most celebrated work, uses scriptural teachings to elaborate (in over four hundred pages) the duties that various members of the household owe to each other. A husband for twenty-one years and the father of thirteen children, Gouge notably promotes the ideal of "companionate marriage" within the godly household. Toward this goal, he denounces not only extreme forms of domestic conflict, such as wife-beating, but also "the rigor and austerity of many husbands, who stand upon the uttermost step of their authority, and yield no more to a wife than to any other inferior" (Treatise 4, sec. 20). In

William Gouge, *Of Domestical Duties* (London, 1622); STC 21119; sigs. Cc8r–Dd1v, Kk5r–Kk6r.

the excerpts below, Gouge advises husbands on caring for their pregnant wives and advises parents on providing for the healthy delivery of their children.

Gouge acknowledges the danger and pain women experience in childbirth; at the same time, however, he indicates that pregnant women should expect to enjoy a greater degree of power, attention, and comfort in the household. In more prosperous households, childbirth could be a "topsy-turvy time when the wife lay in at leisure (provided she was not seriously ill), while the husband temporarily took responsibility for some of the woman's domestic duties" (Cressy, *Birth* 35). Consequently, husbands sometimes came to resent the needs and demands of their wives during pregnancy and after childbirth. Since Gouge writes for a broad audience comprised of the middle and lower ranks of society, his advice on economic matters does not always seem relevant to the situation of a royal family. Under normal circumstances, a king would hardly deny his pregnant wife access to a trained nurse or a room with a fireplace, as Gouge complains of miserly husbands. As the accounts of the birth of Princess Mary presented later in this chapter reveal, King James spent lavishly on preparations for his wife's delivery. Presumably, Hermione would have enjoyed the same comforts had Leontes not imprisoned her for adultery and treason.

Nonetheless, Gouge's account of husbands who neglect their pregnant wives might offer insights into the religious, psychological, and ethical ramifications of Leontes' severe treatment of Hermione. At her trial, Hermione refers to Leontes' "immodest hatred" in denying her the childbed privilege (3.2.99), whereas he describes her as "one / Of us too much beloved" (3.2.3–4). How might Gouge be helpful in evaluating these contradictory assessments of Leontes' affections? Does Leontes seem aware that his treatment of Hermione might endanger her health? Is there any indication that Hermione's health has, in fact, been jeopardized by Leontes' severity?

Although Gouge chastises husbands who jeopardize the physical or emotional well-being of their pregnant wives, he also blames women for miscarriages, which were extremely common in the period: "one in every two conceptions ended in miscarriage" (Cressy, *Birth* 47). Moreover, he believes that some mothers readily abandon or murder their newborns. On what grounds does Gouge assert this maternal propensity for negligence and violence? Are Gouge's assumptions about the kinds of maternal "offenses" women are likely to commit comparable to Leontes' assumptions about the kinds of sexual offenses women are likely to commit? We should also consider the role played by genre and rhetorical style in shaping our response to the charged issue of domestic violence. How might the language and structure of Gouge's treatise affect our assessment of its argument? Do the generic traits of romance in *The Winter's Tale* serve to foreground certain aspects of domestic violence and to occlude others?

From *Of Domestical Duties*

FOURTH TREATISE

Of a husband's provident care for his wife about her child-bearing.

Most proper to this place is that provident[1] care which husbands ought to have of their wives both before and in the time of their travail and child-bed, and that in two things especially:

1. In procuring for their wives to the uttermost of their power and ability, such things as may save their longing, in case they do long (as in all ages women in the time of breeding and bearing child, have been subject thereunto). For it is well known, that it is very dangerous both for mother and child to want her longing: the death sometimes of the one, sometimes of the other, sometimes of both hath followed thereupon.

2. In providing such things as are needful for their travail and lying in child-bed.

This time is especially to be provided for, in many respects:

1. Because it is a time of weakness, wherein the woman cannot well provide for herself.

2. Because her weakness is joined with much pain. The pain of a woman in travail is the greatest pain that ordinarily is endured by any for the time. None know it so well as they that feel it, and many husbands, because they are not subject thereto, think but lightly of it. But if we duly weigh that the Holy Ghost[2] when he would set forth the extremity of any pains and pangs, resembleth them to the pains of a woman in travail, we may well gather, that of all they are the greatest; which is further manifested by the screeks and outcries which not only weak and faint-hearted women utter in the time of their travail, but also are forced from the strongest and stoutest women that be, and that though beforehand they resolve to the contrary. Neither may we wonder thereat, for their body is as it were set on a rack (if at least the travail be sharp) and all their parts so stretched, as a wonder it is they should ever recover their health and strength again; or that they should hold out the brunt[3] and not die with their travail, as Rachel and the wife of Phinehas,[4]

---

[1] **provident:** foreseeing. [2] **Holy Ghost:** in the margin, Gouge provides the following Biblical citations: Psalms 48:6; Isaiah 13:8, 21:3; Jeremiah 4:31, 30:6; Micah 4:9. [3] **brunt:** assault.
[4] **Rachel and the wife of Phinehas:** the wife of Jacob, Rachel dies giving birth to Benjamin (Genesis 35:16–19); upon learning that the Philistines have taken the ark of God, Phinehas's wife goes into labor and dies (1 Samuel 4:19–22).

and many in all ages have done. Surely among ordinary deliverances I know none so near a miracle, none wherein the Almighty doth so evidently manifest his great power and good providence, as in the safe delivery of women. Besides the great pang of travail, women are also after their delivery subject to many after-throws[5] which are very painful. From all these pains and great weakness which befalleth women in child-bed, especially if they nurse their children, men by reason of their sex are freed. Now, then, to apply this point, seeing women are brought to such pains and weakness in bringing forth those children which are the man's as well as hers, and he freed from all; is it not very just and meet[6] that he should provide all things needful for her welfare, ease, and recovery of strength?

3. Because the want of things needful is at that time very dangerous: dangerous to the health and life of the woman and child also.

Of neglecting wives in their weakness.

Contrary to a husband's provident care in general are those vices which were taxed in the treatise of common duties, *as grudging at the charges bestowed on a wife: Covetousness, Prodigality*, and *Idleness*.

But contrary in particular to a husband's care for his wife in child-bed, is the inhumane and more than barbarous unkindness of many husbands, who no whit[7] consider the weakness of their wives in this case, to help, ease, and comfort them, but rather make their burden much more heavy. For,

1. Some through covetousness refuse before hand to afford means to their wife to provide such things as are needful for herself and child: and when the time cometh, if their wife be desirous of a midwife that requireth somewhat more charges than she that is next,[8] she shall have none if she will not have the next. And as for a nurse to tend her, they think their maid will serve the turn well enough: they need not be at the charges to bring a nurse into the house. In regard of convenient lodging some will not stick[9] to say, Cannot my wife be brought to bed in a room without a chimney as well as the Virgin Mary? Why should my wife need more things than she did? Yea, further, there be many that when the time that their wife should be delivered approacheth near, carry her from all her friends into a place where she is not known, lest her friends should by importunity[10] draw him to expend and lay out more upon his wife than he is willing. In the time while their wife is weak in child-bed, many are loath to allow them any other diet than

---

[5] after-throws: violent spasms after delivery. [6] meet: proper. [7] no whit: not in the least. [8] next: closest or most convenient. [9] will not stick: will not hesitate. [10] importunity: persistent urging.

is for themselves and children provided in the house, not considering that her stomach cannot be like theirs.

Many other such bitter fruits of unkind husbands arising from covetousness might be reckoned up, whereby husbands plainly show that they love their wealth better than their wives: they had rather lose *them* than part with *that*.

2. Others through jealous suspicion forbear not even in the time of their wives' pain and weakness, to upbraid them with lightness,[11] and to say that the child is none of theirs. To lay this to a wife's charge unjustly is at any time a most shameful and odious reproach, but in the time of childbirth, whether just or unjust, a thing too too spiteful and revengeful. Some wives are so far overcome thereby (especially in the time of their weakness) as they are not able to bear it, but even faint and die under the reproach. Others more stout vow never to know[12] their husbands again. Many like mischiefs follow on such unkindness.

Sixth Treatise

Of parents' providence for their children.

The head whereunto all the particular duties which parents owe to their children may be referred as *a provident care for their children's good*. This extendeth itself to all times, and to all things.

To all times, as to the infancy, youth, and man-age of their children: and that not only while parents live, but after their departure.

To all things, namely, tending both to the temporal good of their children, and also to their spiritual good.

Children are of the very substance of their parents, and therefore ought parents so far to seek their children's good as their own.

The patterns of holy parents recorded and commended in scripture do lively set forth this provident care.

But this general we will exemplify in the particulars: and in order declare how parents must provide both for the temporal and also for the spiritual good of their children in every degree of their age.

They who at any time in any thing are negligent and careless of their children's good offend in the contrary to this general duty. The heinousness of which offences will appear in the particulars.

---

[11] **lightness:** sexual promiscuity.   [12] **know:** have intercourse with.

Of a mother's care over her child while it is in her womb.

The first age of a child is the infancy thereof. I will therefore show how therein parents must procure the temporal good of their children, and then their spiritual good.

The first part of a child's infancy is while it remaineth in the mother's womb. Here therefore the duty lieth principally upon the mother, who, so soon as she perceiveth a child to be conceived in her womb, ought to have an especial care thereof, that (so much as in her lieth) the child may be safely brought forth. (The heathen philosopher, by light of nature, observed this to be a duty; and prescribed it to mothers.[13]) A mother then must have a tender care over her self when she is with child, for the child being lodged in her and receiving nourishment from her (as plants from the earth), her well-being tendeth much to the good and safety of the child; but the hurt that cometh to her maketh the child the worse, if it be not a means to destroy it. Why was the charge[14] of *abstaining from wine, strong drink, and unclean things* given to Manoah's wife, but because of the child which she conceived?

In this case there is a double bond to make mothers careful of themselves: 1. Their own, 2. Their child's good.

Husbands also in this case must be very tender over their wives and helpful to them in all things needful, both in regard of that duty which they owe to their wives, and also of that they owe to their children. Why was Manoah so desirous to hear himself the forenamed direction which the angel gave to his wife? And why did the angel again repeat it to him, but to show it belonged to him to see her observe it?

They who through violence of passion, whether of grief or anger; or though violent motion of the body, as by dancing, striving, running, galloping on horseback, or the like; or through distemper of the body, by eating things hurtful, by eating too much, by too much abstinence, by too much bashfulness in concealing their desires and longings (as we speak) cause any abortion or miscarriage, fall into the offense contrary to the forenamed duty.

---

[13] **The heathen philosopher . . . mothers:** in the margin, Gouge cites from Aristotle's *Politics,* Book 7: "*Gravidae corpora curare debent. Mens item earum quietem desiderat. Quae enim procreantur a matre in cuius alvo continentur, alimentum capiunt, ut a terra ea quae gignantur ex ea.*" (Pregnant women must take great care of their bodies. Also, they should keep their minds quiet. For the child takes its nature from the womb of the mother in which it has been contained, just as plants take their nature from the earth out of which they grow.)   [14] **the charge:** in Judges 13:2–5, an angel appears to Manoah's wife, who is barren, and charges her to refrain from strong drink and unclean food, for she will conceive a son (Samson, who will become a hero of the Israelites).

If women were persuaded that in conscience they are bound to the fore-named duty, they would, I think, be more careful of themselves. For if through their default they themselves or their child miscarry, they make themselves guilty of that miscarriage; if both miscarry, they make themselves guilty of the blood of both, at least in the court of conscience before God.

But they who purposely take things to make away their children in their womb are in far higher degree guilty of blood: yea, even of willful murder. For that which hath received a soul formed in it by God, if it be unjustly cast away, shall be revenged.

So far forth as husbands are careless of their wives being with child, denying them things needful, they are accessory to the hurt which the woman or child taketh, guilty of the sin, and liable to the judgment.

*Of providing things needful for the child, so soon as it is born:
and of cruelty contrary thereunto.*

The next degree of a child's infancy is while it is in the swaddling bands and remaineth a sucking child. In this also the care especially lieth upon the mother, yet so as the father must afford what help he can.

The first duty here required is that sufficient provision of all things needful for a child in that weakness be beforehand provided. What the particulars be, women better know than I can express. For me, it is sufficient to lay down the duty in general, which is commended unto us in that worthy pattern of the Virgin Mary, who though she were very poor, and forced to travel far, and brought to bed in a strange place, where she was so little respected as she was not afforded a place meet for a woman in her case but was fain[15] to content herself with a stable in a common inn, yet she provided for her child. For it is said, *She wrapped him in swaddling clothes* (Luke 2:7).

Contrary is the practice of such lewd and unnatural women as leave their new-born children under stalls, at men's doors, in church porches, yea many times in open field. It is noted as a point of unnaturalness in the ostrich, *to leave her eggs in the earth, and in the dust*: in which respect she is said to be *hardened against her young ones, as though they were not hers* (Job 39:14, 16). Much more hardened are the foresaid lewd women. The eagle is counted an unnatural bird, because she thrusteth her young ones which she hath brought forth out of her nest. Are not then such mothers much more unnatural? They oft lay their children forth in public places, for others to show that mercy which they themselves have not. The civil law judgeth this to be a kind of murder.

---

[15] **fain:** glad under the circumstances.

→ JOHN NICHOLS

From The Progresses, Processions, and Magnificent Festivities of King James the First   *1828*

Editor of the *Gentleman's Magazine*, a popular monthly journal, John Nichols (1745–1826) was also an avid biographer and antiquarian who produced two comprehensive collections of documents on Renaissance courtly culture: *The Progresses and Public Processions of Queen Elizabeth I* (1788–1823), and *The Progresses, Processions, and Magnificent Festivities of King James the First*, published posthumously in 1828. These collections provide chronological accounts of these monarchs' progresses (visits to the countryside or to residences around London), entertainments, and political affairs, as recorded in a variety of textual forms: letters, inventories, household accounts, excerpts from contemporary historical narratives, personal memoirs, transcriptions of courtly pageants, and so on.

In the excerpts below from the *The Progresses . . . of King James*, Nichols assembles contemporary documents concerning the birth in 1605 of Mary, the first royal child to be born on English soil since 1537. For the royal family, the personal and political aspects of childbirth were deeply entwined. James named his daughter after his late mother, Mary Queen of Scots, and two days after Mary's birth he commissioned elaborate tombs for his mother and for his predecessor on the English throne, Queen Elizabeth (for an image of Queen Elizabeth's monument, see p. 409). Traditionally, a royal birth also served as an occasion on which the monarch honored favored courtiers (Barroll 105). Ceremonies for the bestowal of noble titles were held on May 4, a day before the spectacular christening ceremony described below. Anne's churching ceremony, a public ritual in which a new mother went to church to thank God for her safe delivery (Wilson 78–79), officially concluded the cycle of pregnancy, birth, and recovery, reinserting the queen into her accustomed role as royal consort and mother.

The documents collected by Nichols record how contemporary observers understood the political significance of the royal family's participation in the ceremonies surrounding childbirth. Nichols includes letters written to Ralph Winwood, the king's secretary of state; a letter written to the earl of Shrewsbury, a courtier; and excerpts from a contemporary historical chronicle, *The Annals of England* (1615), by John Stow and Edmund Howes. Consider what these documents reveal about the relationship between the public and private lives of Renaissance monarchs, and how those lives were made accessible, through texts, to courtiers and commoners alike. What, if anything, do these texts indicate about the relationship between Queen Anne and King James? How do these

John Nichols, *The Progresses, Processions, and Magnificent Festivities of King James the First* (London, 1828), vol. 1, pp. 499–500, 504–5, 510–14.

documents serve to display not only Anne's power as mother and queen, but also James's power as patriarch and king? Note as well the differences in tone, style, and level of detail between the letters and the chronicle accounts. In the letters, what kind of news is included alongside news of the queen's impending delivery?

In *The Winter's Tale*, the conditions in which Hermione gives birth stand in stark contrast to the highly scripted, formal rituals of Queen Anne's delivery described below. Leontes violently appropriates the symbolic meanings of royal childbirth by confining the queen to prison, labeling her infant a bastard, and publicly denouncing her transgressions against his authority as husband and king. Leontes' interruption of the spectacular public rituals of childbirth, christening, and churching denies Hermione the privileges and honors usually enjoyed by wives, but how much of the honor and symbolic power of his own sovereignty does he sacrifice in the process? Is it possible that Hermione achieves greater dignity and symbolic power through Leontes' attempts to evacuate her political role as royal mother?

From *The Progresses, Processions, and Magnificent Festivities of King James the First*

The following extract from a letter of Sir Dudley Carleton to Mr. Winwood, dated March 10 [1605]:

... "Here is much ado about the Queen's lying down, and great suit made for offices of carrying the white staff, holding the back of the chair, door-keeping, cradle-rocking, and such like gossips'[1] tricks, which you should understand better than I.

The King is upon his return from Newmarket Heath,[2] and will be here about Saturday next. The tilting[3] this year will be at his place; here is much practicing, and the Duke of Holst[4] is a learner among the rest, whose horse took it so unkindly the last day to be spur-galled on the fore-shoulder, that he laid his *little burden* on God's fair earth." ...

Mr. Samuel Calvert writes thus to Mr. Winwood, March 28, 1605:

"The King, Queen, and all are now at court, and there purposed to be some time. The Queen expects delivery within a month. There is great preparation of nurses, midwives, rockers, and other officers, to the number of forty or more. Yesterday a son of the Earl of Southampton was christened at court; the King and my Lord Cranbourne, with the Countess of Suffolk,

---

[1] **gossips:** originally from "god-sib," or "kin in God," a gossip was a godmother or godfather.
[2] **Newmarket Heath:** a market town north of London known for horseracing.   [3] **tilting:** jousting performed at a tournament.   [4] **Duke of Holst:** brother of Queen Anne.

being gossips. The tilting on Sunday last (Coronation Day) was not performed with the accustomed solemnity; my Lords the Dukes of Holst and Lennox[5] were the chiefest runners, though our English outran them in every respect. The shows were costly and somewhat extraordinary. The King is purposed to take all woods into his hands within the compass of three miles from the water's side, and near unto his houses, and will allow to such as out of time have enjoyed them as their own recompense, according to discretion, which course will breed in many much discontent. The players do not forbear to represent upon their stage the whole course of this present time, not sparing either king, state, or religion, in so great absurdity and with such liberty, that any would be afraid to hear them." . . .

On the 6th of April, Mr. Samuel Calvert thus writes to Mr. Winwood:

"On Easter Tuesday [April 2], one Mr. William Herrick, a goldsmith in Cheapside,[6] was knighted for making a hole in the great diamond the King doth wear. The party little expected the honor; but he did his work so well as won the King to an extraordinary liking of it.

The Court now remains in such quiet form that there is slender subject for discourse, nor doth this town dispute of any new matter or occurrent that hath happened of late. The Queen expects her delivery every hour, and prayers are daily said everywhere for her safety. There is great preparation for the christening chamber, and costly furniture provided for performance of other ceremonies, and in the meanwhile the time of the year forbids the King his common exercise,[7] and somewhat the ordinary complaints of poor country farmers to endure continual wrong, by the hunting spoils and misgovernment of the unruly train.[8] So that there is now a complete court at Greenwich for some months."

On the same day Mr. John Packer also writes to Mr. Winwood:

"The Queen is not yet delivered, but is come to the end of her reckoning;[9] three midwives are here attending, but she will not speak with any of them till she hath need of their help, neither will she yet signify which of them she will employ until the easiness or hardness of her travail[10] doth urge her to it."

In a letter from Greenwich, April 7, Edmund Lascelles writes thus to the Earl of Shrewsbury:

"Upon Friday, the fifth of April, his majesty came from Greenwich to Whitehall, and lay there all night, which made a general report in London that the Queen was in labor; but was not so, for this Sunday, being the 7th,

---

[5] **Lennox:** the Scottish duke of Lennox, Esmé Stewart (1579–1624).   [6] **Cheapside:** commercial district in London.   [7] **common exercise:** i.e., hunting.   [8] **train:** body of followers.   [9] **reckoning:** the calculated period of pregnancy.   [10] **travail:** labor.

her majesty was in the withdrawing-chamber, and therefore I will crave pardon of your lordship to defer the sending of my letters yet a day or two longer, to see if they will prove so happy as to bring your lordship the first good news.

Yesterday there landed an ambassador from the Archduke, that hath brought the king a dozen gallant mares, all with foal,[11] four ambling horses, and two stallions, all coursers of Naples.

On the 9th of this month, my lord of Hartford takes his leave of the king for his Low Country[12] journey, and goeth away on the Friday following.

His majesty hath commanded two stately tombs to be begun at Westminster, one for the Queen Elizabeth, another for his majesty's mother."

[From Howes' *Annals of England*:]

"The lady Mary, born at Greenwich upon the eighth of April about 11 or 12 of the clock at night; for joy whereof, the next day after, the citizens of London made bonfires throughout London, and the bells continued ringing all the whole day. . . .

"On Saturday the 4th, the Hall of Greenwich being richly hanged with arras,[13] and a cloth of estate[14] being there erected, the king's majesty standing thereunder, accompanied with the princes his children, the Duke of Holstein, the Duke of Lennox, and the most part of the great nobility both of England and Scotland, created three earls, one viscount, and four barons, that is to say, Robert Cecil, Viscount Cranbourne, Baron of Egiston, was created Earl of Excester. Sir Philip Herbert, younger brother to the Earl of Pembroke, was created Baron of Shurland and Earl of Montgomery. Robert Sidney, Baron of Penshurst, Lord Chamberlain to the queen, was created Viscount Lisle. Sir John Stanhope, Vice-Chamberlain to the king, was created Lord Stanhope of Harrington. Sir George Carew, Vice-Chamberlain to the queen, was created Lord Carew of Clopton. Master Thomas Arundel, of Devonshire, was created Lord Arundel of Warder. Master William Cavendish was created Lord Cavendish of Hardwick.

The next day, being Sunday, between four and five of the clock in the afternoon, the lady Mary was christened, in manner as followeth.

First, the three courts at Greenwich were railed in and hung about with broadcloth, where the proceeding should pass. The child was brought from the queen's lodgings through both the great chambers, and through the

---

[11] **with foal:** pregnant.   [12] **Low Country:** the Netherlands.   [13] **arras:** tapestry.   [14] **cloth of estate:** a ceremonial canopy.

presence,[15] and down the winding stairs into the conduit-court.[16] At the foot whereof attended a canopy born by eight barons, before which went the Officers of Arms, and divers[17] bishops, barons, and earls. The Earl of Northumberland bore a covered gilt basin; after followed the Countess of Worcester, bearing a cushion covered with lawn,[18] which had thereon many jewels of inestimable price. Under the canopy went the Countess of Derby, bearing the child, and she was supported by the Dukes of Holstein and Lennox. The train of the mantle[19] was born by two of the greatest countesses; then followed the godmothers, the Lady Arabella and the Countess of Northumberland, after whom followed many countesses and other great ladies.

At the entrance to the chapel stood the Lord Archbishop of Canterbury, assisted with the deans of Canterbury, and of the chapel, in rich copes,[20] received the child; and, bringing the child unto the traverse,[21] the choir sung certain anthems, and the lords took one side of the stalls, and the ladies the other.

In the midst of the choir was erected a most stately canopy of cloth of gold, 12 foot square, within the which upon a foot pace of four degrees,[22] stood a very rich and stately font of silver and gilt, most curiously wrought with figures of beasts, serpents, and other antic[23] works, and after a while the gentlemen ushers opening the barriers of the canopy, the Lord Archbishop with the two deans entered the same; then followed the Countess of Derby with the child, the Duke of Holstein godfather, and the two godmothers, attended on each side of the font. During the solemnity of baptism, which in all points was fully read and performed according to the Church of England, naming the child Mary, then the child was carried back into the traverse, and the godfather and godmothers ascending, offered at the altar. The Lord Almoner, Bishop of Chicester, received their offerings. Then the Earl Marshall and the Lord Chamberlain placing Seager, Garter Principal King of Arms, between them, Master Garter making low reverence unto the king's majesty, who stood in the closet[24] window, began to pronounce with a loud voice, these words following: 'Almighty God, of His infinite grace and goodness, preserve and bless with long life, in health, honor, and all happiness, this high and right noble Lady Mary, daughter

---

[15] **presence:** presence-chamber, a room used for ceremonial attendance. [16] **conduit-court:** a connecting room or passage. [17] **divers:** various. [18] **lawn:** a fine linen. [19] **mantle:** a loose cloak or blanket. [20] **copes:** cloaks or capes. [21] **traverse:** a small compartment closed off by a curtain or screen. [22] **a foot pace of four degrees:** a platform of four steps. [23] **antic:** bearing monstrously or grotesquely shaped designs. [24] **closet:** a small room used for private devotions.

to the most high and mighty prince, James, by the grace of God, King of Great Britain, France, and Ireland, defender of the faith, and of the most excellent princess Queen Anne, amen.' Which being ended, then the gentlemen ushers and sewers[25] brought in a voider[26] of wine and confectures;[27] the trumpets sounded, the whole train returned the same way and order that they came, saving that the gifts of their gossips were carried by six earls. . . .

"Upon Whit-Sunday,[28] the 19th of May, the queen's majesty was churched in manner and form following. First, the king, accompanied with the most part of the peers of the realm, went unto the closet, and there heard a sermon preached by Doctor Watson, Almoner, Bishop of Chicester; from thence he went down into the chapel and offered. Then withdrew himself into a rich traverse on the right hand of the altar. Then came the queen from her lodging, and went into her closet, and staying there a while with a great train of ladies, was brought from thence into the chapel by the great lords, supported by the Dukes of Holstein and Lennox, and being come before the altar, she made low reverence and offered her besant,[29] and then went into the traverse, which stood on the left side of the altar; and after the usual prayers and thanksgiving for her health and safe delivery, according to the Book of Common Prayer, and sundry anthems sung with organ, cornets, sackbut,[30] and other excellent instruments of music, the king and queen came both forth of their traverses, and met before the altar, and, embracing each other with great kindness, went hand in hand together, until they came to the king's presence-chamber door, where they parted, doing great reverence to each other. And the same day the king dined openly in the presence-chamber, accompanied with the Archduke's ambassador, Prince Henry, and the Duke of Holstein."

---

[25] **sewers:** attendants at a meal who superintended the arrangement of the table, the seating of guests, and the tasting and serving of the dishes.   [26] **voider:** tray.   [27] **confectures:** preparations of preserved fruits and other sweets.   [28] **Whit-Sunday:** the seventh Sunday after Easter, the feast of Pentecost.   [29] **besant:** a gold coin traditionally given as an offering.   [30] **sackbut:** a brass trumpet.

→ FREDERICK DEVON

From Issues of the Exchequer   *1836*

Frederick Devon worked in the Chapter House Record Office in Westminster Abbey, one of four repositories used since the mid-sixteenth century to store important crown documents such as deeds, wills, and diplomatic treaties. These repositories were known as the Treasury of the Receipt of the Exchequer (the office that administered the crown's revenue). In 1836, Devon published a selection of records relating to expenditures during King James's reign that he culled from the Pell Office, another repository at Westminster Hall. These records detail royal payments for various goods and services, including gifts, clothing, minting, coronation ceremonies, pensions, and household administration. Refuting a long line of biographers and historians, including John Nichols, who had perpetuated the view of James as debauched and uncouth, Devon asserts that these financial records reveal the king's "liberality and fondness for the arts and literature" as well as his "unceasing parental solicitude" toward his children and "kindness and benevolence" to his wife (xviii, xx–xxi).

The records below indicate the enormous cost and care devoted to the birth and christening of Princess Mary. The queen had six midwives, and her bed cost a stunning £15,593. To appreciate the magnitude of this expense, consider that in 1600 the Fortune Theater in London cost £520 to build, and a wage laborer would have done well to make £12 for the year. These account book entries are fascinating not only for what they reveal about the material realities of royal privilege, but also for the radical contrast they provide to *The Winter's Tale* as a type of cultural document. Filled with facts, figures, and dates, these fragmented account book entries could hardly be more different in form and spirit from the human drama of *The Winter's Tale*. Nonetheless, both Shakespeare and the exchequer officer (or officers) who kept these records can provide access into the cultural significance of royal birth in early modern England.

12th of April — By order, 10th of April, 1605. To Maxamilian Powtram, alias Coult, the sum of £150, parcel[1] of a more sum towards the making and erecting of a tomb for a monument of the late Queen Elizabeth, according to an agreement made with him. By writ,[2] dated 4th of March, 1604, and by other direction.

---

[1] **parcel:** a small part.   [2] **writ:** a written command, precept, or formal order.

Frederick Devon, *Issues of the Exchequer; Being Payments Made out of his Majesty's Revenue During Reign of King James I* (London, 1836), pp. 21, 23, 29, 48, 55.

1st of June — By order, 29th of May, 1605. To Alice Dennis, midwife, the sum of £100 for her pains and attendance upon the Queen, as of his Highness' free gift and reward, without account, imprest,[3] or other charge to be set on her for the same. By writ, dated 28th of May, 1605.

7th of February — By order, 7th of February, 1605 [1606]. To Sir Roger Dallison, Knight, the sum of £1,498, 16*d.*, to be by him paid over to divers[4] shopkeepers, artificers,[5] and others, as parcel of a more sum due to them for stuffs[6] taken of them, and for workmanship of divers things made for the childbed of the Queen, according to a list of their particular names and sums, signed by his Majesty. By writ, dated the 22nd of January, 1605 [1606].

21st of October — By order, 11th of October, 1606. — To Philip Jacobson, jeweler, the sum of £880, in full satisfaction and payment of his part of a certain diamond, pearls pendant, and 2 dozen of buttons, taken of him and Arnold Lulles, bestowed by his Majesty upon the Queen at the christening of Lady Mary, amounting in the whole to the sum of £2,530. By writ, dated 18th of May, 1605.

9th of February — By order, 7th of February, 1606 [1607]. To Sir Roger Dallison, Knight, the sum of £3,132, 9*s.*, 10*d.*, in part of payment of the sum of £15,593, 14*s.*, limited to be by him paid over to divers shopkeepers, artificers, and others, for stuffs taken of them, and for workmanship of divers things made for the childbed of the Queen, according to a schedule of assignment,[7] containing as well the names of divers creditors as the several sums due to them, assigned unto them as parcel of their debts; subscribed by me the Lord Treasurer, the Lord Chamberlain, and the Earl of Salisbury, amounting to the sum of £3,132, 9*s.*, 10*d.*

---

[3] **imprest:** money paid in advance. [4] **divers:** different. [5] **artificers:** craftsmen. [6] **stuffs:** goods. [7] **assignment:** allotment of a share.

→ JACQUES GUILLEMEAU

From Childbirth; Or, the Happy Delivery of Women *with* The Nursing of Children   *1612*

A student of Ambrose Paré, considered the founder of modern surgical practice, Jacques Guillemeau (1550–1613) served as royal surgeon to three kings of France and authored influential treatises on childbirth, nursing, and ophthalmology. His treatises on childbirth and nursing were translated into English in 1612 and remained enormously popular throughout the seventeenth century (Bicks 55). Although Guillemeau wrote primarily for other medical professionals, it is likely that his works were read by "anxious fathers and husbands, and perhaps even some women" in search of expert advice (Cressy, *Birth* 38). Guillemeau's theories of childbirth and nursing cannot be regarded as "scientific": he is, after all, writing on events that in this era would have been very difficult for a man to observe firsthand. Nonetheless, the medical idiom in which he writes makes available an important and fascinating set of contexts for the conflicts around gender and sexuality that rend domestic harmony in *The Winter's Tale*.

In *Childbirth*, Guillemeau takes very seriously the task of defining the criteria that make for a good midwife. Based on these criteria, would Guillemeau approve of Paulina as symbolic (if not literal) midwife to Hermione, or would he share Leontes' objections to her behavior and character? Guillemeau also explores the complementary roles that art and nature play in a successful delivery, an issue that Shakespeare presents more obliquely through Paulina's "delivery" of Perdita from jail. Consider how Guillemeau's observations about the midwife's purpose in using "fair and flattering speeches" might shed light on the series of speeches Paulina delivers about Perdita to Hermione's jailer, Leontes, and Antigonus. In particular, pay attention to Paulina's rhetorical appeals to "nature" in making these arguments, and to the factors that account for her success or failure in convincing others to accept her point of view. Finally, we might debate whether or not Paulina, by allowing Leontes to believe that Hermione has perished, employs what Guillemeau calls a "commendable deceit" in the interests of "the patient's good."

Even before the birth of his daughter, Leontes interferes in the female world of childrearing by removing Mamillius from Hermione's care. Leontes regrets that Mamillius has inherited his mother's corrupt "blood," but expresses relief that she "did not nurse him" with her own breast milk (2.1.59, 57). Queens did not nurse their children, since breastfeeding "was widely assumed to be more

---

Jacques Guillemeau, *Childbirth; Or, the Happy Delivery of Women* with *The Nursing of Children* (London, 1612), sigs. L2v–L3v, Ii2r–Ii3v.

difficult as well as more burdensome for the aristocratic woman," who would be required "to remove herself from social circulation, and to risk the premature aging and wrinkling that was commonly associated with suckling" (Paster, *Body* 202). However, in terms of the infant's welfare, Leontes' relief that Hermione did not nurse their son might be misplaced. Given the familiar belief that breast milk could transmit to the child the "moral and bodily character" of the mother or nurse, many medical, religious, and moral authorities in this period worried about the "nurse-milk's competition with and perversion of parentally transmitted identity" (Trubowitz 84).

In *The Nursing of Children*, Guillemeau recommends maternal nursing in the interests of the infant's emotional and physical well-being. Even though Hermione follows the typical practice of royal mothers in not nursing Mamillius, neither has she sent him away shortly after birth to nurse in the household of a host family, the fate of a "significant minority of wellborn infants, male and female" (Paster, *Body* 218). What, then, can we gather about the strength of the psychological and even physical bond between Hermione and Mamillius? Do they enjoy the "natural affection" between mother and child that Guillemeau celebrates? Despite not having nursed her son, does Hermione still fulfill some of Guillemeau's criteria of good motherhood?

From *Childbirth; Or, the Happy Delivery of Women*

WHAT MANNER OF WOMAN A MIDWIFE OUGHT TO BE.

Many things are requisite and needful in a midwife, but they are all referred to her person, to her manners, and to her mind. First, concerning her person. She must be of an indifferent age, neither too young nor too old; well-composed of body, not being subject to any diseases, nor misshapen or deformed in any part thereof; neat in her apparel and person, especially having little hands and not thick, clean, and her nails pared[1] very near and even; neither must she wear rings upon her fingers nor bracelets upon her arms, when she is about her business. She must be pleasant, merry, of good discourse, strong, painful,[2] and accustomed to labor, that she may be able (if need be) to watch[3] two or three nights by the woman.

Concerning her behavior, she must be mild, gentle, courteous, patient, sober, chaste; not quarrelsome nor choleric,[4] neither proud or covetous, nor a blabber or reporter of anything she shall either hear or see in secret, in the

---

[1] **pared:** trimmed.   [2] **painful:** painstaking, diligent.   [3] **watch:** remain awake.   [4] **choleric:** of hot or fiery nature.

house or person of her she hath delivered. For as Terence[5] saith, *It is not fit to commit her into the hands of a drunken or rash woman, that is in travail of her first child.*

As for her mind, she must be wise, discreet, and witty, able to make use sometime of fair and flattering speeches: as Plato reporteth midwives were wont to do in times past, which was done to no other end but only to busy and beguile[6] the poor apprehensive women. And it is a commendable deceit, allowed also in a surgeon when it is done for the patient's good. For as the same Terence saith, *Deceit doth serve oftentimes for a good medicine in extreme diseases.*

Now above all things the said midwife ought to know that nature, the handmaid of this great God, hath given to everything a beginning, increase, state, perfection, and declining, which he doth manifestly and chiefly show (saith Galen[7]) in the birth of a child, when the mother brings him into the world. For Nature surpasseth all, and in that she doth is wiser than either art, or the midwife, whosoever she be, yea, than the best or most cunning workman that may be found, as Galen witnesseth. For it is she that hath set down the day of the child's conformation,[8] and the hour of his birth. And certainly it is a thing worthy of consideration to see how in a little space, yea even in the twinkling of an eye, the neck of the womb, which all the time of the nine months was so perfectly and exactly closed and shut that the point of a needle could not enter therein: how (I say) in an instant it is dilated and enlarged to give passage and way for the child; the which cannot be comprehended (as the same Galen saith) but only wondered at, and admired. The same author in his fifteenth book *De usu partium,*[9] desirous to show the providence of Nature, saith that the faults of Nature are very rare, and that she worketh always and in such order and measure that of a thousand births there is scarce one found that is amiss.

Wherefore neither the midwife nor any of the woman's kinsfolk or assistants ought to do anything rashly, but suffer nature to work; helping her notwithstanding in that which shall be needful, as hereafter shall be declared: dividing the work of their delivery into three several times and seasons.

---

[5] **Terence:** Roman comic playwright (c.190–159 B.C.E.), whose comedy *Andria* features a midwife. In Act 1, scene 4, a maid-servant refers to the midwife as a drunken and rash woman who is not trustworthy enough to care for a woman giving birth to her first child.   [6] **beguile:** divert, amuse.   [7] **Galen:** Greek physician and anatomist (129–99 B.C.E.) whose theories were still influential in the early seventeenth century.   [8] **conformation:** the symmetrical formation of the fetus.   [9] *De usu partium*: *On the Usefulness of the Parts* [of the body], an anatomy text.

From *The Nursing of Children*

Aulus Gellius[10] (in my opinion) did not amiss in putting no difference between a woman that refuses to nurse her own child and one that kills her child, as soon as she hath conceived, that she may not be troubled with bearing it nine months in her womb. For why may not a woman with as good reason deny to nourish her child with her blood in her womb, as to deny it her milk being born? Since the milk is nothing else but blood whitened, being now brought to perfection and maturity.

But some will say that the child may be delivered to some other woman to nurse it, and that the mother may have an eye and care over it. But (gentle ladies) here I desire you to consider with me the great inconveniences that may hence arise, which though they be infinite, yet I will reduce them to four heads:

1. First, there is danger lest the child be changed and another put in his place.

2. Then, that natural affection which should be betwixt the mother and the child by this means is diminished.

3. Thirdly, it may be feared that some bad conditions or inclinations may be derived from the nurse into the child.

4. And lastly, the nurse may communicate some imperfection of her body into the child.

1. As for the first point, which is the changing of the child, that may easily come to pass. Because as soon as the child is born and christened, the mother presently delivers it to the nurse, to be carried into the country, where the child, being wholly left to the discretion of the nurse, may by some ill chance be stifled, over-laid, be let fall, and so come to an untimely death; or else may be devoured, spoiled, or disfigured by some wild beast, wolf, or dog, and then the nurse, fearing to be punished for her negligence, may take another child into the place of it, which can hardly ever be marked and distinguished. And indeed when children grow somewhat big and are brought home from nurse, if they prove not like their parents in body, in conditions, and wit, the proverb goes, *that they are changed at nurse*; which sometimes may be truer, than they are aware of. . . .

2. For the second point, which is natural affection, without doubt that cannot be so earnest either from the mother toward the child or from the child toward the mother if she hath not nursed him and given him suck. For

---

[10] **Aulus Gellius:** ancient Roman author.

if she nurse him, he sucks and draws her own blood, whereupon grows a familiar inwardness, and the child (when he comes to years of discretion) finds himself bound to his mother for many benefits: both in that she hath borne him nine months in her womb, and also because she hath nursed him, watched him, and often made him clean. In recompense whereof, he endeavors to show her a thousand delights, to make her forget or take in good part so much care and pains as she hath taken with him. He plays a number of apish[11] tricks about her; he kisseth her; strokes her hair, nose, and ears; he flatters her; he counterfeits anger and other passions. And as he groweth bigger, he finds other sports with her, which causeth that they bear one another such an affection as cannot be expressed, and makes that they can never be parted. When he is big and comes to be weaned, if one chide his nurse he cries and stamps; and if one offers to take him out of his nurse's arms, he will fly in their faces, and, if it were possible, he would even pull out their heart: and all this proceeds from that inward affection of the child, to which no love can be compared. And hereupon Plato justly said *that children would never love their parents so well, but that their fathers do often bear them in their arms, and the mothers give them suck at their own breasts.*

Conjugal Faultlines

> Should all despair
> That have revolted wives, the tenth of mankind
> Would hang themselves.   (1.2.198–200)

The metaphor of "conjugal faultlines" suggests a submerged flaw awaiting the traumatic event that will shake the foundations of domestic order and harmony. In *The Winter's Tale*, Leontes' jealous accusations traumatically manifest male anxieties about female sexuality that were pervasive in a patriarchal society that placed a great emphasis on women's chastity. The documents that follow reveal the various forms such anxieties could take in the early modern period.

First, an excerpt from John Milton's *Paradise Lost* (p. 203) articulates the fear that male identity could be undermined by sexual intimacy with women. In early modern England, relations with women were considered paradoxically both necessary to and threatening to the accomplishment of adult masculine identity. On the one hand, manhood was associated with becoming a husband and father. On the other hand, the period's dominant gender ideologies assumed the moral and intellectual inferiority of women, and

---

[11] **apish:** ape-like in imitation; silly.

typically portrayed sexual passion for women as emasculating. Consequently, a powerful strain of Renaissance thought celebrated men's bonds with each other as more enduring and affectionate than their bonds with women (Smith, *Homosexual* 33–34; DiGangi 31).

Sometimes, the celebration of male affection in Renaissance texts shades into expressions of same-sex love or even eroticism. One of the most remarkable expressions of the virtue of male same-sex love comes from the French philosopher Michel de Montaigne, whose *Essays* were first translated into English in 1603. In his essay "Of Friendship," Montaigne insists that "affection for women," which flares up like "an impetuous and fickle flame," cannot be compared with affection for a friend, which distributes "a general and universal warmth" that is "all gentleness and smoothness, with nothing bitter and stinging about it" (137). Montaigne defines marriage as a pragmatic contract or "bargain" rather than a bond of true love, since "the ordinary capacity of women is inadequate for that communion and fellowship which is the nurse of this sacred bond; nor does their soul seem firm enough to endure the strain of so tight and durable a knot" (137–38). It is only through the extraordinary intimacy of male friendship that "our souls mingle and blend with each other so completely that they efface the seam that joined them, and cannot find it again" (139).

The notion of a "natural" emotional incompatibility between men and women leads to another conjugal faultline: the belief that women were unable to control their sexual appetite. In early modern culture, the male fear of being sexually betrayed by a woman is seemingly universal — witness the cuckold jokes that sour even Shakespeare's sweetest comedies of love and marriage. The cuckolded husband's loss of personal, domestic, and social authority, addressed in Benedetto Varchi's *Blazon of Jealousy*, helps to account for the suddenness and intensity of Leontes' suspicions. Howsoever we interpret the causes of Leontes' jealousy, Varchi makes clear that the experience of jealousy in early modern culture is caught up with patriarchal assumptions about female sexuality and the proprietary relations of marriage. Thus jealousy in the play need not be understood as a manifestation of Leontes' unique and seemingly pathological psychological makeup, but can be appreciated in all its complexity as a product of the sharply gender-differentiated structure of Shakespeare's society. In this sense, could we regard Leontes as the victim as well as the perpetuator of a patriarchal system that places such extreme emphasis on female sexual purity?

Of course, it is difficult to perceive Leontes as a victim when he is accusing Hermione of betraying him as "an adult'ress" and as "a traitor" who has plotted against his life (2.1.89–90). In the early modern imagination, adultery and murder were often linked. William Gouge warns that through adultery "husbands and wives are stirred up to wish and long after one another's death: and not only inwardly in heart to wish it, but outwardly also in deed to practice it" (sig. P6v). But more to the point than Gouge's conjugal advice is the power Leontes gains over his wife by publicly accusing her of adultery and treason, thereby opening his domestic crisis to juridical intervention. In Renaissance England, a woman who was publicly defamed as an adulteress or "whore" (not literally a prostitute, but a sexually promiscuous woman) could protect her reputation by suing her accuser for sexual slander in an ecclesiastical court (Gowing 60–67). Through the same courts, a husband could seek a judicial separation from his wife on grounds of adultery. However, "women rarely if ever attempted to use this option against their husbands" (102). Moreover, wives accused of crimes against their husbands faced particular legal disadvantages based simply on their status as women.

That even a queen might suffer from the gender bias of the law becomes clear not only from Hermione's trial for adultery and "high treason" (3.2.13), but also from one of the most notorious trials of the sixteenth century. In 1536, Anne Boleyn, wife of Henry VIII (and mother of the future Queen Elizabeth), was tried and executed for adultery and treason. Since it was a legal question as to whether a queen's adultery in itself constituted treason, Henry attempted to evade any ambiguity in the law by linking the charge of adultery with the charge of conspiracy to murder. The success of Henry's strategy was due in part to the fact that, in Renaissance society, accusing a woman of sexual transgression was the most effective way to strip her of authority. Anne Boleyn's career therefore "provides a kind of prototype and a warning for all subsequent slandered women in positions of authority" (Kaplan and Eggert 92). Anne's trial provides a fascinating angle on the real legal and political consequences of early modern gender ideology, and opens up the trial scene in *The Winter's Tale* to an analogous reading of the workings of gender and power in Leontes' Sicilia.

→ JOHN MILTON

From Paradise Lost   *1674*

A prolific writer, John Milton (1608–1674) worked in myriad literary forms, including sonnets, translations, pastoral elegies, tragedy, religious polemic, and treatises on divorce, education, and censorship. He is best known for *Paradise Lost*, his enormously learned epic poem on the fall of Adam and Eve. Milton composed *Paradise Lost* while serving as Latin secretary to Oliver Cromwell's parliamentary government, which took power after the 1649 execution of King Charles I, an act that Milton defended. In 1660, the son of the executed king returned from exile to rule England as King Charles II, and Milton's subsequent political troubles delayed the publication of *Paradise Lost* for four years. The first edition, published in 1667, divided the poem into ten books; the second edition of 1674, cited below, divides it into twelve.

Paradise Lost massively elaborates the biblical account of Adam and Eve's disobedience to God and expulsion from the Garden of Eden (Genesis 1–3). The climactic moment occurs in Book Nine, when Eve, tricked by Satan, eats from the forbidden tree and subsequently tempts Adam to do the same. Though he is aware of the consequences, Adam, determined to share a common fate with Eve, eats the fruit; however, he later regrets his decision and rebukes Eve for having succumbed to Satan's temptation. In the passage below, Adam bitterly vents misogynist sentiments that seem to call into question the very possibility of conjugal harmony. Although in Book One of the poem Milton implies that angels are androgynous — "Spirits when they please / Can either Sex assume, or both" (sig. B8r) — in this passage Adam associates the purity of angels with their maleness, and blames the creation of woman for the existence of suffering in the world.

Adam's complaint points to the contradictory messages that young men in Renaissance England received about the relationships they were expected to form with women and with other men. While Shakespeare's culture celebrated married love between men and women, it also inherited a classical discourse of male friendship that celebrated intimacy between men. Shakespeare voices these idealized sentiments of same-sex love in his *Sonnets* and in several plays, including *The Winter's Tale*. Camillo opens the play by recollecting the childhood friendship that deeply "rooted . . . such an affection" between Leontes and Polixenes, and Polixenes nostalgically elaborates on this youthful affection: "We were as twinned lambs that did frisk i'th' sun, / And bleat the one at th'other" (1.1.17–18, 1.2.67–68). In the passage from *Paradise Lost*, Adam's celebration of "Spirits Masculine" is prompted by his conviction that Eve has tricked him into committing sin (Figure 11). What motivates Polixenes' celebration of male friendship at this early moment in the play? Can we assume that Leontes shares

---

John Milton, *Paradise Lost. A Poem in Twelve Books* (London, 1674); *Book Ten*, sigs. T3r–T3v.

FIGURE II
*Zacharias Dolendo,
after Bartholomeus
Spranger,* The Fall
*(1611). What does
this illustration of
the fall imply about
Adam's motives for
eating the forbidden
fruit? How does
Polixenes' story of
lost childhood inno-
cence draw from this
archetypal story of
lost innocence?*

Polixenes' feelings about male friendship? In her response to Polixenes' tale, what perspective does Hermione provide on the role women are made to play in such narratives of male friendship?

From *Paradise Lost*

Out of my sight, thou Serpent, that name best
Befits thee with him leagu'd,[1] thyself as false
And hateful; nothing wants,[2] but that thy shape,
Like his, and color Serpentine may show
Thy inward fraud, to warn all Creatures from thee   5

---

[1] **leagu'd:** banded together.   [2] **wants:** is lacking.

Henceforth; lest that too heav'nly form, pretended
To hellish falsehood, snare them. But for thee
I had persisted happy, had not thy pride
And wand'ring vanity, when least was safe,
Rejected my forewarning, and disdain'd   10
Not to be trusted, longing to be seen
Though by the Devil himself, him overweening[3]
To over-reach, but with the Serpent meeting
Fool'd and beguil'd, by him thou, I by thee,
To trust thee from my side, imagin'd wise,   15
Constant, mature, proof against all assaults,
And understood not all was but a show
Rather than solid virtue, all but a Rib[4]
Crooked by nature, bent, as now appears,
More to the part sinister[5] from me drawn,   20
Well if thrown out, as supernumerary[6]
To my just number found. O why did God,
Creator wise, that peopl'd highest Heav'n
With Spirits Masculine, create at last
This novelty on Earth, this fair defect   25
Of Nature, and not fill the World at once
With Men as Angels without Feminine,
Or find some other way to generate
Mankind? this mischief had not then befall'n,
And more that shall befall, innumerable   30
Disturbances on Earth through Female snares,
And straight conjunction with this Sex: for either
He never shall find out fit Mate, but such
As some misfortune brings him, or mistake,
Or whom he wishes most shall seldom gain   35
Through her perverseness, but shall see her gain'd
By a far worse, or if she love, withheld
By Parents, or his happiest choice too late
Shall meet, already linkt and Wedlock-bound
To a fell Adversary, his hate or shame: 40
Which infinite calamity shall cause
To Human life, and household peace confound.

---

[3] **overweening:** excessively self-confident.   [4] **Rib:** allusion to Adam's rib from which Eve was created.   [5] **part sinister:** the left side (from Latin *sinister*, left), but also connoting disaster or malice.   [6] **supernumerary:** according to Adam, God created Eve from an extra, and unnecessary, rib.

→ BENEDETTO VARCHI

From The Blazon of Jealousy   *1615*

Translated by Robert Tofte

The Florentine Benedetto Varchi (1503–1565) was a historian and poet best known for *Storie Fiorentine in Sedici Libri* (1527–30), a history of contemporary Florence, and *L'Hercolano* (1570), a treatise about language. He was a member of the Florentine Academy and served as president of the Accademia degli Infiammati (Academy of the Burning Ones) in Padua, where he delivered this lecture on jealousy. In 1615, Varchi's text was translated into English and annotated by Robert Tofte (1562–1620). Born into a family of London fishmongers, Tofte became a traveler and writer. From 1591 to 1594 he lived in Italy, where he wrote pastoral poems, a sonnet sequence, and a treatise about the papacy. Upon his return to London, he produced English translations of satirical Italian texts such as *Of Marriage and Wiving* (1599) and *Ariosto's Satires* (1608); he also translated a French satire on marriage, *Les Quinze Joies de Marriage*, as *The Bachelor's Banquet* (1603).

Varchi's analysis of the various causes of jealousy suggests that Leontes' rash behavior can be explained in multiple, possibly competing, terms, including the medical, psychological, economic, and sociological. For instance, Varchi's description of jealousy as a disease alerts us to the possibility that Leontes might be suffering from melancholy. In the Renaissance, melancholy was frequently blamed for irrational behaviors. Medical theory held that the liver created four liquid substances, called humors, which affected one's natural disposition and state of health. Melancholy was a cold and sluggish humor that could produce "distempered" or erratic behavior when subjected to elevated bodily temperatures (Wood 188). In his *Treatise of Melancholy* (1586), Timothy Bright describes the psychological effects of melancholic spirits or vapors that arise from the spleen, where they

> annoyeth the heart and, passing up to the brain, counterfeiteth terrible objects to the fantasy; and, polluting both the substance and spirits of the brain, causeth it without external occasion to forge monstrous fictions, and terrible to the conceit, which the judgment taking as they are presented by the disordered instrument, deliver over to the heart, which . . . giving credit to the mistaken report of the brain, breaketh out into that inordinate passion, against reason. (sig. G3v)

Bright provides a medical explanation for the "infection of [the] brains" and "*tremor cordis*," or agitation of the heart, that Leontes describes as symptoms of

---

Benedetto Varchi, *The Blazon of Jealousy: A Subject Not Written of by any Heretofore*, trans. Robert Tofte (London, 1615); STC 24593; sigs. C2v–C3v, D2v–D3r, D4v, E1v–E3v, F1r–F3v, H2v–H3r, K2r–K2v; omitting most of Tofte's marginal comments.

his jealousy (1.2.145, 110). Likewise, Robert Burton's description of a melancholic jealous man in his *Anatomy of Melancholy* (1621) could be Leontes: he "pries in every corner, follows close, observes to an hair: besides all those strange gestures of staring, frowning, grinning, rolling of eyes, menacing, ghastly looks, broken pace," and so on (sig. Uu5v). Paulina provides a layperson's medical diagnosis of Leontes' jealousy as a manifestation of "dangerous unsafe lunes" or fits of lunacy (2.2.30). Might our assessment of Leontes' rash behavior be affected by the possibility that it arises from a physical and psychological illness? Given Varchi's account of the psychology of love, is it even possible to read Leontes' jealousy sympathetically, as a melancholic consequence of his "[a]ffection" for Hermione (1.2.138)?

While the onset of Leontes' jealousy might be explained in psychological terms, the economic and social implications of adultery in this period help to explain the vehemence of his rage. If Hermione is an adulteress and Leontes' children are illegitimate, his authority as husband and king will be irreparably subverted, and he will forever be remembered with "[c]ontempt and clamor" (1.2.189). Consider the role that Varchi attributes to feelings of possessiveness in the development of jealousy, and how such feelings might contribute to Leontes' rapidly escalating suspicions. Does Leontes perceive Hermione as an active subject of desire, as an object to be owned and lost, or as both subject and object? If there is a contradiction in his perception of her, how might we account for it?

From *The Blazon of Jealousy*

And certainly, were it not but that Nature (who for many respects is thought by divers[1] to be rather a cruel stepdame[2] than a kind and loving mother) had ordained that all our sweet meats should be (ever) seasoned with sour sauce, then doubtless should every one be most happy, but above all, loyal lovers should be more blessed than the rest. But as no sweetness, no pleasure, nor happiness, are so delightful, so pleasant, nor so much desired, as that which proceedeth from love; even so again, those bitter pills, those intolerable griefs, and those disastrous mischances, or rather mischiefs, which fall out in love, exceed (beyond all comparison) all other torments and tortures whatsoever, as they who have proved,[3] and tried them, find it to be but over-true . . .

Yet will I not deny (but justify what I now speak for a most constant truth) that all those disdainful disgraces, but now spoken of, all those burn-

---

[1] **divers:** many people.   [2] **stepdame:** stepmother.   [3] **proved:** experienced.

ing martyrings, all those insupportable punishments; and to be brief, all those unspeakable bloody passions in love (yea, were they all placed in one body together) are nothing, or rather, passing pleasing and sweet, in respect of that one damned fear, or hellish suspect, or rather incurable plague and deadly poison, cleped[4] jealousy: which (coupled together with love) is no other thing, than (as hath oftentimes been delivered in this place) *a certain eager and earnest desire to enjoy the beauty of one alone, by himself only.* . . . [Varchi cites the Italian poets Ludovico Ariosto and Giovanni della Casa on the topic of jealousy.]

And therefore we will say that jealousy is a certain fear or doubt lest anyone whom we would not should enjoy a beauty that we make account of; and this, for two reasons: either because we ourselves would enjoy the same alone, or else that such a one as we like and desire might have the sole fruition and possession thereof. Nor there is no doubt but that jealousy is a spice or species of envy, and although it followeth not of necessity that wheresoever envy is, there jealousy should be, yet is it necessary that wheresoever jealousy is the precursor, there envy must be the follower always, as that which is a living creature, is not a man, and yet every man is a living creature. [Varchi cites poetry of Francesco Petrarch.] . . .

I say that they [lovers] may be jealous three manner of ways; and that jealousy may be taken after three several fashions: 1. either when we would not have that anyone should obtain that which we ourselves have already gotten; 2. or that which we wish and desire to obtain; 3. or which we have labored and endeavored, following it in chase, and yet could never gain the same. Now this jealousy springing from our own covetous mind and proper greediness to have such a thing, is after a four-fold manner, *viz.*[5]:

By reason
⎧ 1. of *pleasure.*
⎨ 2. of *passion.*
⎪ 3. of *property* or *right.*
⎩ 4. of *Honor.*

Jealousy cometh of pleasure when we estimate and prize the delight we take in the party we love at so high a rate as we would engross it wholly unto ourselves, and when we think, or imagine, it will decrease and wax less if it should be communicated or lent unto another. . . . [Varchi cites the poetry of Tibullus.] . . .

Jealousy proceedeth from passion when we covet to enjoy or possess that which we most love and like, wonderfully fearing lest we should lose the

---

[4] cleped: called.   [5] *viz.*: namely (an abbreviation of Latin, *videlicet*).

possession thereof, as if our mistress should become a secret sweet friend unto another man. And in this pitiful perplexity and case was *Propertius*,[6] as may appear, when he made this mournful and mestful[7] elegy; beginning thus:

Eripitur nobis iampridem cara Puella,
Et tu me lachrymas fundere (Amice) vetas?

My Wench is gone and stolen away,
    Whom I did love so dear,
And art my Friend, and yet forbidst,
    That I from tears forbear?

Thirdly, jealousy springeth from the property or right that we have, when we, enjoying our lady or mistress, would have her solely and wholly unto ourselves; without being able (by any means) to suffer or endure that another man should have any part or interest in her, any way, or at any time. . . . [Varchi cites a poem by Propertius.] And so puissant[8] and potent is this our desire which we have to enjoy that party which we love solely and alone, without the society and company of any other whatsoever, as that (many times) when this our high-prized commodity chanceth to light into some other merchant's hands, and that this our private enclosure proveth to be a common[9] for others, we care no more for it, but give it altogether over, quite extinguishing and quenching in us not alone the jealousy we had of the same, but likewise the hot love and affection we bore it before. . . . [Varchi cites verses of Ovid.]

Lastly, jealousy cometh in respect of a man's reputation and honor, according as his nature is, or as his breeding hath been, or after the fashion and manner of the country in which he is born and liveth, because (in this point) divers are the opinions of men, and as contrary are the customs of countries. Whereupon they say that the southern nations and such as dwell in hot regions are very jealous, either because they are much given and inclined unto love naturally, or else for that they hold it a great disparagement and scandal to have their wives or their mistresses tainted with the foul blot of unchastity, which thing those that are of contrary regions, and such as live under the North Pole, take not so deep at the heart. . . .

---

[6] **Propertius:** Sextus Propertius, a Roman poet (c. 50–c. 16 B.C.E.). *Tofte's marginal note:* When jealousy once seizeth on such weak and resistless souls (as *Propertius* was) it is pitiful to see how cruelly it tormenteth, and how insultingly it tyrannizeth over them, for of all the mind's diseases, that is it whereto most things serve for sustenance, but fewest for remedy; such a furious perturbation and moody agitation it is, which throweth them into extremities, altogether contrary to the cause.   [7] **mestful:** mournful.   [8] **puissant:** powerful.   [9] **common:** public land.

Besides, who knoweth not, but that the more one feareth, the more he is jealous? Ariosto[10] likewise setteth down the quick swiftness and the strange credulity of jealous folks, when he saith that this incurable and mortal wound is so easily imprinted in the heart of a lover. And certainly it is wonderful, and almost incredible to believe, that men should be such deadly enemies unto themselves and of their own lives — as many times they are — through these strange and foolish humors: that for one word only, or for a sign, a beck,[11] or a glance cast upon one, without as much as a thought of any ill. Nay, more, that they will (despite of their own selves) imagine and conceit that which doth so much afflict, gall,[12] and torment them incessantly, and without any rest, as if there were not properly in love other cares and troubles beside than those only, which we ourselves (without any profit or pleasure at all) seek to purchase most unseasonably every hour of the day: a gross error and a token of much insufficiency of wit. [Varchi cites a poem of Petrarch.]

But to come (where I left) to intreat of[13] jealousy, I say that this malignant spirit increaseth and decreaseth according unto the party for whose sake we are jealous. And this we do not alone in respect she is well bred, is pitiful[14] of nature, proper[15] of personage, constant, witty, discreet, modest, of few words, tender of her own reputation and honor, and other such like good parts in her, but withal likewise consider and have an eye unto even her own mother, her nurse, her sisters, and kindred, her familiars, acquaintance, and such neighbors as she converseth withal. . . . [Varchi cites a poem of Petrarch.]

Besides, the mind and condition of the lover towards the woman whom he affecteth importeth very much in this business; for if he be given to choler,[16] or is (by any other accident) discontent and displeased, he will then quickly take occasion to be angry with her, and every mote (as the proverb goeth) is a beam in his eye. . . . And therefore is it very requisite and needful that men should not be over-heady, nor rash, in their humors[17] and proceedings, but rather discreet, wary, and cool, canvassing and measuring every action and behavior of their mistresses with sound discretion and judgment, and not to be over-forward and too much credulous, or too too light of belief, without any just cause given them, which is the only reason (as we daily see) of many gross absurdities, springing and issuing from such like light and idle occasions as these. . . .

---

[10] **Ariosto:** Ludovico Ariosto (1474–1533), Italian poet and author of the romantic epic *Orlando Furioso* (1532). [11] **beck:** a nod or wave. [12] **gall:** vex. [13] **intreat of:** deal with. [14] **pitiful:** compassionate. [15] **proper:** attractive. [16] **choler:** bile, supposed to cause irascibility of temper. [17] **humors:** moods, whims.

[The jealous] always living, as it were, in a continual hell, take no rest in the day, neither can they sleep at all in the nights; but ever grieve and lament, taking on as well for that which is false as for what they stand in doubt[18] of to be true, imagining many times and conceiting[19] divers things that are altogether impossible. For this strange malady engendereth a continual and a perpetual discontentment and disquietness in the mind, so that he is not able nor hath any power to give over from vexing himself, standing always watchful with his ears wide open to hearken and listen to every word, every voice, every sound, and every wind: all which, he taketh in a wrong and sinister sense, conjecturing evermore worse of the same than he need. . . .

[Jealousy] sometimes bursteth out so far and exceedeth beyond her bounds so much as it turneth itself into extreme hatred, and from thence falleth into a frenzy, and madness, not alone against the party it loveth, or his adversary or rival, but as well against all such, who, as he thinks, may be any way an obstacle or let[20] to hinder or cross him in his design and purpose; whereupon have ensued most cruel revengements, and most horrible and savage murders, beyond all common sense and reason. Yea, many times against their own reputations and honors, and against their own proper selves and lives, as we may see and read in histories, as well ancient as modern, and as poets in their fictions and shadows show more at large.

[18] doubt: fear.   [19] conceiting: believing.   [20] let: hindrance.

→ MICHAEL DALTON

From The Country Justice   *1618*

Trained as a lawyer in London's Inns of Court, Michael Dalton left a mark on his profession with the 1618 publication of *The Country Justice*, a legal guidebook for local magistrates and justices of the peace. A very popular text, it was reprinted multiple times during the seventeenth and eighteenth centuries. Dalton cites statutes and offers procedural advice about various crimes and misdemeanors relevant to *The Winter's Tale*, such as bastardy, theft, and murder, but his discussions of treason and petty treason, excerpted below, have particular application to Leontes' legal proceedings against Hermione.

Michael Dalton, *The Country Justice, Containing the Practice of the Justices of the Peace out of Their Sessions* (London, 1618), STC 6205; sigs. S3v, S6r–T1v.

Thanks to its concise style, Dalton's *The Country Justice* articulates the patriarchal assumptions of English Renaissance society in a particularly direct way. The excerpts that follow show that murder was defined and punished differently depending on who killed whom. In which circumstances was murder simply "murder" and in which circumstances was it "petty treason"? What are the implications of defining particular crimes as acts of "petty treason"? Also notice that whereas for men the punishment for petty treason (hanging) was less severe than that for high treason (drawing and quartering), for women the punishments for petty treason and high treason were the same (burning at the stake). What do these discrepancies suggest about the cultural significance attributed to crimes by women?

The hypothetical cases Dalton records of wives and servants who conspire to murder the master of the house starkly reveal cultural anxieties about what Frances Dolan calls "dangerous familiars," threats to patriarchal authority from within the domestic sphere. Do such anxieties seem to inform Leontes' jealous fantasies? How different, after all, are Dalton's formulaic lists of "hypothetical" domestic crimes and Leontes' paranoid rants? If Leontes manifests a "diseased opinion" about domestic treachery (1.2.296), does Dalton provide a reasonable, disinterested perspective on the need for vigilance over one's domestic inferiors?

From *The Country Justice*

HIGH TREASON

High treason (called in law *crimen lese majestatis*[1]) is a grievous offense, done or attempted against the estate regal, *viz.*,[2] against the king (the head, life, and ruler of the commonwealth) in his person, the queen his wife, his children, realm, or authority, as:

To compass[3] the death of the king, the queen his wife, or of their eldest son and heir.

To intend or imagine their or any of their deaths, though they bring it not to effect, *sc.*[4] if they shall declare this by any open act, whereby it may be known, or to utter it by words or letters.

To intend to deprive[5] the king or to say that he will be king after the king's death, etc. . . .

For high treason, the offender shall be hanged, cut down alive and quartered, and he shall forfeit all his lands and goods, etc., to the king, yea at this

---

[1] *crimen lese majestatis*: a crime against the sovereign [Latin]. [2] *viz.*: namely (an abbreviation of *videlicet* [Latin]). [3] **compass**: contrive. [4] *sc.*: that is to say (an abbreviation of *scilicet* [Latin]). [5] **deprive**: depose.

day his lands entailed[6] shall be forfeited . . . and his wife shall lose her dower,[7] and his blood shall be corrupted,[8] saving in certain cases. . . .

PETTY TREASON

Petty treason is when willful murder is committed (in the estate oeconomical[9]) upon any subject by one that is in subjection, and oweth faith, duty, and obedience to the party murdered, as in these cases following:

If a servant maliciously killeth his or her master or mistress; this was petty treason by the Common Law . . .

The wife maliciously killeth her husband; this is petty treason.

The husband maliciously killeth his wife; this is but murder.

The reason of this difference is for that the one is in subjection and oweth obedience, and not the other.

The wife and a servant do conspire to kill the husband, and he[10] killeth him in the wife's absence; this is petty treason in them both.

The wife and a stranger do conspire to kill her husband, and he killeth her husband in the wife's absence; this is no petty treason in the wife, but murder in the stranger, and she shall be hanged as accessory to murder.

Also where the wife or servant (procuring, conspiring, or practicing such murder) at the time of such murder is in the same house, though they be not present thereat but are in another room; yet it is petty treason in them, as it seemeth by two cases reported by Master Crompton[11] in *4 and 5 Marie*.[12]

The wife poisoneth a thing, to the intent to poison her husband therewith, the husband eateth of it and becometh very sick thereof, but recovereth; after, a stranger eateth thereof and dieth thereof; this is only murder in the wife.

The wife poisoneth an apple, to the intent to poison a stranger therewith, and layeth it (to that purpose) in a secret place, and the husband by chance eateth of it and dieth thereof within a year and a day; this is petty treason in the wife, for that she intended murder thereby.

The wife poisoneth an apple or other thing and delivereth it to B. (knowing nothing of the poison) to give to C. and B. giveth it to the husband (without the assent of the wife) who eateth thereof in the wife's absence, and he dieth thereof; this is petty treason in the wife. . . .

---

[6] **entailed:** bequeathed to a series of heirs.   [7] **dower:** the portion of a deceased husband's estate that the law allows to his widow for her life.   [8] **blood shall be corrupted:** "tainted" blood deprived the criminal and his heirs of rank, title, and possession of land.   [9] **oeconomical:** domestic.   [10] **he:** the servant.   [11] **Master Crompton:** Richard Crompton (fl. 1573–1599), London lawyer and legal writer.   [12] *4 and 5 Marie*: statutes passed during the reign of Queen Mary I of England.

The punishment of petty treason is this: the man so offending shall be drawn[13] and hanged; the woman shall be burned alive, in case as well for petty treason, as of high treason. . . . But in case of felonies, the judgment both of the man and woman is to be hanged.

[13] **drawn:** dragged on a hurdle to the place of execution.

⇥ THOMAS BAYLY HOWELL

From A Complete Collection of State Trials   *1809–26*

The excerpt below comes from a chapter on the "Trials of Queen Anna Boleyn, and her Brother Lord Viscount Rochford, for High Treason" in Thomas Bayly Howell's twenty-one-volume *Collection of State Trials*, the standard reference work on trials for high treason in England from 1163 to 1783. The materials for this collection were originally gathered by William Cobbett, an early-nineteenth-century journalist who printed a weekly political newsletter attacking industrialism. When Cobbett was imprisoned for libel in 1810, Howell, a young English lawyer, took over the job of editing the collection. In his chapter on Anne Boleyn's trial, Howell includes passages from three different sources: an anonymous account of the trial in the British Museum's Harleian Manuscripts that was compiled from sixteenth- and seventeenth-century printed chronicles; the *Memorials of Thomas Cranmer, Archbishop of Canterbury* (1694), by church historian John Strype (1643–1737); and the *History of the Reformation in England* (1679) by bishop and historian Gilbert Burnet (1643–1715). Burnet's narrative of the trial itself compiles information not only from sixteenth- and seventeenth-century printed chronicles, but also from several contemporary manuscript sources: various letters, journal entries by the sixteenth-century historian Henry Spelman, and a chronicle of the years 1522–58 by Anthony Anthony, a military administrator in the Tower of London.

The existence of varying accounts of these events foregrounds the problems of evidence and interpretation that often vex the historical record. Our only access to Anne's downfall comes through the mediation of a series of texts, some of which are based on earlier texts. Much like a Shakespearean play, these historical texts shape their raw materials into an intelligible narrative through the selection, arrangement, and omission of various details.

Howell's account of Anne's trial — taken from Burnet's *History* — proves so illuminating for *The Winter's Tale* precisely because it demonstrates the limitations,

Thomas Bayly Howell, *A Complete Collection of State Trials and Proceedings for High Treason and Other Crimes and Misdemeanors*, 21 vols. (London, 1809–26), vol. 1, pp. 411–23.

biases, and ambiguities at work in the process of interpreting the motives, words, and actions of a queen accused of sexual impropriety. Just as Leontes reads erotic meanings into Hermione's words and gestures, Anne's contemporaries made judgments about her chastity based on observations, reports, rumors, and assumptions. In the account below, what kind of evidence is presented to make claims for Anne's guilt or innocence, and how reliable is this evidence? Which factors seem to carry the most weight in ultimately determining Anne's guilt? During her own trial, Hermione shrewdly observes that her self-defense can hardly be persuasive when her judge has already concluded that her "integrity" is "falsehood" (3.2.23–24). Is Anne's trial also a sham, or is it more legitimate than Hermione's?

As queens, Anne and Hermione are exceptional figures, yet it is important to recognize in their trials the association between sexual transgression and social transgression that could be used against any woman in this period. Despite the outlandish elements of *The Winter's Tale*, it is conceivable that certain playgoers identified with Hermione as an unjustly slandered woman. The lessons to be drawn from such identification are harder to determine. Does the play generally indict patriarchal power and its recourse to the law? Or are we left with the impression that Leontes cynically exploits a legal system that might otherwise work to maintain sexual and social order?

From *A Complete Collection of State Trials*

In January 1536, the queen brought forth a dead son. This was thought to have made ill impressions on the king: and that, as he concluded from the death of his sons by the former queen,[1] that the marriage was displeasing to God, so he might upon this misfortune begin to make the like judgment of his marriage. Sure enough, the popish party[2] were earnestly set against the queen, looking on her as the great supporter of heresy[3] . . . But the Duke of Norfolk at court, and Gardiner[4] beyond sea, thought there might easily be found a mean to accommodate the king, both with the emperor[5] and the pope, if the queen were once out of the way; for then he might freely marry any one whom he pleased, and that marriage, with the male issue of it, could not be disputed. Whereas, as long as the queen lived, her marriage, as being

---

[1] **the former queen:** Katherine of Aragon (1485–1536), Henry's first wife.   [2] **popish party:** the Roman Catholic faction at court.   [3] **heresy:** i.e., the Protestant Reformation; Anne's avid evangelicalism challenged Catholic orthodoxy.   [4] **Gardiner:** Stephen Gardiner (c. 1495–1555), bishop of Winchester, who at the time was serving as ambassador to France.   [5] **emperor:** the Holy Roman Emperor, King Charles V of Spain (1500–1558), nephew of Katherine of Aragon.

judged null from the beginning,[6] could never be allowed by the court of Rome, or any of that party.

With these reasons of state, others of affection concurred. The queen had been his wife three years, but at this time he entertained a secret love for Jane Seymour, who had all the charms both of beauty and youth in her person; and her humor was tempered, between the severe gravity of queen Katherine, and the gay pleasantness of queen Anne. The queen, perceiving this alienation of the king's heart, used all possible arts to recover that affection, of whose decay she was sadly sensible. But the success was quite contrary to what she designed. For the king saw her no more with those eyes, which she had formerly captivated; but grew jealous, and ascribed these caresses to some other criminal affections, of which he began to suspect her. . . .

She was of a very cheerful temper, which was not always limited within the bounds of exact decency and discretion. She had rallied[7] some of the king's servants more than became her. Her brother, the Lord Rochford, was her friend as well as brother, but his spiteful wife was jealous of him. And being a woman of no sort of virtue (as will appear afterwards by her serving queen Katherine Howard in her beastly practices, for which she was attainted and executed[8]), she carried many stories to the king, or some about him, to persuade him that there was a familiarity between the queen and her brother, beyond what so near a relation could justify. All that could be said for it, was only this: that he was once seen leaning upon her bed, which bred great suspicion. Henry Norris, that was groom of the stool,[9] Weston, and Brereton, that were of the king's privy-chamber, and one Mark Smeton, a musician, were all observed to have much of her favor; and their zeal in serving her was thought too warm and diligent to flow from a less active principle than love.

Many circumstances were brought to the king, which working upon his aversion to the queen, together with his affection for mistress Seymour, made him conclude her guilty. Yet somewhat which himself observed, or fancied, at a tilting[10] at Greenwich is believed to have given the crisis to her

---

[6] **being judged null from the beginning:** two days before her execution, Anne's marriage to Henry was declared null and void, perhaps on the grounds of incest: Anne's older sister Mary had been Henry's mistress during the king's marriage to Katherine of Aragon; but see below, pp. 218–19.   [7] **rallied:** exchanged pleasantries with.   [8] **Katherine Howard . . . executed:** The fifth wife of Henry VIII, Katherine Howard (c. 1524–1542) was executed for adultery in 1542 under the charge of high treason. The Lady Rochford, widow of Anne Boleyn's brother George, was also executed as Katherine's accomplice.   [9] **groom of the stool:** the chief member of the king's privy chamber, or body of personal servants.   [10] **tilting:** a joust or ceremonial combat.

ruin. It is said that he spied her let her handkerchief fall to one of her gallants to wipe his face, being hot after a course. Whether she dropped it carelessly or of design, or whether there be any truth in that story, the letters concerning her fall making no mention of it, I cannot determine. For Spelman[11] makes no mention of it, and gives a very different account of the discovery in these words: "As for the evidence of this matter, it was discovered by the Lady Wingfield, who had been a servant to the queen, and becoming on a sudden infirm some time before her death, did swear this matter to one of her —" and here unluckily the rest of the page is torn off. By this it seems there was no legal evidence against the queen, and that it was but a witness at second hand who deposed what they heard the Lady Wingfield swear. Who this person was we know not, nor in what temper of mind the Lady Wingfield might be, when she swore it. The safest sort of forgery, to one whose conscience can swallow it, is to lay a thing on a dead person's name, when there is no fear of discovery before the great day;[12] and when it was understood that the queen had lost the king's heart, many, either out of their zeal to popery, or design to make their fortune, might be easily induced to carry a story of this nature. And this it seems was that which was brought to the king at Greenwich, who did thereupon immediately return to Whitehall, it being the first of May.

The queen was immediately restrained to her chamber; the other five were also seized on, but none of them would confess anything but "Mark Smeton, as to any actual thing," so Cromwell[13] writ. Upon this they were carried to the Tower. The poor queen was in a sad condition: she must not only fall under the king's displeasure, but be both defamed and destroyed at once. At first she smiled and carried it cheerfully, and said she believed the king did this only to prove[14] her. But when she saw it was in earnest, she desired to have the sacrament in her closet, and expressed great devotion, and seemed to be prepared for death.

[Several contemporary letters reporting Anne's experiences in the Tower testify to her mental anguish and protestations of innocence. A few members of the king's council convince Anne that Norris and Mark had accused her of infidelity.] The same letter says that Norris had not accused her; and that he said to her almoner[15] that he could swear for her "she was a good woman." But she being made believe that he had accused her, and not being then so free in her thoughts as to consider that ordinary artifice for drawing

---

[11] **Spelman:** Henry Spelman, sixteenth-century historian whose journal entries furnish much of Burnet's information.   [12] **the great day:** Judgment Day.   [13] **Cromwell:** Thomas Cromwell (c. 1485–1540), chief minister to Henry VIII and architect of the English Reformation.   [14] **prove:** test.   [15] **almoner:** a clergyman in the royal household.

out confessions, told all she knew both of him and Mark. Which though it was not enough to destroy her, yet certainly wrought much on the jealous and alienated king. She told them "that she once asked Norris, why he did not go on with his marriage?" Who answered her "that he would yet tarry[16] some time." To which she replied, "You look for dead men's shoes; for if aught come to the king but good, you would look to have me." He answered "if he had any such thought, he would his head were cut off." Upon which she said "she could undo him if she pleased, and thereupon she fell out with him." As for Mark, who was then laid in irons, she said he was never in her chamber, but when the king was last at Winchester; and then he came in to play on the virginals.[17] She said that "she never spoke to him after that, but on Saturday before May-day, when she saw him standing in the window, and then she asked him why he was so sad." He said it was no matter. She answered, "You may not look to have me speak to you, as if you were a nobleman, since you are an inferior person." "No, no, madam," said he, "a look sufficeth me." She seemed more apprehensive of Weston than of anybody. For on Whitsun Monday last he said to her "that Norris came more to her chamber upon her account, than for anybody else that was there." She had observed that he loved a kinswoman of hers, and challenged him for it, and for not loving his wife. But he answered her "that there were women in the house, whom he loved better than them both." She asked, "Who is that?" "Yourself," said he; upon which she said "she defied him."

[Sympathetic towards Anne, Thomas Cranmer, Archbishop of Canterbury, writes a letter to Henry in her defense.] But jealousy, and the king's new affection, had quite defaced all the remainders of esteem for his late beloved queen. Yet the ministers continued practicing to get further evidence for the trial, which was not brought on till the twelfth of May; and then Norris, Weston, Brereton, and Smeton were tried by a commission of oyer and terminer[18] in Westminster-Hall. They were twice indicted, and the indictments were found by two grand juries, in the counties of Kent and Middlesex; the crimes with which they were charged being said to be done in both those counties. Mark Smeton confessed he had known the queen carnally three times. The other three pleaded "not guilty." But the jury, upon the evidence formerly mentioned, found them all guilty, and judgment was given that they should be drawn to the place of execution, and some of them to be hanged, others to be beheaded, and all to be quartered, as guilty of high treason.

---

[16] **tarry:** wait. [17] **virginals:** a keyboard instrument. [18] **commission of oyer and terminer:** a commission authorizing a circuit judge to hold courts; from a variation of the French for "to hear and to determine."

On the fifteenth of May, the queen and her brother the Lord Rochford (who was a peer, having been made a viscount when his father was created Earl of Wiltshire) were brought to be tried by their peers. . . . Here the queen of England by an unheard-of precedent was brought to the bar and indicted of high treason. The crimes charged on her were "that she had procured her brother and the other four to lie with her, which they had done often; that she had said to them that the king never had her heart; and had said to every one of them by themselves that she loved them better than any person whatsoever. Which was to the slander of the issue[19] that was begotten between the king and her." And this was treason, according to the statute made in the twenty-sixth year of this reign (so that the law, that was made for her and the issue of her marriage, is now made use of to destroy her). It was also added in the indictment that she and her complices[20] "had conspired the king's death." But this, it seems, was only put in to swell the charge, for if there had been any evidence for it, there was no need of stretching the other statute; or if they could have proved the violating of the queen, the known statute of the twenty-fifth year of the reign of Edward III had been sufficient.

When the indictment was read, she held up her head and pleaded not guilty, and so did her brother, and did answer the evidence was brought against her discreetly. One thing is remarkable: that Mark Smeton, who was the only person that confessed anything, was never confronted with the queen, nor was kept to be an evidence against her; for he had received his sentence three days before, and so could be no witness in law. But, perhaps, though he was wrought on[21] to confess, yet they did not think he had confidence enough to aver[22] it to the queen's face. Therefore the evidence they brought, as Spelman says, was the oath of a woman that was dead. Yet this, or rather the terror of offending the king, so wrought on the lords that they found her and her brother guilty; and judgment was given that she should be burnt or beheaded at the king's pleasure. Upon which Spelman observes that, whereas burning is the death which the law appoints for a woman that is attainted of treason, yet since she had been queen of England, they left it to the king to determine whether she should die so infamous a death or be beheaded. But the judges complained of this way of proceeding, and said such a disjunctive[23] in a judgment of treason had never been seen. The Lord Rochford was also condemned to be beheaded and quartered.

Yet all this did not satisfy the enraged king, but the marriage between him and her must be annulled, and the issue illegitimated. [To justify an

[19] **the issue:** the princess Elizabeth, future Queen Elizabeth I.   [20] **complices:** accomplices.
[21] **wrought on:** pressured or possibly tortured.   [22] **aver:** declare.   [23] **disjunctive:** alternative.

annulment of his marriage, the king and his counselors had tried to get the earl of Northumberland to confess to a prior promise of marriage to Anne, but he denied it. Nor, before a sentence of death was passed against her, could they get Anne to confess to a previous marriage contract.] But now she lying under so terrible a sentence, it is most probable that either some hopes of life were given her, or at least she was wrought on by the assurances of mitigating that cruel part of her judgment, of being burnt, into the milder part of the sentence, of having her head cut off; so that she confessed a pre-contract. And on the seventeenth of May was brought to Lambeth, and in court, the afflicted archbishop sitting judge, some persons of quality being present, she confessed some just and lawful impediments by which it was evident that her marriage with the king was not valid. Upon which confession, her marriage between the king and her was judged to have been null and void. The record of the sentence is burnt; but these particulars are repeated in the act that passed in the next parliament, touching the succession to the crown. It seems this was secretly done, for Spelman writes of it thus: it was said, there was a divorce made between the king and her, upon her confessing to a pre-contract with another before her marriage with the king; so that it was then only talked of, but not generally known.

The two sentences that were passed upon the queen — the one of attainder[24] for adultery, the other of divorce because of a pre-contract — did so contradict one another, that it was apparent, one, if not both, of them must be unjust. For if the marriage between the king and her was null from the beginning, then since she was not the king's wedded wife there could be no adultery. And her marriage to the king was either a true marriage, or not: if it was true, then the annulling of it was unjust; and if it was no true marriage, then the attainder was unjust, for there could be no breach of that faith which was never given. So that it is plain: the king was resolved to be rid of her, and to illegitimate her daughter, and in that transport of his fury did not consider that the very method he took discovered the injustice of his proceedings against her.

Two days after this, she was ordered to be executed in the green on Tower-Hill. How she received these tidings, and how steadfast she continued in the protestations of her innocence, will best appear by the following circumstances. The day before she suffered, upon a strict search of her past life, she called to mind that she had played the step-mother too severely to Lady Mary,[25] and had done her many injuries. Upon which, she made the

---

[24] **attainder**: condemnation for treason.   [25] **Mary**: Mary Tudor (1516–1558), daughter of Henry VIII and Katherine of Aragon, the future Queen Mary I (1553–1558).

lieutenant of the Tower's lady sit down in the chair of state;[26] which the other, after some ceremony, doing, she fell down on her knees, and with many tears charged the lady, as she would answer it to God, to go in her name and do as she had done to the Lady Mary, and ask her forgiveness for the wrongs she had done her. And she said, she had no quiet in her conscience till she had done that. But though she did in this what became a Christian, the Lady Mary could not so easily pardon these injuries, but retained the resentment of them her whole life.

This ingenuity and tenderness of conscience about lesser matters is a great presumption[27] that, if she had been guilty of more eminent faults, she had not continued to the last day denying them, and making protestations of her innocency. . . .

A little before noon, being the 19th of May, she was brought to the scaffold, where she made a short speech to a great company that came to look on the last scene of this fatal tragedy. . . . "She said, she was come to die, as she was judged by the law; she would accuse none, nor say anything of the ground upon which she was judged. She prayed heartily for the king; and called him a most merciful and gentle prince, and that he had been always to her a good, gentle, sovereign lord, and if any would meddle with her cause, she required them to judge the best. And so she took her leave of them, and of the world; and heartily desired they would pray for her" . . .

These proceedings occasioned as great variety of censures as there were diversity of interests. The popish party said the justice of God was visible: that she who had supplanted Queen Katherine met with the like — and harder — measure by the same means. Some took notice of her faint justifying herself on the scaffold, as if her conscience had then prevailed so far that she could no longer deny a thing for which she was so soon to answer at another tribunal. But others thought her care of her daughter made her speak so tenderly, for she had observed that Queen Katherine's obstinacy had drawn the king's indignation on her daughter. She spake in a style that could give the king no just offense, and as she said enough to justify herself, so she said as much for the king's honor as could be expected. Yet in a letter that she wrote to the king from the Tower (which will be found in the Collection), she pleaded her innocence in a strain of so much wit, and moving passionate eloquence, as perhaps can scarce be paralleled: certainly her spirits were much exalted when she wrote it, for it is a pitch above her ordinary style. Yet the copy I take it from, lying among Cromwell's other papers, makes me believe it was truly written by her.

Her carriage[28] seemed too free, and all people thought that some free-

---

[26] **chair of state:** ceremonial chair or throne. [27] **presumption:** ground for belief. [28] **carriage:** deportment.

doms and levities in her had encouraged those unfortunate persons to speak such bold things of her, since few attempt upon the chastity, or make declarations of love, to persons of so exalted a quality, except they see some invitations, at least in their carriage. Others thought that a free and jovial temper might, with great innocence, though with no discretion, lead one to all those things that were proved against her; and therefore they concluded her chaste, though indiscreet. Others blamed the king, and taxed his cruelty in proceeding so severely against a person whose chastity he had reason to be assured of, since she had resisted his addresses near five years, till he legitimated them by marriage. But others excused him. It is certain her carriage had given just cause of some jealousy, and that being the rage of a man, it was no wonder if a king of his temper, conceiving it against one whom he had so signally obliged, was transported into unjustifiable excesses. Others condemned Cranmer, as a man that obsequiously followed all the king's appetites; and that he had now divorced the king a second time, which showed that his conscience was governed by the king's pleasure as his supreme law. But what he did was unavoidable. For whatever motives drew from her the confession of that pre-contract, he was obliged to give sentence upon it; and that which she confessed, being such as made her incapable to contract marriage with the king, he could not decline the giving of sentence upon so formal a confession. . . .

Some have since that time concluded it a great evidence of her guilt that during her daughter's long and glorious reign there was no full nor complete vindication of her published. For the writers of that time thought it enough to speak honorably of her and, in general, to call her innocent, but none of them ever attempted a clear discussion of the particulars laid to her charge. This had been much to her daughter's honor, and therefore since it was not done, others concluded it could not be done; and that their knowledge of her guilt restrained their pens. But others do not at all allow of[29] that inference, and think rather that it was the great wisdom of that time not to suffer such things to be called in question, since no wise government will admit of a debate about the clearness of the prince's title. For the very attempting to prove it weakens it more than any of the proofs that are brought can confirm it; therefore it was prudently done of that queen and her great ministers never to suffer any vindication or apology to be written. Some indiscretions could not be denied, and these would all have been catched hold of and improved[30] by the busy emissaries of Rome and Spain.

---

[29] **allow of:** accept. [30] **improved:** aggravated; the implication is that England's Catholic enemies (Rome and Spain) would have seized upon any opportunity to impugn Elizabeth's legitimacy as monarch by exaggerating the crimes of her mother.

Death of Children

The Prince your son . . . is gone. (3.2.139–40)

A rare occurrence in Shakespeare's plays, the death of a child is usually marked by impassioned expressions of grief. In *Richard III*, even the "bloody dogs" who murder the king's young nephews "[m]elted with tenderness and mild compassion, / Wept like two children in their deaths' sad story" (4.3.6–8). The murdered children's mother, Queen Elizabeth, poignantly laments, "Ah, my poor princes! Ah, my tender babes! / My unblown flowers, new-appearing sweets" (4.4.9–10). In *Macbeth*, Macduff openly grieves over the murder of his wife and children, despite the military code that regards weeping as unmanly: "All my pretty ones? / Did you say all? O hell-kite! All? / What, all my pretty chickens and their dam / At one fell swoop?" (4.3.217–20).

Although Mamillius's death is certainly less gruesome than that of the children in *Richard III* and *Macbeth*, it is nonetheless a shocking and terrible loss that generates surprisingly little expression of grief. A servant simply reports that the prince "is gone . . . Is dead" (3.2.140). Unlike the grieving parents in *Richard III* and *Macbeth*, Leontes expresses neither sorrow nor amazement at the news of his son's death; instead, he interprets it as a sign of divine anger, confesses the folly of his behavior, and elaborates his regret at the loss of Camillo. While empathizing with Mamillius's suffering, Paulina reserves her sharpest outcry for the supposed death of Hermione: "cry woe! The Queen, the Queen, / The sweet'st, dear'st creature's dead, and vengeance for't / Not dropped down yet" (3.2.195–97). At this point, Leontes acknowledges regret for the deaths of his wife and son, promising to shed daily tears at their graves. There is no more talk of Mamillius until act 5, when Dion addresses the "dangers" the kingdom has incurred by Leontes' "fail of issue" (5.1.27). Throughout the last act, Mamillius is never named but only alluded to in talk of the king's "lost" son and daughter. What do we make of the apparent inconsistency between Leontes' fury at his wife's supposed betrayal and his emotionally taciturn response to his son's death? How might a contemporary audience have expected a prince to be mourned and memorialized?

In 1612, about a year after the first performance of *The Winter's Tale*, Prince Henry, King James's eldest son and heir to the English throne, died suddenly at the age of eighteen. The high expectations for Henry's glorious deeds as future king, bitterly rehearsed in elegies such as Robert Allyne's poem below, recall the laudatory discussion of Mamillius in the first scene of *The Winter's Tale*, yet Mamillius is significantly younger than Henry, who

FIGURE 12 *Marcus Gheeraerts the Younger,* Anne, Lady Pope with Her Children *(1596). From this portrait, what conclusions can be drawn about the cultural construction of children's gender identity in early modern England?*

was seventeen when *The Winter's Tale* was first staged. Although the play never specifies Mamillius's age, we can infer that he is about seven years old — still very much a little boy. It is not entirely clear in what ways this "gallant child" shows such promise as the future king (1.1.29–30). Perhaps Mamillius represents a particular type of prince (as Prince Hal in Shakespeare's *Henry IV, Part 1* can be said to represent the type of the prodigal son). If so, which "princely" qualities does Mamillius seem to represent, and how might his death point to the loss of these qualities in the Sicilian court? Or perhaps the play's original audiences understood Mamillius as a flattering portrait of Henry at a younger age.

Thanks to William Haydon's 1634 biography of Prince Henry, excerpted on p. 229, we do possess an account of Henry's character when he was about the same age as Mamillius. Both Shakespeare and Haydon suggest that an awareness of gender roles significantly marked the childhoods of young boys in early modern England. Mamillius's interactions with his mother and her ladies-in-waiting reflect the association between childhood and femininity in early modern England. Women were responsible for the care of young boys and girls alike, and until about age six or seven, when boys were "breeched" or allowed to wear the short pants that signified male gender, they wore the same skirts as young girls. Observing Mamillius, Leontes recalls his own appearance at that age when he was "unbreeched, / In my green velvet coat, my dagger muzzled" (1.2.155–56). Because of the common gendering of young boys and girls, in Renaissance portraits of children it is sometimes difficult to identify the subject's gender (Figure 12).

Breeching, which formally marked the transition to the next stage of childhood, often coincided in aristocratic families "with a shift from the nursery and women's care to male tutors and attendants" (Snyder 2). Susan Snyder theorizes that delaying breeching until six or seven "allowed for the dissolution of what modern psychologists call symbiosis, the child's early implication with the maternal figure, out of which a separate identity emerges only gradually" (4). Torn from his mother before having formed his own identity, Mamillius never appears again on stage. The documents that follow suggest many different ways of approaching the emotional and political implications of his abiding absence from the play.

ROBERT ALLYNE

From Funeral Elegies upon the Most Lamentable and Untimely Death of the Thrice Illustrious Prince Henry, Prince of Wales *1613*

In contrast to the reticence that greets Mamillius's death, the title page of Allyne's poem eulogizing the death of Prince Henry declares that *"[i]am neque saxa silent"* [now not even the stone will be silent], implying a universal outcry of grief. That Allyne dedicates his *Funeral Elegies* to Sir Thomas Erskene, a gentleman of the privy chamber and hence an intimate of the late prince, indicates that he had some familiarity with affairs at court. In the same year, Allyne also published a poem honoring Henry's sister Elizabeth, who had recently married: *Tears of Joy Shed at the Happy Departure from Great Britain of the Two Paragons of the Christian World, Frederick and Elizabeth, Prince and Princess Palatines* (1613). As no further biographical information about Allyne seems to exist, it is not possible to say with certainty what his precise connection to the royal family might have been. Nonetheless, his *Funeral Elegies* is worthwhile for its vivid analysis of the political consequences of Prince Henry's death.

Henry had provided comfort to English Protestants who resented King James's conciliatory stance towards Catholic powers in Europe, especially Spain, and his death was a severe blow to advocates of a more militant foreign policy. As Roy Strong writes, "The flood of literature that attended his departure far exceeded that for Gloriana [Queen Elizabeth] in quantity, and in theme it matched that which mourned the passing of another quintessential perfect Protestant Knight, Sir Philip Sidney" (220). In contrast to his father, Henry did not enjoy sedentary intellectual pursuits, despised hunting, and delighted in militaristic exercises (Strong 13–15). Like many fathers, Leontes proudly regards his son as a "copy" or "collop" (piece) of himself (1.2.122,137), but King James had reason to be embarrassed and even alarmed by the popularity of a charismatic son whose character, interests, and political positions diverged so sharply from his own. How does Allyne's poem negotiate the fine line between praising Henry and risking offense to King James?

In terms of the patrilineal succession so crucial to the orderly transfer of royal power in Shakespeare's England, Mamillius's death creates a much direr political situation for Sicilia than Henry's death did for England, since it leaves Leontes without an heir. Does the Sicilian court turn to what Allyne calls "true repentance" in the hopes that religious piety might "yet restore / This darkened island to her former glore [glory]"? Do Shakespeare and Allyne have a similar understanding of the relative role of spiritual and political consolations in coming to

Robert Allyne, *Funeral Elegies upon the Most Lamentable and Untimely Death of the Thrice Illustrious Prince Henry, Prince of Wales* (London, 1613); STC 384; sigs. A4r–B1v.

terms with the death of a prince? In the face of tragic loss, where can consolation be found: in time, in faith, in the symbolic power of the monarchy, in the hope offered by another heir, in collective mourning, or even in silence?

From *Funeral Elegies*

Go death, and mount in victories amain,[1]
Disperse thy conquests in a woeful volume
Amongst th'insulting sons of Ottomain,[2]
How Christendom hath lost her chiefest column.
    Haply those paynims[3] shall applaud the same,
    And raise eternal trophies of thy shame.   5
Go dull the ears of antichristian[4] Rome
With sweeter music than the earth can yield,
Whose bowels did late within her breast consume
To see great Britain's heir to brave the field   10
    Against proud Babel, and her champion Spain,
    T'have brought the Gospel in request again.
Tell thou hast brought to his untimely tomb
One who in time had comed[5] t'have worn the crown
Of Britain, and thrown down the walls of Rome,   15
And laid them level with the lowest ground.
    And all that envied at great Britain's bliss
    Shall change their mourning, and rejoice at this.
But Britain shall consume her self in tears,
And bathe her woeful face in floods of brine,[6]   20
Nor shall the date[7] of days, nor months, nor years
Confine her grief, until by grace divine
    Our young succeeding Prince[8] express in time
    The high worth which the world expect'd of him.
And oh (God grant) he may perform no less,   25
Nay rather may so far exceed his brother,

---

[1] **amain:** with full force. [2] **Ottomain:** referring to the Ottoman Empire established by Othman I in the thirteenth century and expanded to include all of Asia Minor, the Balkans, the Crimea, Iraq, Syria, Palestine, west and south Arabia, Egypt, Libya, and Tunisia until its collapse during World War I (1914–18). [3] **paynims:** pagans, non-Christians. [4] **antichristian:** because Catholic, not Protestant. [5] **had comed:** would have come. [6] **brine:** salt water, tears. [7] **date:** duration. [8] **our young succeeding Prince:** the twelve-year-old Charles, who became heir to the throne upon his brother Henry's death; Charles succeeded to the throne when King James died in 1625.

As he in highest gifts of hopefulness
And princely virtues did surpass all other.
    That once great Britain and the world may utter
    That Henry died but to admit his better.   30
And truly if the eye, and brow, and face,
Do not deceive the sense with false conceits,
Which bear I know not what majestic grace,
But greater far than shines in lower states.
    How far the lion's looks exceeds the lamb's,   35
    So far thy show, brave Prince, excels a man's.
If these deceive not, as indeed they do not,
These rules of phisnomy[9] cannot wrong inform.
What though thy years do promise what they owe not,
Yet more than they have promised they'll perform.   40
    And (oh would God) I might but live to see
    That hope effect'd which all conceive of thee.
That yet our barbarous en'mies in the East,
Within the empire of old Babylon,
And that proud mystic Babel in the West,   45
That holds the cup of fornication[10]
    By whose vile dregs the kings on earth are drunk,
    May be in deep of dark confusion sunk.
. . . .

God grant our sins procure[11] no greater wrath
Upon our heads, but that we once may turn   80
To true repentance, by a lively faith,
And for our many sins sincerely mourn,
    That God may in his mercy yet restore
    This darkened island to her former glore.
And in the person of our tender prince   85
Renew those lamps of discontinued light,
Which have been drowned in darkness ever since
That worthy prince did bid the world goodnight.
    Let never this small isle, while heavens remain,
    Be dark'd with such a dire eclipse again.   90
And though the bravest branch be cut away,

---

[9] **phisnomy:** physiognomy, the art of judging character from studying the face. [10] **cup of fornication:** an allusion to the Whore of Babylon described in Revelation 17–18, which English Protestants typically interpreted as a figure of the Roman Catholic Church (that "proud mystic Babel"). [11] **procure:** bring about.

Yet seat the root most steadfast in his place,
To shine from Thames, to Trent, to Forth, and Tay,[12]
Eternal in his never ruined race.[13]
From whence while earth endures may still be one
To rule th'united Isle of Albion.[14]   95
So long as Tay, and Forth, and Trent, and Thames
Irrigates this isle with crystal streams.

[12] **Thames, Trent, Forth,** and **Tay:** rivers in England.   [13] **race:** lineage.   [14] **Isle of Albion:**
Great Britain.

→   WILLIAM HAYDON [W. H.]

From The True Picture and Relation of Prince Henry His Noble and Virtuous Disposition   *1634*

The True Picture and Relation of Prince Henry offers a tantalizing glimpse into
the behavior and speeches of a young Renaissance prince. According to its title
page, the book was written by "a famous doctor of physic in French, and newly
translated into English." Its author "is almost certainly William Haydon, the
most senior Groom of the Bedchamber" (Strong 11). Roy Strong describes *The
True Picture* as "a disconnected compilation of anecdotes lacking narrative structure . . . clearly written by someone close to the Prince's circle but not cognizant
of its inner political affiliations and workings" (11). Whether or not Haydon
accurately reports what Prince Henry literally said and did, he provides a fascinating record of the kind of conduct and outlook that might plausibly be attributed to a prince of about Mamillius's age.

Like Mamillius, Prince Henry spent the first years of his life in the care of
women, until his father decided that he was old enough to be placed with a male
tutor. In *The Life and Death of Our Most Incomparable and Heroic Prince Henry*
(1641), Charles Cornwallis writes that when Henry was six years old, "the
women being put from about his highness, divers of good sort were appointed
to attend upon his person" and "in the 7th, 8th, and 9th years of his age, leaving
those childish and idle toys, . . . he began to delight in more active and manly
exercises" (quoted in Bergeron, *Romances* 52). Mary Ellen Lamb explains that
young boys were expected to outgrow the "natural" femininity associated with
early childhood: "Not yet old enough to assume the social power defining their

---

William Haydon, *The True Picture and Relation of Prince Henry his Noble and Virtuous Disposition* (Leyden, 1634), STC 12581; sigs. B2v–B3v, B4v, C1r, C4v.

masculinity, boys younger than the age of seven were not yet considered fully rational, either; and so, much like women, young boys were perceived as creatures more of their bodies than their minds" ("Engendering" 530). Haydon's biography suggests that, at seven years old, Henry already had some insight into the "social power" of masculinity.

When reading Haydon, consider what kind of picture he wishes to present of Prince Henry's intellect, values, and sense of self. Both Haydon and Shakespeare show young princes interacting with their fathers and with ladies at court, and these episodes are well worth comparing. Although Haydon's text is not a coherent narrative but a loose collection of anecdotes, for that very reason it productively calls our attention to the fragmentary, partial, and constructed nature of all biographical portraits, including Shakespeare's "biographies" of the characters in his plays. How might the particular choices Shakespeare makes in presenting Mamillius affect our response to the tragedy of the Sicilian court?

I come now to the rehearsal of sundry[1] of his pleasant and witty speeches during his young and tender years, wherein the pregnancy of his wit and virtuous disposition do appear.

When he was but a little past seven years of age, a son of the Earl of Mar something younger then himself falling out with one of his pages, to whom (as his highness was informed) he had done some little wrong, he reproved him therefore, saying, "I love you because you are my lord's son and my cousin, but if you be not better conditioned, I will love such a one better," naming the child that complained of him.

Being asked very young what instruments of music he liked best, he answered, a trumpet.

On a time that he saw some hunting on a deer, being asked whether he loved that hunting well he answered, "Yes, but I love another kind of hunting better." One asking him what manner of hunting that was, he answered, "Hunting of thieves and rebels with brave men and horses." And turning him to one of his pages descended of highland parents, who were bruited[2] to be thieves, he added, "And such thieves as I take shall be hanged, the great ones higher than the rest, and you, sirrah,[3] (if you be a thief) highest of all."

Once in his childhood, in a merry humor taking up strawberries with two spoons when one might suffice, he said, "The one I use as a rapier, and the other as a dagger."[4]

---

[1] **sundry:** various.   [2] **bruited:** reputed.   [3] **sirrah:** term of address to a social inferior.   [4] **rapier and dagger:** duels were sometimes fought with a rapier, or light sword, in one hand and a dagger in the other.

Being asked of a nobleman whether after his father he had rather be king of England or Scotland, he demanded whether of them was best. And answer being made that it was England, then (said he) "Would I have both." . . .

Eating in the king's presence a dish of milk, his majesty asked him why he ate so much child's meat.[5] "Sir," quoth he, "it is man's meat also." And immediately after fed well of a partridge, the king said to him, "That meat will make you a coward." Whereunto he answered, "Though it be a cowardly bird, yet it shall not make me a coward."

The king asking him whether he loved Englishmen or Frenchmen better, he answered, "Englishmen." The king demanded the cause thereof; because, said he, "I am kin to more noble persons of England, than of France." Then the king asked him whether he loved the English or the Germans better; he answered, "The English." Whereunto the king replying that his mother was a German, he answered, "Sir, you are the cause thereof."

At the same time, his Majesty asked him upon some mention made of Queen Elizabeth whether she had any children. He answered he understood of none. "And hath she none," said the king, "that may be called her son"? He said, "Yes, sir, yourself." "And who next after me?" said his Majesty. "Sir," said he, "your son." Another standing by saying that was Duke Charles, "No, sir," said his highness, "it must be the eldest," wherein his discretion and modesty in not once naming himself is worth the noting. . . .

A certain courtly and merrily conceited[6] lady who had a husband whom she could not well enjoy, in presence of as pleasant a conceited gentleman who was then a widower, jesting with his highness, requested him that he would send her beyond seas in embassage[7] to court a certain prince's daughter for him. "Marry,"[8] (said his highness) "I am contented so to do, upon condition that when your husband shall die you marry this gentleman, who being well traveled and languaged will serve you for a good guide." . . .

On a time as he was walking in the heat of the day, one told him that the sun would scorch his face. To whom he answered, "It is no matter; I am not a woman." . . .

His highness once playing him after the manner of children, his schoolmaster, desirous to draw him to some more man-like exercise, amongst other things said unto him jesting, "God send you a wise wife"; his highness added, "that she may govern you and me." His schoolmaster saying that he had one of his own, the prince thereto answered, "But mine (if I had one) would govern your wife, and by that means would govern both you and me."

---

[5] **meat:** food.   [6] **conceited:** witty.   [7] **embassage:** an ambassador's mission.   [8] **Marry:** a mild oath sworn to the Virgin Mary.

FIGURE 13 *Anonymous artist*, Sir Walter Raleigh *(1602). A soldier, poet, and fa-vorite of Queen Elizabeth, Sir Walter Raleigh poses here with his son Walter, aged eight years. In what ways does this portrait imagine the son as a "copy" of his father (1.2.122)?*

→ BEN JONSON

On My First Daughter *and* On My First Son   *1616*

A professional poet and playwright, Ben Jonson turned to poetry to express his grief over the deaths of his first daughter, Mary, and his first son, Benjamin. Mary died at six months of age; Benjamin, born in 1596, died of plague in 1603, at the age of seven. While presumably written shortly after each child's death, "On My First Daughter" and "On My First Son" were published much later: they were part of a collection of 133 short poems, *Epigrams*, that was included in the large folio edition of Jonson's collected *Works* (1616). Jonson's *Works* also included another collection of poems, *The Forest*, as well as nine plays and over a dozen masques.

Jonson's inclusion of these two epitaphs on his children's deaths in his *Works* reminds us not to read these poems simply as heartfelt expressions of a father's grief. While they might be so, they are also carefully crafted literary artifacts meant to display Jonson's mastery of the epigram: usually a short poem with a clever twist or witty comment at the end. "On My First Daughter," for instance, was published between an epigram "On a Reformed Gamester," which ridicules a reformed gambler, and an epigram "To John Donne," which praises a fellow poet. Immediately before encountering Jonson's tender poem about the infant Mary's death, therefore, a reader of the *Works* could enjoy his scorn for the modish gambler who decides to live soberly (by cutting his long hair and wearing unfashionable clothes) only because he has received a humiliating beating. Despite their differences in tone, the two poems even use similar imagery: in his epitaph on Mary, Jonson acknowledges that his daughter's soul will outlive her buried flesh; in his satire on the gambler, he ironically comes to realize that "[t]he body's stripes . . . the soul may save."

Even though we have access to Jonson's sentiments only in the highly mediated form of published poetry, he nonetheless draws upon culturally specific ways of coming to terms with the death of children that prove relevant for a reading of *The Winter's Tale*. In Jonson's poems and in *The Winter's Tale*, how does the gender and age of the child affect the emotions attached to its loss? What role do Jonson and the characters in *The Winter's Tale* attribute to supernatural agents in their attempts to make sense of these deaths? How do notions of innocence and guilt enter into these contemplations? Jonson claims that he has learned a lesson from the loss of his son. What, if anything, does Leontes learn from the loss of Mamillius and Perdita?

Ben Jonson, *The Works of Benjamin Jonson* (London, 1616); STC 14752; sigs. Ttt3v, Ttt6v–Uuu1r.

On My First Daughter

Here lies to each her parents' ruth,[1]
Mary, the daughter of their youth:
Yet, all heaven's gifts, being heaven's due,
It makes the father, less, to rue.[2]
At six month's end, she parted hence   5
With safety of her innocence;
Whose soul heaven's queen, (whose name she bears)
In comfort of her mother's tears,
Hath placed amongst her virgin train:
Where, while that severed doth remain,   10
This grave partakes[3] the fleshly birth.
Which cover lightly, gentle earth.

On My First Son

Farewell, thou child of my right hand,[4] and joy;
My sin was too much hope of thee, loved boy,
Seven years thou wert lent to me, and I thee pay,
Exacted by thy fate, on the just day.
Oh, could I lose all father,[5] now. For why   5
Will man lament the state he should envy?
To have so soon 'scaped[6] world's, and flesh's rage,
And, if no other misery, yet age?
Rest in soft peace, and, asked, say here doth lie
Ben Jonson his best piece of poetry.   10
For whose sake, henceforth, all his vows be such,
As what he loves may never like too much.

---

[1] ruth: sorrow.   [2] to rue: to grieve.   [3] partakes: takes share in, receives.   [4] child of my right
hand: the meaning of the name "Benjamin" in Hebrew.   [5] could I lose all father: if only I could
cease to feel the emotional attachment of a father.   [6] 'scaped: escaped.

CHAPTER 3

Authority and Resistance

————————————————————— >‹ ———————————————

W hen Paulina warns Leontes that his cruel treatment of Hermione "something savors / Of tyranny" (2.3.119–20), she treads dangerously on a vexed political question in Shakespeare's England: namely, what are the limits of the sovereign's authority? In which circumstances might the sovereign's exercise of power "savor of" tyrannical abuse, and who can claim the right to draw the distinction between legitimate and illegimate uses of power?

In early modern Europe, *tyrant* was an incendiary term. It usually meant either an illegitimate monarch — one who violently or treacherously usurped the throne — or a legitimate monarch who ruled unjustly. In *De Republica Anglorum* (1583), Sir Thomas Smith vividly defines a tyrant as an "evil king" who "hath no regard to the wealth of his people, but seeketh only to magnify himself . . . and to satisfy his vicious and cruel appetite, without respect of God, of right, or of the law" (sig. C1r). For his violent seizure of the throne of Scotland, Shakespeare's Macbeth is vilified as an "untitled tyrant bloody-sceptered" (4.3.105). Given the overwhelmingly negative connotations of tyranny, then, it is not surprising that Leontes sharply refutes Paulina's accusation: "Were I a tyrant, / Where were her life? She durst not call me so / If she did know me one" (2.3.122–24). Were he indeed a cruel tyrant rather than a just king, Leontes reasons, he would have summarily executed Paulina for daring to challenge his authority.

The first part of this chapter will explore the rich culture of debate about monarchical authority in early modern England, focusing on topics such as the privileges and limits of royal power, the role of counselors in advising the king, and the legitimacy of resistance to the king. During the reign of King Charles I (1625–1649), escalating conflict over the monarch's broad exercise of royal prerogative ultimately contributed to the outbreak of civil war between Parliamentary and Royalist forces; in 1649, Parliament executed the king. If, under King James I, ideological disputes about the limits of monarchical authority did not reach such a drastic climax, they nonetheless deeply informed political theory and practice, as well as many London stageplays. The first document excerpted in this chapter, King James's *The True Law of Free Monarchies*, advances several intertwined arguments to justify the wide powers he enjoyed as monarch. Whereas James and Leontes similarly insist on royal prerogative, they also make use of significantly different strategies in defining and exercising their power. The next document, Francis Bacon's essay on the benefits of political counsel, defines the king's counselors not as those who would limit the king's power, but as those who help him to rule more wisely. Unfortunately, Leontes' counselors have little success convincing their king of the wisdom of their advice. In the third document, the influential republican political theorist George Buchanan goes further than either Bacon or Leontes' courtiers in arguing that subjects are sometimes justified in removing a wicked king.

While questions of monarchical power are central to Shakespeare's English history plays, tragedies, and romances, *The Winter's Tale* also explores the analogy between subjects' resistance to monarchical authority and women's resistance to patriarchal authority. Because of the stigma attached to women who voiced their views loudly and publicly, Paulina faces intense scrutiny for criticizing Leontes. The second part of the chapter opens with William Whately's sermon *A Bride-Bush*, which presents an orthodox argument about the virtues of female silence and obedience. A few years after the first performances of *The Winter's Tale*, a series of pamphlets appeared in London bookshops that fiercely debated the intellectual capacities of women and the legitimacy of their speech. We will consider the notoriously misogynist pamphlet of Joseph Swetnam, which ignited this debate, as well as the response by Rachel Speght, in which an educated young woman expresses a firm conviction in her right to speak on all women's behalf. Like Leontes, Swetnam rehearses misogynist commonplaces when he attacks women as aggressive shrews; like Paulina, Speght boldly defends women's wisdom and virtue. Finally, we will look at a popular ballad that depicts marriage as a negotiation between husband and wife for shared authority, not as the struggle for dominance that Leontes reads into the marriage of

Paulina and Antigonus. Collectively, the documents in the second part of this chapter demonstate that just as some voices in Shakespeare's culture were reiterating traditional prejudices that branded outspoken women as shrews or whores, other voices, male and female alike, were passionately arguing against the orthodox insistence on female silence and obedience.

Monarch and Ministers

Our prerogative
Calls not your counsels,   (2.1.164–65)

Leontes' vigorous defense of his prerogative recalls King James's fundamental philosophy of sovereignty, which held that the "free monarch" was "free from coercive human jurisdiction" (Burgess 41). Before discussing the theories of sovereignty that inform *The Winter's Tale*, however, it will be helpful to consider how the practical structures of governance in Leontes' kingdom compare to those in early modern England.

As political historian Glenn Burgess explains, English government under the Tudor and Stuart monarchs was "constitutionalist," meaning that the king was "bound to govern through the common law"; he "could rule *absolutely* in spheres where the law was silent, or spoke only to give voice to the king; but in crucial matters — above all, property and liberty," he could rule only according to the written law (211–12). The legislative institution of the English government was Parliament, which was comprised of a House of Commons and a House of Lords. Members of the House of Commons were independently elected representatives from boroughs and counties: only wealthy and elite citizens were eligible to vote, and only knights were eligible to serve in the county seats. The House of Lords was comprised of Lords Temporal (noblemen), who served through hereditary right, and Lords Spiritual (bishops). Parliament sat infrequently, since the monarch could summon it at will — usually to request money — and could dissolve it at will.

In *The Winter's Tale*, Leontes has a group of counselors, but there is no indication that a parliamentary government exists in either Sicilia or Bohemia, which are presumably modeled after the ancient kingdoms of Greece and Rome. Unlike the government of England, in which the monarch was limited by his allegiance to national laws, the governments of Sicilia and Bohemia appear to be truly absolutist, in that their kings "*alone* could give laws to their people (and thus alter existing law)." As an absolute sovereign,

Leontes "could not only change laws, he could act without need to obey the law" (Burgess 29). The threat of absolutism was a source of great anxiety in a constitutionalist monarchy such as England, and King James's habit of asserting his sovereign rights did little to assuage these anxieties in his subjects.

Occasionally, James did attempt to appease his subjects by declaring his commitment to uphold English laws, but tensions still flared up between the king and members of Parliament, especially in the House of Commons. In a 1610 speech to Parliament, for instance, James tried to quell the outrage provoked by a law dictionary called *The Interpreter* (1607) that vigorously justified absolutism. Written by John Cowell, a professor of civil law at Cambridge University, *The Interpreter* defined the king as "above the law by his absolute power" and went on to assert that "he may alter or suspend any particular law that seemeth hurtful to the public estate" (quoted in *Proceedings* 38 n.2, n.6). The resentment generated by Cowell's baldly absolutist positions came at an unfortunate time for James, who was trying to persuade Parliament to grant him a yearly income. James denounced Cowell's book, claiming that it

> had mistaken the fundamental points and constitutions of parliament and waded more curiously in them than a subject ought, which if his Majesty had known before (though out of parliament) he would have suppressed, as he intends to do this and give order for prevention of the like hereafter. But as we are curious or rather careful to preserve the privileges of parliament, to live under the protection of law, which is our birthright, so is it both a tender and dangerous thing to submit the power of a king to definition. (*Proceedings* 49)

This was a rhetorical gesture James would make many times: acknowledging that a good king was bound to uphold the law, but insisting nonetheless that it was seditious for subjects not only to challenge but even to *define* the nature of his power. Only the king had the authority to determine whether or not he was fulfilling his duty to his subjects.

Of course, the king could always seek out the advice of his counselors. In *The Winter's Tale*, Paulina discovers that getting the king to listen to her unsolicited counsel is more difficult than she had anticipated. Those who found themselves in the position of advising Queen Elizabeth or King James might well have understood Paulina's frustration. Queen Elizabeth "often felt the need to remind parliament of the limits of its authority to advise a prince" (Crane 8). Early in her reign, in response to a Parliamentary bill urging her to marry, Queen Elizabeth used the analogy of the body politic to marvel that "the foot should direct the head in so weighty a cause" (quoted in Crane 9). King James warned the House of Commons not to show undue zeal in voicing subjects' grievances, as if the House were eager to demonstrate that "there are many abuses in the government, and many causes of complaint" (James, *Political* 189). James further admonished Parliament not to "meddle with the main points of Government; that is my craft: . . . to meddle with that, were to lesson me: . . . I must not be taught my Office" (190–91). As Curtis Perry observes, James's "confidence in the science of kingcraft, together with his insistence that subjects can never fathom the drifts of kings, tended to de-emphasize the importance of counsel" (91).

Although in *The Winter's Tale* Shakespeare does not attempt to reproduce the multilayered hierarchy of the Jacobean court, the conflict between Leontes and his counselors nevertheless speaks to contemporary doubts about James's willingness to receive and to accept honest counsel. Much like James, perhaps, Leontes does not hesitate to admonish his counselors for overstepping their place: "Why, what need we / Commune with you of this, but rather follow / Our forceful instigation? Our prerogative / Calls not your counsels, but our natural goodness / Imparts this" (2.1.162–66). On what grounds does Leontes reject the advice of his counselors, and how reasonable are those grounds? Are the Sicilian lords trustworthy counselors who give their king honest advice, or are they self-serving flatterers who tell him only what he wants to hear? According to Francis Bacon in his essay "Of Counsel," what kinds of strategies might a monarch in Leontes' position use to solicit, evaluate, and implement wise counsel?

Camillo, Antigonus, and Paulina might all be regarded as different kinds of counselors who use particular rhetorical strategies to accomplish particular aims. The experiences of Camillo and Paulina reveal the moral and political pitfalls of advising the king. Although Camillo at first insists on Hermione's innocence, he finally promises Leontes that he will assassinate Polixenes; instead of keeping his word, however, he surreptitiously flees Sicilia, leaving Hermione to face Leontes' wrath on her own. Does Camillo act prudently? Does he act justly or ethically? Does he act for his own good or for that of the kingdom? Paulina believes that her bold speech and the sight of Hermione's newborn infant will "soften" Leontes' severity toward Hermione (2.2.40); however, her interference only stokes his wrath. Does Paulina's miscalculation perhaps reveal that she has unleashed her "red-looked anger" not simply for the king's benefit, as she claims, but also to vent her own rage against him (2.2.34)? Paulina's deception in keeping Hermione's survival a secret for sixteen years is also difficult to judge. On the one hand, Paulina might be thought to serve the king and queen faithfully by making Leontes wait for the fulfillment of Apollo's oracle before reuniting him with his wife. On the other hand, this deception allows Paulina to prolong the extraordinary influence she enjoys over the king, queen, and kingdom — a power that will come to an end once Leontes and Hermione are reunited.

When Shakespeare was writing *The Winter's Tale*, most political thought in England was "constitutionalist rather than republican," meaning that it "drew on the notion of a mutually beneficial union of monarch and people in which the government of the former was enhanced and made possible by the counsel and consent of the latter, insofar as they were represented in Parliament and especially by the Commons" (Jordan 18). The Scottish scholar George Buchanan could be considered "republican" in his insistence that monarchs were subject to the laws made by and in the interests of the people. Buchanan insists that the king is not only a ruler but a man, liable to error and passion; hence the law must act as a "curb upon his arbitrary will." If a king violates the laws, he becomes a "tyrant," a "public enemy," and as such the people are justified in deposing him by trial or by force, if necessary. In *The Winter's Tale*, how far are Paulina and Leontes' courtiers willing to go to curb their monarch's "arbitrary will"? According to what criteria do they measure the limits of legitimate monarchical power and legitimate opposition to it? Do Leontes' subjects voice positions that might be regarded as absolutist on one end of the political spectrum, or as republican on the other end?

→ KING JAMES I OF ENGLAND

From The True Law of Free Monarchies   *1598*

As King of Scotland, James published two major works expounding his political philosophies. *The True Law of Free Monarchies* (1598) justifies the broad powers of a king; *Basilikon Doron* (The King's Testament) (1603), a guide on statecraft addressed to his son, declares at the outset that "God gives not kings the style of gods in vain, / For on his throne his scepter do they sway" (sig. 3r) Defining the monarch as a little god instead of a great man, James elevated himself far above those subjects who also participated in the political process, such as members of Parliament, magistrates, and counselors. If James considered himself a god, would he be willing to conform himself to the customary laws of the nation? If

King James I, *The True Law of Free Monarchies: or the Reciprock and Mutual Duty Betwixt a Free King and His Natural Subjects* (Edinburgh, 1598), STC 14409; sigs. B1r–B5r, C5r–C5v, C8v–D1v, D3r–D6v, E3r–E4r.

he believed, as he once instructed Parliament, that kings have the God-like power to "make and unmake their subjects, . . . to exalt low things, and abase high things" (James, *Political* 181), then what would prevent him from making and unmaking the laws to suit his own interests?

King James expounds his own definitions of the rights and responsibilities of monarchical authority in *The True Law of Free Monarchies*. Originally published in Scotland in 1598, this important treatise was reprinted in London in 1603, when James was crowned as king of England. Although *The True Law* examines the "mutual duty and allegiance" between monarch and subjects, the bulk of the work is devoted to elaborating the grounds of subjects' obedience to the monarch. James explains that he undertook to justify the "truth" of monarchy because preachers in Scotland and France had been advocating rebellion against kings on the grounds of religious freedom. Glenn Burgess usefully reminds us that the central theme of *The True Law* "was defensive and not aggressive. . . . James needed to demonstrate, not that kings were unlimited, but rather that their being limited did not imply that there was on earth any power superior to them" (41).

James's description of the free monarch in the *The True Law* exists in a complicated and oblique relationship to Shakespeare's depiction of sovereignty in *The Winter's Tale*. Both James and Leontes make rhetorical arguments on behalf of monarchical power, but whereas the "defensive" James presents carefully ordered claims supported by textual citations, the "aggressive" Leontes is less concerned to justify the theoretical basis of the royal authority to which he demands obedience. When reading *The True Law*, consider how James constructs his theory of kingship from sets of interlocking or analogous "laws" derived from different sources of authority. These laws and the particular roles they assign to members of the commonwealth determine both the duties and the powers of the king. How effective are James's individual arguments? Are some more convincing than others? The formality of James's rhetorical strategies and the overtness of his political positions can help us to identify Leontes' more spontaneous rhetorical strategies and implict political positions. In his lectures to his counselors, does Leontes ground his absolute power on the same ideological "foundations" as James (2.1.102)? According to the theories of monarchical authority elaborated in *The True Law*, is Leontes acting within his rights as a king? If not, what recourse do his subjects have?

From *The True Law of Free Monarchies*

As there is not a thing so necessary to be known by the people of any land, next the knowledge of their God, as the right knowledge of their allegiance, according to the form of government established among them, especially in a monarchy (which form of government, as resembling the divinity, approacheth nearest to perfection, as all the learned and wise men from the beginning have agreed upon, unity being the perfection of all things), so hath the ignorance, and (which is worse) the seduced opinion of the multitude blinded by them, who think themselves able to teach and instruct the ignorants, procured the wrack and overthrow of sundry flourishing commonwealths, and heaped heavy calamities, threatening utter destruction upon others. . . . I have chosen then only to set down in this short treatise the true grounds of the mutual duty and allegiance betwixt a free and absolute monarch, and his people; not to trouble your patience with answering the contrary propositions, which some hath not been ashamed to set down in writ, to the poisoning of infinite number of simple souls, and their own perpetual and well deserved infamy. For by answering them, I could not have eschewed whiles to pick[1] and bite well saltly[2] their persons: which would rather have bred contentiousness among the readers (as they had liked or misliked) than sound instruction of the truth. Which I protest to him, that is the searcher of all hearts, is the only mark that I shoot at herein.

First then, I will set down the true grounds, whereupon I am to build, out of the scriptures, since monarchy is the true pattern of divinity, as I have already said. Next, from the fundamental laws of our own kingdom, which nearest must concern us. Thirdly, from the law of nature, by divers similitudes drawn out of the same. And will conclude syne[3] by answering the most weighty and appearing incommodities[4] that can be objected.

The prince's duty to his subjects is so clearly set down in many places of the scriptures, and so openly confessed by all the good princes, according to their oath in their coronation, as, not needing to be long therein, I shall as shortly as I can run through it.

Kings are called gods[5] by the prophetical King David, because they sit upon God his[6] throne in the earth, and have the count[7] of their administration to give unto him. Their office is "to minister justice and judgment to their people," as the same David saith; "to advance the good, and punish the evil,"[8] as he likewise saith; "to establish good laws to his people, and procure obedience to the same," as divers good kings of Judah[9] did; "to procure the peace of the people,"[10] as the same David saith; "to decide all controversies that can arise among them,"[11] as Solomon did; "to be the minister of God

---

[1] **eschewed whiles to pick:** avoided sometimes to find fault with.   [2] **bite well saltly:** speak bitterly against.   [3] **syne:** then.   [4] **incommodities:** inconveniences.   [5] **Kings are called gods:** "I have said, Ye are gods; and all of you are children of the most High" (Psalm 82:6).   [6] **God his:** God's.   [7] **count:** account.   [8] **to minister justice . . . and punish the evil:** Psalm 101.   [9] **kings of Judah:** e.g., Hezekiah (2 Kings 18, 2 Chron. 29) and Josiah (2 Kings 22, 2 Chron. 34–35).   [10] **to procure the peace . . . :** Psalm 72.   [11] **to decide all controversies . . . :** 1 Kings 3:16–28.

for the weal of him that doth well, and as the minister of God to take vengeance upon them that do evil,"[12] as Saint Paul saith. And finally, "as a good pastor, to go out and in before his people,"[13] as is said in the first of Samuel; "that through the prince's prosperity the people's peace may be procured,"[14] as Jeremy saith.

And therefore in the coronation of our own kings, as well as of every Christian monarch, they give their oath first to maintain the religion presently professed within their country, according to their laws whereby it is established, and to punish all those that should press to alter or disturb the profession thereof. And next, to maintain all the allowable and good laws made by their predecessors: to see them put in execution, and the breakers and violators thereof to be punished, according to the tenor of the same. And lastly, to maintain the whole country, and every state therein, in all their ancient privileges and liberties, as well against all foreign enemies as among themselves. And shortly,[15] to procure the weal[16] and flourishing of his people, not only in maintaining and putting to execution the old allowable laws of the country, and by establishing of new (as necessity and evil manners will require), but by all other means possible to foresee and prevent all dangers that are likely to fall upon them; and to maintain concord, wealth, and civility among them, as a loving father and careful watchman, caring for them more than for himself, knowing himself to be ordained for them, and they not for him; and therefore countable to that great God who placed him as lieutenant over them, upon the peril of his soul to procure the weal of both souls and bodies, as far as in him lieth, of all of them that are committed to his charge. And this oath in the coronation is the clearest civil and fundamental law, whereby the king's office is properly defined.

By the law of nature the king becomes a natural father to all his lieges at his coronation. And as the father of his fatherly duty is bound to care for the nourishing, education, and virtuous government of his children, even so is the king bound to care for all his subjects. As all the toil and pain that the father can take for his children will be thought light and well bestowed by him, so that the effect thereof redound to their profit and weal, so ought the prince to do towards his people. As the kindly father ought to foresee all inconvenients and dangers that may arise towards his children, and though with the hazard of his own person press to prevent the same, so ought the king towards his people. As the father's wrath and correction upon any of his children that offendeth ought to be by a fatherly chastisement seasoned with pity, as long as there is any hope of amendment in them, so ought the

---

[12] to be the minister . . . : Romans 13:4.   [13] as a good pastor . . . : 1 Samuel 8.   [14] that through the prince's prosperity . . . : Jeremiah 29.   [15] shortly: in short.   [16] weal: welfare.

FIGURE 14 *Simon de Passe,* Anne of Denmark, Prince Charles, and King James I of England *(after 1612). Whereas Queen Elizabeth never married or had children, King James's status as husband and father accorded with the patriarchal conception of the Renaissance monarch.*

king towards any of his lieges that offends in that measure. And shortly, as the father's chief joy ought to be in procuring his children's welfare, rejoicing at their weal, sorrowing and pitying at their evil, to hazard for their safety, travail for their rest, wake for their sleep: and in a word, to think that his earthly felicity and life standeth and liveth more in them, nor in himself, so ought a good prince think of his people.

As to the other branch of this mutual and reciprock[17] band, it is the duty and allegiance that the lieges owe to their king. The ground whereof I take out of the words of Samuel, dited[18] by God's spirit, when God had given him commandment to hear the people's voice in choosing and anointing them a king. . . . [Here James cites and explicates 1 Samuel 8:9–20.]

Shortly then to take up in two or three sentences, grounded upon all these arguments, out of the law of God, the duty and allegiance of the people to their lawful king. Their obedience, I say, ought to be to him as to God's lieutenant in earth, obeying his commands in all things, except directly against God, as the commands of God's minister; acknowledging him as a judge set by God over them, having power to judge them, but to be judged only by God, whom to only he must give count of his judgment; fearing him as their judge; loving him as their father; praying for him as their protector; for his continuance, if he be good; for his amendment, if he be wicked; following and obeying his lawful commands, eschewing and flying his fury in his unlawful, without resistance, but by sobs and tears to God, according to that sentence used in the primitive church in the time of persecution: *preces & lachrimae sunt arma ecclesiae.*[19] . . .

[Scottish subjects owe allegiance to their king on the grounds that the first laws of Scotland were formulated by kings.]

And for conclusion of this point that the king is overlord over the whole lands, it is likewise daily proved by the law of our hoards,[20] of want of heirs, and of bastardies.[21] For if a hoard be found under the earth, because it is no more in the keeping or use of any person, it of the law pertains to the king. If a person, inheritor of any lands or goods, die without any sort of heirs, all his lands and goods return to the king. And if a bastard die unrehabled[22] without heirs of his body (which rehabling only lies in the king's hands) all that he hath likewise returns to the king. And as ye see it manifest that the king is overlord of the whole land, so is he master over every person that inhabiteth the same, having power over the life and death of every one of them. For although a just prince will not take the life of any of his subjects without a clear law, yet the same laws whereby he taketh them are made by himself, or his predecessors. And so the power flows always from himself. As by daily experience we see, good and just princes will from time to time make new laws and statutes, adjoining the penalties to the breakers thereof, which

---

[17] **reciprock:** reciprocal. [18] **dited:** inspired. [19] *preces & lachrimae sunt arma ecclesiae:* prayers and tears are the weapons of the church. [20] **hoards:** hidden treasures. [21] **bastardies:** illegitimate births. [22] **unrehabled:** not made legitimate.

before the law was made had been no crime to the subject to have committed. Not that I deny the old definition of a king and of a law, which makes the king to be a speaking law, and the law a dumb king: for certainly a king that governs not by his law can neither be countable to God for his administration, nor have a happy and established reign. For albeit it be true that I have at length proved that the king is above the law, as both the author and giver of strength thereto, yet a good king will not only delight to rule his subjects by the law, but even will conform himself in his own actions thereunto, always keeping that ground that the health of the commonwealth be his chief law. And where he sees the law doubtsome or rigorous, he may interpret or mitigate the same: lest otherwise *summa jus* be *summa injuria.*[23] And therefore general laws, made publicly in parliament, may upon known respects to the king by his authority be mitigated, and suspended upon causes only known to him.

As likewise, although I have said a good king will frame all his actions to be according to the law, yet is he not bound thereto but of his good will, and for good example-giving to his subjects. . . .

[Because the king is overlord and master of all his subjects, it is always unlawful for subjects to "control or displace" a monarch.]

And the agreement of the law of nature in this our ground with the laws and constitutions of God and man, already alleged, will by two similitudes easily appear. The king towards his people is rightly compared to a father of children, and to a head of a body composed of divers members. For as fathers the good princes and magistrates of the people of God acknowledged themselves to their subjects. And for all other well ruled commonwealths, the style of *Pater Patriae*[24] was ever and is commonly used to kings. And the proper office of a king towards his subjects agrees very well with the office of the head towards the body, and all members thereof. For from the head, being the seat of judgment, proceedeth the care and foresight of guiding, and preventing all evil that may come to the body, or any part thereof. The head cares for the body: so doth the king for his people. As the discourse and direction flows from the head, and the execution according thereunto belongs to the rest of the members, every one according to their office, so is it betwixt a wise prince and his people. As the judgment coming from the head may not only employ the members, every one in their own office, as long as they are able for it; but likewise, in case any of them be

---

[23] *summa jus* be *summa injuria*: the highest justice be the greatest harm.   [24] *Pater Patriae*: father of the fatherland.

affected with any infirmity, must care and provide for their remedy in case it be curable, and if otherwise, gar cut them off[25] for fear of infecting the rest: even so is it betwixt the prince and his people. And as there is ever hope of curing any diseased member by the direction of the head, as long as it is whole; but by the contrary, if it be troubled, all the members are partakers of that pain, so is it betwixt the prince and his people.

And now first for the father's part (whose natural love to his children I described in the first part of this my discourse, speaking of the duty that kings owe to their subjects) consider, I pray you, what duty his children owe to him, and whether, upon any pretext whatsoever, it will not be thought monstrous and unnatural to his sons to rise up against him, to control him at their appetite, and when they think good to slay him, or to cut him off, and adopt to themselves any other they please in his room. Or can any pretence of wickedness or rigor on his part be a just excuse for his children to put hand into him? And although we see by the course of nature that love ever useth to descend more than to ascend, in case it were true that the father hated and wronged the children never so much, will any man endued with the least spunk[26] of reason think it lawful for them to meet him with the like? Yea, suppose the father were furiously following his sons with a drawn sword, is it lawful for them to turn and strike again, or make any resistance but by flight? I think surely, if there were no more but the example of brute beasts and unreasonable creatures, it may serve well enough to qualify and prove this my argument. We read often the piety that the storks have to their old and decayed parents. And generally we know that there are many sorts of beasts and fowls that with violence and many bloody strokes will beat and banish their young ones from them, how soon they perceive them to be able to fend themselves. But we never read or heard of any resistance on their part, except among the vipers: which proves such persons as ought to be reasonable creatures, and yet unnaturally followed this example, to be endued with their viperous nature.

And for the similitude of the head and the body, it may very well fall out that the head will be forced to gar cut off some rotten member (as I have already said) to keep the rest of the body in integrity. But what state the body can be in if the head, for any infirmity that can fall to it, be cut off, I leave it to the reader's judgment.

So as (to conclude this part) if the children may, upon any pretext that can be imagined, lawfully rise up against their father, cut him off, and choose any other whom they please in his room; and if the body, for the weal of it, may for any infirmity that can be in the head strike it off, then I can not

---

[25] **gar cut them off:** cause them to be cut off.   [26] **spunk:** spark.

deny that the people may rebel, control, and displace, or cut off their king at their own pleasure, and upon respects moving them. And whether these similitudes represent better the office of a king, or the offices of masters or deacons of crafts, or doctors in physic (which jolly comparisons are used by such writers, as maintain the contrary proposition) I leave it also to the reader's discretion.

And in case any doubts might arise in any part of this treatise, I will (according to my promise) with the solution of four principal and most weighty doubts, that the adversaries may object, conclude this discourse. And first it is casten up[27] by divers that employ their pens upon apologies for rebellions and treasons, that every man is born to carry such a natural zeal and duty to his commonwealth, as to his mother, that seeing it so rent and deadly wounded as whiles it will be by wicked and tyrannous kings, good citizens will be forced, for the natural zeal and duty they owe to their own native country, to put their hand to work for freeing their commonwealth from such a pest.

Whereunto I give two answers. First, it is a sure axiom in theology that evil should not be done that good may come of it. The wickedness therefore of the king can never make them that are ordained to be judged by him to become his judges. And if it be not lawful to a private man to revenge his private injury upon his private adversary (since God hath only given the sword to the magistrate) how much less is it lawful to the people, or any part of them (who all are but private men, the authority being always with the magistrate, as I have already proved) to take upon them the use of the sword, whom to it belongs not, against the public magistrate, whom to only it belongeth.

Next, in place of relieving the commonwealth out of distress (which is their only excuse and color[28]) they shall heap doubt, distress, and desolation upon it. And so their rebellion shall procure the contrary effects that they pretend it for. For a king can not be imagined to be so unruly and tyrannous, but the commonwealth will be kept in better order, notwithstanding thereof, by him, than it can by his way-taking.[29] For first, all sudden mutations are perilous in commonwealths, hope being thereby given to all bare men to set up themselves and fly with other men's feathers, the reins being loosed to all the insolencies that disordered people can commit by hope of impunity, because of the looseness of all things.

And next, it is certain that a king can never be so monstrously vicious, but he will generally favor justice and maintain some order, except in the particulars, wherein his inordinate lusts and passions carry him away; where,

---

[27] **casten up:** spewed out (as in vomiting).   [28] **color:** pretense.   [29] **way-taking:** taking away.

FIGURE 15 *Thomas Scott,* Vox Regis *(1624). In this image of national unity, James sits enthroned in the House of Lords, above the kneeling figures of his son Prince Charles, his daughter Princess Elizabeth, and her husband Frederick V, the Protestant Elector Palatine (a German principality). In 1618, Frederick had accepted the crown of Bohemia from Protestant Bohemians who had rebelled against the Austrian Holy Roman Emperor, Ferdinand II. This action precipitated the Thirty Years' War (1618–48). Although James had tried to resolve the crisis through diplomacy, the threat*

The Frontispiece Explained.

PEerelesse Prince *Charles*, his *Sister* doth present
With her lou'd *Spouse* in publike *Parliament* :
Pleads their *Iust cause*, in honourable hight
Of *Speech* and *Passion*, vnto which, their sight
in *Sable Weedes*, adds flame ; as Flint with Steele,
When nimble Tinder doth the quicke sparkes feele.
    And in affection first, the *King*, to heare
And see *Himselfe*, in his owne *Flesh* (so deere,
Louing, and loued) abused, His angry Sword
Drawes, and to Armes, the *Signall* giues and *Word*.
    The *Nobles*, with this sight prouok'd, and led
By him who now pursues, what earst he fled,
Make hast to follow, Each his Fauchion reares
Aboue his head, cryes, *Therefore we are Peeres*.
    The *Clergie* pray ; The *Commons* for their parts
Seale their consent with *Purses, Tongues, Hands, Hearts*.
    O all ye *Prouder Nations* who by swarmes,
Like stinging Wasps, haue *forc'd* vs to these Armes,
Shew now that *Personall odds* you so much vaunt,
And with stout braggs, the boulder *Britanes* daunt,
Challenge the single Combate man to man,
And prooue whose *Head Heart, Hand*, the Conquest can
Winne from each other, Enuie to conuince,
And honour bring to *Countrey, Nation, Prince*.
    See now when *Drummes* doe beat, and *Tabers* cease,
If you in *Warre* can wrong vs as in *Peace*.

of an expanded Austrian empire finally convinced him in 1624 to join with the Dutch and French against Catholic Austrian-Spanish forces.

    A Protestant polemicist, Thomas Scott wrote Vox Regis (The King's Voice) after Parliament had voted to supply James's military campaign. Both the engraving and the accompanying poem on the frontispiece promote an ideal of familial and national unity. Moved by the suffering of his daughter and son-in-law, King James raises his sword to signal the call to arms. He is supported by the nobles and clergy in the House of Lords, and by the House of Commons, represented by the cheering crowd holding burning hearts. Although the image places the King, the House of Lords, and the House of Commons in a shared space, the monarch never actually sat in the House of Commons.

by the contrary, no king being, nothing is unlawful to none. And so the old opinion of the philosophers proves true, that better it is to live in a commonwealth where nothing is lawful than where all things are lawful to all men: the commonwealth at that time resembling an undaunted young horse that hath casten[30] his rider. For as the divine poet Du Bartas[31] sayeth: "Better it were to suffer some disorder in the estate and some spots in the commonwealth, than, in pretending to reform, utterly to overthrow the republic." . . .

[James addresses three other objections to his position.]

Not that by all this former discourse of mine, and apology for kings, I mean that whatsoever errors and intolerable abominations a sovereign prince commit, he ought to escape all punishment, as if thereby the world were only ordained for kings, and they without controlment to turn it upside-down at their pleasure. But by the contrary, by remitting them to God (who is their only ordinary judge) I remit them [to] the sorest and sharpest schoolmaster that can be devised for them. For the further a king is preferred by God above all other ranks and degrees of men, and the higher that his seat is above theirs, the greater is his obligation to his maker. And therefore, in case he forget himself (his unthankfulness being in the same measure of height) the sadder and sharper will his correction be; and according to the greatness of the height he is in, the weight of his fall will recompense the same. For the further that any person is obliged to God, his offense becomes and grows so much the greater than it would be in another. Jove's thunderclaps light oftener and sorer upon the high and stately oaks than on the low and supple willow trees. And the highest bench is sliddriest[32] to sit upon. Neither is it ever heard that any king forgets himself towards God, or in his vocation, but God with the greatness of the plague revengeth the greatness of his ingratitude. Neither think I by the force and argument of this my discourse so to persuade the people, that none will hereafter be raised up and rebel against wicked princes. But remitting to the justice and providence of God to stir up such scourges as pleaseth him for punishment of wicked kings (who made the very vermin and filthy dust of the earth to bridle the insolency of proud Pharaoh).

---

[30] casten: thrown.   [31] Du Bartas: Guillaume de Salluste Du Bartas (1544–1590), French poet.
[32] sliddriest: slipperiest.

SIR FRANCIS BACON

Of Counsel   *1612*

Francis Bacon's essay "Of Counsel" presents an informed analysis of the fraught power relations between king and counselors that Shakespeare explores in the imaginary world of *The Winter's Tale*. Bacon writes in the tradition of sixteenth-century humanist educators, who aimed "to train young men in the serious moral purpose and copious Latin style that they needed to become authoritative advisors and public servants" (Crane 3). Under the Tudor monarchs, humanists such as Sir Thomas Elyot, who wrote *The Governor* (1531), and Roger Ascham, who wrote *The Schoolmaster* (1570), promulgated the values of classical education that would train young men for roles in government. A product of this educational system, Bacon (1561–1626) wrote many important works of philosophy and science (mostly in Latin), even as he had a long public career as a member of Parliament and adviser to two monarchs. Although in 1596 Queen Elizabeth appointed him to an official position as Learned Counsel Extraordinary, it was not until King James knighted him in 1603 that Bacon truly prospered, ascending through a series of prominent posts as Solicitor General, Attorney General, Privy Councillor, Lord Keeper of the Seal, and finally Lord Chancellor. Bacon's glorious career was shattered in 1621, when he was accused of accepting bribes.

Bacon's *Essays* have a complex publication history. In 1597, Bacon published a collection of ten essays; in 1612, a second edition of thirty-eight essays; and in 1625 a third edition of fifty-eight *Essays or Counsels*. Not only did Bacon continue to produce essays on new topics, he expanded and revised previous essays; hence, several of them exist in different versions. "Of Counsel" first appeared in the 1612 edition, among essays on topics as diverse as beauty, atheism, marriage, and empire. In his dedication of the 1597 *Essays* to his brother Anthony, Bacon describes the essays as "fragments of [his] conceits" and declares them "medicinable," that is, useful, and free of anything "contrary or infectious to the state of religion, or manners" (sigs. A3r–A3v). In *The Winter's Tale*, Paulina will use the same language when claiming that her "medicinal" counsel will cure the king and restore justice to the state (2.3.37). What other similarities (or differences) in attitudes about providing counsel emerge from reading Bacon with an eye to Paulina, Antigonus, Camillo, or Leontes?

The greatest trust between man[1] is the trust of giving counsel. For in other confidences men commit the parts of their life, their lands, their goods, their child, their credit, some particular affair. But to such as they make their

---

[1] **between man:** the 1625 edition of this essay has "between man and man."

Francis Bacon, "Of Counsel," *The Essays of Sir Francis Bacon Knight, the King's Solicitor General* (London, 1612), STC 1141, sigs. E2v–F1r.

counselors, they commit the whole: by how much the more they are obliged to all faith and integrity.

The wisest princes need not think it any diminution to their greatness or derogation to their sufficiency, to rely upon counsel. God himself is not without, but hath made it one of the great names of his blessed Son: "The Counselor."[2] Solomon hath pronounced that "in counsel is stability."[3] Things will have their first or second agitation: if they be not tossed upon the arguments of counsel, they will be tossed upon the waves of fortune, and be full of inconstancy, doing, and undoing, like the reeling of a drunken man. Solomon's son[4] found the force of counsel, as his father saw the necessity of it. For the beloved kingdom of God was first rent and broken by ill counsel, upon which counsel there are set for our instruction the two marks whereby bad counsel is forever best discerned: that it was young counsel, for the persons, and violent counsel, for the matter.

The ancient times do set forth in figure both the incorporation and inseparable conjunction of counsel with kings, and the wise and politic use of counsel by kings. The one, in that they say Jupiter[5] did marry Metis[6] (which signifieth counsel) so as Sovereignty or Authority is married to Counsel. The other in that which followeth, which was thus: they say after Jupiter was married to Metis, she conceived by him and was with child, but Jupiter suffered her not to stay till she brought forth, but ate her up; whereby he became with child, and was delivered of Pallas, armed, out of his head. Which monstrous fable containeth a secret of empire: how kings are to make use of their council of state. That first they ought to refer matters to them, which is the first begetting or impregnation. But when they are elaborated, molded, and shaped in the womb of their council, and grow ripe and ready to be brought forth, that then they suffer not their council to go through with the resolution and direction, as if it depended on them, but take the matter back into their own hand, and make it appear to the world that the decrees and final directions (which, because they come forth with prudence and power, are resembled to Pallas armed) proceeded from themselves, and not only from their authority, but (the more to add reputation to themselves) from their head and device.

---

[2] The Counselor: "his name shall be called Wonderful, Counsellor" (Isaiah 9:6). [3] in counsel is stability: "in multitude of counsellors there is safety" (Proverbs 24:6). [4] Solomon's son: Rehoboam, who reigned for seventeen years. [5] Jupiter: in Roman mythology, the king of the gods, known as Zeus in Greek mythology. [6] Metis: Jupiter's first wife and the personification of wise counsel. She aided her husband in the war against his father Kronos. After the war, Metis became pregnant and Gaia, the earth goddess, predicted that she would give birth to a deity wiser than Jupiter. To avoid this outcome, Jupiter consumed his wife and, therefore, her wisdom, and later gave birth to Pallas Athena, the goddess of wisdom, from his own head.

The inconveniences that have been noted in calling and using counsel are three. First, the revealing of affairs, whereby they become the less secret. Secondly, the weakening of the authority of princes, as if they were less of themselves. Thirdly, the danger of being unfaithfully counseled, and more for the good of them that counsel than of him that is counseled. For which inconveniences the doctrine of Italy and practice of France hath introduced cabinet councils,[7] a remedy worse than the disease.

But for secrecy, princes are not bound to communicate all matters with all counselors, but may extract and select. Neither is it necessary that he that consulteth what he should do should declare what he will do. But let princes beware that the unsecreting of their affairs come not from themselves. And as for cabinet counsel, it may be their motto, *plenus rimarum sum.*[8] One futile person that maketh it his glory to tell will do more hurt than many that know it their duty to conceal.

For weakening of authority, the fable showeth the remedy; neither was there ever prince bereaved of his dependences by his council, except where there hath been an over-greatness in one, or an over-strict combination in divers.[9]

For the last inconvenience, that men will counsel with an eye to themselves, certainly, *non inveniet fidem super terram*[10] is meant of the nature of times, and not of all particular persons. There be that are in nature faithful and sincere, and plain and direct, not crafty and involved. Let princes, above all, draw to themselves such natures. Besides, counsels are not so commonly united, but that one keepeth sentinel over another. But the best remedy is if princes know their counselors as well as their counselors know them: *principis est virtus maxima nosse suos.*[11] And of the other side, counselors should not be too speculative into their sovereign's person. The true composition of a counselor is rather to be skillful in their master's business than in his nature, for then he is like to advise him and not to feed his humor.[12] It is of singular use to princes if they take the opinions of their council, both separately and together. For private opinion is more free, but opinion before others is more reverent. In private, men are more bold in their own humors, and in consort men are more obnoxious to others' humors. Therefore it is good to take both, and of the inferior sort rather in private, to preserve freedom;

---

[7] **cabinet councils:** small groups of ministers who meet secretly or privately with the prince. [8] *plenus rimarum sum:* "I am full of cracks"; a quotation from the ancient Roman playwright Terence also cited in Michel de Montaigne's essay "Of Presumption" (1578–80). [9] **divers:** many. [10] *non inveniet fidem super terram:* "he shall not find faith upon the earth" (see Luke 18:8). [11] *principis est virtus maxima nosse suos:* "the greatest virtue of a prince is to know his followers" (Martial, *Epigram* 8.15), also quoted by Montaigne in "Of the Art of Discussion" (1585–88). [12] **humor:** whim or disposition.

of the greater rather in consort, to preserve respect. It is in vain for princes to take counsel concerning matters if they take no counsel likewise concerning persons, for all matters are as dead images, and the life of the execution of affairs resteth in the good choice of persons. Neither is it enough to consult concerning persons *secundum genera*,[13] as in an idea or mathematical description, what kind of person should be in *individuo*:[14] for the greatest errors and the greatest judgments are shown in the choice of individuals. It was truly said, *optimi consiliares mortui*.[15] Books will speak plain when counselors blanch.[16] Therefore it is good to be conversant in them, specially the books of such as themselves have been actors upon the stage.[17]

[13] *secundum genera*: according to types.　[14] in *individuo*: as an individual.　[15] *optimi consiliares mortui*: the best counselors are the dead.　[16] **blanch**: suppress the truth, whitewash.　[17] **books of such as themselves have been actors upon the stage**: books written by those who have been statesmen (Bacon is using a theatrical metaphor).

→ GEORGE BUCHANAN

From De Jure Regni apud Scotos

1579

King James wrote his defense of sovereign power in *The True Law of Free Monarchies* as a direct response to the republican ideas expressed by his former tutor, George Buchanan, in *De Jure Regni apud Scotos* (1579). Born in Scotland, Buchanan (1506–1582) studied at St. Andrews University and at the University of Paris. After a few years teaching in Paris, he returned to Scotland, where he was jailed for Protestant heresies; he escaped, and fled to London and eventually to France, where he wrote and taught. Upon his return to Scotland, Buchanan served in various government posts during the 1560s and 1570s. Along with *De Jure Regni*, he composed several plays in Latin; in 1582, the year of his death, he published the *History of Scotland*.

Originally written in Latin, *De Jure Regni apud Scotos* was first translated into English in 1680 as *The Due Privilege of the Scots Government*, from which the excerpts below are taken. Upon its initial appearance in 1579 and long thereafter, *De Jure Regni* provoked controversy. Throughout the sixteenth and seventeenth centuries, its republican arguments influenced radical Protestant and antiabsolutist thinkers, including John Milton, who borrowed Buchanan's ideas for

---

George Buchanan, *De Jure Regni apud Scotos. Or A Dialogue Concerning the Due Privilege of Government in the Kingdom of Scotland, Betwixt George Buchanan and Thomas Maitland, by the Said George Buchanan. And Translated out of the Original Latin into English by Philalethes* (Edinburgh, written in Latin, 1579; trans. 1680); Wing B5275; sigs. B4v–B5r, B5v–B6r, D4r–D6v, F8r–F9r.

his *Defense of the People of England* (Arrowood 15). Unsurprisingly, Buchanan's anti-absolutist sentiments also met with open hostility. In 1584, the Parliament of Scotland condemned *De Jure Regni* as seditious (Arrowood 16). The fact that the first English translation of *De Jure Regni* appeared a hundred years after its initial publication, and that even then its translator remained anonymous, attests to its status as a politically radical text.

Buchanan's description of the tyrant provides perspective on Paulina's condemnation of the "tyrannous passion" that will make Leontes "ignoble" and "scandalous to the world" (2.3.28, 120–21). After Apollo's oracle pronounces Leontes a "jealous tyrant," Paulina directly accuses him of being such, even goading him to gratify his sadistic passions through torture: "What studied torments, tyrant, hast for me?" (3.2.130, 170). As Rebecca Bushnell observes, Renaissance humanists argued that "tyranny lies not so much in power itself but in desire as a form of power" (53). In what ways does Buchanan's portrait of the tyrant emphasize "passion" or "desire as a form of power," and to what extent does this view of the tyrant accurately describe Leontes? When Paulina calls Leontes a "tyrant," is she exaggerating for rhetorical effect, or is Leontes clearly recognizable as the stereotypical tyrant excoriated by Buchanan?

The problem of how subjects should respond to a wicked king is directly addressed both in *The Winter's Tale* and in *De Jure Regni*. Buchanan argues that subjects can (and should) resist a wicked monarch in various ways. Consider how far the Sicilian courtiers are willing to go in resisting Leontes, and what assumptions or beliefs inform their notions of appropriate resistance. *The Winter's Tale*, of course, is not a political tract, but Buchanan's text (like those of King James and Francis Bacon) can help to identify those moments in the play that evoke theories of obedience and resistance circulating in the early modern period. For instance, whereas Buchanan argues that kings are subject to law, Paulina seems to deny that avenue of redress when she laments that Leontes "cannot be compelled" by law to recant his slander against the queen (2.3.89). Why can't Leontes be compelled by law? What are the factors that limit the Sicilian courtiers' desire or ability to impose stricter constraints on Leontes' power? What might Buchanan recommend as a legitimate response to Leontes' conduct?

As its English title implies, Buchanan's *Dialogue* takes the form of a Socratic dialogue, in which Buchanan uses deductive reasoning and carefully phrased questions to guide his interlocutor, Thomas Maitland, to a greater understanding of the issues at hand. When reading this text, pay attention to how Buchanan rhetorically stacks the deck in leading his reader to accept certain conclusions as self-evidently true.

The first excerpt appears in the context of a discussion about a king's duty to govern according to law.

From *De Jure Regni apud Scotos*

BUCHANAN: And because we fear he[1] be not firm enough against inordinate affections, which may and for the most part use to decline men from truth, we shall adjoin to him the law, as it were a colleague, or rather a bridler of his lusts.

MAITLAND: You do not, then, think that a king should have an arbitrary power over all things?

BUCHANAN: Not at all. For I remember that he is not only a king, but also a man, erring in many things by ignorance, often failing willingly, doing many things by constraint: yea, a creature easily changeable at the blast of every favor or frown, which natural vice a magistrate useth also to increase. So that here I chiefly find that of the comedy made true, "All by licence become worse."[2] Wherefore the most prudent have thought it expedient to adjoin to him a law, which may either show him the way, if he be ignorant, or bring him back again into the way, if he wander out of it. . . .

BUCHANAN: . . . We must therefore always stand to what we spoke at first: that kings at first were instituted for maintaining equity. If they could have holden that sovereignty in the case they had received it, they might have holden and kept it perpetually, but this is free and loosed by laws. But (as it is with human things) the state of affairs tending to worse, the sovereign authority which was ordained for public utility degenerated into a proud domination. For when the lust of kings stood in stead of laws, and men being vested with an infinite and immoderate power did not contain themselves within bounds but connived at many things out of favor, hatred, or self-interest, the insolency of kings made laws to be desired. For this cause, therefore, laws were made by the people, and kings constrained to make use not of their own licentious wills in judgment, but of that right or privilege which the people had conferred upon them. For they were taught by many experiences that it was better that their liberty should be concredited[3] to laws than to kings, whereas the one might decline many ways from the truth, but the other being deaf both to entreaties and threats might still keep one and the same tenor. . . .

[Buchanan explains the differences between the governments of kings and tyrants.]

---

[1] **he:** the generic king of whom they are speaking. [2] **All . . . worse:** a quotation from the Roman playwright Terence: "Where there is license, everything goes from bad to worse" (Arrowood 56). [3] **concredited:** entrusted.

BUCHANAN: But they who bear rule not for their country's good but for their own self interests, have no regard to the public utility but to their own pleasure and lust, they place the stability of their authority in the people's weakness, and think that a kingdom is not a procuration[4] concredited to them by God, but rather a prey put into their hands. Such are not joined to us by any civil bond or bond of humanity, but should be accounted the greatest enemies of God and of all men. For all the actions of kings should aim at the public safety of their subjects, and not at their own wealth. By how much kings are raised above other men, so much should they imitate the celestial bodies, which having no good offices of ours given to them yet do infuse on human affairs a vital and bountiful virtue of heat and light. Yea, the very titles wherewith we have honored kings (if you remember) might put them in mind of their munificence.[5]

MAITLAND: Methinks I remember, namely, that they should use a paternal indulgence towards their subjects committed to them as towards children; the care of a shepherd in procuring their profit; as generals in maintaining their safety; as governors in excellency of virtues; and as emperors commanding those things which might be useful.

BUCHANAN: Can he then be called a father who accounts his subjects slaves? Or a shepherd, who doth not feed his flock, but devoureth them? Or a pilot, who doth always study to make shipwreck of the goods in his ship, and who (as they say) makes a leak in the very ship wherein he sails?

MAITLAND: By no means.

BUCHANAN: What is he then who doth not rule for the people's good but still doth all for himself, who doth not strive with good men in virtue, but contendeth to exceed the most flagitious[6] wretch in vices? Who leadeth his subjects into manifest snares?

MAITLAND: Indeed such shall not be by me accounted either a general, or emperor, or governor.

BUCHANAN: If you then shall see any usurping the name of a king, and in no kind of virtue excelling any of the people but inferior to many therein, not fatherly affectionate towards his subjects but rather oppressing them by arrogant domineering, and that thinketh the people is concredited to him for his own gain and not for their safeguard, will you imagine that such a man is truly a king? Albeit he goes vaporing[7] with a great many in guard about him, and openly be seen with gorgeous apparel, and make a show of punishments; can he conciliate[8] the people, and catch their applause by rewards, games, pompous shows, and even mad underminings,

---

[4] **procuration:** administration.   [5] **munificence:** great generosity.   [6] **flagitious:** guilty of atrocious crimes.   [7] **vaporing:** swaggering.   [8] **conciliate:** pacify.

and whatever is thought to be magnificent. Will you, I say, account such a man a king?

MAITLAND: Not indeed if I would understand myself aright, but void of all human society.

BUCHANAN: Within what limits do you circumscribe human society?

MAITLAND: Within the very same limits wherein by your preceding discourse you seemed to include it, namely within the hedge of laws, which whosoever transgress, be they robbers, thieves, or adulterers, I see them publicly punished; and that to be accounted a just cause of their punishment, because they transgressed the limits of human society.

BUCHANAN: What say you of those who would never once enter within these hedges?

MAITLAND: I think they should be accounted enemies to God and men, and reckoned amongst wolves, or some other kind of noisome[9] beasts, rather than amongst men: which whosoever doth nourish, he nourisheth them for his own destruction and others', and whosoever killeth them, doth not only good to himself but to all others. But if I had power to make a law, I would command (which the Romans were wont to do with monsters) such kind of men to be carried away into solitary places or to be drowned in the depths of the sea afar from the sight of any land, lest by the contagion of their carcasses they might infect other men. And rewards to the killers of them to be discerned not only by the whole people, but by every particular person, as useth to be done to those who have killed wolves or . . . bears, or apprehended their whelps.[10] For if such a monster should be born and speak with a man's voice, and have the face of a man and likeness of other parts, I would have no fellowship with him. Or if any man divested of humanity should degenerate into such cruelty as he would not meet with other men but for their destruction, I think he should be called a man no more than satyrs, apes, or bears, albeit they should resemble man in countenance, gesture, and speech.

BUCHANAN: Now, if I mistake not, you understand what a king, and what a tyrant the wisest ancients meant in their writings. Will it please you then that we propose some idea of a tyrant also, such as we gave in speaking of a king?

MAITLAND: Yes, that I do earnestly desire, if it be not a trouble to you.

BUCHANAN: You have not forgot, I suppose, what by the poets is spoken of the Furies, and by our divines of the nature of evil spirits: [that they] are

---

[9] noisome: harmful.   [10] whelps: cubs.

enemies of mankind, who whilst they are in perpetual torments, yet do rejoice in the torments of men. This is indeed the true idea of tyranny. But because this idea can only be discerned in the imagination but not by any of the senses, I shall set before you another idea, which not only the mind may discern but the senses also perceive, and as it were represented to the very eye. Imagine you see a ship tossed by waves in the sea, and all the shores round about not only without haven or harbor but also full of most cruel enemies, and the master of the ship in contest with the company, and yet to have no other hope of safety than in their fidelity, and the same not certain, as knowing well that he puts his life into the hands of a most barbarous kind of men and void of all humanity, whom by money he may hold trusty and who for greater gain may be conduced to fight against him. Such indeed is that life which tyrants embrace as happy. They are afraid of enemies abroad and of their subjects at home, and not only of their subjects but of their domestics, kinsfolk, brethren, wives, children, and near relations. And therefore they have always war — either a foreign war with their neighbors, civil war with their subjects, or a domestic war within doors — or else they are still in fear thereof. Neither do they expect aid anywhere but by a mercenary way: they dare not hire good men, nor can they trust bad men. What then in all their life can be to them pleasant? Dionysius[11] would not let his daughters, once become women, to trim him, fearing to let the razor come to his throat. Timoleon was killed by his own brother, Alexander Pheraeus by his own wife, and Sp. Cassias by his own father.[12] He that still hath such examples set before his eyes, what a torture do you imagine he carryeth about in his breast, seeing he thinks that he is the mark set for all mankind to shoot at? Neither is he only while awake tormented with these tortures of conscience, but also is awakened out of his sleep by terrifying sights both of the living and dead, and agitated by the fire brands of hellish furies. For the season which nature doth grant for rest to all creatures and also to men for relaxation of their cares to him is turned into horrors and punishment. . . .

[Buchanan has been arguing that a king is subject to trial by law.]

---

[11] **Dionysius:** A despotic Sicilian tyrant (ca. 432–367 B.C.E.) who was so afraid of being assassinated that he had his daughters shave him until he grew fearful even of them. [12] **Timoleon . . . father:** actually, the Greek general Timoleon (4th century B.C.E.) was involved in the assassination of his brother, the Corinthian tyrant Timophanes; Alexander was despot of Pherae, in Thessaly (4th century B.C.E.); Spurius Cassius was a consul of the Roman Republic (5th century B.C.E.) who was executed on the charge of attempting to make himself king.

MAITLAND: What if a king will not willingly compear[13] nor by force can be compelled to compear?

BUCHANAN: Then the case is common with him as with all other flagitious persons, for no thief or warlock[14] will willingly compear before a judge to be judged. But I suppose you know what the law doth permit, namely to kill any way a thief stealing by night and also to kill him if he defend himself when stealing by day. But if he cannot be drawn to compear to answer but by force, you remember what is usually done. For we pursue by force and arms such robbers as are more powerful than that by law they can be reached. Nor is there almost any other cause of all the wars betwixt nations, people, and kings than those injuries which, whilst they cannot be determined by justice, are by arms decided.

MAITLAND: Against enemies indeed for these causes wars used to be carried on, but the case is far otherwise with kings, to whom by a most sacred oath interposed we are bound to give obedience.

BUCHANAN: We are indeed bound: but they do first promise that they shall rule in equity and justice.

MAITLAND: It is so.

BUCHANAN: There is then a mutual paction[15] betwixt the king and his subjects.

MAITLAND: It seems so.

BUCHANAN: Doth not he who first recedes from what is covenanted and doth contrary to what he hath covenanted to do break the contract and covenant?

MAITLAND: He doth.

BUCHANAN: The bond then being loosed which did hold fast the king with the people, whatever privilege or right did belong to him by that agreement and covenant who looseth the same, I suppose is lost.

MAITLAND: It is lost.

BUCHANAN: He then with whom the covenant was made becometh as free as ever he was before the stipulation.

MAITLAND: He doth clearly enjoy the same privilege and the same liberty.

BUCHANAN: Now if a king do those things which are directly for the dissolution of society, for the continuance whereof he was created, how do we call him?

MAITLAND: A tyrant, I suppose.

BUCHANAN: Now a tyrant hath not only no just authority over a people, but is also their enemy.

---

[13] compear: appear in court.   [14] warlock: traitor, reprobate.   [15] paction: pact, convenant.

MAITLAND: He is indeed an enemy.

BUCHANAN: Is there not a just and lawful war with an enemy for grievous and intolerable injuries?

MAITLAND: It is forsooth[16] a just war.

BUCHANAN: What war is that which is carried on with him who is the enemy of all mankind, that is, a tyrant?

MAITLAND: A most just war.

BUCHANAN: Now a lawful war being once undertaken with an enemy, and for a just cause, it is lawful not only for the whole people to kill that enemy but for every one of them.

MAITLAND: I confess that.

BUCHANAN: May not every one out of the whole multitude of mankind assault with all the calamities of war a tyrant who is a public enemy, with whom all good men have a perpetual warfare?

[16] forsooth: truly.

Women's Speech: Attacks and Defenses

If I prove honeymouthed, let my tongue blister.   (2.2.33)

In *The Winter's Tale*, women's speech is both a source of the crisis at the Sicilian court and also part of its solution. The trouble starts when Leontes urges Hermione to persuade Polixenes to remain in Sicilia: "Tongue-tied, our Queen? Speak you" (1.2.27). When the "heartiness" and "bounty" of Hermione's eloquence overcome Polixenes, her success ironically arouses Leontes' suspicions about her fidelity (1.2.113). In Shakespeare's England, excessive or public female speech could easily be perceived as disorderly; moreover, it was a common belief that a woman who was open with her mouth was likely to be open with her body as well. Because the "connection between speaking and wantonness was common to legal discourse and conduct books," a man accused of slandering a woman as a "whore" could defend himself "by claiming that he meant 'whore of her tonge,' not 'whore of her body'" (Stallybrass 126, citing Houlbrooke 80). We might therefore assume that Hermione's eloquence triggers Leontes' anxiety about her sexual promiscuity, even though he does not directly articulate this connection between a loose tongue and a loose body.

Leontes does call attention to the transgressive implications of female speech in his effort to delegitimize Paulina's challenge to his political and

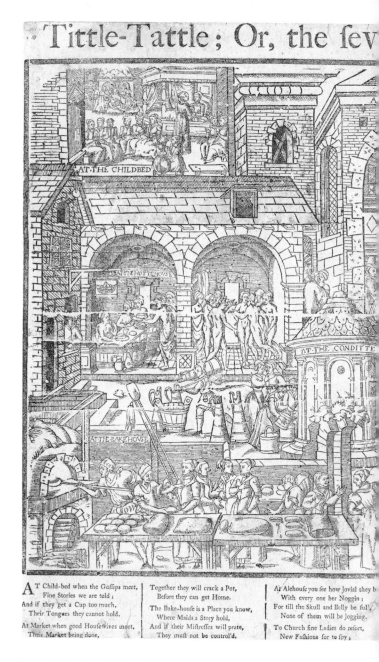

FIGURE 16 *"Tittle-Tattle; Or, the Several Branches of Gossipping," a woodcut print from 1750 that derives from an Elizabethan original from around 1603. That this image has kept its currency for so long suggests the conventionality of its depiction of*

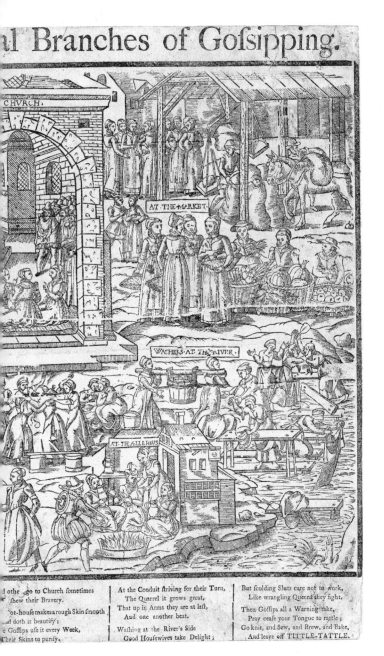

CHVRCH.

AT·THE·MARKET

WAÍHERS·AT·THE·RIVER·

AT·THE·ALE·HOVS·

...othe ...go to Church ſometimes ...ſhew their Bravery. ...ot-houſe makes a rough Skin ſmooth ...d doth it beautify ; ...e Goſſips uſe it every Week, Their Skins to puriſy,	At the Conduit ſtriving for their Turn, The Quarrel it grows great, That up in Arms they are at laſt, And one another beat. Waſhing at the River's Side Good Houſewives take Delight ;	But ſcolding Sluts care not to work, Like wrangling Queans they fight. Then Goſſips all a Warning take, Pray ceaſe your Tongue to rattle ; Go knit, and Sew, and Brew, and Bake, And leave off TITTLE-TATTLE.

women. How does the illustration combine details of everyday life with stereotypical portraits of unruly women? With which kinds of activities are women associated?

domestic authority. Paulina initially requests simply to be heard as a faithful, if painfully blunt, adviser:

> Good my liege, I come —
> And, I beseech you hear me, who professes
> Myself your loyal servant, your physician,
> Your most obedient counselor, yet that dares
> Less appear so in comforting your evils
> Than such as most seem yours — (2.3.52–57)

Despite Paulina's declaration of loyalty, Leontes attacks her as a "mankind witch" — an unnaturally aggressive woman in collusion with demonic powers — and a "most intelligencing bawd" (2.3.68–69) — a spying pander, or sexual go-between. Leontes deploys the common cultural association between female speech and female promiscuity to disarm Paulina's political critique of his own unruly speech, his stinging slander of the queen.

Although Paulina certainly does not deserve to be called Hermione's bawd, by publicly accusing the king of being ignorant, mad, unworthy, and unnatural, she does expose herself to the charge of scolding. Ridiculing Paulina as a "callet / Of boundless tongue, who hath late beat her husband," and identifying her as "Dame Partlet" and "Lady Margery," comical names for hens, Leontes reduces Paulina to the stereotype of the nagging, domineering wife (2.3.91–92, 76, 160). The absurd comedy of the conflict between Paulina and Leontes derives in part from the disjunction between the dignified royal setting and the allusions to scolding: a domestic offense associated with women of middling and lower classes, such as Katherine in Shakespeare's *Taming of the Shrew* (Jardine 105). It is important to understand what kind of associations the figure of the scold might have evoked for the original audiences of *The Winter's Tale*. Does Paulina in fact correspond to the contemporary stereotypes of the scold, shrew, or gossip (see Figure 16 on p. 262)?

In early modern England, women from the middling and lower ranks of society were subject to humiliating and brutal public punishments for scolding. Through an examination of local court records between 1560 and 1640, David Underdown finds "an intense preoccupation with women who are a visible threat to the patriarchal system," including those defined as scolds, witches, or whores (119). Lynda Boose further observes that "the punishments meted out to women are much more frequently targeted at suppressing women's speech than they are at controlling their sexual transgressions"; the "chief social offenses seem to have been 'scolding,' 'brawling,' and dominating one's husband" (184–85). Scolds could be punished with the "cucking stool," a chair attached to a lever used to dunk the victim repeatedly into a lake or river, or with the "scold's bridle," an iron headpiece with a metal bit that pressed down on the victim's tongue, preventing her from speaking and possibly causing gagging or lacerations. The cucking stool appears in legal records as well as in ballads and plays. Since the scold's bridle was not legally recognized as a form of punishment, it rarely appears in official documents, and thus it is difficult to determine the regularity of its use. However, Boose argues both from literary evidence and town records that its use was more

FIGURE 17 *Bridling of Ann Bidlestone, from Ralph Gardiner,* England's Grievance Discovered *(1655). Gardiner's tract attacks the mayor and burgesses of the town of Newcastle for various abuses of trade and law. He complains that local magistrates' regular use of the scold's bridle "is not granted by their charter" and is "repugnant to the known laws of England." According to Gardiner, scolds should not be bridled but "ducked head and ears into the water in a ducking-stool" (sig. P4r).*

widespread than has been acknowledged. One mid-seventeenth-century visitor to the town of Newcastle reported that "he saw one Ann Bidlestone drove through the streets by an officer of the same corporation, holding a rope in his hand, the other end fastened to an engine called the branks, which is like a crown, it being of iron, which was muffled over the head and face, with a great gap or tongue of iron forced into her mouth, which forced the blood out. And that is the punishment which the magistrates do inflict upon chiding and scolding women, and that he hath often seen the like done to others" (sigs. P3v–P4r) (see Figure 17 on p. 265).

The husbands of scolding or domineering wives were also sometimes punished for their failure to maintain proper order within the household, and by extension, within the larger community. The shaming ritual known as charivari or skimmington featured a carnivalesque procession in which neighbors publicly ridiculed the disorderly domestic behavior of the targeted couple. To the playing of percussive "rough music," the offending husband (or a neighbor impersonating him) was placed backwards on a horse or donkey, thus symbolizing the inversion of domestic order. As the husband (or his surrogate) was paraded through the streets, a cross-dressed man representing his wife sometimes followed behind, beating him with a ladle (Underdown 129–32). In the image of a skimmington in Figure 18, the husband, riding backwards, carries a distaff in his hand and wears cuckold's horns on his head. The poem reads: "Well worth to scourge, so weak a patch [fool], / Who with so strong a whore should match, / And cause the boys thereat make games / By riding thus, to both their shames." As Diane Purkiss explains, ritual punishments such as the skimmington "depend on the replication of a source of social disorder in a symbol of disorder"; hence, "a perceived inversion of the social order is both represented and corrected by another, different inversion" (81).

Since the cucking-stool, scold's bridle, and skimmington were not used against members of the gentle and noble classes, Leontes implicity degrades the social status of Paulina and Antigonus by defining them as if they were an unruly village couple. Leontes berates Antigonus as a husband who cannot "rule" and even "dreads" his wife, and has consequently become effeminate: "Thou dotard, thou art woman-tired, unroosted / By thy Dame Partlet here" (2.3.46, 80, 75–76). Peter Erickson suggests that in attacking Antigonus, Leontes might be expressing "self-accusations and self-doubts" about his own masculinity (155). When Paulina is finally ejected, however, Leontes accuses Antigonus not of a failure to control his wife, but of inciting her to disorder. According to Leontes, then, Antigonus is either a weak husband who cannot control his wife or a strong husband who is a traitor. Either way, Leontes judges Antigonus based on his wife's unruly speech.

FIGURE 18 *An illustration of the shaming ritual known as skimmington from* English Customs *(1628).*

The four documents below represent the range of styles, motives, and genres that early modern writers used to address the controversial issue of female speech. Whereas some of these texts indicate how Leontes' accusations of scolding might effectively undermine Paulina's moral authority, others articulate strategies of resistance against attempts to shame or coerce women into silence. Of the four documents, the most orthodox is the marriage sermon by the puritan minister William Whately that uses biblical examples to illustrate the virtues of wifely submission and silence. Next we will consider two popular pamphlets that are directly linked: Joseph Swetnam's *Arraignment of Lewd, Idle, Froward, and Unconstant Women*, and Rachel Speght's *A Muzzle for Melastomus*. Swetnam's misogynist pamphlet provoked responses from several writers, including Speght, a minister's daughter, who defends women's honor and intelligence against the slanders of this blasphemous, ignorant ranter. In our last text, a ballad by Martin Parker, a husband and wife debate the mutual duties of marriage. Offering conversation and negotiation as models of domestic communication, Parker's ballad suggests that the contentious issue of women's speech need not be addressed solely through the antagonistic rhetorical strategies of attack and defense.

→ WILLIAM WHATELY

From A Bride-Bush:
Or, A Direction for Married Persons   *1619*

A puritan minister in Oxfordshire, William Whately published many sermons, as well as two popular treatises on marriage, *A Bride-Bush* and *A Care-Cloth* (1624). In the dedication of the second edition of *A Bride-Bush* (1619), Whately explains that he had preached a marriage sermon "some ten or eleven years since and delivered a copy thereof unto a friend"; a forty-nine-page version of this sermon had been published without his permission in 1617 (sig. A1r). For the 1619 edition (reprinted in 1623), Whately used some "larger notes" on the topic of marriage to expand his original sermon into a 220-page treatise. Whately named his treatise after a traditional village custom, in which a bush would be hung out at an alehouse to honor a wedding. Despite the allusion to local customs in its title, *A Bride-Bush* controversially advocated divorce on the grounds of desertion and adultery, a position that contradicted the doctrine of the Church of England.

The title page of *A Bride-Bush* recommends the book to all spouses who find marriage a "little hell." Whately aims to purge his readers of the pride and passion that cause woeful marriages by explicating the mutual duties of husbands and wives. Whereas both partners have the duties of remaining chaste and demonstrating benevolence, faithfulness, and helpfulness, they also have "peculiar" duties. The husband's charge is "to govern or rule" and "to maintain" his wife. Like other Protestant marriage manuals (such as William Gouge's *Of Domestical Duties*, see p. 180), *A Bride-Bush* admonishes the wife "to acknowledge her inferiority," "to practice the virtue of subjection," and to "show reverence" towards her husband through her "gestures, countenances, and whole behavior." Placing particular emphasis on unruly speech as a sign of disrespect that inverts domestic authority, Whately rebukes wives who "chase and scold with their husbands, railing upon them and reviling them" (p. 270).

In *The Winter's Tale*, Paulina vigorously chastises Leontes for his folly, but does her criticism amount to the "railing" and "reviling" that Whately finds so "loathsome and unwomanly" (p. 270)? To answer this question, we might consider Paulina's motives for confronting Leontes and the success of her strategy. When she declares that the task of defending Hermione's innocence "[b]ecomes a woman best," does Paulina mean that a woman can best sympathize with the queen's plight and hence function most effectively as "[h]er advocate to th'loud'st" (2.2.32, 39)? Or does she mean that a woman should confront Leontes because, according to a famililar stereotype, nothing is more fearsome than an angry, sharp-tongued woman? Describing her tongue as a trumpet blasting out

---

William Whately, *A Bride-Bush: Or, A Direction for Married Persons. Plainly Describing the Duties Common to Both, and Particular to Each of Them* (London, 1619), STC 25297; sigs. Cc2r–Dd2r.

fiery indignation, Paulina announces her intention to speak aggressively: "If I prove honeymouthed, let my tongue blister / And never to my red-looked anger be / The trumpet any more" (2.2.33–35). Is Paulina here self-consciously embracing the role of the furious scold? Paulina's arrival at court is indeed unruly and disruptive. Ignoring her husband's command to remain silent, she insists on her duty to cure the king with "medicinal" words (2.3.37). Leontes, of course, perceives only the "noise" of an "audacious lady" who meddles in political affairs and disobeys her husband (2.3.39, 42). Does the play allow us to sympathize both with Paulina's insistence on speaking and with Leontes' insistence that she hold her tongue?

By the end of the play, the question of the relative merits of female speech and female silence has not been resolved. Whatley affirms that "a simple woman holding her peace shall have more honor than one of more wit if she be full of tongue" (p. 272). Does the play uphold Whatley's claim that a woman earns more honor from silence than from speech? Paulina's determination to tell the truth eventually does earn her the respect of Leontes, who admits that he deserves "[a]ll tongues to talk their bitt'rest"; nonetheless, a Lord still chastises Paulina for the "boldness of [her] speech" (3.2.211, 213). To what degree are these assessments of appropriate or inappropriate speech based specifically on considerations of gender? How does Paulina respond to these contradictory assessments of the value of her speech?

It is finally not clear what lessons are to be drawn from *The Winter's Tale* about the legitimacy of female speech. While Paulina continues to advise Leontes, Hermione remains virtually silent during the final scene of the play, speaking only briefly to her daughter, and not at all to her husband. At the end of act 3, Paulina says, "I'll say nothing" (3.2.227), but Hermione, sequestered from the public world of men for sixteen years and returned to her husband in the form of a statue, comes closer than Paulina to embodying that ideal of womanly virtue — and to revealing the steep price paid for achieving it.

From *A Bride-Bush*

The husband is to the wife the image and glory of God. The power that is given to him is God's originally and his by God's appointment. Look not therefore on the gifts and qualities of thine husband but upon his place, and know that thou canst not neglect or despise him but that the contempt redoundeth[1] unto God's dishonor, who hath ordained him to be thine head. So if religion hath seasoned thine heart with the fear of God, thou shalt fear thine husband also for his commandment sake.

But as the wife's heart must be affected with this loving fear, so must her

---

[1] redoundeth: returns.

outward carriage also savor thereof and show it forth, and that in two special things. First, in her words; secondly, in her gestures and behavior. Her words are either to himself in person, of him behind his back, or to others before him. All must have a taste of reverence. First, her speeches to himself must neither be cutted,[2] sharp, sullen, passionate, tetchy,[3] nor yet rude, careless, unmannerly, and contemptuous, but all such as carry the stamp of fear upon them, testifying that she well considers who herself is and to whom she speaketh. The wife's tongue toward her husband must neither be keen[4] nor loose, neither such as argues rage nor neglect, but savoring of all lowliness and quietness of affection that if another should stand by and hear them he might perceive (though he knew not otherwise) that these are the words of an inferior to her better. Look what kind of words thyself wouldest dislike from thy servant or child, those must not thou dare to give unto thine husband: for the same duty of fear is in the same words and in the same plainness commanded to thee that unto them.

Herein Sarah once faulted. She was aloft and in the boughs (as we speak). "Thou dost me wrong," saith she, "and God be judge between me and thee" (Genesis 16:5). Herein also Rachel offended, that came to her husband fuming, and in a pelting chafe must needs chide with him for children, saying, "Give me children, or else I die." Though Jacob loved Rachel tenderly, yet (you know) he could not brook this rudeness without anger, for his wrath was kindled and he said, "Am I in God's place, that hath denied to thee the fruit of the womb?" (Genesis 30:1–2). Herein also Michol, Saul's daughter and David's wife, though a Queen, yet was much out of the way, for she came scoffing and flouting to the King her husband — a thing of the two less tolerable than wrath and rage, because it shows a more allowed contempt — and, "How glorious" saith she, "was the King of Israel this day, etc." (2 Samuel 6:20). When her husband, in her conceit (though not indeed), had carried himself somewhat unfittingly for the place of a King, she cannot tell him of it in good and respective fashion, but with a bitter taunting must needs break a jest upon him. These examples tend to show how subject women are to disreverent[5] passages of speech, and withal how loathsome and unwomanly they be.

Yet for all these examples and warnings, we want[6] not women (if the name of a woman be not wronged in giving it to such shameless creatures) that chase and scold with their husbands, railing upon them and reviling them, and shaking them up with such terms as were nothing sufferable towards a neighbor or towards a servant. Stains of womankind; blemishes

---

[2] **cutted:** curt or snappish. [3] **tetchy:** quick to take offense. [4] **keen:** sharp. [5] **disreverent:** disrespectful. [6] **want:** lack.

of their sex; monsters in nature; botches[7] of the family; rude, shameless, graceless; next to[8] harlots, if not the same with them. Let such words leave a blister behind them, and let the canker eat out such tongues. And what remedy a husband should use for such a festering sore, we delivered you before. If patient forbearing and admonitions will not bring them to reformation, let the words of Solomon[9] be hearkened unto, "a rod is for the fool's back," and strike a scorner. Why this precept should be limited with any limitation tending to safeguard a scornful, foolish, graceless woman from the execution of it I can verily see no reason; neither, I think, can any man render any.

But besides these notorious ones, women otherwise virtuous must be content to be told of a fault in this behalf. They can sometimes take up[10] their husbands with quick speeches sharply set on, they can set them down short[11] with a cutted answer, and weary their ears with tumultuous brawling. Is this seemly for a Christian woman? Should a daughter of Sarah govern her tongue no better? Why wilt thou teach thy children to be rebellious and show thy servants the trade of swelling, fuming, and rudeness? Thinkest thou that such behavior is not infectious? Shall not they use it to thee when they see thee use it to thine husband? Or is it more tolerable in them to thyself than in thee to thine head? Set not those of thy family so bad a copy; teach them rather that reverent and dutiful carriage which thou wouldst have them practice to thyself. For be sure the woman shall make herself vile that sets her husband at naught, and those that abuse their superiors do but embolden their inferiors to pay themselves home with the like abuse. . . .

[A wife should not use overly familiar language, calling her husband by his first name; she should call him "husband," or a name of like dignity.]

She must also look to her speeches directed to others in his presence that they be such and so framed as may witness a due regard of him. His company must make her more respective of her behavior to any other before him than otherwise she need to be. Her words to children and servants in his sight and hearing ought not to be loud and snappish. If she perceive a fault in them, she must yet remember that her better stands by, and therefore must not speak but upon necessity, and then utter that reproof in a more still and mild manner which in his absence she might set on with more roundness.[12] No woman of government will allow her children and servants to be

---

[7] **botches:** blemishes or sores.   [8] **next to:** similar to.   [9] **Solomon:** in Proverbs 26:3.   [10] **take up:** rebuke.   [11] **set them down short:** respond curtly.   [12] **roundness:** plainness or severity.

loud and brawling before her, and shall she herself be so before her husband? What then is become of the remembrance of inferiority? Nay, verily, this reverence doth enjoin the woman silence when her husband is present: I mean not an utter abstinence from speech, but using fewer words (and those mild and low) not loud and eager. The Apostle commands the woman to be in silence or in quietness, wherein he enjoins not alone a public but a general silence to hold in the house and other private meetings (1 Timothy 2:10). For why should that place of Scripture be needlessly restrained which is fitly capable of a larger interpretation. . . .

[The duty of women's silence is grounded on the difference between the sexes, the female being inferior to the male.]

And if in anything this inferiority be to be acknowledged, then doubtless in this particular whereof we are speaking, than which there cannot be a less nor yet a fitter demonstration of it, and which is also required of younger people toward their ancients, if other things do also agree, to abstain from many and high words, and to speak little and low before them. Wherefore, let women either excuse chat and loudness in youth before their ancients or in their children and servants before them, or else let them condemn it in themselves before their husbands, and not alone so, but before men in general. I know this duty goes against the hair, and there are but a very few women that can persuade themselves to show their thoughts of inferiority by fewness of words. For where is suddenness of wit and scarcity of wisdom — as in the greater number of this sex comparatively — there is likely forwardness to speak and multitude of words. But at all times, amongst all wise folk, the talkativeness of women before men (chiefly their husbands, and most of all when it comes to loud and earnest speaking) hath gone in the reckoning of a fault and a sign of self-conceitedness and indiscretion. And contrarily, silence hath been highly accounted of as a comely[13] ornament to that sex, who then are best liked and most worthy to be liked when they show least liking of themselves by not loving to hear themselves speak. You know of what woman it was of whom Solomon saith, "She is loud and stubborn," and again, "She is clamorous" (Proverbs 7:11, 9:13). Doubtless, a simple woman holding her peace shall have more honor than one of more wit if she be full of tongue. Wherefore let womankind learn silence — this is one part of the quietness of spirit commended to them by Peter — and suffer the due and reverent esteem of their husbands to work in them a special moderation of speech, whilst they be in place.

[13] **comely:** pleasing.

➜ JOSEPH SWETNAM

From The Arraignment of Lewd, Idle, Froward, and Unconstant Women   *1615*

Given the aggressive temper of his writing, it is fitting that Joseph Swetnam (d. 1621) might have worked as a fencing-master and a soldier. Little is known of his life, but Swetnam has earned a place in literary history as the author of *The Arraignment of Lewd, Idle, Froward, and Unconstant Women*, a misogynist diatribe that sparked a vigorous contemporary debate about gender ideology. Swetnam's treatise, which "gathered together misogynist commonplaces from the debate over women throughout the preceding century in England" (Jones 45), was popular not only in its own time, but throughout the seventeenth century, during which it was reprinted thirteen times.

In 1617, three responses to Swetnam's attack were published: Rachel Speght's *A Muzzle for Melastomus*, Esther Sowernam's *Esther hath Hanged Haman*, and Constantia Munda's *The Worming of a Mad Dog: Or, a Sop for Cerberus, the Jailor of Hell*. The names Esther Sowernam (*Sour*nam, the inverse of *Swe[e]t*nam) and Constantia Munda ("Moral Constancy") are clearly pseudonyms, and the writers behind them were possibly men speaking through female personas. All three pamphlets portray Swetnam as an ignorant, idle, shameful, and blasphemous railer. In 1620, an anonymous comedy called *Swetnam the Woman-Hater, Arraigned by Women* (see Figure 19) was staged at the Red Bull, a popular London theater. In it, Swetnam is humiliated by a tribunal of "extremely aggressive" women who bind, gag, and prick him with their needles (Woodbridge 312). At the end of the play, Swetnam recants his misogyny.

As Linda Woodbridge tartly observes, Swetnam's *Arraignment* is a "gallimaufry of proverb, sermon, anecdote, moral maxim, [and] invective": it "suffers from verbal diarrhea and is irritating to read" (85). Swetnam addresses his treatise both to "the common sort of women," from whom he anticipates a counterattack, and to "the ordinary sort of giddy-headed young men," whom he invites to enjoy his baiting of women. The treatise itself is divided into three parts: chapter 1 portrays women as proud and lazy; chapter 2 focuses on women's sexual vices; chapter 3 provides advice on how to choose a good wife. Swetnam ends by describing marriage to a widow as a state of hell. *The Arraignment* might well be derivative, contradictory, "patched and misshapen," as Constantia Munda, one of its contemporary critics, described it, yet precisely these shortcomings fruitfully opened its conventional misogynist positions to critique. As Ann Rosalind Jones explains, "[u]nlike the arguments of theologians and humanists whose erudition lent their pronouncements on women the authority of

---

Joseph Swetnam, *The Arraignment of Lewd, Idle, Froward, and Unconstant Women: Or the Vanity of Them, Choose You Whether* (London 1615), STC 23534; sigs. A2r–A2v, A4r, B1r–B1v, B4v–C1r, C2r–C2v, F1r, F2r–F2v, F4r–G2r.

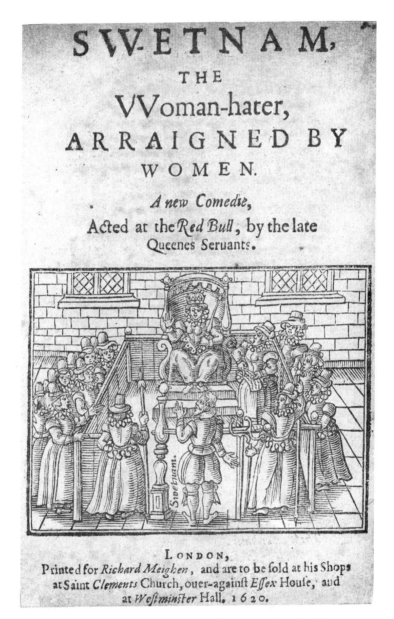

SVV-ETNAM,

THE

VVoman-hater,

ARRAIGNED BY

WOMEN.

A new Comedie,
Acted at the *Red Bull*, by the late
Queenes Seruants.

LONDON,
Printed for *Richard Meighen*, and are to be sold at his Shops
at Saint *Clements* Church, ouer-againſt *Eſſex* Houſe, and
at *Weſtminſter* Hall. 1620.

FIGURE 19 *Title page,* Swetnam the Woman-Hater, Arraigned by Women *(1620).*

wisdom and reason, Swetnam's tract could be dissected as evidence of how irrational and self-interested misogyny was" (46). Swetnam's own admitted resentment against women and the mocking, irreverent, and excessive language he uses to slander them undermined the legitimacy of his critique.

We might make a similar point about Leontes' criticism of Paulina. When reading *The Arraignment*, look for the points of correspondence and the points of divergence between Swetnam and Leontes in their roles as critics of women. On what grounds do they base their criticism of women? What purposes do they have in airing such views of women? Is Leontes as "irrational and self-interested" a misogynist as Swetnam?

From *The Arraignment of Lewd, Idle, Froward, and Unconstant Women*

Neither to the best nor yet to the worst; but to the common sort of women.

Musing with myself being idle, and having little ease to pass the time withal; and I being in a great choler[1] against some women, I mean more than one; and so in the ruff[2] of my fury, taking my pen in hand to beguile the time withal, indeed I might have employed myself to better use than in such an idle business, and better it were to pocket up[3] a pelting injury than to entangle myself with such vermin. For this I know — that because women are women, therefore many of them will do that in an hour which they many times will repent all their whole life time after; yet for any injury which I have received of them, the more I consider of it, the less I esteem of[4] the same.

Yet perhaps some may say unto me that I have sought for honey and caught the bee by the tail, or that I have been bit or stung with some of these wasps; otherwise I could never have been expert in bewraying[5] their qualities, for the mother would never have sought her daughter in the oven but that she was there herself. Indeed I must confess I have been a traveler this thirty and odd years, and many travelers live in disdain of women. The reason is, for that their affections are so poisoned with the heinous evils of unconstant women which they happen to be acquainted with in their travels: for it doth so cloy[6] their stomachs that they censure hardly[7] of women ever afterwards. Wronged men will not be tongue-tied: therefore, if you do

---

[1] **choler:** anger. [2] **ruff:** highest degree. [3] **pocket up:** accept without resentment. [4] **esteem of:** think well of. [5] **bewraying:** speaking badly about. [6] **cloy:** to overfill, so as to cause disgust. [7] **censure hardly:** judge harshly.

ill, you must not think to hear well; for although the world be bad, yet it is not come to that pass that men should bear with all the bad conditions that are in some women.

I know I shall be bitten by many, because I touch many. But before I go any further, let me whisper one word in your ears, and that is this: whatsoever you think privately, I wish you to conceal it with silence, lest in starting up to find fault you prove yourselves guilty of these monstrous accusations, which are here following against some women. And those which spurn if they feel themselves touched prove themselves stark fools in bewraying their galled[8] backs to the world, for this book toucheth no sort of women but such as when they hear it will go about to reprove it. For although in some part of this book I trip at your heels, yet I will stay you by the hand, so that you shall not fall further than you are willing. Although I deal with you after the manner of a shrew, which cannot otherwise ease her curst heart but by her unhappy tongue, if I be too earnest, bear with me a little, for my meaning is not to speak much of those that are good, and I shall speak too little of those that are naught.

But yet I will not altogether condemn the bad, but hoping to better the good by the naughty examples of the bad: for there is no woman so good, but hath one idle part or other in her which may be amended. For the clearest river that is, hath some dirt in the bottom; jewels are all precious, but yet they are not all of one price, nor all of one virtue; gold is not all of one picture: no more are women all of one disposition. Women are all necessary evils, and yet not all given to wickedness; and yet many so bad that, in my conceit,[9] if I should speak the worst that I know by some women, I should make their ears glow that hear me, and my tongue would blister to report it. But it is a great discredit for a man to be accounted for a scold, for scolding is the manner of shrews; therefore, I had rather answer them with silence which find fault, than strive to win the cucking-stool[10] from them.

Now me thinks I hear some curious[11] dames give their rash judgments, and say that I, having no wit, descant upon[12] women, which have more wit than men. To answer you again: if I belie you, judge me unkind, but if I speak the truth I shall be the better believed another time. And if I had wrote never so well, it is unpossible to please all, and if never so ill, yet I shall please some. Let it be well or ill, I look for no praise for my labor. I am weaned from my mother's teat, and therefore never more to be fed with her

---

[8] **galled:** sore from chafing.   [9] **conceit:** conception.   [10] **cucking-stool:** an instrument of punishment, consisting of a chair in which the offender was fastened and exposed to the jeers of the bystanders, or conveyed to a pond or river and repeatedly submerged.   [11] **curious:** unduly inquisitive or precise.   [12] **descant upon:** criticize.

pap. Wherefore say what you will, for I will follow my own vein in unfolding every pleat, and showing every wrinkle of a woman's disposition. . . .

Read it if you please, and like as you list: neither to the wisest clerk,[13] nor yet to the starkest fool, but unto the ordinary sort of giddy-headed young men I send this greeting.

If you mean to see the bear-baiting of women, then trudge to this bear-garden apace and get in betimes,[14] and view every room where thou mayest best sit, for thy own pleasure, profit, and heart's ease; and bear with my rudeness, if I chance to offend thee. But before I do open this trunk full of torments against women, I think it were not amiss to resemble those which in old time did sacrifices to Hercules, for they used continually first to whip all their dogs out of their city; and I think it were not amiss to drive all the women out of my hearing, for doubt[15] lest this little spark kindle into such a flame, and raise so many stinging hornets humming about my ears, that all the wit I have will not quench the one nor quiet the other. For I fear me that I have set down more than they will like of, and yet a great deal less than they deserve. And for better proof, I refer myself to the judgment of men which have more experience than myself. For I esteem little of the malice of women, for men will be persuaded with reason, but women must be answered with silence. For I know women will bark more at me than Cerberus the two-headed dog did at Hercules, when he came into hell to fetch out the fair Proserpina[16]. . .

CHAPTER I

This first chapter showeth to what use women were made; it also showeth that most of them degenerate from the use they were framed unto, by leading a proud, lazy, and idle life, to the great hindrance of their poor husbands.

Moses[17] describeth a woman thus: at the first beginning (saith he) a woman was made to be a helper unto man, and so they are indeed: for she helpeth to spend and consume that which man painfully getteth. He also saith that

---

[13] **clerk:** scholar.   [14] **betimes:** early.   [15] **doubt:** fear.   [16] **Cerberus . . . Proserpina:** Swetnam gets his Greek mythology wrong. Cerberus was a *three*-headed dog that guarded the gate to Hades; the last of Hercules' twelve labors was to capture Cerberus. While in Hades, Hercules also freed Theseus, who had been imprisoned there during his attempt to kidnap Proserpina.
[17] **Moses:** Swetnam alludes to the creation of Eve and the fall of Adam and Eve from Genesis, chapters 2–3.

they were made of the rib of a man, and that their froward[18] nature showeth. For a rib is a crooked thing, good for nothing else, and women are crooked by nature, for small occasion will cause them to be angry. Again, in a manner, she was no sooner made but straightway her mind was set upon mischief, for by her aspiring mind and wanton will she quickly procured man's fall, and therefore ever since they are and have been a woe unto man, and follow the line of their first leader.

For, I pray you, let us consider the times past, with the time present: first, that of David and Solomon. If they had occasion so many hundred years ago to exclaim so bitterly against women, for the one of them said that it was better to be a door-keeper and better dwell in a den amongst lions, than to be in the house with a froward and wicked woman. And the other said that the climbing up of a sandy hill to an aged man was nothing so wearisome as to be troubled with a froward woman. And further he saith that the malice of a beast is not like the malice of a wicked woman, nor that there is nothing more dangerous than a woman in her fury.[19] The lion being bitten with hunger, the bear being robbed of her young ones, the viper being trod on — all these are nothing so terrible as the fury of a woman.

A buck may be enclosed in a park, a bridle rules a horse, a wolf may be tied, a tiger may be tamed: but a froward woman will never be tamed, no spur will make her go, nor no bridle will hold her back. For if a woman hold an opinion, no man can draw her from it. Tell her of her fault, she will not believe that she is in any fault; give her good counsel, but she will not take it. If you do but look after another woman, then she will be jealous; the more thou lovest her, the more she will disdain thee. And if thou threaten her, then she will be angry; flatter her, and then she will be proud; and if thou forbear her, it maketh her bold; and if thou chasten her, then she will turn to a serpent. At a word, a woman will never forget an injury, nor give thanks for a good turn. What wise man then will exchange gold for dross, pleasure for pain, a quiet life for wrangling brawls, from the which the married men are never free?

. . . [F]or do but cross a woman, although it be never so little, she will straightway put finger in the eye and cry. Then presently many a foolish man will flatter her and entreat her to be quiet, but that mars all, for the more she is entreated she will pour forth the more abundance of deceitful tears, and

---

[18] **froward:** ungovernable.   [19] **for the one of them said . . . in her fury:** Swetnam is thinking of biblical passages such as the following: "I had rather be a door-keeper in the house of my God, then to dwell in the tents of wickedness" (Psalm 84); "It is better to dwell in the wilderness, than with a contentious and an angry woman" (Proverbs 21:19); "It is better to dwell in the corner of the housetop, than with a brawling woman and in a wide house" (Proverbs 25:24)

therefore no more to be pitied than to see a goose go barefoot. For they have tears at command, so have they words at will, and oaths at pleasure; for they make as much account of an oath, as a merchant doth, which will forswear himself for the getting of a penny. I never yet knew woman that would deny to swear in defense of her own honesty, and always standing highly upon it, although she be ashamed to wear it in winter for catching of cold, nor in summer for heat, fearing lest it may melt away. . . .

When a woman wanteth any thing, she will flatter and speak fair, not much unlike the flattering butcher, who gently claweth[20] the ox when he intendeth to knock him on the head. But the thing being once obtained and their desires gained, then they will begin to look big, and answer so stately, and speak so scornfully, that one would imagine they would never seek help nor crave comfort at thy hands any more. But a woman is compared unto a ship, which being never so well rigged, yet one thing or other is to be amended: even so, give a woman all that she can demand today, yet she will be out of reparations tomorrow and want one thing or other.

Women are called night crows, for that commonly in the night they will make request for such toys as cometh in their heads in the day. For women know their time to work their craft, for in the night they will work a man like wax, and draw him like as the adamant doth the iron, and having once brought him to the bent of their bow, then she makes request for a gown of the new fashion stuff, or for a petticoat of the finest stammell,[21] or for a hat of the newest fashion. Her husband being overcome by her flattering speech, partly he yieldeth to her request, although it be a grief to him, for that he can hardly spare it out of his stock; yet for quietness' sake he doth promise what she demandeth, partly because he would sleep quietly in his bed. Again, every married man knows this: that a woman will never be quiet if her mind be set upon a thing till she have it.

Now, if thou drive her off with delays, then her forehead will be so full of frowns as if she threatened to make clubs trump,[22] and thou never a black card in thy hand. For except a woman have what she will, say what she list,[23] and go where she please, otherwise thy house will be so full of smoke that thou canst not stay in it.

It is said that an old dog and a hungry flea bite sore; but in my mind, a froward woman biteth more sorer. And if thou go about to master a woman, in hope to bring her to humility, there is no way to make her good with stripes except thou beat her to death. For do what thou wilt, yet a froward

---

[20] **claweth:** scratches, i.e., flatters or cajoles.   [21] **stammell:** a shade of red.   [22] **trump:** in cards, a suit that temporarily dominates the other three, with pun on "clubs" as weapons.   [23] **list:** wish.

woman in her frantic mood will pull, haul, swerve, scratch, and tear all that stands in her way. . . .

CHAPTER 3

This third chapter showeth a remedy against love; also many reasons
not to be too hasty in choice of a wife. But if no remedy but thou wilt
marry, then how to choose a wife, with a commendation
of the good, virtuous, and honest women.

. . . If thou marriest a still and a quiet woman, that will seem to thee that thou ridest but an ambling horse to hell; but if with one that is froward and unquiet, then thou wert as good ride a trotting horse to the devil. Herein I will not be my own carver,[24] but I refer you to the judgment of those which have seen the troubles and felt the torments. For none are better able to judge of women's qualities than those which have them; none feels the hardness of the flint but he that strikes it; none knows where the shoe pincheth but he that wears it. It is said that a man should eat a bushel of salt with one which he means to make his friend, before he put any great confidence or trust him. And if thou be so long in choosing a friend, in my mind thou hadst need to eat two bushels of salt with a woman, before thou make her thy wife. Otherwise, before thou hast eaten one bushel with her thou shalt taste of ten quarters[25] of sorrow; and for every dram[26] of pleasure an ounce of pain; and for every pint of honey a gallon of gall;[27] and for every inch of mirth an ell[28] of moan. In the beginning, a woman's love seemeth delightful, but endeth with destruction. Therefore, he that trusteth to the love of a woman shall be as sure as he that hangeth by the leaf of a tree in the later end of summer: and yet there is great difference betwixt the standing pool and the running stream, although they are both waters.

. . . Some with sweet words undermine their husbands, as Delilah did Samson,[29] and some with chiding and brawling are made weary of the world, as Socrates[30] and others. Socrates when his wife did chide and brawl would go out of the house till all were quiet again. But because he would not scold with her again, it grieved her the more; for on a time she watched his

---

[24] **be my own carver:** speak from my own authority or expertise.   [25] **ten quarters:** the equivalent of eighty bushels.   [26] **dram:** an eighth of an ounce.   [27] **gall:** poison.   [28] **ell:** forty-five inches.   [29] **Delilah . . . Samson:** Delilah cajoled Samson into revealing that his strength came from his hair; Delilah had his head shaved and then betrayed him to the Philistines, who blinded and imprisoned him (Judges 16).   [30] **Socrates:** Xanthippe, the wife of the ancient Greek philosopher Socrates, was reputed to be a shrew.

going out, and threw a chamber-pot out of a window on his head. "Ha, ha," quoth he, "I thought after all this thunder there would come rain."

There is an history maketh mention of one named Annynious, who invited a friend of his to go home with him to supper; but when he came home, he found his wife chiding and brawling with her maidens, whereat his guest was very much discontented. Annynious turning to him, said, "Good Lord, how impatient art thou? I have suffered her these twenty years, and canst not thou abide her two hours?" By which means he caused his wife to leave chiding and laughed out the matter.

There is no woman but either she hath a long tongue or a longing tooth, and they are two ill neighbors if they dwell together: for the one will lighten thy purse, if it be still pleased, and the other will waken thee from thy sleep, if it be not charmed. Is it not strange of what kind of metal a woman's tongue is made of, that neither correction can chastise nor fair means quiet? For there is a kind of venom in it, that neither by fair means nor foul they are to be ruled. All beasts by man are made tame, but a woman's tongue will never be tame; it is but a small thing, and seldom seen, but it is often heard, to the terror and utter confusion of many a man.

Therefore, as a sharp bit curbs a froward horse, even so a curst woman must be roughly used: but if women could hold their tongues, then many times men would hold their hands. As the best mettled[31] blade is mixed with iron, even so the best woman that is, is not free from faults: the goodliest gardens are not free from weeds, no more is the best nor the fairest woman from ill deeds. . . .

Divers[32] beasts and fowl by nature have more strength in one part of the body than in another, as the eagle in the beak, the unicorn in the horn, the bull in the head, the bear in his arms, the horse in his breast, the dog in his teeth, the serpent in his tail. But a woman's chief strength is in her tongue. The serpent hath not so much venom in his tail as she hath in her tongue; and as the serpent never leaveth hissing and stinging, and seeking to do mischief, even so some women are never well except they be casting out venom with their tongues, to the hurt of their husbands or of their neighbors. Therefore, he that will disclose his secrets to a woman is worthy to have his hair cut with Samson, for if thou unfoldest anything of secret to a woman, the more thou chargest her to keep it close, the more she will seem as it were to be with child till she have revealed it amongst her gossips. Yet if one should make doubt of her secrecy, she would seem angry and say, "I am no such light huswife[33] of my tongue, as they whose secrets lie at their tongues' ends, which flies abroad so soon as they open their mouths; therefore, fear

[31] **mettled:** tempered.   [32] **Divers:** different.   [33] **huswife:** hussy.

not to disclose your secrets to me, for I was never touched with any stain of my tongue in all my life." Nay, she will not stick to swear that she will tread it under foot or bury it under a stone. Yet for all this believe her not, for every woman hath one especial gossip at the least, which she doth love and affect above all the rest, and unto her she runneth with all the secrets she knoweth.

There is a history making mention of one Lyas, whom King Amasis commanded to go into the market and to buy the best and profitablest meat he could get; and he bought nothing but tongues. The king asked him the reason why he bought no other meat, who made this answer, "I was commanded to buy the best meat, and from the tongue came many good and profitable speeches." Then the king sent him again and bade him buy the worst and unprofitablest meat; and he likewise bought nothing but tongues. The king again asked him the reason. "From nothing," said he "cometh worse venom than from the tongue, and such tongues must women have."

Roman history maketh mention of one of the chief governors of Rome that had a son whose name was Papirius, whose father took him with him to the council-house that thereby he might learn wisdom, wishing him withal to keep their secrets. His mother was divers times asking of the boy what they did at the council-house, and what the cause was of their often meeting. On a time young Papirius, fearing to displease his father and hoping to satisfy his mother, told her this: "Mother," said he, "there is hard hold[34] amongst them about making of a law that every man shall have two wives or every woman two husbands; and so far as I can perceive, it is likely to be concluded upon, that every man shall have two wives."

The next day, when his father and he were gone to the council-house, she bestirred herself, and got most of the chief women of the city together, and told them what a law was like to be made, if it were not prevented. And so to the council-house they went a great flock of them. But when they came in, the governors were all amazed, and asked the cause of their coming. And one of the women having leave to speak, said thus: "Whereas you are about to make a law that every man shall have two wives, consider with yourselves what unquietness and strife thereby will arise; but," said she, "it were better that one woman should have two husbands, that if the one were on business abroad, the other might be at home." Now when the governors heard this speech, they marveled whereupon it should arise. Then young Papirius requested that he might speak, who presently resolved them the cause of the women's coming, so they greatly commended the boy, and laughed the women to scorn.

[34] **hard hold:** contention.

↛ RACHEL SPEGHT

From A Muzzle for Melastomus, the Cynical Baiter of, and Foul-Mouthed Barker against, Eva's Sex
1617

With *A Muzzle for Melastomus*, the first published response to Joseph Swetnam's *Arraignment of Lewd . . . Women* (and possibly the only one written by a woman), Rachel Speght (b. 1597) enjoys the distinction of being the first Englishwoman to have published a treatise, using her own name, on the controversy about women. In 1621, she also published *Mortality's Memorandum*, a verse meditation on death, along with *The Dream*, an allegorical poem recounting the obstacles she encountered in pursuit of education. Speght had "acquired a classical education very rare for seventeenth-century women of any class; she knew Latin and had some training in logic and rhetoric, and had at least encountered a wide range of learned authorities" (*Dictionary of National Biography*). In fact, Speght's publication of *Mortality's Memorandum* was partially motivated by her desire to refute those who believed that not she but her father, a Calvinist minister in London, had written *A Muzzle*.

In *The Arraignment*, when Swetnam jocularly invites his male readers to witness his "bear-baiting of women" (see p. 277), he alludes to a popular pastime in which a bear was tied to a post and set upon by dogs (see Chapter 4, p. 300). Speght understands that if women are the baited bears, then Swetnam himself is the vicious, biting cur: the name Melastomus in the title of her pamphlet comes from the Greek for "black mouth," or slanderer. In the play *Swetnam the Woman-Hater Arraigned by Women* (1620) (see p. 273), the idea of using a scold's bridle to punish Swetnam might have been suggested by Speght's central image of the muzzled dog.

Characterizing Swetnam as "irreligious and illiterate," Speght marshals impressive biblical knowledge in defense of women's worth. In the second part of her treatise, separately entitled *Certain Queries to the Baiter of Women, with Confutation of some Part of his Diabolical Discipline*, Speght directly cites and refutes Swetnam's individual claims. The *Muzzle* proper does not directly engage Swetnam's argument, choosing instead to address larger theological and moral debates about the nature of women and biblical interpretation. One critic describes Speght's tactic as an attempt "to negotiate a position for woman to speak, write and defend herself from within the discourses of morality which insisted on her silence, to oppose Swetnam by abducting authority from the

---

Rachel Speght, *A Muzzle for Melastomus, the Cynical Baiter of, and Foul-Mouthed Barker against, Eva's Sex. Or an Apologetical Answer to that Irreligious and Illiterate Pamphlet Made by Jo. Sw. and by him Entitled The Arraignment of Women* (London, 1617), STC 23058; sigs. A3r–B4r, D1v–D3v, D4v–E3r.

very discourse he disrupts" (Purkiss 93). How do Speght's particular rhetorical strategies "negotiate a position" or clear a space for women to speak? For instance, what role do her theological citations or her characterizations of male authority figures play in these strategies? How does Speght manage to defend her right to speak from "within the discourses of morality" that insisted on female silence, and how successful is that defense?

As the only known woman to have participated in the debate about Swetnam's *Arraignment*, Speght provides a compelling parallel to Shakespeare's Paulina. For instance, both Paulina and Speght describe their zealous defense of female honor in terms of a trial by combat, a mode of judicial redress open only to men (2.3.61–62). Although Paulina and Speght thereby risk casting themselves as overly aggressive, masculine women, they take steps to balance their threats of aggression with more humble claims about the limits of their own authority and their virtuous intentions. Consider, for instance, how both women appeal to the authority of nature in making arguments for harmonious domestic relations. In act 3, scene 2, after Mamillius and (apparently) Hermione have died, Paulina delivers a "long speech of accusation" that one critic regards an an example of "female satire": a legitimate use of rough speech to expose and to correct social and moral disorder (Brown 197). Does Speght provide any indication that she regards herself as a female satirist, producing disorderly speech for the purpose of restoring social order?

Of course, there are also important differences of status and situation between Speght, a citizen-class young maiden addressing a popular audience, and Paulina, a married noblewoman addressing her king. Paulina accuses Leontes of "slander," whose "sting is sharper than the sword's" (2.3.86–87), but she dare not accuse the king of being a rabid dog who needs to be muzzled; nor does she have the opportunity to develop the richly metaphoric imagery with which Speght paints a vivid portrait of her antagonist's folly. When reading *A Muzzle*, take account of how its form, style, and mode of address affect what kinds of arguments Speght can advance regarding female speech. Observe, for instance, how Speght not only quotes biblical passages, but includes precise citations to chapter and verse. How did the medium of print provide a new opportunity for women not only to express themselves, but self-consciously to justify their right to express themselves?

It is tempting to wonder if outspoken stage characters such as Paulina might have contributed to the determination of young women like Speght to defend their right to speak. Mihoko Suzuki has argued that the long and successful reign of Queen Elizabeth, a female monarch in a strictly patriarchal society, had the effect of empowering regular women who "sought to overturn gender norms by asserting a woman's right to inherit titles and estates, by contesting orthodox interpretations of the Bible that justified the subordination of women, and by intervening in the public sphere and participating in political discussion" (234). Likewise, even if Paulina could not safely accuse her king, as Speght does Swetnam, of having an "idle corrupt brain," is it possible that Paulina's moral courage might have inspired Speght to risk being branded as an intemperate scold for publishing such harsh words about her misogynist adversary?

From *A Muzzle for Melastomus*

To all virtuous ladies honorable or worshipful, and to all other of Eva's sex fearing God and loving their just reputation, grace and peace through Christ, to eternal glory

It was the simile of that wise and learned Lactantius[1] that if fire, though but with a small spark kindled, be not at the first quenched, it may work great mischief and damage; so likewise may the scandals and defamations of the malevolent in time prove pernicious, if they be not nipped in the head at their first appearance. The consideration of this, right honorable and worshipful ladies, hath incited me (though young, and the unworthiest of thousands) to encounter with a furious enemy to our sex, lest if his unjust imputations[2] should continue without answer he might insult and account himself a victor; and by such a conceit deal, as historiographers report the viper to do, who in the winter time doth vomit forth her poison and in the spring time sucketh the same up again, which becometh twice as deadly as the former. And this our pestiferous[3] enemy, by thinking to provide a more deadly poison for women than already he hath foamed forth, may evaporate,[4] by an addition unto his former illiterate pamphlet (entitled *The Arraignment of Women*), a more contagious obtrectation[5] than he hath already done and indeed hath threatened to do. Secondly, if it should have had free passage without any answer at all (seeing that *tacere* is *quasi consentire*[6]), the vulgar ignorant might have believed his diabolical infamies to be infallible truths not to be infringed; whereas now they may plainly perceive them to be but the scum of heathenish brains, or a building raised without a foundation (at least from sacred scripture) which the wind of God's truth must needs cast down to the ground. A third reason why I have adventured to fling this stone at vaunting Goliath[7] is to comfort the minds of all Eva's sex, both rich and poor, learned and unlearned, with this antidote: that if the fear of God reside in their hearts, maugre[8] all adversaries, they are highly

---

[1] Lactantius: early Christian writer and rhetorician (c. 240–c. 320 C.E.) [2] imputations: accusations. [3] pestiferous: morally or socially harmful. [4] evaporate: give vent to. [5] obtrectation: slander. [6] *tacere* is *quasi consentire*: to be silent is almost to consent. [7] Goliath: Philistine giant slain by the young David with a stone (1 Samuel 17); throughout this document, biblical citations not provided in the text by Speght will be provided in the footnotes. [8] maugre: in spite of.

esteemed and accounted of in the eyes of their gracious Redeemer, so that they need not fear the darts of envy or obtrectators. For shame and disgrace (saith Aristotle[9]) is the end of them that shoot such poisoned shafts. Worthy therefore of imitation is that example of Seneca,[10] who when he was told that a certain man did exclaim and rail against him, made this mild answer: some dogs bark more upon custom than cursedness;[11] and some speak evil of others, not that the defamed deserve it, but because through custom and corruption of their hearts they cannot speak well of any. This I allege as a paradigmatical pattern for all women, noble and ignoble, to follow: that they be not enflamed with choler[12] against this our enraged adversary, but patiently consider of him according to the portraiture which he hath drawn of himself, his writings being the very emblem of a monster.

This my brief apology, right honorable and worshipful, did I enterprise not as thinking myself more fit than others to undertake such a task, but as one who, not perceiving any of our sex to enter the lists[13] of encountring with this our grand enemy among men — I being out of all fear because armed with the truth, which though often blamed yet can never be shamed, and the word of God's spirit, together with the example of virtue's pupils for a buckler[14] — did no whit[15] dread to combat with our said malevolent adversary. And if in so doing I shall be censured[16] by the judicious to have the victory, and shall have given content unto the wronged, I have both hit the mark whereat I aimed and obtained that prize which I desired. But if Zoilus[17] shall adjudge me presumptuous in dedicating this my chirograph[18] unto personages of so high rank, both because of my insufficiency in literature and tenderness in years, I thus apologize for myself: that seeing the Baiter of Women hath opened his mouth against noble as well as ignoble, against the rich as well as the poor; therefore meet[19] it is that they should be joint spectators of this encounter. And withal in regard of my imperfection both in learning and age, I need so much the more to impetrate[20] patronage from some of power to shield me from the biting wrongs of Momus,[21] who oftentimes setteth a rankling[22] tooth into the sides of truth. Wherefore I being of Decius[23] his mind, who deemed himself safe under the shield of Caesar, have presumed to shelter myself under the wings of you, honorable personages, against the persecuting heat of this fiery and

---

[9] **Aristotle:** ancient Greek philosopher (384–322 B.C.E.).　[10] **Seneca:** Roman dramatist and philosopher (c. 4 B.C.E.–65 C.E.).　[11] **cursedness:** ill temper.　[12] **choler:** anger.　[13] **lists:** space in which titling combats were held.　[14] **buckler:** small shield.　[15] **no whit:** not at all.　[16] **censured:** judged.　[17] **Zoilus:** Greek philosopher (fourth century B.C.E.) notorious for attacking Isocrates, Plato, and Homer.　[18] **chirograph:** formally written document.　[19] **meet:** proper.　[20] **impetrate:** procure.　[21] **Momus:** Greek god of ridicule.　[22] **rankling:** festering.　[23] **Decius:** Decius Junius Brutus Albinus (died 43 B.C.E.), military commander under Julius Caesar.

furious dragon; desiring that you would be pleased not to look so much *ad opus* as *ad animum*.[24] And so, not doubting of the favorable acceptance and censure of all virtuously affected, I rest your honors' and worships' humbly at commandment,

Rachel Speght

I f reason had but curbed thy witless will,
O r fear of God restrained thy raving quill,
S uch venom foul thou would'st have blushed to spew,
E xcept that grace have bidden thee adieu.
P rowess disdains to wrestle with the weak,
H eathenish affected care not what they speak.

S educer of the vulgar sort of men,
W as Satan crept into thy filthy pen,
E nflaming thee with such infernal smoke,
T hat (if thou had'st thy will) should women choke?
N efarious fiends thy sense herein deluded,
A nd from thee all humanity excluded.
M onster of men, worthy no other name,
　For that thou didst essay our sex to shame.

Ra[chel] Sp[eght]

**Not unto the veriest idiot that ever set pen to paper,
but to the Cynical Baiter of Women,
or metamorphosed Misogynes,[25]
Joseph Swetnam**

From standing water, which soon putrifies, can no good fish be expected, for it produceth no other creatures but those that are venemous or noisome, as snakes, adders, and such like. Semblably,[26] no better stream can we look should issue from your idle corrupt brain, than that whereto the ruff[27] of your fury (to use your own words) hath moved you to open the sluice. In which excrement of your roaring cogitations[28] you have used such irregularities touching concordance,[29] and observed so disordered a method, as I doubt not to tell you that a very accidence scholar[30] would have quite put you down in both. You appear herein not unlike that painter who, seriously

---

[24] *ad opus* as *ad animum*: at the work as at the spirit (of the work).　[25] **Misogynes**: misogynist.
[26] **Semblably**: similarly.　[27] **ruff**: pride; pun on "rough"; also, a small freshwater fish with prickly scales.　[28] **cogitations**: reflections.　[29] **concordance**: grammatical agreement between words.　[30] **accidence scholar**: student learned in grammar.

endevoring to portray Cupid's bow, forgot the string; for you, being greedy to botch up your mingle-mangle invective against women, have not therein observed in many places so much as grammar sense. But the empriest[31] barrel makes the loudest sound, and so we will account of you.

Many propositions have you framed which (as you think) make much against women, but if one would make a logical assumption, the conclusion would be flat against your own sex. Your dealing wants so much discretion, that I doubt whether to bestow so good a name as the dunce upon you. But minority[32] bids me keep within my bounds, and therefore I only say unto you that your corrupt heart and railing tongue hath made you a fit scribe for the devil.

In that you have termed your virulent foam "The Bear-baiting of Women," you have plainly displayed your own disposition to be cynical,[33] in that there appears no other dog or bull to bait them but yourself. Good had it been for you to have put on that muzzle which Saint James would have all Christians to wear: "Speak not evil one of another" (James 4:11); and then had you not seemed so like the serpent Porphyrus[34] as now you do, which, though full of deadly poison, yet being toothless hurteth none so much as himself. For you having gone beyond the limits not of humanity alone, but of Christianity, have done greater harm unto your own soul than unto women, as may plainly appear. First, in dishonoring of God by palpable blasphemy, wresting and perverting every place of scripture that you have alleged, which by the testimony of Saint Peter is to the destruction of them that so do (1 Peter 3:16). Secondly, it appears by your disparaging of, and opprobrious[35] speeches against, that excellent work of God's hands, which in his great love he perfected for the comfort of man. Thirdly and lastly, by this your hodgepodge of heathenish sentences, similes, and examples, you have set forth yourself in your right colors unto the view of the world. And I doubt not but the judicious will account of you according to your demerit. As for the vulgar sort, which have no more learning than you have showed in your book, it is likely they will applaud you for your pains.

As for your bugbear[36] or advice unto women, that whatsoever they do think of your work they should conceal it, lest in finding fault, they bewray[37] their galled[38] backs to the world — in which you allude to that proverb, *rub a galled horse, and he will kick* — unto it I answer by way of apology, that though every galled horse, being touched, doth kick, yet every one that kicks

---

[31] **empriest:** emptiest. [32] **minority:** youthfulness. [33] **cynical:** resembling the misanthropic Cynic philosophers; etymologically, "doglike, currish." [34] **Porphyrus:** legendary serpent from India that, although toothless, spewed poisonous vomit. [35] **opprobrious:** scornful. [36] **bugbear:** hobgoblin, or imaginary terror. [37] **bewray:** expose. [38] **galled:** sore from chafing.

is not galled. So that you might as well have said that because burnt folks dread the fire, therefore none fear fire but those that are burnt, as made that illiterate conclusion which you have absurdly inferred.

In your title leaf, you arraign none but lewd, idle, froward and unconstant women, but in the sequel (through defect of memory as it seemeth) forgetting that you had made a distinction of good from bad, condemning all in general, you advise men to beware of, and not to match with, any of these six sorts of women, *viz.*[39] good and bad, fair and foul, rich and poor. But this doctrine of devils Saint Paul, foreseeing would be broached in the latter times, gives warning of (1 Timothy 4:3).

There also you promise a commendation of wise, virtuous, and honest women, whenas in the subsequent, the worst words and filthiest epithets that you can devise you bestow on them in general, excepting no sort of women. Herein may you be likened unto a man which upon the door of a scurvy[40] house sets this superscription, "Here is a very fair house to be let," whereas, the door being opened, it is no better then a dog-hole and dark dungeon.

Further, if your own words be true that you wrote with your hand but not with your heart, then are you a hypocrite in print. But it is rather to be thought that your pen was the bewrayer of the abundance of your mind, and that this was but a little mortar to daub up against the wall which you intended to break down.

The revenge of your railing work we leave to Him who hath appropriated vengeance unto himself, whose penman[41] hath included railers in the catalogue of them that shall not inherit God's kingdom, and yourself unto the mercy of that just Judge, who is able to save and to destroy.

Your undeserved friend,
Rachel Speght

In praise of the Author and her Work

If little David that for Israel's sake
    esteemed neither life nor limb too dear,
In that he did adventure without dread
    to cast at him, whom all the host did fear,
A stone, which brought Goliath to the ground,
Obtained applause with songs and timbrels' sound.

Then let another young encombatant
    receive applause and thanks as well as he:

---

[39] *viz.*: that is to say.   [40] **scurvy**: shabby.   [41] **penman**: divinely inspired writer of scripture.

For with an enemy to womenkind
  she hath encountered, as each wight[42] may see;
And with the fruit of her industrious toil,
To this Goliath she hath given the foil.

Admire her much I may, both for her age
  and this her Muzzle for a black-mouthed wight,
But praise her and her work to that desert
  which unto them belongs of equal right
I cannot; only this I say, and end,
She is unto her sex a faithful friend.
          Philalethes[43]

[Following two more laudatory poems, the treatise proper begins. After a demonstration of "women's excellency," Speght uses the language of classical philosophy to demonstrate the four "causes" of women's creation: the first cause is the "efficient" or creative cause, God; the second cause is the "material" cause, or the matter from which woman was made, Adam's rib.]

Thirdly, the formal cause, fashion, and proportion of woman was excellent. For she was neither like the beasts of the earth, fowls of the air, fishes of the sea, or any other inferior creature, but man was the only object which she did resemble. For as God gave man a lofty countenance that he might look up toward heaven, so did he likewise give unto woman. And as the temperature of man's body is excellent, so is woman's. For whereas other creatures, by reason of their gross humors[44] have excrements for their habit[45] — as fowls, their feathers; beasts, their hair; fishes, their scales — man and woman only have their skin clear and smooth (Genesis 1:26). And (that more is) in the image of God were they both created; yea, and to be brief, all the parts of their bodies, both external and internal, were correspondent and meet each for other.

Fourthly and lastly, the final cause or end for which woman was made was to glorify God, and to be a collateral companion for man to glorify God, in using her body and all the parts, powers, and faculties thereof as instruments for his honor. As with her voice to sound forth his praises, like Mariam,[46] and the rest of her company (Exodus 15:20); with her tongue not to utter words of strife, but to give good counsel unto her husband, the which he must not despise. For Abraham was bidden to give ear to Sarah his

---

[42] **wight:** person. [43] **Philalethes:** "lover of truth," from Greek *phil* (lover) + *aletheia* (truth). [44] **gross humors:** coarse bodily fluids. [45] **excrements for their habit:** outgrowths (such as hair or nails) for their outer covering. [46] **Mariam:** the prophetess who celebrated the Israelites' safe passage out of Egypt.

wife (Genesis 21:12). Pilate was willed by his wife not to have any hand in the condemning of Christ, and a sin it was in him that he listened not to her (Matthew 27:19). Leah and Rachel counseled Jacob to do according to the word of the Lord (Genesis 31:16). And the Shunammite put her husband in mind of harboring the prophet Elisha (2 Kings 4:9). Her hands should be open according to her ability in contributing towards God's service and distressed servants, like to that poor widow, which cast two mites[47] into the treasury (Luke 8); and as Mary Magdalene, Susanna, and Joanne[48] the wife of Herod's steward, with many other, which of their substance ministered unto Christ. Her heart should be a receptacle for God's word, like Mary that treasured up the sayings of Christ in her heart (Luke 1:51). Her feet should be swift in going to seek the Lord in his sanctuary, as Mary Magdalene made haste to seek Christ at his sepulcher (John 20:1). Finally, no power external or internal ought woman to keep idle, but to employ it in some service of God, to the glory of her Creator, and comfort of her own soul.

The other end for which woman was made was to be a companion and helper for man. And if she must be a helper, and but a helper, then are those husbands to be blamed which lay the whole burden of domestical affairs and maintenance on the shoulders of their wives. For as yokefellows they are to sustain part of each other's cares, griefs, and calamities. But as if two oxen be put in one yoke, the one being bigger than the other, the greater bears most weight; so the husband being the stronger vessel is to bear a greater burden than his wife. And therefore the Lord said to Adam, "In the sweat of thy face shalt thou eat thy bread, till thou return to the dust" (Genesis 3:19). And Saint Paul saith "that he that provideth not for his household is worse than an infidel" (1 Timothy 5:8). Nature hath taught senseless creatures to help one another, as the male pigeon, when his hen is weary with sitting on her eggs and comes off from them, supplies her place, that in her absence they may receive no harm until such time as she is fully refreshed. Of small birds the cock always helps his hen to build her nest, and while she sits upon her eggs he flies abroad to get meat for her, who cannot then provide any for herself. The crowing cockerel helps his hen to defend her chickens from peril, and will endanger himself to save her and them from harm. Seeing then that these unreasonable creatures by the instinct of nature bear such affection each to other, that without any grudge they willingly, according to their kind, help one another, I may reason *a minore ad maius*[49] that much more should man and woman, which are reasonable creatures, be helpers

---

[47] **mites:** coins of small value. [48] **Mary Magdalene, Susanna, and Joanne:** these women "ministered" to Jesus "out of their substance" (Luke 8:3). [49] *a minore ad maius:* from the lesser to the greater.

each to other in all things lawful, they having the law of God to guide them, his word to be a lantern unto their feet and a light unto their paths, by which they are excited to a far more mutual participation of each other's burden than other creatures. So that neither the wife may say to her husband, nor the husband unto his wife, "I have no need of thee" (1 Corinthians 12:21), no more then the members of the body may so say each to other, between whom there is such a sympathy that if one member suffer, all suffer with it. Therefore, though God bade Abraham forsake his country and kindred,[50] yet he bade him not forsake his wife, who being "flesh of his flesh, and bone of his bone"[51] was to be copartner with him of whatsoever did betide him, whether joy or sorrow. Wherefore Solomon saith, "Woe to him that is alone" (Ecclesiates 4:10); for when thoughts of discomfort, troubles of this world, and fear of dangers do possess him, he wants a companion to lift him up from the pit of perplexity into which he is fallen. For a good wife, saith Plautus,[52] is the wealth of the mind and the welfare of the heart; and therefore a meet associate for her husband. And "Woman," saith Paul, "is the glory of the man" (1 Corinthians 11:7). . . .

Yet a truth ungainsayable[53] is it, that the "Man is the woman's head" (1 Corinthians 11:3). By which title yet of supremacy, no authority hath he given him to domineer, or basely command and employ his wife as a servant, but hereby is he taught the duties which he oweth unto her. For as the head of a man is the imaginer and contriver of projects profitable for the safety of his whole body, so the husband must protect and defend his wife from injuries. For he is her head "as Christ is the head of his church" (Ephesians 5:23), which he entirely loveth, and for which he gave his very life (Job 2:4): the dearest thing any man hath in this world. "Greater love than this hath no man, when he bestoweth his life for his friend," saith our Savior (John 15:13). This precedent passeth all other patterns: it requireth great benignity and enjoineth an extraordinary affection, for "men must love their wives, even as Christ loved his church."[54] Secondly, as the head doth not jar or contend with the members, which "being many," as the Apostle saith, "yet make but one body" (1 Corinthians 12:20); no more must the husband with the wife, but, expelling all bitterness and cruelty (Colossians 3:19), he must live with her lovingly and religiously, honoring her as the weaker vessel (1 Peter 3:7). Thirdly, and lastly, as he is her head, he must by instruction bring her to the knowledge of her creator (1 Corinthians 14:35), that so she may be a fit stone for the Lord's building. Women for this end must have an

---

[50] **God bade Abraham forsake . . . :** Genesis 12:1.   [51] **"flesh . . . bone":** Adam's words upon the creation of Eve out of his rib (Genesis 2:23).   [52] **Plautus:** ancient Roman playwright (c. 254–184 B.C.E.)   [53] **ungainsayable:** unquestionable.   [54] **"men . . . church":** Ephesians 5:25.

especial care to set their affections upon such as are able to teach them, that as they "grow in years, they may grow in grace, and in the knowledge of Christ Jesus our Lord" (2 Peter 3:18).

Thus if men would remember the duties they are to perform in being heads, some would not stand a tip-toe as they do, thinking themselves lords and rulers, and account every omission of performing whatsoever they command, whether lawful or not, to be matter of great disparagement and indignity done them. Whereas they should consider that women are enjoined to submit themselves unto their husbands no otherways than as to the Lord (Ephesians 5:22). So that, from hence, for man ariseth a lesson not to be forgotten: that as the Lord commandeth nothing to be done but that which is right and good, no more must the husband. For if a wife fulfill the evil command of her husband, she obeys him as a tempter, as Sapphira did Ananias[55] (Acts 5:2). But lest I should seem too partial in praising women so much as I have (though no more than warrant from scripture doth allow) I add to the premises, that I say not all women are virtuous, for then they should be more excellent than men, sith of Adam's sons there was Cain as well as Abel,[56] and of Noah's, Cham as well as Shem.[57] So that of men as of women, there are two sorts, namely, good and bad, which in *Matthew* the five and twenty chapter, are comprehended under the name of "sheep" and "goats."[58] And if women were not sinful, then should they not need a Savior. But the Virgin Mary, a pattern of piety, "rejoiced in God her Savior" (Luke 1:47): *ergo*,[59] she was a sinner. In the *Revelation* the church is called the spouse of Christ;[60] and in *Zechariah*, wickedness is called a woman (Zechariah 5:7–8), to show that of women there are both godly and ungodly. For Christ would not "purge his floor"[61] if there were not chaff among the wheat; nor should gold need to be fined,[62] if among it there were no dross. But far be it from anyone to condemn the righteous with the wicked, or good women with the bad (as the Baiter of Women doth). For though there are some scabbed sheep in a flock, we must not therefore conclude all the rest to be mangy. And though some men, through excess, abuse God's creatures, we must not imagine that all men are gluttons, the which we may with as good reason do as condemn all women in general for the offenses of some particulars. Of the good sort is it that I have in this book spoken, and so would I that all that read it should so understand me. For if

---

[55] **Sapphira did Ananias:** Sapphira sinfully conspires with her husband Ananias to deceive the apostle Peter (Acts 5:1–10). [56] **Cain as well as Abel:** Cain murdered his brother Abel (Genesis 4:8). [57] **Cham as well as Shem:** Noah cursed Cham (or Ham) and blessed Shem (Genesis 9:25–26). [58] **"sheep" and "goats":** Matthew 25:33. [59] *ergo:* therefore. [60] **church . . . Christ:** Revelation 21:2. [61] **"purge his floor":** Matthew 3:12. [62] **fined:** refined.

otherwise I had done, I should have incurred that woe which by the prophet Isaiah is pronounced against them that "speak well of evil" (Isaiah 5:20), and should have "justified the wicked, which thing is abominable to the Lord" (Proverbs 17:15).

THE EPILOGUE OR UPSHOT OF THE PREMISES

Great was the unthankfulness of Pharaoh's butler unto Joseph; for though he had done him a great pleasure, of which the butler promised requital, yet was he quite forgotten of him (Genesis 40:23).[63] But far greater is the ingratitude of those men toward God that dare presume to speak and exclaim against woman, whom God did create for man's comfort. What greater discredit can redound to a workman, than to have the man for whom he hath made it say it is naught? Or what greater discourtesy can be offered to one that bestoweth a gift, than to have the receiver give out that he cares not for it, for he needs it not? And what greater ingratitude can be showed unto God than the opprobrious speeches and disgraceful invectives which some diabolical natures do frame against women?

Ingratitude is and always hath been accounted so odious a vice, that Cicero[64] saith, "If one doubt what name to give a wicked man, let him call him an ungrateful person, and then he hath said enough." It was so detested among the Persians, as that by a law they provided that such should suffer death as felons which proved unthankful for any gift received. And "Love," saith the Apostle, "is the fulfilling of the law" (Romans 13:10). But where ingratitude is harbored, there love is banished. Let men therefore beware of all unthankfulness, but especially of the superlative ingratitude, that which is towards God, which is no way more palpably declared than by the contemning of and railing against women. Which sin, of some men (if to be termed men) no doubt but God will one day avenge, when they shall plainly perceive that it had been better for them to have been born dumb and lame than to have used their tongues and hands — the one in repugning, the other in writing — against God's handiwork, their own flesh, women I mean, whom God hath made equal with themselves in dignity, both temporally and eternally, if they continue in the faith. Which God for his mercy's sake grant they always may, to the glory of their creator and comfort of their own souls, through Christ, amen.

To God only wise be glory now and for ever, amen.

---

[63] **Pharaoh's butler . . . :** Imprisoned with Pharaoh's butler, Joseph comforts him by predicting that he will be forgiven; once restored to his position, the butler forgets to speak to Pharaoh on Joseph's behalf.   [64] **Cicero:** Roman orator and statesman (106–43 B.C.E.).

→ MARTIN PARKER

A Merry Dialogue Betwixt a Married Man and His Wife, Concerning the Affairs of This Careful Life
1628

Little is known about Martin Parker (fl. 1624–1647), who was probably a Londoner and possibly an alehouse-keeper. Nonetheless, he was "the most famous and popular ballad writer of the seventeenth century" (Watt 54). A ballad was comprised of song lyrics printed on a single sheet of paper, often including a stock or generic illustration that could be used over and over (a kind of early modern clip-art). The music was not printed; instead the reader was directed to sing the lyrics to the tune of another familiar song. This particular ballad simply indicates, "To an excellent tune," but its opening line, "I have for all good wives a song," identifies the name of the popular tune to which music "A Merry Dialogue" was also to be sung. In any case, peddlers such as Autolycus typically sang ballads in the streets as a way of advertising their wares. Since ballads were mass-produced and usually sold for only a penny, they were accessible to a wide range of readers and listeners, who could have heard them sung by peddlers even if they did not purchase them.

Although it is sometimes difficult to establish authorship for such ephemeral publications, Parker is credited with writing nearly one hundred ballads and chapbooks, which were small, inexpensive books that "offered abridged and illustrated versions of chivalric tales and jests" (Watt 296). Parker's ballads reported a variety of sensationalistic and newsworthy events, as well as debating gender relations. As in the two-part "Merry Dialogue," Parker addresses the problem of conjugal strife in a pair of matched ballads published in 1634: in "Keep a Good Tongue in Your Head," a husband complains of his wife's scolding; in the accompanying ballad "Hold Your Hands, Honest Men," a wife complains that her husband beats her. Both the scolding wife and the violent husband are shown to be responsible for household disorder (Wiltenburg 109).

The generic wife in the "Merry Dialogue" who laments "the women's wrong" is written in the tradition of the "scold's privilege," in which the figure of the "disorderly scold" provides "an outlet for grievance in a female guise" (Jardine 116). For instance, Edward More's *The Defense of Women* (1560), an early contribution to the Elizabethan pamphlet controversy about women, argues that "wives' remonstrances over husbandly vices such as drinking should not be interpreted as scolding: they are, in fact, justified rebukes" (Woodbridge 51). In *The Winter's Tale*, Antigonus describes Paulina's moral outrage in terms of justified shrewishness when he admits, "When she will take the rein I let her run, / But she'll not stumble" (2.3.51–52). Antigonus's image of his wife as an unreined

Martin Parker, "A Merry Dialogue Betwixt a Married Man and his Wife, Concerning the Affairs of this Careful Life" (London, 1628), STC 6809; 266–67.

horse might recall the scold's bridle used to punish excessively talkative women (see p. 265), but his intention is to praise Paulina for her independent and well-governed speech. When Leontes later tells Antigonus that he deserves to be hanged for his failure to "stay [Paulina's] tongue," Antigonus jocularly observes that this failure is the common lot of husbands: "Hang all the husbands / That cannot do that feat, you'll leave yourself / Hardly one subject" (2.3.110–12). If husbands universally fail to rule their wives' tongues, then perhaps it is foolish even to try. Perhaps, Antigonus implies, a successful marriage depends on a degree of mutual trust and independence, especially when one's partner has demonstrated virtue and good judgment in the past.

Parker's "Merry Dialogue" also suggests that marriage might be understood in terms of a negotiated balance of power between husband and wife. Sandra Clark notes that for all the ballads from this period that attack wives as scolds, shrews, and cuckolders, "an equally extensive selection" sympathetically present the wife's perspective on the ingredients of a happy marriage, such as affection, patience, and understanding (106). In certain ballads, the wife urges her husband to avoid jealousy or to save money; others, such as "A Merry Dialogue," stage a debate over which partner makes the greatest contributions to the household. "A Merry Dialogue" presents a fitting analogue for *The Winter's Tale* because the debate explicitly raises the issue of female speech: whereas the husband complains that his wife bosses him around — "Your tongues will get the upper hand" — the wife insists on her right to speak: "My tongue's mine own." Does the husband seem justified in complaining about his wife's sharp tongue? Does the wife always speak sharply, or does her tone shift according to the kind of argument she is making about domestic relations? After their public dispute in the court, Antigonus and Paulina apparently never have the opportunity to reconcile before Antigonus is sent off, with Perdita, to what will be his death. How do the husband and wife in Parker's ballad resolve their domestic dispute, and how satisfying is this resolution?

A Merry Dialogue Betwixt a Married Man and His Wife

WOMAN:

> I have for all good wives a song —
> I do lament the women's wrong,
> And I do pity them with my heart,
> To think upon the women's smart.[1]
> Their labor's great, and full of pain,   5
> Yet for the same they have small gain.

MAN:

> In that you say cannot be true,

---

[1] smart: pain.

For men do take more pains than you;
We toil, we moil,[2] we grieve and care,
When you sit on a stool or chair.   10
Yet let us do all what we can,
Your tongues will get the upper hand.

WOMAN:

We women in the morning rise
As soon as day breaks in the skies;
And then to please you, with desire,   15
The first we do is make a fire.
Then other work we straight begin,
To sweep the house, to card,[3] or spin.

MAN:

Why, men do work at plough and cart,
Which soon would break a woman's heart;   20
They sow, they mow, and reap the corn,
And many times do wear the horn.[4]
In praise of wives speak you no more,
For these were lies you told before.

WOMAN:

We women here do bear the blame,   25
But men would seem to have the same.
But trust me, I will never yield,
My tongue's mine own, I thereon build.
Men may not in this case compare
With women, for their toil and care.   30

MAN:

Fie, idle woman! How you prate![5]
'Tis men that get you all your state.[6]
You know 'tis true in what I say;
Therefore you must give men the way,
And not presume to grow too high.   35
Your speeches are not worth a fly.

WOMAN:

You men could not tell how to shift,[7]
If you of women were bereft;[8]
We wash your clothes, and dress your diet,
And all to keep your minds in quiet.   40

---

[2] **moil:** drudge.   [3] **card:** prepare wool for spinning.   [4] **wear the horn:** sprout horns on their heads, the fabled fate of cuckolds (husbands with unfaithful wives).   [5] **prate:** chatter.   [6] **state:** prosperity.   [7] **shift:** get by.   [8] **bereft:** deprived.

Our work's not done at morn nor night;
To pleasure men is our delight.

MAN:

Women are called a house of care:
They bring poor men unto despair.
That man is blest that hath not been   45
Inlured[9] by a woman's sin.
They'll cause a man, if he'll give way,
To bring him to his life's decay.

The Second Part

WOMAN:

If we, poor women, were as bad
As men report, being drunk or mad,   50
We might compare with many men,
And count ourselves as bad as them.
Some oft are drunk, and beat their wives,
And make them weary of their lives.

MAN:

Why, women they must rule their tongues   55
That bring them to so many wrongs.
Sometimes, their husbands to disgrace,
They'll call him knave and rogue to's face.
Nay, worse than that, they'll tell him plain,
His will he shall not well obtain.   60

WOMAN:

We women in childbed take great care —
I hope the like sorrow will fall to your share;
Then would you think of women's smart,
And seem to pity them with your heart.
So many things to us belong,   65
We oftentimes do suffer wrong.

MAN:

Though you in childbed bide some pain,
Your babes renew your joys again.
Your gossips come, unto your joy,
And say, "God bless your little boy."   70

[9] **Inlured:** caught.

They say, "The child is like the dad,"
When he but little share in't had.

WOMAN:

You talk like an ass, you are a cuckoldly fool;
I'll break thy head with a [three]-leg'd stool!
While you poor women thus abuse   75
Our tongues and hands we need to use.
You say our tongues do make men fight —
Our hands must serve to do us right.

MAN:

Then I to you must give the way,
And yield to women in what they say.   80
All you that are to choose a wife,
Be careful of it as your life!
You see that women will not yield
In any thing to be compelled.

WOMAN:

You maids, I speak the like to you,   85
There's many dangers do ensue.
But howsoever fortunes serve,
See that my rules you do observe.
If men once have the upper hand,
They'll keep you down, do what you can.   90

MAN:

I will not seem to urge no more —
Good wives, what I did say before
Was for your good, and so it take.
I love all women, for my wife's sake.
And I pray you, when you are sick and die,   100
Call at my house, and take my wife wi'ye.

WOMAN:

Well, come, sweetheart, let us agree.

MAN:

Content, sweet wife, so let it be.
Where man and wife do live at hate,
The curse of God hangs o'er the gate.   105
But I will love thee as my life,
As every man should love his wife.

CHAPTER 4

Encountering Nature

————————————⟩⟨————————————

The first two acts of *The Winter's Tale* take place entirely indoors. During these early scenes, we hear brief references to the outside world: Polixenes recalls frisking "i'th'sun" (1.2.67) with Leontes, Hermione leaves to stroll "i'th' garden" (1.2.178), Mamillius begins a tale of a man who dwelt "by a churchyard" (2.1.30), and a Lord reports Polixenes' escape from "[b]ehind the tuft of pines" (2.1.34). Sicilia, we discover, has pleasant gardens as well as eerie graveyards, but we experience Leontes' winter kingdom only as a collection of enclosed interiors: the court, the chamber, the prison, the courtroom.

In *The Winter's Tale*, the temperance and sweetness of the natural world are found well beyond Sicilia, first in the paradisal tranquility of Delphos, and later in the lush bounty of Bohemia. Delphos contains divine truth as well as earthly beauty: "The climate's delicate, the air most sweet, / Fertile the isle" (3.1.1–2). Significantly, Shakespeare does not represent Delphos on stage: we are permitted neither to witness the "solemn, and unearthly" ceremonies of the priests nor to hear the "ear-deaf'ning voice" of the oracle (3.1.7, 9), perhaps because Delphos represents a mythical realm of sanctified authority far removed from the postlapsarian worlds of Sicilia and Bohemia. Whereas Shakespeare paints Sicilia in the grey, chill shades of winter, however, he adorns Bohemia with the bright, warm tones of summer. Ironically,

Shakespeare's fertile Bohemian countryside thus recalls the Sicily praised by ancient poets and contemporary travelers alike for its natural riches. After a visit to Sicily, English travel writer George Sandys extolled it as "the Queen of the Mediterranean Islands" (sig. X3v). Although Sandys acknowledges Sicily's violent political history of tyrants and colonizers, he also celebrates its abundant store of "[v]ines, sugar-canes, honey, saffron, and fruits of all kinds ... mulberry trees ... quarries of porphyry, and serpentine; hot baths, rivers, and lakes replenished with fish" (sig. X4r). Sandys's admiring catalogue of Sicily's natural resources sounds much like the list of goods that Shakespeare's Clown plans to buy for the sheep-shearing festival: "sugar," "currants," "rice," "saffron," "mace," "nutmegs," "ginger," "prunes," and "raisins o'th' sun" (4.3.34–35, 40–42).

Although Shakespeare associates Sicilia with the chill indoors and Bohemia with the warm outdoors, the two kingdoms are not starkly antithetical locales, for just as Sicilia contains both gardens and graveyards, so Bohemia contains places of delight as well as danger. The play's first Bohemian scene is set in the coastal "deserts" during a raging tempest (3.3.2). Yet for all its fierceness, this stormy Bohemian coast seems quite conventional. Tempests and bears, in fact, carry overtly theatrical associations that might ameliorate the horror evoked by the deaths of Antigonus and the Sicilian mariners. In Shakespeare's romances *Pericles* and *The Tempest*, terrifyingly chaotic shipwrecks turn out to be pivotal events in the ultimately comic fortunes of the plays' protagonists. Shakespeare's audience might have associated bears with fantastic narratives of travel to exotic lands or, conversely, with the familiar sport of bearbaiting, which took place in the same part of town as public stage plays. Appropriately, then, the scene on the Bohemian coast concludes with a nod towards both the theatrical and the magical. When the Old Shepherd identifies the abandoned Perdita as "some changeling" (3.3.101), he recalls popular Elizabethan fairy lore, as well as Shakespeare's use of such lore in the early comedy *A Midsummer Night's Dream.*

The documents in this chapter address the multiple ways in which Shakespeare's contemporaries thought about and physically engaged with the natural environment. As Edward Topsell's "Of the Bear" indicates, bears were regarded not simply as savage predators, but as creatures capable of interacting with humans at various levels of intimacy and empathy. Focusing on the danger and excitement of travel to unknown territories, Gerrit de Veer's account of Dutch voyages to the North Seas provides a unique perspective on bears as occupying one side of consistently violent encounters between human explorers and native predators. While confrontations with nature in de Veer's text are often fatal, George Puttenham's *Art of English Poesy* considers how human art — whether that of the poet or of the gardener — might alter or even improve nature. Renaissance pastoral poetry made art out of the humble matter of shepherds' lives and loves. Outside the pages of pastoral verse, of course, actual shepherds lived by the dirty work of keeping sheep. We will explore the stark contrast between pastoral play and rural labor through Michael Drayton's lyrical *Eclogues* and John Fitzherbert's pragmatic *Book of Husbandry*. Drayton's idealization of pastoral play occludes not only the labor of sheep-shearing, but also the opposition to rural festivities voiced by moralists such as Philip Stubbes in his satirical *Anatomy of Abuses*. One objection that moralists sometimes raised against rural celebrations was their allure to con-men and vagabonds such as Autolycus. Through two official documents — a parliamentary statute and a royal proclamation — and two popular cony-catching pamphlets by Robert Greene, we will examine contemporary attitudes toward socially marginal figures such as peddlers, rogues, and cutpurses, who sometimes occupied overlapping roles as entertainers, laborers, and criminals.

Pursued by a Bear

and how the poor gentleman roared and the bear mocked him . . .

(3.3.87–88)

In one of the most notorious deaths in all of Shakespeare, Antigonus is devoured by a bear. The bear's appearance and impact in this scene have generated much debate. Did Shakespeare's company use an actual bear or an actor in a costume? Did playgoers find the bear frightening or funny? What did London playgoers know about bears?

We simply do not know whether the deadly bear in *The Winter's Tale* was played by a man in costume or by an actual bear. Those who argue for the latter cite the physical proximity of the public theaters to the bearbaiting arenas in Jacobean London. The Globe Theater, the Rose Theater, and the Bear Garden were all located in the same area of the Bankside on the south side of the Thames. That impresario Philip Henslowe managed both the Rose Theater and the Bear Garden supports the view that bearbaiting was generally regarded not as a spectacle of animal cruelty but as a theatrical entertainment, "a showpiece of controlled violence under the auspices of a master-producer" (Ravelhofer 288). In a bearbaiting match, four to six mastiff dogs were set loose upon a bear chained to a post (see Figure 20). If the

FIGURE 20 *William Horman*, Antibossicon *(London, 1521). Horman (1457–1535) was a grammarian and schoolmaster at Eton College, Oxford. In* Antibossicon *("Against Bossus"), Horman attacks a rival grammarian, Robert Whittington, who had attacked a previous book of Horman's using the pseudonym Bossus. The image of the bearbaiting refers to the provocation and satirical "biting" of this rivalry.*

bear killed or mauled any of the dogs, fresh ones would be supplied until the bear was either overcome or kept the dogs at bay long enough to have been deemed victorious. While this sport might strike us as grotesquely cruel, Stephen Dickey argues from contemporary accounts that "the audience was pleased by what it saw, cheered it on, and laughed at it" (259). Challenging Dickey's claim that bearbaiting matches elicited purely lighthearted reactions from spectators, Gail Paster cites contradictory evidence of spectators who expressed sympathy for the animals' suffering (*Humoring* 148–50). Either way, it is clear that famous bears such as Harry Hunks and Sackerson garnered the kind of celebrity associated with famous London actors.

Although some critics of *The Winter's Tale* have doubted that an actual bear could have been safely and effectively used on the London stage, bears might have been featured in other theatrical performances. Ben Jonson's court masque *Oberon* (1611) calls for two white bears to draw a chariot. In the pastoral comedy *Mucedorus* (1598), the titular hero rescues a princess by killing a bear (offstage) and returning with its head, or at least with a prop replica of a bear's head. A 1610 revival of *Mucedorus* included additional scenes for the bear, perhaps to showcase one of the two polar bears that Philip Henslowe had acquired in 1609 from an expedition to Greenland (Ravelhofer 287). As for the problem of controlling a bear on stage, Barbara Ravelhofer cites the tradition of dancing and performing bears to posit that a trained bear would have had little difficulty simply chasing an actor across the stage, especially if enticed by some strategically placed bait on the other side.

While it is not necessary for our purposes to determine whether or not an actual bear appeared in original performances of *The Winter's Tale*, the question of original performance practices does raise the problem of tone. Is Antigonus's death tragic, comic, or tragicomic? We might assume that a man in a bear suit would tilt the tone of the scene toward comedy, and that a real bear would tilt it toward tragedy, but we should be wary about making absolute judgments about audience response. For a majority of the audience, seeing a real bear on stage might have immediately evoked the sport of bearbaiting. Alternatively, whereas an actor in a bear suit might strike us as farcical, Jacobean playgoers, who were accustomed to accepting boy actors as women, might have been better able to accept a human actor as a ravenous beast. Andrew Gurr speculates that original audiences might have experienced a kind of "double-take" reaction: the sudden appearance of a bear on stage might have inspired terror, but once playgoers realized that they were seeing an actor or a trained animal (who would also, in this context, be an "actor"), their fear might have given way to an appreciation of the scene's comic potential (424). Aware that the actor playing Antigonus was not really in danger, that is, playgoers might have taken pleasure in recognizing that what they initially accepted for reality (a wild bear) was really only a theatrical illusion (an actor or a trained bear) — precisely the situation they would confront again at the end of the play when a statue seemingly comes to life.

It might simply be that the bear produced an ambivalent response, mixing horror and delight, the feelings appropriate to tragedy and comedy. As such, the bear would effectively function as the pivot for the play's generic transition from tragedy to comedy — a transition underscored by the Old Shepherd's sententious pronouncement to his son, "Thou met'st with things dying, I with things newborn" (3.3.98). Gurr argues that the Shepherd's balancing of death and birth alludes to the familiar distinction between tragedy and comedy drawn by the ancient Roman rhetorician Evanthius (421): *in tragoedia fugienda vita, in comedia capessanda exprimitur* (tragedy shows the taking of life; comedy shows the making of life). Despite the deaths of Antigonus and the mariners, the predominant mood of this scene might be comic, or some mixture of comic and tragic. Moreover, educated members of the audience might have known of the association of bears with tragicomedy in Italian pastoral drama. Pastoral dramas typically used particular animals to elicit particular emotional responses: lions were considered majestically terrifying, wolves insidiously murderous, and boars brutishly destructive (Clubb 145–46). The bear "seems both more and less terrible than the other wild beasts, because it is humanoid, capable of upright posture, ambiguous in reputation and habitat" (Clubb 147). Because of the common belief that bears were born unformed and had to be licked into proper shape by their mothers, they acquired an "inherent versatility of character" that "must therefore have seemed almost emblematic of the tragicomic genre" (Clubb 148–49). With its ambiguous status between the strange and the familiar, the destructive and the nurturing, a bear thus fits the scene of Antigonus's death and Perdita's survival better than, say, a lion or a wolf.

As the texts that follow suggest, the bear that kills Antigonus can be understood from a surprising variety of contemporary perspectives. Edward Topsell's "Of the Bear" provides a detailed catalogue of Renaissance beliefs about the nature and behavior of actual bears, as well as the symbolic attributes associated with them. Gerrit de Veer's popular narrative about Dutch sailors who squared off with deadly polar bears in the Antarctic sea underscores the vulnerability of Antigonus and Perdita to the "creatures / Of prey" that stalk the savage landscape on which their ship alights (3.3.11–12). Alone and unarmed, Antigonus suffers a violent death. Perdita's survival in such an inhospitable place seems all the more miraculous when viewed in the context of the Dutch sailors' encounters with the ferocious beasts they met in exotic wintry lands.

→ EDWARD TOPSELL

From Of the Bear   1607

How do we read a "history" of animals? According to its title page, the *History of Four-Footed Beasts* treats not only "the true and lively figure" of animals, but also their "love and hate to mankind" and "the wonderful work of God in their creation, preservation, and destruction." A curate in the Church of England, Edward Topsell (c. 1572–1625) propounds the view that, beyond their individual features and habits, animals are to be understood in terms of their position within an orderly, providential universe. The study of nature thereby yields spiritual as well as pragmatic knowledge that can be applied to the conduct of our own lives. As Topsell explains in his Epistle Dedicatory or prefatory letter to the book, we can learn from mice "a foreknowledge of things to come," from ants a "providence against old age," and from bears "the love of young" (sig. A4r). Especially in biblical contexts, animals also convey moral knowledge, for "the Lord compare[s] the Devil to a lion; evil judges to bears; false prophets to wolves," and so forth (sig. A4v). Such allegorical reading habits seem to invite contradiction: bears can represent nurturing mothers as well as corrupt judges. But these contradictions can also be attributed to Topsell's habit of synthesizing information from potentially incompatible sources, including "scriptures, [church] fathers, philosophers, physicians, and poets" (sig. A2r). Indeed, *The History of Four-Footed Beasts* largely comprises an amalgamation of passages copied directly from the *Historia Animalium* (1551–58) of Swiss naturalist Conrad Gesner, with additions from various English naturalists and Topsell's own commentary.

The contradictory definitions of bears in Topsell's Epistle prompt us to look for a similar multiplicity of meanings in his chapter "Of the Bear." When reading the excerpt below, consider how Topsell's gathering of examples from scripture, history, literature, mythology, folklore, and natural history — a broad discipline comprising botany, zoology, and geology — provides different kinds of knowledge about bears that might illuminate Antigonus's death in *The Winter's Tale*. For instance, to the degree that Leontes can be considered responsible for Antigonus's death, might Topsell support an interpretation of the bear as a symbol for Leontes? How do the descriptions of ravenous bears compare in Topsell and Shakespeare, through the Clown's report of Antigonus's death? Also consider the possible significance of the bear's appearance just after Antigonus has related his dream-vision of Hermione. Do any of Topsell's observations justify drawing connections between Antigonus's vision of Hermione and the manner of his death? Finally, we should not overlook the significance of Perdita's presence in this scene. Since Antigonus's flight prevents the bear from

---

Edward Topsell, "Of the Bear" in *The History of Four-Footed Beasts* (London, 1607); STC 24123; sigs. E1r–E1v, E2r, E3r, E4r.

noticing Perdita, should we understand his death as some kind of sacrifice? According to Topsell, what might the bear have done with the infant?

A bear is of a most venereous[1] and lustful disposition, for night and day the females with most ardent inflamed desires do provoke the males to copulation, and for this cause at that time they are most fierce and angry.

Phillipus Gillius of Constance[2] did most confidently tell me that in the mountains of Savoy a bear carried a young maid into his den by violence, where in venereous manner he had the carnal use of her body, and while he kept her in his den he daily went forth and brought her home the best apples and other fruits he could get, presenting them unto her for her meat[3] in very amorous sort, but always when he went to forage, he rolled a huge great stone upon the mouth of his den that the virgin should not escape away. At length her parents with long search found their little daughter in the bear's den, who delivered her from that savage and bestial captivity.

The time of their copulation is in the beginning of winter, although sometime in summer (but such young ones seldom live), yet most commonly in February or January. The manner of their copulation is like to a man's, the male moving himself upon the belly of the female, which lyeth on the earth flat upon the back, and either embraceth other with their forefeet: they remain very long time in that act, inasmuch as if they were very fat at their first entrance, they disjoin not themselves again till they be made lean.

Immediately after they have conceived, they betake themselves to their dens, where they (without meat) grow very fat (especially the males) only by sucking their forefeet. When they enter into their den, they convey themselves in backward, so that they may put out their footsteps from the sight of the hunters. The males give great honor to the females great with young during the time of their secrecy, so that although they lie together in one cave, yet do they part it by a division or small ditch in the midst, neither of them touching the other. The nature of all of them is to avoid cold, and therefore in the winter time do they hide themselves, choosing rather to suffer famine than cold, lying for the most part three or four months together and never see the light, whereby their guts grow so empty that they are almost closed up and stick together.

. . . And whereas it hath been believed and received that the whelps of bears at their first littering are without all form and fashion, and nothing but a little congealed blood like a lump of flesh, which afterward the old one[4]

---

[1] **venereous:** venereal; lustful.   [2] **Constance:** city in southwest Germany.   [3] **meat:** food.   [4] **the old one:** i.e., the mother.

frameth[5] with her tongue to her own likeness, as Pliny, Solinus, Aelianus, Orus, Oppianus, and Ovid[6] have reported, yet is the truth most evidently otherwise, as by the eye witness of Joachimus Rhetichus[7] and other is disproved. Only it is littered without eyes, naked without hair, and the hinder legs not perfect, the forefeet folded up like a fist, and other members deformed by reason of the immoderate humor[8] or moistness in them which also is one cause why the womb of the bear cannot retain the seed to the perfection of her young ones.

They bring forth sometimes two, and never above five, which the old bear daily keepeth close to her breast, so warming them with the heat of her body and the breath of her mouth, till they be thirty days old, at what time they come abroad, being in the beginning of May, which is the third month from the spring. . . .

If a she-bear having young ones be hunted, she driveth her whelps before her until they be wearied, and then if she be not prevented, she climbeth upon a tree, carrying one of her young in her mouth and the other on her back. . . .

A prince of Lithuania nourished a bear very tenderly, feeding her from his table with his own hand, for he had used her to be familiar in his court, and to come into his own chamber when he listed,[9] so that she would go abroad into the fields and woods, returning home again of her own accord, and would with her hand or foot rub the king's chamber door to have it opened when she was hungry, it being locked. It happened that certain young noblemen conspired the death of this prince and came to his chamber door, rubbing it after the custom of the bear; the king, not doubting[10] any evil and supposing it had been his bear, opened the door and they presently slew him. . . .

They will bury one another being dead, as Tzetzes[11] affirmeth, and it is received in many nations that children have been nursed by bears. Paris, thrown out of the city, was nourished by a bear. There is in France a noble house of the Ursons, whose first founder is reported to have been certain years together nourished by a bear, and for that cause was called Urson.[12] And some affirm that Arcesius was so, being deceived by the name of his mother who was called Arctos, a bear, as among the Latins was Ursula. And it is reported in the year of our Lord 1274 that the concubine of Pope Nicholas (being with child as was supposed) brought forth a young bear,

---

[5] **frameth:** fashions. [6] **Pliny . . . Ovid:** ancient poets, naturalists, and historians. [7] **Joachimus Rhetichus:** sixteenth-century Austrian astronomer. [8] **humor:** bodily fluid. [9] **listed:** desired. [10] **doubting:** fearing, suspecting. [11] **Tzetzes:** twelfth-century Byzantine scholar. [12] **Urson:** *ursus* is Latin for bear.

which she did not by any unlawful copulation with such a beast, but only with the most holy pope; and conceived such a creature by strength of imagination, lying in his palace, where she saw the pictures of many bears. So that the Holy Father being first put in good hope of a son, and afterward seeing this monster (like himself *Revel.* 13)[13] for anger and shame defaced all his pictures of those beasts. . . .

Great is the fierceness of a bear, as appeareth by Holy Scripture (*Hosea* 13): "I will meet them as a bear robbed of her whelps (saith the Lord) and will tear in pieces their forward heart." And Chusai[14] telleth Absalom (2 *Samuel* 17), "Thou knowest that thy father and the men that be with him be most valiant and fierce like a she-bear robbed of her whelps." For a she-bear is more courageous than a male. . . .

Vitoldus, King of Lithuania, kept certain bears of purpose to whom he cast all persons which spoke against his tyranny, putting them first of all into a bear's skin. Whose cruelty was so great that if he had commanded any of them to hang themselves, they would rather obey him than endure the terror of his indignation. In like sort did Alexander Phaeraeus[15] deal with his subjects, as is reported by Textor Valentintanus: the Emperor nourished two bears, devourers of men, one of them called golden Mica, the other Innocentia, which he lodged near his own chamber. At length after many slaughters of men, he let Innocentia go loose in the woods for her good deserts in bringing so many people to their funerals.

---

[13] *Revel.* **13:** Revelation 13 describes a seven-headed beast with the feet of a bear.   [14] **Chusai:** Hushai, a court official under King David.   [15] **Alexander Phaeraeus:** tyrant of Pherae, Greece, 369–358 B.C.E.

→ GERRIT DE VEER

From The True and Perfect Description of Three Voyages
1609

Translated by William Phillip

Gerrit de Veer's account of three Dutch sea voyages to discover a northern passage to China was first published, with over thirty illustrations, in 1598. Its popularity is indicated by the subsequent publication of multiple editions of the Dutch text as well as translations into French, Latin, German (all in 1598), and

---

Gerrit de Veer, *The True and Perfect Description of Three Voyages* (London, 1609), tr. William Phillip; STC 24628; sigs. B4v-C1r, F2v–F3r, G3v, J4v–K1r.

Italian (1599). The 1609 English translation was prepared by William Phillip, who translated several other Dutch books into English between 1596 and 1619. In the nineteenth century, Dutch nationalist poets promoted the story of the sixteenth-century travelers' arduous winter in Nova Zembla as a legend of national heroism, and many children's books based on the tale have been written (Groesen). This famous tale of winter has, in effect, become a winter's tale.

By the time it was translated into English, de Veer's story was already known as an adventure "so strange and wonderful, that the like hath never been heard of before" (sig. A1r). The sailors' encounters with "cruel bears, and other monsters of the sea" play a large role in creating that aura of adventure (sig. A1v). But de Veer's book was also used to promote mercantile and nationalistic agendas. Tellingly, William Phillip dedicated his English translation to Sir Thomas Smith, governor of the English Muscovy Company, the mercantile organization licensed to trade with Russia. Phillip explains that he translated de Veer's book to assist any of his countrymen who wished to attempt the same voyage, as well as to promote national pride: having read de Veer's account of the "congealed climates" of the North, English subjects will no doubt thank God for "planting [them] in so temperate, so civil, and so religious a part of the world as this blessed island" (sig. A2v).

The younger son of a prominent Dutch family, de Veer was not present on the initial voyage made by four ships in 1594; presumably, he drew his account of this voyage from the notes of William Barents, an experienced navigator and the pilot for all three expeditions (Beke cvi). After the first expedition failed to find a route to China, Barents set out again in 1595; in a show of optimism, five of the seven ships were laden with merchandise intended to be sold upon their arrival. A third and final attempt was made in 1596. This time, the United Provinces of the Netherlands offered a reward for the discovery of a northern passage, and only two ships sailed, de Veer again accompanying Barents, as he had on the second voyage. When the mariners became trapped in the ice around the island of Nova Zembla, they were forced to spend the winter among polar bears in a log cabin they constructed with wood from their ship. Several men, including Barents, did not survive this trip, and de Veer's narrative serves to memorialize their pilot's resolution and courage. Although their mission failed, de Veer refutes detractors' claims that their "proceeding therein was wholly unprofitable and fruitless; which peradventure in time to come may turn unto our great profit and commodity" (sig. B2r).

The differences between de Veer's narrative and Shakespeare's play are perhaps more instructive than the similarities. Unlike the Sicilian sailors, the Dutch sailors know their destination from the start (even if they never reach it), and they have very different motives for undertaking their voyage. How do the different purposes and expectations of Shakespeare's and de Veer's travelers affect how they respond to crisis? Does the encounter with bears seem more terrifying in one text than in the other? The Dutch explorers' treatment of their fallen shipmates alerts us to the possible significance of Antigonus's solitary death. In terms of purpose, tone, or style, how does the Clown's account of Antigonus's death — and of his dying words — compare to de Veer's accounts of his companions' deaths?

From *The True and Perfect Description of Three Voyages*

[The first voyage into the North Seas, 1594. Since de Veer was not present for this voyage, the narrative is presented in the third person.]

The 9th of July they entered into Beeren-fort[1] upon the road under Williams Island, and there they found a white bear, which they perceiving presently entered into their boat and shot her into the body with a musket, but the bear showed most wonderful strength, which almost is not to be found in any beast, for no man ever heard the like to be done by any lion or cruel beast whatsoever. For notwithstanding that she was shot into the body, yet she leapt up and swam in the water; the men that were in the boat rowing after her cast a rope about her neck, and by that means drew her at the stern of the boat, for that not having seen the like bear before, they thought to have carried her alive in the ship and to have showed her for a strange wonder in Holland. But she used such force that they were glad that they were rid of her and contented themselves with her skin only, for she made such a noise, and strove in such sort, that it was admirable, wherewith they let her rest and gave her more scope with the rope that they held her by, and so drew her in that sort after them, by that means to weary her. Meantime, William Barents made nearer to her, but the bear swam to the boat and with her forefeet got hold of the stern thereof, which William Barents perceiving said she will there rest herself, but she had another meaning, for she used such force that at last she had gotten half her body into the boat, wherewith the men were so abashed that they ran into the further end of the boat, and thought verily to have been spoiled[2] by her. But by a strange means they were delivered from her, for that the rope that was about her neck caught hold upon the hook of the rudder, whereby the bear could get no further but so was held back and hanging in that manner. One of the men boldly stepped forth from the end of the scute[3] and thrust her into the body with a half-pike,[4] and therewith she fell down into the water, and so they rowed forward with her to the ship, drawing her after them, till she was in a manner

---

[1] **Beeren-fort:** Bear Creek.   [2] **spoiled:** destroyed.   [3] **scute:** forepart of the boat.   [4] **half-pike:** a small staff with a spike or point.

dead, wherewith they killed her outright, and having flayed her, brought the skin to Amsterdam.

[The second voyage, 1595.]

The 6th of September, some of our men went on shore upon the firm land to seek for stones, which are a kind of diamond, whereof there are many also in the States Island. And while they were seeking the stones, two of our men lying together in one place, a great lean white bear came suddenly stealing out and caught one of them fast by the neck, who not knowing what it was that took him by the neck cried out and said, "Who is that that pulls me so by the neck?" Wherewith the other that lay not far from him lifted up his head to see who it was, and perceiving it to be a monstrous bear, cried and said, "Oh mate, it is a bear," and therewith presently rose up and ran away.

The bear at the first falling upon the man bit his head in sunder and sucked out his blood, wherewith the rest of the men that were on land, being about 20 in number, ran presently thither, either to save the man or else to drive the bear from the dead body. And having charged their pieces[5] and bent their pikes set upon her that still was devouring the man, but perceiving them to come towards her, fiercely and cruelly ran at them, and got another of them out from the company which she tore in pieces, wherewith all the rest ran away.

We perceiving out of our ship and pinnace[6] that our men ran to the seaside to save themselves, with all speed entered into our boats and rowed as fast as we could to the shore to receive our men. Where being on land, we beheld the cruel spectacle of our two dead men that had been so cruelly killed and torn in pieces by the bear. We seeing that encouraged our men to go back again with us, and with pieces, curtal-axes,[7] and half-pikes to set upon the bear, but they would not all agree thereunto: some of them saying, our men are already dead, and we shall get the bear well enough, though we oppose not ourselves into so open danger; if we might save our fellows' lives, then we would make haste, but now we need not make such speed, but take her at an advantage with most security for ourselves, for we have to do with a cruel, fierce, and ravenous beast. Whereupon three of our men went toward the bear still devouring her prey, not once fearing the number of our men, and yet there were thirty at the least. The three that went forward in that sort were Cornelius Jacobson, Master of William Barents' ship; William Gysen, pilot of the pinnace; and Hans van Nufflen, William Barents'

---

[5] **pieces:** muskets. [6] **pinnace:** a small boat. [7] **curtal-axes:** short, broad swords.

FIGURE 21 *Illustration from Gerrit de Veer,* Waerachtighe Beschryvinghe van Drie Seylagien *(1598). This image from* True Accounts of Three Sea Voyages *depicts the events of September 15, 1596, in which Dutch sailors trapped on the island of Nova Zembla encountered three polar bears. Why might the engraver have chosen to represent this particular moment in the story?*

purser. And after that the said master and pilot had shot three times and missed, the purser stepping somewhat further forward and seeing the bear to be within the length of a shot, presently leveled his piece, and discharging it at the bear, shot her into the head, between both the eyes, and yet she held the man still fast by the neck and lifted up her head with the man in her mouth. But she began somewhat to stagger, wherewith the purser and a Scottish man drew out their curtal-axes and struck at her so hard that their curtal-axes burst, and yet she would not leave the man. At last William Geysen went to them and with all his might struck the bear upon the snout with his piece, at which time the bear fell to the ground, making a great noise, and William Gyson leaping upon her, cut her throat. The seventh of September we buried the dead bodies of our men in the States Island, and having flayed the bear, carried her skin to Amsterdam.

[Third voyage, 1596–97]

The 12th of June in the morning we saw a white bear which we rowed after with our boat, thinking to cast a rope about her neck, but when we were near her, she was so great that we durst not do it, but rowed back again to our ship to fetch more men and our arms, and so made to her again with muskets, harquebuses,[8] halberds,[9] and hatchets, John Cornelyson's men coming also with their boat to help us. And so being well furnished of men and weapons we rowed with both our boats unto the bear, and fought with her while four glasses[10] were run out, for our weapons could do her little hurt. And amongst the rest of the blows that we gave her, one of our men struck her into the back with an axe, which stuck fast in her back, and yet she swam away with it; but we rowed after her, and at last we cut her head in sunder with an axe, wherewith she died. And then we brought her into John Cornelyson's ship, where we flayed her and found her skin to be twelve foot long; which done, we ate some of her flesh, but we brooked[11] it not well. This island we called the Bear Island. . . .

The 15th of September, in the morning, as one of our men held watch, we saw three bears, whereof the one lay still behind a piece of ice, the other two came close to the ship, which we perceiving, made our pieces ready to shoot at them. At which time there stood a tub full of beef upon the ice, which lay in the water to be seasoned, for that close by the ship there was no water. One of the bears went unto it and put in his head to take out a piece of the beef, but she fared therewith as the dog did with the pudding,[12] for as she was snatching at the beef she was shot into the head, wherewith she fell down dead and never stirred. The other bear stood still and looked upon her fellow, and when she had stood a good while she smelled her fellow, and perceiving that she was dead, she ran away. But we took halberds and other arms with us and followed her, and at last she came again towards us, and we prepared ourselves to withstand her, wherewith she rose up upon her hind feet, thinking to ramp at us, but while she reared herself up, one of our men shot her into the belly, and with that she fell upon her forefeet again, and roaring as loud as she could, ran away. Then we took the dead bear and ripped her belly open; and taking out her guts, we set her upon her four feet, that so she might freeze as she stood, intending to carry her with us into Holland, if we might get our ship loose. And when we had set the bear upon her four feet, we began to make a sled, thereon to draw the wood to the place where we went to build our house, at that time it froze two fingers thick in the salt water, and it was exceeding cold, the wind blowing north-east.

---

[8] **harquebuses:** portable guns supported on a tripod or trestle.   [9] **halberds:** a combination of spear and battle-axe.   [10] **four glasses:** four hourglasses, or two hours.   [11] **brooked:** digested.   [12] **as the dog did with the pudding:** in a Dutch proverb, a dog is beaten for stealing a sausage ("pudding").

Pastoral Preoccupations

> This your sheep-shearing
> Is as a meeting of the petty gods ... (4.4.3–4)

Unlike some of his contemporaries, Shakespeare was not overly preoccupied with pastoral. The most noted sixteenth-century English writers of pastoral were Edmund Spenser and Sir Philip Sidney, authors respectively of *The Shepheardes Calender* (1579), a collection of twelve eclogues (or verse dialogues), and *The Arcadia* (1590), a prose romance. For Sidney and Spenser, the *Eclogues* of the ancient Roman poet Virgil provided the primary classical model for both the style and the subject matter of pastoral. Although ostensibly about shepherds, pastoral writing was often used to comment allegorically on sensitive social, moral, or political matters. As the English literary critic George Puttenham acknowledged in his *Art of English Poesy*, classical pastorals do not accurately record how ancient shepherds actually spoke. Rather, Puttenham explains, "the poet devised the eclogue long after the other dramatic poems" such as comedy and tragedy, "not of purpose to counterfeit or represent the rustical manner of loves and communication: but under the veil of homely persons and in rude speeches to insinuate and glance at greater matters, and such as perchance had not been safe to have been disclosed in any other sort" (sigs. F3v–F4r). Medieval and Renaissance commentators on Virgil's first eclogue typically interpreted its contrast between the happy shepherd Tityrus and the exiled shepherd Meliboeus as an allegory of the fate of different political factions under the emperor Augustus (O'Callaghan 308).

Renaissance poets understood that pastoral, with its apparently humble language, figures, and situations, might be effectively used to comment indirectly upon current political, social, and religious affairs. Louis Montrose demonstrates how the April eclogue from Spenser's *Shepheardes Calender* shrewdly fuses classical and Christian pastoral traditions to construct a flattering image of Queen Elizabeth as "Elisa," the lovely "goddess" and "Queen of shepherds" (61). Transforming conventionally simple images of rural life into a "pastoral of power," courtier-poets such as Spenser promoted the illusion that Queen Elizabeth was "approachable and knowable, lovable and loving, to lords and peasants, courtiers and citizens alike" (Montrose 61). Offering a visual image of the incongruously elevated social concerns of Renaissance pastoral, the title page of a Jacobean text by the popular writer John Taylor unrealistically depicts shepherds as fashionably dressed gentlemen (Figure 22). According to Taylor, the "noble antiquity" of shepherds originated with the biblical Abel: "a prince, a patriarch, a figure of the true church, a type of Christ, and a shepherd" (sig. B1v).

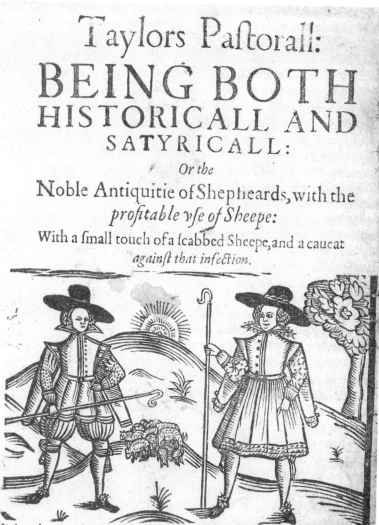

Taylors Paſtorall:
BEING BOTH
HISTORICALL AND
SATYRICALL:

Or the
Noble Antiquitie of Shepheards, with the
profitable vſe of Sheepe:
With a ſmall touch of a ſcabbed Sheepe, and a caueat
againſt that infection.

Printed at London by *G.P.* for *Henrie Goſſon,* and are to be ſold at *Edward Wrights* ſhop neere Chriſts Church Gate. 1624.

FIGURE 22 *Frontispiece from John Taylor,* Taylor's Pastoral: Being Both Historical and Satirical: or the Noble Antiquity of Shepherds, with the Profitable Use of Sheep *(1624).*

Puttenham's insight that pastoral writers use humble figures to glance at "greater matters" can help to link the seemingly disparate environments of *The Winter's Tale*. As the setting of the play shifts from the Sicilian court to the Bohemian countryside, its focus does not correspondingly shift from serious business to rustic play, for the pastoral landscape of Bohemia is also a site of deep social, sexual, and political conflict. Perdita's ambivalence about getting "pranked up" (4.4.10) in the costume of the Roman goddess Flora seems to reflect her understandable anxiety about the risks of a romantic entanglement with the prince. In Ovid's poem *Fasti*, the god of the west wind Zephyrus rapes the nymph Chloris, who is then transformed into Flora, the goddess of flowers and spring (Figure 23). Explaining that Zephyrus "made amends" for having raped her, Flora asserts: "I cannot blame my life. / My spring is constant; all my season's good: / My trees with leaves, my ground is clad with food" (*Ovid's Festivals* 5.206–8). Perdita's impersonation of a nymph who was raped by a god disturbingly parallels her own circumstances as a humble shepherdess wooed by a prince. Indeed, Florizel justifies disguising himself in a shepherd's habit on the grounds that the classical gods took the form of animals to seduce mortal women: "Jupiter / Became a bull, and bellowed; the green Neptune / A ram, and bleated" (4.4.27–29). This is not to say that Florizel intends to rape Perdita, or that Perdita fears being raped, although it is worth pondering Simon Palfrey's observation that "Florizel aestheticizes, without quite banishing, the will to rape" (227). In any case, the apparent difference in rank between the prince and the shepherdess presents a serious obstacle to their marital union. "To me the difference forges dread" (4.4.17): so Perdita confesses her trepidation about being the prince's mate, even — or especially — when falsely costumed as a "queen" (4.4.5).

Politics also intrude more directly into the sheep-shearing festival. Polixenes and Camillo disguise themselves in modest garb not to mingle in a spirit of communal festivity with humble subjects, but to spy on Prince Florizel, who has been frequenting the home of a "most homely shepherd" (4.2.30). Even Autolycus, whose opening song introduces the traditional pastoral imagery of daffodils blossoming and birds chirping in "the sweet o'the year" (4.3.3), is a displaced courtly figure, a disgraced former servant of the prince. Having begun in the context of a political intrigue surrounding the prince, the sheep-shearing scene concludes by gesturing toward a crisis of succession that threatens to replicate the crisis of the heirless Sicilian court. Enraged that his son would stoop to marry a mere shepherdess, Polixenes threatens to bar his sole heir from inheriting the throne. Florizel vows that he will renounce his political title before betraying his love: "From my

FIGURE 23 Occidens (West Wind), *an engraving by Jan Sadeler (1550–1600), after a painting by Marten de Vos (c. 1532–1603). Chased by Zephyrus, god of the west wind, Flora drops her flowers.*

succession wipe me, father; I / Am heir to my affection" (4.4.460–61). Just as Leontes has lost his son and heir, so Polixenes stands to lose his.

Yet the sheep-shearing feast does not simply become the unfortunate occasion of another political disaster, for the pastoral energies the feast embodies — the generative resources of "great creating nature" (4.4.88) — carry the promise of a more harmonious resolution to the kinds of conflicts that generated tragedy in Sicilia. By revealing the diverse meanings that Shakespeare's contemporaries attached to the notion of the "country," the documents below illuminate how Bohemian pastoral both reflects and offers an alternative to the political tensions of Leontes' Sicilia. In Shakespeare's depiction of Bohemia, a traditional view of the country as a place of simple virtue is belied by those aspects of courtly life (embodied in Florizel, Polixenes, and Camillo) and urban life (embodied in Autolycus, who resembles a London con artist) that are also present. Nor are the social and moral meanings of the "country" stable. For instance, Perdita's moral purity might be attributed either to the innocence of her rural upbringing or to the innate nobility of her royal blood. Does the vulgarity of the country girls Mopsa and Dorcas prove the inherent difference between the morals of "low-born lass[es]" (4.4.156) and those of a high-born lass such as Perdita who only happens to be raised in a humble environment? Finally, in the midst of all this natural beauty, what role does artifice play in forging bonds of love and fidelity? In the more expansive Bohemian environment, can theatrical artifice shed some of the negative associations that it accumulated in Leontes' wintery court?

→ GEORGE PUTTENHAM

From The Art of English Poesy   *1589*

George Puttenham (1529–1590) was the author of the first full-scale work of poetic criticism in English. While tracing poetry back to its ancient roots, Puttenham also argues that contemporary writers deserve honor for poetic accomplishments that have "so much beautified our English tongue" (sig. H4v). Among the English authors he singles out for praise are Geoffrey Chaucer; the early-sixteenth-century sonneteers Thomas Wyatt and Howard Surrey; Arthur Golding, the translator of Ovid; and the Elizabethan poets Philip Sidney and Walter Raleigh. Puttenham divides his long treatise into three books. "Of Poets and Poesy" defines the subject matter and forms of poetry; "Of Proportion Poetical" describes the rules of meter, accent, and rhyme; and "Of Ornament" treats the correct use of rhetorical and figurative language, such as metaphor, irony, and hyperbole. The final chapter of *The Art of English Poesy*, excerpted below,

George Puttenham, *The Art of English Poesy* (London, 1589), STC 20519.5; sigs. Ll 1r–Ll 2r, pp. 253–55.

considers "in what cases the artificial is more commended than the natural, and contrariwise" (sig. Ll 1r)."

In the "natural" world of the Bohemian countryside, art and artifice are surprisingly prominent, and ambivalent, presences. Even though Polixenes harshly accuses Perdita of using artifice to seduce Florizel, the sheep-shearing episode generally displays the more affirmative view of artifice found in comedy, in which theatricality serves for entertainment, courtship, and the celebration of nature's fertility. Camillo, for instance, offers disguise and role-playing as a strategy for Florizel, Perdita, and himself to evade the repressive power of Polixenes. Nonetheless, Perdita's reluctance to "bear a part" in Camillo's "play" (4.4.274) emphasizes her ambivalent participation in the festival atmosphere of the sheep-shearing scene. From the outset, Perdita has been playing a part as queen of the festival, yet one of her most distinctive traits is a resistance to artifice in its various forms. As hostess of the festival, Perdita reluctantly observes the custom of donning an elaborate costume that she complains does not suit her: what Florizel admiringly calls her "unusual weeds" she pejoratively calls her "borrowed flaunts" (4.4.1, 23).

It is precisely Perdita's resistance to artifice that leads to one of the great rhetorical set pieces of the play, her debate with Polixenes about the virtues of art and nature. The debate begins when Perdita declares her refusal to grow "carnations and streaked gillyvors, / Which some call nature's bastards" (4.4.82–83). Gillyflowers might be considered "nature's bastards" because they were "thought to produce cross-breeds without human aid" and to display the greatest variety of colors (Pafford 170). In his *Herbal* (1597), an encyclopedic natural history of plants, John Gerard explains that under the name of "stock gilloflowers are comprehended many kinds of violets, which differ especially in the color of the flowers" (sig. Aa2v). Yet even if gillyflowers were thought to generate hybrid or multiple varieties naturally, Perdita also attributes their "piedness" to the intervention of an "art" such as grafting, in which a gardener cuts a cultivated plant into a wilder stock, thereby adulterating or bastardizing nature (4.4.87). Polixenes counters that nature itself makes the art that the gardener uses to improve upon nature. The art of grafting might "mend" or even "change" nature, but the "art itself is nature" (4.4.96–97).

An analogue for Polixenes' defense of "natural" artifice appears in the excerpt below from *The Art of English Poesy*, in which Puttenham justifies the poet's use of rhetorical arts to enhance natural eloquence. Puttenham's treatment of the topic reveals that Perdita and Polixenes are engaged not in a dry philosophical meditation about art and nature, but in a lively debate about the social value of different skills and abilities. To pursue this line of thought, we can examine how "art" and the "artificial" are defined and evaluated in Puttenham and Shakespeare. In *The Art of English Poesy* and *The Winter's Tale*, under what circumstances is art most likely to receive "great praise"? Is Perdita simply naïve in championing "nature" over "art"? Perhaps Perdita recognizes a danger to art that Puttenham ignores or minimizes. If so, what might that danger be?

From *The Art of English Poesy*

And yet for all that our maker[1] may not be in all cases restrained, but that he may both use and also manifest his art to his great praise, and need no more be ashamed thereof, than a shoemaker to have made a cleanly[2] shoe or a carpenter to have built a fair house; therefore to discuss and make this point somewhat clearer, to wit,[3] where art ought to appear and where not, and when the natural is more commendable than the artificial in any human action or workmanship, we will examine it further by this distinction.

In some cases we say art is an aid and coadjutor[4] to nature, and a furtherer of her actions to good effect, or peradventure[5] a mean to supply her wants,[6] by reinforcing the causes wherein she is impotent and defective, as doth the art of physic, by helping the natural concoction,[7] retention, distribution, expulsion, and other virtues, in a weak and unhealthy body. Or as the good gardener seasons his soil by sundry sorts of compost: as muck[8] or marl,[9] clay or sand, and many times by blood, or less of oil or wine, or stale,[10] or perchance with more costly drugs: and waters his plants, and weeds his herbs and flowers, and prunes his branches, and unleaves his boughs to let in the sun: and twenty other ways cherishes them, and cureth their infirmities, and so makes that never, or very seldom any of them miscarry, but bring forth their flowers and fruits in seasons. And in both these cases it is no small praise for the physician and gardener to be called good and cunning artificers.

In another respect art is not only an aid and coadjutor to nature in all her actions, but an alterer of them, and in some sort a surmounter of her skill, so as by means of it her own effects shall appear more beautiful or strange and miraculous, as in both cases before remembered. The physician by the cordials he will give his patient shall be able not only to restore the decayed spirits of man, and render him health, but also to prolong the term of his life many years over and above the stint[11] of his first and natural constitution. And the gardener by his art will not only make an herb, or flower, or fruit, come forth in his season without impediment, but also will embellish the same in virtue, shape, order and taste, that nature of herself would never have done: as to make the single gillyflower, or marigold, or daisy, double; and the white rose, red, yellow, or carnation; a bitter melon sweet; a sweet apple, sour; a plum or cherry without a stone;[12] a pear without core or kernel; a gourd or cucumber like to a horn, or any other figure he will: any of

---

[1] **maker:** poet.   [2] **cleanly:** neatly made.   [3] **to wit:** that is.   [4] **coadjutor:** assistant.   [5] **peradventure:** perhaps.   [6] **wants:** deficiencies.   [7] **concoction:** digestion.   [8] **muck:** manure.   [9] **marl:** an earthy deposit.   [10] **stale:** urine.   [11] **stint:** limit.   [12] **stone:** pit.

which things nature could not do without man's help and art. These actions also are most singular,[13] when they be most artificial.

In another respect, we say art is neither an aider nor a surmounter, but only a bare imitator of nature's works, following and counterfeiting her actions and effects, as the marmoset[14] doth many countenances and gestures of man, of which sort are the arts of painting and carving, whereof one represents the natural by light, color, and shadow in the superficial or flat, the other in a body massy[15] expressing the full and empty, even, extant,[16] rabbeted,[17] hollow, or whatsoever other figure and passion of quantity. So also the alchemist counterfeits gold, silver, and all other metals; the lapidary[18] pearls and precious stones by glass and other substances falsified, and sophisticate by art. These men also be praised for their craft, and their credit is nothing impaired, to say that their conclusions and effects are very artificial. Finally in another respect art is as it were an encounterer[19] and contrary to nature, producing effects neither like to hers, nor by participation with her operations, nor by imitation of her patterns, but makes things and produceth effects altogether strange and diverse, and of such form and quality (nature always supplying stuff) as she never would nor could have done of herself, as the carpenter that builds a house, the joiner that makes a table or a bedstead, the tailor a garment, the smith a lock or a key, and a number of like, in which case the workman gaineth reputation by his art, and praise when it is best expressed and most apparent, and most studiously.

[13] **singular:** remarkable. [14] **marmoset:** small monkey. [15] **massy:** three-dimensional. [16] **extant:** protruding. [17] **rabbeted:** grooved. [18] **lapidary:** one who cuts and polishes precious stones. [19] **encounterer:** adversary.

➔ JOHN FITZHERBERT

From Fitzherbert's Book of Husbandry   *1598*

First printed in 1523, John Fitzherbert's *Book of Husbandry* went through many editions throughout the sixteenth century. It was eventually supplanted by more recent Elizabethan writings on the topic. The passages below come from the 1598 edition, the last to be published prior to the first performances of *The Winter's Tale*. Fitzherbert also wrote *The Book of Surveying* (1523), a handbook of estate management. The oldest son of a landed gentry family, Fitzherbert headed the family estate in Norbury, Derbyshire, and the *Book of Husbandry*

John Fitzherbert, *Fitzherbert's Book of Husbandry* (London, 1598), STC 11004; sigs. H2v–H4r.

derives from his experience of being a "householder this forty years and more" (sig. Cc4r).

As Andrew McRae explains, Fitzherbert assumed that his reader would be, like himself, "a gentleman in charge of a sizeable estate, and his recommended routine is one of supervision rather than manual labour" (137–38). In this way, Fitzherbert's "insistence on the order of a large estate aligns with classical traditions of husbandry writing" going back to the *Oeconomicus* (meaning "household economy") of the ancient Greek writer Xenophon (McRae 138). Fitzherbert provides advice on many aspects of estate management, including plowing and sowing; breeding and maintaining cattle; planting, chopping, and grafting trees; and running an orderly household. Reflecting the broader classical definition of "economy," Fitzherbert concludes with essays on moral and religious precepts, such as "What Riches Are," "What Things Pleaseth God Most," and "A Mean to Avoid Temptation."

The *Book of Husbandry* describes the difficult labor of sheep-shearing, which is not shown in *The Winter's Tale*, even though Shakespeare stages a festival that takes place during the sheep-shearing season. In seventeenth-century England, the washing, clipping, and winding required to shear the flock of 1,500 sheep owned by Perdita's father would have involved enormous labor from a great number of agricultural workers. First, washers would remove dirt from the wool. A skilled washer might have been able to wash more than one hundred sheep per day (Bowden 22). Just this preliminary stage of the Old Shepherd's sheep-shearing operation, then, would have taken five men at least three days to perform. According to a farm account from 1676, it took twelve clippers and three wool collectors three days to round up and shear a comparable flock of 1,560 sheep (Bowden 23). Great quantities of tar had to be on hand to apply to the skin of any sheep that were accidentally cut. Finally, the clipped fleeces were carefully "wound," or folded up to be brought to market. The Old Shepherd's son calculates that every eleven sheep will produce a tod (28 pounds) of wool, and each tod will sell for 21 shillings. If this is accurate, then Perdita's family stands to make approximately £143 — an enormous profit. Even subtracting the cost of labor and supplies for the sheep-shearing — perhaps £25 — the Old Shepherd will add considerably to his already "unspeakable estate" (4.2.31–32).

In emphasizing pastoral festivity over rural labor, Shakespeare discourages us from thinking through these calculations. For one thing, the Clown himself admits that the figures are too complex to determine. More important, the excitement of Autolycus's scams and the ebullience of the festival distract us from calling to mind the toil of agricultural wage laborers responsible for the daily upkeep of flocks. The different treatment of economic issues provides a good index to the difference between the pragmatic aims of the *Book of Husbandry* and the romantic fantasy of *The Winter's Tale*. Though Fitzherbert shows that the proper care of sheep can generate "exceeding profit," the Old Shepherd's excessive wealth comes not from his labor as a shepherd but from the "fairy gold" he discovers with Perdita (3.3.105). With this gold he purchases a large flock and the land on which to graze it, and presumably hires the workers who will prepare the wool for highly profitable sale. When reading the excerpts below, consider in what other ways Shakespeare transforms the work involved in sheep husbandry into the play of the Bohemian sheep-shearing festival.

From *Fitzherbert's Book of Husbandry*

CHAPTER 11: HOW TO CURE THE WORM IN A SHEEP'S FOOT

Many times it happeneth among sheep that they have a worm in their foot which maketh them to halt.[1] Take that sheep and look between his claws, and there you shall find a little hole, as much as a great pin's head, and therein groweth five or six black hairs, about an inch long, or somewhat more. Take a sharp pointed knife, and slit the skin a quarter of an inch long above the hole, and as much beneath, and put thy one hand in the hollow of the foot under the hinder claw, and set thy thumb above, almost at the slit, and thrust thy finger underneath forward, and with your other hand take the black hair by the end, or with the knife's point take hold thereof. Then pull the hair by little and little, and thrust after thy other hand with thy finger and thy thumb, and there will come out a worm like a piece of fleam,[2] as much as a little finger, and when it is out, put a little tar in the hole, and it will be quickly well.

CHAPTER 12: OF THE BLOOD, AND REMEDY IF ONE COME BETIME[3]

Amongst sheep there is a sickness called the blood. That sheep which hath it will die suddenly, but ere he die he will stand still and hang down his head, and another while stand and quake. If the shepherd do espy him, let him take him and rub him about the head, and especially about his ears and under his eyes, and with a knife cut of his ears in the midst, and also let him blood in a vein under his eye; and if he bleed well he is likely to live. And if he bleed not then kill him and save his flesh, for if he die by himself the flesh is utterly lost, and the skin will be far ruddier like blood, more than any other skin will be, to the great hindrance of the sale. And this disease for the most part taketh the fattest and best liking[4] sheep.

---

[1] **halt:** be lame. [2] **fleam:** i.e., phlegm, mucus. [3] **betime:** early. [4] **best liking:** healthiest.

Chapter 13: Of the Pox and Remedy Therefore

This disease of the pox in a sheep appeareth upon the skin, and is like red pimples, as broad as a farthing,[5] and therefore die many. The remedy therefore is to handle all thy sheep, and to look on every part of their bodies, and as many as you find taken therewith, put them in fresh new grass, and keep them from their fellows. And also look your flock oft, and draw[6] them as they need, and if it be summer time that there be no frost then wash them; but if you cannot wash them, then let them blood in the roofs of the mouth, and after they have left bleeding, give them a supping[7] of milk and saffron mingled together. Divers[8] shepherds have other medicines, but this is the most approved that may be.

Chapter 14: Of the Wood Evil and Remedy Therefore

There is also a sickness amongst sheep is called the wood evil, and that cometh in the spring of the year, and taketh them most commonly in the legs or in the neck, and maketh them to halt and hold their necks awry. The most part that have that sickness will die shortly in a day or two. The best remedy is to wash them a little, and to change their ground, and to bring them to low ground and fresh grass, for that sickness is most commonly on hilly ground, lay ground,[9] and ferny ground. And some men use to let them blood under the eye in a vein for the same cause.

Chapter 15: How to Wash Sheep

In June is the best time to shear sheep, yet ere they be shorn they must be very well washed, which shall be to the owner's great profit in the sale of his wool, and also to the cloth maker. But yet beware thou put not too many sheep in a pen at one time, neither at the washing nor at the shearing, for fear of smothering or oppressing of their fellows; and that none go away till they be clean washed; and regard that they which hold the sheep by the head in the water hold his head high enough for fear of drowning. Wash your sheep in running rivers, for standing ponds are ill.

---

[5] **farthing:** a small coin.   [6] **draw:** set apart from the flock.   [7] **supping:** broth.   [8] **Divers:** different.   [9] **lay ground:** untilled land.

Chapter 16: How to Shear Sheep

Take heed of the shearers in shearing for twitching[10] the sheep with his shears, and specially of pricking him with the point of his shears; and that the shepherd be always ready with his tarbox,[11] or bronne[12] salve to dress them; and see that they be well marked, both ear mark, pitch mark,[13] and raddle[14] mark. Let your wool be well folded or wound with a wool-winder that hath good skill in that faculty, which shall do much good, and be exceeding profitable in the sale of the same.

Chapter 17: How to Draw and Sever the Bad Sheep from the Good

When you have shorn all your sheep, it is then the best time to draw[15] them, and to sever them in divers sorts: those sheep which thou wilt feed by themselves, the ewes by themselves, the shear-hogs[16] and theaves[17] by themselves, the lambs by themselves, the wethers[18] and rams by themselves, if thou have so many pastures for them, for the biggest will beat the weakest with his head. And of every sort of sheep it may fortune there be some that like not and be weak: those would be put in fresh grass by themselves, and when they are somewhat mended sell them, for oft change of grass shall mend all manner of cattle.

[10] twitching: pinching.   [11] tarbox: box used to hold tar.   [12] bronne: brand.   [13] pitch mark: mark of ownership made with pitch.   [14] raddle: red ochre.   [15] draw: select and set apart. [16] shear-hog: a lamb between the first and second shearings.   [17] theave: a ewe between the first and second shearings.   [18] wether: a castrated male sheep.

➜ MICHAEL DRAYTON

The Ninth Eclogue   *1606*

The son of a tradesman, Michael Drayton (1563–1631) entered as a young man into the service of a noble family in Nottinghamshire. There is no evidence that he attended a university. By 1590 he was living in London, where he began a long career as a poet and playwright. Proficient in many literary modes, Drayton wrote pastoral eclogues, satires, sonnets, verse letters, and poems on historical and biblical topics. After an unsuccessful bid for patronage from King James,

Michael Drayton, "The Ninth Eclogue" in *Poems, Lyrical and Pastoral: Odes, Eclogues, The Man in the Moon* (London, 1606); STC 7225.5; sigs. G2r–G6r.

FIGURE 24 *An engraving of "Summer," by Aegidius Sadeler (c. 1570–1629), based on a series of drawings of* The Four Seasons *by Pieter Stevens (1567–1624). How does this image of summer compare to the depiction of sheep-shearing festivities in Drayton and Shakespeare?*

Drayton attached himself to a young knight, Sir Walter Aston. Drayton's most impressive work is *Poly-Olbion* (1612), a massive "chorography" or description of the natural features, legends, and history of the countryside. *Poly-Olbion* constituted an "extremely ambitious project to mythologize the English countryside," which Drayton associated with moral virtue (Norbrook 185). The folio volume *Poems by Michael Drayton*, published in 1619, collected all his verse except *Poly-Olbion*.

In the early 1590s, responding to Spenser's *Shepheardes Calender*, Drayton wrote a collection of pastoral eclogues called *Idea, The Shepheardes Garland* (1593). He significantly revised the eclogues for their publication in 1606 (Perry 67); they were subsequently reprinted in the 1619 *Poems*. David Norbrook describes Drayton as one of a group of poets "who were alienated from the court" of King James "and sometimes used the traditional symbolism of Protestant pastoral to voice their discontent" (175). Some of Drayton's eclogues glance critically at King James and at Sir Robert Cecil, his powerful secretary of state. In Drayton's first eclogue, for instance, Rowland laments that only base flatterers win advancement (Perry 71). The ninth eclogue represents a festive rural world far removed from courtly intrigues and disappointments. However, the sudden appearance of the shepherdess Idea, an idealized figure of the late Queen Elizabeth, expresses the "nostalgia of a whole community" for a golden age under a beloved monarch (Perry 73).

In his translation of pastoral festivity to the stage, Shakespeare both borrows from and modifies the conventions of pastoral poetry exemplified by Drayton. Consider how Drayton and Shakespeare use similar pastoral conventions — floral imagery, romantic intrigue, praise of female beauty, feasting and singing — to different ends. At the most basic level, it is worth comparing the kinds of people who attend the festivals in the two texts, and the kinds of activities in which they engage. Also telling is the different treatment of gender and sexuality in the two texts. For instance, how do Shakespeare and Drayton acknowledge the possible threat that sexual rivalry poses to communal harmony? As queen of the sheep-shearing feast, is Perdita comparable to Drayton's Idea, "the shepherds' queen"? Finally, although both Drayton and Shakespeare incorporate royal figures into their depictions of rural festivity, the interaction between social ranks produces different consequences. In each text, what is the relationship between cross-rank interaction and the way in which the pastoral festivities come to an end?

The Ninth Eclogue

Late 'twas in June, the fleece when fully grown,
In the full compass¹ of the passed year,
That them provide immediately to shear.
The season well by skillful shepherds known,

Their lambs late waxed so lusty² and so strong,   5
That time did them their mothers' teats forbid,
And in the fields the common flocks among,
Eat of the same grass that the greater did.

Now not a shepherd anything that could,
But greased his start-ups³ black as autumn's sloe,⁴   10
And for the better credit of the wold,⁵
In their fresh russets⁶ every one doth go.

---

¹ **compass:** course. ² **lusty:** healthy. ³ **start-ups:** rustic boots. ⁴ **sloe:** black-thorn, a black shrub. ⁵ **wold:** a piece of open country. ⁶ **russets:** garments made of homespun woolen cloth.

Who now a posy[7] pins not in his cap?
And not a garland baldric-wise[8] doth wear?
Some of such flowers as to his hand doth hap,   15
Others, such as a secret meaning bear:

He from his lass him lavender hath sent,
Showing her love, and doth requital crave,
Him rosemary his sweetheart, whose intent,
Is that, he her should in remembrance have.   20

Roses, his youth and strong desire express,
Her sage doth show his sovereignty in all,
The July-flower[9] declares his gentleness,
Thyme truth, the pansy, hearts-ease maidens call.

In cotes[10] such simples,[11] simply in request,   25
Wherewith proud courts in greatness scorn to mell,[12]
For country toys become the country best,
And please poor shepherds, and become them well.

When the new-washed flock from the river's side,
Coming as white as January's snow,   30
The ram with nosegays[13] bears his horns in pride,
And no less brave, the bell-wether[14] doth go.

After their fair flocks in a lusty rout,
Came the gay swains[15] with bagpipes strongly blown,
And busied though this solemn sport about,   35
Yet had each one an eye unto his own.

And by the ancient statutes of the field,
He that his flocks the earliest lamb should bring,
(As it fell out now Rowland's charge to yield)
Always for that year was the Shepherds' King.[16]   40

And soon preparing for the shepherd's board,[17]
Upon a green that curiously[18] was squared,

---

[7] **posy**: a small bunch of flowers.   [8] **baldric-wise**: like a baldric, a belt worn diagonally across the chest.   [9] **July-flower**: queen's gillyflower.   [10] **cotes**: cottages.   [11] **simples**: plants or herbs. [12] **to mell**: to associate.   [13] **nosegays**: bunches of flowers.   [14] **bell-wether**: the leading sheep of a flock, to whose neck a bell was attached.   [15] **swains**: shepherds.   [16] **Shepherd's King**: this time it was the shepherd Rowland's turn to be the Shepherd King.   [17] **board**: meal.   [18] **curiously**: skillfully.

With country cates[19] that plentifully stored:
And 'gainst[20] their coming handsomely prepared.

New whig,[21] with water from the clearest stream,   45
Green plums, and wildings,[22] cherries chief of feast,
Fresh cheese, and dowsets,[23] curds and clouted cream,
Spiced syllabubs,[24] and cider of the best:

And to the same down solemnly they sit,
In the fresh shadow of their summer bowers,   50
With sundry sweets which every way to fit,
Which neighboring vale not spoiled of her flowers.

And whilst together merry thus they make,
The sun to west a little 'gan[25] to lean,
Which the late fervor soon again did slake,   55
When as the nymphs[26] came forth upon the plain.

Here might you many a shepherdess have seen,
Of which no place as Cotswold[27] such doth yield,
Some of it native, some for love[28] I ween,[29]
Thither were come from many a fertile field.   60

There was the widow's daughter of the Glen,
Dear Rosalind, that scarcely brooked compare,
The Moreland maiden, so admired of men,
Bright Goldy-locks, and Phillida the fair.

Lettice and Parnell, pretty lovely peats,[30]   65
Cusse of the fold,[31] the virgin of the well,
Fair Anbrie with the alabaster teats,
And more, whose names were here too long to tell,

Which now came forward following their sheep,
Their batt'ning[32] flocks on grassy leas to hold   70
Thereby from scathe,[33] and peril them to keep,
Till evening come that it were time to fold.

---

[19] cates: delicacies.   [20] 'gainst: against, in preparation for.   [21] whig: a beverage made from fermented whey.   [22] wildings: wild apples.   [23] dowsets: sweet dishes.   [24] syllabubs: drinks made of sweetened milk.   [25] 'gan: began.   [26] nymphs: young women.   [27] Cotswold: a range of hills in Gloucestershire.   [28] some for love: some came from other towns to be with their sweethearts.   [29] I ween: I believe.   [30] peats: young women.   [31] Cusse of the fold: a shepherdess's nickname (fold = sheepfold).   [32] batt'ning: battening, growing fat.   [33] scathe: harm.

When now, at last, as liked[34] the Shepherds' King
(At whose command they all obedient were)
Was 'pointed[35] who the roundelay[36] should sing,   75
And who again the under-song[37] should bear:

The first whereof he Batte doth bequeath,
A wittier wag on all the wold's not found,
Gorbo the man that him should sing beneath,
Which his loud bagpipe skillfully should sound.   80

When amongst all the nymphs that were in sight,
His best beloved Daffadill he missed,
Which, to inquire of, doing all his might,
Whom his companion kindly doth assist.

BATTE: Gorbo, as thou cam'st this way   85
   By yonder little hill,
   Or as thou through the fields didst stray,
   Saw'st thou my Daffadill?
   She's in a frock of Lincoln green,[38]
   The color maids delight,   90
   And never hath her beauty seen
   But through a veil of white.
   Than roses richer to behold
   That trim up lovers' bowers,
   The pansy and the marigold,   95
   Though Phoebus'[39] paramours.
GORBO: Thou well describ'st the Daffadill,
   It is not full an hour
   Since by the spring near yonder hill
   I saw that lovely flower.   100
BATTE: Yet my fair flower thou didst not meet,
   Nor news of her didst bring,
   And yet my Daffadill more sweet
   Than that by yonder spring.
GORBO: I saw a shepherd that doth keep   105
   In yonder field of lilies,

---

[34] liked: pleased. [35] 'pointed: appointed. [36] roundelay: a simple song with a refrain.
[37] under-song: a song accompanying another song. [38] Lincoln green: a bright green.
[39] Phoebus': Phoebus Apollo, the sun god.

Was making (as he fed his sheep)
A wreath of daffodillies.

BATTE: Yet Gorbo thou delud'st me still,
My flower thou didst not see,   110
For know my pretty Daffadill
Is worn of none but me.
To show itself but near her seat[40]
No lily is so bold,
Except to shade her from the heat   115
Or keep her from the cold.

GORBO: Through yonder vale as I did pass,
Descending from the hill,
I met a smirking bonny lass,
They call her Daffadill: 120
Whose presence as she went along
The pretty flowers did greet,
As though their heads they downward bent
With homage to her feet.
And all the shepherds that were nigh   125
From top of every hill
Unto the valleys low did cry,
There goes sweet Daffadill.

BATTE: Aye, gentle shepherd, now with joy
Thou all my flocks dost fill,   130
That's she alone, kind shepherd's boy,
Let us to Daffadill.

The easy turns and quietness of the song,
And slight occasion whereupon 'twas raised,
Not one this jolly company among   135
(As most could well judge) highly that not praised.

When Motto next with Perkin pay their debt,
The Moreland maiden Sylvia that espied,
From th'other nymphs a little that was set,
In a near valley by a river's side.   140

Whose sovereign flowers her sweetness well expressed,
And honored sight a little them not moved:
To whom their song they reverently addressed,
Both as her loving, both of her beloved.

[40] **seat**: abode.

MOTTO: Tell me, thou skilful shepherd's swain,   145
      Who's yonder in the valley set?
PERKIN: Oh, it is she whose sweets do stain
      The lily, rose, or violet.
MOTTO: Why doth the sun against his kind[41]
      Stay his bright chariot in the skies?   150
PERKIN: He pauseth, almost strooken blind
      With gazing on her heavenly eyes.
MOTTO: Why do thy flocks forbear their food,
      Which sometime was their chief delight?
PERKIN: Because they need no other good   155
      That live in presence of her sight.
MOTTO: How come these flowers do flourish still,
      Not withering with sharp winter's breath?
PERKIN: She hath robbed nature of her skill,
      And comforts all things with her breath.   160
MOTTO: Why slide these brooks so slow away,
      As swift as the wild roe that were?
PERKIN: Oh, muse not shepherd, that they stay,
      When they her heavenly voice do hear.
MOTTO: From whence come all these goodly swains   165
      And lovely nymphs attir'd in green?
PERKIN: From gathering garlands on the plains,
      To crown thy Sylvia shepherd's queen.
MOTTO: The sun that lights this world below,
      Flocks, brooks, and flowers, can witness bear.   170
PERKIN: These shepherds and these nymphs do know
      Thy Sylvia is as chaste as fair.

Lastly it came unto the clownish[42] king,
Who to conclude this shepherds' yearly feast,
Bound as the rest his roundelay to sing   175
As all the other him were to assist.

When she (whom then, they little did expect,
The dearest nymph that ever kept in field)
Idea, did her sober pace direct
Towards them, with joy that every one beheld.   180

And whereas other drave[43] their careful keep,
Hers did follow, duly at her will,

---

[41] **kind**: nature.   [42] **clownish**: rustic.   [43] **drave**: drove.

For through her patience she had learned[44] her sheep
Where ere she went to wait upon her still.

A milk-white dove upon her hand she brought, 185
So tame, t'would go, returning at her call,
About whose neck, as in a collar wrought,
"Only like me, my mistress hath no gall."[45]

To whom her swain (unworthy though he were)
Thus unto her his roundelay applies, 190
To whom the rest the under-part did bear,
Casting upon her their still-longing eyes.

ROWLAND: Of her pure eyes (that now is seen)
CHORUS: Help us to sing that be her faithful swains.
ROWLAND: Oh, she alone the shepherds' queen, 195
CHORUS: Her flock that leads,
   The goddess of these meads,
   These mountains and these plains.
ROWLAND: Those eyes of hers that are more clear
CHORUS: Than silly shepherds can in song express, 200
ROWLAND: Than be his beams that rules the year.
CHORUS: Fie on that praise,
   In striving things to raise
   That doth but make them less.
ROWLAND: That do the flowery spring prolong, 205
CHORUS: So much the earth doth in her presence joy,
ROWLAND: And keeps the plenteous summer young:
CHORUS: And doth assuage
   The wrathful winter's rage
   That would our flocks destroy. 210
ROWLAND: Jove[46] saw her breast that naked lay,
CHORUS: A sight alone was fit for Jove to see:
ROWLAND: And swore it was the milky way,
CHORUS: Of all most pure,
   The path (we us assure) 215
   Unto Jove's court to be.
ROWLAND: He saw her tresses hanging down,
CHORUS: That to and fro were moved with the air,

---

[44] **learned:** taught.   [45] **gall:** bitterness.   [46] **Jove:** in Roman mythology, king of the gods.

ROWLAND: And said that Ariadne's[47] crown,
CHORUS: With those compared   220
    The gods should not regard,
    Nor Berenice's[48] hair.
ROWLAND: When she hath watched my flocks by night,
CHORUS: Oh, happy were the flocks that she did keep:
ROWLAND: They never needed Cynthia's[49] light,   225
CHORUS: That soon gave place,
    Amazed with her grace
    That did attend thy sheep.
ROWLAND: Above where heavens high glories are,
CHORUS: When as she shall be placed in the skies,   230
ROWLAND: She shall be called the shepherds' star,
CHORUS: And evermore,
    We shepherds will adore
    Her setting and her rise.

---

[47] **Ariadne:** in Greek mythology, the princess of Crete who helped Theseus to escape from the labyrinth of the Minotaur.   [48] **Berenice:** third century B.C.E. Egyptian queen who offered her hair for the safe return of her husband from a voyage; according to legend, the hair was stolen and placed in the heavens.   [49] **Cynthia:** the Greek goddess Artemis (equivalent to the Roman Diana), associated with the moon.

→   PHILIP STUBBES

From The Anatomy of Abuses   *1583*

Little is known about the background of Philip Stubbes (c.1555–c.1610). By the late 1580s, however, he had earned a reputation as a writer of ballads and pamphlets on moral and religious themes, such as *The Theater of the Pope's Monarchy* (1585) and *A Crystal Glass for Christian Women* (1591). His most popular work was *The Anatomy of Abuses*, a harsh satire printed in four editions between 1583 and 1595. Stubbes structures the *Anatomy* as a dialogue between two interlocutors, Philoponus ("hard worker") and Spudeus ("earnest scholar"), who discuss the manifold vices afflicting the famous island of "Ailgna" — Anglia (i.e., England) in reverse.

Philip Stubbes, *The Anatomy of Abuses: Containing a Discovery or Brief Summary of such Notable Vices and Imperfections as now Reign in Many Christian Countries of the World, but (especially) in a Very Famous Island Called Ailgna* (London, 1583¹); STC 23376; sigs. C4r–C5v, E7v–E8v, F1v–F2r, M4r–M5r.

The excerpts below come from three different sections of the *Anatomy*. In the first, Stubbes censures rich attire; in the second, an excerpt from a chapter on the excesses of women's apparel, he denounces the use of cosmetics. Stubbes's disdain for immoderate luxury and artifice provide a context for Perdita's anxiety about wearing "borrowed flaunts" (4.4.23). At one point, Perdita confesses, "Methinks I play as I have seen them do / In Whitsun pastorals. Sure this robe of mine / Does change my disposition" (4.4.133–35). Does Perdita share Stubbes's moral and religious objections to excessive finery, or are her objections based on different principles?

In the third excerpt, Stubbes rails against the custom of church-ales, in which the community sold food and drink to raise money during religious holidays such as Christmas and Whitsuntide (Pentecost, the seventh Sunday after Easter). Although the sheep-shearing festival in *The Winter's Tale* is a seasonal, not a religious, observation, Perdita alludes to the plays, games, and dances traditionally enjoyed at "Whitsun pastorals" (4.4.134). To some contemporary observers, even these traditional rural pastimes were impious and "inherently idolatrous" (Jensen 283). In a sermon of 1570, for example, William Kethe attacked church-ales on the grounds that they encouraged people to dishonor the Sabbath with "bull-baitings, bear-baitings, bowlings, dicing, carding, dancings, drunkenness, and whoredom" (quoted in Brand 278). Other critics censured rural celebrations on social and economic grounds. In O. B.'s *Questions of Profitable and Pleasant Concernings* (1594), an old gentleman accuses sheep-shearing feasts of excessive wastefulness, in that they provide "fresh cates, besides spices and saffron pottage" worth three shepherds' wages (sig. B3r). He also blames the "unmeasurable house keepings," or unlimited hospitality of festivals at great estates, for drawing "loitering disposed persons from labor to ease," thus encouraging them to become rogues and vagrants such as Autolycus (sig. B2v).

It is tempting to speculate about how Stubbes or O. B. might have responded to Perdita's sheep-shearing festival. One critic has observed that Perdita bestows "lavish expenditure" on her feast. Since rice was "one of the very few commodities" that could not be grown in England, Shakespeare's audience would have regarded it as an exotic luxury item. Moreover, Perdita buys sugar instead of using "the honey widely available in the countryside in early summer" (Bristol 165). The Old Shepherd corroborates the abundance of food and liquor customarily served at the festival when he recalls that his late wife acted as "pantler, butler, [and] cook" for the occasion (4.4.56). Does Shakespeare give any indication that we are to regard the excessive cost and consumption of Perdita's feast with disapproval? Might Perdita's timidity in entertaining her guests in fact derive from a reluctance to preside over the kind of celebration Stubbes would attack as gluttonous and profane? Does Stubbes's description of the "swilling and gulling" (see p. 340) revelers at church-ales correspond to the behavior of the revelers at this sheep-shearing festival?

From *The Anatomy of Abuses*

PHILOPONUS: . . . Then seeing our apparel was given us of God to cover our shame, to keep our bodies from cold, and to be as pricks in our eyes, to put us in mind of our frailties, imperfections, and sin, of our backsliding from the commandments of God and obedience of the highest, and to excite us the rather to contrition, and compunction of the spirit, to bewail our misery, and to crave mercy at the merciful hands of God, let us be thankful to God for them, be sorry for our sins (which were the cause thereof) and use them to the glory of our God, and the benefit of our bodies and souls, against the great day[1] of the Lord appear. But (alas) these good creatures,[2] which the Lord our God gave us for the respects before rehearsed, we have so perverted, as now they serve in stead of the devil's nets, to catch poor souls in: for everyone nowadays (almost) covet to deck and paint their living sepulchers or earthly graves (their bodies I mean) with all kind of bravery,[3] whatsoever can be devised, to delight the eyes of the unchaste beholders, whereby God is dishonored, offense is increased, and much sin daily committed, as in further discourse shall plainly appear.

SPUDEUS: Did the Lord clothe our first parents in leather as not having anything more precious to attire them withal, or for that it might be a permanent rule or pattern unto us (his posterity) for ever, whereafter we are of force to make all our garments, so as it is not now lawful to go in richer array, without offending his majesty?

PHILOPONUS: Although the Lord did not clothe them so meanly for that he had nothing else more precious to attire them withal (for "*Domini est terra, et plenitudo ejus*" — "the earth is the Lord's and the fullness thereof" — saith the Lord by his Psalmist;[4] and by his Prophet,[5] "Gold is mine, silver is mine, and all the riches of the world is my own") yet no doubt but he would that this their mean and base attire should be as a rule or pedagogy unto us, to teach us that we ought rather to walk meanly and simply than gorgeously or pompously: rather serving present necessity than regarding the wanton appetites of our lascivious minds. Notwithstanding, I suppose not that his heavenly majesty would that those garments of leather should stand us as a rule or pattern of necessity unto us, whereafter we should be bound to shape all our apparel forever, or else grievously to offend: but yet by this, we may see his blessed will is that we should rather go an ace[6] beneath our degree, than a jot above.

---

[1] **great day:** judgment day.   [2] **creatures:** garments created by God for human comfort.   [3] **bravery:** finery.   [4] **Psalmist:** David, in Psalms 24:1.   [5] **Prophet:** Haggai 2:8.   [6] **ace:** jot.

And that any simple covering pleaseth the godly, so that it repel the cold and cover the shame, it is more than manifest as well by the legends both of profane historiographers, chronologers,[7] and other writers, as also by the censures, examples, and lives of all godly, since the beginning of the world. And if the Lord would not that the attire of Adam should have been a sign or pattern of mediocrity to us, he both in mercy would and in his almighty power could have invested[8] them in silks, velvets, satins, grograms,[9] gold, silver, and whatnot. But the Lord our God foresaw that if he had clothed man in rich and gorgeous attire (such is our proclivity to sin) he would have been proud thereof as we see it is come to pass at this day (God amend it) and thereby purchase to himself, his body, and soul eternal damnation.

A Particular Description of the Abuses of Women's Apparel in Ailgna

Thus having given thee a superficial view or small taste (but not discovered the hundredth part) of the guises of Ailgna in men's apparel and of the abuses contained in the same, now will I with the like celerity[10] of matter impart unto thee the guise and several abuses of the apparel of women there used also: whereof give attentive ear. . . .

The women of Ailgna use to color their faces with certain oils, liquors, unguents and waters made to that end, whereby they think their beauty is greatly decored.[11] But who seeth not that their souls are thereby deformed, and they brought deeper into the displeasure and indignation of the Almighty, at whose voice the earth doth tremble and at whose presence the heavens shall liquefy and melt away. Do they think thus to adulterate the Lord his workmanship, and to be without offense? Do they not know that he is *zelotypus*,[12] a jealous God, and cannot abide any alteration of his works, otherwise than he hath commanded?

If an artificer or craftsman should make anything belonging to his art or science and a cobbler should presume to correct the same: would not the other think himself abused, and judge him worthy of reprehension? And thinkest thou (oh woman) to escape the judgment of God, who hath fashioned thee to his glory, when thy great and more than presumptuous audacity dareth to alter and change his workmanship in thee? . . .

---

[7] **chronologers:** historians who assign events to their correct dates. [8] **invested:** dressed. [9] **grogram:** coarse fabric of silk, mohair, and wool. [10] **celerity:** speed. [11] **decored:** decorated, adorned. [12] *zelotypus*: a jealous man (Latin).

Saint Ambrose[13] saith that from the coloring of faces springs the entice-
ments to vices, and that they which color their faces do purchase to themselves the blot and stain of chastity.

For what a dotage is it (saith he) to change thy natural face which God
hath made thee, for a painted face which thou hast made thyself? If thou
beest fair, why paintest thou thyself to seem fairer? And if thou be not fair,
why dost thou hypocritically desire to seem fair, and art nothing less? Can
those things which besides that they be filthy, do carry the brand of God his
curse upon their backs forever, make thee to seem fairer? I could show you
the sharp invections and grounded reasons of many more, as of Augustine,
Jerome, Chrysostome, Gregory, Calvin, Peter Martyr, Gualter,[14] and of an
infinite number more: yea of all generally since the beginning of the world
against this whorish and brothelous painting and coloring of faces; but to
avoid prolixity,[15] I will omit them, deferring them to further opportunity, for
pauca sapienti, to a wise man few words are sufficient. . . .

THE MANNER OF CHURCH-ALES IN AILGNA

PHILOPONUS: The manner of them is thus. In certain towns where
    drunken Bacchus[16] bears all the sway, against[17] a Christmas, an Easter,
    Whitsunday, or some other time, the churchwardens[18] (for so they call
    them) of every parish, with the consent of the whole parish, provide half
    a score[19] or twenty quarters[20] of malt, whereof some they buy of the
    church stock, and some is given them of the parishioners themselves,
    everyone conferring somewhat, according to his ability, which malt being
    made into very strong ale or beer, it is set to sale, either in the church or
    some other place assigned to that purpose.

    Then when the nippitatum, this huff-cap[21] (as they call it) and this
    nectar of life, is set aboard, well is he that can get the soonest to it, and
    spend the most at it, for he that sitteth the closest to it, and spends the
    most at it, he is counted the godliest man of all the rest; but who either

---

[13] **Saint Ambrose:** fourth-century bishop of Milan and one of the Doctors of the Church in
Roman Catholicism, a saint whose writings have significantly contributed to the Christian
Church; "Doctor" refers to "teacher," from Latin *docere,* to teach.   [14] **Augustine . . . Gualter:**
St. Augustine, Jerome, and Pope Gregory I were fourth-century Doctors of the Church;
St. John Chrysostom, fourth-century Christian bishop of Constantinople; John Calvin,
sixteenth-century Protestant theologian; Peter Martyr, thirteenth-century Dominican friar;
Gualter is Walter Map, a twelfth-century English churchman and writer of *De Nugis Curial-
ium* (Courtiers' Trifles).   [15] **prolixity:** wordiness.   [16] **Bacchus:** Roman god of wine.
[17] **against:** in preparation for.   [18] **churchwardens:** lay officers in a parish church.   [19] **half a
score:** ten.   [20] **quarters:** eight bushels.   [21] **nippitatum, this huff-cap:** strong ale.

cannot for pinching poverty, or otherwise will not stick to it, he is counted one destitute both of virtue and godliness. In so much as you shall have many poor men make hard shift[22] for money to spend thereat, for it being put into this corban,[23] they are persuaded it is meritorious and a good service to God. In this kind of practice they continue six weeks, a quarter of a year, yea half a year together, swilling and gulling,[24] night and day, till they be as drunk as apes, and as blockish as beasts.

SPUDEUS: Seeing they have so good utterance,[25] it should seem they have good gains. But, I pray you, how do they bestow that money which is got thereby?

PHILOPONUS: Oh, well, I warrant you, if all be true which they say: for they repair their churches and chapels with it, they buy books for service, cups for the celebration of the sacrament, surplices[26] for Sir John, and such other necessaries. And they maintain other extraordinary charges in the parishes besides. These be their exceptions, these be their excuses, and these be their pretended allegations, whereby they blind the world and convey themselves away invisibly in a cloud. But if they dance thus in a net,[27] no doubt they will be espied.

For if it were so, that they bestowed it as they say, do they think that the Lord will have his house built with drunkenness, gluttony, and such like abomination? Must we do evil that good may come of it? Must we build this house of lime and stone with the desolation and utter overthrow of his spiritual house, cleansed and washed in the precious blood of our savior Jesus Christ?

---

[22] **make hard shift:** make a strenuous effort.   [23] **corban:** church treasury.   [24] **gulling:** guzzling.
[25] **utterance:** sale.   [26] **surplices:** white linen vestments worn by clerics.   [27] **if they dance thus in a net:** if they so poorly disguise their true intentions (since a net can be seen through).

Rogues and Peddlers

> What maids lack from head to heel,
> Come buy of me, come.   (4.4.219–20)

Entering the play singing about how the "winter's pale" gives way to the "sweet o'the year," Autolycus is a fitting herald for rural festivity (4.3.3–4). An embodiment of holiday license, he frequents parish festivals, fairs, and bearbaitings; he plays the parts of traveler, peddler, and courtier; and he offers entertaining ballads as well as gifts for lovers. Selling "ribbons of all the colors i'th' rainbow" and more points (laces) than the points (legal arguments) that "all the lawyers in Bohemia can learnedly handle" (4.4.199–200), Autolycus ushers holiday abundance into *The Winter's Tale*.

At the same time, however, Autolycus embodies social disorder, moral vice, and political corruption. He haunts rural fairs not to participate in communal sports, but to pick purses. Although he blames his dishonesty on his birth under the sign of Mercury, the patron god of thieves, Autolycus's poverty comes not from low birth but from a fall from grace at court. As a former servant to the prince, Autolycus, we can assume, is at least a gentleman's son. Had he not been expelled from court for vicious behavior, he might have earned advancement and honor there; instead, having "flown over many knavish professions," he has determined to be a "rogue" (4.3.81–82). Nevertheless, Autolycus still considers himself superior to the rural folk from whom he steals.

Autolycus's presence at the sheep-shearing festival is central to understanding the overall significance of this pastoral episode. Do we admire Autolycus for his rhetorical skills, his facility at playing different roles, and his wit in duping the gullible shepherds? Or is he the wolf in the sheepcote: the reminder that, in the fallen world of the play, corruption infects not only the court but also the countryside, even among the daffodils, in the sweet of the year? Providing various perspectives on the place of rogues and peddlers in the social order of early modern England, the following documents suggest why Autolycus might evoke such contradictory associations.

The first documents that we will examine are a parliamentary statute and a royal proclamation concerning vagrancy. Before considering the relevance of these documents to *The Winter's Tale*, it is necessary to understand the difference between a statute and a proclamation, and to consider what kind of evidence they might offer about social order in early modern England. The legislative branch of government was parliament, composed of a House of Commons (representing counties, towns, and cities) and a House of Lords (comprising the nobility and clergy). Parliament introduced and debated bills that, upon consent of both houses and the monarch, became law in the form of statutes or acts of Parliament. Laws, however, did not necessarily have a visible impact on the everyday lives of subjects. As D. M. Palliser cautions, "while statutes are a good guide to the intentions" of the monarch and parliament, "they are a hazardous guide to the behaviour of their subjects" (316). Some statutes were difficult to enforce, and in certain cases, the local officials responsible for enforcement simply neglected or refused to do so. Even though monarchs and ministers "took the trouble to justify their actions and to urge loyalty through proclamations, addresses and pamphlets," enforcement of laws seems to have been sporadic and uneven (Palliser 319).

Unlike a statute, a proclamation was a "public ordinance issued by the sovereign in virtue of the royal prerogative, with the advice of the Privy

Council" (Larkin and Hughes, 2: xvii). Proclamations were accompanied by a "writ" addressed to local officials such as mayors and sheriffs that provided instructions about when and where to read the proclamation. Sometimes proclamations were issued to enforce obedience to an already existing statute or to institute a new policy, often in response to an immediate local need, in the absence of a statute. In short, the mere existence of a statute or proclamation does not provide any clear evidence about how widespread was the kind of transgression it targeted or about how thoroughly such transgressions would be prosecuted.

Nonetheless, statutes and proclamations do provide evidence of the *perception* of social and economic disorder by the nation's rulers. Hence, the documents that follow can provide valuable insight into the fears and anxieties elicited by figures such as the peddler, rogue, or "masterless man," a contemporary term for someone without a home or legitimate job (and consequently without a "master"). English statutes detailing punishments for "wandering beggars" extend as far back as the reign of Richard II in the fourteenth century. A particularly noteworthy statute for our purposes is the *Act for Tinkers and Peddlers* passed in 1552 during the reign of Edward VI. Defining tinkers (itinerant craftsmen) and peddlers (itinerant sellers of small wares) as "vagrant persons" who "are more hurtful than necessary to the commonwealth," the statute forbids such people from "wander[ing]" from place to place selling "pins, points, laces, gloves, knives, glasses, tapes, or any such kind of wares whatsoever" — the contents of Autolycus's pack, essentially — without a license issued by two justices of the peace (Great Britain, *Statutes* 5 & 6 Edw. VI. c. 21, p. 155). This early statute associates peddlers with vagrancy in a way that will continue to inform depictions of peddlers up to and including Autolycus.

Yet, as Barbara Mowat argues, Shakespeare's contemporaries might have regarded the "unemployed vagrant" as either "scandalously evil" or "truly pitiable" ("Rogues" 69). Since the mid-sixteenth century, the number of homeless poor in England had risen steeply due to the practice of enclosure: the privatization of common fields that had once served as a source of timber and arable land for rural populations. As landowners converted communal property into sheep pasture in order to profit from the sale of wool, poor families who had once lived off this land sometimes turned to theft as a means of survival. A sympathetic perspective on the plight of displaced families is presented in Thomas More's *Utopia*. More's narrator observes that "England is overrun by thieves, not because thieves enjoy stealing . . . but because people have lost their livings: serving men out of work, returned soldiers, evicted farm laborers thrown out of work when farms are sold — these are the men and women frantic for food and driven to begging and stealing" (Mowat, "Rogues" 67–68). With his flock of 1,500 sheep, the Old Shepherd in *The Winter's Tale* might evoke the kind of wealthy landowner whom social satirists condemned for fattening their sheep while their neighbors starved. Nonetheless, vagrancy laws did not acknowledge the legitimate reasons, such as dispossession or unemployment, that forced some of the poor into a migrant life.

→ *From* An Act for Punishment of Rogues, Vagabonds and Sturdy Beggars   *1597*

An Elizabethan statute of 1572 was the first to define a criminal class of "rogues, vagabonds, and sturdy beggars" — a formula that would appear in every subsequent vagrancy statute through the reign of James I. According to the 1572 statute, a "rogue" is an able-bodied person who has no land, no master, and no "lawful merchandize, craft, or mystery whereby he or she might get his or her living"; unlicensed peddlers, tinkers, and petty chapmen (itinerant sellers of small wares) thus come under the definition of rogue. The statute also requires local magistrates to punish offenders in the following manner: the rogue is to be "grievously whipped, and burnt through the gristle of the right ear with a hot iron of the compass of an inch about, manifesting his or her roguish kind of life, and his or her punishment received for the same" (Great Britain, *Statutes* 14 Eliz. c. 5, p. 591). Although the 1597 *Act for Punishment of Rogues, Vagabonds and Sturdy Beggars* excerpted below rescinds the ear-boring punishment, in 1604 James's first parliament passed a new statute that reinstituted a body-marking punishment on the grounds that

> the said rogues having no mark upon them to be known by, notwithstanding such judgment of banishment may return or retire themselves into some other parts of this realm where they are not known, and so escape the due punishment which the said statute did intend to inflict upon them. For remedy thereof be it ordained and enacted, that such rogues as shall . . . be adjudged as aforesaid incorrigible or dangerous, shall also . . . be branded in the left shoulder with an hot burning iron of the breadth of an English shilling, with a great Roman R upon the iron, and the branding upon the shoulder to be so thoroughly burned and set on upon the skin and flesh, that the letter R be seen and remain for a perpetual mark upon such rogue during his or her life . . . (Great Britain, *Statutes* 1 Jac. I c. 7, p. 1025)

An Act for Punishment of Rogues, Vagabonds and Sturdy Beggars (39 Elizabeth, c. 4), 1597, in *Tudor Economic Documents*, ed. R. H. Tawney (London: Longman, 1951), 354–55.

Branding the rogue's flesh with a permanent sign of his or her criminal identity seems designed to thwart the kind of shape-shifting that is so integral to Autolycus's success. In what terms does the 1597 act describe the social and geographical mobility of rogues? How might Shakespeare's portrait of Autolycus exceed the statute's attempt to identify and define the generic "rogue"?

From *An Act for Punishment of Rogues, Vagabonds and Sturdy Beggars*

I. For the suppressing of rogues, vagabonds, and sturdy beggars, be it enacted by the authority of this present Parliament, that from and after the feast of Easter next coming, all statutes heretofore made for the punishment of rogues, vagabonds, or sturdy beggars, or for the erection or maintenance of houses of correction, or touching the same, shall for so much as concerneth the same be utterly repealed. . . .

II. And be it also further enacted by the authority aforesaid, that all persons calling themselves scholars going about begging, all seafaring men pretending losses of their ships or goods on the sea going about the country begging, all idle persons going about in any country either begging or using any subtle craft or unlawful games and plays, or feigning themselves to have knowledge in physiognomy, palmistry, or other like crafty science, or pretending that they can tell destinies, fortunes, or such other like fantastical imaginations; all persons that be or utter themselves to be proctors,[1] procurers,[2] patent gatherers, or collectors for jails, prisons, or hospitals; all fencers, bearwards,[3] common players of interludes and minstrels wandering abroad (other than players of interlude belonging to any baron of this realm, or any other honorable personage of greater degree, to be authorized to play under the hand and seal of arms of such baron or personage); all jugglers, tinkers, peddlers, and petty chapmen wandering abroad; all wandering persons and common laborers being persons able in body using loitering and refusing to work for such reasonable wages as is taxed or commonly given in such parts where such persons do or shall happen to dwell or abide, not having living otherwise to maintain themselves; all persons delivered out of jails that beg for their fees, or otherwise do travel begging; all such persons as shall wander abroad begging, pretending losses by fire or otherwise; and all such persons not being felons wandering and pretending themselves to be

---

[1] **proctor:** one with a license to collect alms.   [2] **procurer:** a legal agent or estate manager.
[3] **bearward:** a bear keeper.

Egyptians,[4] or wandering in the habit, form, or attire of counterfeit Egyptians; shall be taken, adjudged, and deemed rogues, vagabonds, and sturdy beggars, and shall sustain such pain and punishment as by this Act is in that behalf appointed.

III. And be it enacted by the authority aforesaid that every person which is by this present Act declared to be a rogue, vagabond, or sturdy beggar, which shall be at any time after the said feast of Easter next coming, taken begging, vagrant, wandering, or misordering themselves in any part of this realm or the dominion of Wales, shall upon their apprehension by the appointment of any Justice of the Peace, constable,[5] headborough, or tithingman[6] of the same county, hundred,[7] parish, or tithing[8] where such person shall be taken, the tithingman or headborough being assisted therein with the advice of the minister and one other of that parish, be stripped naked from the middle upwards and shall be openly whipped until his or her body be bloody, and shall be forthwith sent from parish to parish by the officers of every the same the next straight way to the parish where he was born, if the same may be known by the party's confession or otherwise; and if the same be not known, then to the parish where he or she last dwelled before the same punishment by the space of one whole year, there to put him or her self to labor as a true subject ought to do; or not being known where he or she was born or last dwelled, then to the parish through which he or she last passed without punishment. After which whipping the same person shall have a testimonial subscribed with the hand and sealed with the seal of the same Justice of the Peace, constable, headborough, or tithingman and of the minister of the same parish, or any two of them, testifying that the same person hath been punished according to this Act, and mentioning the day and place of his or her punishment, and the place whereunto such person is limited to go, and by what time the said person is limited to pass thither at his peril. And if the said person through his or her default do not accomplish the order appointed by the said testimonial, then to be eftsoons[9] taken and whipped, and so as often as any default shall be found in him or her contrary to the form of this Statute, in every place to be whipped till such person be repaired to the place limited; the substance of which testimonial shall be registered by the minister of the parish in a book to be provided for that purpose, upon pain to forfeit five shillings for every default thereof: and the party so whipped and not known where he or she was born or last

---

[4] **Egyptians:** i.e, gypsies.   [5] **constable:** parish or township officer charged with keeping the peace.   [6] **headborough, or tithingman:** petty constable.   [7] **hundred:** subdivision of a county or shire.   [8] **tithing:** a rural division (a tenth of a hundred).   [9] **eftsoons:** again.

dwelled by the space of a year, shall by the officers of the said village where he or she so last passed through without punishment be conveyed to the house of correction of the limit wherein the said village standeth, or to the common jail of that county or place, there to remain and be employed in work until he or she shall be placed in some service, and so to continue by the space of one whole year, or not being able of body until he or she shall be placed, to remain in some almshouse in the same county or place.

→ *From* A Proclamation Inhibiting All Persons after Bartholomew-tide Next, to Use the Trade of a Peddler or a Petty Chapman   *1618*

Whereas the 1597 vagrancy statute implies that all peddlers are actually or potentially vagabonds, King James's 1618 *Proclamation Inhibiting All Persons . . . To Use the Trade of a Peddler or a Petty-Chapman* distinguishes legitimate from illegitimate peddlers. The proclamation acknowledges that "industrious" peddlers provide a useful service to English subjects who live far from centers of commerce. Nonetheless, in practice it might be difficult to tell an "industrious honest" tradesman from a "dissolute and dissembling wanderer" (see p. 347), especially considering that industry and honesty are exactly the qualities that a dissolute wanderer might try to dissemble. Autolycus's criminal behavior would certainly seem to justify the proclamation's complaint about thieves wandering the countryside under the guise of officially licensed peddlers. At the same time, the proclamation's stipulations of a steep bond fee and of the need to acquire the testimony of two justices of the peace might have discouraged even the "better sort" of otherwise legitimate peddlers from obtaining an official license.

Autolycus's own commentary upon his knavery puts an ironic spin on the official language of legitimate industry one finds in James's proclamation. Referring to the many opportunities he finds for theft, Autolycus claims that "[e]very lane's end, every shop, church, session, hanging, yields a careful man work" (4.4.649–50). When he speaks of his "traffic" in sheets, he means not that he works as a draper, who buys and sells linens, but that he nabs linens drying on hedges (4.3.23). Autolycus openly admits his knavery to us, but we might ask why it is so easy for him to deceive his victims. Is there anything about his

A Proclamation Inhibiting All Persons after Bartholomew-tide Next, To Use the Trade of a Peddler or a Petty Chapman, Unless They Be Licensed According to a Course Lately Taken by Us in that Behalf, Windsor Castle, 6 July 1618. In *Stuart Royal Proclamations,* ed. James F. Larkin and Paul L. Hughes (Oxford: Clarendon, 1973), 1: 393–95

behavior or merchandise that should alert the shepherds to the possibility of an "idle" rogue beneath the seemingly "industrious" peddler? Might Autolycus confound the very distinctions that official statutes and proclamations attempted to draw between the "idle" and the "industrious"? Does the play encourage us to mock the shepherds for being so easily seduced by Autolycus, or does it suggest that such seduction is truly appealing and difficult to resist? It might even be worth considering that in contrast to Leontes, who wrongly suspects his wife and closest friend of betrayal, the shepherds' faith in the word of a stranger represents a kind of virtue.

Whereas, by an Act of Parliament made in the nine and thirtieth year of the reign of our late dear sister Queen Elizabeth of famous memory, entitled, *An Act for Punishing of Rogues, Vagabonds, and Sturdy Beggars*, it was (amongst other things) enacted that all peddlers and petty chapmen wandering abroad should be taken, adjudged, and deemed rogues, vagabonds, and sturdy beggars, and should sustain such pain and punishment, as by the said Act was imposed: which statute was in the seventh year of our reign ratified, and confirmed, and the same enacted to be put in due execution. And whereas the trade of a peddler or petty chapman hath heretofore been used for the benefit and ease of our loving subjects dwelling remote from cities and market towns, and for that cause the industrious and well-disposed petty chapman, as well before the said statutes as sithence,[1] hath been in some sort permitted to travel and use his trade; and whereas under color[2] of using the said trade, many rogues and idle wandering persons, carrying about trifles in the habit of peddlers or petty chapmen, so misbehave themselves, as they are indeed no other but sturdy beggars, thieves, and absolute dissolutes, and many of them being of no religion, or infected with popery,[3] carry abroad and disperse superstitious trumperies,[4] unknown and unsuspected, to the prejudice and wrong of us and our loving subjects: Whereupon, We (in our princely care of the commonwealth) desiring redress and reformation of all abuses in this kind, in such sort as our kingdom might be purged of all dissolute and dissembling wanderers; and yet the industrious honest peddler or petty chapman be tolerated and encouraged to travail in his vocation: and finding no better way to effect the same, than by licensing such as should be known to be of good and honest conversation;[5] did, by our letters patents bearing date the nine and twentieth day of March, in the

---

[1] **sithence:** since. [2] **color:** pretense. [3] **popery:** i.e., Roman Catholicism. [4] **trumperies:** rubbish. [5] **conversation:** behavior.

fifteenth year of our reign, ordain an office to be kept in some convenient place within our city of London, and in any other two or more cities or towns corporate within this our realm of England, or the principality of Wales, for the licensing of peddlers or petty chapmen. . . .

[To obtain a license, a peddler has to seal a bond of £40 and get testimonials of his honesty from two justices of the peace. Although not specified in the proclamation, the peddler must also pay the patent officer a fee for his license. All licenses not issued by the king's patent office are void.]

And because in our princely judgment we conceive that the former abuses will not be clean taken away, nor the intended good and quiet of our loving subjects be fully perfected, without the suppressing of the said dissolute and obstinate vagrants, which shall use the said trade without such license: And for that the said peddlers and petty chapman of the better sort, have not yet so fully conformed themselves to our will and pleasure formerly declared by our said officers by publications, notified by them, nor have sought licenses accordingly, for that no precise day was appointed for their conformity in that behalf. We therefore hereby do straightly charge and command, prohibit and forbid, that no person or persons whatsoever (other than such as shall be licensed by force of, and according to the true meaning of our said letters patents), do attempt or presume to wander, travel, or go abroad in the habit of a peddler or petty chapman, nor to buy, sell, or utter[6] any manner of wares or commodities whatsoever, in any place or places whatsoever within this our realm of England, or dominion of Wales, or in any part of them, or either of them from and after the feast of St. Bartholomew the Apostle[7] next after the date of this our proclamation, upon the pains and penalties in the said statutes made in the said nine and thirtieth year of the reign of the said late Queen Elizabeth mentioned and expressed. . . .

[All justices and officers of the realm are exhorted to execute the terms of the statute.]

---

[6] **utter**: offer for sale.   [7] **feast of St. Bartholomew the Apostle**: August 24.

➜ ROBERT GREENE

From The Second and Last Part of Cony-Catching *and* The Third and Last Part of Cony-Catching   *1592*

Having studied at Cambridge and Oxford Universities, Robert Greene (c. 1558–1592) moved to London, where he enjoyed a brief but fruitful career as "England's first celebrity author" (*DNB*). In the 1580s, Greene published several romances, including *Pandosto* (1588), the main source for *The Winter's Tale* (see pp. 150–65); he then turned to autobiographical narratives of repentance such as *Greene his Farewell to Folly* (1587) and *Greene's Mourning Garment* (1590). In 1591 he began to publish cony-catching pamphlets, which described the tricks used by London criminals to steal from unsuspecting gulls or "conies" (rabbits).

Autolycus is recognizable not only as a rural peddler, but also as a figure from popular pamphlets such as Greene's devoted to exposing England's criminal underworld. In fact, the word "rogue" first entered the English language in John Awdeley's *Fraternity of Vagabonds* (1561), where it describes a vagrant who travels the countryside under the pretext of seeking out a kinsman. In 1567, Thomas Harman's *A Caveat for Common Cursitors, Commonly Called Vagabonds* defined "rogue" as a con artist who feigns illness in order to receive alms from passers-by (Mowat, "Rogues" 65). Popular throughout the sixteenth and early seventeenth centuries, books such as Harman's offered to reveal criminals' con games and secret dialect, known as "peddler's French" or cant. Autolycus implicitly associates himself with the fraternity of vagabonds when he uses canting terms such as "doxy" (mistress) and "pugging" (thieving) in his opening song (4.3.2, 7).

The excerpts below from two of Greene's cony-catching pamphlets describe pickpocketing scams similar to those used by Autolycus. Greene's tales of clever London criminals provide an important context for evaluating the social, moral, and dramatic significance of Autolycus's role in the play. For instance, how might we describe the social status of rogues such as the "foist" (cutpurse) or Shakespeare's Autolycus? Elsewhere in the same pamphlet, Greene explains that whereas a "nip" uses a knife to cut purses, a "foist" uses only his hands. More skilled in their methods, foists regard themselves as superior artists: the "[f]oist holdeth himself of the highest degree, and therefore, they term themselves Gentlemen foists, and so much disdain to be called cutpurses, as the honest man that lives by his hand or occupation" (*Second Part*, sig. C2r). In Greene's tale of the cutpurse who feigns illness in order to rob a wealthy farmer, do we sympathize with the farmer or with the "gentleman foists" who regard him as a "churl" worthy to be duped? Reflecting on his loss, the farmer makes a wry joke at his own expense, provoking laughter among spectators. In the parallel scene in *The Winter's Tale*, is Autolycus's robbery of the Clown an occasion for laughter or

---

Robert Greene, *The Second and Last Part of Cony-Catching* (London, 1592), STC 12282, sigs. D1r–D1v; *The Third and Last Part of Cony-Catching* (London, 1592), STC 12283.5, sigs. C3v–C4v.

A vpright man Nicolas Blunt.

The coūterfet Nicolas

Cranke. Genings.

FIGURE 25 *An illustration of an "Upright Man" and a "Counterfeit Crank" from Thomas Harman's* A Caveat for Common Cursitors, Commonly Called Vagabonds *(1573). A vagabond "of great authority" among beggars, an "upright man" haunts fairs, asking for charity and stealing goods. A "counterfeit crank" pretends to have the falling sickness and wears filthy clothes in order to elicit more generous alms. The accompanying poem explains that the two figures shown here are actually the same man:*

> These two pictures lively set out
> One body and soul, God send him more grace:
> This monstrous dissembler, a crank all about.
> Uncomely coveting of each to embrace,
> Money or wares, as he made his race.
> And sometime a mariner, and a serving man,
> Or else an artificer, as he would feign then.
> Such shifts he used, being well tried,
> Abandoning labor till he was espied.
> Condign punishment for his dissimulation,
> He surely received with much exclamation.

At the end of his book Harman records the names of all the vagabonds he has met; under the category "Rogues" he identifies "Nicholas Jennings" as the alias of "Nicholas Blunt." Like Nicholas Blunt/Jennings, Autolycus appears both in fine courtly dress and in rags.

outrage? Shakespeare does not stage the scene in which the Clown discovers that he has been robbed. What is the effect of this omission?

Whereas Greene's tale about the foist focuses on the gulling of a single victim, his tale of the ballad-singing rogues in the second excerpt below focuses on the pickpockets' ability to rob an entire group. This tale ends not with laughter, but with the angry crowd's retaliation against the cutpurses. Greene's report of the rogues' "journey westward" implies that they were hanged. How do we feel about the demise of these ballad-singing thieves? Although Autolycus too fears hanging, he manages to avoid any punishment, even the lesser punishment of whipping stipulated by the Elizabethan statute against rogues and vagabonds. Does Autolycus's escape from punishment point to a troubling failure of justice in Bohemia or rather to a utopian suspension of harsh laws — a softening of strict social and economic divisions in accord with the communal ethos of pastoral?

From *The Second and Last Part of Cony-Catching*

A Kind Conceit[1] of a Foist[2] Performed in Paul's[3]

While I was writing this discovery of foisting, and was desirous of any intelligence that might be given me, a gentleman, a friend of mine, reported unto me this pleasant tale of a foist, and as I well remember it grew to this effect. There walked in the middle walk a plain country farmer, a man of good wealth, who had a well-lined purse, only barely thrust up in a round slop,[4] which a crew of foists[5] having perceived, their hearts were set on fire to have it, and every one had a fling at him, but all in vain, for he kept his hand close in his pocket and his purse fast in his fist like a subtle churl, that either had been forewarned of Paul's or else had aforetime[6] smoked[7] some of that faculty.[8] Well, howsoever, it was impossible to do any good with him, he was so wary. The foists spying this, strained their wits to the highest string how to compass[9] this bung,[10] yet could not all their politic conceits[11] fetch the farmer over; for, jostle him, chat with him, offer to shake him by the hand, all would not serve to get his hand out of his pocket.

At last, one of the crew that for his skill might have been doctorate in his mystery[12] amongst them all chose out a good foist, one of a nimble hand

---

[1] **kind conceit:** pleasant tale.   [2] **foist:** trick.   [3] **Paul's:** St. Paul's Cathedral, in which shops were set up.   [4] **round slop:** baggy breeches.   [5] **crew of foists:** group of pickpockets.   [6] **aforetime:** previously.   [7] **smoked:** smoked out, exposed.   [8] **faculty:** profession.   [9] **compass:** attain.   [10] **bung:** thieves' cant for a purse.   [11] **conceits:** wits.   [12] **mystery:** occupation or craft.

and great agility, and said to the rest thus: "Masters, it shall not be said such a base peasant shall slip away from such a crew of gentlemen foists as we are and not have his purse drawn, and therefore this time I'll play the stale[13] myself, and if I hit him not home, count me for a bungler forever." And so left them and went to the farmer and walked directly before him and next him three or four turns; at last standing still, he cried, "Alas, honest man, help me, I am not well," and with that sank down suddenly in a swoon. The poor farmer seeing a proper young gentleman (as he thought) fall dead afore him, stepped to him, held him in his arms, rubbed him and chafed him: at this there gathered a great multitude of people about him, and the whilst the foist drew the farmer's purse and away. By that the other thought the feat was done, he began to come something to himself again, and so half staggering, stumbled out of Paul's, and went after the crew where they had appointed to meet, and there boasted of his wit and experience.

The farmer little suspecting this villainy, thrust his hand into his pocket and missed his purse, searched for it, but lining[14] and shells[15] and all was gone, which made the country man in a great maze,[16] that he stood still in a dump[17] so long, that a gentleman perceiving it asked what he ailed. "What ail I, sir?" quoth he. "Truly, I am thinking how men may long[18] as well as women." "Why dost thou conjecture that, honest man?" quoth he. "Marry, sir," answers the farmer, "the gentleman even now that swooned here, I warrant him, breeds[19] his wife's child, for the cause of his sudden qualm[20] that he fell down dead grew of longing." The gentleman demanded how he knew that. "Well enough, sir," quoth he, "and he hath his longing too, for the poor man longed for my purse, and thanks be to God he hath it with him." At this all the hearers laughed, but not so merrily as the foist and his fellows that then were sharing his money.

---

[13] **stale:** decoy.   [14] **lining:** the purse's contents.   [15] **shells:** cant for money.   [16] **maze:** amazement.   [17] **dump:** dazed or puzzled state.   [18] **long:** yearningly desire.   [19] **breeds:** is pregnant with.   [20] **qualm:** sudden fit of illness.

From *The Third and Last Part of Cony-Catching*

ANOTHER TALE OF A COZENING COMPANION, WHO WOULD NEEDS TRY HIS CUNNING IN THIS NEW INVENTED ART, AND HOW BY HIS KNAVERY (AT ONE INSTANT) HE BEGUILED HALF A DOZEN AND MORE.

Of late time there hath a certain base kind of trade been used, who though divers[21] poor men, and doubtless honest, apply themselves only to relieve their need, yet are there some notorious varlets do the same, being compacted[22] with such kind of people, as this present treatise manifesteth to the world. And what with outward simplicity on the one side, and cunning close treachery on the other, divers honest citizens and day-laboring men that resort to such places as I am to speak of only for recreation as opportunity serveth, have been of late sundry times deceived of their purses. This trade, or rather unsufferable loitering quality, in singing of ballads and songs at the doors of such houses where plays are used, as also in open markets and other places of this city, where is most resort, which is nothing else but a sly fetch[23] to draw many together, who listening unto a harmless ditty, afterward walk home to their houses with heavy hearts. From such as are hereof true witnesses to their cost, do I deliver this example.

A subtle fellow, belike emboldened by acquaintance with the former deceit, or else being but a beginner to practice the same, calling certain of his companions together, would try whether he could attain to be master of his art or no, by taking a great many of fools with one train.[24] But let his intent and what else beside remain to abide the censure after the matter is heard, and come to Gracious Street, where this villainous prank was performed. A roguing mate, and such another with them, were there got upon a stall singing of ballads, which belike was some pretty toy,[25] for very many gathered about to hear it, and divers buying, as their affections served, drew to their purses, and paid the singers for them. The sly mate and his fellows, who were dispersed among them that stood to hear the songs, well noted where every man that bought put up his purse again, and to such as would not buy, counterfeit warning was sundry times given by the rogue and his associate, to beware of the cutpurse, and look to their purses, which made them often feel where their purses were, either in sleeve, hose, or at girdle, to know whether they were safe or no. Thus the crafty copesmates[26] were acquainted with what they most desired, feigning to let fall something, and other wily tricks fit for their purpose. Here one lost his purse, there another

---

[21] **divers:** several. [22] **compacted:** joined together. [23] **fetch:** trick. [24] **train:** trap. [25] **toy:** lively tune. [26] **copesmates:** companions.

had his pocket picked, and to say all in brief, at one instant, upon the complaint of one or two that saw their purses were gone, eight more in the same company found themselves in like predicament.

Some angry, others sorrowful, and all greatly discontented, looking about them, knew not who to suspect or challenge, in that the villains themselves that had thus beguiled them made show that they had sustained like loss. But one angry fellow more impatient than all the rest, he falls upon the ballad singer, and beating him with his fists well-favoredly,[27] says, if he had not listened his singing, he had not lost his purse, and therefore would not be otherwise persuaded but that they two and the cutpurses were compacted together. The rest that had lost their purses likewise and saw that so many complain together, they jump in opinion with the other fellow, and begin to tug and hale the ballad singers when, one after one, the false knaves began to shrink away with the purses. By means of some officer then being there present, the two rogues were had before a justice, and upon his discreet examination made, it was found that they and the cutpurses were compacted together, and that by this unsuspected villainy they had deceived many. The fine fool-taker himself, with one or two more of that company, was not long after apprehended, when I doubt not but they had their reward answerable to their deserving. For I hear of their journey westward, but not of their return: let this forewarn those that listen singing in the streets.

[27] **well-favoredly:** severely.

↣ # The Description of a Rare or Rather Most Monstrous Fish Taken on the East Coast of Holland   *1566*

Performing at markets, street corners, and fairs, ballad-mongers relied upon sensationalism and "showmanship" to attract customers (Würzbach 17). Like Autolycus's ballads about the usurer's wife who gives birth to money bags and the maid who is transformed into a singing fish, the document below belongs to a genre of popular printed texts that focused on monsters and monstrous births. According to David Cressy, "[m]ore than two dozen publications describing monstrous births survive from the mid-sixteenth to the mid-seventeenth century" (*Travesties* 32). Titles of such texts published around the time of *The Winter's Tale* include *Strange News out of Kent, of a Monstrous and Misshapen Child, Born*

The Description of a Rare or Rather Most Monstrous Fish Taken on the East Coast of Holland the xvii of November, Anno 1566 (London, 1566), STC 6769.

in *Old Sandwich* (1609); *Strange News of a Prodigious Monster, Born in the Township of Adlington* (1613); and *God's Handiwork in Wonders, Miraculously Shown upon Two Women, Lately Delivered of Two Monsters* (1615).

Stories about monsters were part of a tradition of "Protestant 'providence' tales that documented God's presence on earth through unnatural events explained by natural laws" (Kitch 57). *The Description of a Rare or Rather Most Monstrous Fish* — a "broadside," or cheaply printed single sheet — provides an apt example of these texts' strange blend of sensationalism and moralism. With its grotesque illustration, eyewitness report, and didactic poem, even the form of this broadside reveals multiple and possibly contradictory ways of reading the significance of the monstrous fish. As with *The Description of a Rare or Rather Most Monstrous Fish*, we can approach Autolycus's ballads in terms of entertainment as well as didactic value. For instance, does the ballad of the usurer's wife teach religious or economic lessons, or does it simply provide a voyeuristic thrill? Is there any wisdom to be gleaned from the ballad about the maid who turns into a "cold fish" (4.4.262)?

The interpretive problems raised by Autolycus's ballads reflect upon the larger issue of the truth value of "old tales," including the winter's tale that comprises Shakespeare's play. On the one hand, the providentialism behind monstrous birth tales seems to be at work in the play's romance narrative, which reaches its conclusion only when Apollo's oracle has been fulfilled by Perdita's miraculous return. Autolycus himself derives not only from popular accounts of rogues, but also from the elite genre of "providential romance": he is associated with the wandering, chance, and good fortune that typically guide romance protagonists to a happy conclusion (Mentz 82–83). By bringing the Old Shepherd to Florizel's ship, Autolycus inadvertently brings the romance plot of the play to fruition.

On the other hand, just as we might regard Autolycus's ballads as sensationalistic lies rather than imaginative tales, we might doubt that there is any deep truth behind the equally sensationalistic turns of Shakespeare's plot. Does the reunion of Leontes' family really provide any insight into the operations of faith, providence, or repentance? Perhaps the reunion comes about through the lucky conjunction of Camillo's scheming, Autolycus's knavery, Paulina's resourcefulness, and pure chance. As Cressy observes, monstrous birth texts often advertised themselves as "true reports" and cited credible witnesses to their wonderful events, much as Autolycus corroborates the credibility of his ballads through the testimony of eyewitnesses such as "Mistress Taleporter" (4.4.253). But a savvy customer would be leery of the testimony of anyone named "Taleporter": a porter of tales. Through crafty Autolycus, Shakespeare shares this insight with us at the expense of the naïve rustics who believe that a "ballad in print" must be "true" (4.4.245–46). Is the truth value of *The Winter's Tale* any more stable than the truth value of Autolycus's ballads or of *The Description of a Rare or Rather Most Monstrous Fish*?

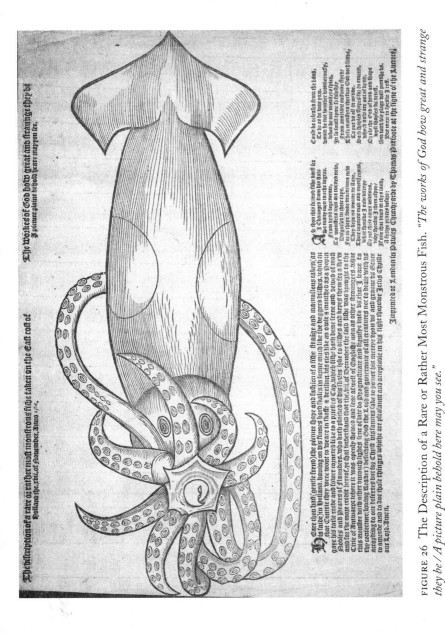

FIGURE 26 The Description of a Rare or Rather Most Monstrous Fish. *"The works of God how great and strange they be / A picture plain behold here may you see."*

The Description of a Rare or Rather Most Monstrous Fish Taken on the East Coast of Holland

Here thou hast, gentle friend, the picture, shape, and fashion of a fish strange and marvelous taken (as is said) in Holland, having on his fins hard scales in form much like the beggars' dishes[1] which in that country they were wont to wear in scoff and derision; his eyes like an owl and mouthed as a popinjay;[2] his tail red and four-cornered like to a priest's cap. Which fish hath been seen and viewed of most nobles and peers of Flanders, who hath plucked off his scales like to dishes and keep them for a show. And for the more credit hereof, ye shall understand that the 7th of December the said fish was brought to the city of Antwerp where it was openly showed and seen as well of English men as other strangers. What this monster with other uncouth[3] sights seen of late do prognosticate and signify unto us, that I leave to thy conjecture (loving reader), beseeching God the Lord and governor of all creatures not to deal with us according to our deserts but for Christ his son's sake to pour his mercy upon us and grant us grace to amend and to do those things which are pleasant and acceptable in his sight through Jesus Christ our Lord. Amen.

As thou this formed fish dost see
Y-changed[4] from his state,
So many men in each degree[5]
From kind[6] degenerate.
To monsters men are turned now,   5
Disguised in their ray.[7]
For in their fond[8] inventions new
They keep no mean ne stay,[9]
Their manners mad and monstrous,
What should I now descry?[10]   10
Or yet their cates[11] delicious,
Why should I them espy?[12,13]
If one that lived in this land
A forty years before
Could be released from the band[14]   15

---

[1] beggars' dishes: dishes for collecting alms.   [2] popinjay: parrot.   [3] uncouth: strange.
[4] Y-changed: changed (y- is an archaic form indicating past tense).   [5] degree: social rank.
[6] kind: nature.   [7] ray: array.   [8] fond: foolish.   [9] no mean ne stay: neither moderation nor restraint.   [10] descry: disclose.   [11] cates: delicacies.   [12] espy: examine closely.   [13] Or yet . . . them espy: What good would it do to criticize the contemporary appetite for fine foods?
[14] band: bond, i.e., of death.

To be as he was yore,
Would he not wonder wondrously,
When he our monsters spied,
In so small time so foolishly
From ancient custom flied?   20

CHAPTER 5

Hermione's Statue

———————————————— >< ————————————————

The Winter's Tale ends with a stunning spectacle that falls somewhere on the spectrum between a trick and a miracle. Hermione's return from death as a statue that comes to life before our eyes has long been admired as a brilliant stroke of stagecraft. Perhaps more than any other scene Shakespeare wrote, this one seems designed to elicit wonder: the sense of astonishment that confounds rational expectations and explanations.

Not all readers of *The Winter's Tale*, however, have been able or willing to yield to wonder's charms. The eighteenth-century critic Charlotte Lennox found utterly implausible the idea that a woman such as Hermione would behave so perversely as to sequester herself for sixteen years and then return as a piece of marble. In *Shakespeare Illustrated* (1753), Lennox writes:

> Shakespeare seems to have preserved the queen alive for the sake of her representing her own statue in the last scene, — a mean and absurd contrivance: for how can it be imagined that Hermione, a virtuous and affectionate wife, would conceal herself during sixteen years in a solitary house, though she was sensible that her repentant husband was all that time consuming away with grief and remorse for her death: and what reason could she have for choosing to live in such a miserable confinement when she might have been happy in the possession of her husband's affec-

tion and have shared his throne? How ridiculous also in a great Queen, on so interesting an occasion, to submit to such buffoonery as standing on a pedestal, motionless, her eyes fixed, and at last to be conjured down by a magical command of Paulina. (quoted in Furness 353)

Throughout the two and a half centuries since Lennox expressed dismay at Shakespeare's apparent lapse of judgment, the statue scene has continued to arouse impassioned sentiments, from complaints about its absurdity and artificiality to celebrations of its sublime spirituality and psychological depth.

Jacobean playgoers might have experienced a comparably broad range of responses to Hermione's statue. Taking a historical perspective, Bruce Smith argues that Shakespeare's contemporaries tended to respond to statues in one of three ways: they revered them as objects of religious devotion, interpreted them as embodiments of philosophical ideas, or marveled at their verisimilitude. Smith observes that "[a]ll three Renaissance perspectives on sculpture converge on Hermione in Paulina's gallery/chapel" ("Sermons" 18). The documents in this chapter suggest some of the many social, ideological, and aesthetic contexts in which Hermione's statue might be understood.

As an object of hushed admiration in a chapel, Hermione's statue resembles the images of saints (particularly the Virgin Mary) to which early modern Catholics paid devotion. For Protestant reformers, such practices amounted to superstitious idolatry. Theological controversies will inform the first two sets of documents that follow, which focus on doctrinal debates about faith, repentance, and the miraculous, as well as on the sacrilegious practices of witchcraft, fraudulent "resurrections," and the desecration of corpses. These transgressions represent the illicit horizon of Paulina's apparent ability to bring a statue to life. The line between devotion and desecration is similarly blurred by Leontes' sensual response to the ivory image of his wife, a scenario that recalls the Ovidian myth of the sculptor Pygmalion, who falls in love with the statue of a beautiful woman he has carved. Moved by his devotion, the goddess Venus gives the statue life. The social value that attaches to Hermione's statue as a work of art — fashioned by a famous Italian artist, owned by Paulina, and unveiled before a courtly audience in a gallery — will be addressed through Henry Peacham's discussion of art patronage and collecting in early modern England. Finally, we will consider three notable performances of the statue scene from the nineteenth, twentieth, and twenty-first centuries. The very different stage interpretations of Hermione's wonderful revivification provide insight not only into the dramatic potential of the last scene of *The Winter's Tale*, but also into the different cultural values that directors and actors have brought to the play in different historical eras.

Repentance, Devotion, and the Miraculous

> And do not say 'tis superstition, that
> I kneel and then implore her blessing. (5.3.43–44)

Although *The Winter's Tale* is set in pre-Christian antiquity, its story of a banished infant whose miraculous return brings about the "resurrection" of her dead mother evokes an archetypal Christian pattern of death and rebirth. Leontes' tyrannical violence against his newborn daughter resonates with the Christian feast of Innocents' Day (December 28), which commemorates King Herod's slaughter of all the newborns in Bethlehem in an attempt to destroy the infant Christ. For Innocents' Day, the *Book of Common Prayer* (1559) appoints Gospel passages to be read at Anglican church services that address themes of "error, confusion, and of the destruction of innocence" — themes that aptly describe Leontes' behavior in the first part of the play (Laroque 30). A record of a court performance of *The Winter's Tale* on Easter Tuesday in 1618 suggests that contemporaries also recognized a parallel between the resurrection of Christ and the apparent resurrection of Hermione. In the appointed Gospel reading for Easter Tuesday (Luke 24:39–40), the resurrected Jesus reveals the materiality of his body to his disciples: "Behold my hands and my feet, that it is even I myself. Handle me and see, for a spirit hath no flesh and bones, as ye see me have. And when he had thus spoken, he showed them his hands and his feet" (*Book of Common Prayer* 158). Paulina's name and her commandment that brings Hermione back to life — "Bequeath to death your numbness, for from him / Dear life redeems you" (5.3.102–03) — might also evoke St. Paul's teachings about redemption through Christ: "But now is Christ risen from the dead, and was made the first fruits of them that slept. For since by man came death, by man came also the resurrection of the dead" (Romans 15:20–21).

The play's allusions to Christian notions of redemption and new life raise the question of whether Leontes will be able to make the spiritual journey from a Herod-like tyrant to a reformed penitent. The debate between Paulina and Cleomenes over the efficacy of Leontes' "saintlike sorrow" (5.1.2) points to competing beliefs about repentance and salvation held by Catholics and Protestants in Renaissance England. For Catholics, salvation came from faith in God and the performance of good works: God would have mercy on those who showed mercy to others through charitable deeds, such as feeding the hungry and giving alms (Duffy 357–62). For Protestants, salvation came from faith alone. Cleomenes' focus on the efficacy of what Leontes has "done" and "performed" resembles the Catholic emphasis on good works as a path to forgiveness and sanctity, even though Leontes has not literally performed charitable works of mercy. By contrast, Paulina's insistence on Leontes' accountability to the "secret purposes" (5.1.36) of the gods corresponds to the Protestant insistence on salvation through inner faith.

Yet the distinction between Catholic and Protestant doctrines in the play is not as sharp as the dispute between Cleomenes and Paulina might imply, for Paulina is also associated with certain beliefs and practices that Protestants branded as Catholic "superstitions": the belief in ghosts and the practice of praying to saints. According to Catholic doctrine, the spirits of souls in Purgatory sometimes appeared on earth as ghosts to ask loved ones to "remember them," or say prayers that would reduce their time doing penance before entering heaven. Since Protestants rejected the existence of Purgatory, they regarded ghosts not as the spirits of the dead, but as illusions of the devil. Thomas Cranmer, archbishop of Canterbury and architect of the Protestant Reformation in England, writes in his *Confutation of Unwritten Verities* (1556) that the devil sometimes counterfeits the voices of dead souls in order to lure the gullible into sin. Cranmer insists that tales of ghosts walking the earth "ought to be taken as old wives' fables, the words of liars, and fraybugs of children" (44) — that is, as winter's tales. Paulina thus appears to take a "Catholic" position when she encourages Leontes to believe that, were he to remarry, Hermione's "sainted spirit" would "possess her corpse" and haunt him (5.1.57–58). Evoking the pleas of Purgatorial ghosts who cried "Remember me," Paulina imagines that Hermione's ghost would challenge Leontes to justify the appeal of his new wife's eyes by enjoining him to "Remember mine" (5.1.67). Moreover, when Paulina brings the court to her chapel to admire Hermione's statue, she creates a scenario that evokes Catholic devotion to statues of the saints, particularly the Virgin Mary (Figure 27).

According to Frances Dolan, controversy over Marian devotion escalated in England after the 1605 Gunpowder Plot, a failed Catholic attempt to assassinate members of the royal family and Parliament. Marian devotion was fiercely debated again in the 1620s and 1630s, during the reign of King Charles and Queen Henrietta Maria, who was Catholic (Dolan, *Whores* 103). That the initial surge in publication of pro-Marian and anti-Marian treatises coincides with the first performance of *The Winter's Tale* in 1610 or

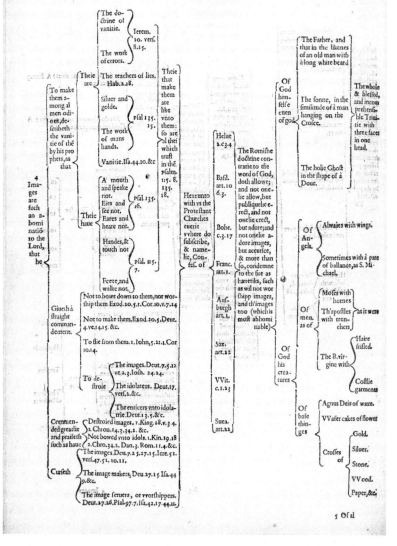

The truth.　　　*The English Creede.*　　　Errors

22　Article.

FIGURE 27 *Tables from Thomas Rogers,* The English Creed . . . Second Part *(London, 1587). From the chapter "Of Purgatory," Article 22 of the 39 Articles of the Church of England. Bracketed tables expounding the prohibition of images attack the "Romish doctrine" of adoring statues as "repugnant to the word of God." Prohibited images include those of God, Christ, angels, the apostles, the Virgin Mary, and crosses (see Aston 454–57).*

1611 suggests that the play's original audiences might have been particularly attuned to controversies over devotion and idolatry.

Such controversies might have been evoked as well by the parallels between the play and Catholic saint's legends. Especially since her statue becomes the object of a kind of pilgrimage to a chapel, Hermione can be seen as the type of the "virtuous martyr" celebrated and memorialized in these tales. Legends of female saints "usually involved torture and death at the hands of tyrannical kings," who were then "converted by the spectacle of the saints' courage, patience, and faith" (Vanita 317). Saint Dorothea, for example, succeeded in converting "the very tyrant who had mocked her" (Lupton 210). When Leontes threatens to burn Paulina, she casts herself in the role of the sainted martyr willing to die for her faith in Hermione: "It is an heretic that makes the fire, / Not she which burns in't" (2.3.115–16). Paulina also casts Leontes as the cruel "tyrant" who would torture her with "wheels, racks, fires, . . . flaying, boiling / In leads or oils" (3.2.171–72). Sixteen years later, Leontes grants Paulina an extraordinary influence over the kingdom when he vows not to marry without her permission, "so be blest [his] spirit" (5.1.71). Paulina thus comes to function as a kind of spiritual confessor to Leontes as well as a protector to Hermione: in saints' legends, female saints often assist faithful women in distress, much as Paulina "provides Hermione with a sanctuary away from men" (Vanita 316).

The Protestant and Catholic perspectives on repentance and devotion addressed in the documents that follow exist in a complicated relationship to *The Winter's Tale*. From an orthodox Anglican perspective, the Elizabethan *Homily of Repentance* expounds the role of faith in true repentance. The opposed Catholic and Protestant positions on devotional practices and miracles are represented by A. G.'s *The Widow's Mite* and William Crashaw's *The Jesuits' Gospel*. Whereas the Catholic A. G. argues that the scriptures warrant paying devotion to Mary, the Protestant minister Crashaw scathingly refutes the doctrine of miracles espoused by Catholic devotees of Mary. *The Winter's Tale*, of course, is neither a sermon nor a religious polemic. When thinking about these texts in relation to *The Winter's Tale*, it is important to resist the temptation to read a particular character, such as Paulina or Hermione, as embodying one or another of these polarized doctrinal views. These texts are useful not because they allow us to derive a singular and stable religious meaning from a character or episode from the play, but because they reveal how contested and fluid religious meanings could be in this period. The multivalent theological concepts and practices under scrutiny in these documents — faith, repentance, forgiveness, the miraculous, truth, belief, devotion — illuminate the rich tensions, ambiguities, and contradictions that animate the statue scene.

→ *From* An Homily of Repentance　　　　　*1563*

During the reign of King Edward VI (1537–1553), Anglican bishops and arch-
bishops produced a collection of sermons intended to disseminate official
church doctrine to the realm. First published in 1547, *Certain Sermons, or Homilies, Appointed by the King's Majesty, to be Declared and Read, by All Parsons, Vicars,
or Curates Every Sunday in Their Churches* was reprinted in many successive editions throughout the sixteenth and seventeenth centuries. The *Homily of Repentance* first appeared in *The Second Tome of Homilies* (1563). Every church in
England was required to have available to the public a copy of the *Homilies*, the
Bible, and the *Book of Common Prayer*. Since church attendance was mandatory,
the official Anglican positions conveyed by sermons such as the *Homily of
Repentance* would have received an extremely wide hearing.

　　As the official doctrine of the Anglican Church, the *Homily of Repentance*
provides an orthodox standard against which to evaluate the sincerity and ef-
fectiveness of Leontes' repentance. According to the homily, true repentance
requires an "outward profession of repentance" but does not "consist in outward
weeping and mourning only." What distinguishes true repentance from false
repentance is the "lively faith" that God will forgive our sins. Leontes certainly
professes his repentance outwardly. Receiving the news of Hermione's death,
he vows that his only "recreation" will be to perform a daily ritual of penitence and commemoration at the tomb of his wife and son (3.2.235). Yet Paulina
has already argued that no amount of penitence could ever redeem the wrongs
Leontes has committed. She goes so far as to advise him to despair, a terrible
sin in Christian theology, because it denies the efficacy of God's redemptive
grace:

> But, O thou tyrant!
> Do not repent these things, for they are heavier
> Than all thy woes can stir. Therefore betake thee
> To nothing but despair. A thousand knees
> Ten thousand years together, naked, fasting,
> Upon a barren mountain, and still winter
> In storm perpetual, could not move the gods
> To look that way thou wert.　(3.2.202–09)

Although her counsel to despair is extreme, Paulina does raise valid concerns
about the efficacy of rituals of penance. Outward signs of devotion and self-
mortification might effectively express inner sorrow; then again, they might
constitute false shows of regret. Nor is it clear if such rituals can elicit divine forgiveness. If no amount of repentance can move the gods, then Leontes and his

Church of England, *The Second Tome of Homilies of Such Matters as Were Promised and Entitled
in the Former Part of Homilies* (London, 1563), *An Homily of Repentance and of True Reconciliation unto God;* STC 13663.3; sigs. Nnn3v–Nnn5r, Nnn6v–Nnn8r, Ooo7v–Ooo8v.

kingdom appear doomed to live in the perpetual winter of grief brought about by his tyrannical violence.

Sixteen years later, Cleomenes insists that Leontes has, in fact, redeemed himself through his rituals of devotion:

> Sir, you have done enough, and have performed
> A saintlike sorrow. No fault could you make
> Which you have not redeemed — indeed, paid down
> More penitence than done trespass. At the last,
> Do as the heavens have done: forget your evil.
> With them, forgive yourself. (5.1.1–6)

Cleomenes uses key terms in the Christian discourse of repentance: "redeemed," "penitence," "trespass," and "forgive." He claims that Leontes has so purified himself through his excessive penance that he has earned the status of a saint. Nonetheless, some doubts remain. For instance, when admitting his past sins, Leontes cites his "blemishes" against Hermione's "virtues" (5.1.8, 7), not against Apollo's sacred authority; he also mourns that he will never again see Hermione's "full eyes" or take "treasure from her lips" (5.1.53–54). Does Leontes' focus on absent physical and emotional comforts indicate that he feels more regret about what he has lost than what he has done? Might Leontes' daily visits to Hermione's tomb be understood not as a sign of true repentance and amendment of life, but as evidence that he lacks "lively faith" in divine forgiveness of his sins? It is even arguable that Leontes is more concerned with earning the forgiveness not of Apollo but of Paulina, whose habit of bluntly recalling his past sins implies that such forgiveness has not yet been granted. When Paulina insists that Leontes must "awake [his] faith" (5.3.95) before she can make Hermione's statue move, are we to understand "faith" in a religious sense (as faith in Apollo) or in a secular sense (as faith in Paulina, Hermione, or himself)?

Perhaps the fulfillment of Apollo's oracle through the finding of what has been lost — not only Perdita, but also Hermione — does indicate divine forgiveness of Leontes' sins, including his role in Mamillius's death. Nonetheless, no miracle brings Mamillius back to life. The incomplete reunion of the royal family requires us to ask if such a loss can ever be truly redeemed. Will Leontes continue to perform his "saintlike sorrow" at his son's tomb? Should he?

From *An Homily of Repentance*

There is nothing that the Holy Ghost doth so much labor in all the Scriptures to beat into men's heads, as repentance, amendment of life, and speedy returning unto the Lord God of hosts. And no marvel why. For we do daily and hourly by our wickedness and stubborn disobedience horribly fall away from God, thereby purchasing unto ourselves (if he should deal with us according to his justice) eternal damnation. So that no doctrine is so necessary in the church of God as is the doctrine of repentance and amendment of life. . . .

I might here allege very many places out of the prophets in the which this most wholesome doctrine of repentance is very earnestly urged, as most needful for all degrees[1] and orders of men: but one shall be sufficient at this present time. These are the words of Joel the prophet:[2] "Therefore, also now, the Lord saith: Return unto me with all your heart, with fasting, weeping, and mourning, and rent your hearts, and not your clothes, and return unto the Lord your God, for he is gracious and merciful, slow to anger, and of great compassion, and ready to pardon wickedness." Whereby it is given us to understand that we have here a perpetual rule appointed unto us, which ought to be observed and kept at all times, and that there is none other way whereby the wrath of God may be pacified and his anger assuaged, that the fierceness of his fury and the plagues or destruction which by his righteous judgment he had determined to bring upon us, may depart, be removed, and taken away. Where he saith, "But now therefore, saith the Lord, return unto me," it is not without great importance, that the prophet speaketh so. For he had afore set forth at large unto them the horrible vengeance of God, which no man was able to abide, and therefore he doth move them to repentance, to obtain mercy, as if he should say: "I will not have these things to be so taken as though there were no hope of grace left. For although ye do by your sins deserve to be utterly destroyed, and God by his righteous judgments hath determined to bring no small destruction upon you, yet now that ye are in a manner on the very edge of the sword, if ye will speedily return unto him, he will most gently and most mercifully receive you into favor again."

Whereby we are admonished that repentance is never too late, so that it be true and earnest, for, sith[3] that God in the scriptures will be called our father, doubtless he doth follow the nature and property of gentle and merciful fathers, which seek nothing so much than the returning again and amendment of their children, as Christ doth abundantly teach in the parable of the prodigal son.[4] Doth not the Lord himself say by the Prophet:[5] "I will not the death of the wicked, but that he turn from his wicked ways and live?" And in another place:[6] "If we confess our sins, God is faithful and righteous to forgive us our sins, and to make us clean from all wickedness." Which most comfortable promises are confirmed by many examples of the scriptures. When the Jews did willingly receive and embrace the wholesome counsel of the prophet Isaiah, God by and by did reach his helping hand

---

[1] **degrees:** social ranks.   [2] **Joel the prophet:** Joel 2:12–13.   [3] **sith:** since.   [4] **prodigal son:** Luke 15:11–32.   [5] **Prophet:** Ezekiel 18:23.   [6] **another place:** 1 John 1:9.

unto them, and by his angel did in one night slay the most worthy and valiant soldiers of Sennacherib's camp.[7] Whereunto may king Manasseh[8] be added, who after all manner of damnable wickedness returned unto the Lord, and therefore was heard of him, and restored again into his kingdom. The same grace and favor did the sinful woman Magdalene, Zacchaeus, the poor thief,[9] and many other feel. All which things ought to serve for our comfort against the temptations of our consciences, whereby the devil goeth about to shake or rather to overthrow our faith. For every one of us ought to apply the same unto himself, and say: "Yet now return unto the Lord, neither let the remembrance of thy former life discourage thee; yea, the more wicked that it hath been, the more fervent and earnest let thy repentance or returning be, and forthwith thou shalt feel the ears of the Lord wide open unto thy prayers. . . ."

[The homily explores four points in greater detail: from what we must return (sin); to whom we must return (God); by whom we must return (Christ); the manner of return — the passage reproduced below.]

Fourthly, this holy prophet Joel doth lively express the manner of this our returning by repentance, comprehending all the inward and outward things that may be here observed. First he will have us to return unto God with our whole heart, whereby he doth remove and put away all hypocrisy, lest the same might justly be said unto us: "This people draweth near unto me with their mouth, and worshipeth me with their lips: but their heart is far off from me." Secondly, he requireth a sincere and pure love of godliness, and of the true worshipping and service of God; that is to say, that forsaking all manner of things that are repugnant and contrary unto God's will, we do give our hearts unto him, and all the whole strength of our bodies and souls, according to that which is written in the law:[10] "Thou shalt love the Lord thy God with all thy heart, with all thy soul, and with all thy strength." Here, therefore, nothing is left unto us that we may give unto the world and unto the lusts of the flesh. For sith that the heart is the fountain of all our works, as many as do with their whole heart turn unto the Lord do live unto him only. Neither do they yet repent truly that, halting on both sides, do otherwhiles[11] obey God, but by and by[12] do think that, laying him aside, it is lawful for them to serve the world and the flesh. And because that we are letted[13] by the natural corruption of our own flesh and the wicked affections

---

[7] **by his angel . . . camp:** Isaiah 37.   [8] **Manasseh:** 2 Chronicles 33:1–16.   [9] **Magdalene, Zacchaeus, the poor thief:** Mary Magdalene (Luke 7:37–50), Zacchaeus the tax-collector (Luke 19:1–10), the poor thief crucified with Christ (Luke 23: 40–43).   [10] **the law:** Deuteronomy 6:5. [11] **otherwhiles:** occasionally.   [12] **by and by:** before long.   [13] **letted:** hindered.

of the same, he doth bid us also to return with fasting: not thereby understanding a superstitious abstinence and choosing of meats, but a true discipline or taming of the flesh, whereby the nourishments of filthy lusts and of stubborn contumacy[14] and pride may be withdrawn and plucked away from it. Whereunto he doth add weeping and mourning, which do contain an outward profession of repentance, which is very needful and necessary that so we may partly set forth the righteousness of God, when by such means we do testify that we deserved punishments at his hands, and partly stop the offence that was openly given unto the weak. This did David see, who being not content to have bewept and bewailed his sins privately, would publicly in his Psalms[15] declare and set forth the righteousness of God in punishing sin and also stay[16] them that might have abused his example to sin the more boldly. Therefore, they are farthest from true repentance that will not confess and acknowledge their sin nor yet bewail them, but rather do most ungodly glory and rejoice in them.[17]

Now lest any man should think that repentance doth consist in outward weeping and mourning only, he doth rehearse that wherein the chief of the whole matter doth lie, when he saith: "Rent your hearts, and not your garments, and turn unto the Lord your God." For the people of the East part of the world were wont to rent their garments if anything had happened unto them that seemed intolerable. This thing did hypocrites sometime counterfeit and follow, as though the whole repentance did stand in such outward gesture. He teacheth them that another manner of thing is required, that is, that they must be contrite in their hearts, that they must utterly detest and abhor sins, and being at defiance with them, return unto the Lord their God, from whom they went away before. For God hath no pleasure in the outward ceremony, but requireth a contrite and humble heart, which he will never despise, as David doth testify.[18] There is therefore none other use of these outward ceremonies but as far forth as we are stirred up by them, and do serve to the glory of God, and to the edifying of other.

Now doth he add unto this doctrine or exhortation certain goodly reasons, which he doth ground upon the nature and property of God, and whereby he doth teach that true repentance can never be unprofitable or unfruitful. . . .

[The remainder of the first part of the sermon elaborates on God's mercy to those who are truly repentant. The second part of the homily elaborates the four

---

[14] contumacy: resistance to authority.　[15] Psalms: Psalms 25, 35, 51, 103.　[16] stay: stop.
[17] rejoice in them: Psalm 52.　[18] as David doth testify: Psalm 51.

parts of repentance: contrition; unfeigned confession; faith; and amendment of life. The passage on faith is excerpted below.]

The third part of repentance is faith, whereby we do apprehend and take hold upon the promises of God touching the free pardon and forgiveness of our sins, which promises are sealed up unto us with the death and blood shedding of his son Jesus Christ. For what should avail and profit us to be sorry for our sins, to lament and bewail that we have offended our most bounteous and merciful father, or to confess and acknowledge our offences and trespasses, though it be done never so earnestly, unless we do steadfastly believe and be fully persuaded that God for his son Jesus Christ's sake will forgive us all our sins, and put them out of remembrance and from his sight?

Therefore, they that teach repentance without a lively faith in our savior Jesus Christ do teach none other but Judas' repentance, as all the schoolmen[19] do, which do only allow these three parts of repentance: the contrition of the heart, the confession of the mouth, and the satisfaction of the work.[20] But all these things we find in Judas' repentance,[21] which in outward appearance did far exceed and pass the repentance of Peter. For first and foremost, we read in the gospel that Judas was so sorrowful and heavy, yea, that he was filled with such anguish and vexation of mind for that which he had done, that he could not abide to live any longer. Did not he also, afore he hanged himself, make an open confession of his fault, when he said: "I have sinned, betraying the innocent blood"? And verily this was a very bold confession, which might have brought him to great trouble. For by it, he did lay to the high priests' and elders' charge the shedding of innocent blood, and that they were most abominable murderers. He did also make a certain kind of satisfaction when he did cast their money unto them again.

No such thing do we read of Peter, although he had committed a very heinous sin, and most grievous offense, in denying of his master.[22] We find that he went out and wept bitterly, whereof Ambrose[23] speaketh on this matter: "Peter was sorry and wept, because he erred as a man." I do not find what he[24] said; I know that he wept. I read of his tears, but not of his satisfaction. But how chance that the one was received into favor again with God and the other cast away, but because that the one did by a lively faith in him whom he had denied take hold upon the mercy of God, and the other

---

[19] **schoolmen:** medieval (Catholic) scholars.   [20] **satisfaction of the work:** performance of penal and meritorious acts.   [21] **Judas' repentance:** Matthew 27:3–5.   [22] **denying of his master:** Matthew 26: 69–75.   [23] **Ambrose:** Saint Ambrose, fourth-century bishop of Milan and Doctor of the Church, in *De Penitentia* [*Of Repentance*].   [24] **he:** Peter.

wanted[25] faith, whereby he did despair of the goodness and mercy of God? It is evident and plain, then, that although we be never so earnestly sorry for our sins, acknowledge, and confess them, yet all these things shall be but means to bring us to utter desperation, except we do steadfastly believe that God our heavenly father will for his son Jesus Christ's sake pardon and forgive us our offenses and trespasses, and utterly put them out of remembrance in his sight. Therefore, as we said before, they that teach repentance without Christ and a lively faith in the mercy of God do only teach Cain's[26] or Judas' repentance.[27]

---

[25] wanted: lacked.   [26] Cain's: Genesis 4:13–14.   [27] only teach Cain's or Judas' repentance: an outward show of repentance without true faith in God's mercy.

→ **A. G.**

From The Widow's Mite   *1619*

Although the author of *The Widow's Mite* remains anonymous, we can confidently place this treatise among a group of early-seventeenth-century Marian devotional texts that emerged from Catholic presses such as the Jesuit College in St. Omer, France. The College at St. Omer was founded in 1592–93 by the English priest Robert Parsons, who had fled England to avoid laws that defined Catholic priests, particularly Jesuits, as traitors and spies. Whether originally composed in English or later translated into English, several of these treatises were available to English readers, including Philippe Numan's *Miracles Lately Wrought by the Intercession of the Glorious Virgin Mary, at Mont-aigu* (Antwerp, 1606; trans. Robert Chambers); Orazio Torsellino's *The History of Our Blessed Lady of Loreto* (St. Omer, 1608; trans. Thomas Price); and John Floyd's *Overthrow of the Protestants' Pulpit-Babels* (St. Omer, 1612) and *Purgatory's Triumph over Hell* (St. Omer, 1613).

The Catholic associations of the statue scene in *The Winter's Tale* are particularly important because of the moral and spiritual power Catholics attributed to female saints. In *The Widow's Mite*, A. G. denounces Calvinists who afford the Virgin Mary no greater respect than to treat her as the inert vessel who carried Christ. A. G. insists that Mary "did most eminently cooperate as a most elevated, active, and lively instrument" of God's will; she was not passive like "a very stock or stone," but lived an actively virtuous life as the mother of Christ (sig. C7r). Analogously, he argues, it is lawful to pray to sculpted and painted

---

A. G., *The Widow's Mite, Cast into the Treasure-house of the Prerogatives and Praises of our Blessed Lady, the Immaculate and Most Glorious Virgin Mary, the Mother of God* (St. Omer, 1619); STC 11490; sigs. H6v–I4v.

images of Mary because such images are not merely inert matter or idols: they serve as vehicles through which the saints hear our prayers and act as our intermediaries in heaven. A. G. expounds on both the corporal and spiritual miracles wrought by God at the intercession of Mary on behalf of the faithful who pay devotion at her chapels and shrines.

If *The Widow's Mite* suggests that Paulina and Hermione can be interpreted as saintly figures capable of producing physical and spiritual miracles, it simultaneously raises questions about the consequences of such an interpretation. Consider what it might mean to read Hermione as an analogue to the Virgin Mary or to the "virtuous martyr" of saints' legends. Is it fitting to cast Hermione as a martyr and Leontes as a tyrant, or does that analogy exaggerate her victimization at his hands? Does the violent opposition between martyr and tyrant imply a moral and spiritual distance between Hermione and Leontes that renders unlikely any prospect of marital reconciliation, or does the conversion of tyrants in saints' legends point to just such a possible reconciliation? Catholics attributed to the "all-compassionate" Mary the desire to "forgive and protect the worst sinners" (Vanita 313). Does seeing Hermione as the "Blessed Lady" turn her into a flat allegorical figure of virtue, or does it bring out a genuine spiritual dimension of her character (Figure 28)? Can we assume that Hermione has indeed forgiven Leontes? Finally, we might debate how much spiritual agency Hermione has in the play's final scene. As a statue, is Hermione merely a passive "stock or stone," or does she operate as an active agent of divine providence, as Catholics claimed of Mary?

From *The Widow's Mite*[1]

There is no article of our religion which is more impugned by the enemy of mankind[2] than this of saints. And I could name a great Calvinist, and a great man that lived not long ago, who could patiently enough be told that he was not truly called to the place he held, who yet when there was speech of the invocation of the Blessed Virgin, grew abruptly into such a passion, or rather fury, as that he seemed to be little better than possessed. And as all of them are extremely averse in the generality[3] of praying to saints, so particularly it hath place when there is no question of[4] honoring or imploring the aid of our Blessed Lady. But it hath pleased almighty God in his goodness,

---

[1] **The Widow's Mite:** the title refers to a parable told by Jesus in which a poor widow donates two mites, coins of very small value, to the temple treasury. Jesus explains that the poor widow "hath cast more in, than all they which have cast into the treasury: For they did cast in of their abundance, but she of her want did cast in all that she had, even all her living" (Mark 12:43–44).
[2] **enemy of mankind:** Satan.   [3] **in the generality:** on the general point.   [4] **no question of:** no room for doubt about.

FIGURE 28 *"The Coronation of Our Blessed Lady," M. de Vos*, The Rosary of Our Lady *(1600).*

that after the rate of[5] their malice who impugn this article, so is the evidence whereby they are to be convinced plain, and testified not only by the practice of the Church, the express inference of Holy Scripture, the conformity with nature and reason, but with infinite arguments of miracles which God hath set as so many seals upon this truth.

It is strange (and would be incredible, if we were told by less than experience itself) that there should be such a deal of infidelity in the world as to make men doubt, and of impudence as to make them deny, that the power and gift of miracles is still in the Church, and that they have been abundantly wrought by the providence and power of God in proof of invocation of saints, and above all of the glorious and immaculate Virgin: the mother, the daughter, and the spouse of God. There is no corner of the Christian Catholic world which is not full of them; but no time or place will be able more readily to rise up in judgment against our Calvinists, than the mercy of this kind which God hath showed in honor of the sacred Virgin in these very days of ours, and even in the next confines of our country.

For they are great numbers of most certain miracles which have been wrought in Brabant[6] near to Sichem,[7] in a chapel there devoted to our Blessed Lady. The stories of the men and women that have received miraculous cure by the prayers of the Blessed Virgin, to whom they recommended themselves, after exact and severe examination of the parties themselves, of the persons who knew them both before and after, of whole colleges of physicians and surgeons who had been formerly privy to[8] their infirmities, have been proved and enrolled in the records of principal cities. Yea, and the providence of God hath been such as to make some one of these miracles fall upon the most known begging cripple of a whole country, and of whom for his notorious deformity from his mother's womb, together with the importunity of his begging, all the states[9] of the court and town from the Archduke and Infanta[10] themselves, to the meanest tradesman in Brussels[11] have taken precise and perfect knowledge. There was, I say, a most impotent lame creature who came deformed out of his mother's womb (and by occasion thereof he was her death) whose knees by continual cleaving to his breast had made deep holes therein, whose legs hung down like a couple of drum sticks, and who in his life had never made one pace,[12] but on his hands and hips. This man (if he was not rather a monster) they all saw when he

---

[5] **after the rate of:** in proportion to.   [6] **Brabant:** a duchy in the Low Countries (Netherlands).
[7] **Sichem:** town in Brabant, today in Belgium.   [8] **privy to:** privately aware of.   [9] **states:** social ranks.   [10] **Archduke and Infanta:** Archduke Albert of Austria and his wife Isabella of Spain (the *infanta,* or daughter of Spanish King Phillip II) ruled the Seventeen Provinces of the Low Countries, including the Duchy of Brabant.   [11] **Brussels:** city in Brabant, today the capital of Belgium.   [12] **pace:** step.

was thus, and within a fortnight after, when he had been miraculously and in an instant cured by the prayers of the most gracious and glorious Queen of heaven in that chapel devoted to herself, they saw him again of a good stature, of good proportion, of good health and strength. And not only he was seen by them, but many of those noble English gentlemen who accompanied the Earl of Hartford in his embassage to that court did also see him and speak with him, and so may yet as many more as will in Brussels, where he continueth to this day, and his name is John Clement.

They are wont[13] to tell us I know not what of counterfeited miracles, and I doubt not but divers[14] may have been counterfeited, and that even in the apostles' days, as well as ours. But so far off is that from proving that there are no true miracles as this would be a ridiculous inference: the king's hand[15] is counterfeited; therefore the king knoweth not how to write his name. It would rather hold on the other side, that because sometimes either for pride or profit some men are so wicked as to counterfeit miracles, it is an evident sign that true miracles are wrought sometimes, which no man would else be so sottish[16] as to counterfeit, as no man would counterfeit the king's hand if the king could not write.

But howsoever, I assure the reader in the word of a Christian and as in the presence of God, who needeth not that any man should tell a lie in his behalf and who will grievously punish such impostures wheresoever he findeth them, that the Church our Mother detesteth all such impotent and impure proceeding, and excommunicateth such as concur to the countenancing[17] thereof. And, as by occasion of the frequent miracles wrought lately in divers parts of Brabant, there have been some found so wicked as to the uttermost of their power to make some very few false miracles pass for true ones, so (the providence of God working by the prudence of such as have the office of looking into those matters) they have been detected and grievously punished with whipping, having their tongues bored through, and being banished out of their country, as appeareth upon record in Brussels.

And in those parts where miracles have been so frequently seen in these later times, the examination of the truth of them doth not (as God would have it) lie there in the hands of ecclesiastical persons, whom the rage[18] of heresy is wont to charge with at least connivency[19] in this point, if not collusion, but the custom hath been of many years for the secular magistrates to take knowledge thereof, who will not be pretended even by our adversaries to be so partial as those others.

---

[13] **wont:** likely. [14] **divers:** various. [15] **hand:** signature. [16] **sottish:** foolish. [17] **countenancing:** encouraging. [18] **rage:** mania, violent passion [19] **connivency:** connivance, tacit permission.

Now, for as much as concerneth the truth or falsehood of our miracles, although it should be true that the most part of them are wholly false (which yet is no more possible than that the whole world except our adversaries should be all grown fools or knaves), yet if all that were granted, and that yet either they shall confess or it may be justified that any one miracle was ever wrought by God upon the prayers made to our Blessed Lady, with the invocation of her aid (which truth the devil himself is not so dogged[20] or so damned as to deny), one of these two things will follow: that either almighty God hath cooperated so far to a false doctrine as to credit it by supernatural means (which cannot be conceived without blasphemy); or else that the invocation of saints, and in particular of the immaculate and most glorious Virgin, cannot be impugned or denied without heretical impiety.

And if the inference of one true miracle be so pregnant,[21] what will that be which may be made from so many hundreds? Which howsoever they be most evidently true and most easily known to be so, we are the less to wonder at the incredulity of our adversaries through the doctrine which is delivered in the person of Abraham, and recorded by the Evangelist St. Luke, where he sayeth that the friends of Dives, who then survived, *had Moses among them and the prophets, and if they refused to hear them, neither would they believe though one should rise to them from the dead.*[22] By changing only the terms it falleth out to be the Calvinists' case, who having the Church of Christ in such a visible and undoubted manner before their eyes, do yet contest, yea, and detest the authority thereof. For the punishment of which perverseness, the most undoubted miracles which are wrought by God, in confirmation of the doctrine which she[23] teacheth, are denied to be true by them who have eyes and see not, who have hearts and understand not, but are incapable of all instruction; and which daily ripen towards damnation if they free them not from sinning thus against their conscience, as the Jews did notwithstanding the infinite miracles of our Savior Christ, which yet they would never be drawn to acknowledge, but did impute those arguments of his omnipotency either to collusion with the parties who were cured or to the use of sorcery in casting out some devils by the help of others.

The corporal miracles wrought by God at the intercession of our Blessed Lady are in a manner innumerable, yet are they few in comparison of the spiritual miracles, which are daily seen by the conversion of souls to God's

---

[20] dogged: malicious. [21] pregnant: obvious. [22] Abraham ... *the dead*: in Luke 16:19–31, Jesus tells the parable of a rich man (*Dives* is Latin for "rich man") who dies and finds himself in hell. Dives asks Abraham to send Lazarus, a beggar who has died and gone to heaven, back from the dead in order to warn Dives' brothers about hell. Abraham replies as quoted here. [23] she: the Church.

service through the prayers of the Mother of God and us. It is most certainly true, and known to be so, that innumerable sinners have been reduced to penance before their death, to which grace they were never known to have had any other disposition, but by some tenderness of devotion, though imperfect, which in their hearts they ever carried to our Blessed Lady. Innumerable they are who, only coming into those sanctuaries where God hath been most honored in the devotion borne to his Blessed Mother (as particularly in that Holy House of Loreto[24]), and there having recommended themselves (though unworthily enough) to our Blessed Lady, they have yet found themselves sometimes stricken down with the horrible fear of God's judgments, sometimes raised up with an extraordinary hope of mercy, sometimes stricken through with reflecting upon the ugliness and baseness of sin as that in the same very instant they have resolved upon a whole change of their lives, without taking any longer time than of so many minutes as might conduct them and cast them at the feet of a ghostly father,[25] for the making of entire restitutions, the quitting of sensual conversations,[26] the disposing of mortal or rather immortal enmities, and the performing of such other heroical, and high acts of mind. Which as they cannot be purchased but by the infinite merit of Christ's passion, so that is never more comfortable and effectually applied than by the means of our Blessed Lady's sacred protection and dear prayers. And although the acts and records of these spiritual miracles be not so well kept in parchment as are the corporal, yet I appeal to the conscience of observing and curious[27] Catholics, which cannot fail to bear witness with me of this truth, that the bowels of our Blessed Lady's compassion do by the providence of God extend themselves as much more frequently to the strange cure of souls than of bodies, as the body is less considerable[28] than the soul. In so much as a whole city in Italy[29] hath been found upon some devotion which it hath taken to our Blessed Lady to make within the space of a few years such a total change from vice to virtue and piety, as there is difference between a disorderly tavern and a devout church.

In the same manner, if the state of Brabant and the provinces adjoining (for as much as concerneth morality or religion) be considered, and the difference well weighed concerning the great example of virtue and manners, and the integrity of faith, to the contrary in both these respects, whereby those countries were endangered until the miracles (wrought by the intercession of our Blessed Lady, near Sichem, and other places) made them cast

---

[24] **Holy House of Loreto:** a famous shrine in Loreto, Italy.   [25] **ghostly father:** a confessor.   [26] **conversations:** behaviors, habits.   [27] **curious:** discerning.   [28] **considerable:** important.   [29] **city in Italy:** in Lucca, a congregation of the Blessed Virgin was founded in 1574 in the church of Santa Maria della Rosa.

a quicker eye of humble devotion towards her. If it be considered, I say, how all the states of people are admirably improved since that time, all such as together with common sense have not the poison of prejudicate passion in their hearts and heads will acknowledge the powerful and gracious hand of our Blessed Lady in this heavenly work, and will not fail to esteem it for a spiritual miracle.

It is time that I grow to a conclusion, and I will procure to tie it up in as straight a compass[30] as I can. I have endeavored to show how highly our Blessed Lady is honored by the testimony of holy scripture and to remove such objections as her adversaries take from thence, whereby to do her disparagement. I have showed her genealogy, her beauty, her perfection of virtue which filled the whole world with heroical actions. I have accompanied that discourse with showing how the whole Church hath employed itself in her devotion and how the ancient, most holy, and most learned Fathers[31] have endeavored to excel one another in piety towards her, wherein the sectaries[32] of our time are as wholly unlike them as in other things. I have offered to the reader's consideration the authority both of corporeal and spiritual miracles, whereby almighty God hath as it were laboriously concurred in this age of ours towards the planting of a trophy to our Blessed Lady in the hearts of all men. Happy are they who mean to take occasion hereby either to begin or to increase in a most reverend and filial affection towards her: and most happy should I accompt[33] myself if the little which I have been able to say or do might cause some few mites, after the example of this of mine, to be cast into the rich treasury of her praises.

[30] **straight a compass:** direct a course.   [31] **Fathers:** the fourth-century fathers of the Church.   [32] **sectaries:** members of a sect, here Protestants.   [33] **accompt:** account.

→ WILLIAM CRASHAW

From The Jesuits' Gospel   *1610*

A clergyman in the Church of England, William Crashaw (1572–1626) authored strongly Puritan sermons and treatises. Having earned several degrees at Cambridge University, he returned to his native Sheffield to preach and eventually secured a position as preacher for the London law schools. In tracts such as *Romish Forgeries and Falsifications* (1606), Crashaw attacked what he regarded as the scriptural errors and abuses advocated by Roman Catholic theologians.

William Crashaw, *The Jesuits' Gospel* (London, 1610); STC 6016; sigs. D1v–D3v, E1r–E3r.

Ironically, his son Richard converted to Catholicism and expressed his beliefs through powerfully sensual devotional poetry that is still studied today.

The Jesuits' Gospel constitutes Crashaw's reply to *Amphitheatrum Honoris*, an encomium of the Virgin Mary published by Carolus Scribanius in 1606 (*DNB*). The excerpt below is taken from Crashaw's "Discourse on the Ladies of Halle and Sichem," which precedes his line-by-line refutation of Scribanius's encomium. In the "Discourse," Crashaw is primarily concerned with refuting another continental Catholic writer, Justus Lipsius, who had published reports of the miraculous events that had occurred before images of Mary in Halle and Sichem, towns in the Duchy of Brabant (now Belgium).

Crashaw's tirade against idolatry expresses in an overtly antagonistic mode what the visitors to Paulina's chapel experience as concern about the appropriateness of paying devotion to a statue. Perdita kneels to the statue of Hermione, implores its blessing, and addresses it as "Dear Queen," as if the stone were indeed sentient (5.3.45). As Ruth Vanita points out, the "[t]raditional devotional practices of kneeling to statues and kissing them had been expressly forbidden" from the time of Henry VIII, "although many people continued surreptitiously to perform these actions" (321). Perdita even recognizes that such devotion might be criticized as "superstition" (5.3.43). When Perdita and Leontes offer to kiss the statue, Paulina forbids such physical contact, as if to defend against a taboo manifestation of the "superstitious" idolatry that she has otherwise encouraged. On what grounds does Crashaw excoriate such devotional practices? Why does he consider them so dangerous? Might his objection to belief in the miraculous power of images shed light on the caution with which Paulina manages the encounter between Hermione's statute and its audience? Crashaw describes Catholic accounts of miracles as "ridiculous legend[s]," fraught with "improbabilities and impossibilities" (p. 382). When Paulina admits that the story of Hermione's statue coming to life would "be hooted at / Like an old tale" (5.3.117–18), is she similarly denying the presence of a true miracle? Without a belief in the miraculous, does the statue scene lose its emotional power, or might the false miracles that Crashaw dismissively calls "tricks" and "lying wonders" still have the power to move us?

From *The Jesuits' Gospel*

Amongst the late devices[1] that Romish policy hath forged to uphold their hierarchy, a principal is their art of miracles, which they pretend to have so ordinary, that in many churches they have more miracles than sermons. But, alas, daily experience showeth that they be lying wonders and no true mir-

---

[1] **devices:** stratagems.

acles. Now, because such tricks are most effectual to delude the common people, and that they find themselves and their cause to have lost much of late in many parts of Christendom; therefore to recover themselves and to gain credit to their forlorn cause, they have most busily applied this point of late, and have by the craft of Machiavellian Jesuits[2] (as Watson[3] their brother priest often styles them) so far prevailed, that there scarce passeth a month wherein some new Image of our Lady is not found, or some strange miracle and wonders heard of.

Two years ago they caused a story to be written and published wherein they blush not to make their people believe that more miracles and greater than Christ did have been and are daily done at Halle (a town in the borders of Brabant and Hainaut[4]) by the Virgin Mary at a picture of hers in a chapel there. And this is set out by no vulgar or trivial fellow, but by that famous apostate Lipsius,[5] that the tale may carry the more credit. And the miracles are not of ordinary but of the highest nature: for healing of frenzies, fevers, convulsions, is nothing, nay. Sight is given to the blind, and whereas Christ raised but three from the dead (that we know of), our Lady of Halle (saith Lipsius) gave life to seven at least that were dead. Lo, hear how far short Christ himself is of his mother. And now we marvel no more if they have written that *St. Francis did all that Christ did and more than Christ did*, seeing the picture of his mother can do more than he did.

I say the picture of his mother, because Georgius Fabricus, the Pope's censor of books,[6] in his allowance of this legend of Lipsius saith that God giveth and communicateth down power to work miracles not only to the Virgin Mary and the saints, but even to their images or pictures. Behold, good reader, a worthy piece of new refined popery: *God's divine power is communicated to the very pictures of creatures.* And if any man object that miracles are not in these days to be expected, Lipsius hath a learned and catholic[7] answer: that now indeed in respect of Christ, or[8] to aver his doctrine or to maintain his honor, they need not;[9] but the case is otherwise (saith he) with

---

[2] **Machiavellian Jesuits:** a Machiavellian is a supposed follower of the principles found in Niccolò Machiavelli's treatise on statecraft, *The Prince.* The English associated Machiavelli (1469–1527) with political expediency and duplicity. Jesuits were members of a Roman Catholic order founded by St. Ignatius Loyola (1491–1556); they vigorously promoted the Catholic faith against Protestant reformers. [3] **Watson:** William Watson, an English Catholic priest and opponent of the Jesuits. [4] **Brabant and Hainaut:** the Duchy of Brabant and County of Hainaut were provinces of the Low Countries, or Netherlands. [5] **Lipsius:** Justus Lipsius, sixteenth-century Flemish scholar who openly converted to Catholicism in 1590. [6] **censor of books:** from the mid-sixteenth century, the Roman Catholic Church regularly published indexes of forbidden books. [7] **catholic:** universally applicable. [8] **or:** either. [9] **they need not:** i.e., miracles are not necessary.

saints, for many do refuse to worship them, and grudge at the honor that in the Romish Church is given them, and therefore to defend them in this point and to establish that worship which they do unto them, God suffreth so many miracles to be done even by their images. Which answer being well considered of, what a kind of doctrine it containeth, I leave to the learned and judicious reader. . . .

Now therefore surely we must needs believe (else we are unbelieving heretics) that one was before this dispossessed of a devil without any other means, for so he saith, and that ten at least were delivered from present death by but calling or thinking upon Our Lady at Halle, and that seven were raised from death to life being but laid before the image. And all these within the space of twenty years, and in one country, so ordinary a matter is it in popery[10] to raise the dead. Nay, we must believe (or else we are infidels) that when a falconer should have been hanged for losing his lord's falcon, and had the rope about his neck, and did but call to mind the Lady of Halle, forthwith the hawk came flying home again and light[11] upon the falconer's shoulder, and so saved his life. For this is not Lipsius ashamed to report. Which if it be true, then we shall less wonder hereafter at that in the legend, where it is reported how a parrot having got abroad out of her cage and sporting herself in the air, was by and by espied by a hawk, who being ready to seize upon her, instantly the parrot seeing herself in danger to be surprised, cried out "Saint Thomas a Becket, save me!" And presently the hawk fell down dead and the parrot was delivered.[12] . . .

But hath not Lipsius recanted, or the Romish Church reformed this since then? Alas, Lipsius was so far from that, that the year after [the publication of his book about Our Lady of Halle], very near unto his death, as though he intended nothing but *to heap up wrath against the day of wrath*,[13] he added *drunkenness to thirst*, as the Prophet[14] saith. For heaping sin upon sin instead of revoking and recanting his former collusion, he published another pamphlet, a more ridiculous legend and fraught with more improbabilities and impossibilities than the former. It bears this title: *Justus Lipsius his History of Our Lady of Sichem, or of Our Lady's Picture, of the Craggy-Rock or Sharp Hill, and of Her New Miracles and Benefits* (at Antwerp, 1605).

At this image, saith he, are wrought miracles of all sorts. Apoplexies, epilepsies, gouts, and all kind of diseases are healed; lame are restored to limbs; blind to sight; deaf to their hearing: and all these by heaps, not seldom or extraordinarily, but yearly, monthly, daily. Almost 60 are registered

---

[10] popery: i.e., Roman Catholicism.   [11] light: alighted.   [12] delivered: saved.   [13] *to heap up . . . day of wrath*: Romans 2:5.   [14] Prophet: Moses, Deuteronomy 29:19.

by Lipsius besides many more omitted, and all to be done in two or three years, insomuch as if his report be true, God makes miracles far more ordinary for the honor of saints and their images, than he did for confirming the doctrine of Christ and his apostles. But what credit hath the story of Our Lady of Sichem? Even as good as hath Our Lady of Halle, else let the reader judge.

Near to the little, poor (but old) town of Sichem, saith Lipsius, there is a mount barren, rough, and craggy, on one side whereof there is a little hillock. On it grows an oak, and in it or fastened to it is a little image of Our Lady, which hath done great miracles in time past, and was therefore worshipped of the people there. But how is that proved? Thus: above 100 years ago, a shepherd found that image and put it in his bosom, thinking to carry it home to worship it, but as he was in these thoughts, he was suddenly stricken and astonished in his senses, and benumbed in his whole body, insomuch as he could not stir one foot, but stood still like a dead trunk, not knowing what to think of it, nor how to help himself. His master wanting both his shepherd and his sheep, sought them, and found him so standing, who told him the whole matter. His master taking the image, went with great devotion and set it up in the oak again, and forthwith the shepherd had his limbs restored, and went and worshipped it. And so by their reports all the country heard of it, who came by heaps and were healed of all diseases, but agues[15] especially, and so it continued (saith he) till within these 20 years, about which time the blessed image was stolen or lost, no man can tell how. (But is it not strange that if it could do these miracles, they would let it be lost so carelessly?) Well, lost it was. But what, though? People went as fast then as afore, and still as great cures were there done as when the image was there. And in want[16] of the image the people worshipped the oak, and why might they not, said Lipsius? The holy image had hallowed the tree, so that it might lawfully be worshipped (behold popish devotion!). Yet, saith he, we worshipped not the tree, but in it the image, and in it our Lady, and in her God. Mark, good reader, God gets his worship at last, though it be at the fourth hand: they tender it to the tree, the tree yields it to the image, the image conveys it to Our Lady, and she presents it to God. So then by popish doctrine and devotion God is served and honored after his creatures, and so at last gets his own. If they say that the worship is intended to God, and is not ended but in him, I answer: but were it not better that the worship were offered immediately from the heart and hands of the worshipper to God himself, and to pass through no hands but

[15] agues: fevers.   [16] want: absence.

of his son the mediator? But this is heresy. Let it pass, or else it must pass the fire.

To return to the story. Our Lady of Sichem is lost, but what then? Must the poor town lose her traffic and living? (Nay, rather we will make another, for that is no hard nor unusual thing in that religion.) And so, saith he, seven years after, an honest and devout alderman of Sichem (perceiving how well his and his neighbors' gains came in, and how the poor town lived), like a good townsman, made another image, put it in a box of wood, and fastened the box to the oak, that so their Lady might not be lost so carelessly as afore.

This new image thus made did as many miracles as the other, and why should it not, for was it not as good as the other? Nay, it may be it was more curiously[17] carved and better wrought. Thus it continued certain years till at last the parish priest perceiving they began to be well customed,[18] bestowed some cost on their Lady which got them so much, and built her a little chapel of boards, and there placed her. But still their custom growing greater, they showed themselves thankful to their patroness, and as she filled their purses they sought her honor, and built her a fair chapel of stone some two years ago, and in that resteth the image, working miracles every day. But what became of the holy oak? It was so cut away by pieces by devout persons and carried away that it was in danger of falling, and a council was called in the town what were to be done with it (as in so great a matter it is requisite); and there, after serious consideration, it was gravely concluded that it should be cut up by the roots and with much solemnity brought into the town of Sichem. Where, when it came, forthwith happy was he that could get a piece of the holy wood, whereof (saith Lipsius, and blusheth not to write it) divers made them little images, and with much piety do worship them. Others that were sick of grievous diseases shaved it into their drink and drunk it, and so were healed. See what an excellent religion this is. One image hath begot many, and the first image being but fastened to the tree so sanctified the whole oak that every image made of the whole tree should be as good as itself, and every crumb of the wood should work miracles, as fast as the image did.

Lo, here the history of our Lady of Sichem, or of the sharp hill. And this legend is not Lipsius ashamed to thrust upon the world for a true and undoubted story. Such are the times we be fallen into, that to set fast the crown upon the Pope's head, truth must stand aside and lies must pass for

---

[17] **curiously:** artfully.   [18] **customed:** patronized by customers.

current without control. And such a cause is popery as cannot continue in credit before the people but by forging a continued succession of lying wonders. For now we are made believe that the Virgin Mary hath two images within few miles together which have done more miracles in a few years by passed, than God himself did in the Old, or Christ and his apostles in the New Testament. Such idols of indignation doth the Romish harlot advance against the sovereign majesty of God, to provoke him withal. For what is it but an idol of indignation that not a creature only, but the very image of a creature, should be made partaker of the divine power and majesty of God?

Death and Desecration

> No longer shall you gaze on't, lest your fancy
> May think anon it moves. (5.3.60–61)

A common Protestant strategy for delegitimizing Catholicism was to define its rituals and ceremonies as merely "theatrical spectacles" (O'Connell 33). For instance, reformers claimed that pilgrims at holy shrines witnessed not true miracles but merely illusions created by the devil or by impious priests (Lim 323). When she offers to make Hermione's statue speak, Paulina seeks to disarm such accusations by disavowing the assistance of any "wicked powers" (5.3.91). Although Paulina finds it prudent to protect herself from charges of witchcraft, growing skepticism and the emergence of empirical science in early modern England made available other, more rational, explanations for ostensibly supernatural phenomena. Thus, in the first document, Reginald Scot argues that witches, much like Catholic priests, use theatrical trickery to fool the gullible into believing that they possess supernatural powers. Scot would doubtless have regarded Paulina's "resurrection" of Hermione as the feat of a crafty illusionist.

Whereas Paulina hopes to defend herself from suspicion of witchcraft, the characters in Thomas Middleton's contemporary play *The Second Maiden's Tragedy* passionately indulge in all manner of socially and theologically taboo behavior, including suicide, tomb desecration, fetishism, necrophilia, and corpse painting. With its sensationalistic display of horrors, Middleton's tragedy suggests that the difference between a tragic desecration and the kind of comic miracle that appears to occur in Paulina's chapel has much to do with the suppression of violent passions and the cultivation of temperance, patience, and restraint.

→ REGINALD SCOT

From The Discovery of Witchcraft
1584

Reginald Scot (c. 1538–1599) attended Oxford University and went on to a varied career as a public servant. He helped to engineer a dam, collected subsidies, served as a captain in the defenses against the Spanish Armada, and was elected to Parliament in 1589. Although three works by Scot survive, he is best known for *The Discovery of Witchcraft* — "discovery" here meaning the exposure of a fraudulent practice. *The Discovery of Witchcraft* is a remarkably erudite refutation of witchcraft belief as enshrined both in popular consciousness and in learned accounts such as Jean Bodin's 1580 treatise *La Démonomanie des Sorciers* (On Witchcraft). Scot attributes both past and present belief in the supernatural power of witches to prejudice, storytelling, superstition, and gullibility.

In the excerpts below from Book Seven of *The Discovery of Witchcraft*, Scot's skeptical reading of the biblical story of the witch of Endor refutes the blasphemous claim that witches can raise the dead. In this story, Saul, king of Israel, asks a witch for insight into an impending war. He requires her to conjure up the spirit of the prophet Samuel, who appears to him and prophesies his defeat by the Philistine army (1 Samuel 28: 7–25). Scot's skeptical analysis of this story helps to define what Paulina stands to gain and to lose in her staging of the pseudo-miraculous spectacle of Hermione's resurrection. Scot accuses the witch of practicing "abuse," being a "counterfeit," and speaking with the "lying corporal tongue of a cozener, that careth neither for God nor the devil" (p. 387). In *The Winter's Tale*, no-one makes such charges against Paulina, but is her manipulation of Leontes' emotions and expectations any less egregious than the witch's manipulation of Saul's? What, ultimately, differentiates Paulina's deceptive illusionism from that of the witch of Endor?

It is worthwhile to explore how Paulina herself understands the ethics of her participation in the resurrection of Hermione. On the one hand, Paulina takes steps to protect herself from charges of witchcraft or blasphemous trickery. On the other hand, she associates her ability to animate Hermione's statue with the kind of silly "old tale" typically told by an untrustworthy, garrulous old woman (5.3.118), the same kind of woman whom Scot blames for telling superstitious winter's tales to gullible children. Is Paulina indirectly admitting that she is a kind of con artist playing on the fears and desires of a naïve audience? In yet another connection with *The Winter's Tale*, Scot argues that the priests of Apollo at Delphos "abused and cozened" great philosophers and princes with their doubtfully worded oracles. From Scot's skeptical perspective, does Paulina's insistence that Leontes await the fulfillment of Apollo's oracle look less like an

Reginald Scot, *The Discovery of Witchcraft, Wherein the Lewd Dealing of Witches and Witchmongers is Notably Detected* . . . (London, 1584); STC 21864; sigs. M2v–M3v, M4v–M6r.

assertion of religious faith, and more like a shrewd attempt to control the king until Hermione is ready to reclaim her sovereignty?

The residue of 1 Samuel 28 expounded: wherein is declared how cunningly this witch brought Saul resolutely to believe that she raised Samuel, what words are used to color[1] the cozenage,[2] and how all might also be wrought by ventriloquy.

THE THIRTEENTH CHAPTER

Now cometh in Samuel to play his part. But I am persuaded it was performed in the person of the witch herself, or of her confederate. He saith to Saul, "Why hast thou disquieted me, to bring me up?" as though without guile or packing[3] it had been Samuel himself. Saul answered that he was in great distress, for the Philistines made war upon him. Whereby the witch, or her confederate priest, might easily conjecture that his heart failed and direct the oracle or prophecy accordingly, especially understanding by his present talk, and also by former prophecies and doings that were past, that God had forsaken him and that his people were declining[4] from him. For when Jonathan (a little before) overthrew the Philistines, being thirty thousand chariots and six thousand horsemen, Saul could not assemble above six hundred soldiers.

Then said Samuel (which some suppose was Satan, and as I think was the witch, with a confederate, for what need so far fetches, as to fetch a devil supernaturally out of hell, when the illusion may be here by natural means deciphered? And if you note the words well, you shall perceive the phrase not to come out of a spiritual mouth of a devil, but from a lying corporal tongue of a cozener that careth neither for God nor the devil, from whence issueth such advice and communication as greatly disagreeth from Satan's nature and purpose). For thus (I say) the said Samuel speaketh: "Wherefore dost thou ask me, seeing the Lord is gone from thee, and is thine enemy? Even the Lord hath done unto him as he spake by mine hand: for the Lord will rent thy kingdom out of thine hand, and give it to thy neighbor David, because thou obeyedst not the voice of the Lord, etc." This (I say) is no phrase of a devil, but of a cozener, which knew before what Samuel had prophesied concerning Saul's destruction. For it is the devil's condition to allure the people into wickedness, and not in this sort to admonish, warn,

---

[1] **color:** disguise. [2] **cozenage:** deception. [3] **packing:** conspiring. [4] **declining:** turning away.

and rebuke them for evil. And the popish[5] writers confess that the devil would have been gone at the first naming of God. If it be said that it was at God's special commandment and will that Samuel or the devil should be raised to propound[6] this admonition, to the profit of all posterity, I answer that then he would rather have done it by some of his living prophets and that Satan had not been so fit an instrument for that purpose. After this, falleth the witch (I would say Samuel) into the vein of prophesying, and speaketh to Saul on this wise:[7] "The Lord will rent thy kingdom out of thine hand, and give it to thy neighbor David, because thou obeyedst not the voice of the Lord, nor executedst his fierce wrath upon the Amalekites: therefore hath the Lord done this unto thee this day. Moreover, the Lord will deliver thee into the hands of the Philistines, and tomorrow shalt thou and thy sons be with me, and the Lord shall give the host of Israel into the hands of the Philistines." What could Samuel have said more?

Methinks the devil would have used another order,[8] encouraging Saul rather than rebuking him for his evil. The devil is craftier than to leave such an admonition to all posterities, as should be prejudicial unto his kingdom and also be void of all impiety. But so divine a sentence maketh much for the maintenance of the witch's credit and to the advancement of her gains. Howbeit, concerning the verity of this prophecy, there be many disputable questions. First, whether the battle were fought the next day; secondly, whether all his sons were killed with him; item,[9] whether they went to heaven or hell together, as being with Samuel they must be in heaven, and being with Satan they must be in hell. But although every part of this prophecy were false, as that all his sons were not slain (Ishbosheth living and reigning in Israel two years after Saul's death) and that the battle was not on the morrow, and that wicked Saul, after that he had killed himself, was not with good Samuel; yet this witch did give a shrewd guess to the sequel. Which whether it were true or false pertains not to my purpose, and therefore I will omit it. But as touching the opinion of them that say it was the devil because that such things came to pass, I would fain know of them where they learn that devils foreknow things to come. If they say he guesseth only upon probabilities, the witch may also do the like. . . . And if this exposition like you not, I can easily frame[10] myself to the opinion of some of great learning, expounding this place, and that with great probability, in this sort: to wit, that this pythonist[11] being ventriloqua, that is, speaking as it were from the bottom of her belly, did cast herself into a trance and so

---

[5] **popish:** i.e., Roman Catholic. [6] **propound:** put forth. [7] **on this wise:** in this manner. [8] **order:** method. [9] **item:** likewise. [10] **frame:** conform. [11] **pythonist:** deceiving ventriloquist, soothsayer.

abused Saul, answering to Saul in Samuel's name in her counterfeit hollow voice as the wench of Westwell[12] spake, whose history I have rehearsed before at large. . . .

[In chapter 14 Scot argues that miracles have ceased in the modern world, despite the attempts of knavish priests to pass off their tricks as actual ghosts.]

Of vain apparitions; how people have been brought to fear bugs,[13] which is partly reformed by preaching of the gospel; the true effect of Christ's miracles.

THE FIFTEENTH CHAPTER

But certainly, some one knave in a white sheet hath cozened and abused many thousands that way, specially when Robin Goodfellow[14] kept such a coil[15] in the country. But you shall understand that these bugs specially are spied and feared of sick folk, children, women, and cowards, which through weakness of mind and body are shaken with vain dreams and continual fear. The Scythians,[16] being a stout and a warlike nation (as divers writers report) never see any vain sights or spirits. It is a common saying: a lion feareth no bugs. But in our childhood our mothers' maids have so terrified us with an ugly devil having horns on his head, fire in his mouth, and a tail in his breech, eyes like a basin, fangs like a dog, claws like a bear, a skin like a Niger,[17] and a voice roaring like a lion, whereby we start and are afraid when we hear one cry "boo." And they have so fraid[18] us with bull-beggars,[19] spirits, witches, urchins,[20] elves, hags, fairies, satyrs,[21] pans,[22] fauns, sylens,[23] Kit with the canstick,[24] tritons,[25] centaurs, dwarfs, giants, imps,[26] calkers,[27] conjurors, nymphs,[28] changelings,[29] incubus,[30] Robin Goodfellow, the spoorn,[31] the mare,[32] the man in the oak,[33] the hell-wain,[34] the

---

[12] **wench of Westwell:** earlier, Scot tells the story of a young woman from Westwell in Kent, who in 1574 practiced "diabolical witchcraft and ventriloquy" by pretending to be possessed by Satan and answering questions in his voice. [13] **bugs:** bugbears, hobgoblins. [14] **Robin Goodfellow:** a mischievous fairy or goblin believed to haunt the English countryside. [15] **kept such a coil:** made such a disturbance. [16] **Scythians:** ancient nomadic people from what is today Russia. [17] **Niger:** African, Negro. [18] **fraid:** frightened. [19] **bull-beggars:** specters. [20] **urchins:** goblins who took the form of hedgehogs. [21] **satyrs:** part-human, part-bestial woodland demons. [22] **pans:** in Greek mythology, Pan was a faun (half-man, half-goat) and shepherd. [23] **sylens:** kinds of satyrs. [24] **Kit with the canstick:** Jack-o'-lantern (literally, Christopher with the candlestick). [25] **tritons:** sea-gods or sea-monsters. [26] **imps:** little devils. [27] **calkers:** astrologers. [28] **nymphs:** female spirits. [29] **changelings:** children left by fairies in exchange for stolen children. [30] **incubus:** evil spirit. [31] **spoorn:** phantom. [32] **mare:** spirit that produces a feeling of suffocation in a sleeping person (nightmare). [33] **man in the oak:** spirit supposed to inhabit an oak tree. [34] **hell-wain:** phantom wagon seen in the sky at night.

fire-drake,[35] the puckle,[36] Tom Thumb,[37] hobgoblin, Tom tumbler,[38] boneless,[39] and such other bugs, that we are afraid of our own shadows. In so much as some never fear the devil but in a dark night, and then a polled[40] sheep is a perilous beast, and many times is taken for our father's soul, specially in a churchyard, where a right hardy man heretofore scant[41] durst[42] pass by night but his hair would stand upright. For right grave writers report that spirits most often and specially take the shape of women appearing to monks, etc.; and of beasts, dogs, swine, horses, goats, cats, hares; of fowls, as crows, night owls, and shriek owls; but they delight most in the likeness of snakes and dragons. Well, thanks be to God, this wretched and cowardly infidelity,[43] since the preaching of the gospel, is in part forgotten, and doubtless the rest of those illusions will in short time (by God's grace) be detected and vanish away. . . .

Witches' miracles compared to Christ's; that God is the creator of all things; of Apollo, and of his names and portraiture.

THE SIXTEENTH CHAPTER

If this witch of Endor had performed that which many conceive of the matter, it might have been compared with the raising up of Lazarus.[44] I pray you, is not the converting of water into milk as hard a matter as the turning of water into wine? And yet, as you may read in the gospel, that Christ did the one, as his first miracle;[45] so you may read in *M. Mal.*[46] and in Bodin,[47] that witches can easily do the other, yea, and that which is a great deal more, of water they can make butter. But to avoid all cavils,[48] and lest there should appear more matter in Christ's miracle than the others, you shall find in *M. Mal.* that they can change water into wine, and what is it to attribute to a creature the power and work of the creator, if this be not? Christ saith, "Opera quae ego facio nemo potest facere."[49] Creation of substance was never granted to man nor angel; ergo,[50] neither to witch nor devil. For God

---

[35] **fire-drake:** will-o'-the-wisp.   [36] **puckle:** evil spirit or demon.   [37] **Tom Thumb:** dwarf of popular fable.   [38] **Tom tumbler:** imp or devil.   [39] **boneless:** boneless spirit, perhaps in the form of a snake.   [40] **polled:** shorn.   [41] **scant:** hardly.   [42] **durst:** dares.   [43] **infidelity:** lack of true religious faith.   [44] **Lazarus:** Jesus raised Lazarus from the dead (John 11:41–44).   [45] **first miracle:** Jesus turns water into wine at a wedding celebration (John 2:1–11).   [46] **M. Mal.:** *Malleus Maleficarum,* or "The Hammer of Witches," a late-fifteenth-century treatise on witchcraft.   [47] **Bodin:** Jean Bodin (1530–1596), French political philosopher who wrote *La Démonomanie des Sorciers* (On Witchcraft)   [48] **cavils:** frivolous objections.   [49] **Opera . . . facere:** "The work that I do nobody can do" (Latin); loose paraphrase of John 10:25, in which Jesus says, "the works that I do in my Father's name, they bear witness of me."   [50] **ergo:** therefore (Latin).

is the only giver of life and being, and by him all things are made, visible and invisible. Finally, this woman of Endor is in the scripture[51] called Pythonissa, whereby it may appear that she was but a very cozener. For Pytho[52] himself, whereof pythonissa is derived, was a counterfeit. And the original story of Apollo, who was called Pytho because he killed a serpent of that name, is but a poetical fable. For the poets say he was the god of music, physic, poetry, and shooting. In heaven he is called Sol,[53] in earth Liber Pater,[54] in hell Apollo. He flourisheth always with perpetual youth, and therefore he is painted without a beard: his picture was kept as an oracle-giver, and the priests that attended thereon at Delphos were cozeners, and called pythonists of[55] Pytho, as papists of Papa.[56] And afterwards all women that used that trade were named pythonissae, as was this woman of Endor. But because it concerneth this matter, I will briefly note the opinions of divers learned men, and certain other proofs which I find in the scripture, touching the ceasing of miracles, prophecies, and oracles.

[51] **in the scripture:** in the Latin Vulgate Bible, 1 Chronicles 10:13.   [52] **Pytho:** in the Latin Vulgate Bible, *pythones* are demons or the soothsayers possessed by them (Isaiah 19:3); in Greek mythology, Pytho is also the name of the serpent-god of Delphi, whom Apollo slew before establishing his oracle there.   [53] **Sol:** the sun.   [54] **Liber Pater:** the "Free [Unrestrained] Father" (Latin), actually identified with Bacchus, god of wine.   [55] **of:** after.   [56] **Papa:** the Pope.

→ THOMAS MIDDLETON

From The Second Maiden's Tragedy   *1611*

Thomas Middleton (1580–1627) was one of the most prolific and important playwrights of the early seventeenth century. While still a student at Oxford University, he published two poems, and by 1602 he had begun writing for the Admiral's Men, the chief rivals of Shakespeare's playing company, the Chamberlain's Men. As the *Dictionary of National Biography* observes, "Middleton and Shakespeare were the only writers of the English Renaissance who created plays that are still considered masterpieces in all four major dramatic genres: comedy, history, tragedy, and tragicomedy." Middleton specialized in satirical comedies set in contemporary London, such as *The Roaring Girl* (1611) and *A Chaste Maid in Cheapside* (1613), as well as tragedies of courtly vice, such as *The Revenger's Tragedy* (1606), *Women Beware Women* (1621), and *A Game at Chess* (1624).

Thomas Middleton, *The Second Maiden's Tragedy,* ed. Anne Lancashire (Baltimore: Johns Hopkins University Press, 1978), 208–17, 249–55, 259–60.

The Second Maiden's Tragedy, which exists in a single untitled and unattributed seventeenth-century manuscript, was first published in the nineteenth century. The strange title by which the play has come to be known derives from an annotation on the manuscript by the seventeenth-century dramatic censor, Sir George Buc. Although other candidates, including Shakespeare, have been advanced as the author of the play, scholarly consensus has settled on Middleton.

The Second Maiden's Tragedy delves deeper than *The Winter's Tale* into the troubling implications of paying devotion to a dead woman. At the beginning of the play, the "Tyrant" has usurped the rightful king, Govianus, and sets about to marry Govianus's betrothed, the "Lady." The Lady commits suicide to preserve her chastity, but, refusing to be denied his pleasures, the Tyrant removes her corpse from the tomb and brings it to his chamber, where he embraces and kisses it. The Tyrant decides to employ an artist to paint the Lady's corpse so that it will have the appearance of life. After the Ghost of the Lady informs Govianus of the Tyrant's outrageous behavior, Govianus disguises himself as an artist and applies poisoned paint to the corpse's face; when the Tyrant kisses the corpse, he dies and Govianus is restored to the throne. A violent revenger in the tradition of Hamlet, Govianus thus occupies ambiguous moral ground. As Susan Zimmerman argues, Govianus's "attachment to a spirit he envisages in material terms and to whom he has an overtly sensual devotion compromises his outrage at the Tyrant's necrophilia" (99).

In the scenes below, consider how Govianus's and the Tyrant's expressions of desire for the deceased Lady compare with Leontes' expressions of desire for Hermione. Are Leontes' longings any less sensual than those of the men in Middleton's tragedy? In *The Second Maiden's Tragedy*, there is no Paulina figure. What is the significance of Paulina's role in shaping the encounter between Leontes and his (supposedly) dead wife? How does the different use of artistic resources by Paulina and Govianus reflect their different motives in staging a theatrical spectacle centered on a dead woman?

Significantly, Hermione implies that she herself has used some form of artifice to wait out the time until her daughter's return. In her final lines, Hermione claims that she has "preserved" herself in the hope of being reunited with her daughter (5.3.128). To be "preserved" means to be "kept safe" or "kept in existence," but also has a more specialized meaning derived from cooking: "treated so as to resist putrefaction," as in preserved fruit (*Oxford English Dictionary*). Might Hermione's ascetic preservation of her own body — sealing herself away for sixteen years from contact with the outside world, as if she were indeed living all that time as a statue — be understood as an attempt to freeze time? If so, how does Hermione's desire to freeze time compare with the Tyrant's attempt to disguise the putrefaction of his mistress's corpse by having her face painted in lifelike colors? In fact, the Tyrant uses the same language as Hermione when he recalls the precedent of Herod, who "preserved . . . in honey" the dead body of Mariamne (4.3.119; see p. 396). Do Paulina and Hermione use theatrical artifice to arrest the processes of nature and time? If so, is their attempt at preserving time fully restorative and redemptive, or is there something pathetic, perhaps even tragic, about it?

From *The Second Maiden's Tragedy*

[ACT 4, SCENE 3]

Enter the Tyrant [with Soldiers] again at a farther door, which opened, brings them to the tomb where Lady lies buried. The tomb here discovered,[1] richly set forth.

TYRANT: Softly, softly.
Let's give this place the peace that it requires.
The vaults e'en chide our steps with murmuring sounds,
For making bold so late. — It must be done.
1ST SOLDIER: I hear nothing but the whorish ghost of a quean[2] I   5
kept once. She swore she would so haunt me I should
never pray in quiet for her,[3] and I have kept myself from
church this fifteen year to prevent her.
TYRANT: The monument woos me; I must run and kiss it.
Now trust me if the tears do not e'en stand   10
Upon the marble. What slow springs[4] have I!
'Twas weeping to itself before I came.
How pity strikes e'en through insensible things
And makes them shame our dullness!
Thou house of silence, and the calms of rest   15
After tempestuous life, I claim of thee
A mistress, one of the most beautiful sleepers
That ever lay so cold, not yet due to thee
By natural death, but cruelly forced hither
Many a fair year before the world could spare her.   20
We miss her 'mongst the glories of our court
When they be numbered up. All thy still strength,
Thou grey-eyed monument, shall not keep her from us.
[*To 2nd Soldier*] Strike, villain, though the echo rail[5] us all
Into ridiculous deafness! Pierce the jaws   25
Of this cold, ponderous creature.
2ND SOLDIER: Sir!
TYRANT: Why strik'st thou not?

---

[1] **discovered:** revealed.   [2] **quean:** prostitute.   [3] **for her:** because of her.   [4] **springs:** i.e., for weeping.   [5] **rail:** speak abusive language.

2ND SOLDIER: I shall not hold the axe fast,⁶ I'm afraid, sir.

TYRANT: O shame of men! A soldier, and so limber?⁷

2ND SOLDIER: 'Tis out of my element⁸ to be in a church, sir.
  Give me the open field and turn me loose, sir.   30

TYRANT: True, there thou hast room enough to run away.
  [*To 1st Soldier*] Take thou the axe from him.

1ST SOLDIER: I beseech your grace,
  'Twill come to a worse hand. You'll find us all
  Of one mind for⁹ the church, I can assure you, sir.

TYRANT: [*To 3rd Soldier*]   Nor thou?

3RD SOLDIER: I love not to disquiet ghosts,   35
  Of any people living; that's my humor,¹⁰ sir!

TYRANT: O slaves of one opinion! [*To 2nd Soldier*] Give me't from thee,
  Thou man made out of fear! [*Seizes axe.*]

2ND SOLDIER: [*Aside*]   By my faith, I'm glad
  I'm rid on't. I that was ne'er before in cathedral
  And have the batt'ring of a lady's tomb   40
  Lie hard upon my conscience at first coming —
  I should get much by that! It shall be a warning to me;
  I'll ne'er come here again.

TYRANT: [*Striking at tomb*]   No, wilt not yield?
  Art thou so loath to part from her?

1ST SOLDIER: [*Aside*]   Life, what means he?
  Has he no feeling with him?¹¹ By this light, if I be   45
  not afraid to stay any longer, I'm a stone-cutter. Very
  fear will go nigh¹² to turn me of¹³ some religion or other,
  and so make me forfeit my lieutenantship.

TYRANT: [*Loosening stone*]   O, have we got the mastery? Help, you vassals!¹⁴
  Freeze you in idleness and can see us sweat?   50

2ND SOLDIER: We sweat with fear as much as work can make us.

TYRANT: Remove the stone that I may see my mistress.
  Set to your hands, you villains, and that nimbly,
  Or the same axe shall make you all fly open!

SOLDIERS: O, good my lord!

TYRANT: I must not be delayed.   55

---

⁶ **fast:** firmly.   ⁷ **limber:** limp.   ⁸ **out of my element:** outside of my usual experience or surroundings.   ⁹ **for:** regarding.   ¹⁰ **humor:** disposition.   ¹¹ **feeling with him:** capacity for emotion.   ¹² **nigh:** near.   ¹³ **turn me of:** make me convert to.   ¹⁴ **vassals:** slaves.

IST SOLDIER: This is ten thousand times worse than en'tring upon a
    breach.[15]
    'Tis the first stone that ever I took off
    From any lady; marry, I have brought 'em many:
    Fair diamonds, sapphires, rubies. [*They remove the stone.*]
TYRANT: O blessed object!
    I shall never be weary to behold thee;   60
    I could eternally stand thus and see thee.
    Why, 'tis not possible death should look so fair;
    Life is not more illustrious when health smiles on't.
    She's only pale, the color of the court,[16]
    And most attractive; mistresses most strive for't   65
    And their lascivious servants best affect[17] it.
    Where be these lazy hands again?
SOLDIERS: My lord!
TYRANT: Take up her body.
IST SOLDIER: How, my lord!
TYRANT: Her body!
IST SOLDIER: She's dead, my lord!
TYRANT: True; if she were alive,
    Such slaves as you should not come near to touch her.   70
    Do't, and with all best reverence; place her here.
IST SOLDIER: Not only, sir, with reverence, but with fear.
    You shall have more than your own asking once.
    I am afraid of nothing but she'll rise
    At the first jog,[18] and save us all a labor.   75
2ND SOLDIER: Then we were best take her up and never touch her!
IST SOLDIER: Life, how can that be? Does fear make thee mad?
    I've took up[19] many a woman in my days,
    But never with less pleasure, I protest!
TYRANT: O, the moon rises! What reflection   80
    Is thrown about this sanctifièd building
    E'en in a twinkling! How the monuments glister,
    As if death's palaces were all massy[20] silver
    And scorned the name of marble! Art thou cold?
    I have no faith in't yet; I believe none.   85

---

[15] **en'tring upon a breach:** entering through a hole in an enemy fortification.   [16] **color of the court:** pale skin was the ideal of feminine beauty.   [17] **best affect:** most strongly desire.   [18] **jog:** shake.   [19] **took up:** had sex with.   [20] **massy:** solid, not hollow.

Madam! 'Tis I, sweet lady. Prithee speak!
'Tis thy love calls on thee — thy king, thy servant.
No? Not a word? All prisoners to pale silence?
I'll prove[21] a kiss.

1ST SOLDIER: [*Aside*] Here's a fine chill venery!
    'Twould make a pander's heels ache.[22] I'll be sworn   90
    All my teeth chatter in my head to see't.

TYRANT: By th'mass, thou'rt cold indeed! Beshrew thee for't!
    Unkind to thine own blood? Hard-hearted lady!
    What injury hast thou offered to the youth
    And pleasure of thy days! Refuse the court   95
    And steal to this hard lodging: was that wisdom?
    O, I could chide thee with mine eye brimful,
    And weep out my forgiveness when I ha' done.
    Nothing hurt thee but want[23] of woman's counsel.
    Hadst thou but asked th'opinion of most ladies,   100
    Thou'dst never come to this! They would have told thee
    How dear a treasure life and youth had been.
    'Tis that they fear to lose; the very name
    Can make more gaudy tremblers in a minute
    Than heaven or sin or hell: those are last thought on.   105
    And where got'st thou such boldness from the rest
    Of all thy timorous sex, to do a deed here
    Upon thyself, would plunge[24] the world's best soldier
    And make him twice bethink him, and again,
    And yet give over? Since thy life has left me,   110
    I'll clasp the body for the spirit that dwelt in't,
    And love the house still for the mistress' sake.
    Thou art mine now, spite of destruction
    And Govianus, and I will possess thee.
    I once read of a Herod,[25] whose affection   115
    Pursued a virgin's love, as I did thine,
    Who for the hate she owed him killed herself
    (As thou too rashly didst), without all pity.
    Yet he preserved her body dead in honey,
    And kept her long after her funeral.   120
    But I'll unlock the treasure house of art

---

[21] **prove:** try. [22] **'Twould make a pander's heels ache:** even a pimp would flee from this sexual encounter. [23] **want:** lack. [24] **plunge:** overpower, confound. [25] **Herod:** king of Judaea (first century B.C.E.).

With keys of gold, and bestow all on thee.
Here, slaves, receive her humbly from our arms.
Upon your knees, you villains! All's too little,
If you should sweep the pavement with your lips.   125
IST SOLDIER: [Aside]   What strange brooms he invents!
TYRANT: So, reverently
Bear her before us gently to our palace.
Place you the stone again where first we found it.

Exeunt [with body]. Manet [26] *1 Soldier.*

IST SOLDIER: Life, must this on now to deceive all comers,
And cover emptiness? 'Tis for all the world   130
Like a great city-pie[27] brought to a table
Where there be many hands that lay about;
The lid's shut close when all the meat's picked out.
Yet stands to make a show and cozen people.   *Exit.*

.   .   .   .

[In the last scene of the play, Govianus, disguised as an artist, offers his services to the Tyrant.]

[ACT 5, SCENE 2]

TYRANT: Let but thy art hide death upon her face,
That now looks fearfully on us, and but strive
To give our eye delight in that pale part
Which draws so many pities[28] from these springs,
And thy reward for't shall outlast thy end,[29]   85
And reach to thy friend's fortunes, and his friend.[30]
GOVIANUS: Say you so, my lord? I'll work out my heart, then,
But I'll show art enough.
TYRANT: About it, then.
I never wished so seriously for health
After long sickness.   90
GOVIANUS: [Aside]   A religious trembling shakes me by the hand
And bids me put by such unhallowed business,
But revenge calls for't, and it must go forward.

---

[26] **Manet:** remains.   [27] **city-pie:** pie baked in London.   [28] **pities:** i.e., tears of pity.   [29] **outlast thy end:** continue past your death.   [30] **friend:** friend or kinsman.

'Tis time the spirit of my love[31] took rest;
Poor soul, 'tis weary, much abused and toiled.

                                                              [Paints the face of the body.]   95

TYRANT: Could I now send for one to renew heat
    Within her bosom, that were a fine workman!
    I should but too much love him. But alas,
    'Tis as unpossible for living fire
    To take hold there,   100
    As for dead ashes to burn back again
    Into those hard, tough bodies whence they fell.
    Life is removed from her now, as the warmth
    Of the bright sun from us when it makes winter
    And kills with unkind coldness. So is't yonder;   105
    An everlasting frost hangs now upon her.
    And as in such a season men will force
    A heat into their bloods with exercise,
    In spite of extreme weather, so shall we
    By art force beauty on yon lady's face   110
    Though death sit frowning on't a storm of hail
    To beat it off. Our pleasure shall prevail.

GOVIANUS: My lord!

TYRANT: Hast done so soon?

GOVIANUS: That's as your grace
    Gives approbation.

TYRANT: O, she lives again!
    She'll presently speak to me. Keep her up;   115
    I'll have her swoon no more; there's treachery in't.
    Does she not feel warm to thee?

GOVIANUS: Very little, sir.

TYRANT: The heat wants cherishing,[32] then. Our arms and lips
    Shall labor life into her. Wake, sweet mistress!
    'Tis I that call thee at the door of life.
                   [Kisses the body.] Ha!   120
    I talk so long to death, I'm sick myself.
    Methinks an evil scent still follows me.

GOVIANUS: Maybe 'tis nothing but the color, sir,
    That I laid on.

TYRANT: Is that so strong?

GOVIANUS: Yes, faith, sir.

---

[31] **my love:** i.e., my lover, the Lady.   [32] **cherishing:** keeping warm, caressing.

'Twas the best poison I could get for money.   125

                        [*Throws off his disguise.*]

TYRANT: Govianus!
GOVIANUS: O thou sacrilegious villain!
  Thou thief of rest, robber of monuments!
  Cannot the body after funeral
  Sleep in the grave, for thee?[33] Must it be raised
  Only to please the wickedness of thine eye?   130
  Does all things end with death, and not thy lust?
  Hast thou devised a new way to damnation,
  More dreadful than the soul of any sin
  Did ever pass yet between earth and hell?
  Dost strive to be particularly plagued   135
  Above all ghosts beside? Is thy pride such
  Thou scorn'st a partner in thy torments too?

. . . .

[As Govianus defends his dedication to his mistress, the Ghost of the Lady enters *"in the same form as the (body of the) Lady is dressed in the chair."*]

GOVIANUS: Welcome to mine eyes
  As is the dayspring[34] from the morning's womb   155
  Unto that wretch whose nights are tedious,
  As liberty to captives, health to laborers,
  And life still to old people, never weary on't!
  So welcome art thou to me! The deed's done,
  Thou queen of spirits; he has his end upon him.   160
  Thy body shall return to rise again,[35]
  For thy abuser falls, and has no pow'r
  To vex thee farther now.
LADY: My truest love,
  Live ever honored here, and blessed above.   [*Exit.*]

. . . .

[As the Tyrant dies, the Nobles enter and proclaim Govianus their king.]

GOVIANUS: Well, he's gone,
  And all the kingdom's evils perish with him.

---

[33] **for thee:** because of you.   [34] **dayspring:** dawn.   [35] **return to rise again:** i.e., return to the grave to be resurrected on judgment day.

And since the body of that virtuous lady   195
Is taken from her rest, in memory
Of her admirèd mistress, 'tis our will
It receive honor dead, as it took part
With us in all afflictions when it lived.
Here place her in this throne; crown her our queen,   200
The first and last that ever we make ours,
Her constancy strikes so much firmness in us.
That honor done, let her be solemnly borne
Unto the house of peace from whence she came
As queen of silence.

The Spirit [of the Lady] enters again and stays to go out with the body, as it were attending it.

              O, welcome, blessed spirit!   205
Thou need'st not mistrust me; I have a care
As jealous[36] as thine own. We'll see it done
And not believe report. Our zeal is such
We cannot reverence chastity too much.
Lead on!   210
I would those ladies that fill honor's rooms
Might all be borne so honest to their tombs.

Recorders or other solemn music plays them out.

FINIS.

[36] **jealous:** devoted.

Eroticizing the Statue

          O, she's warm!
If this be magic, let it be an art
Lawful as eating.   (5.3.109–111)

Can statues be sexy? They could be, according to the Puritan clergyman John Rainolds, who attacked the London theater by comparing the erotic appeal of cross-dressed boy actors to the erotic appeal of beautiful statues. In *The Overthrow of Stage Plays* (1599), Rainolds warns that "men may be ravished with love of stones, of dead stuff, framed by cunning gravers to beautiful women's likeness . . . [so also] the cladding of youths in such attire is an occasion of drawing and provoking corruptly minded men to most heinous wickedness" (quoted in Zimmerman 93). In short, feminine trappings could move men to lust, even if a male body or a piece of stone lay beneath that lovely exterior. Rainolds might have illustrated this theory through Ovid's myth of Pygmalion, the "cunning graver" who falls in love with a statue of his own making — except for the fact that Pygmalion's "wicked" desire appears to be justified when Venus transforms the statue into a living woman, who then becomes Pygmalion's wife. The Pygmalion myth seems an indisputable analogue for the statue scene in *The Winter's Tale*, but how are we to understand the implications of the parallel between Pygmalion and Leontes? Is Leontes also "ravished with love of stones"? Is such a love necessarily wicked or transgressive?

→ OVID

From Metamorphoses

1567

Translated by Arthur Golding

The great Roman poet Publius Ovidius Naso (43 B.C.E.–17 C.E.), or Ovid, tells the story of Pygmalion in Book 10 of the *Metamorphoses*, his enormous verse account of the transformations undergone by the deities and mortals of classical mythology. The *Metamorphoses* was a staple text in the grammar school curriculum of Shakespeare's England. In 1565, Arthur Golding published an English translation of the first four books of *Metamorphoses*; two years later he published the first complete English translation of all fifteen books. Reprinted in 1575, 1584, 1587, 1593, 1603, and 1612, Golding's version exerted a wide influence on Elizabethan authors, including Spenser, Marlowe, and, of course, Shakespeare.

When Golding explains that Book 10 of the *Metamorphoses* "chiefly doth contain one kind of argument / Reproving most prodigious lusts," he links Pygmalion with other figures of sexual transgression who appear in this book: Apollo, who loves the boy Hyacinth, and Myrrha, who commits incest with her father. Moreover, as Lynn Enterline observes, Ovid frames the tale of Pygmalion with various misogynist narratives that tarnish "the luster of a story that otherwise seems to be about love for beautiful form" (19). For instance, Pygmalion's story is related by Orpheus, who persuades men to reject women and love boys; and it is Pygmalion's disgust at the sexual licentiousness of prostitutes that drives him to renounce all women and to seek companionship with an ivory statue.

Ovid, *The XV Books of P. Ovidius Naso, Entitled Metamorphoses, Translated out of Latin into English Meter by Arthur Golding, Gentleman, a Work Very Pleasant and Delectable* (London, 1567); STC 18956; sigs. R7r–R7v.

Nonetheless, Ovid's tale of a man who falls in love with a statue has a more positive outcome than one might have thought possible, for Pygmalion winds up in a satisfying relationship with the object of his desire. Shakespeare's contemporary John Marston expresses both admiration and contempt for Pygmalion in his erotic poem *The Metamorphosis of Pygmalion's Image* (1598). Opening the poem with the announcement that his "wanton Muse lasciviously doth sing / Of sportive love," Marston elaborates Pygmalion's attraction to his statue's cheeks, lips, breasts, and thighs. At one point, Marston satirically compares Pygmalion's dotage to the folly of "peevish Papists" (Roman Catholics) who "crouch, and kneel / To some dumb Idol with their offering / As if a senseless carved stone could feel." Nonetheless, in Marston's overtly erotic poem as in Ovid's more modest tale, Pygmalion's idolatry ends happily — and rather conventionally — when his prayers persuade Venus to transform the statue into the living woman who will become his wife.

The moral and sexual ambiguities of the Pygmalion myth richly contextualize the ambiguities of Leontes' encounter with Hermione's statue. Leonard Barkan argues that before his statue can "achieve the miracle of life," Pygmalion must demonstrate his "faith in Venus" and his "capacity for love" ("Living" 644). Likewise, Paulina informs Leontes that in order for Hermione's statue to move, "It is required / You do awake your faith" (5.3.94–95). What kind of faith must Leontes awaken? Does the restoration of Hermione indicate that Leontes has indeed demonstrated a capacity for love? Possibly, but in the overall context of *The Winter's Tale*, the parallel between Pygmalion and Leontes might seem troubling as well as touching. Disgusted with the brazen sexuality of women, Pygmalion devotes himself to a statue that represents his ideal of femininity. What does it mean when an ivory statue represents the ideal woman? Has Hermione returned to Leontes as the male fantasy of the perfect wife? It is important to remember that, unlike Pygmalion's statue, Hermione's "statue" is fashioned not by a man — neither by Leontes nor by the artist Giulio Romano — but by Paulina and Hermione. Does the women's agency in fashioning the statue suggest that they are teaching Leontes a lesson about judging a flesh and blood woman against an impossible standard of perfection?

From *Metamorphoses*

Whom for because Pygmalion saw to lead their life in sin,
Offended with the vice whereof great store is packed within
The nature of the womankind, he led a single life.
And long it was ere[1] he could find in heart to take a wife.
Now in the while by wondrous art an image he did grave   5

---

[1] **ere**: before.

Of such proportion, shape, and grace as nature never gave
Nor can to any woman give. In this his work he took
A certain love. The look of it was right[2] a maiden's look,
And such a one as that ye would believe had life, and that
Would moved be,[3] if womanhood[4] and reverence letted[5] not: 10
So artificial was the work. He wondreth at his art
And of his counterfeited corse[6] conceiveth love in heart.
He often touched it, feeling if the work that he had made
Were very flesh or ivory still. Yet could he not persuade
Himself to think it ivory. For he oftentimes it kissed   15
And thought it kissed him again.[7] He held it by the fist,
And talked to it. He believed his fingers made a dint
Upon her flesh, and feared lest some black or bruised print
Should come by touching overhard. Sometime with pleasant bourds[8]
And wanton toys[9] he dallyingly doth cast forth amorous words.   20
Sometime (the gifts wherein young maids are wonted to delight)
He brought her ouches,[10] fine round stones, and lilies fair and white,
And pretty singing birds, and flowers of thousand sorts and hue,
And painted balls, and amber from the tree distilled new.
In gorgeous garments furthermore he did her also deck,   25
And on her fingers put me[11] rings, and chains about her neck.
Rich pearls were hanging at her ears, and tablets[12] at her breast.
All kind of things became her well. And when she was undressed,
She seemed not less beautiful. He laid her in a bed
The which with scarlet dyed in Tyre[13] was richly overspread,   30
And terming her his bedfellow, he couched down her head
Upon a pillow soft, as though she could have felt the same.
    The feast of Venus hallowed through the isle of Cyprus,[14] came
And bullocks[15] white with gilden horns were slain for sacrifice,
And up to heaven of frankincense the smoky fume did rise.   35
When as Pygmalion having done his duty that same day,
Before the altar standing, thus with fearful heart did say:
"If that you, goddess, can all things give, then let my wife, I pray,"
(He durst not say "be yon same wench of ivory," but) "be like
My wench of ivory." Venus (who was nought at all to seek[16]   40

---

[2] **right**: exactly.   [3] **moved be**: affected by emotion.   [4] **womanhood**: feminine modesty.   [5] **letted**: prevented.   [6] **corse**: body.   [7] **again**: back.   [8] **bourds**: jests.   [9] **toys**: frivolous speeches.
[10] **ouches**: brooches.   [11] **put me**: put ("me" adds emphasis).   [12] **tablets**: jewelry.   [13] **Tyre**: an ancient Phoenician city famous for rare dyes.   [14] **Cyprus**: mythical birthplace of Venus, goddess of love.   [15] **bullocks**: young bulls.   [16] **was nought at all to seek**: i.e., understood very well.

FIGURE 29 *Pieter van der Borcht,* P. Ovidii Nasonis Metamorphoses Expositae *(Antwerp, 1591). This three-part illustration of the Pygmalion myth shows the sculptor carving his statue and praying to a statue of Venus in the background. In the third scene to the right, does Pygmalion lie in bed with the statue or with the living woman into whom Venus has transformed the statue? What is the effect of this ambiguity in our reading of the tale?*

What such a wish as that did mean) then present at her feast,
For handsel[17] of her friendly help did cause three times at least
The fire to kindle and to spire thrice upward in the air.
As soon as he came home, straight way Pygmalion did repair[18]
Unto the image of his wench, and leaning on the bed,
Did kiss her. In her body straight[19] a warmness seemed to spread.   45
He put his mouth again to hers, and on her breast did lay
His hand. The ivory waxed soft: and putting quite away
All hardness, yielded underneath his fingers, as we see
A piece of wax made soft against the sun, or drawn to be   50
In divers[20] shapes by chafing it between one's hands, and so

---

[17] **handsel:** good omen.   [18] **repair:** return.   [19] **straight:** immediately.   [20] **divers:** various.

To serve to uses. He amazed stood wavering to and fro
'Tween joy, and fear to be beguiled; again he burnt in love,
Again with feeling he began his wished hope to prove.[21]
He felt it very flesh indeed. By laying on his thumb,   55
He felt her pulses beating. Then he stood no longer dumb
But thanked Venus with his heart and at the length he laid
His mouth to hers who was as then become a perfect maid.
She felt the kiss, and blushed thereat: and lifting fearfully
Her eyelids up, her lover and the light at once did spy.   60
The marriage that herself had made the goddess blessed so,
That when the moon with fulsome light nine times her course had go,[22]
This lady was delivered of a son that Paphus hight,[23]
Of whom the island[24] takes that name.

[21] **to prove:** to experience.   [22] **go:** gone.   [23] **hight:** was called.   [24] **the island:** Paphos (the modern Cyprus), birthplace of Venus.

Artists, Patrons, and Collectors

> Masterly done.
> The very life seems warm upon her lip.   (5.3.65–66)

Having lived in seclusion for sixteen years, Hermione returns as a spectacular work of art created by "that rare Italian master, Julio Romano" (5.2.74). Romano enters the world of the play as a celebrity, the viewing of his new masterpiece eagerly anticipated by savvy courtiers with the "benefit of access" (5.2.84) to Paulina's gallery. Consequently, the perfection of Hermione's statue reflects not only the skill of the artist, but also the taste of those who commission and admire it, namely, Paulina and the Sicilian court. Paulina's presentation of Hermione as a valuable artwork thus raises questions about the cultural status of Giulio Romano and of art collecting more generally in early modern England.

To begin with, Romano hardly seem likes the obvious choice for the carver of Hermione's statue. Whereas the play takes place in ancient Sicilia, Romano (c.1499–1546) was a sixteenth-century artist who was born in Rome and worked in Rome and in the northern town of Mantua. Moreover, Romano was known primarily as a painter and architect, not as a sculptor; his contemporary Michelangelo, who was famous for his lifelike work in stone, would have been a more fitting choice as the creator of Hermione's statue. Most surprisingly, Romano's fame during Shakespeare's lifetime derived in large part from his contributions to *I Modi* (The Positions), a collection of pornographic images engraved in 1524 from Romano's original drawings. Shakespeare might well have known of Romano's responsibility for these scandalously frank depictions of couples enjoying sex in various positions (Sokol 102–04). Romano's association with pornography almost seems designed to challenge the image of cold chastity conveyed by Hermione's embodiment in stone (Figure 30).

Shakespeare might also have encountered Romano in a more respectable source, Giorgio Vasari's biography of the most prominent Italian artists of the age, *The Lives of the Most Eminent Painters, Sculptors, and Architects*, originally published in 1550. Vasari praises Romano for his "almost incredible" ability to "imitate nature," as with the picture of a cat "that was so natural that it appeared to be truly alive" (124, 123). As Leonard Barkan observes, "To a reader of Vasari — especially one who had never seen any of the artist's work — Giulio Romano would appear as a great and godlike creator, master of many arts and worthy opponent of Nature herself as a creator" ("Living" 657). One of Leontes' courtiers asserts that could Romano "put breath into his work," he "would beguile Nature of her custom, so perfectly he is her ape" (5.2.75–76). That Hermione's statue is described as newly "performed" by Romano also associates the sculptor's naturalistic art with Shakespeare's living art of theater (5.2.74).

It is difficult to say what Shakespeare knew about Romano's work. There was no English translation of Vasari's *Lives* prior to 1622, when Henry Peacham included a few of its biographical sketches in his educational treatise, *The Complete Gentleman* (Ziegler 205). According to Georgiana Ziegler, however, Shakespeare might have come across Romano's name in an earlier educational treatise, *The Necessary, Fit, and Convenient Education of a Young Gentlewoman*, which was translated into English in 1598 from an Italian text by Giovanni Michele Bruto. At one point, Bruto advises parents to choose a tutor who can model virtuous behavior for their daughter, in the same way that they would show the "patterns" of Romano or Michelangelo to "an excellent painter that should paint the hall and chambers of your house" (quoted in Ziegler 206). Whether or not Shakespeare was familiar with Bruto's treatise, it is significant that writers such as Bruto and Peacham considered knowledge of fine art an important component of an elite education — and of the cultural privilege such an education bestowed. In *The Winter's Tale*, Romano's celebrity as a "rare Italian master" suggests that the meaning of the court's encounter with Hermione's statue cannot be separated from the matter of the social, political, and economic value of fine art.

The social value of Hermione's statue as a commissioned piece of statuary displayed in a gallery would have been especially noteworthy in early-seventeenth-century England, before collecting statues had become a

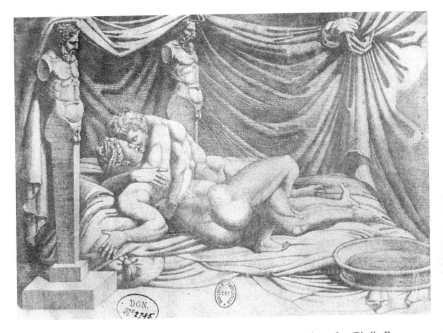

FIGURE 30 *Marcantonio Raimondi,* I Modi, *Position 1, engraving after Giulio Romano (Bibliothèque national de France). One of the less graphic illustrations in* I Modi, *this drawing provides a gloss on the eroticism of the Pygmalion story, as well as suggesting a bawdy connotation to Leontes' admiration of the "natural posture" of Hermione's statue (5.3.23).*

common aristocratic pursuit. As Stephen Orgel remarks, "Paulina is presented in the play as a connoisseur, the owner of a collection of artistic rarities; she knows what she's doing, and her expertise reminds us that the collecting instinct was starting to burgeon in the England of 1610" (Orgel, "Idols" 251). Leontes praises the "many singularities" (5.3.12) or rare artworks that fill Paulina's gallery. Despite her modesty in referring to Hermione's statue as "my poor image," Paulina declares that it is *her* possession — even "the stone is mine" (5.3.57–58). Orgel proposes a contemporary model for Paulina in the countess of Arundel. The earl and countess of Arundel owned "the greatest collection of art works in Jacobean England," including several of Romano's drawings (Orgel, "Idols," 251). Moreover, prior to the earl of Arundel's collection of Greek and Roman marbles, "not a single ancient statue — not even a single *copy* of an ancient statue — had been imported into England" (Smith, "Sermons" 1). Orgel makes the crucial point about the social significance of such collections: "Increasingly in this period great art was felt, in a way that was at once pragmatic and mystical, to be a manifestation of the power and authority of its possessor," especially when that possessor was an aristocrat or monarch (*Imagining* 122). Through her ownership of Hermione's statue, does Paulina achieve a "power and authority" that competes with Leontes' power and authority as king?

The unique circumstances surrounding Paulina's display of Hermione's statue enhance the remarkable aesthetic experience she provides the Sicilian court. Although it is displayed in a gallery like a "royal piece" of ancient Roman statuary (5.3.38), Hermione's statue differs in many respects from the archeological treasures collected by the earl of Arundel. As Leonard Barkan explains, the ancient Roman statuary widely excavated during the Renaissance was almost always broken; consequently, "the sheer plurality of possibilities" for identifying a stone fragment as one figure or another meant that "statues were places of disputed and disputable signification" (*Unearthing* 128). Hermione's statue is not an excavated work from an ancient culture but a newly commissioned work; it depicts not a mythological personage whose identity might be disputed but an actual person intimately known to its audience; and it is an original piece with no copies.

In all these ways, Hermione's statue displays the salient characteristics of Renaissance tomb statuary. Early modern English sculptors were almost exclusively employed in making statues for tombs, not for galleries. Like Hermione's statue, presumably a marble figure adorned with "oily painting" to give the illusion of "ruddiness upon her lip" (5.3.83, 81), Renaissance tomb sculptures were painted in colors. For these reasons, Catherine Belsey argues that Hermione's statue might have been presented on stage as if it were a tomb effigy. Unlike Hermione, who is clearly standing, most tomb effigies in the period were kneeling or recumbent figures. Nonetheless, Belsey observes a tantalizing parallel to *The Winter's Tale* in the 1605 play *The Trial of Chivalry*, in which a character who is thought to be dead poses as a kneeling marble effigy on a funeral monument and comes to life after the woman he loves expresses remorse at his death. Belsey concludes that the "moment would be spectacular indeed if Hermione's monumental body rose from her tomb to be reunited with her husband and child" (120).

Although Hermione's statue resembles Renaissance tomb effigies in certain respects, the simplicity of its presentation does not correspond to the design of funeral monuments intended to commemorate aristocratic families. Such tombs were elaborate structures typically featuring "a Gothic canopy" or a "classical 'triumphal arch'" in which the effigy posed (Smith, "Sermons" 3). The statue of the deceased was usually surrounded with "as many armorial bearings as the family could decently muster"; in this way, "the house was rendered immortal, whatever the fate of individuals" (Howarth 156). Excellent examples of such elaborate monuments are the tombs that King James commissioned in 1605 for his mother, Mary, Queen of Scots, and for Queen Elizabeth. Completed in 1606, Elizabeth's tomb is a massive structure adorned with numerous symbols, arms, and inscriptions (Figure 31). If we take Queen Elizabeth's heavily ornamented monument as

FIGURE 31 *A 1620 engraving by Willem de Passe or Magdalena de Passe of the tomb of Queen Elizabeth I, completed by Maximilian Colte in 1606, Henry VII Chapel, Westminster Abbey.*

a model, Queen Hermione's statue — a free-standing figure ostensibly carved by a famous painter and displayed in a noblewoman's art gallery — hardly resembles a tomb effigy commemorating a member of the royal family.

In Hermione's statue, therefore, Shakespeare has fashioned a remarkably hybrid figure that combines characteristics of an ancient ruin displayed in a gallery and a contemporary tomb effigy displayed in a chapel. Paulina emphasizes the uniqueness of Hermione's statue:

> As she lived peerless,
> So her dead likeness, I do well believe,
> Excels whatever yet you looked upon
> Or hand of man hath done. Therefore I keep it
> Lonely, apart. (5.3.14–18)

What really sets this statue apart, of course, is its incredible fidelity to its subject. Unlike either ancient sculptures or modern funerary sculptures, which fix their subjects at a particular moment in time, Hermione's statue, with its wrinkled face, apparently warm lips and blood-bearing veins, seems impossibly to exist in the present. At once familiar and strange, Hermione's statue is an uncanny work of theatrical art.

→ HENRY PEACHAM

Of Antiquities

1634

A minister's son, Henry Peacham (c. 1576–c. 1643) became a schoolteacher after earning degrees at Cambridge University, but his passion was for the visual arts. His notable works include the *Art of Drawing* (1606); the emblem book *Minerva Britanna* (1612); *The Period of Mourning* (1613), an elegy on the death of Prince Henry; and *The Complete Gentleman* (1622). Having spent several years in Europe, Peacham wrote *The Complete Gentleman* to promote in England the kind of sophisticated education young gentlemen received on the continent: the book covers topics as diverse as the arts and sciences ("Of Poetry," "Of Geometry"), recreation ("Of Fishing"), and comportment ("Of Reputation and Carriage"). The first edition of *The Complete Gentleman*, published in 1622, included a chapter on "Drawing and Painting in Oil," but not on statuary. The book was published in a second edition of 1627, but only in the third edition of 1634 did Peacham include a chapter advocating the nobility of studying and collecting

Henry Peacham, "Of Antiquities" in *The Complete Gentleman, Fashioning Him Absolute in the Most Necessary and Commendable Qualities Concerning Mind or Body that May Be Required in a Noble Gentleman* (London, 1634), STC 19504; sigs. P2v–Q2r.

ancient statues. In "Of Antiquities," excerpted below, Peacham celebrates the first English collectors of ancient Greek and Roman statues, including ruins from Apollo's Temple at Delos.

According to Peacham, the identification of figures was the primary challenge facing the connoisseur anxious to display his artistic knowledge. In the excerpt below, Peacham advises his reader to visit statues "in company of such as are learned in them, and by their help to grow familiar with them, and so practice their acquaintance." How does Paulina help Perdita and Leontes "grow familiar" with Hermione's statue? Would Peacham approve or disapprove of Leontes' and Perdita's responses to Hermione's statue? Peacham's opinions on the "profit of knowing" ancient statuary might also prompt the larger question of what Paulina accomplishes by presenting Leontes with a stone image of Hermione before delivering her to him in her natural state. Why, in short, does she "mock" him "with art" (5.3.68)? What does Paulina have to gain by transforming Hermione into an object of high aesthetic value?

Out of the treasury and storehouse of venerable antiquities, I have selected these three sorts: statues, inscriptions, and coins, desiring you to take a short view of them ere you proceed any further.

The pleasure of them is best known to such as have seen them abroad in France, Spain, and Italy, where the gardens and galleries of great men are beautified and set forth to admiration with these kinds of ornaments. And indeed the possession of such rarities, by reason of their dead[1] costliness, doth properly belong to princes, or rather to princely minds. But the profitable necessity of some knowledge in them will plainly appear in the handling of each particular. Sure I am that he that will travel must both heed them and understand them, if he desire to be thought ingenious, and to be welcome to the owners. For next[2] men and manners,[3] there is nothing fairly more delightful, nothing worthier of observation, than these copies and memorials of men and matters of elder times, whose lively presence is able to persuade a man that he now seeth two thousand years ago. Such as are skilled in them are by the Italians termed *virtuosi*,[4] as if others that either neglect or despise them were idiots or rake-hells.[5] And to say truth, they are somewhat to be excused if they have all *liefhebbers*[6] (as the Dutch call them) in so high estimation, for they themselves are so great lovers of them (and *similis simili gaudet*[7]) that they purchase them at any rate,[8] and lay up mighty treasuries of money in them. Witness that exchequer[9] of metals in the cabinets of the

---

[1] **dead**: absolute. [2] **next**: aside from. [3] **manners**: the customs of a particular society. [4] *virtuosi*: connoisseurs. [5] **rake-hells**: scoundrels. [6] *liefhebbers*: aficionados. [7] *similis simili gaudet*: like takes pleasure in like (Latin proverb). [8] **rate**: price. [9] **exchequer**: treasury.

great Duke of Tuscany, for number and rarity absolutely the best in the world, and not worth so little as 100,000 pounds. For proof whereof, do but consider the number of those which Peter de Medicis[10] lost at Florence upon his banishment and departure thence, namely, a hundred thousand pieces of gold, and silver, and brass, as Philip de Commines[11] reporteth, who mentioneth them as an infinite treasure. And yet Peter was but a private man, and not to be any way compared with the dukes of his house that have been since all of them great and diligent gatherers of all manner of antiquities. And for statues, the Diana of Ephesus[12] in the marble chamber at Paris; Laocoon[13] and Nilus[14] in Belvedere[15] at Rome; and many more, are pieces of inestimable value. But the matchless and never too much admired Toro[16] in Cardinal Farnese's garden outstrippeth all other statues in the world for greatness and workmanship. It comprehendeth[17] a great bull, and (if my memory fail me not) seven or eight figures more as great as the life, all of one entire piece of marble, covered with a house[18] made of purpose, and estimated at the wealth of a kingdom, as the Italians say, or all other statues put together.

And now to spend a few lines on statues in general. I began with them, because I suppose them of greater standing[19] and antiquity than either inscriptions or coins. For, not to speak of inscriptions but of the genus[20] of them, writing and letters, they seem to be so much the later invention of the two (I mean in regard of statues) as it was more obvious and easier for man to figure and represent his outward body than his inward mind. We hear of Laban's idols,[21] long before the two tables[22] of the commandments, and they are the first of either kind mentioned in the holy scriptures. And in the stories of the East and West Indies, we find idols among those savages that had neither writing nor money. Coins I place in the rear, because they are made up of both the other. For most commonly they consist (I speak not of the material but formal part) either of an inscription, or an image, or both; so that the other two may justly claim precedency of coins, seeing they are the ingredient simples[23] that compound them. . . .

---

[10] **Peter de Medicis:** Piero di Lorenzo de' Medici (1471–1503), who was exiled from Florence after an invasion by the French King Charles VIII in 1494. [11] **Philip de Commines:** Philippe de Commines, diplomat and political writer whose *Mémoires* recount events under Kings Louis XI and Charles VIII of France. [12] **Diana of Ephesus:** goddess of virginity and motherhood whose temple stood in the ancient Asian city of Ephesus. [13] **Laocoon:** mythical Trojan priest; a famous ancient Greek statue depicts Laocoon and his two sons being strangled by sea serpents. [14] **Nilus:** in Greek mythology, the god of the Nile river. [15] **Belvedere:** courtyard attached to the Vatican that housed the sculpture collection of Pope Julius II. [16] **Toro:** massive ancient sculpture displayed, in the sixteenth century, in the Palazzo Farnese, Rome. [17] **comprehendeth:** comprises. [18] **house:** framing structure. [19] **standing:** age, status. [20] **genus:** general class. [21] **Laban's idols:** clay or stone images of household gods (Genesis 31). [22] **tables:** the stone tablets on which the Ten Commandments were written. [23] **ingredient simples:** singular components.

To return to our statues. They, I propound, are chiefly Greek and Roman, and both these either of deities or mortals. And where should the magazine[24] of the best of these be, but where the seat of the last empire was? Even at Rome. Where though they be daily found and digged for, yet are they so extremely affected[25] and sought after, that it is (as with jennets[26] in Spain) felony to convey them thence without special license. But in Greece and other parts of the Grand Signior's[27] dominions (where sometime there were more statues standing than men living, so much had art out-stripped nature in those days) they may be had for digging and carrying. For by reason of the barbarous religion[28] of the Turks, which alloweth not the likeness or representation of any living thing, they have been for the most part buried in ruins or broken to pieces; so that it is a hard matter to light upon any there, that are not headless and lame, yet most of them venerable for their antiquity and elegancy. And here I cannot but with much reverence mention the every way right honorable Thomas Howard,[29] Lord High Marshall of England, as great for his noble patronage of arts and ancient learning, as for his birth and place. To whose liberal charges[30] and magnificence, this angle of the world oweth the first sight of Greek and Roman statues with whose admired presence he began to honor the gardens and galleries of Arundel House about twenty years ago, and hath ever since continued to transplant old Greece into England. King Charles also ever since his coming to the crown[31] hath amply testified a royal liking of ancient statues, by causing a whole army of old foreign emperors, captains, and senators all at once to land on his coasts, to come and do him homage, and attend him in his palaces of Saint James, and Somerset House. A great part of these belonged to the late Duke of Mantua,[32] and some of the old Greek marble-bases, columns, and altars were brought from the ruins of Apollo's temple at Delos,[33] by that noble and absolutely complete gentleman Sir Kenelm Digby,[34] Knight. In the garden at St. James there are also half a dozen brass statues, rare ones, cast by Hubert Le Sueur,[35] his Majesty's servant now dwelling in Saint Bartholomew's London, the most industrious and excellent statuary in all materials that ever this country enjoyed.

---

[24] magazine: storehouse.   [25] affected: desired.   [26] jennets: small Spanish horses.   [27] Grand Signior: the Sultan of Turkey.   [28] barbarous religion: i.e., Islam.   [29] Thomas Howard: the earl of Arundel (1585–1646) was a courtier under James I and Charles I; he collected hundreds of paintings, sculptures, and other antiquities.   [30] liberal charges: generous expenditures.   [31] coming to the crown: Charles became king of England in 1625.   [32] Duke of Mantua: Vincenzo I of Gonzaga, duke of Mantua from 1587–1612, a major art patron.   [33] Delos: Greek island and mythological birthplace of Apollo.   [34] Kenelm Digby: seventeenth-century scientist and courtier.   [35] Hubert Le Sueur: French sculptor who in 1625 accompanied Charles I's new wife, Henrietta Maria, to England.

[Peacham describes the statues in the garden at St. James and in York House.]

It is not enough for an ingenuous[36] gentleman to behold these with a vulgar eye, but he must be able to distinguish them, and tell who and what they be. To do this, there be four parts: first, by general learning in history and poetry, whereby we are taught to know Jupiter by his thunderbolt; Mars by his armor; Neptune by his trident; Apollo by his harp; Mercury by his wings on his cap and feet, or by his caduceus;[37] Ceres by a handful of corn; Flora by her flowers; Bacchus by his vine leaves; Pomona by her apples; Hercules by his club or lion's skin; Hercules infans[38] by his grasping of snakes; Comedy by a vizard[39] in her hand; Diana by a crescent; Pallas[40] by her helmet and spear; and so generally of most of the deities. Some mortals also are known by their cognizances,[41] as Laocoon by his snakes stinging him to death, Cleopatra by a viper, Cicero by his wart, and a great many more.

But because all statues have not such properties and badges, there is a second way to discern them, and that is by their coins. For if you look upon them sideways and consider well their half-faces, as all coins show them, you will easily know them. For this is certain (which also witnesseth the exquisite diligence of ancient works) that all the faces of any one person, whether on old coins or stones, in greater or lesser volume, are all alike. Insomuch as if you bring an old rusty coin to any reasonable antiquary, if he can see but a nose upon it, or a piece of the face, he will give you a shrewd guess at him, though none of the inscription be to be seen.

A third and very good way to distinguish them, is by the book of collection of all the principle statues that are now to be seen at Rome, printed there with the title *Icones statuarum quae hodie visuntur Romae.*[42] He that is well acquainted with this book will easily discover at first sight a great many of them. For there are a number of statues of one and the same person: and he that knows one of them knows all the rest.

The fourth and last help, and without which the rest are weak, is to visit them in company of such as are learned in them, and by their help to grow familiar with them, and so practice their acquaintance.

Now, besides the pleasure of seeing and conversing with these old heroes (whose mere presence, without any farther consideration, reared on their

---

[36] ingenuous: honorable. [37] caduceus: winged staff with two serpents. [38] Hercules infans: the infant Hercules. [39] vizard: mask. [40] Pallas: Athena. [41] cognizances: characteristic emblems or properties. [42] *Icones . . . Romae*: images of statues that can be seen today in Rome (Latin).

several pedestals, and ranked decently, either *sub dio*,[43] where they show best, or in a stately gallery, cannot but take any eye that can but see), the profit of knowing them, redounds to all poets, painters, architects, and generally to such as may have occasion to employ any of these, and by consequent to all gentlemen. To poets for the presentation of comedies, tragedies, masques, shows, or any learned scene whatsoever, the properties whereof can neither be appointed nor judged of but by such as are well seen[44] in statue-craft. To painters, for the picturing of some exquisite arm, leg, torso, or wreathing of the body, or any other rare posture, whether smooth or forced.

Besides, rounds (so painters call statues and their fragments) may be had when the life cannot, and have the patience to stand when the life will not. And this is a maxim among artists in this kind: that a round is better to draw by and comes nearer the life, than any flat or painting whatsoever. And if a painter will meddle with history, then are old statues to him the only life itself. I call Rubens[45] to witness (the best story-painter of these times) whether his knowledge in this kind hath not been his only making. But his statues before named and his works do testify it for him, yea, while he is at work, he useth to have some good historian or poet read to him, which is rare in men of his profession, yet absolutely necessary. And as for architects, they have great use of statues for ornaments for gates, arches, friezes and cornices, for tombs and divers[46] other buildings.

And therefore I may justly conclude that the study of statues is profitable for all ingenuous gentlemen, who are the only men that employ poets, painters, and architects, if they be not all these themselves. And if they be not able to judge of their works, they well deserve to be cozened.[47]

[43] *sub dio*: in the open air (Latin). [44] **well seen**: proficient. [45] **Rubens**: Peter Paul Rubens (1577–1640), Flemish painter patronized by Charles I. [46] **divers**: various. [47] **cozened**: duped.

Performing the Statue

> Strike all that look upon with marvel. (5.3.100)

Although this edition has explored the cultural contexts of *The Winter's Tale* through the lens of contemporary texts, performance history can also reveal interpretative possibilities. Examining some notable performances of the statue scene from different eras demonstrates how acting and staging choices can substantially alter an audience's experience of the play. For instance, the staging of the reunion between Hermione and Leontes might tilt the play toward the comic or the tragic, or it might produce a delicate tragicomic equilibrium. Moreover, the decisions made by directors, actors, and designers can elicit particular symbolic, emotional, or political meanings from the figure of the living statue. Below, we will consider three performances of act 5, scene 3 from three different centuries: John Philip Kemble's Drury Lane production (1802), Harley Granville-Barker's Savoy Theater production (1912), and Edward Hall's Propeller Shakespeare company production (2005).

When reading these accounts, keep in mind the unique difficulty of describing a live performance, and try to decipher the subjective or cultural values revealed by the kinds of judgments the writer makes. What details of the production does a particular writer emphasize, elaborate, or minimize? What details are omitted? Consider too the kind of language used to evaluate the impact of an actor's performance of Hermione. From these accounts, can you gather whether or not the actors and director wished to convey a dominant idea about the statue scene? Do the various cultural prisms through which we have examined Hermione's statue — as a religious icon, a theatrical illusion, an erotic fixation, or an aesthetic artifact — centrally inform any of these stage interpretations?

JOHN PHILIP KEMBLE'S DRURY LANE PRODUCTION (1802)

The Winter's Tale went unperformed from the mid-seventeenth to the mid-eighteenth century, and its successful return to the stage came in the severely adapted forms of Macnamara Morgan's *The Sheep-Shearing, or Florizel and Perdita* (1754) and David Garrick's *Florizel and Perdita, a Dramatic Pastoral* (1756). As their titles indicate, both productions marginalized the Leontes-Hermione plotline, Morgan eliminating those characters altogether, and Garrick setting the entire play (including the statue scene) in Bohemia. Garrick also rewrote the statue scene by adding lines in which Hermione warmly and generously forgives Leontes.

John Philip Kemble's production of 1802, which restored the play's early scenes, provided a somewhat more faithful adaptation of Shakespeare's text. Kemble (1757–1823) built his reputation at London's Drury Lane Theatre playing Shakespearean tragic heroes such as Hamlet, Macbeth, and Coriolanus. Drury Lane was one of London's two premiere theaters — the other being Covent Garden, to which Kemble moved in 1803 — and when Kemble took over as the manager of Drury Lane in 1788, he mounted a series of spectacular Shakespearean productions there. In his 1802 revival of *The Winter's Tale*, Kemble played Leontes to the Hermione of Sarah Siddons, his sister.

→ JAMES BOADEN

From Memoirs of the Life of John Philip Kemble   *1825*

James Boaden (1762–1839) was a playwright and prolific theatrical biographer. Drawing on his personal acquaintance with his subjects, he wrote biographies not only of Kemble (whom he had known for almost thirty years), but also of the actresses Sarah Siddons, Dorothy Jordan, and Elizabeth Inchbald. Boaden's comprehensive two-volume *Memoirs* spans Kemble's life, from his birth, education, and early theatrical career in York and Dublin, to his ascendancy as lead actor and manager at Drury Lane Theatre, to his later career at Covent Garden Theatre, his retirement, and death.

It was on the 24th of this month [March, 1802] that Mr. Kemble presented his revival of *The Winter's Tale*, in all the splendor of decoration and power of acting, that he could impress upon it. In Paulina's chapel Mrs. Siddons stood as one of the noblest statues that even Grecian taste ever invented. The figure composed something like one of the Muses,[1] in profile. The drapery was ample in its folds, and seemingly stony in its texture. Upon the magical words, pronounced by Paulina: "Music; awake her! strike!" the sudden action of the head absolutely *startled*, as though such a miracle really vivified the marble; and the descent from the pedestal was equally graceful and affecting.

[1] **Muses:** in Greek mythology, the nine goddesses of the arts.

James Boaden, *Memoirs of the Life of John Philip Kemble* (London, 1825), ii, 314; qtd. *A New Variorum Edition of Shakespeare, The Winter's Tale*, ed. Horace Howard Furness (Philadelphia, 1898), 389–90.

→ THOMAS CAMPBELL

From Life of Mrs. Siddons   *1834*

Sister of John Philip Kemble, Sarah Siddons (1755–1831) is widely regarded as the greatest tragic actress of her time. After her disastrous 1775 London stage debut as Portia in *The Merchant of Venice*, Siddons performed widely in the provinces, where her talent for tragic roles — including Hamlet — became evident. She achieved phenomenal success at London's Drury Lane Theatre in

Thomas Campbell, *Life of Mrs. Siddons* (London, 1834), ii, 264; qtd. *A New Variorum Edition of Shakespeare, The Winter's Tale*, ed. Horace Howard Furness (Philadelphia, 1898), 390.

FIGURE 32 *Adam Buck*, Mrs. Siddons as Hermione.

roles such as Volumnia (*Coriolanus*), Hermione, and, most famously, Lady Macbeth. In 1834, the poet and magazine editor Thomas Campbell (1777–1844) published an appreciative biography of Siddons, whom he had known for thirty years.

From *Life of Mrs. Siddons*

On the 25th of March, 1802, Mrs. Siddons for the first time performed Hermione. . . . She must have long foreseen the transcendent charm which her performance would bestow on [this part]; yet there was a policy[1] in reserving it for the years of her professional appearance when her form was becoming too matronly for the personation of juvenile heroines. At the same time, she still had beauty enough left to make her so perfect in the statuescene, that assuredly there was never such a representative of Hermione. Mrs. Yates[2] had a sculpturesque beauty that suited the statue, I have been told, as long as it stood still; but when she had to speak, the charm was broken, and the spectators wished her back to her pedestal. But Mrs. Siddons looked the statue, even to literal illusion; and, whilst the drapery hid her lower limbs, it showed a beauty of head, neck, shoulders, and arms, that Praxiteles[3] might have studied. This statue-scene has hardly its parallel for enchantment even in Shakespeare's theatre. The star of his genius was at its zenith when he composed it; but it was only a Siddons that could do justice to its romantic perfection. The heart of every one who saw her when she burst from the semblance of sculpture into motion, and embraced her daughter, Perdita, must throb and glow at the recollection.

[1] **policy:** strategem. [2] **Mrs. Yates:** Mary Ann Yates, eighteenth-century English tragic actor.
[3] **Praxiteles:** renowned fourth-century B.C.E. Greek sculptor.

GRANVILLE-BARKER'S SAVOY THEATER PRODUCTION (1912)

Harley Granville-Barker (1877–1946), who went by the name "Barker" until 1918, was one of the most innovative English theater directors of the early twentieth century. As a young man living in London he acted and wrote plays. In 1903 he began directing at the Court Theatre, where his productions of the socially radical drama of Shaw, Ibsen, and others made a sharp break from the banal theatrical entertainments of the day. Following his move to the larger and more established Savoy Theatre, Barker mounted a landmark production of *A Midsummer Night's Dream* that emphasized the expressive power of Shakespeare's language and made striking use of non-representational stage imagery. In 1918, Granville Barker retired from the theater, although he continued to write plays; he eventually settled into teaching positions at various English and American universities.

→ BRIAN PEARCE

From Granville Barker's Production of *The Winter's Tale* (1912)

1996

Barker's 1912 production of *The Winter's Tale*, like his famous 1914 production of *A Midsummer Night's Dream*, boldly rejected the excessive stage spectacle and pictorial realism typical of late Victorian productions of Shakespeare. In this essay, Brian Pearce shows how Barker made various directorial choices in direct opposition to the 1906 production of *The Winter's Tale* directed by Sir Herbert Beerbohm Tree. Tree earned an international reputation by mounting lavish, spectacularly visual Shakespeare productions that appealed to popular audiences. For instance, Tree's set for Act 4 of *The Winter's Tale* featured a pastoral landscape with a shepherd's cottage and running brook. Barker's reaction to Tree's staging of the statue scene is described below.

Another example of Barker's direct "reaction" to Tree's production was in his staging of the statue scene. Tree, using his mastery of illusionism in this scene, placed the statue, together with "real" statues, well up-stage[1] amidst an imposing classical setting. Barker, in dialectically minded response, placed the statue on the forestage, in front of the drop curtain. Kennedy[2] writes:

> This scene, the last of the play, with all its opportunities for illusion — special lighting, music, a statue that comes to life — is even today regularly mounted in full set with Hermione well upstage. Indeed it seems made for the tricks of the theatre, and Shakespeare himself may have taken advantage of some of them, especially in the performances at the court of James I where sophisticated stage machinery was available. It is therefore especially significant that Barker was confident enough in his

[1] **up-stage:** at the back of the stage.   [2] **Kennedy:** Dennis Kennedy, in *Granville Barker and the Dream of the Theatre* (Cambridge: Cambridge UP, 1985), pp. 126–27.

Brian Pearce, "Granville Barker's Production of *The Winter's Tale* (1912)," *Comparative Drama* 30 (Fall 1996): 395–411, 406.

non-illusionist methods to place it in front of a drop, downstage of the proscenium, a few feet from the spectators' eyes. The Account Book records that the arc lights and the dress-circle[3] lights were on full.

Barker was defiant in his reaction to Tree's illusionistic staging, even down to flooding the statue with light.

[3] **dress-circle:** gallery of seats next above the floor.

↘ **HARLEY GRANVILLE-BARKER**

From Preface to *The Winter's Tale* (1912)   *1974*

Having retired from the theater, Granville-Barker spent years writing his *Prefaces to Shakespeare* (1927–45) as a pragmatic guide for actors and directors. The *Prefaces* are still widely appreciated for their acute insights into Shakespearean dramaturgy. The passage below discusses the dramatic pacing and tension of the final scene of *The Winter's Tale*.

The crude stage effect is so good that hasty naked handling might have spoiled it. Raw material at its richest is also the hardest to work in. But Shakespeare goes about the business with great care. He prepares the audience, through Paulina's steward, almost to the pitch of revelation, saving just so much surprise, and leaving so little, that when they see the statue they may think themselves more in doubt than they really are whether it is Hermione herself or no. He prepares Leontes, who feels that his wife's spirit might walk again; who is startled by the strange air of Hermione that the yet unknown Perdita breathes out; who, his egotism killed, has become simple of speech, simple-minded, receptive. The scene is elaborately held back by the preceding one, which though but a preparation, actually equals it in length, and its poetry is heightened by such contrast with fantastic prose and fun. While from the moment the statue is disclosed, every device of changing color and time, every minor contrast of voice that can give the scene modeling and beauty of form, is brought into easy use. Then the final effect of the music, of the brisk stirring trumpet sentences in Paulina's speech, of the simplicity of Leontes' "let it be an act lawful as eating." Then the swift contrast of the alarmed and skeptical Polixenes and Camillo, then

Harley Granville-Barker, *Preface to* The Winter's Tale (1912), *More Prefaces to Shakespeare,* ed. Edward M. More (Princeton: Princeton University Press, 1974), 22.

Paulina's happiness breaking almost into chatter. And then the perfect sufficiency of Hermione's eight lines (oh, how a lesser dramatist might have
overdone it with Noble Forgiveness and what not!) — it all really is a wonderful bit of work.

→ DENNIS BARTHOLOMEUSZ

From *The Winter's Tale* in Performance
in England and America, 1611–1976 *1982*

Dennis Bartholomeusz's indispensable stage history of *The Winter's Tale* spans
over three hundred and fifty years and treats notable performances from England, Canada, and the United States. He focuses on how different productions
have handled the play's central interpretative problems, such as the motivation
for Leontes' jealousy, the figures of Time and the bear, and the presentation of
Hermione's statue. Arguing that eighteenth- and nineteenth-century stagings
of *The Winter's Tale* tended to simplify its generic and tonal complexities,
Bartholomeusz praises Barker's 1912 Savoy Theatre production for its sensitive
approach to the play's mixture of realism and romanticism. How does the passage below address the mixed realism and romanticism in Barker's staging of the
statue scene?

In the first two acts Lillah McCarthy showed great charm and dignity, and
in the fifth act, during her descent from the pedestal in grey silk brocade,
and in her recognition of Perdita she showed an "exquisite" tact, a "sudden
piercing tenderness," as she embraced the kneeling girl and spoke . . . The
critic writing for the *Stage* (26 September 1912) detected no haste here, but
"simplicity, largeness, freedom."

In his preface, comparing Hermione with Desdemona, and Paulina with
Emilia, Barker wrote: "though interest is not centered throughout on
Hermione . . . , she is to me a most attractive and for a 'good' woman a
remarkably interesting figure." Acknowledging that goodness in drama is,
technically, one of the most difficult things to present with success, Barker
argues that the playwright had succeeded remarkably well with Hermione,
as well as with Paulina and Perdita, pointing out quite rightly that no play of

Dennis Bartholomeusz, The Winter's Tale *in Performance in England and America, 1611–1976*
(Cambridge: Cambridge University Press, 1982), 155.

FIGURE 33 *Photograph of Lillah McCarthy as Hermione in Harley Granville Barker's 1912 production of* The Winter's Tale, *Savoy Theatre, London.*

Shakespeare's "boasts three such women." For him they were not arche-types, or echoes of archetypes, these aspects he did not see; they possessed for him a human reality and a considerable dramatic complexity. If the set was "decorative," the costumes "mythical," the characters were approached, to start with, in the spirit of realism.

→ MARIO DIGANGI

An Account of Edward Hall's Watermill Theatre Production by Propeller
2005

What follows is my own account of the statue scene from Edward Hall's pro-duction of *The Winter's Tale*, which originated at the Watermill Theatre (UK), the residence of the Propeller company, and then toured to the Brooklyn Acad-emy of Music (BAM). I attended the BAM performance in November 2005, and subsequently reviewed it at the Theater on Film and Tape library of the New York Public Library. The recorded performance took place at BAM on November 3, 2005.

Propeller is an all-male company, and in this production the same actor played Mamillius and Perdita. The set consisted of a simple back wall, with a central doorway. Instead of side walls, a few white columns were arranged at either side of the back wall. A piano, which was occasionally played by a cast member, was placed against the back wall near the doorway.

The statue scene opens serenely with the stage bathed in a deep blue light, as if it were night. Above the back wall, little white lights shimmer like stars. A gentle melody comes from the on-stage piano. Leontes, Polixenes, Florizel, Perdita, Camillo, the Old Shepherd, and his son gather at center stage, while Paulina appears at stage right, elegantly dressed in a black blouse, black pants and a light shawl draped over her arms, and holding a candle. Except for the piano, the stage is bare.

As Paulina informs Leontes that she keeps Hermione's statue "[l]onely, apart" (5.3.18), she takes him by the hand and, holding out the candle, leads him and the rest of her visitors upstage towards the back wall. Tracing an arc around the stage, Paulina and her visitors sweep by the back wall and circle up to the front of the stage; the visitors stop in a tight group at downstage left, Leontes remains alone at center stage, and Paulina continues walking until she reaches the columns at stage right. Telling her guests to "[p]repare / To see the life as lively mocked as ever / Still sleep mocked death" (5.3.18–20), Paulina gestures behind her, as if about to reveal the statue perched atop one of the columns. But suddenly, with the words "Behold, and say 'tis well," Paulina holds out the candle toward Leontes (5.3.20). The piano melody that has been playing all this while ends on a decisive chord, punctuating Paulina's command. As Leontes spins around to follow the sight line of Paulina's outstretched arm, which leads directly to the group standing downstage, they (and we) suddenly realize that the statue of Hermione is right there, concealed among the visitors themselves, as if it had miraculously materialized in their midst. (In fact, the actor playing Hermione had snuck on stage behind the visitors as Paulina led them past the doorway at the back of the set.) Gasping in surprise, the stunned visitors quickly scatter, leaving Hermione alone, bathed in a white light. Hermione appears as she had earlier in the play, in a simple light grey dress, with a long cloth draped over her head, and barefoot. She stands with her back to the audience. She holds out her left arm, turned up at the elbow.

When the moment finally comes for Paulina to animate the statue, she again holds out the candle toward Hermione. At her command "Music, awake her; strike!" (5.3.98) the pianist begins to play chords in a regularly spaced sequence, enhancing the suspense. The upstage lights go down, again plunging the stage into deep blue except for the white light illuminating Hermione from behind. Paulina tells the visitors to "[a]pproach," and they tentatively move toward the statue (5.3.99). When Paulina instructs Hermione to "[b]equeath to death your numbness, for from him / Dear life redeems you," Hermione suddenly lowers her arm, producing cries of astonishment from the visitors as they quickly retreat (5.3.102–03).

In this production, the reunion between Hermione and Leontes feels tentative and strained; the genuinely emotional connection occurs between Hermione and Perdita. While Leontes stays at center stage, Hermione walks toward him slowly, her head lowered, as if dazed — or as if she really were waking up after a sixteen-year slumber. Stiffly, almost mechanically, she places one arm around his neck and the other arm around his torso. As Leontes embraces her tightly, she does not look him in the face. When Paulina, addressing Hermione, says "Turn, good lady; / Our Perdita is found" (5.3.121–22), Hermione releases Leontes and looks directly at her daughter, who is dressed in the same manner as she. Overwrought with feeling, Hermione and Perdita passionately embrace each other. After this bittersweet reunion, Paulina seems ready to end her (and Shakespeare's) play. She directs her visitors to "Go together" to share their "exaltation" and blows out her candle, at which the piano music stops (5.3.132–33). Paulina then turns to the audience and describes herself as an "old turtle" who has lost her mate, but her wryly self-deprecating tone elicits gentle, sympathetic laughter (5.3.134). It is a poignant yet light moment on which the play might satisfyingly end.

But precisely at this point, Leontes takes over. As he desperately attempts to wrap up the loose ends, Paulina's delicately achieved harmony begins to unravel. When Leontes awkwardly offers to find Paulina a new husband, she kneels down, hunches over, and lowers her head, as if to weep. Despite his efforts to comfort Paulina, Leontes seems more eager to avert an impending crisis than to soothe her pain. With improvisational haste and a tinge of panic, he seizes Camillo by the hand, haling him downstage to stand with pained discomfort next to Paulina, who remains crouched over. "Let's from this place," Leontes directs, clearly expecting the company to follow him as he walks off stage (148). But nobody moves. Hermione clings to Perdita. Camillo kneels down by Paulina. Turning back, Leontes makes a final plea for a harmonious ending on his terms. Addressing Hermione, he asks her pardon; she takes Polixenes' hand but says nothing. Leontes then shifts attention to the joyful "trothplight" between Florizel and Perdita (153), but instead of rejoining her fiancé Perdita buries her head in Hermione's neck, as if unwilling to be separated again from her mother.

Now Leontes perceives that he is in serious trouble. He is visibly nervous, wringing his hands, moving in starts and jerks, desperately wanting to end this scene. Finally, he seeks Paulina's help: "Lead us from hence" (154). At this point Leontes is the only parent not united with his child: the Old Shepherd and his son are facing each other, embracing; Polixenes has his arm around Florizel's shoulders; Hermione, clinging to Perdita, fixes Leontes with a cold look as he refers to the time since they were first "dissevered" (157).

The end of the scene is devastating. With his final words, "Hastily, lead away," Leontes extends his arm to Paulina, who rises from her crouch and walks toward him (5.3.157). A soft, rapid chime begins to sound, and the lights begin to dim. Paulina appears ready to take Leontes' outstretched hand, but at the last moment she snatches her hand away and drops her arm; then she spins around and walks off. As the lights drop to a dim blue glow, the stage rapidly clears: Perdita and Hermione retreat to the back of the stage, and Florizel exits. We can barely perceive Leontes as he walks towards Camillo, who turns away from him and exits. Leontes attempts to embrace Polixenes, who also abandons him, as do the Old Shepherd and his son. Leontes spies Hermione at the back of the stage and offers her his hand, but she, too, walks away.

In the meantime, the actor playing Perdita has changed back into costume as Mamillius, wearing the pajamas he had on at the start of the play. Alone

FIGURE 34 *Simon Scardifield as Hermione in Edward Hall's Propeller Company production of* The Winter's Tale, *Brooklyn Academy of Music, NY, November 2005. Also in the foreground are Vince Leigh as Leontes and Tam Williams, who played both Perdita and Mamillius.*

with Leontes, Mamillius walks to the front of the stage and lights a candle. The steadily tolling chime now gives way to a lullaby melody. Leontes turns to face Mamillius. Smiling warmly, Leontes approaches his son, waving him over for a hug. Mamillius stands holding the candle in his outstretched arm, like Paulina at the beginning of the scene. Leontes stops about ten feet from Mamillius, both arms out, leaning his body toward him and eagerly waving him closer. Mamillius blows out the candle and the stage goes dark.

Bibliography

➤⬗

Primary Sources

A. G. *The Widow's Mite, Cast into the Treasure-house of the Prerogatives and Praises of Our Blessed Lady.* St. Omer, 1619.

Allyne, Robert. *Funeral Elegies upon the Most Lamentable and Untimely Death of the Thrice Illustrious Prince Henry, Prince of Wales.* London, 1613.

An Act for Punishment of Rogues, Vagabonds and Sturdy Beggars (39 Elizabeth, c. 4), 1597. In *Tudor Economic Documents.* Ed. R. H. Tawney. London: Longman, 1951.

The Bachelor's Banquet. Trans. Robert Tofte. London, 1613.

Bacon, Francis. *The Essays of Sir Francis Bacon.* London, 1612.

———. *Essays, Religious Meditations, Places of Persuasion and Dissuasion.* London, 1597.

Boaden, James. *Memoirs of the Life of John Philip Kemble.* London, 1825.

The Book of Common Prayer, 1559: The Elizabethan Prayer Book. Ed. John E. Booty. Charlottesville: UP of Virginia, 1976.

Brand, John. *Observations on the Popular Antiquities of Great Britain.* London: Bell, 1900–02.

Bright, Timothy. *A Treatise of Melancholy.* London, 1586.

Buchanan, George. *A Dialogue Concerning the Due Privilege of Government in the Kingdom of Scotland.* 1680. Trans. of *De Jure Regni apud Scotos.* 1579.

Burton, Robert. *The Anatomy of Melancholy*. Oxford, 1621.

Campbell, Thomas. *Life of Mrs. Siddons*. London, 1834.

Church of England. *The Book of Common Prayer*. London, 1559.

——. *The Second Tome of Homilies of Such Matters as Were Promised and Entitled in the Former Part of Homilies*. London, 1563.

A Collection of Sundry Statutes. London, 1636.

Cranmer, Thomas. *A Confutation of Unwritten Verities*. In *The Works of Thomas Cranmer*. Ed. John Edmund Cox. 2 vols. Cambridge: Cambridge UP, 1844–46.

Crashaw, William. *The Jesuits' Gospel*. London, 1610.

Dalton, Michael. *The Country Justice*. London, 1618.

The Description of a Rare or Rather Most Monstrous Fish Taken on the East Coast of Holland the xvii of November, Anno 1566. London, 1566.

Devon, Frederick. *Issues of the Exchequer*. London, 1836.

Drayton, Michael. *Poems, Lyrical and Pastoral: Odes, Eclogues, The Man in the Moon*. London, 1606.

Fitzherbert, John. *Fitzherbert's Book of Husbandry*. London, 1598.

Fletcher, John. *The Faithful Shepherdess*. London, 1610.

The Geneva Bible: A Facsimile of the 1560 Edition. Introduction by Lloyd E. Berry. Madison: U of Wisconsin P, 1969.

Gerard, John. *The Herbal or General History of Plants*. London, 1597.

Gouge, William. *Of Domestical Duties*. London, 1622.

Granville-Barker, Harley. *More Prefaces to Shakespeare*. Ed. Edward M. Moore. Princeton: Princeton UP, 1974.

Great Britain. *The Statutes of the Realm*. 1810–28. Vol. 4. London: Dawson's, 1963. 11 vols.

Greene, Robert. *Pandosto. The Triumph of Time*. London, 1588.

——. *The Second and Last Part of Cony-Catching*. London, 1592.

——. *The Third and Last Part of Cony-Catching*. London, 1592.

Guillemeau, Jacques. *Childbirth; Or, the Happy Delivery of Women* with *The Nursing of Children*. London, 1612.

Harman, Thomas. *A Caveat for Common Cursitors, Commonly Called Vagabonds*. London, 1573.

Haydon, William [W. H.]. *The True Picture and Relation of Prince Henry his Noble and Virtuous Disposition*. Leyden, 1634.

Howell, Thomas Bayly. *A Complete Collection of State Trials*. 21 vols. London, 1809–26.

James I of England. *Basilikon Doron, Or His Majesty's Instruction to his Dearest Son, Henry the Prince*. London, 1603.

——. *King James VI and I: Political Writings*. Ed. Johann P. Sommerville. Cambridge: Cambridge UP, 1994.

——. *The True Law of Free Monarchies*. Edinburgh, 1598.

Jonson, Ben. *Bartholomew Fair*. Ed. E. A. Horsman. Revels Plays. Manchester: Manchester UP, 1979.

———. *The Works of Benjamin Jonson*. London, 1616.

Marston, John. *The Metamorphosis of Pygmalion's Image and Certain Satires*. London, 1598.

Middleton, Thomas. *The Second Maiden's Tragedy*. 1611. Ed. Anne Lancashire. Manchester: Manchester UP, 1978.

Milton, John. *Paradise Lost*. London, 1674.

Montaigne, Michel de. *The Complete Essays of Montaigne*. Trans. Donald M. Frame. Stanford: Stanford UP, 1958.

Nichols, John. *The Progresses, Processions, and Magnificent Festivities of King James the First*. 1828. 4 vols. New York: B. Franklin, 1967.

O. B. *Questions of Profitable and Pleasant Concernings*. London, 1594.

Ovid. *The Fifteen Books of P. Ovidius Naso, Entitled Metamorphoses*. Trans. Arthur Golding. London, 1567.

———. *Ovid's Festivals, or Roman Calendar*. Trans. John Gower. Cambridge, 1640.

Parker, Martin. "A Merry Dialogue Betwixt a Married Man and his Wife, Concerning the Affairs of this Careful Life." London, 1628.

Peacham, Henry. *The Complete Gentleman*. London, 1634.

Proceedings in Parliament 1610. Ed. Elizabeth Read Foster. Vol. 2: House of Commons. New Haven: Yale UP, 1966.

A Proclamation Inhibiting All Persons after Bartholomew-tide Next, To Use the Trade of a Peddler or a Petty Chapman, Unless They Be Licensed According to a Course Lately Taken by Us in that Behalf. Windsor Castle, 6 July 1618. In *Stuart Royal Proclamations*. Vol. 1. Ed. James F. Larkin and Paul L. Hughes. 2 vols. Oxford: Clarendon, 1973. 393–95.

Puttenham, George. *The Art of English Poesy*. London, 1589.

Rogers, Thomas. *The English Creed . . . Second Part*. London, 1587.

Sandys, George. *A Relation of a Journey Begun Anno Domini 1610*. London, 1615.

Scot, Reginald. *The Discovery of Witchcraft*. London, 1584.

Shakespeare, William. *Mr. William Shakespeare's Comedies, Histories, and Tragedies*. London, 1623.

———. *The Norton Shakespeare*. Ed. Stephen Greenblatt et al. New York: Norton, 1997.

Sidney, Sir Philip. *The Defense of Poesy*. London, 1595.

Smith, Thomas. *De Republica Anglorum*. London, 1583.

Speed, John. *A Prospect of the Most Famous Parts of the World*. London, 1631.

Speght, Rachel. *A Muzzle for Melastomus, the Cynical Baiter of, and Foul-Mouthed Barker against, Eva's Sex*. London, 1617.

Stubbes, Philip. *The Anatomy of Abuses*. London, 1583.

Swetnam, Joseph. *The Arraignment of Lewd, Idle, Froward, and Unconstant Women*. London, 1615.

Taylor, John. *Taylor's Pastoral, Being both Historical and Satirical: Or the Noble Antiquity of Shepherds, with the Profitable Use of Sheep*. London, 1624.

Topsell, Edward. *The History of Four-Footed Beasts*. London, 1607.

Varchi, Benedetto. *The Blazon of Jealousy*. Trans. Robert Tofte. London, 1615.

Vasari, Giorgio. *Lives of the Painters, Sculptors, and Architects.* 1568. Trans. Gaston du C. de Vere. New York: Knopf, 1996.

Veer, Gerrit de. *The True and Perfect Description of Three Voyages.* Trans. William Phillip. London, 1609.

———. *Waerachtighe Beschryvinghe van Drie Seylagien.* Amsterdam, 1598.

Whately, William. *A Bride-Bush: Or, A Direction for Married Persons.* London, 1619.

The Winter's Tale. By William Shakespeare. Dir. Edward Hall. Perf. Propeller. Brooklyn Academy of Music, Brooklyn, N.Y. 5 Nov. 2005.

———. By William Shakespeare. Dir. Edward Hall. Perf. Propeller. Brooklyn Academy of Music, Brooklyn, NY. 3 Nov. 2005. DVD. Character Generators, Inc., 2005.

Secondary Sources

Arrowood, Charles Flinn, trans. *The Powers of the Crown in Scotland* [*De Jure Regni Apud Scotos*]. By George Buchanan. Austin: U of Texas P, 1949.

Aston, Margaret. *England's Iconoclasts.* Oxford: Clarendon, 1988.

Barkan, Leonard. "'Living Sculptures': Ovid, Michelangelo, and *The Winter's Tale.*" *ELH* 48 (1981): 639–67.

———. *Unearthing the Past: Archaeology and Aesthetics in the Making of Renaissance Culture.* New Haven: Yale UP, 1999.

Barroll, Leeds. *Anna of Denmark, Queen of England: A Cultural Biography.* Philadelphia: U of Pennsylvania P, 2001.

Bartholomeusz, Dennis. *The Winter's Tale in Performance in England and America, 1611–1976.* Cambridge: Cambridge UP, 1982.

Beke, Charles T., ed. *The Three Voyages of William Barents to the Arctic Regions.* 1853. By Gerrit de Veer. New York: Burt Franklin, 1964.

Belsey, Catherine. *Shakespeare and the Loss of Eden: The Construction of Family Values in Early Modern Culture.* New Brunswick: Rutgers UP, 1999.

Bergeron, David M. "The Apollo Mission in *The Winter's Tale.*" *The Winter's Tale: Critical Essays.* Ed. Maurice Hunt. New York: Garland, 1995. 361–79.

———. *Shakespeare's Romances and the Royal Family.* Lawrence. UP of Kansas, 1985.

Bicks, Caroline. "Midwiving Virility in Early Modern England." *Maternal Measures: Figuring Caregiving in the Early Modern Period.* Ed. Naomi J. Miller and Naomi Yavneh. Aldershot: Ashgate, 2000. 49–64.

Boose, Lynda E. "Scolding Brides and Bridling Scolds: Taming the Woman's Unruly Member." *Shakespeare Quarterly* 42 (1991): 179–213.

Bowden, Peter J. *The Wool Trade in Tudor and Stuart England.* London: Macmillan, 1962.

Bristol, Michael D. "In Search of the Bear: Spatiotemporal Form and the Heterogeneity of Economies in *The Winter's Tale.*" *Shakespeare Quarterly* 42 (1991): 145–67.

Brown, Pamela Allen. *Better a Shrew than a Sheep: Women, Drama, and the Culture of Jest in Early Modern England.* Ithaca: Cornell UP, 1993.

Burgess, Glenn. *Absolute Monarchy and the Stuart Constitution.* New Haven: Yale UP, 1996.

Bushnell, Rebecca. *Tragedies of Tyrants: Political Thought and Theater in the English Renaissance.* Ithaca: Cornell UP, 1990.

Clark, Sandra. "The Broadside Ballad and the Woman's Voice." *Debating Gender in Early Modern England, 1500–1700.* Ed. Cristina Malcolmson and Mihoko Suzuki. New York: Palgrave Macmillan, 2002. 103–20.

Clubb, Louise George. *Italian Drama in Shakespeare's Time.* New Haven: Yale UP, 1989.

Crane, Mary Thomas. "'Video et Taceo': Elizabeth I and the Rhetoric of Counsel." *SEL* 28 (Winter 1998): 1–15.

Crawford, Patricia. "The Construction and Experience of Maternity in Seventeenth-Century England." *Women as Mothers in Pre-Industrial England: Essays in Memory of Dorothy McLaren.* Ed. Valerie Fildes. London: Routledge, 1990. 3–38.

Cressy, David. *Birth, Marriage, and Death: Ritual, Religion, and the Life-Cycle in Tudor and Stuart England.* Oxford: Oxford UP, 1997.

———. *Travesties and Transgressions in Tudor and Stuart England: Tales of Discord and Dissention.* New York: Oxford UP, 2000.

Cunningham, J. V. *Woe or Wonder: The Emotional Effect of Shakespearean Tragedy.* Denver: U of Denver P, 1951.

Cunnington, Phillis. *Children's Costume in England.* New York: Barnes and Noble, 1965.

Dickey, Stephen. "Shakespeare's Mastiff Comedy." *Shakespeare Quarterly* 42 (1991): 255–75.

DiGangi, Mario. *The Homoerotics of Early Modern Drama.* Cambridge: Cambridge UP, 1997.

Dolan, Frances E. *Dangerous Familiars: Representations of Domestic Crime in England, 1550–1700.* Ithaca: Cornell UP, 1994.

———. *Whores of Babylon: Catholicism, Gender, and Seventeenth-Century Print Culture.* Ithaca: Cornell UP, 1999.

Duffy, Eamon. *The Stripping of the Altars: Traditional Religion in England, c. 1400–c. 1580.* New Haven: Yale UP, 1992.

Ellison, James. "*The Winter's Tale* and the Religious Politics of Europe." *Shakespeare's Romances.* Ed. Alison Thorne. New York: Palgrave Macmillan, 2003. 171–204.

Enterline, Lynn. "'You Speak a Language that I Understand Not': The Rhetoric of Animation in *The Winter's Tale*." *Shakespeare Quarterly* 48 (1997): 17–44.

Erickson, Peter. *Patriarchal Structures in Shakespeare's Drama.* Berkeley: U of California P, 1985.

Felperin, Howard. *Shakespearean Romance.* Princeton: Princeton UP, 1972.

Fildes, Valerie. "Maternal Feelings Re-Assessed: Child Abandonment and Neglect in London and Westminster, 1550–1800." *Women as Mothers in Pre-Industrial England: Essays in Memory of Dorothy McLaren.* Ed. Valerie Fildes. London: Routledge, 1990. 139–78.

Fletcher, Anthony. *Gender, Sex, and Subordination in England, 1500–1800.* New Haven: Yale UP, 1995.

Fox, Adam. *Oral and Literate Culture in England 1500–1700.* Oxford: Clarendon, 2000.

Frye, Northrop. *The Myth of Deliverance: Reflections on Shakespeare's Problem Comedies.* Toronto: U of Toronto P, 1983.

Furness, Horace Howard, ed. *A New Variorum Edition of Shakespeare: The Winter's Tale.* Philadelphia: Lippincott, 1898.

Gillespie, Stuart. "Shakespeare and Greek Romance: 'Like an Old Tale Still.'" *Shakespeare and the Classics.* Ed. Charles Martindale and A. B. Taylor. Cambridge: Cambridge UP, 2004. 225–37.

Gowing, Laura. *Domestic Dangers: Women, Words, and Sex in Early Modern London.* Oxford: Clarendon, 1996.

Groesen, Michiel von. "The Winter at Novaya Zemlya." University College London. http://www.ucl.ac.uk/dutch/novaya_zemlya.html.

Gurr, Andrew. "The Bear, the Statue, and Hysteria in *The Winter's Tale.*" *Shakespeare Quarterly* 34 (1983): 420–25.

Hattaway, Michael, ed. *The New Inn.* By Ben Jonson. Revels Plays. Manchester: Manchester UP, 2001.

Henke, Robert. *Pastoral Transformations: Italian Tragicomedy and Shakespeare's Late Plays.* Newark, Del.: U of Delaware P, 1997.

Houlbrooke, Ralph. *Church Courts and the People during the English Reformation, 1520–1570.* Oxford: Oxford UP, 1979.

Howarth, David. *Images of Rule: Art and Politics in the English Renaissance, 1485–1649.* Berkeley: U of California P, 1997.

Hunt, Maurice. "Romance and Tragicomedy." *A Companion to Renaissance Drama.* Ed. Arthur F. Kinney. Oxford: Blackwell, 2002. 384–98.

Iwasaki, Soji. "Veritas Filia Temporis and Shakespeare." *English Literary Renaissance* 3 (1973): 249–63.

Jardine, Lisa. *Still Harping on Daughters: Women and Drama in the Age of Shakespeare.* New York: Columbia UP, 1989.

Jensen, Phebe. "Singing Psalms to Horn-pipes: Festivity, Iconoclasm, and Catholicism in *The Winter's Tale.*" *Shakespeare Quarterly* 55 (2004): 279–306.

Jones, Ann Rosalind. "Counterattacks on 'the Bayter of Women': Three Pamphleteers of the Early Seventeenth Century." *The Renaissance Englishwoman in Print: Counterbalancing the Canon.* Ed. Anne M. Hazelkorn and Betty Travitsky. Amherst: U of Massachusetts P, 1990. 45–62.

Jordan, Constance. *Shakespeare's Monarchies: Ruler and Subject in the Romances.* Ithaca: Cornell UP, 1997.

Kaplan, M. Lindsay, and Katherine Eggert. "'Good queen, my lord, good queen': Sexual Slander and the Trials of Female Authority in *The Winter's Tale*." *Renaissance Drama* 25 (1994): 89–118.

Kennedy, Dennis. *Granville Barker and the Dream of Theatre.* Cambridge: Cambridge UP, 1985.

Kitch, Aaron. "Bastards and Broadsides in *The Winter's Tale*." *Renaissance Drama* ns 30 (2001): 43–71.

Lamb, Mary Ellen. "Engendering the Narrative Act: Old Wives' Tales in *The Winter's Tale, Macbeth,* and *The Tempest*." *Criticism* 40 (Fall 1998): 529–53.

———. "Old Wives' Tales, George Peele, and Narrative Abjection." *Critical Survey* 14.1 (2002): 28–43.

Larkin, James F., and Paul L. Hughes, eds. *Stuart Royal Proclamations.* 2 vols. Oxford: Clarendon, 1973.

Laroque, François. "Pagan Ritual, Christian Liturgy, and Folk Customs in *The Winter's Tale*." *Cahiers Elisabethains* 22 (1982): 25–33.

Lim, Walter. "Knowledge and Belief in *The Winter's Tale*." *SEL* 41 (2001): 317–34.

Loewenstein, Joseph. "Guarini and the Presence of Genre." *Renaissance Tragicomedy: Explorations in Genre and Politics.* Ed. Nancy Klein Maguire. New York: AMS, 1987. 33–55.

Lupton, Julia Reinhard. *Afterlives of the Saints: Hagiography, Typology, and Renaissance Literature.* Stanford: Stanford UP, 1996.

Marrapodi, Michele. "'Of That Fatal Country': Sicily and the Rhetoric of Topography in *The Winter's Tale*." *Shakespeare's Italy: Functions of Italian Locations in Renaissance Drama.* Ed. Michele Marrapodi. Manchester: Manchester UP, 1993. 213–28.

McRae, Andrew. *God Speed the Plough: The Representation of Agrarian England, 1500–1660.* Cambridge: Cambridge UP, 1996.

Mendelson, Sara, and Patricia Crawford. *Women in Early Modern England, 1550–1720.* Oxford: Clarendon, 1998.

Mentz, Steven. "Wearing Greene: Autolycus, Robert Greene, and the Structure of Romance in *The Winter's Tale*." *Renaissance Drama* ns 30 (2001): 73–92.

Miller, Naomi. "Mothering Others: Caregiving as Spectrum and Spectacle in the Early Modern Period." *Maternal Measures: Figuring Caregiving in the Early Modern Period.* Ed. Naomi J. Miller and Naomi Yavneh. Aldershot: Ashgate, 2000. 1–25.

Montrose, Louis Adrian. "'Eliza, Queene of shepheardes,' and the Pastoral of Power." *Renaissance Historicism: Selections from English Literary Renaissance.* Ed. Arthur F. Kinney and Dan S. Collins. Amherst: U of Massachusetts P, 1987. 34–63.

Mowat, Barbara A. "Rogues, Shepherds, and the Counterfeit Distressed: Texts and Infracontexts of *The Winter's Tale* 4.3." *Shakespeare Studies* 22 (1994): 58–76.

———. "'What's in a Name?' Tragicomedy, Romance, or Late Comedy." *A Companion to Shakespeare's Works. Volume IV: The Poems, Problems Comedies, Late*

Plays. Ed. Richard Dutton and Jean E. Howard. Oxford: Blackwell, 2003. 129–49.

Newcomb, Lori Humphrey. *Reading Popular Culture in Early Modern England.* New York: Columbia UP, 2002.

Norbrook, David. *Poetry and Politics in the English Renaissance.* Rev. ed. Oxford: Oxford UP, 2002.

O'Callaghan, Michele. "Pastoral." *A Companion to English Renaissance Literature and Culture.* Ed. Michael Hattaway. Oxford: Blackwell, 2000. 307–16.

O'Connell, Michael. *The Idolatrous Eye: Iconoclasm and Theater in Early Modern England.* New York: Oxford UP, 2000.

Orgel, Stephen. "Idols of the Gallery: Becoming a Connoisseur in Renaissance England." *Early Modern Visual Culture: Representation, Race, and Empire in Renaissance England.* Ed. Peter Erickson and Clark Hulse. Philadelphia: U of Pennsylvania P, 2000. 251–83.

———. *Imagining Shakespeare: A History of Texts and Visions.* New York: Palgrave Macmillan, 2003.

———, ed. *The Winter's Tale.* By William Shakespeare. New York: Oxford UP, 1996.

Pafford, J. H. P., ed. *The Winter's Tale.* By William Shakespeare. Arden Shakespeare. London: Routledge, 1966.

Palfrey, Simon. *Late Shakespeare: A New World of Words.* Oxford: Clarendon, 1997.

Palliser, D. M. *The Age of Elizabeth: England under the Later Tudors, 1547–1603.* London: Longman, 1983.

Paster, Gail Kern. *The Body Embarrassed: Drama and the Disciplines of Shame in Early Modern England.* Ithaca: Cornell UP, 1993.

———. *Humoring the Body: Emotions and the Shakespearean Stage.* Chicago: U of Chicago P, 2004.

Pearce, Brian. "Granville Barker's Production of *The Winter's Tale* (1912)." *Comparative Drama* 30 (Fall 1996): 395–411.

Perry, Curtis. *The Making of Jacobean Culture: James I and the Renegotiation of Elizabethan Literary Practice.* Cambridge: Cambridge UP, 1997.

Pettet, E. C. *Shakespeare and the Romance Tradition.* Brooklyn: Haskell House, 1976.

Purkiss, Diane. "Material Girls: The Seventeenth-Century Woman Debate." *Women, Texts and Histories, 1575–1760.* Ed. Clare Brant and Diane Purkiss. London: Routledge, 1992. 69–101.

Ravelhofer, Barbara. "'Beasts of Recreation': Henslowe's White Bears." *English Literary Renaissance* 32 (2002): 287–323.

Smith, Bruce R. *Homosexual Desire in Shakespeare's England: A Cultural Poetics.* Chicago: U of Chicago P, 1991.

———. "Sermons in Stones: Shakespeare and Renaissance Sculpture." *Shakespeare Studies* 17 (1985): 1–24.

Snyder, Susan. "Mamillius and Gender Polarization in *The Winter's Tale.*" *Shakespeare Quarterly* 50 (1999): 1–8.

Sokol, B. J. *Art and Illusion in* The Winter's Tale. Manchester: Manchester UP, 1994.

Stallybrass, Peter. "Patriarchal Territories: The Body Enclosed." *Rewriting the Renaissance: The Discourses of Sexual Difference in Early Modern Europe.* Ed. Margaret W. Ferguson, Maureen Quilligan, and Nancy J. Vickers. Chicago: U of Chicago P, 1986.

Staub, Susan C. "Early Modern Medea: Representations of Child Murder in the Street Literature of Seventeenth-Century England." *Maternal Measures: Figuring Caregiving in the Early Modern Period.* Ed. Naomi J. Miller and Naomi Yavneh. Aldershot: Ashgate, 2000. 333–47.

Strong, Roy. *Henry, Prince of Wales and England's Lost Renaissance.* London: Thames and Hudson, 1986.

Suzuki, Mihoko. "Elizabeth, Gender, and the Political Imaginary of Seventeenth-Century England." *Debating Gender in Early Modern England, 1500–1700.* Ed. Cristina Malcolmson and Mihoko Suzuki. New York: Palgrave Macmillan, 2002. 231–53.

Trubowitz, Rachel. "'But Blood Whitened': Nursing Mothers and Others in Early Modern Britain." *Maternal Measures: Figuring Caregiving in the Early Modern Period.* Ed. Naomi J. Miller and Naomi Yavneh. Aldershot: Ashgate, 2000. 82–101.

Underdown, David E. "The Taming of the Scold: The Enforcement of Patriarchal Authority in Early Modern England." *Order and Disorder in Early Modern England.* Ed. Anthony Fletcher and John Stevenson. Cambridge: Cambridge UP, 1985.

Vanita, Ruth. "Mariological Memory in *The Winter's Tale* and *Henry VIII*." *SEL* 40 (Spring 2000): 311–37.

Watt, Tessa. *Cheap Print and Popular Piety, 1550–1640.* Cambridge: Cambridge UP, 1991.

Wilson, Adrian. "The Ceremony of Childbirth and Its Interpretation." *Women as Mothers in Pre-Industrial England: Essays in Memory of Dorothy McLaren.* Ed. Valerie Fildes. London: Routledge, 1990. 68–105.

Wiltenburg, Joy. *Disorderly Women and Female Power in the Street Literature of Early Modern England and Germany.* Charlottesville: UP of Virginia, 1992.

Wood, David Houston. "'He Something Seems Unsettled': Melancholy, Jealousy, and Subjective Temporality in *The Winter's Tale*." *Renaissance Drama* 31 (2002): 185–213.

Woodbridge, Linda. *Women and the English Renaissance: Literature and the Nature of Womankind, 1540–1620.* Urbana: U of Illinois P, 1984.

Würzbach, Natascha. *The Rise of the English Street Ballad, 1550–1650.* Trans. Gayna Walls. Cambridge: Cambridge UP, 1990.

Ziegler, Georgiana. "Parents, Daughters, and 'That Rare Italian Master': A New Source for *The Winter's Tale*." *Shakespeare Quarterly* 36 (1985): 204–12.

Zimmerman, Susan. *The Early Modern Corpse and Shakespeare's Theatre.* Edinburgh: Edinburgh UP, 2005.

Suggestions for Further Reading

ROMANCE AND TRAGICOMEDY

Bishop, T. G. *Shakespeare and the Theatre of Wonder.* Cambridge: Cambridge UP, 1996.

Foster, Verna A. *The Name and Nature of Tragicomedy.* Aldershot: Ashgate, 2004.

Frey, Charles H. *Shakespeare's Vast Romance: A Study of* The Winter's Tale. Columbia: U of Missouri P, 1980.

Hackett, Helen. *Women and Romance Fiction in the English Renaissance.* Cambridge: Cambridge UP, 2000.

Hartwig, Joan. *Shakespeare's Tragicomic Vision.* Baton Rouge: Louisiana State UP, 1972.

Maguire, Nancy Klein, ed. *Renaissance Tragicomedy: Explorations in Genre and Politics.* New York: AMS, 1987.

McDonald, Russ. "Fashion: Shakespeare and Beaumont and Fletcher." *A Companion to Shakespeare's Works. Volume IV: The Poems, Problem Comedies, Late Plays.* Ed. Richard Dutton and Jean E. Howard. Oxford: Blackwell, 2003. 150–174.

McMullan, Gordon, and Jonathan Hope, eds. *The Politics of Tragicomedy: Shakespeare and After.* London: Routledge, 1992.

Mowat, Barbara A. *The Dramaturgy of Shakespeare's Romances.* Athens: U of Georgia P, 1976.

Peterson, Douglas L. *Time, Tide, and Tempest: A Study of Shakespeare's Romances.* San Marino, CA: Huntington, 1973.

Platt, Peter G. *Reason Diminished: Shakespeare and the Marvelous.* Lincoln: U of Nebraska P, 1997.

GENDER, SEXUALITY, AND THE FAMILY

Adelman, Janet. *Suffocating Mothers: Fantasies of Maternal Origin in Shakespeare's Plays,* Hamlet *to* The Tempest. New York: Routledge, 1992.

Alfar, Cristina León. *Fantasies of Female Evil: The Dynamics of Gender and Power in Shakespearean Tragedy.* Newark: U of Delaware P, 2003.

Barton, Anne. "Leontes and the Spider: Language and Speaker in Shakespeare's Last Plays." *Essays, Mainly Shakespearean.* Cambridge: Cambridge UP, 1994. 161–81.

Cavell, Stanley. "Recounting Gains, Showing Losses: Reading *The Winter's Tale.*" *Disowning Knowledge in Seven Plays of Shakespeare.* Updated edition. Cambridge: Cambridge UP, 2003. 193–221.

Felperin, Howard. "'Tongue-Tied, Our Queen?': The Deconstruction of Presence in *The Winter's Tale.*" *The Uses of the Canon: Elizabethan Literature and Contemporary Theory.* New York: Oxford UP, 1990. 35–55.

Gowing, Laura. *Common Bodies: Women, Touch and Power in Seventeenth-Century England.* New Haven: Yale UP, 2003.

Johnson, Nora M. "Ganymedes and Kings: Staging Male Homosexual Desire in *The Winter's Tale.*" *Shakespeare Studies* 26 (1998): 187–217.

Maus, Katharine Eisaman. "Horns of Dilemma: Jealousy, Gender, and Spectatorship in English Renaissance Drama." *ELH* 54 (1987): 561–83.

Neely, Carol Thomas. *Broken Nuptials in Shakespeare's Plays.* New Haven: Yale UP, 1985.

Ward, David. "Affection, Intention, and Dreams in *The Winter's Tale.*" *Modern Language Review* 82 (1987): 545–54.

AUTHORITY AND RESISTANCE

Goldberg, Jonathan. *James I and the Politics of Literature: Jonson, Shakespeare, Donne, and Their Contemporaries.* Baltimore: Johns Hopkins UP, 1983.

Kurland, Stuart M. "'We need no more of your advice': Political Realism in *The Winter's Tale.*" *SEL* 31 (1991): 365–86.

Morse, William R. "Metacriticism and Materiality: The Case of Shakespeare's *The Winter's Tale.*" *ELH* 58 (1991): 283–304.

Palmer, Daryl. "Jacobean Muscovites: Winter, Tyranny, and Knowledge in *The Winter's Tale.*" *Shakespeare Quarterly* 46 (1995): 323–39.

Strier, Richard. *Resistant Structures: Particularity, Radicalism, and Renaissance Texts.* Berkeley: U of California P, 1995.

Tylus, Jane. *Writing and Vulnerability in the Late Renaissance.* Stanford: Stanford UP, 1993.

ENCOUNTERING NATURE

Alpers, Paul J. *What Is Pastoral?* Chicago: U of Chicago P, 1996.

Dionne, Craig, and Steve Mentz, eds. *Rogues and Early Modern English Culture.* Ann Arbor: U of Michigan P, 2004.

Hunt, Maurice. "'Bearing Hence': Shakespeare's *The Winter's Tale.*" *SEL* 44 (2004): 333–46.

Kinney, Arthur F., ed. *Rogues, Vagabonds, and Sturdy Beggars.* Amherst: U of Massachusetts P, 1990.

Kitch, Aaron. "Bastards and Broadsides in *The Winter's Tale.*" *Renaissance Drama* 30 (1999–2001): 43–71.

Randall, Dale B. J. "'This is the Chase': or the Further Pursuit of Shakespeare's Bear." *Shakespeare Jahrbuch* 121 (1985): 89–95.

Spufford, Margaret. *The Great Reclothing of Rural England: Petty Chapmen and Their Wares in the Seventeenth Century.* London: Hambledon, 1984.

Tayler, Edward W. *Nature and Art in Renaissance Literature.* New York: Columbia UP, 1964.

Woodbridge, Linda. *Vagrancy, Homelessness, and English Renaissance Literature.* Urbana: U of Illinois P, 2001.

HERMIONE'S STATUE

Cox-Rearick, Janet, ed. *Giulio Romano, Master Designer: An Exhibition of Drawings in Celebration of the Five Hundredth Anniversary of His Birth.* Seattle: U of Washington P, 1999.

Diehl, Huston. *Staging Reform, Reforming the Stage: Protestantism and Popular Theater in Early Modern England.* Ithaca: Cornell UP, 1997.

Eaton, Sara. "'Content with Art?': Seeing the Emblematic Woman in *The Second Maiden's Tragedy* and *The Winter's Tale.*" In *Shakespearean Power and Punishment: A Volume of Essays.* Ed. Gillian Murray Kendall. Madison: Fairleigh Dickinson UP, 1998. 59–86.

Gross, Kenneth. *The Dream of the Moving Statue.* Ithaca: Cornell UP, 1992.

Hunter, Robert G. *Shakespeare and the Comedy of Forgiveness.* New York: Columbia UP, 1965.

Jankowski, Theodora A. ". . . in the Lesbian Void: Woman-Woman Eroticism in Shakespeare's Plays." *The Feminist Companion to Shakespeare.* Ed. Dympna Callaghan. Oxford: Blackwell, 2000. 299–319.

Knapp, James A. "Visual and Ethical Truth in *The Winter's Tale.*" *Shakespeare Quarterly* 55 (2004): 253–78.

Marshall, Cynthia. *Last Things and Last Plays: Shakespearean Eschatology.* Carbondale: Southern Illinois UP, 1991.

Newcomb, Lori Humphrey. "'If that which is lost be not found': Monumental Bodies, Spectacular Bodies in *The Winter's Tale.*" *Ovid and the Renaissance Body.* Ed. Goran V. Stanivukovic. Toronto: U of Toronto P, 2001. 239–59.

Salingar, L. G. "Time and Art in Shakespeare's Romances." *Renaissance Drama* 9 (1966): 3–35.

Traub, Valerie. "Jewels, Statues, and Corpses: Containment of Female Erotic Power." *Desire and Anxiety: Circulations of Sexuality in Shakespearean Drama.* New York: Routledge, 1992. 25–49.

Acknowledgments

INTRODUCTION

Figure 1. Frontispiece, from Charles Perrault, *Histoires ou contes du temps passé* (London, 1786). Reprinted by permission of Houghton Library, Harvard College Library. Call number: 26234.2.

Figure 2. Portrait of *Thomas Howard 2nd Earl of Arundel and Surrey*, by Daniel Mytens (1618). Reprinted by permission of National Portrait Gallery, London.

Notes to *The Winter's Tale* from *The Complete Works of Shakespeare*, 5th ed. Ed. David Bevington. Copyright 2004 by Pearson Education, Inc. Reprinted by permission.

CHAPTER 1

Figure 3. Frontispiece, from Achilles Tatius, *The Loves of Clitophon and Leucippe*, tr. Anthony Hodges (Oxford, 1638). Reprinted by permission of the Folger Shakespeare Library, Washington, D.C.

Figure 4. "Catalogue of the Several Comedies, Histories, and Tragedies contained in this Volume," from *Mr. William Shakespeare's Comedies, Histories, and Tragedies* (London, 1623). Reprinted by permission of the Folger Shakespeare Library, Washington, D.C.

Figure 5. Map of Bohemia, from John Speed, *A Prospect of the Most Famous Parts of the World* (London, 1631). Reprinted by permission of the British Library, MAPS C.7.c.6, pp. 18–19.

Figure 6. Frontispiece, from Ben Jonson, *The Works of Benjamin Jonson* (London, 1616). Reprinted by permission of the British Library, C.39.h.9.

Figure 7. Map of the Mediterranean Sea, from George Sandys, *A Relation of a Journey Begun An. Dom. 1610* (London, 1621). Reprinted by permission of the Folger Shakespeare Library, Washington, D.C.

Figure 8. Woodcut by Jost Amman, *Allegory of Truth and Time* (1562). Reprinted by permission of Albertina, Vienna.

Figure 9. *The Rape of Proserpina*, by Alessandro Varotari (Il Padovanino). Permission to reprint by Cameraphoto Arte, Venice / Art Resource, NY.

CHAPTER 2

Figure 10. Titlepage, *De Conceptu et Generatione Hominis*, by Jacob Rüff (Frankfurt, 1580). Reprinted by permission of the Folger Shakespeare Library, Washington, D.C.

Figure 11. *The Fall*, Engraving by Zacharias Dolendo, after Bartholomeus Spranger (1611). Reprinted by permission of Rijksmuseum Amsterdam.

Figure 12. *Anne, Lady Pope with her children Henry, 3rd Baron Wentworth (d. 1593), Thomas (1591–1667, later Earl of Cleveland), Jane (later wife of Sir John Finet) and Henry (d. 1644, a major-general in the King's army)*, by Marcus Gheeraerts the Younger (1596). Reprinted by permission of National Portrait Gallery, London. Private Collection courtesy of Nevill Keating Pictures.

Figure 13. *Sir Walter Raleigh*, by Unknown Artist (1602). Reprinted by permission of National Portrait Gallery, London.

CHAPTER 5

Figure 27. From *The English Creed . . . Second Part,* by Thomas Rogers (London, 1587). Reprinted by permission of the Folger Shakespeare Library, Washington, D.C.

Figure 28. "The Coronation of Our Blessed Lady," from M. de Vos, *The Rosary of Our Lady* (Antwerp, 1600). Reprinted by permission of Keble College Library.

Figure 29. From P. *Ovidii Nasonis Metamorphoses Expositae,* by Pieter van der Borcht (Antwerp, 1591). Reprinted by permission of Rijksmuseum Amsterdam.

Figure 30. *I Modi, Position 1 or Amours d'un Dieu et d'une Deesse,* by Marcantonio Raimondi, after an engraving by Giulio Romano. Reprinted by permission of Bibliothèque national de France.

From *The Second Maiden's Tragedy,* ed. by Anne Lancashire, 1978, Manchester University Press, Manchester, UK.

Figure 31. *Monument to Queen Elizabeth I in Westminster Abbey,* by Willem de Passe, after Maximilian Colte, 1620. Reprinted by permission of National Portrait Gallery, London.

Figure 32. *Mrs. Siddons as Hermione,* by Adam Buck, from Forrest Collection Volume. Reproduced by permission of Birmingham Library and Information Services.

Figure 33. *Lillah McCarthy as Hermione,* Savoy Theatre, 1912. THE SKETCH, 2.10.1912, Supp. 4. Reprinted by permission of The Illustrated London News Picture Library.

Figure 34. *Simon Scardifield as Hermione,* from Edward Hall's Propeller company production, BAM, 2005. Photo by Richard Termine. Reprinted by permission of Richard Termine.

Index